MAYA
SOCIETY
UNDER COLONIAL
RULE

MAYA
SOCIETY
UNDER COLONIAL
RULE

*The Collective Enterprise
of Survival*

By Nancy M. Farriss

Princeton University Press

CONTENTS

CONTENTS

ILLUSTRATIONS

All illustrations are reproduced by permission.

TABLES, FIGURES, AND
MAPS

PREFACE

This is a study of the Maya Indians of Yucatan, Mexico, from late preconquest times through the end of Spanish colonial rule (ca. 1500-1820). It takes the form of an historical ethnography, which attempts to reconstruct the Maya world in as comprehensive a fashion as possible—by relating ecology and modes of subsistence to social forms and belief systems—and to trace changes in that world within the larger colonial context.

The choice of subject and format was influenced by various motives, starting with a personal desire (by no means uncommon among visitors to Yucatan) to learn more about the Maya than the guidebooks tell us. What I especially wanted to know was how the pre-Hispanic Maya, who built the stone monuments for which Yucatan is so famous, became the modern Maya, whose villages and maize fields surround the archaeological sites—in close physical proximity to them but with a causal relationship that is not immediately discernible. Here even the scholarly literature was for the most part silent. One aim of this study, then, is to help fill the large chronological gap that has separated the extensively studied ancient Maya past from the present, and, not incidentally, to offer an historically based model of Maya social organization. A second, overlapping aim in choosing this particular time frame is to look at the Spanish conquest and colonization in America from a relatively neglected point of view, that of the colonized. Finally, I have had in mind a more general, comparative goal: to relate the specific Maya example to certain broad issues concerning both the nature and functioning of complex agrarian societies and the processes of sociocultural change within them, especially under the impact of colonial rule.

The clearest precedents for this combination of aims lie in the regional fields of Africa, South Asia, and Southeast Asia, where much recent scholarship has merged history's interest in change over time with anthropology's comparative perspectives and insights on culture. The *Annales* school's dual tradition of total history over the "long duration" and the history of mentalities has provided another source of inspiration and basis for comparison; the literature on Afro-American culture history within the Anglophone slave societies of the southern United States and the Caribbean has provided still another.

Within Latin American studies I have been able to draw on an extensive body of scholarship in social, economic, and demographic history for regional comparisons of colonial regimes. Very little exists on the

ix

Indian side of the story: that is, how they viewed and responded to European domination as opposed to what merely happened to them. But the exceptions, if few, are impressive. I am especially indebted, in roughly equal measure, to Charles Gibson's monumental study of the Aztecs and to Eric Wolf's synthesis of Mesoamerican culture history. Besides providing a wealth of information and insights, the former has inspired this similarly detailed study of the Maya, and the latter has lent a holistic framework for the study that adds an ecological and cultural dimension to the analysis of social behavior.

In attempting to present a many-faceted and at the same time detailed account of Maya history, analyzing not only social structure and proc-esses but also the systems of meaning that informed them, I have by necessity taken an equally eclectic approach to the choice and use of sources. The bulk of the material consists of colonial manuscript re-cords. Most of these are in Spanish, but Yucatec Maya documents have supplied much valuable linguistic and historical evidence far out of pro-portion to their small number. To supplement and help interpret the historical sources, I have also drawn heavily on archaeological and eth-nographic data from my own fieldwork as well as from the published literature. The contributions flow in both directions, for patterns dis-cerned from the colonial records have suggested new interpretations of much of the pre-Hispanic and modern material. A more detailed dis-cussion of sources and methods is included as an appendix to this study.

Finally, a note on Spanish and Yucatec Maya words and names. Spell-ing has been modernized, and for Yucatec Maya this means modern local spelling, without accents and without the tone marks used in some phonetic transcriptions. Maya nouns are given the English plural ending of "s" rather than the Maya "ob" or Spanish "es" (thus, *batabs* rather than *batabob* or *batabes*), except in the few cases where the Maya plural has become common usage in Spanish and English (e.g., *cruzob*). A glossary is provided only for frequently used words; others are defined where they appear in the text.

Philadelphia
May 1983

ACKNOWLEDGMENTS

Many institutions and individuals have helped me in the preparation of this study. Summer grants from the American Philosophical Society, the American Council of Learned Societies, the College of William and Mary, and the University of Pennsylvania, as well as a fellowship from the National Endowment for the Humanities, enabled me to carry out archival research, interspersed with ethnographic work. Grants from the National Geographic Society supported archaeological surveys and excavations carried out in 1974 and 1975. For access to manuscript collections I owe thanks to the directors and staffs of the following archives and libraries: the Archivo del Estado, the Archivo de Notarías, the Archivo General del Arzobispado, and the Carrillo y Ancona library of the Instituto Yucateco de Antropología e Historia, in Merida, Yucatan; the Archivo General de la Nación, the Biblioteca Nacional, and the library of the Museo de Antropología e Historia, in Mexico City; the Archivo General de Indias in Seville; and the Latin American Library of Tulane University in New Orleans.

Many of the documents most valuable to this study are located in private collections and in ecclesiastical archives that were not (and some of them are still not) ordinarily accessible to researchers. I owe an incalculable debt to Joaquín de Arrigunaga Peón, through whose good offices I was granted permission to consult the administrative records of the archdiocese of Yucatan (Archivo del Arzobispado, Secretaría); diocesan and parish archives in the bishopric of Campeche, and a number of colonial *títulos*, or estate records, owned by members of his extended family. I take this opportunity to thank all of those who made their estate records available to me and who also arranged for me to explore the same haciendas firsthand during many enjoyable sojourns. Don Joaquín himself has been the direct source of much information on, and many insights into, the Spanish side of local history, in which his family has played a major role since the time of his most prominent ancestor, Francisco de Montejo, who led the Spanish conquest of Yucatan. Don Joaquín has shared documents in his collection, the results of his own research, and his large store of memories from the early part of this century, on a range of topics from upper-class household organization to commercial logwood cutting on the Campeche coast.

The archaeological projects undertaken on the east coast of Yucatan, in collaboration with Arthur Miller, would have aborted in the planning stages without the encouragement and deft guidance through bureaucratic labyrinths provided by Pilar Luna Erreguerena and Norberto

González Crespo, both of the Instituto Nacional de Antropología e Historia. Arlen Chase, Harold Egerton, John Gifford, Francisco Hau, Pilar Luna, and Secundino Sabido all contributed brain and brawn to the fieldwork itself. Pablo Bush Romero and Elsy Betancourt de Bush, gracious hosts in Yucatan for many years, donated logistical support; Joann McManus Andrews and her Maya friends at Quinta Mari helped in countless ways in all phases of the research.

Much knowledge of present-day Maya life was acquired through travels around the peninsula undertaken with other purposes in mind. My more systematic efforts have benefited greatly from the guidance of Celinda Gómez, Víctor Segovia, and the late Alfredo Barrera Vázquez (who also aided in deciphering colonial Maya texts). Walter Winrich, of the Maryknoll order, introduced me to his widespread mission territory in the old Caste War region of central Quintana Roo, and José González Avilés provided hospitality at Rancho Tancah along with a fund of knowledge gained from a lifetime of trading and ranching among the eastern Maya. Last and far from least are the many Maya who welcomed me to their homes and fiestas with a warmth that no amount of linguistic and cultural ineptness seems capable of diluting.

Much of the theoretical and methodological orientation of this study developed out of workshop discussions and joint teaching ventures in the Ethnohistory Program at the University of Pennsylvania. Particular thanks are due to Sandra Barnes, Lee Cassanelli, and Igor Kopytoff for their advice and criticisms, and to my student Kevin Gosner for ideas and information from his own work on Yucatan and Chiapas. The manuscript has also benefited from suggestions made by Woodrow Borah, Charles Gibson, Robert Hartwell, Grant Jones, Charles Rosenberg, Robert Sharer, and Jan Vansina, with the usual caveat that they are not responsible for any of the errors and blunders that remain. Diane Chase prepared the final version of the maps, and Cecilia Blewer gave much appreciated help with the index. Finally, I owe a special debt to my husband and colleague, Arthur Miller, who understands the Maya, past and present, better than any quasi outsider (being partly Mayanized himself) I can think of. His insights have contributed much to this study; his empathetic encouragement in a seemingly endless project, even more.

MAYA
SOCIETY
UNDER COLONIAL
RULE

INTRODUCTION

Most of the world's population has lived until recently in complex but small-scale agrarian societies. In Asia, Latin America, and North Africa most people still do, although now they are encapsulated within larger state structures and an even larger world economy that are increasingly shaped by industrial production. Because of the relative isolation in which all such societies have developed and because of their primitive level of technology, there tends to be great cultural and ecological variation among them. All have evolved their own peculiar interpretations of the world around them (a world that they, lacking the means to transform, have had to take largely as they find) and their own peculiar social forms in consonance with these interpretations. Yet certain structural similarities underlie the heterogeneity. Perhaps most basic to them is the same all-pervasive concern with wresting a living from the soil by largely unaided human effort, a common preoccupation that gives certain stand-ard outlines to the particular cultural configurations and social arrange-ments. This preoccupation is of course shared by all agricultural peoples. What distinguishes the particular type of society I refer to here from simpler forms of agrarian-based organization is social stratification: a basic division into peasants, who supply the vast bulk of the goods and labor, and an elite, who manage by one means or another to extract a surplus from the peasantry to support themselves and a small number of dependents who serve them in specialized ways.

The Maya Indians of Yucatan and adjoining regions of Mexico and Central America have lived under this type of social system for several millennia. Their society has developed its own distinctive features even within the general culture area of Mesoamerica, while sharing the same basic structure outlined above as well as the only slightly less common historical experience of European colonial rule. The present study is an analysis of this society over roughly three hundred years of its recent past. It is a study of survival, in two senses and within two overlapping environments. The first sense is material and refers to the strategies the Maya devised for survival within their tropical lowland habitat. The second is sociocultural and refers to the ways in which Maya society and culture adapted, or failed to adapt, to the new social environment created by Spanish conquest. Central to the analysis is the working hy-pothesis that both types of environment are influential but not deter-minant and that they are themselves modified by the adaptive responses they elicit.

3

Social Bonding

The underlying theme of this study is the nature of the social bond: what forms it takes, how it relates to the ecological and ideational systems in which the forms are embedded, and how both social order and sustaining ideology are affected by colonial rule. What holds people together in groups is a basic sociological question that has especially intrigued students of pre-Hispanic Maya history. According to standard theories of early sociopolitical evolution, Maya civilization should not have happened, or rather, it should not have happened where it did—in a physical setting that is allegedly unfavorable to the development of complex societies. Such societies, it has been argued, are most likely to emerge in circumscribed, diversified environments that restrain people from spreading out in search of new resources or looser social controls.[1] Maya civilization (as well as the Khmer of Southeast Asia) is considered a puzzling anomaly, arising in a tropical forest setting without significant barriers or limitations on resources to keep people literally and figuratively in their place.[2] The issue is not so much the rise of advanced civilizations as the kinds of social systems that supported them. Yet premodern history offers many such examples of societies that are perhaps smaller in scale and with less impressive material remains, but are similarly composed of small agrarian communities stratified internally and linked hierarchically into a larger structure (whether called city-state, or principality, or by some other label) and occurring in some relatively open, undifferentiated environment.

Various refinements on the basic ecological model have been offered to account for the organization of Maya society, based on one kind of material stimulus or another that, however plausible in theory, still fails to fit the facts of the case.[3] They still leave unanswered the question of why the Maya should have coalesced into relatively compact territorial units under the authority of a ruling elite, when their environment, their shifting mode of cultivation (variously called swidden, slash-and-burn, or milpa) and their lack of economic interdependence all seem to suggest they would have done better living on their own in widely dispersed settlements, with no one to provide for but their own families. Such an inquiry is not a search for origins. These are probably untraceable, since it would be difficult to recover the historical particulars of what happened in late Preclassic times (600 B.C. to A.D. 250), when the basic outlines of the social system first took shape. It is a search for explanation. And if we cannot say what originally persuaded the Maya farmers to choose or accept this social arrangement, we can explore what held it together during the historically more accessible late Postclassic and colonial periods (ca. 1500-1820), in the same ecological setting, with similar population densities and the same mode of subsistence, and therefore the same apparent lack of material necessity or advantage.

At first sight the study of Maya society during the Spanish colonial period would seem to do little to illuminate the basic issue of social bonding. According to the model of postconquest Mesoamerican social organization that has been in vogue for several decades—Eric Wolf's "closed corporate peasant communities"—colonial Indian society was an artifact of the new conditions imposed by conquest and is thus by implication irrelevant to any understanding of indigenous social forms.[4] This model offers a variant of environmental circumscription to explain social cohesion: the communities are surrounded and held together not by mountains or deserts but by Spanish haciendas; because land is scarce, the social boundaries of the communities are closed and they adopt a corporate, tightly knit internal structure to defend themselves against further Spanish encroachments. As it turns out, this elegant formulation fits the Maya case no better than the standard variety of ecological model. Spanish haciendas developed and expanded so slowly in Yucatan that for most of the colonial period (and well beyond it in some regions) there was plenty of land and empty space. The Maya could and did move around with ease, and Indians in other regions of Mesoamerica seem to have enjoyed a similar mobility, although to a lesser degree. If the conquest did not create closed communities, neither did it create corporate ones, since, among the Maya at least, the corporate structure already existed. Whatever effect colonial rule had on Maya social organization—and much of this study is concerned in one way or another with this question—it did not create an environmental circumscription that the natural habitat lacked.

All the explanations of social solidarity alluded to so far are based on the presence of some kind of external boundary. People stay in groups because they have no choice. The basic premise in this as in much sociological analysis is that fissioning is a natural tendency; people seek to escape the social constraints and competition for (or unequal access to) resources that inevitably build up in any group. This may be so, but it does not follow that natural or social boundaries, beyond which lie hostile or unfamiliar territory, provide the only or even the main check on this tendency. In any case, people as often as not draw the boundaries around themselves, deciding what constitutes a hostile environment or an obstacle to movement, and the boundaries then shift from the category of cause to one of effect or instrument. The image of people all locked in a prison who must make the best of it is one way of looking at social cohesion and no doubt valid for some groups. For others that are firmer at the center than at the edges, such as the Maya communities, a more appropriate image would seem to be one of a magnetic field, holding people together in a more positive way through some internal force of attraction. The starting point for the present inquiry into social bonding among the Maya is an effort to identify some sort of magnetic field within Maya society.

The alternative explanation for Maya social integration presented here also has an ecological base, but one of a different kind—one that offers a particular Maya perspective and suggests a general approach to the analysis of preindustrial agrarian societies. Maya society was organized into a corporate and at the same time hierarchical structure, replicated at each level of society from kin group to the larger units that formed and reformed according to the ebb and flow of political centralization. The difficulty in explaining what integrates people into this kind of structure, in Maya society or elsewhere, often comes from applying a supposedly objective—that is, our own—definition of need and advantage. The answer must surely lie in how the people themselves view these criteria, and this ultimately depends on how they perceive the world around them and the best way to survive in it. In other words, the physical environment will exert a strong influence on social forms, but the influence is mediated through a society's particular interpretations of the way the environment functions. As can be expected of an agricultural people inhabiting a tropical forest environment where biological recycling is especially rapid and obvious, the Maya ecological model was an organic, circular one, in which all creation was seen as mutually dependent, feeding on itself in endless cycles of decay and renewal. In a region where the life-renewing rains are so uncertain, it is also not surprising that this cyclical rhythm was not to be taken for granted and that man as part of the system was expected to do his share to keep it going. The Maya conceived of survival as a collective enterprise in which man, nature, and the gods are all linked through mutually sustaining bonds of reciprocity, ritually forged through sacrifice and communion. This collective enterprise provided the organizing principle of Maya society, incorporating the individual in widening networks of interdependence from extended family through community and state and ultimately to the cosmos. The elite directed this enterprise in all its aspects. Above all, they ensured the flow of offerings and benefits between society and the sacred order, and thus the survival of both.

COLONIAL RULE

The model of Maya social organization offered in this study draws on evidence from both the pre-Hispanic and colonial periods. It is not, however, a static model. Colonial rule presented new challenges to Maya strategies for survival, and created new demands and new forms of unpredictability to add to existing insecurities. The conquering group also brought with them a very different, in some ways antithetical, set of beliefs and norms. Interaction between two different cultures can reveal much about both, often illuminating the most fundamental patterns and principles that, precisely because they are fundamental, lie buried under the routine of ordinary social life. At the same time the confrontation is a force for change; thus the same responses to an alien system that reveal underlying patterns also represent a form of innovation.

The impact of colonial rule is one of the most important issues in the recent history of a large part of the non-European world. For the Maya and other native peoples of America, much more so than in the excolonial areas of Africa and Asia, the issue is a very basic one of sociocultural survival. Did the Spanish leave behind anything recognizable as indigenous culture when they were ousted from their empire after three centuries? Opinions vary widely. At one extreme is the contention that conquest and colonization reduced all Indians to a deculturated peasantry on the fringes of Spanish society.[5] At the other extreme is the view—more implicit than explicit and more prevalent regarding the Maya than their neighbors in central Mexico—that Spanish customs have merely been superimposed on a basically unmodified indigenous system.[6] Most observers detect some degree of change, whether seen as a substitution of Spanish traits for native ones or a blending of the two, and merely differ on how complete or profound it has been. There is no lack of ethnographic evidence on the end product of the cultural interaction, only a lack of agreement on what it means. The main problem would seem to be an emphasis on measuring the results rather than on seeing how they were reached. A better way to assess their significance would be to look at the processes of change themselves and, most importantly, look at them within the larger perspective of sociocultural change in general. The colonial setting gives certain parameters, but the processes are not necessarily unique. Cultures are always changing, inasmuch as the material and social conditions that shape and reflect culture are themselves inherently unstable. We would therefore expect to find in pre-Hispanic Mesoamerica, as the evidence amply confirms, that indigenous sociocultural systems were not sealed in wax until the Europeans arrived. Shifting trade patterns, changing modes of exploiting the environment, conquests, migrations, the rise and fall of states, urban growth and decline, new religious cults and transformations of old ones—these and many other changes were all part of the rich texture of preconquest history. It is only when the Spanish break into this *dynamic* scene that we question the compatibility between change and cultural survival.

7

And in doing so, we also ignore the fact that the conquest itself was partly shaped by the pre-Columbian systems, their internal relationships, and their particular patterns of response to new challenges.

If change is a constant, not all change is of an equal order of value. Without some guidelines for judging the order, the same set of facts could lead equally well to the conclusion that a culture has been transformed beyond all recognition as to the conclusion that it has been only superficially modified. We need to identify the thing itself that is being measured, and "culture" may be too loose a concept for analytical purposes, encompassing as it does everything from hair styles to world views. The approach I suggest in analyzing change (and the standard for assessing its significance) is based on the notion that each culture or cultural configuration contains a central set of ideas about the way things are and ought to be—in other words, a core of general explanations and norms around which the shared cognitive map and the social order are organized. These ideas comprise the most stable part of the system both because they are central and because, being general rather than specific, they are open to varying interpretations in the ancillary concepts that flow from them and in the way they are expressed through social action. As core concepts, they provide not only the principles according to which change will take place but also the measure of its extent; they indicate whether we are dealing merely with variations on a theme or an altogether new theme.

Clearly some changes can occur in a culture's general environment that are too massive to be accommodated within the existing framework of basic principles. In the minds of many, the Spanish conquests in America represent just such a culture shock in its most extreme form, so completely and abruptly obliterating the past that any reinterpretation or adjustment along existing lines is out of the question.[7] But was this in fact the case? The answer seems to be a qualified no: not entirely, not everywhere, not all at once. For some groups, in particular the advanced pre-Hispanic societies of the Andes and Mesoamerica, the immediate break with the past was only partial, occurring primarily at the level of the larger state systems that were of far less significance in the lives of most people than the local cults and the local power structures.[8] Further innovations came at a much slower pace. The cumulative effect would eventually be cultural extinction for some groups through assimilation into the dominant Spanish-mestizo society. For others, including the Yucatec Maya, it is still possible to speak of cultural survival—but survival of a particular sort. It is not the preservation of an unmodified cultural system under a veneer of Spanish customs, but the preservation of a central core of concepts and principles, serving as a framework within which modifications could be made and providing a distinctive shape to the new patterns that emerged. What this meant for the Maya was the persistence throughout the colonial period and beyond of a cultural configuration that became transformed under Spanish influence, but along Maya lines and in accordance with Maya principles. And thus it remained, for all the transformations, distinctively and identifiably Maya.

Such durability is possible only through creative adaptation—the capacity to forge something new out of existing elements in response to changing circumstances. The Maya's collective approach to survival continued to sustain the cosmic order and the social order, but by way of new forms of social action more acceptable to their colonial masters. The fact that adaptation and not total disintegration was the Maya response to conquest can be accounted for partly by their own resources, which included a cognitive framework for assimilating conquest and a set of strategies for accommodation, developed during a long pre-Hispanic history of foreign domination. But it was also (and perhaps primarily) due to the nature of the newly imposed conditions. If the Maya preserved more of their traditional way of life than many other similarly organized indigenous groups, the difference would seem to lie less in any inherent strength or staying power of Maya culture than in the more favorable environment of the particular colonial regime that was established in Yucatan.

THIS study begins with a discussion of the Spanish colonial regime in Yucatan (chapters 1-3) as the context for what will be an essentially Maya story. The regime itself is seen as a product of interaction, shaped as much by the local environment—including its human element—as by Spanish goals and institutions. In the economic sphere, lack of exportable resources and a consequently low level of Spanish immigration combined with a relative abundance of labor (despite the devastating effects of recurring plagues and famines) to retard the shift from a tribute economy to a market economy. In the political sphere, the heavy demographic imbalance served to favor a system of indirect rule; even the clergy, the principle agents of Spanish control, left much of the parish administration in the hands of the Maya elite. Less formal pressures for change were also weak, for, although much interaction and intermixture occurred across the boundaries of caste, the influence was not all in one direction. In language, diet, and many other domestic patterns, it was the Spanish who became assimilated into Maya culture.

Chapter 4 turns to the problem of Maya social bonding, as raised by various ecological, demographic, and economic models that fail to fit

9

the Maya case. An alternative model is offered, based on the collective conception of survival outlined above, with a discussion of the elite's role in warfare and divine mediation as the ideological foundation of dominance.

Chapters 5 to 7 analyze the disintegrating effects of colonial rule on an already fragile social order. The larger political structures of the Maya were fragmented into autonomous communities; within these communities and their component kin groups, cohesion was further undermined by Spanish demands and the ways these demands were imposed. Signs of strain were visible not so much in overt conflict as in the alternative and favored Maya response of flight: to the cities, across the colonial frontier, and to maize fields scattered in the bush. Movement to the embryonic Spanish haciendas—the small cattle ranches—was part of this dispersal process, offering for most of the colonial period far less onerous burdens than community life.

Chapters 8 to 11 provide an extended analysis of why, despite apparently ample cause and clear signs, the Maya social bond did not give way completely. One key was the territorial, genealogical, and functional continuity of the Maya nobility, even within outwardly changing political forms. Another, related key was the collective enterprise of survival, under elite management, which included techniques for mobilizing community resources and for defending these resources against Spanish threats. The forced introduction of Christianity presented the most serious challenge to the sociopolitical order. Chapters 10 and 11 analyze the effects of evangelization on Maya religious beliefs and rituals, not as a process of conversion but as an interchange on three levels, dealing with three types of sacred beings: private negotiation with lesser spirits; corporate support of tutelary deity-saints; and a more or less elaborated cult of homage to a supreme being. Mutually adaptable at the second level, Maya religion and Christianity merged into a syncretistic cult of the saints, which enabled the Maya elite, through the development of *cofradías* (parish confraternities) and the annual round of village fiestas, to recapture their control of public ritual and thus validate their continued control of wealth and power.

The final chapter is presented by way of a coda and a prelude. It outlines an accelerated thrust during the closing decades of Spanish rule to incorporate the conquered Maya more fully into the wider imperial system that had first cast its net over them almost three centuries before. This renewed assault, which I compare to a second conquest, met a delayed and ultimately unsuccessful resistance in a protracted war waged by the Maya during the latter half of the nineteenth century. The Caste War, as it is called, falls outside the chronological scope of this study but is in many ways its logical conclusion, feeding on three centuries of bitterness engendered by the first conquest and inflamed by the more recent impingements of the second. The second conquest inaugurated the Maya's confrontation with the modern world, a world shaped by economic developments far beyond their borders, yet one that reached out through rapidly expanding export demand to engulf Maya land and Maya labor. In retrospect, the original encounter with sixteenth-century Spain appears to be the much less devastating of the two.

PROLOGUE

Conquest

A case for the comparatively mild effects of Spanish colonization in Yucatan rests ultimately on the entire record of the colonial regime. Throughout most of the colonial period, Yucatan's position on the periphery of the Spanish empire preserved for the Maya a degree of isolation and autonomy that the Aztecs and other groups in the economic and political core had lost within decades of the conquest. But differences are apparent from the start, in the first confrontations between Indians and Spaniards in what is present-day Mexico. The conquest of Yucatan was a lengthy affair. The prolonged warfare produced much material devastation. Yet by the same token it represented a less abrupt and therefore a less traumatic break with the past than the rapid overthrow of the Aztec empire. Indeed, for large areas of Yucatan it is difficult to say exactly when the conquest ended and colonial rule began.

Yucatan was discovered in 1517 during a voyage of exploration out of Cuba. This first encounter with the more sophisticated Indians of the American mainland, who wore clothes, had stone buildings, and above all possessed gold, stimulated Spanish plans to colonize the new territory. But Yucatan itself was bypassed. A second voyage had received a friendlier reception and hints of more substantial wealth to the west. A third expedition, organized by Hernán Cortés in 1519, touched only briefly at Yucatan on the way to Veracruz and ultimately to Cortés's rendezvous with Moctezuma at Tenochtitlan.[1]

Only in 1527, after campaigns throughout the Mesoamerican highlands and into Honduras, did the Spanish turn their attention to Yucatan, under the leadership of one of Cortés's lieutenants, Francisco de Montejo. It took two full decades to conquer Yucatan, in contrast with a bare two years to subdue the Aztecs. The Maya had no overarching imperial structure that could be toppled with one swift blow to the center. Yucatan was divided into at least sixteen autonomous provinces with varying degrees of internal unity. Each of the provinces, and sometimes the subunits within them, had to be negotiated with, and failing that, conquered separately.

At times Yucatan must scarcely have seemed worth the trouble of conquest. Discontent with lack of gold thinned Montejo's ranks. The dense bush and pot-holed terrain of Yucatan proved difficult for horses and ill-suited to the pitched battles that favored Spanish weapons and tactics. Resistance was fierce in some areas and, worst of all, the Maya refused to stay conquered.

12

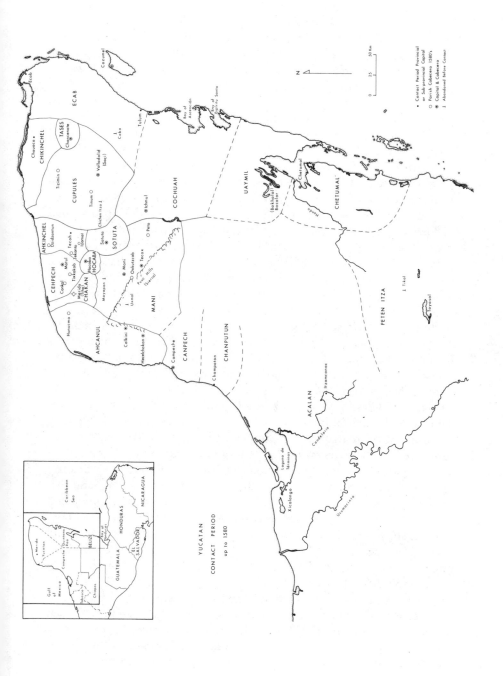

The conquest of Yucatan is generally considered to have ended with the suppression in 1547 of the Great Revolt, a large-scale uprising by the Maya of the entire central and eastern regions. The Spanish hold over the peninsula was never again seriously challenged, but it was incomplete and remained so throughout the colonial period. In a low-key and sporadic way, the conquest was to continue for centuries.

The initial thrust had stopped at the southern borders of the provinces of Mani and Cochuah. Beyond them lay a vast, barely explored region stretching through the Montaña district and the Peten to the settled foothills of Guatemala and Chiapas, a region bypassed and largely ignored after Cortés's brief swing through the heart of the area on his march from central Mexico to Honduras in 1525.[2] An isolated missionary outpost was founded in the Montaña district but lasted only from 1604 to 1614. In the east along the Caribbean coast the Spanish had subdued the provinces of Ecab, Uaymil, and Chetumal but failed to occupy them permanently, except for the fortified settlement of Bacalar at the base of the peninsula. For the first century and a half after the colony was established, the Spanish actually lost ground, pulling back from territory that they still nominally claimed but lacked the means and the incentive to control.

The colonists had settled in the most hospitable part of the peninsula, the northwest, where the Indians were more numerous and the drier climate proved more attractive to Europeans. Spanish influence remained concentrated in this region for the same related combination of factors. The rain forests of the Montaña and the Peten, once the teeming heartland of Classic Maya civilization, had already suffered a severe population decline (although exactly how severe is still debated) long before the Spanish arrived. The depopulation of the eastern and southwestern coastal provinces was their unwitting handiwork. Except for Uaymil and Chetumal, these provinces had all submitted to Spanish rule with little or no resistance, so that losses through warfare and disruptions in food production were minimal in most areas. Climate and strategic location, which had been the basis of their prosperity, now contributed to their decline. The moist climate, with heavier rainfall and more surface water, produced good crop yields but was also particularly congenial to many of the Old World pathogens introduced by the Spanish and their African slaves.

Equally devastating in its effects, though perhaps more difficult to measure, was the collapse of the Maya economy, which had been based largely on long-distance trade. At the time of contact vigorous commercial centers nearly ringed the peninsula from Chauaca in the north, down through Cozumel and Tulum on the Caribbean to Nito on the

14

1. View of Tulum, a late Postclassic "Putun" site on the east coast of Yucatan, near where Montejo's forces landed in 1527. Note the region's characteristically flat terrain in the background. (Photo by Arthur G. Miller)

Bay of Honduras, and across the base to the gulf coast. All were controlled by or affiliated with the "Putun," or Chontal Maya, in southwestern Campeche, who have been called the "Phoenicians of the New World."[3] Strategically located, they funneled goods between the peninsula and the highlands of Mexico and Central America. Even before the actual conquest of Yucatan, their traditional trade networks had been disrupted by the overthrow of the Aztec empire in central Mexico and of other trading partners in Guatemala and Honduras.[4]

By the time the Spanish turned their attention back from the northwestern part of the peninsula to these peripheral regions that had been so quickly and easily won (again, with the exception of Uaymil and Chetumal, which were virtually destroyed in a late, fierce campaign), they found them already in severe decline. What once had been flourishing zones were reduced to a few scattered settlements well before the

15

end of the sixteenth century. By the latter part of the seventeenth century these regions had been officially abandoned. Their strategic location had contributed to their further decline; for they were exposed to attack by French, Dutch, and English pirates who had been attracted to the Caribbean by Spanish wealth and had already begun to harass ships and settlements along Yucatan's coasts by the 1560s. Faced with the impossibility of defending the peninsula's long, exposed shoreline, except for the major port of Campeche (itself sacked several times), the Spanish decided to move the remnant Maya populations well inland and abandon the coasts to the "Lutheran corsairs."[5]

In the mid-seventeenth century the colonial frontier had contracted to a line curving from below Champoton up to the Puuc hills, across to Peto and Tihosuco, and then angling northeast to the Caribbean along a line now marking the boundary between the states of Yucatan and Quintana Roo. The territory beyond that frontier was officially referred to as *despoblado*, or uninhabited. In fact, it became the home of large numbers of refugees who fled colonial rule to form independent settlements of their own or to join their unconquered cousins, who held out in small pockets in the east and controlled all the territory to the south. They were never left totally in peace. Every so often a wave of evangelistic fervor would sweep through the local Franciscans, and a missionary or two would be dispatched into the bush to make or renew contact with any unconverted or apostate Maya they could locate. The Indians generally received them peacefully. On occasion they became exasperated into discourtesy and even threats, but only three unescorted missionaries are on record as having won the "crown of martyrdom" in the entire unpacified area.[6] The Maya were aware that resistance would provoke armed reprisals and they found it more prudent to feign submission, and then relocate their settlements or simply revert to former habits once the friars had left.[7]

Military expeditions were also undertaken sporadically by the Spanish to round up fugitives by force and resettle them in the pacified areas, and these raids seem to have cleared out a large part of the eastern region.[8] The Spanish could not, however, mount guard along the entire frontier, and as long as the large and accessible territory to the south remained unsubdued, the conquest of the rest of the peninsula could not be considered complete.

The existence of totally independent Maya polities, the largest and most powerful of them the Itza kingdom centered at Lake Peten, blurred the boundary between pre-Columbian and colonial, pagan and Christian, unconquered and conquered. The effect was analogous in kind if not in degree to that of the Inca state in exile that held out on the

16

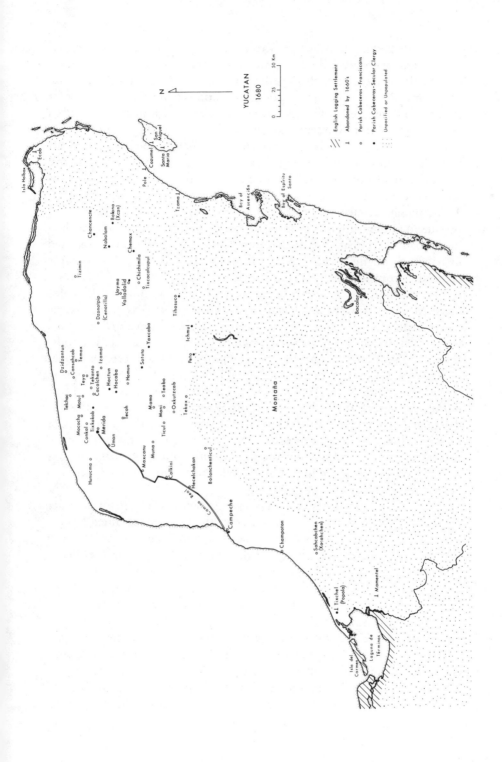

YUCATAN
1680

0   25   50 Km

/// English Logging Settlement

1   Abandoned by 1660's

o   Parish Cabeceras — Franciscans

•   Parish Cabeceras — Secular Clergy

∴   Unspecified or Unpopulated

N

Isla Holbox
Ecab 1

Cozumel 1
San Miguel 1
Santa Maria

Pole
Izamal 1

Bay of Ascención

Bay of Espíritu Santo

Chancenote o

Nabolam •
Boloná (Kaan) •

Chemax •

Tizimin o

Chichimila •
Tixcacalcupul •

Uayma o
Valladolid

Dzonotpip
(Cenotillo) o

Tihosuco o

Bacalar

Ichmul •

Peto •

Dzidzantun
o Cansahcab
Temax

Telchac
Mocochá
Conkal o
Tixkokob •
Merida
Úman o

Teya o
o Tekanto
Cacalchen
Hoctun •
Hocabá •
o Homun

Izamal
o

Montaña

Maxcanu o

Muna o

Teabo
o Oxkutzcab

Tekax o

Pecoh

Mama
Mani o

Tecoh •

Ticul o

Calkini •

Hecelchakan

Bolonchenticul •

Camino Real

Campeche

Champoton •

Sahcabchen
(Kcabchen) •

Tixchel
(Popola) 1 •

Montaña

Laguna de
Términos

Isla del
Carmen

1 Mamantel

borders of the kingdom of Peru for decades after the initial overthrow. In Yucatan, as in Peru, there was no clean break with the past on either side of the frontier, which the Maya found highly permeable in both directions. Refugees, raiding parties, delegations from the Itza and other groups, and, above all, traders moved back and forth in steady if often clandestine contact. We have no way of measuring the volume of the illicit trade, about which the Spanish had some notion but could not stop. Interregional commerce had been brisk in pre-Columbian times; it became reinforced by the new demand among both pagan and apostate Maya for the steel axes and other tools introduced by the Spanish. Trade in salt, which the west and north coasts of the peninsula had presumably long supplied to the interior, continued after conquest. It is more than likely that part of the honey and wax the Spanish collected in tribute from the pacified Maya for export to central Mexico came originally from the unconquered interior.[9]

The unconquered zones were an escape hatch for some of the colonized Maya; they were a cultural and political as well as an economic factor in the lives of all of them. Contact between separated kinsmen was not entirely broken, for news traveled rapidly with the trade goods. Even for the great majority of Maya who did not flee there, the zones of refuge were an ever-present and familiar (if only by hearsay) option rather than a frightening unknown. Masses of them chose this option during the latter part of the seventeenth century. They swelled the unconquered settlements in the south that seemed to be coalescing under a native "king." These groups became increasingly bold, raiding pacified border towns and making the not wholly bombastic claim of sovereignty over them.[10] Long at a standstill, the conquest now seemed to be going into reverse.

Despite some inconclusive forays into the Peten from Spanish settlements in Tabasco, Chiapas, and Yucatan, the interior remained largely outside Spanish control until 1697, when a combined expedition from Yucatan and Guatemala conquered the Itza kingdom.[11] Another series of expeditions in the early 1700s finally expelled the English from the Laguna de Términos, where a military outpost was established to protect Spanish settlements along the gulf en route toward Tabasco.[12] A new mission was founded in the interior west of Bacalar, and thin archipelagos of pacified villages grew up along the trails linking Yucatan with Bacalar and a new outpost at Lake Peten. The much acclaimed conquest of the Peten did not, however, destroy the zones of refuge. The groups of fugitives and unpacified Maya merely moved further into the bush, harassed by occasional raids but never totally reduced to Spanish rule.[13] Deep in the interior, the Lacandon Maya, survivors of this population, have never, strictly speaking, been conquered to this day.

When did the conquest of Yucatan actually end? In 1547, with the suppression of the Great Revolt? In 1697, with the conquest of the Peten? Some might consider the nineteenth-century Caste War as the final chapter, but then the conclusion of the Caste War itself is difficult to fix. Drawn into the factional strife of postindependence Yucatan and regaining a long dormant taste for military victory, the Maya launched their own struggle in 1847 to rid themselves of what they still regarded as foreign domination. For a brief time it looked as if they might succeed. From the east around Valladolid, Tihosuco, and Sotuta (the same regions that had united in the Great Revolt three hundred years earlier), the rebellion spread south to Bacalar and, much more menacingly, began to close in on Merida. The city and the whites who had taken refuge there were saved only by the "grace of God," the Maya term for maize. Reaching within attacking distance of Merida just as the rainy season was approaching, the Maya troops—farmers all—retreated to their villages and their maize fields. First things first: the maize had to be planted, tended, and harvested, and only then could they return to finish the war. But they had lost their chance. The *dzuls* (foreigners) were not, after all, to be driven out of Yucatan. On the other hand, the Maya never admitted defeat, either. They only retreated east again and established a rebel state around a Maya-Christian cult of a Speaking Cross, acquiring the name of *cruzob* Maya from the *Santa Cruz* or Holy Cross they worshiped. They actually managed to push the old colonial frontier back to its mid-seventeenth-century position, where it was to remain, with minor advances and retreats, for the next fifty years.[14]

In 1901 Chan Santa Cruz, the *cruzob* capital, fell to federal troops from central Mexico. Does this defeat mark the end of the Caste War and, along with it, the conquest of Yucatan? Or did both the war and the conquest continue for another sixty years or so? During this time the *cruzob* Maya still controlled the district into which they had retreated and which encompassed a large portion of the present state of Quintana Roo in eastern Yucatan. But perhaps the conquest was not complete until 1969, with the death of the chief of the *cruzob* town of Chumpom and the last of the Caste War leaders. His successors decided after much deliberation not to carry out their threat to attack the highway crew that pushed its way into the formerly isolated territory. Federal troops had been sent to guard the crew and the Maya had been unsuccessful in obtaining modern carbines to replace their antiquated firearms. The road was completed and the *cruzob* Maya, like it or not, are now being incorporated into the fabric of national society. Some of them hold jobs

19

with the national archaeological institute as custodians of the pre-Columbian sites in their areas; others have already been tapped for military service in the army that their grandfathers held off for so long.

MAYA PERCEPTIONS OF THE CONQUEST

The Yucatec Maya have left several accounts of the sixteenth-century Spanish conquest, accounts that differ markedly in tone and perspective from the Aztec versions. Their narratives of the arrival and military campaigns of the Spanish are spare and matter of fact.[15] And while there is a certain poignancy in the later chronicles that record the evil times ushered in by the conquest,[16] they lack the immediacy and grief-stricken anguish of the Aztec elegies for a world that had been suddenly and irrevocably shattered.[17] The contrast reflects, in part, different experiences: swift and total military defeat with the leveling of a mighty city to a heap of rubble, as opposed to a drawn-out series of skirmishes and battles carried on for the most part outside the population centers. It also reflects different perceptions of the significance of defeat and foreign domination.

The Spanish conquest was a particularly rude shock to the Aztecs because of their own mystique of invincibility based on a long, virtually unbroken record of military success. Foreign domination was an unfamiliar experience in the central highlands, where the pattern was conquest from within. The Aztecs, and the Toltecs before them, were outsiders originally, but they had arrived as humble migrants who gradually assimilated into and then dominated the local scene before expanding outward.

If the Mexican highlands were the dynamic center of expansion within Mesoamerica, Yucatan was a favored target, and the Maya had a long history of conquest to prepare them psychologically and cognitively for the arrival of the Spanish. The well-known "Toltec" invasion, which brought the cult of the Feathered Serpent (Quetzalcoatl-Kukulcan) and other distinctively highland influences to the peninsula in the late tenth century, was once thought to be unique. It is now seen by scholars as simply one of a series of more or less warlike intrusions into the lowlands, ranging in time from at least the early centuries of the Christian era down to the Spanish conquest itself.[18] The Spanish invasion could take its place in that series with little stretch of the imagination.

These intrusions were not always or necessarily full-scale invasions directly from the highlands. The lowland Maya engaged in much local warfare among themselves. Border conflicts and civil strife provided ideal opportunities for small groups of foreign adventurers, either Mex-

ican or Mexicanized intermediaries, to gain a foothold. Rather than replace the local contenders entirely, the foreigners joined in the fray,
jockeying for position by strategic alliances and eventually merging with
the local rulers through intermarriage. The struggle for control of the
late Postclassic center of Mayapan, abandoned in 1441, provides one of
the better-known examples, involving at least three different foreign
groups of varying antiquity in the peninsula. The Cocom lineage, identified with the former rulers of Chichen Itza, was overthrown by the
more recently established Xiu, despite the aid of Mexican troops, and
these latest arrivals were then able to establish themselves as local rulers
in the Ah Canul province.[19]

The record of these past invasions was well preserved in the Maya's
written chronicles and oral traditions.[20] The memory was kept fresh by
the expansionist activities of the Chontal Maya traders and by the continued presence of Mexican troops in their trading enclave at Xicalango
on the shores of the Laguna de Términos (the source of the earlier Cocom allies). At the time of the Cortés expedition the Aztecs are reported
to have assembled a large force in Xicalango under Moctezuma's brother
for yet another major invasion, a plan that was thwarted only by the
collapse of the Aztec empire at the center.[21]

Whether or not the Maya were expecting this particular invasion,
Spanish actions followed patterns familiar enough to suggest that history was repeating itself. And since the Maya's entire view of time was
based on the conviction that each of their twenty-year *katun* periods
repeated itself with the same recurring events at 256-year intervals (with
no doubt some ex post facto juggling to make the proper fit), the suggestion must have had compelling force. The Spanish arrived in small
numbers, invading the peninsula both via the east coast into the interior
around Chichen Itza as the Itza had done perhaps eight centuries before,
and then via Tabasco into Campeche, the route of more recent penetra-
tions. They quickly adopted the local stiffened cotton quilting for armor
instead of steel cuirasses. In their second invasion they even brought
central Mexican (Aztec and Tlaxcalan) troops, whose participation in
the conquest meant in a sense that Moctezuma's original scheme was
not totally aborted. These auxiliaries, like their predecessors, settled in
Yucatan as conquerors. They retained throughout the colonial period
the special privileges granted them by the Spanish for their services, and
they followed precedent by merging genetically and culturally with the
conquered Maya.[22] Thus it was not only due to the Maya's cyclical view
of time, in which history and prophecy are intertwined in recurring
patterns, that the major pre-Columbian invasions (called "descents" by

the Maya) are often hard to distinguish from the Spanish in the native chronicles.

The Maya did not confuse the fair-skinned bearded Spaniards with Mexicans, whom they knew well as trading partners as well as potential conquerors. But neither did they take them for gods. The Spaniards must have been a strange and frightening sight with their "thunder sticks," their horses, and their fierce hunting dogs. But the Maya were not troubled by the same perceptual problems that initially paralyzed the Aztecs, who were at first unsure whether the newcomers were gods, emissaries of gods, or mere men and therefore vacillated in their reactions to them.[23] We find no supernatural overtones in the Maya's responses. They seem to have accepted the Spanish simply as some kind of human strangers and to have acted on purely pragmatic political grounds in dealing with them, according to how they calculated their best interests.[24]

In view of the fragmented political structure of the lowland Maya, it is not surprising that their interests were narrowly conceived, often in terms of possible advantages to be gained against neighboring groups. Interprovincial rivalries, sometimes based on centuries-old traditions of enmity, prevented the Maya from uniting against the intruders. Foreign conquerors throughout history have profited from this kind of provincialism that, with hindsight, seems so myopic. The Maya leaders, like many others in similar circumstances, sought to place the newcomers into the existing framework of the region's politics, without realizing that the new element would destroy the framework and thus render obsolete the basis of their calculations.

Some of the Maya lords chose a policy of active cooperation, joining the invaders in the conquest of neighboring provinces. Such alliances seem to have been a traditional expedient in local warfare. Many of the Maya lords were of foreign origin themselves and at least some had gained ascendancy through similar means. In theory, all the lowland Maya dynasties traced descent from one or another earlier group of conquerors as part of their claim to rulership, no matter how remote the ancestral ties. Some were, however, of more recent stock, and it is among these comparative newcomers, such as the Chontal Maya on the gulf and east coasts, the Pech, Chel, and Canul dynasties, and most notably the Xiu rulers of Mani province, that the Spanish found the friendliest receptions.[25]

In the interior of the peninsula, among the Cupul, the Cochuah, and the Cocom (of Sotuta), the Spanish met with unrelenting resistance from beginning to end—and beyond. For these same provinces joined forces again in the Great Revolt of 1546-1547. The antecedents of the Cochuah have not been recorded, but it is perhaps no coincidence that the most unequivocal enemies of the Spanish were the Cupul and the Co-com, the two most ancient ruling lineages in Yucatan, who traced their ancestry back to the Itza invaders who had established their capital at Chichen Itza.[26] They were presumably more thoroughly Mayanized, certainly more isolated from foreign influences, and possibly for that reason more hostile to outsiders, especially Mexican outsiders.

Only in retrospect does the policy of resistance seem the more astute choice or at least the more farsighted one. We cannot credit Nachi Co-com, the lord of Sotuta, with any clearer insights into the consequences of Spanish victory than his neighbor and enemy, Tutul Xiu of Mani, who chose to ally himself with the Spaniards. All the Maya rulers drew on more or less the same historical traditions, and all of them must have been dealing in their calculations, based on the region's past experience, with questions of political power, not cultural survival. They merely reached different conclusions about how best to preserve or enhance their own power.

However unwelcome domination by foreigners had been in the past, leaving a legacy of resentment that can be detected in the later chroni-cles, it does not seem to have been coupled in the minds of the Maya with devastating culture shock. Mexicans, after all, were part of the larger Mesoamerican civilization that had come to share many basic features through centuries of interaction. Some of the influences trickled in through the peaceful vehicle of long-distance trade; some were im-posed by force. Foreigners had left traces of their impact in the style of public monuments, in Nahuatl words incorporated into the vocabulary, in new deities added to the local pantheon, and in other innovations.[27] There is evidence that the old guard continued to find some of these innovations very distasteful.[28] But the Yucatec Maya had shown a ca-pacity again and again to absorb alien influences without being over-whelmed by them.

Immediate impressions of the Spanish were in this context reassuring, giving the Maya little hint that anything drastically different was in store for them. Aside from bringing familiar Mexican auxiliaries with them, with their familiar central Mexican *atl-atls*, or spear throwers, and aside from following the usual invasion routes, the Montejos (father, son, and nephew all confusingly bearing the same name of Francisco) pursued prudent and—again—familiar policies in their dealings with the Maya lords. They always sought to negotiate a peaceful agreement first, often sending ahead native emissaries. They offered, and initially hon-ored, highly reasonable terms that left the local power structure intact under Spanish overlordship.[29] None of the native rulers was deposed. Even the implacable Nachi Cocom retained his position, as did the other leaders of the Great Revolt, despite the fact that they, having once taken an oath of fealty to the Crown, were all in Spanish eyes guilty of treason.

The terms of submission to Spanish authority included, along with the loss of autonomy and the exaction of tribute (a galling but predictable price of conquest), the acceptance of Christianity. It is unlikely that this acceptance implied for the Maya lords any radical break with the past. The introduction of new religious cults by a conquering group—cults that would coexist along with the old—was a Mesoamerican tradition. That Christianity was an exclusive religion, one that demanded the total extinction of the Maya's own beliefs and deities, would not have been immediately apparent. Montejo, though by all accounts a devout Christian, was no religious zealot. Neither he nor the chaplains who accompanied his forces were given to dramatic scenes of idol smashing of the sort indulged in by Cortés. This was in part because Maya idolatries, which did not involve human sacrifice on any large scale, outraged Spanish sensibilities considerably less than the gory spectacles of the Aztecs. But only in part, for Cortés had already started his iconoclastic activities on the Maya island of Cozumel.

Evangelization was a decidedly low-key affair in Yucatan during the initial stages of contact. Several local lords, we are told, sought baptism, although it is hard to say what significance they attached to this ceremony, since none of the few clergymen who accompanied the Spanish forces ever learned the Maya language, and all confined themselves almost exclusively to their duties as military chaplains.[30] The old cults persisted virtually unchallenged in practice. No churches were built for the Indians and no organized program of conversion was undertaken until a handful of Franciscan missionaries arrived at the end of 1544 or early in 1545.[31]

The conquest itself brought much suffering, as any protracted military struggle will do. Reprisals and systematic devastation were, however, limited to the Uaymil and Chetumal districts under the desperate and semi-independent campaign of the Pachecos, although other provinces also resisted as stubbornly. Montejo had rivals and enemies within his own ranks, and if he had countenanced or committed similar acts of cruelty and indiscriminate slaughter (which also characterized Spanish campaigns in the Caribbean islands, in Panama, and in Mexico under Cortés's successor, Nuño de Guzmán), his accusers would have mentioned them in the detailed inquiry into his conduct ordered by the Crown. The one major accusation against him that involved the Indians, as opposed to acts deemed detrimental to the interests of the Crown or his fellow Spaniards, was the shipment of prisoners of war to central

Mexico for sale as slaves.[32] Whether consciously or not, Montejo had merely followed local tradition. Slaves had been one of Yucatan's principal exports in pre-Columbian times, and slave taking a major incentive for the endemic border warfare in the region. Montejo's local allies were induced to aid in suppressing the Great Revolt (and most likely to aid in the original conquest) with the promise that they could continue their custom of enslaving the prisoners they captured.[33] Far more objectionable and portentous from the Maya rulers' point of view than Montejo's slave trading must have been the Crown's subsequent order emancipating all slaves in the recently conquered territory, whether owned by Indians or Spaniards.

During the first decades of confrontation with the Spanish, then, the Maya had little cause to believe that this latest incursion would not take its place in the same recurrent pattern of earlier conquests. Logically, this small band of warriors, vastly outnumbered and far from their home base, would be assimilated into the local elite like their Mexican predecessors. A few adjustments would have to be made: some loss of autonomy, new gods added to the local pantheon, extra tribute. Disagreeable, perhaps, but hardly intolerable. If some of the Maya lords expected a replay of previous episodes of foreign hegemony, the prohibition against slavery, which represented an important source of their wealth, was simply one of the many unpleasant surprises in store for them as the new overlords set about turning the conquered territory into a colony organized according to entirely alien principles.

Perhaps the Maya never perceived or acknowledged the full significance of the Spanish conquest. Along with a sense of grievance and loss, their later accounts of the conquest reveal that they retained from the pre-Columbian past their cyclical view of time, which under the circumstances must have been a great source of comfort. According to this view, all human history repeats itself in the same orderly fashion as the recurrent movement of the heavenly bodies. All things, good and bad, have their appointed time to end and to be repeated in an endless cycle, in which past is prophecy and prophecy is the past.[34] The persistence of this sustaining cosmology (when it was lost, if ever, is uncertain)[35] is symptomatic of the resilience of Maya culture. Some of the resilience rested on a history of accommodation already sketched out. Much, however, was due to the circumstances of colonial rule itself. Conquest, which was less immediately catastrophic for the Maya than for the Aztecs—less literally world shattering as an event—was also to prove less destructive in its long-term implications.

25

PART ONE
THE IMPLICATIONS
OF CONQUEST

· 1 ·

A COLONIAL REGIME

The Spanish carried with them to America a shared system of values and a shared set of social institutions that had been distilled from the rich diversity of forms throughout the Iberian homeland.[1] Yet from this common colonial blueprint regional differences quickly emerged in the New World in response to particular local conditions, and the colonial experience of the indigenous peoples varied accordingly.

Two basic goals stimulated the enterprise of the Indies. The soldier–chronicler Bernal Díaz del Castillo has expressed them in his customarily plain-spoken fashion: "To bring light to those in darkness, and also to get rich, which is what all of us men commonly seek."[2] In offering this epitaph for his comrades killed in the conquest of Mexico, Díaz summarized the guiding principles of the Spanish imperial system for the next three centuries. Only the order of priorities is in question. For all the complexities and contradictions that this system contained, it is hard to escape the conclusion that the dominant principle—the least dependent of all the variables that shaped the colonial regimes—was the search for wealth.

No one familiar with the history of Spanish colonization in the New World can doubt the sincerity of the first motive. Saving Indian souls was a genuine concern, not only to the friars who devoted their lives to this task, but also to the Crown and in varying degrees to the majority of conquerors, bureaucrats, and ordinary settlers who migrated to America. Despite the famous theological debates carried on during the sixteenth century over the morality of the conquest and the methods of conversion, few Spaniards saw any contradiction between the spiritual and material goals of colonization. And there is a certain logic to their position. Spain's relentless pursuit of wealth in America did not preclude the expenditure of considerable effort, and even some financial subsidies, to bring the Indians into the Christian fold.[3] That the Spaniards' economic interests came into conflict with the Indians' temporal welfare is, theologically speaking, another matter altogether. The boon of eternal salvation remains no less valid for being accompanied by economic exploitation. Rather, the risk of damnation is borne by the soul of the exploiter, not the exploited. The fact that all but a small proportion of Spaniards in America were prepared to take this risk in no way nullified the spiritual efficacy of the mission.

29

This mission was, however, functionally if not ideologically subordinate to Bernal Díaz's second goal—getting rich. Fray Bartolomé de Las Casas, the most ardent champion of Indian interests, never argued that the missionary effort in America could be sustained without colonization. And as Las Casas learned himself, colonization required the incentive of economic gain. The same incentive fueled the colonizing ventures of other European nations. They simply felt no need to apologize for it.

If the goal of wealth was the prime mover within the Spanish imperial system, without regard to time or place, ideas on how best to obtain it and spend it were also universally shared. Economic concepts were enviably simple, unclouded by theoretical subtleties and competing econometric models. Wealth consisted of gold and silver and ultimately what they could buy in the European market. One either amassed gold and silver in order to return home to live in a grand manner,[4] or one exported these same commodities, along with other less valuable but still salable products, in exchange for European goods, so that a similar manner of life could be recreated in America. Wealth was intimately bound up with the concept of *hidalguía*, a nobility of style as well as of birth that required among other things that one's wealth be produced by the labor of the lower orders.[5] Since every Spaniard, regardless of social origin, obtained a psychological patent of nobility on his passage to the New World, the lower orders came to mean in the colonial system the Indians, imported Africans, and any mixed-blood descendants of the two.

For the Indians, then, as for all groups brought under European domination, the primary consequence of the domination on which all others hinged was incorporation into a global commercial system. Major variations in the colonial experience, including the degree to which other aspects of Spanish rule impinged on the lives and consciousness of the Indians, can ultimately be traced to differences in the pace and mode of incorporation. These differences in turn depended on how the local environment, both human and physical, modified the more or less standard colonial model the Spanish sought to apply.

A COLONIAL BACKWATER

Yucatan, to the good fortune of the Maya Indians and the sore disappointment of their conquerors, was extremely poor in what Europeans then or now would define as natural resources. However much some colonial eulogists might emphasize the rich variety and abundance of the exotic local flora and wildlife,[6] they could not disguise the fact that the region contained scarcely any commercially exploitable resources—

30

that is, anything in demand on the European market. Above all, it lacked precious metals. The early Spanish explorers found a few gold ornaments in the Maya temples, which at first had aroused visions of great riches in the area. The gold, as it turned out, was all imported from the highlands. Yucatan is an ancient coral reef exposed by a subsiding sea; had the explorers possessed even the most elementary geological knowledge available today, one glance at Yucatan's karst limestone would have told them that nowhere on the peninsula would they find gold or any other valuable mineral.

The local climate was also uncongenial. Aside from the steamy heat, which the Spanish found enervating, and the teeming population of noxious insects, all the lowlands of the Caribbean and Pacific coasts gained a deserved reputation as deathtraps. Malaria and a daunting variety of other tropical fevers and parasites, either indigenous to the region or imported from Africa, weakened resistance to other diseases when they did not kill outright. Most European crops and animals fared worse than the human migrants. Wheat cannot be grown in Yucatan. Sheep do not thrive. Cattle, horses, and mules will survive but are stunted by parasites and poor pasture. It is little wonder that the Spanish preferred to settle in the cooler, drier valleys and plateaus of the highlands, where they could live more comfortably, grow wheat, and raise large herds of sheep and beef cattle with little effort.

If climate were the only consideration, they also would have flocked to the temperate pampas of Argentina and Uruguay, now among the world's major producers of beef and wheat. But the highlands, as it happened, also contained exceedingly rich deposits of high-grade silver ore mixed with some gold. The great silver-mining industries that developed in Mexico and Peru and, to a lesser extent, the gold fields of Colombia (the colonial Nueva Granada) fueled the entire colonial economy. Silver attracted Spanish immigrants and stimulated most of the auxiliary enterprises that they and the mining industry demanded— transportation, construction, commercial agriculture, and manufacturing. Bullion exports paid for the luxury goods the Spanish imported from Europe and Asia. They largely determined the location of administrative centers and commercial routes. And these routes in turn determined what other export products would find an outlet.

Precious metals also paid for the expressions of colonial grandeur, public and private, that are the architectural and artistic legacy of Spanish rule. If anyone doubts the disparity in wealth between Yucatan and central Mexico, Peru, or even Colombia, a brief stroll around a few central plazas will provide ample visual proof. The colonial architecture of Merida, impressive sometimes in its sturdy bulk, contrasts in its plainness and crudity with the baroque splendors of a Puebla, a Oaxaca, a Popoyán—to say nothing of the magnificent monuments of Mexico City or Lima. Only one carved façade is to be found in the whole city, that of the Montejo residence situated at right angles to the cathedral;[7] not a single gilded retable in the whole province. None of the testaments or inventories from the period hints of the prodigal displays of wealth characteristic of the central Mexican magnates. If any of the local elite had palaces filled with silver platters and candelabra, or a gorgeous coach flanked by a large retinue of liveried servants, they have guarded the secret well from posterity. A slave or two, a modest amount of gold jewelry, some silver forks and spoons, and perhaps a two-wheeled calash: these were the signs of opulence in colonial Merida and Campeche.[8]

The lack of precious metals, more than any disadvantages of climate, is what condemned the region to poverty. Yucatan managed to achieve the status of colonial backwater even before it became a colony, when news of the riches found by Francisco Pizarro in Peru caused mass desertions among the forces Montejo had recruited for his own campaigns.[9] The Spanish empire contained many poor, peripheral areas that failed to attract large numbers of settlers. Indeed, the majority of the colonies would fall into that category. What distinguished Yucatan from the rest was the combination of a dearth of natural resources with a relative abundance of human resources.

The advanced pre-Columbian civilizations with their large sedentary populations were confined for the most part to the highlands. The Maya lowlands, along with the southern gulf coast of Mexico and the river valleys of coastal Peru, were the exceptions. How much more densely settled Yucatan was to begin with, compared to other tropical lowland areas, is unknown. Certainly the demographic decline that followed contact (to be discussed in the next chapter) was considerably less severe. With this one exception, the ethnic map of Spanish America became increasingly divided by altitude. Africans and mulattoes virtually replaced Indians in the lowlands. Europeans and mestizos came to predominate in the plateaus; and Indians remained the major ethnic group only in the highlands. Yucatan's peculiar combination of lack of economic opportunity and a large labor force (only Chiapas comes to mind as remotely comparable) explains its particular type of backwardness: the long reliance on Indian tribute in various forms as the colonists' economic base.

All the Spanish colonial regimes were initially founded on tribute. In all of them, the Spanish extracted directly from the Indian economy whatever local commodities they could trade overseas, as well as the goods and services they needed to sustain themselves. In most regions this primitive system soon proved inadequate, as the Indian populations declined rapidly and the ranks of the conquerors were swelled by new arrivals intent on gaining a share of the spoils. In order to generate wealth, sometimes merely to feed their growing numbers, the Spanish had to organize production themselves. Even in the areas where Indians survived in large numbers, tribute was relegated to a very minor role in the total economy compared to the mining enterprises, the haciendas, and the small factories producing textiles for the colonial market, all of them using Indian labor but owned and operated by Spaniards.[10]

The Spanish in Yucatan (where all those of Spanish descent, whether born in Spain or America, were designated as "Spaniards") lacked equivalent incentives to transform the native economy. They faced no risk of starvation. Except during the periodic droughts that assailed the peninsula, the Indians continued to supply a sufficient surplus of the traditional foodstuffs from their own system of subsistence agriculture. However distasteful maize and beans may have been to the European palate, they happened to be the only staple crops the region could produce.

Out of preference, not necessity, the colonists began to establish cattle ranches soon after the conquest in order to supplement the local diet with beef. For almost two centuries, stock raising remained the only agrarian enterprise they engaged in on a commercial scale, and a very minor one at that. In Yucatan, as elsewhere within the empire, the landed estate was to be the principal vehicle for incorporating the Indians into the market economy, eventually absorbing most of the land and along with it most of the rural population. When not drawn fully into the hacienda's orbit as resident peons, Indians served either by legal obligation or economic necessity as a reserve pool of part-time and seasonal labor. This process of absorption was virtually complete in central Mexico by the beginning of the seventeenth century.[11] In Yucatan it stretched well past independence and in some parts of the peninsula scarcely advanced at all.

Appearing first in the immediate vicinity of Merida by the 1580s, cattle ranches, or *estancias*, spread outward along the three main routes of Spanish penetration into the Maya countryside: east to the secondary Spanish center of Izamal, southwest through the Sierra or Mani district to Peto, and south along the *camino real* (royal road) that linked Merida with the port of Campeche.[12] Wherever Spaniards settled, *estancias* followed, even reaching the remote and isolated districts around the military outposts of Bacalar and, in the eighteenth century, Peten Itza and Laguna de Términos.[13]

Stock raising met with few obstacles in Yucatan. If the climate was not ideal, land was at least abundant and therefore cheap. The initial investment of about one hundred pesos to purchase a parcel of land, several cows, a bull, a horse, and a few accoutrements was small even in local terms.[14] Primitive methods of animal husbandry demanded little in the way of labor. The animals roamed semiwild through the bush, requiring hand watering wherever surface sources of water were scarce but otherwise receiving little attention except at the annual roundups for branding and head counts. Nevertheless, as a commercial enterprise ranching also found little stimulus for growth. *Estancias* remained concentrated along the original lines of expansion in the north and west, close to such internal markets and export outlets as the colony offered, and even there they developed at a laggardly pace.

For much of their history the *estancias* in Yucatan were modest operations by almost any standards, pitifully so by those of central and northern Mexico. In the district of Guadalajara, two ranchers were reported to have branded a total of 75,000 calves on their estates in one year, 1586.[15] Two centuries later the entire colony of Yucatan could not have equalled this production. Only a handful of late colonial estates possessed herds numbering more than a thousand; more commonly they included only a few hundred cattle and a dozen or so horses and mules.[16]

Inventories of the period reveal how very primitive these ranching establishments tended to be. The *planta*, as the central core of the *estancia* was called in Yucatan, normally consisted of a few corrals, some watering troughs, a *noria* (a bucket-type water wheel powered by mules or horses), and a few pole-and-thatch dwellings for the small, full-time staff of foreman and one or two ranch hands.[17] The main house was as often as not of the same simple construction. Although stone buildings began to appear on the larger estates before independence, the imposing structures that now form the decaying hacienda centers almost all date from the era of henequen, the hemplike fiber that brought such prosperity to Yucatan in the nineteenth century.

A key measure of Yucatan's lag behind the core colonies is the retarded development of the landed estate.[18] Exactly how retarded is open to some question,[19] depending upon the particular yardstick one uses. The relevant one here is the role of the estate within the local economy. For much of its history that role was a distinctly minor one. The Spanish relied on the independent Indian producer for most of what they consumed and exported. *Estancias* increased in size and number; some of the larger ones began to grow maize, not only to feed the cowhands and the owner's household, but also for the urban market. Yet as late as 1763 the public granary in Campeche obtained 77 percent of its maize

34

2. Colonial hacienda. The main house and gate are of typical late colonial
construction, with the addition of a chimney stack for the henequen mill and
a windmill replacing the original *noria*. (Photo courtesy of *National Geographic Magazine*, Otis Imboden)

from independent milpa farmers—that is, Indians and, increasingly in
this district, mulattoes and mestizos. And some undetermined portion
of the maize supplied by the Spanish estates was also purchased from
the small producers.[20]

Only in the final decades before independence did landed estates begin
to dominate the agricultural production and, by extension, the economy
of the region, both of which began to expand dramatically during the
last quarter of the eighteenth century. This late spurt of growth, which
will be discussed in chapter 12, was impressive only in comparison with
the slow, if not to say altogether sluggish, tempo of the preceding centuries, and the transformation of Yucatan's agrarian structures was still
far from complete. The eastern part of the peninsula was scarcely touched,
and something like two-thirds of the colony's Indian population still

lived as independent milpa farmers in their own communities at the turn of the century.[21]

The lack of export opportunities that for so long inhibited Yucatan's development was the result of commercial rather than geographical isolation. The province was well placed between the two principal sea routes linking the colonies with Spain. Both the silver fleets, one with its depot in Panama and the other in nearby Veracruz, had to sail almost within hailing distance of the peninsula's northern tip to reach their homeward rendezvous in Havana. Only bad weather or navigational error caused any of the trans-Atlantic ships to stop in Yucatan, more often than not piled up on one of its reefs.[22] Yucatan was singularly unsuccessful in gaining any share in the overseas trade, in part because nature had endowed the region so poorly but also because the resulting commercial isolation simply reinforced itself.

Local soil and climate, it is true, were ill-suited for some tropical cash crops like cacao, which brought a modest prosperity to the adjacent province of Tabasco and the Pacific coasts of Central America. Still, Yucatan could produce several items eminently salable in Europe but which the colony somehow failed to exploit. A short-lived experiment with indigo began within a few decades of the conquest and was abandoned before the end of the century.[23] The Franciscan missionaries strongly opposed the use of Indian labor in this enterprise because of its exceedingly unhealthy effects. Indigo releases a highly toxic substance during processing but presumably no more toxic in Yucatan than in other areas where similar opposition had little effect. One can only surmise that the colonists capitulated so easily on this issue because of competition from Guatemala. Cochineal, another dyestuff introduced in the early 1600s, met a similar fate, although its production aroused no humanitarian objections. Here the source of competition was Oaxaca, which had easier access to the major commercial axis of Mexico City and Veracruz.[24]

Competition from another quarter accounted for the failure to profit from the extensive stands of *palo de campeche*, or dyewood, which were found exclusively on the coasts of Yucatan. It was the English who supplied this valuable commodity to the textile industry in Europe, including to Spain itself.[25] Their logging camps and bases along the coast were left in peace, as Spain's declining naval forces concentrated on protecting the more valuable bullion exports. Not until the mid-eighteenth century, after the English had been expelled from southern Campeche, could the Spanish begin logging operations on any significant scale. Even then they made only a minor dent in the English monopoly, which still controlled the main source of supply around Belize and could ship directly to the major European markets, thus bypassing the restrictions that inhibited the flow and raised the price of Spanish colonial goods.

Whether or not these restrictions were deliberately designed by Spanish merchants to keep volume low and prices high, as the English alleged,[26] they were a great inducement to smuggling. The volume of contraband trade is impossible to calculate; like any undercover activity, only its failures and not its successes found their way into official records. Two inspectors reporting in 1766 on the state of the colony were able to collect only circumstantial but nonetheless damning evidence. The latest official port registers of 1764 had recorded no legal entry of fine linens, cambrics, and other European textiles, and yet the colony was amply supplied with these and other undeclared imports.[27] They are precisely the type of goods that Jamaican merchants listed as being transshipped to the Bay of Honduras, where the miserable little English settlements of dyewood loggers managed to sustain a brisk commerce in luxury goods out of all proportion to their size and wealth.[28]

By the end of the seventeenth century, when other European nations had become firmly settled in the area, the Caribbean was a smuggler's paradise. And so it remains today. Detection is difficult and officials have always been accommodating, for a price, when they have not organized the smuggling networks themselves. It has been suggested that this was the case in colonial Central America.[29] In Yucatan, the post of *vigía*, or coastal lookout—a job with low pay, primitive living conditions, and few Indians to exploit as an added enticement—did not, revealingly, suffer from any lack of well-connected applicants.[30]

Nevertheless, it would be difficult to assign contraband trade more than a minor role in Yucatan's economy. Without it Yucatan, like the Río de la Plata and other peripheral regions, would have been even more isolated, but it could not provide the same stimulus for development as legal trade. The reasons why are no doubt complex. Any patriotic distaste for dealing with the enemy would be strongly reinforced among Spaniards living in the New World by a well-founded antipathy toward and distrust of foreigners who might as easily come to raid as to trade. More basically, contraband trade may have been limited by the same factors that contributed to neglect under the rigidly controlled flota system in the first place—the paucity of easily marketable export goods. Contraband trade could not alter the dismal fact that Yucatan had nothing to offer the foreigners in Europe or the New World, or at any rate nothing profitable enough to justify the added risks and uncertainties entailed in circumventing the law on both sides of the exchange.[31] Clandestine trade is always attended by a certain amount of

37

extra bother and risk and therefore favors items of low bulk and high value. In our own day gold and gems, narcotics and small arms fit the bill. It is hard to imagine similar enthusiasm for an illicit trade in palm oil or bauxite.

Perhaps Yucatan supplied some of the cheap provisions that the English sugar islands preferred to import rather than devote their valuable acreage to feeding slaves, although it is doubtful that Yucatan could have competed with legal imports from the North American colonies.[32] The spurt in Yucatan's legal trade in the late colonial period, after the lifting of trade restrictions within the empire,[33] was based mainly on such unglamorous commodities as maize, beans, salt beef, and pork, tallow, lard, lumber, and cordage—all exported to ports in the Spanish Caribbean.[34] Liberalized trade within the Spanish orbit was the key to Yucatan's economic expansion, reinforced later by concessions granted to neutral shipping. These innovations, by increasing the volume and lowering the costs and risks of trade, could finally make Yucatan's bulky, low-profit goods competitive.

Spanish officials occasionally complained that the local elite lacked enterprise.[35] It is true that after the immediate postconquest period, marked by optimism and experimentation, a certain entrepreneurial torpor settled on the colony. The fault would seem to lie mainly with the larger commercial system of the empire. When trade restrictions were loosened toward the end of colonial rule and then lifted altogether after independence and new markets opened up for Yucatan's products, this same elite found no difficulty in rousing themselves to take advantage of the new opportunities.

Not until the nineteenth century did Yucatan finally find in henequen fiber a product that the economically advanced areas of the world wanted and which was not more easily available elsewhere. Before then its participation in the global economy was almost entirely indirect, through interregional trade, and mainly through the secondary metropolis of central Mexico. For much of the colonial period its external trade followed the pattern already established in pre-Columbian times, exchanging raw or only slightly processed materials from the lowlands for manufactured goods from the highlands to be consumed by the local elite. The tastes of the new elite differed, and many of the goods they imported originated in Europe (more rarely in Asia via the Manila galleon) rather than in the highland manufacturing centers. The products that Yucatan shipped out were the same: *mantas*, or lengths of cotton cloth, and beeswax,[36] followed by honey and salt—all traditional tribute goods that the Indians continued to supply in the traditional way.

Using Indian corvée labor, the Spanish eventually took over the principal coastal salt flats.[37] Except for salt and stock raising, they were content to leave production in the hands of the Indians once the fledgling indigo and cochineal industries had died out. No textile factories were established during the entire colonial period. The Maya women wove the cotton *mantas*, by far the chief export item, at home on their backstrap looms. Maya milpas and gardens supplied the raw cotton, as well as most of the maize, beans, chile, and poultry that fed the town dwellers. Maya apiaries supplied a portion of the beeswax and honey, and the rest was gathered wild in the forests along with such minor exports as deer hides and sarsaparilla root.[38]

These humble, everyday articles were hardly the stuff to sustain fantasies of El Dorado. But they were all that Yucatan had, or could sell, at the time. And tribute would continue to be the Spaniards' main source of wealth and basic sustenance long after the core colonies had shifted to a more complex commercial economy.

TRIBUTE AND ITS VARIANTS

Tribute took a variety of guises. There was, first of all, the ordinary tribute that Indians paid to individual Spaniards under the *encomienda* system, or to the Crown when *encomiendas* were transferred to direct royal control. *Encomiendas* were in most areas a transitional institution, grants of Indians to conquerors and other early settlers, under which the Spaniards obtained material support in return, supposedly, for tutelage and the supervision of the Indians' conversion to Christianity. The long and stable history of the *encomienda* in Yucatan is symptomatic of the region's backwardness in general and most especially its feeble economic growth. This the Crown openly acknowledged. With the sole exception of the Montejo family's grants, confiscated within decades of the conquest, the private *encomienda* was allowed to continue in Yucatan until 1786.[39] By then abolition raised only a subdued murmur of protest, since over the years ordinary tribute had come to represent a smaller and smaller share of the colonists' income. Very early on, with the first *tasación*, or official assessment, of 1549,[40] tribute had become a fixed quota of goods, which, after several reductions, became set at a rate equivalent in cash to fourteen reales (eight reales = one peso) a year for men and eleven reales for women.[41] The number of Indian tributaries declined during the sixteenth and seventeenth centuries, in absolute terms and even more so in proportion to the number of Spaniards, all seeking to live one way or another from Indian labor. At the same time the Crown ate steadily into the dwindling *encomienda* revenues with an increasing burden of taxes on the income.[42]

The decline in the gross and net income from *encomiendas* did not, however, stimulate a corresponding shift to a market economy to take up the slack. For in the meantime the Spanish, *encomenderos* and non-*encomenderos* alike, had been turning their creative energies to expanding the original tribute system. When I say that Yucatan's colonial economy was based on tribute, I mean tribute in this larger sense of all the substitutes and supplements devised to bypass the strict royal laws regulating what was officially termed tribute. This official tribute was sacrosanct and not to be tampered with. The royal conscience could rest easily so long as these laws were strictly enforced, while it ignored the fact that some kind of direct appropriation from the Indians was all that stood between the local Spaniards and a totally threadbare existence.

The clergy exacted their own form of tribute, which the Franciscan missionaries tactfully called *limosnas* (alms) in keeping with the order's rule that its members should be supported solely by voluntary contributions from the faithful. Unlike civil tribute, *limosnas* remained for long a matter for negotiation between the local Indian officials and the individual friars and secular priests who served the Indian parishes.[43] By the early eighteenth century, after intense and almost continuous conflict between the Franciscans and various civil officials who sought to regulate and limit ecclesiastical exactions,[44] *limosnas* had become a uniform head tax, too, under the title of *obvenciones*. The diocesan tax schedule, which remained basically unmodified for the rest of the colonial period, was set at twelve and a half reales for men and nine reales for women.[45]

Both church and state added a variety of lesser taxes to their basic tribute (see table 1.1). The *holpatan* was levied to support the colony's special Indian court, the Tribunal de Indios (sometimes called Tribunal de Naturales), which provided legal service to the Indians otherwise free of charge.[46] The *comunidades* tax was instituted as a local levy to defray community expenses but was often diverted into the needy provincial exchequer. The parish clergy increased their income with fees for baptisms, marriages, and burials—carefully graded according to a scale of lavishness—and a weekly tuition charge for each Indian child attending the obligatory catechism classes (*doctrina*). And to these must be added an eight-real fee paid to the bishop for each confirmation. The Bull of the Holy Crusade, which Indians were obliged to buy, provided a papal indulgence permitting the purchaser to eat meat on fast days, a privilege the Indians were rarely in a position to take advantage of; it was one of those hermaphroditic taxes characteristic of the Spanish colonial system, with an ecclesiastical character but earmarked for the royal Treasury by papal grant.

TABLE 1.1. SCHEDULE OF ANNUAL TAXES OWED BY AN INDIAN FAMILY
IN COLONIAL YUCATAN (IN REALES)

Civil		Ecclesiastical	
Tribute (male)	14	*Obvención mayor* (male)	12½
Tribute (female)	11[a]	*Obvención mayor* (female)	9
Comunidades	8[b]	*Doctrina*	8[c]
Holpatan (at ½ real)	1	*Obvenciones menores*	
Bula de la Santa Cruzada	4	Baptisms (@ 3 reales)	
		Confirmations (@ 8 reales)	
		Weddings (@ 10 reales)	
		Matrimonial Inquiries (@ 4 reales)	
		Burials, adult (@ 8-20 reales)	
		Testamentos (@ 4 reales)	
		Burials, infant (@ 4 reales)	
		Annual Average	5[d]
Total	38		34½
Total Taxes Owed		72½ reales	

Sources: On ecclesiastical contributions, see IY, Sínodo Diocesano, 1721-1722, ff 217-225; AA, Aranceles, 1737 and 1756; AA, Estadística, Relación jurada que hacen los curas . . . , 1774. On civil contributions, see AGI, Mexico 3132, Cargo y data, Campeche, 1761; BN, Archivo Franciscano 55, no. 1150, Discurso sobre la constitución de Yucatan, 1766; AGI, Mexico 3139, Reglamento, 28 July 1786. On *comunidades*, see AGI, Mexico 158, Abogado de Indios to Crown, 28 July 1668; and AA, Oficios y decretos 4, Abogado de Indios to Governor, 25 Sept. 1781. On the *Bula de la Santa Cruzada*, see AA, Real cedulario no. 27, Instrucción . . . , 1753.

Note: Averaged over the lifetime of an Indian couple with three surviving children and three dying in infancy.

[a] Paid by all females between the ages of 12 and 55, regardless of marital status; abolished in 1760.

[b] Varied in the seventeenth century, reaching a high of 10 reales each adult, but officially fixed toward the end of the century at 4 reales each.

[c] Calculated on the basis of one egg and one jar of *higuerilla* per week, the standard *doctrina* fee for each child.

[d] Based on an average (over a 20-year span) of one wedding with matrimonial inquiries, six baptisms, three confirmations, and two adult burials with *testamentos* (prescribed bequests for various pious works) for the couple's parents (assuming an equal share with other siblings).

The church imposed almost as heavy a burden of taxes on the Indians as did the state. In aggregate, the supplementary levies far exceeded the original tributary assessment, even more so after 1760, when the Crown relieved Indian women from civil tribute. The basic tax table moreover does not take into account another set of extra contributions that all members of both the civil and ecclesiastical bureaucracies imposed when transacting any official business with the Indians. Under such euphemistic titles as fees, alms, gifts, and fines, they ranged from certain standard gratuities (like a few chickens offered when presenting a petition),[47] which came to be sanctioned by custom if not by law, to ad hoc and blatantly extortionate exactions devised by especially enterprising individuals.

All these unscheduled additions are by nature unquantifiable. Usually our only hint of their existence is some passing mention—a reference in 1629, say, to a fee that was being collected from Indians for the privilege of owning a horse or a mule.[48] The reference does not specify either the amount of the fee, how consistently it was imposed, or for how long it was in effect. And we have no way of telling whether it was the brainchild of that particular governor or a practice so taken for granted that no one else bothered to mention it. Only when competition over the spoils became intense enough to elicit an inquiry by church officials into the "excesses" of the royal bureaucrats, or vice versa, do details of these practices surface in the written records.

The bishops received no share of the parish clergy's *obvenciones*. Their official income was derived entirely from tithes, woefully small so long as commercial agriculture remained undeveloped. Like everyone else, they turned to the Indians, who were exempt from tithes, to rescue them from penury. In addition to persuading the Crown to subject *encomienda* income to tithes, the first resident bishop set up his own tribute system on the side, organized partly around the diocesan visitations (*visitas pastorales*).[49] He set a precedent for bishops and governors alike. The latter, while deploring episcopal greed, themselves found tours of inspection a most lucrative source of income.[50]

One such tour could pick the colony clean. Governors and bishops both traveled with advance parties and large entourages, all having to be fed in style at the expense of the Maya. The grossest gluttony, however, could not account for the lists of provisions demanded. The surplus was simply another form of tribute to be shipped back to Merida as part of the tour's net receipts, along with the regular fees and fines collected. Because it was official business, the Indians also had to provide free transport for goods and people. This was not, it should be noted, an easy way to turn a profit. The distances were long and the roads rough (the more delicate or less able equestrians favored travel by litter, also provided free by the Indians); the food and accommodations, if free, were hardly first class. Governors understandably preferred to rely on their agents sent out from Merida, and bishops rarely made more than one diocesan tour during their term in office.

Other ecclesiastical institutions that in the core colonies were supported entirely by endowments from wealthy Spaniards in Yucatan depended on some form of Indian tribute. Responding to pleas based on the region's extreme poverty, the Crown assigned a portion of the tribute from royal *encomiendas* as annuities for the Jesuit College in Merida, the convent of Concepcionist nuns (the Jesuits and the Concepcionists were among the two wealthiest religious orders in central Mexico) and the hospital order of San Juan de Dios.[51] The orders were further subsidized by quotas of maize assessed on the Crown's *encomiendas*.

These subsidies, the *obvenciones*, the minor head taxes, and the myriad extra perquisites of office are easy to recognize as simple extensions of the original tribute system. Other exactions, because they bear a superficial resemblance to trade, are less clear-cut but nevertheless should be placed in the same category.

The Spanish in Yucatan, officeholders and private citizens alike, engaged in a variety of what at first sight may appear to be commercial transactions with the Indians, either through agents or on their own behalf. They found it convenient to subsume these activities under the heading of *tratos* or *grangerías* (business dealings) for the benefit of the Crown and no doubt for their own self-justification. But whatever label was current at the time should not obscure the difference between appropriation by force and genuine commercial exchange, in which prices may be distorted by inequalities in power between the parties involved but the exchange itself is in some degree voluntary. The Spaniards' own moral unease about these activities, no matter what interpretation they offered to the Crown, is revealed in the number of endowed masses and other pious bequests in favor of the Indians "with whom I have had business dealings, in case I may have done them some harm," in addition to the usual masses for the benefit of the testator's soul.[52]

Only the loosest definition of trade, to the point of being meaningless, could include the *repartimiento* system, which rapidly became the principal device for extracting exportable goods from the Indians and thus the chief means of generating wealth. I find little evidence for the forced sale of goods similar to the notorious *repartimiento de efectos* in Peru, where sickly mules and other useless items were unloaded on the Indians at exorbitant prices.[53] In Yucatan the *repartimiento* most commonly operated in reverse, forcing cash advances on the Indians for the delivery of a specified amount of goods within a stipulated period.[54] Almost any kind of local product might be obtained this way, from sarsaparilla root and copal gathered in the forest to maize, cotton, and other basic commodities. The most desired goods and the most common *repartimiento* items were beeswax and cotton cloth, for which the raw cotton as well as the cash was advanced. As practiced by the provincial governors and their agents, these transactions were so unfavorable to the Indians that only outright physical coercion could induce the Indians to accept them.[55]

Despite frequent and vehement denunciations against the *repartimientos*, the Crown tolerated them for the same reason that the *encomienda* was allowed to persist—in recognition of the colony's otherwise fragile economic base. The governors and other interested parties also claimed that the *repartimiento* was beneficial to the Indians, enabling them to earn money to pay their tribute. No matter that the vast weight of evidence pointed to its pernicious effects, the telling argument was the destitution the Spanish would suffer if it were abolished.[56]

The Indians were well aware of the various means used to cheat them in these transactions. *Repartimiento* agents invested the motto "buy cheap and sell dear" with a special meaning. Cash was advanced for the cloth and wax well below the market price. Also the standard amount of raw cotton advanced was short-weighted, so that the Indians had to supply not only the labor but part of the material as well. In addition, fraudulent weights and measures were used when collecting the goods, so that the "pound" of wax demanded was heavier than standard, and the length of cloth longer. The Indians were also aware that when they had to buy cotton or wax themselves to fill the quotas, the Spaniards, who controlled most local trade, sold it to them at two or three times the purchase price they offered. The great discrepancy in prices, always in the Spaniards' favor, was of course one reason that the latter had to rely on force to extract goods from the Maya in the first place.

When these abuses were especially gross or the quotas so excessive that they interfered with food production, the parish priests and *encomenderos*, who had their own financial stake in the Indians' survival, protested on the Indians' behalf. The official *repartimiento* agents acting for the governors and their lieutenants were the worst offenders. Unofficial *repartimientos*, by which the rest of the colonial elite tapped the same source, seem to have offered somewhat better terms, or less unfavorable ones, presumably because they had to. Almost any Spaniard could physically abuse any Indian with impunity. But a few kicks and cuffs, humiliating as these were to the native leaders, lacked the same coercive effect as the imprisonments and whippings administered by official agents for noncompliance with their quotas or complaints about the terms. Ordinary merchants sometimes made allowances and deferred collection, just as curates and *encomenderos* sometimes let tax payments pile up. The governors' agents were implacable, for they had to render account to their employers, who sought to make or recoup their fortunes during their short term in office.

Some of the economic exchanges that were carried on between Indians and non-Indians can legitimately be defined as trade.[57] Spaniards, and sometimes mestizos and mulattoes, controlled the distribution of the few items the Maya needed or developed a taste for but did not produce themselves. These were chiefly metal tools, gunpowder (which came to be regarded as a requirement for any fiesta, besides its use in hunting), and cane liquor. They also supplied at least part of the salt and cacao consumed by the Maya and the small quantity of European-style luxury goods owned by the native elites. All these items seem to have been genuinely desired and freely purchased by the Maya. The ordinary Maya rarely had any cash. These transactions were similar in operation to the private *repartimientos* in that the buyer contracted for later delivery of maize, cotton, beeswax, or some other product in return for the purchased item. The distinction was in the voluntary (so far as we can tell) nature of the exchange.[58]

It is impossible to calculate the extent of this trade. If the activities of peddlars and merchants in the countryside could be quantified, however, I suspect we would find that most took the form of forced *repartimientos* or some other kind of appropriation, with genuine trade confined largely to other non-Indians. Poverty, combined with a certain cultural bias against European goods, made Indians poor customers. They bought little, and tools and trinkets once purchased were passed on through generations as treasured heirlooms.[59] The Spanish commonly voiced frustration with and bewilderment at the Maya's imperviousness to the blandishments of a market economy. Apparently the lack of purchasing power as an explanation for low demand had not yet achieved the status of economic verity.

One form of exchange that would seem to depart from the general pattern of coercion was the purchase of foodstuffs for the colony's urban markets as a supplement to ordinary tribute goods. We have no reason to doubt that the Indians resident in the barrios of Merida and other Spanish centers willingly raised pigs and grew vegetables and fruit on their household plots for sale in the cities. The native elite who produced maize, beans, cotton, fruit, and cacao as cash crops also engaged in a genuine commercial exchange.[60] The elite had certain advantages not available to the ordinary subsistence farmer; they were able to produce substantial surpluses, which they could carry directly to the marketplace because they controlled the colony's transport, and they had the experience and knowledge to negotiate directly with the officials in charge of the public granaries.

The ordinary Maya dealt with Spanish middlemen—the grain merchants and agents of the provincial and municipal governments who traveled the countryside buying up small lots from the villagers. An element of coercion underlay even these apparently innocuous transactions, by which Indian farmers could earn cash through the sale of maize grown above and beyond their own subsistence needs and tribute quotas. If some portion of the grain represented a genuine surplus sold freely on a more or less open market, it was not produced freely, since we are told that each Indian was compelled to cultivate a certain quantity of milpa a year; otherwise they "would not grow food for the *vecinos* [non-Indians]."[61] And the purchases made by governors' agents seem to have been merely another type of appropriation under the pretext of provisioning the urban markets. Even if some payment was received, the transactions were made under duress and at confiscatory prices.[62]

During times of famine the guise of trade dropped completely as commissioners scoured the villages to requisition whatever stores of maize the Indians were unable to conceal.[63] The justification offered for these forced sales was that they prevented hoarding and shortages and ensured supplies for the cities at stable prices. Some critics complained that they were merely the device of a few to corner the grain market for their own profit. Whoever gained more from the system, the urban consumer or the middlemen, it is safe to say that the losses were borne by the Indian producer.

Feeding the cities has always been a high priority with any government, if only to discourage urban unrest. The policy of ensuring a steady, cheap supply of grain for the urban population at the expense of the rural producer was not a colonial or even a Spanish innovation but a well-established Mediterranean tradition with roots in the Roman past. One could perhaps see the system in Yucatan as merely an extension of the same policy that municipal governments applied in Spain and in various parts of the empire and which has been blamed in part for the impoverishment of the Castilian countryside and the decadence of its agriculture in the seventeenth century.[64] There is, I think, a significant difference between efforts to control or manipulate market forces through price ceilings and export restrictions, as in Castile, and a complete short circuit of the usual demand-supply-price mechanisms through the simple expedient of overt coercion or the threat of it. For all the commercial terminology with which Spaniards in Yucatan surrounded their grain requisitions and other "business dealings" with the Indians, these dealings still look more like tribute than trade.

The distinction may seem a petty one. All these relationships, whether in Spain or the Indies, can be reduced to a basic formula that repeated itself in other stratified agrarian societies around the world: a simple pattern of dominance in which a ruling group backed by the authority of the state is able to tap the resources of an otherwise marginal peasantry and thus draw them into the orbit of a market economy. Yet it is worthwhile to discriminate among the various methods used to extract the surpluses, for tribute, unequal market exchange, wage labor, and other kinds of direct employment all require different behavioral and cognitive adaptations on the part of the subordinate group.

Much more significant than the distinction between trade and tribute is the fact that the Spanish merely made use of the native economy, leaving the means of production for the most part in Indian hands. The struggle over land between the Indian community and the landed estates came late to Yucatan, not because the Spanish in Yucatan were peculiarly respectful of Indian property rights but because they had little incentive to violate them. During most of the colonial period, until a dramatically expanding market in the late eighteenth century stimulated the development of commercial agriculture on a large scale, there was more than enough land in the colony to satisfy Spanish demands and Indian needs.[65]

Labor Systems

Labor was always a far scarcer commodity in colonial Yucatan than land, but not scarce enough, it would seem, to stimulate a shift to more efficient methods of exploiting this resource. Although the Spanish constantly bemoaned the shortage of manpower, they continued to rely on cumbersome rotating labor drafts to extract most of the labor they required beyond the production of tribute goods. The system of state-controlled corvées, instituted when forced labor was separated from the tribute obligations of the *encomienda,* operated in much the same way throughout the colonies. Only the titles differed. In Yucatan what was called *servicio personal* does not seem to have differed significantly from the *mita* of the Andean colonies and the labor *repartimiento* (not to be confused with the *repartimiento* of goods or cash) in the rest of New Spain. The principal difference in Yucatan as with so many other aspects of the colonial regime was the lack of further innovation. In Peru and Mexico the Spanish turned increasingly to wage labor and peonage as the gap between labor supply and demand widened. In Yucatan they responded, characteristically, by merely expanding the original corvée system.

Every able-bodied adult member of an Indian community was subject to a variety of forced labor drafts, some established by law, some by custom, and some unsanctioned by either. Out of this welter of demands, three main categories can be distinguished. First were the local *tequios* (from the Nahuatl *tequitl*), a community residence tax of one day's labor a week for local projects, such as the construction and repair of churches, and for services to their own native leaders. These tasks seem to have been well-established obligations from pre-Columbian times.[66] If not always explicitly confirmed by the colonial authorities, they nevertheless continued to be performed without their interference. Added to them was a second level of civic obligations imposed by the state, consisting of major public works (roads, forts, the cathedral, and other public buildings), a postal service of relay runners from town to town, the maintenance of hostels in each town for travelers, and the transport of any people and goods connected with official business. The church exacted similar services for the movement of its messages, goods, and personnel. Any time a priest, for example, traveled outside of his residence in the parish's principal town to say mass or perform the last rites in a dependent village, the Indians had to send a horse or litter for him as well as provide food during his stay.[67]

The third category of labor draft, *servicio personal*, was designed to satisfy the colony's private labor requirements, functioning in theory as a government-regulated employment exchange. Each community was assessed a weekly quota of male and female workers called *semaneros*, who were assigned to individual Spaniards by official permits that specified the number of workers each was entitled to employ from the general labor pool.

Servicio personal vied with the *repartimiento* as the most detested feature of colonial rule, if we are to believe the local champions of Indian interests. Despite the Crown's reiterated insistence that Indians were not to be compelled to work for Spaniards against their will,[68] no one bothered to pretend that *servicio personal* was anything but forced labor. Yet why it should have been found so objectionable is not immediately apparent. By the end of the sixteenth century indigo production had ceased and mules and horses had largely replaced Indian porters in local transport.[69] The system had ostensibly evolved into the minor obligation of approximately one week's domestic service a year for each tributary, for which he was to be paid a stipulated minimum wage.

The minimum wage, to be sure, was far from princely: set originally at two reales a week, it was raised to three reales for men in the late sixteenth century; in the early eighteenth century it was raised to four reales for men and three for women, plus food rations during service away from home.[70] One of the justifications offered for the labor drafts, like *repartimiento*, was that it enabled Indians to earn money to pay their taxes. Yet, based on the stipulated wage, it would have taken an Indian man twelve weeks to pay his legal tax assessment in the seventeenth century (see table 1.1) and a woman eighteen weeks, without counting the many unauthorized supplements devised by the fertile colonial mind.

But it is only as one moves from the realm of regulation to practice that the truly objectionable features of *servicio personal* become apparent. Payment below the official wage rate and failure to pay any wages at all were common complaints. The usual stint of service turned out to be three or four weeks instead of one, or it might extend to any period at the whim of the employer unless the *semanero* managed to run away.[71] To this must be added the extra, unremunerated time for each journey on foot between village and work site. Indians were normally drawn from a radius of 20 leagues, or 80 kilometers, for work in Merida, but I have also found mention of Indians coming from Oxkutzcab and Tix-cacaltuyu, about 100 kilometers away.[72] In addition, there was an extra day's labor, also unpaid, and the "gratuity" of one bundle of firewood, both exacted from each *semanero* by the official in charge of labor allocations in the cities; and also, women who served in urban households were usually accompanied by their children and by their husbands, who were then pressed into extra, unpaid service in addition to their regular stints.[73] With each new detail *servicio personal* looks less and less like anything one would ordinarily call "wage labor."

Spaniards justified the labor drafts the standard arguments relied on by any group that tries to extract cheap labor from unwilling subordinate groups. The Maya suffered an affliction common to Indians in the rest of Latin America, other colonized people, slaves, and the lower orders in general: they were "naturally prone to idleness," disinclined to work regardless of the incentives offered.[74] For some of the observers the explanation lay less in the vice of idleness than in an almost saintly disregard for worldly goods, an asceticism that, however laudable in theory or when practiced by only a few anchorites, presented a serious obstacle to economic progress if shared by the mass of laboring poor. Spaniards in Yucatan found something perverse if not passively defiant in the Maya's ability to content themselves with a handful of tortillas and beans, a miserable hut, and no more possessions than they could carry on their backs.

Historians have come increasingly to see these elite pronouncements on the sloth and/or asceticism of the masses as a general if not to say predictable feature of class relations in the transition from precapitalist to capitalist systems of production, whether in an interracial colonial setting or not.[75] The pronouncements reflect a profound conflict between the concepts, values and lifeways attuned to subsistence agriculture and the demands of an expanding capitalist economy—or so the argument goes. Complaints about the ingrained aversion to work dis-

played by the lower orders voice the common frustrations of agricultural and industrial entrepreneurs of whatever nationality seeking to create a disciplined and reliable labor force from the unpromising material
of premodern agrarian populations. Peasants the world over, we are
told, value surplus time over surplus goods, and therefore will not work
for others unless forced nor work more than is necessary to satisfy their
own needs—as defined by themselves.

While in sympathy with any attempt to inject the dimension of culture into the often simplistic analyses of economic relations, I find some
problems with this one. If peasants will not work beyond the minimum
to satisfy their own needs, then the conflict, although most commonly
placed within the particular historical context of the rise of industrial
capitalism, is a much more fundamental one; it is a conflict over surplus
which must arise in any complex society—precapitalist, capitalist, or
socialist—that relies on one portion of the population to produce food
or any other agricultural surplus for another. A propensity to household
autarky will be as intolerable to a feudal lord or socialist planner as to a
sugar planter or textile manufacturer. Some form of coercion will always be necessary, either exercised directly through political means
(tribute, bondage, corvée) or indirectly through economic pressure—
reinforced more often than not by political power. The economic pressure takes the form of creating a gap between the peasantry's perceived
needs and their ability to satisfy them. Either peasants can be deprived
of their land so that they have no choice but to work for others, or the
needs themselves can be redefined by taxation and, in more sophisticated economies, by the lure of consumer goods. Or both processes,
aided sometimes by population increases, may combine to force peasants into the labor market.

The ubiquity of the use of force in the elite's dealings with peasants
suggests that indeed a basic, if not inherent, conflict exists. It also raises
some questions about the role of values or mentalities. The case of Yucatan, among many others that could be offered, suggests that the translation into cultural terms of the moralistic arguments proffered by contemporary elites—that is, the substitution of precapitalist or peasant
mentality for laziness and fecklessness—may continue to obscure the
nature of the conflict.

Ruling groups in Yucatan since before the conquest have resorted at
one time or another to most of the standard methods of extracting surpluses from the local peasantry, all within the context of what must be
considered a premodern economy. (It is not clear that even at the height
of the henequen boom of the late nineteenth century one can talk of a
capitalist mode of production in any orthodox sense of the term.)[76] A

long reliance on tribute and corvée labor, which spanned the conquest divide, eventually gave way to direct control of land and labor as the tempo of external trade increased. But the terms under which tenant farmers and peons labored on the landed estates, however harsh or benevolent, were a far cry from wage-earning employment. Throughout the various modifications in the local economy, involving changes in systems of land tenure and labor recruitment, a simple conflict of interests rather than of mentalities runs as a constant.

It is in fact impossible to say whether peasant values made the colonial Maya immune to ordinary economic incentives, since the Spanish never put their version of this hypothesis to the test. They did not offer the Indians either the going market prices for their goods or the going rate for their labor. A free market existed in both, but it excluded the Indians as active participants and beneficiaries. Spaniards with the power to command tribute goods in one form or another turned around and sold them at many times the "purchase" price. Similarly, those able to secure a larger allotment of *semaneros* than they needed themselves would hire out the surplus to less influential neighbors, charging the standard daily wage for unskilled labor (which at two reales plus rations was three times the *servicio personal* rate) and then pocket the difference.[77]

The official rationale offered for *servicio personal* and the other hybrid systems of compulsory wage labor in the Spanish empire was that they should serve as a transition to completely free wage labor while the Indians became accustomed to a money economy. That may have been the Crown's original intention. It also may be that in some colonies the Indians were viewed as potential employees who must be lured or forced into selling their labor. Some historians have even seen the shift to cash payments of tribute and taxes in general as an alternative recruiting device, one among "a range of strategies to bring people with a precapitalist mentality into the labor market."[78]

Such interpretations based on subtle analyses of market forces are perhaps appropriate to the complex structures of a modern economy. They do not easily apply to colonial Yucatan and only obscure what was essentially a very simple colonial regime—simple in concept and in practice. Accustomed as we are to seeing European colonization as part of the process by which Europe and the rest of the world have been moving into the modern era, we may sometimes forget that Spanish overseas expansion was also an extension of its medieval, reconquest past. The colonial regime in Yucatan (and I would guess in many other similarly isolated regions) remained close to that past despite the modernizing influences at work in the larger imperial and global systems to which they were linked.

The colonizers were no more capitalistic than the colonized in the way they conceived relations between the two groups. Tribute and other taxes retained their original purpose, which was simply to extract wealth from the Indians. Despite the prevailing rhetoric, the Spanish in Yucatan gave no sign that they sought to create a wage-earning labor force. When they needed permanent estate labor, the *hacendados* preferred to bind the Indians, except for a tiny proportion of skilled workers, in a kind of manorial tenantry arrangement that offered neither wages nor credit advances. They also clung tenaciously to *servicio personal* to the end of the colonial period and beyond, and in unguarded moments revealed a conception of the system that was much closer to feudal rights and obligations than to any incipient employer-employee relationship:

> *Servicio personal* is one of the privileges and immunities that Your Royal Highness has granted to the inhabitants of Yucatan for defending the province at no cost to the Treasury and with risk of their lives against the continuous invasions of enemy pirates.[79]

Without ever wavering from the official stance that *servicio personal* was only a temporary expedient, the Crown acknowledged it as a local necessity (if not the inalienable right of colonial fantasy) and extended it or reinstated it after brief suspensions,[80] even when the system had been all but abolished and replaced by other labor systems elsewhere in the viceroyalty of New Spain. Whether or not the Maya were impervious to any wage incentives, they gave ample proof of being impervious to the ones the Spanish were willing to offer. And if they were unlikely to starve unless compelled to work, as their colonial masters alleged,[81] the argument that the Spanish would surely perish without forced Indian labor was a compelling one. Tribute in some form supplied most of their food as well as exports. They relied on the labor drafts to transport their goods (pack animals replaced human carriers only on the main roads, and even there not entirely), to construct their houses, and to provide all the domestic services without which the colonists were convinced—and succeeded in convincing the Crown—that they literally could not survive in that alien land.

Service in the households of Spaniards and the more prosperous mestizos and mulattoes occupied the major portion of the weekly labor drafts.[82] The most modest establishment required at least one *semanera* in order to prepare the cornmeal dough that formed such a large part of everyone's daily diet. Only Indian women were capable of the arduous work of grinding the maize by hand because, it was explained, "they are used to it."[83] Larger households, pursuing the local version of the seigneurial ideal, were supported by a swarm of draftees from the villages to help the cooks, nursemaids, gardeners, footmen, stablehands, laundresses, and other servants that comprised the permanent staff. Each Franciscan friary, in all the austerity of the order's rule, was judged able to manage with an allotment of only twelve to seventeen male *semaneros* (depending on the size of the parish) to look after three or four friars. The total for most friaries, when female servants and caretakers for the church were included, was estimated at over one hundred Indians.[84] The bishop employed twelve *semaneros* simply to keep his patio weeded.[85]

Such profligate use of manpower in service occupations suggests how low the demand was for productive activities. No figures have been found, if they were ever recorded, for the number of Indians drafted for work in the salt industry, which was for long the only significant Spanish-directed enterprise besides ranching. My guess is that the number was small and probably drawn only from adjacent areas immediately inland from the coastal pans. I cannot otherwise explain why these labor drafts figured so minimally in the usual litany of grievances that the Indians and their local spokesmen intoned against the colonial regime. There would have been ample cause for complaint. The work season was short, confined to the few months immediately preceding the summer rains. But this also coincided precisely with the most crucial period of the agricultural cycle, when the Maya were busy clearing and burning their milpas for planting and particularly disinclined to tolerate extra demands. The work itself was notoriously unpleasant. The workers toiled all day up to their waists in the briny slush of the salt pans during the hottest part of the year, half their flesh pickled and the other half parched. The wages for *indios compelidos*, or forced laborers, though half again the ordinary rate for the usual kind of *servicio personal*, were well below the earnings of the mestizo and mulatto workers who contracted freely at a piece rate with the Spanish concessionaires.[86]

Ranching required only a small number of cowhands, who worked as free contract laborers for cash wages and rations. The slow growth of Spanish agriculture meant a correspondingly low demand for labor in that sphere. This demand was satisfied by two different types of recruitment within two different types of agrarian structures. From the earliest postconquest years until the end of the colonial period, Spaniards used allotments of corvée labor to raise cash crops on parcels of land rented or simply requisitioned from the Indian communities. Some maize was grown this way, but the system was used mainly for the production of indigo (during the brief experiment with this crop shortly after conquest), cotton, and, later, tobacco and sugar. These crops were best suited to the more fertile and more humid districts to the east and south, where land was especially plentiful and labor scarce. Operating

3. Salt pans, west coast of Yucatan. The salt is still collected by hand from the shallow salt ponds (background); the wheeled cart for transport along the shore is a post-conquest innovation. (Photo by the author)

outside the framework of an organized hacienda system could be quite profitable for the few locals with enough political influence to requisition the necessary draft labor. Tithe payments could also be evaded more easily, and the later royal *estancos* (monopolies) of tobacco and cane liquor made these unregistered agricultural enterprises that much more attractive.[87]

In the more densely populated core area of the northwest, where the landed estates predominated, rotating labor drafts played a minimal role in the gradual shift from Indian peasant production to commercial agriculture. For agricultural labor, as opposed to the semiskilled tasks involved in stockraising, the estates relied almost solely on a resident labor force of tenant farmers who contributed one day of work per week to the owner as their land rent. (In chapter 7 I shall discuss the incentives that drew Indians to the *estancias*.) At no time did the estates experience much difficulty recruiting an ample supply of resident labor; for much of the colonial period it probably well exceeded the need, and one reason is that the estates generally offered a de facto escape from the more onerous labor burdens imposed on pueblo residents.[88]

Neither *servicio personal* nor resident estate labor, whatever their comparative advantages in the terms of service offered, involved severe disruptions in native life. The absence of mines and tropical plantations meant that the long-term and large-scale population displacements that forced labor imposed in many other colonies were unnecessary. The main centers of Spanish population and of economic activity—such as it was—also coincided with the areas of densest Indian population. The Maya, therefore, could remain firmly embedded in the traditional collective life of their communities under the supervision of their own leaders. The labor drafts were mediated entirely through the village officials who rounded up the weekly quotas, escorted the draftees to the city or the work site, and collected them and their wages—supposedly as credit toward the individual's tax obligation—when the stint of service was completed.

The work assigned under the forced labor drafts was invariably physically demanding but also almost invariably very familiar. Cultivating milpas, hauling stones and mortar for construction, trotting along rough trails with sacks of grain on their backs, or scooping out salt from coastal salt flats thickly populated with sand flies: these were the same tasks that, for their sins, the Maya peasantry had been performing for a millennium or so before the Spanish arrived. Domestic service in the cities where most Spaniards resided, however objectionable for the physical dislocation involved and the risk of prolonged absence from home, did not plunge the Maya into a wholly alien environment. Surrounded as often as not by a platoon of other *semaneras*, the women were set to work grinding maize and preparing tortillas and the men were sent out to gather firewood and fodder and to weed and water the orchards and kitchen gardens—the kinds of chores with which they were all too familiar in their own daily routine.

Commercial agriculture was also for long less disruptive of traditional ways than one might expect. Under the rudimentary agrarian structure that persisted in the marginal zones of low population density, the adjustments were minimal. Workers were temporarily drafted in rotation and otherwise remained within the orbit of the Indian pueblos. The Indians who moved to the *estancias* and haciendas did not thereby wholly detach themselves from their pueblos either. They created small, scattered settlements on *estancia* lands that were very similar to the other outlying hamlets that formed part of the Indian communities. And like them, they remained social and administrative appendages of the pueblo.[89]

The tenant laborers on the estates occupied a position quite apart from the salaried cowhands, who were directly dependent on their employers for food and housing as well as wages. The tenants continued to subsist as milpa farmers and merely transferred their residence tax, or *tequio*, of one day's labor a week from pueblo to *estancia*. Monday (*lunes*) was traditionally the day set aside for *tequios* in the pueblos and presumably on the *estancias*, and hence the local designation of *luneros* for unsalaried estate residents. It was not the movement to the estates in itself but their expansion and transformation into full-fledged agricultural enterprises that eventually marked the *luneros'* complete transition from *indios de pueblo* to *peones de hacienda*.

The Maya of Yucatan were spared by the region's economic backwardness from the profound dislocations that the more rapid and thorough shift to a market economy produced in the dynamic core colonies. The local variant of colonial rule was not necessarily milder in material terms. Corvée labor was probably higher in physical costs than direct, full-time employment would have been, because the cumbersome, rotating drafts made less efficient use of the available manpower. The social costs, however, were comparatively low. Labor drafts and tribute had been customary obligations in pre-Columbian times. Even if the Spanish made greater demands, and we have no precise basis for comparison, these demands differed only in degree, without requiring serious modifications of either the Maya's work habits or their social arrangements. It would also be difficult to compare the material burdens of Spanish rule from colony to colony. The rate of tribute varied but so did prices and wages. That in any case is not the issue. The comparison I am making is in the effect on indigenous society: the difference between a parasite that invades and destroys the host organism—in this case a social organism—and one that merely fastens itself on the organism and weakens it. The colonial regime in Yucatan was the latter variety.

· 2 ·

INDIAN REACTIONS
AND SPANISH
MODIFICATIONS

Any system of rule, colonial or otherwise, takes shape as a dialogue, in which the responses of the subject group may be more or less muted but must be taken into account. The Maya Indians of Yucatan had, from the first, exerted an influence on the type of colonial regime the Spanish established. The presence of a large sedentary population organized into a well-defined social hierarchy meant that the conquerors could settle down as overlords without having to exploit the environment themselves or create an entirely new structure of social and political control. Demography, in particular the ratio of Indians to Spaniards, was to continue to play a major role in defining the range of options open to Spaniards and Indians in their mutual relations.

COLONIAL DEMOGRAPHY

The Indian population of Yucatan, as everywhere in the New World, declined drastically during the first century or so after the coming of the Europeans. The exact extent of the decline will never be known. It seems likely that the heaviest losses occurred in the early years before the first colonial censuses were taken and in some cases before actual conquest itself, when diseases were spread by Indian carriers through areas that had had little or no direct contact with Spaniards or Portuguese. Scholars disagree radically on the size of America's preconquest population.[1] Figures offered for central Mexico, for example, vary from 25 million, which many find greatly inflated, down to well under 4.5 million, which an even larger number of scholars would reject as too low.[2] Estimates for Yucatan range widely, too, from what to many would seem an implausibly high total of 8 million, down to 300,000; a recent figure of 2.3 million seems acceptable only if one also accepts the proposition that the population was not entirely dependent on slash-and-burn agriculture at the time.[3]

For all the intricate and often ingenious calculations on which these estimates are based, they remain at best informed guesses, and all one can do is to choose whichever figure strikes one's fancy or preconceptions. Fortunately for our particular purpose, which is to analyze the development of the colonial regime, the total extent of population decline from precontact times is far less crucial than the patterns of demographic change subsequent to the colony's establishment; and there we are on firmer ground, with documentation that is frustratingly incomplete and often equivocal, to be sure, but abundant enough to allow us to see some general outlines.

Regional differences in the patterns of demographic change can be seen as symptomatic of the differences in the colonial regimes. In particular, they reflect the contrast between central Mexico and Yucatan, where conquest was more protracted but less devastating in its immediate effects. Population losses were massive in both areas and of a magnitude to qualify as a "demographic catastrophe" by any standard, regardless of which estimates one accepts for the precontact point of departure. It is useful, nevertheless, to distinguish degrees of catastrophe. Even leaving aside the heavily disputed early figures, which would merely sharpen the contrast between the two regions, we find that the decline was considerably less severe in Yucatan and also proceeded at a slower and more uneven pace.

Two major demographic studies of colonial Yucatan have appeared during the last decade, neither of which ventures a guess on the precontact population (although one estimates that it had already fallen to about 800,000 by 1528).[4] They are in substantial agreement—by the standards of historical demography—on the losses occurring between 1549, when the first general tributary count was made, and 1580-1586 (see table 2.1); the losses represent a rate of decline less than half that of central Mexico during the same period.[5]

In central Mexico the decline continued unabated until the early seventeenth century, reaching a low of slightly over one million (a long-term ratio of 5.7:1) before leveling out and finally starting what was to be a steady recovery by the middle of the century. In Yucatan, on the other hand, the downward trend actually seems to have been reversed temporarily during the first part of the seventeenth century. Then, in the 1640s, the Indian population started on a second and much more severe decline, which reached a nadir sometime around the end of the century (representing a long-term ratio of 2.4:1). Recovery proceeded during the eighteenth century, attaining the 1549 level by the 1790s, and continued at an accelerated pace into the nineteenth century.

These are only the gross outlines of demographic trends. They are fairly accurate as such trends go, but the curves are misleadingly smooth and need to be broken up into the jagged peaks and valleys of shorter-range oscillations that are often of most interest.[6] If we had no census figures between 1549 and 1794, for example, we might assume that the

TABLE 2.1. INDIAN POPULATION OF YUCATAN, 1549-1809

Year	García Bernal	Cook and Borah	Other
1549-50	232,567	240,000	
1580-85		140,000	
1586	170,000		
1606-07	164,064		
1609		176,320	
1639	207,497	210,000	
1643	209,188		
1688	99,942		
1700	130,000	182,500	
1710			156,788
1736		127,000	126,722
1761			184,998
1765			194,300
1773			128,761
1780			175,287
1794		254,000	
1806		281,012	272,925
1809			291,096

Sources: García Bernal, Yucatán, 163, table 11; Cook and Borah, Essays 2: 48, 69, 72, 93, 94, 112. The remaining figures are derived from the following manuscript sources: AGI, Mexico 1037, Governor of Yucatan to Crown, 15 Sept. 1711; AGI, Mexico 3168, Bishop of Yucatan to Crown, 28 July 1737, with enclosed report; BN, Archivo Franciscano 55, no. 1150, Discurso sobre la constitución de Yucatan, 12 July 1766; AGI, Mexico 3057, Estado general de todos los indios tributarios, 10 Feb. 1774 (comparing the tributary population in 1765 and 1773); Mexico 3061, Demostración del número de poblaciones que comprende la provincia de Yucatan, 15 April 1781; AA, Estadística 1 and 2, Parish censuses, 1806 (see appendix 1 for a detailed breakdown by parish); AGI, Mexico 3168, Oficiales reales to Crown, 22 April 1813 (citing the 1809 matrícula de tributarios).

Indian population had remained almost stable for over two centuries. Or if we leapt from 1765 to 1794 we would see only a steady increase, masking the drastic losses of the 1769-1774 famine and the subsequent recovery. Similarly, it now seems that 1736, the year that had previously looked like the low point in Indian population for the whole colonial period, merely represented a temporary reversal—caused by another severe famine a decade earlier—in a process of recovery that had already begun by 1700.[7]

Historical demographers expect to find many sharp dips in premodern population curves.[8] What needs explaining in colonial Yucatan, and the rest of Latin America, is why the population failed to recover, why the cumulative effect of high mortality followed different patterns over time in different places, and why this long-term trend eventually reversed itself. Information on some of the short-term, episodic variations in population could provide some of the answers and especially help to clarify the complex relationships among demography, biology, and sociocultural change. Old World epidemic diseases, such as smallpox and measles, against which the Indians had no immunity, were the most obvious and perhaps the major killers. But disease alone will not account for the population declines nor for the variations in pace.

Famine also took a very heavy toll in Yucatan. The region was subject to tropical storms, which could destroy an entire year's crop, as well as periods of drought when the annual summer rains were too light or failed altogether; and dry spells were often accompanied by plagues of locusts to compound the colony's woes. Single crop failures were a frequent occurrence in colonial Yucatan. The true famines were produced by successive years of poor or nonexistent harvests. They caused exceedingly heavy losses among the Maya, with estimates running up to one-third or more of the population.[9]

According to the native chronicles,[10] famine had a venerable history in the peninsula. One might expect the effect to be less devastating in colonial times. Famines, we are told, are merely malfunctions in distribution, since shortages in one place will always be matched by surpluses in another. And the Spanish colonial system, with more centralized rule and the superior means of transport for bulk goods (large sailing ships, wheeled vehicles, and pack animals versus canoes and human carriers) should have been able to distribute supplies more evenly. The pre-Columbian inhabitants lacked the administrative apparatus to coordinate famine relief from one region to another even if they had possessed the appropriate technology.

Several factors combined to nullify these advantages. First and foremost was the introduction of European diseases, which often worked in tandem with famines. Sometimes epidemics disrupted normal food production, resulting in poor harvests even without a drought or preventing the later sowing of a type of fast-ripening maize (called *xmehenal* or *iximmehen* = small corn) that was often resorted to when a delay in the rains or a bad storm ruined the first planting of the slower-growing, preferred variety.[11] (*Xmehenal* matures in half the time but produces a smaller ear and harder kernels.) More commonly the epidemics followed in the wake of crop failures, raging through a population weakened by lack of food. In either case, the combination of epidemics and crop failures was far more devastating than the effects of adverse weather alone.

In the second place, the Spanish system of supply was only potentially

TABLE 2.2. EPIDEMICS AND FAMINES IN COLONIAL YUCATAN, 1535–1810

Year	Occurrence	Source
1535–41	*Famine (drought; locusts)	Landa, *Relación*, 54–56
1564	Drought	Cook and Borah, *Essays* 2: 115
1566	Epidemic	AGI, Mexico 359, Bishop to Crown, 18 July 1566
1569–70	Epidemic	Molina Solís, *Historia de Yucatán* 1: 114–115
1571–72	Famine	Cogolludo, *Historia de Yucatan*, Lib. 6, cap. 9
1575–76	Epidemic + famine (drought)	Molina Solís, 1: 166
1604	Famine	Cook and Borah, 2: 115
1609	Epidemic (typhus)	Cogolludo, Lib. 9, cap. 1
1618	Famine (locusts)	Cárdenas Valencia, *Relación historial*, 68
1627–31	*Famine (storm; locusts)	Cogolludo, Lib. 10, caps. 7, 17
1648–50	*Epidemic (yellow fever; smallpox)	Cogolludo, Lib. 12, caps. 12–14
1650–53	*Famine (drought)	Cogolludo, Lib. 12, caps. 17, 21
1659	Epidemic (measles; smallpox)	AGI, Mexico 360, Governor to Crown, 20 Nov. 1659
1692–93	Famine and epidemic (hurricane; locusts)	AGI, Mexico 369, Bishop to Crown, 18 Apr. 1693
1699	Epidemic	AGI, Mexico 1035, Fr. Diego Gallardo, 30 Nov. 1699
1700	Famine	AGI, Mexico 1035, Definitorio franciscano, 16 June 1700
1726–27	*Famine; epidemic	Molina Solís, 3: 178–181
1730	Famine	AGI, Mexico 898, Oficiales reales to Crown, 20 Oct. 1745
1742	Famine	AGI, Mexico 898, Oficiales reales to Crown, 20 Oct. 1745
1765–68	Famine (hurricane; drought; locusts)	AGI, Mexico 3054, Governor to Julián de Arriaga; Mexico 3057, Encomenderos to Oficiales reales, 11 Sept. 1770
1769–74	*Famine (drought; locusts; hurricane)	AGI, Mexico 3057, Governor to Audiencia, 1 March 1774; Informe Ayuntamiento Merida, 1775
1787	Epidemic (*bola*)	AA, Oficios y decretos 3, Pedro Brunet to Bishop, 2 July 1787
1795	Famine	AGN, Intendentes 75, Autos sobre escaceses de víveres, 1795

TABLE 2.2 (cont.)

Year	Occurrence	Source
1799	Epidemic (vómito de sangre)	AGN, Intendentes 75, no. 10, and 78, no. 5, 1799
1800–1804	*Famine (drought; locusts)	AGN, Intendentes 75, Governor to Viceroy, 10 Aug. 1800; AA, Oficios y decretos 5, Cabildo Merida to Bishop, 31 July 1804
1807	Famine (hurricane)	AGI, Mexico 1975, Comercio de Campeche to Crown, 21 Jan. 1808
1809–10	Famine; epidemic	AA, Oficios y decretos 7, Governor to Bishop, 20 July 1810

*Severe

superior, hampered in practice by trade restrictions and ineffective administration. Only in the late colonial period, under the more efficient and activist Bourbon bureaucracy, was the provincial government able to organize emergency grain imports that were both timely and substantial. Relief supplies came from New Spain and from as far away as New Orleans and Charleston, South Carolina.[12]

Finally, the colonial system of supply, insofar as it functioned, did so generally without benefit to the rural, largely Indian masses, and often to their distinct disadvantage. Emergency grain shipments were destined exclusively for Campeche and Merida, and the same held true for available local supplies. At the first sign of a shortage, private grain merchants and officials of the provincial and municipal governments fanned out into the countryside to buy up, by force, all the maize they could find. Hoarding and profiteering were rife, and the urban poor suffered, too, but not as much as their country cousins. At least in the cities, where supplies were concentrated, there was some access to private charity and the public distribution of grain.[13]

In reading the contemporary accounts, one is struck by the apparent helplessness of the Spanish in the face of these recurrent famines. There was much hand wringing, and many Spanish expressed deep concern over the fate of the Indians.[14] For the most part their concern was sincere; encomenderos, curates, royal officials—most Spaniards in the colony, in fact—acknowledged that both private and public prosperity was dependent on Indian labor. Yet they seemed unable to translate that concern into any effective action to help combat the combined effects of natural disaster and the greed of some of their fellows, and some of the official measures that were taken simply made matters worse.

During periods of crop failure, the lowland Maya customarily took to the bush to forage for wild food, some of which has been listed in colonial texts:[15] a kind of bread made from the fruit of the *pich* tree, which resembles pine nuts; various fruits such as *zapotes* (sapodillas or naseberries); *corazón de bonete* (*cumche* in Maya, a squashlike fruit that yields meal for bread); and the roots of the *cup*, a kind of *jícama*, which is "practically a symbol for famine in the prophecies of the Books of Chilam Balam."[16] The Spanish first contributed to the grain shortages by allowing grain merchants and official agents to raid the villages. They then made every effort to round up the scattered Maya, fearing (with some reason, as we shall see) that they would become permanent fugitives. Many of the foragers, who were lured back to the villages with premature assurances that the crisis was past or by false promises that food supplies were available, might have survived if they had stayed in the bush.[17]

We have no way of comparing the mortality caused by famines before and after the conquest. But it is difficult to escape the conclusion that the Maya would have fared better without the sometimes well meaning but almost invariably disastrous intervention of the Spanish. Later chapters of this study deal with a variety of Spanish innovations, and Maya responses to them, that in one way or another may have helped to raise the rate of mortality or lower the rate of fertility (or both) among the colonial Maya. Among these are the physical dislocation suffered in the massive congregation program of the early 1550s; interference with marriage customs and family residential patterns; and destruction of crops by free-ranging cattle. Their effect is difficult to calculate, but they must be taken into account along with the totality of sociocultural and economic pressures exerted by Spanish rule.

Population decline seems to have proceeded at a slower rate in Yucatan than in any other region in New Spain and the Caribbean. Certainly the decline was more precipitous in central Mexico, even more so in other lowland areas, where the native populations were rapidly reduced to a tiny remnant when not extinguished altogether. The colonial demography of Central America has not been studied with the same intensity as central Mexico's or Yucatan's, but one gets the impression that from Panama to Guatemala, population declines were both rapid and massive, the main difference being that the Guatemalan highlands started with a much larger base.[18]

As important as the rate of decline, and perhaps more so, was the ratio of Spaniards to Indians in any given region. The more densely populated highland areas of both Mesoamerica and the Andes had always contained many more Indians than Yucatan, but they also attracted proportionately even greater numbers of Spaniards. As a consequence the ratio of the two groups was particularly unbalanced in Yucatan. Spaniards remained overwhelmingly outnumbered by Indians throughout the region's colonial history. No full, reliable count of the non-Indian population (that is, including the mixed bloods as well as whites) before the late eighteenth century has survived. It is more than likely that none was ever made, since the colonial authorities lacked the same fiscal incentive that existed for keeping careful track of tribute-paying Indians.[19] A few general estimates made by contemporaries and extrapolations from some partial figures provide a rough basis for my calculations; for all their imprecision, they show clearly enough how strong a numerical preponderance the Maya retained even during the period of most severe population decline.

In 1586 the governor estimated that the colony contained four hundred Spaniards (male heads of households), compared to some fifty thousand male Indian tributaries,[20] a ratio of 1:125, or 0.8 percent. By 1671 the number of Spaniards (which included creoles, or those of Spanish descent born in the colonies) had grown to thirteen hundred, while the Indian population had declined considerably, yielding a ratio of perhaps 1:28, or 3.6 percent.[21] Other non-Indians—Africans, *pardos* (a category that included both mulattoes and *zambos*, or those of Indian-African descent), and mestizos—were also increasing, especially the mixed bloods. The estimates oscillated so wildly, and the division of categories within the general category of *vecinos* (as all non-Indians were designated) was so capricious that no specific trend is discernible. This entire group of *vecinos* has been estimated at approximately 5.5 percent of the total population in 1639;[22] it could well have doubled by the end of the century, since the numbers of *vecinos* continued to grow while the Indian population curve reached its nadir.[23]

During the eighteenth century the growth rate among non-Indians rose markedly, far outstripping even the rapid increase among the Indian population during this period. A census taken in 1780 gives a total population for the province, excluding Tabasco, of 210,472, of which non-Indians accounted for 28.8 percent.[24] More detailed records for the period 1802-1806 show an increase to 388,752, with a further rise in the proportion of non-Indians to 29.8 percent.[25] They would, however, account for only 23.8 percent of the population outside Merida and Campeche; 19.3 percent if we also excluded the heavily mestizo and *pardo* (65.2 percent) southwestern coastal strip from Campeche to Isla del Carmen. Some portion of the apparently dramatic increase in the number of non-Indians may also have been more apparent than real, reflecting a shift in boundaries to include in the legal categories of *pardos* and

TABLE 2.3. SPANISH POPULATIONS IN NEW SPAIN: COMPARATIVE RATIOS, 1777-1810

District	Date	Total Population	Percentage of Spaniards
Puebla	1777	71,366	25.6
Tlaxcala	1794	59,158	13.7
Central Plateau	1794	371,253	3.5
Mexico (excluding Mexico City)	1794	1,043,223	13.1
Mexico City	1794	104,760	50.3
Oaxaca	1794	411,336	6.5
Yucatan	1780	210,472	7.9
New Spain	1810	5,764,731	18.6

Sources: All the regional figures except Yucatan are taken from Cook and Borah, Essays 2: 214-215, table 2.4. The figure for Yucatan is from AGI, Mexico 3061, Demostración del número de poblaciones, 15 April 1781 (the total given in the document's summary—214,974—does not tally with the total from the breakdown according to pueblos and castes—210,472). The figure for New Spain is from AGI, Guadalajara 323-A, Estadística del Reino de Nueva España, años de 1810-1811, sent by Fernando Navarro y Noriega. The population figures here differ from those in his Memoria sobre la población del Reino de Nueva España (Mexico, 1814), but the percentage of whites (18.3) is almost the same.

mestizos an increasing number of people who by any cultural as well as genetic criterion were in fact thoroughly Maya. I shall return to this point in the following chapter. No matter how inflated the figures for non-Indians may have been, they still fall far short, even at the end of the colonial period, of challenging the Maya's demographic supremacy. And it was well past the midway point of colonial rule, perhaps sometime in the early eighteenth century, before their share of the total population fell below 90 percent.

The imbalance is even greater when one separates Spaniards from the large vecino category—that is, when one looks at the ratio of conquerors to conquered. Considering the well-documented fecundity of the Spanish colonial elite, we must assume that peninsular immigration to Yucatan was extremely low. It took this group more than a century after conquest, despite sharp Indian declines, to reach 3.6 percent of the total population by 1671. This figure rose to 7.9 percent in 1790.[26] Mestizos at 11 percent and pardos at 9.3 percent accounted for most of the non-Indian increases, with negros or pure Africans, at 0.6 percent. A comparison with some of the districts in central Mexico, as shown in table 2.3, will underscore the extent of the imbalance in Yucatan. Only in Oaxaca does the proportion of Spaniards fall below that of Yucatan. The exceedingly low percentage in the "central plateau" jurisdiction is more than counterbalanced by the massive presence of Spaniards in the province, and especially in the city of Mexico.

Aggregate numbers do not tell the whole story. The uneven geographical distribution of non-Indians, and especially of Spaniards, further heightened the imbalance. The early settlers clustered in the three urban centers of Merida, Campeche, and Valladolid and the outpost of Bacalar. With few exceptions their descendants and the immigrants who followed them showed the same preference.[27] Such a settlement pattern reflected the traditional Spanish taste for urban living and a defensive strategy reinforced by the lessons of the Great Revolt of 1546-1547, in which Spaniards who lived in or visited their *encomienda* districts at the time had been the main casualties.[28]

The Spaniards had good reason to feel less than complacent about their security against both internal and external threats. But for its strategic position near the route of the treasure fleets and its large reserve of native labor, Yucatan might well have been abandoned entirely in the seventeenth century to Spain's European rivals, who infested the coasts, raided far inland at will, and even established their own logging settlements at the base of the peninsula. As it was, the colonists found themselves in an exceedingly precarious position not shared by their neighbors in either the core colonies or any of the other peripheral zones. They faced the unique triple threat represented by foreign incursions, an adjacent frontier zone of unconquered Indians, and a conquered population within their borders comparable in size to that of some core colonies but without comparable manpower to assimilate or control them. Added to that was the fear that the foreigners and both groups of Maya would all combine against them.[29] We have no evidence that either the "Lutheran corsairs" or the logwood cutters ever concerted any anti-Spanish plan with the Maya on either side of the colonial frontier. The leader of a short-lived Maya revolt in central Yucatan in 1761, who is reported to have assured his followers that "thousands of English" supporters would be joining them,[30] undoubtedly was indulging in wishful thinking or propaganda, or more likely the report represents more of Spanish fears than Maya hopes. But it is hard to dismiss it as a totally paranoid fantasy in view of the friendly relations the English maintained with the Indians in Belize and along the Central American coast and later with the Caste War Maya in the nineteenth century.

Defense of the colony was left exclusively to the colonists themselves until the late eighteenth century, except for a token force of regular soldiers stationed at Campeche and Bacalar. Clearly the Spanish were incapable of mounting guard over the entire colony, and it was moreover unsafe to spread themselves too thin. Instead they chose to concentrate their forces and to make Merida, Campeche, Valladolid, and Bacalar garrison towns from which mounted troops could be dispatched to any trouble spot.[31] Considering their resources and the size of the territory, this was probably the only feasible strategy, and on the whole it proved successful. The foreigners failed to gain a permanent foothold except in Belize; the colonial frontier was more or less contained and eventually pushed forward; and the conquered Maya presented no serious challenge to the authority of their masters.

FIGHT OR FLIGHT

The words and deeds of the participants in the Caste War of the nineteenth century demonstrate that a significant proportion of the Yucatec Maya remained unreconciled to what after three centuries they still regarded as foreign domination.[32] The Caste War has received its name precisely because it was not a simple peasant rebellion seeking to redress grievances—one that called merely for "bread and land," as did the later agrarian movements of the Mexican Revolution. It was, rather, a conscious attempt to restore the preconquest status quo by annihilating or at least driving away the whites. The Caste War reveals not only the profound resentment against the *dzuls* (foreigners) long harbored by the Maya, but also the social and cultural vitality that had enabled them to sustain through the centuries of colonial rule such a strong sense of their own identity, with an independent even if not fully remembered past and a vision of an independent future.

Both the hostility and the sociocultural matrix, which ensured that the hostility would find expression in their own version of an independence movement rather than in unfocused outbursts, were equally strong during the colonial period proper. In the colonial Maya texts called the books of Chilam Balam, which combined chronicle with prophecy, Spanish rule was assigned its place among the other evils the Maya were expected to endure, one from which they would be delivered at the proper time if the cosmos continued to operate in its orderly way. That the Maya not only hoped for but fully expected this emancipation from the Spanish by some means or another was no secret to their colonial masters. This conviction fueled the Maya's hopes of deliverance when the yellow fever epidemic of 1648-1650 initially struck only the Spanish cities and spared the Indian pueblos;[33] the leader of an eighteenth-century uprising gained adherents to his cause by proclaiming that "the time has come for the Spanish to be destroyed."[34] Although few Spaniards may have actually seen any of the books of Chilam Balam, they were familiar with the prophecies in the oral traditions of the Maya who surrounded them and had raised them from infancy on tales of imminent and bloody desolation that "froze the blood in our veins."[35]

Yet for all the jittery wariness with which the Spanish contemplated the mass of conquered but not wholly subdued Indians surrounding them, the colonial Maya displayed remarkably little overt opposition. A recent anthology of readings on native rebellions in colonial Mexico contains accounts of six uprisings in Yucatan, the highest number for any province in the viceroyalty.[36] Only one of them, however, can be defined legitimately as a colonial rebellion. Of the other five, four should be considered part of the process of conquest itself: two were merely maneuvers during the extended period of warfare; one was the Great Revolt of 1546–1547, really the last gasp of concerted resistance after a lull of only a few years; and the other was an example of the numerous confrontations along the colonial frontier between unconquered and apostate Maya on the one hand and Spanish missionaries and soldiers on the other.[37] The fifth "rebellion" was no more than a minor plot discovered in embryonic form in 1585;[38] the handful of conspirators involved might have moved from talk to action at some point if they had gone undetected, but we shall never know. Colonial documents refer to several similar "uprisings," which, according to evidence in the same documents, turn out to be equally illusory.[39]

That leaves us with one genuine colonial rebellion on record. This was a small uprising in 1761, centered in the village of Cisteil in the Sotuta district of central Yucatan and led by a partly Hispanized Maya, José Jacinto Uc de los Santos, better known by the self-endowed royal Itza surname of Canek.[40] The Canek rebellion threw the entire Spanish community, still so outnumbered even at that date, into a state of panic that hardly seems justified in retrospect. The number of rebels is unknown but probably never exceeded one thousand at the peak. The movement did not spread much beyond Cisteil itself and was quelled quickly, lasting barely a week from Canek's first rallying call to his capture along with the remnants of his followers. Still, there were elements to feed the Spaniards' ever-present sense of unease and vulnerability: hints and rumors of widespread plans that, had they come to fruition, would have seriously jeopardized the Spaniards' hold on the colonies and indeed their lives as well. The judicial proceedings in this case were uncharacteristically swift and perfunctory, seemingly more concerned with a speedy verdict against Canek and his lieutenants than with a full enquiry into the supposedly aborted larger-scale movement. Allegations were made that arsenals of weapons and munitions were being amassed in various locations, that native leaders from the barrios outside Merida and Campeche were involved in the plot, and that the *semaneros* performing domestic service in Merida had all been primed to set fire to their master's houses and slaughter the inhabitants on the preconcerted night set for a general uprising. Unfortunately, the evidence needed to sort out fact from hysterical conjecture is missing.

My own reading is that the implacable hatred felt by the Maya toward the whites (who were aware of this at some level of consciousness) always represented a potential threat that could not be dismissed lightly, but at the same time, a full-scale, coordinated movement was highly unlikely. The idea for the 1761 uprising seems to have originated entirely with Canek. His personal history and his marginal position at the interstices of Maya and Spanish society (a position that will be analyzed in the following chapter) probably provide the chief explanation for the timing of the revolt, in the absence of any general developments that would account for an increase in unrest at that particular time. More important is the Maya response to his plans. There is no reason to doubt that the Spanish intercepted some of Canek's messengers bearing invitations to towns throughout the colony to join him. However, there is reason to doubt that more than a handful, if that many, would have answered his summons. Canek was a visionary. If he was not acting completely alone, he at least did so without any large network of support, although he claimed to have traveled extensively around the peninsula before his call to arms in Cisteil. He also seems to have established ties with some of the local leaders who congregated during their official visits to Merida at a neighborhood bakery where he had once been employed. His uprising was, I think, an historical accident, ignited by his own peculiar circumstances and fueled briefly by the deep sense of grievance that the Maya nurtured but which they ordinarily did not translate into overt resistance.

Historians and political scientists have been much more concerned with explaining why rebellions occur than with the more tantalizing question of why they do not. What seem to be sufficient motives are rarely hard to find. Much of mankind has lived under conditions that the vast majority of scholars would find intolerable. Mindful of Hamlet's dictum that "there's nothing either good or bad but thinking makes it so," some scholars have recently begun to shift their attention from the actual conditions to the participants' perceptions of them. There can be no objective measure of oppression; it occurs only when a group's own standards of what is just and fair—its "moral economy"—are violated.[41] Yet even a sense of oppression does not always lead to active confrontation with the oppressors.

That the Maya often found Spanish rule oppressive is unquestionable, even if they did not all share the conviction that the rule itself was ipso facto illegitimate. But as we have seen, the grievances engendered only Canek's rather modest uprising. Colonial Yucatan was on the whole a tranquil place, insecure on its coasts and frontiers but internally peaceful. No evidence survives to suggest anything like the high incidence of local riots and other forms of direct, violent protest that are reported for the highland regions of Mesoamerica.[42] Besides the Canek revolt, only one other disturbance is on record—a riot in 1610 in the town of Tekax, directed against the local Maya officials and not the Spaniards.[43]

One explanation for the tranquillity is the lowland Maya's almost obsessively cyclical concept of time, in which Spanish rule, like everything else, was seen as a finite though repeatable part of an endlessly recurring cycle. A Spanish envoy to the Peten Itza kingdom in 1697 is said to have prepared the way for the region's conquest by persuading the Itza lord, Canek, that, according to the Maya's own *katun* (twenty-year cycle) prophecies the time was ripe for submission.[44] Without denying that a similar cosmological fatalism might possibly have fostered in the conquered Maya a kind of passive acceptance of Spanish domination, linked with the expectation of future deliverance, one can also find several explanations of a less transcendental nature.

Simple prudence was one reason. The Spaniards may have been greatly outnumbered, but they still held the upper hand in the superiority of their coercive power. The colonial Maya had some access to European technology. By the eighteenth century many owned firearms for hunting, despite official prohibitions.[45] They could buy powder and knew how to use it, and steel machetes were an item of everyday use. Horses were no longer the frightening creatures of conquest times. Most members of the colonial Maya elite mounted a horse or mule; the colony's transport was largely in Maya hands, and the Maya provided most of the ranch hands on the *estancias*. However, they lacked experience in the military use of the new technology. The Tekax rioters in 1610, numbering over five hundred, melted away merely at the sound of a harquebus shot fired into the air on the outskirts of the town by a band of eight mounted Spaniards.[46] The Cisteil rebels were not so easily intimidated in 1761. They resisted the Spanish siege of the village church, although six hundred of them were killed, as compared to forty of the attackers—at least according to the Spanish reports.[47] What is certain is that the Spanish managed to suppress the revolt swiftly. If the Maya were justifiably pessimistic about succeeding in any rebellion, they could have had a few illusions about clemency if they were defeated, in view of the punishments to which they were accustomed for much less serious offenses. In fact, the usual colonial policy was to pardon the rank and file and reserve "exemplary" punishment for the leaders. Such punishment could range from two hundred lashes and forced labor for life to drawing and quartering—with luck, preceded by execution. The severed heads and quartered corpses were displayed in prominent spots as grisly warnings to would-be imitators.[48]

The near certainty of defeat, to be followed by swift, severe punishment, cannot in itself explain the paucity of violent resistance. The certainty of failure was itself the effect of a more basic cause: the political fragmentation of the Maya that contributed to their conquest in the first place. Interprovincial rivalries had prevented the Maya from joining forces against the intruders initially, as well as during the Great Revolt of 1546-1547. Nor was the common experience of colonial domination sufficient to unite them. Even if traditional enmities (and these persisted along some boundaries long after the conquest) would not necessarily cause some groups to hold back or even to cooperate with the Spanish as they had done earlier, the Maya lacked both the habit of and the mechanisms for cooperation on a large scale. The possibility of concerted action was further weakened by the dissolution of the larger political units existing at the time of the conquest.[49] The nineteenth-century Caste War later demonstrated what the Maya could accomplish— if not victory, at least for a time something close to it—with greater skill in the military use of European weapons and with more coordinated action, both of which they developed by service in the state militias after independence. It is also noteworthy that by that time the local whites had lost some of the edge of superior organization they had enjoyed throughout the colonial period. With the state decentralized, local government in disarray, and political factions taking to the battlefield, the whites could no longer unite against any challenge from the Maya as easily and quicky as they had done in 1761.[50]

The level of panic generated by Canek's revolt, out of all proportion to its actual size, must be accounted for partly by the element of surprise (Spanish distrust of the Maya had not, in fact, been confirmed by any overt action since 1547) and partly, perhaps mainly, by the frightening specter of a widespread rebellion.[51] The evidence for this, as I have noted, is far from convincing. In particular, the suggestion that all the *semaneros*, converging on Merida from one hundred or more villages, had been mobilized to attack the Spaniards at a prearranged signal stretches credibility to the breaking point.[52] Nevertheless, although the Spanish considered Canek a lunatic, they also became convinced that he, or someone linked to him, had enough organizational skill to make widespread contacts and preparations. If such a conspiracy did exist, it obviously remained only that—a conspiracy. The Maya were not as atomized as the Spanish wished, but neither were they as well organized as the Spanish feared at this time. An excellent communications network was maintained from community to community and region to region. It was, so far as we can tell, a network of information only, not of orders or coordinated planning. News could be shared and invitations issued, but no leadership and no structure, even an informal one, existed for making and enforcing decisions beyond each individual pueblo. The Maya's potential for collective resistance on a large scale was never realized during colonial times. I suspect that a pragmatic assessment of their own organizational limitations and of the futility of any uncoordinated action did much to keep them in check.

ANOTHER and equally potent motive for not rebelling was the existence of a more attractive alternative. Like most dominated groups, the Maya resorted to a variety of strategies short of violent confrontation in an effort to improve their lot. Petitions, litigation, payoffs and accommodations with government agents, playing off one patron against another, concealment, conveniently muddled financial records, and other forms of evasion were all, as we shall see, part of the repertoire, that native leaders developed to survive within the system.[53] The Maya leaders' own subjects, as we shall also see, could relieve some of the pressures on them by moving to another pueblo or into dispersed settlements. But these tactics were at best ameliorative, and there was another more drastic choice available: the Maya could escape from the system altogether by fleeing into the unpacified regions to the east and south, where Spanish sovereignty was only nominal.

Running away was as radical a form of protest against the colonial regime as rebellion, but considerably less risky. It is an option that any dissatisfied group might prefer but one not always available where the physical or sociopolitical environment is more circumscribed. To outsiders the lowland Maya appear to be (and consider themselves to be) much less bellicose in temperament than the peoples of highland Mesoamerica. This may be because for so long in their history they have had (and still have, to a large extent) the choice of flight over fight when faced with intolerable circumstances. The colonial Maya were certainly not trapped in a tightly controlled system like North American slavery, from which permanent escape was difficult, even if the plantations are no longer seen as sharing some of the hermetic qualities of modern concentration camps.[54] Within the more lax regimes of Latin America (lax in practice if not always in precept), Yucatan offered better opportunity for escape than many other colonies where no unpacified territory existed nearby or where, as on the eastern slopes of the Andes, the colonial frontiers also divided sharply contrasting ecological zones and were often boundaries between distinctive ethnolinguistic groups as well. The sparsely populated zones of refuge in the southern Maya lowlands presented neither geographical nor cultural barriers to flight. The fact that roads in the colonial period were few and bad and connected only the major population centers was an inconvenience only for the mounted Spanish traveler. A maze of footpaths along which the Maya moved freely crisscrossed the entire peninsula even in the supposedly uninhabited bush. The bush seems impenetrable and disorienting only to the uninitiated. Trails abound that mules and clumsy *dzuls* may stumble along, when they can follow them at all, but which the Maya traverse with astonishing speed at a steady, ground-eating trot, even with heavy loads.

The very simplicity of the ordinary Maya's material existence enhanced their freedom. The colonial Spaniards recognized this and in exasperated moments suspected the Maya of deliberately cultivating poverty so that they could escape easily, unencumbered as they were with wordly goods.[55] A grinding stone for preparing corn meal was all a woman needed to start a new home, and these stone implements can be chopped out of the soft limestone almost anywhere; for the man the necessities were a machete and seed for new crops. The forest would provide the rest. Refugees, it was reported, lived on game and the same wild fruits and roots that have been identified as "famine food" until a new milpa could be harvested. And everywhere, in new settlements and old, in suburban barrios, villages, or *ranchos*, the nearby bush in any case provided all the materials for the common Maya dwellings and their meager furniture and utensils.

The relatively well-documented migrations resulting from the Caste War serve to illustrate this ease of movement. From the mid-nineteenth century until well into the twentieth, much of the eastern half of the peninsula and almost the entire southern lowlands were in a state of flux. Refugees crisscrossed the area and entire polities shifted residence with the readiness of nomads. All wars are disruptive to some degree. The point here is the scale of these movements and especially the apparent facility with which the Maya, including women and children, were able to move long distances quickly, set up new households and plant new crops, and then move on again when necessary, baffling both their government adversaries and the historians who have since sought to trace their moves through the written records.[56]

Such movements were a long-established Maya habit dating from well before the Spanish conquest, which itself displaced many people. Native chronicles and oral traditions record a number of pre-Columbian

4. Preparing tortillas. A square of sheetmetal has replaced the traditional baked–clay griddle (*comal*). (Photo by the author)

migrations within the region,[57] as well as the series of alien incursions that have already been mentioned. One group, the Itza, is supposed to have relocated itself all the way from Chichen Itza at the northern tip of the peninsula to its base in the Peten. The influx of Yucatec Maya refugees from the north both during and after conquest thoroughly changed the ethnic composition of the central and southern Maya lowlands, frustrating any attempt by scholars to reconstruct pre-Columbian ethnic boundaries on the basis of modern ethnographic data.[58]

The refugee Maya apparently had little difficulty adjusting to life on the other side of the frontier. If they moved in large enough numbers, they might occasionally reestablish their own communities; but they were also easily integrated into existing ones. Many of the settlements contacted over the centuries by visiting Spaniards contained both unpacified and apostate Maya.[59] They spoke the same language, maintained the same patterns of subsistence and economic organization and continued to share roughly the same sociopolitical system and, to a large extent, the same beliefs, despite the influence of Christianity on the pacified Maya. Because of the steady communication across the frontiers, they possessed a single cultural system with gradations of Spanish influence, which neither permeated the culture of the conquered Maya thoroughly nor left the unconquered Maya totally untouched.

Only recently have scholars begun to explore the colonial history of the unpacified regions. When it was considered at all in the past, this history was seen as the tail end of the pre-Columbian period rather than as one having a dynamic of its own. The two-way movement of people, goods, and information across the frontiers clearly had a profound effect on the unpacified areas long before they were actually conquered.[60] Here we shall concern ourselves with the effect of the zones of refuge on the area under Spanish control.

For one thing, the zones provided a safety valve. Flight, temporary or permanent, has been the characteristic Maya response to crises throughout their recorded history. In colonial times famines and epidemics, political troubles, or personal conflicts could send individuals, family groups, or whole villages into the bush.[61] Many would not go far, only to their milpas or some nearby *cenote* where they would camp out to weather the crisis. Some might drift to another community. Others presumably found conditions too intolerable to return; they chose to remain permanently outside the colonial orbit, and most of them eventually made their way across the frontier.

Intolerability is of course a subjective judgment. The ease of escape may have lowered the Maya's level of tolerance, and it may also have checked their pugnacity, predisposing them to a certain docility, but one with definite limits. We have no way of knowing because there is no record indicating how many Maya chose to flee, let alone what particular circumstances spurred the decision in each case.[62] Even if all the colonial parish registers of baptisms and burials had been preserved, we could only calculate from them the number of people who are unaccounted for. The colonial authorities themselves had no way of telling how many of these were escapees and how many had perished somewhere in the bush, or how many were among the nameless thousands who died along roads and in city streets during famines and epidemics. Word sometimes filtered through to Spanish officials that some missing person had "gone to the Peten."[63] The Maya themselves probably had a fairly good idea of the general whereabouts of most of the other survivors but they understandably did not communicate this information to the Spaniards.

The zones of refuge shrank gradually as the Spanish extended their control into the Montaña region of southern Campeche and further south into the Peten after the conquest of the Itza in 1697. They established a permanent mission at Chichanha on the southwest frontier, a line of communications from Campeche to Lake Peten, a *vigía* (lookout station) at the Bay of Ascención on the east coast, a military outpost at Isla del Carmen, and a string of towns along the gulf coast—all in the eighteenth century. It is difficult to say to what extent these new settlements may have discouraged flight. Certainly the escape routes became constricted and evasion was made more difficult for the refugee groups, but it was not impossible. All the new settlements continued to be surrounded until the end of the colonial period (even before the Caste War Maya had pushed back the frontier once again) by large areas of unsubdued bush that were penetrated infrequently and uneasily by the Spaniards. They were still only islands, at best archipelagos, in a hostile Maya sea.

The Spanish were well aware that many Maya chose to "vote with their feet" against colonial rule, although they rarely ventured to estimate their numbers.[64] They did receive some indication via the Maya's own grapevine, however, and whenever missionaries or soldiers came across groups of Maya during forays into the unpacified areas, a high proportion of them were not unconquered, pagan Maya but apostates with Christian names who had, in Spanish eyes, perversely renounced the benefits of civilized life and the hope of eternal salvation. Though perverse, the choice to move across the frontier was not considered wholly irrational: that is, the Spanish were also well aware that they often had only themselves to blame if the Maya fled. Since flight was

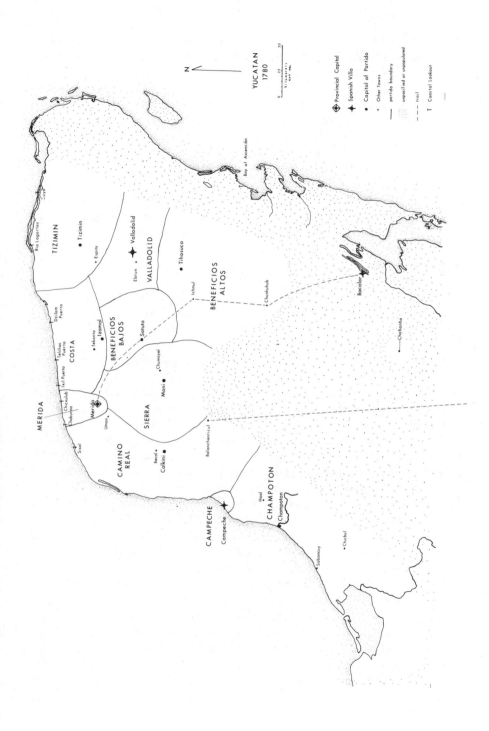

MERIDA

TIZIMIN

VALLADOLID

BENEFICIOS ALTOS

BENEFICIOS BAJOS

COSTA

CAMINO REAL

SIERRA

CAMPECHE

CHAMPOTON

Rio Lagartos

Cuyo

Tizimin

Espita

Ebtun ✦ Valladolid

Tihosuco

Ichmul

Chunhuhub

Bacalar

Chichanha

Dzilam Puerto

Telchac Puerto

Tekonto

Izamal

Sotuta

Chumayel

Mani

Tixil Puerto

Chicxulub

Merida ◈

Chuburna

Uman

Bolonchenticul

Becal

Calkini

Sisal

Hool

Campeche ✦

Champoton

Chicbul

Sabancuy

Bay of Ascención

almost as harmful as rebellion to Spanish interests, the availability of this option could serve as a check on the worst excesses of the regime.

The gap between royal precept and colonial practice has become a commonplace in Spanish American history. It was especially wide in provinces like Yucatan that were remote even from viceregal control. However, if royal decrees, *visitadores* (inspectors), and *residencias* (the judicial inquiry mandated at the end of each official's term in office) could provide little effective protection for the Indians against determinedly greedy local officials who exploited the Indians directly and connived at private exploitation in return for bribes, the fear of losing large numbers of exploitable Indians sometimes could. Both royal revenues and private incomes in the colony were tied directly or indirectly to the size of the Indian population. All suffered financial losses when uncommonly heavy burdens on the Indians swelled the trickle of refugees to a stream.

The perception of this causal link was particularly acute when someone else's greed was to blame. In 1784 the curate of Nabalam, located near the eastern frontier, reported that the leaders of one of his villages had warned him that their village was planning to decamp en masse because of ill treatment from a local Spanish official. The curate sought to have the official replaced, alleging that he forced the Indians to cultivate so many cotton fields for him that they had no time to raise food for themselves and that the parish had already lost many Indians because of these and other abuses.[65] No countercharge from the official is on record, and in this particular case the curate himself may have been blameless. But competition over Indian labor was one of the more common sources of discord between royal officials and the clergy, with each side accusing the other of responsibility for Indian runaways because of unauthorized and excessive demands.[66]

Self-interest might be expected to place some limitation on the demands of most of the agents of church and state. Few were transients in the colony. Except for the bishops, the clergy soon came to be drawn almost exclusively from local families, and the middle and lower ranks of the state bureaucracy, when not creoles (locally born) themselves, tended to be permanent immigrants who remained in their posts for long periods, intermarried with the local elite, and acquired a stake in the colony's general prosperity.[67] The same considerations would not hold for the governors and their immediate circle of assistants, whose terms in office were limited and who, if unscrupulous, could calculate that the consequences of their abuses might be delayed long enough for them to make their fortunes and move on. The most notorious example in colonial Yucatan was Rodrigo Flores de Aldana, whose *repartimientos*, grain requisitions, *residencias* of native officials (with appropriate fines imposed for dereliction of duty), and other unsanctioned stratagems for extracting goods and cash from the Indians were so excessive, and the means his agents employed to force payment so brutal, that thousands of Indians fled their villages during his years in office (1664–1665 and 1667–1669). Two entire parishes in southern Campeche, Popola and Sahcabchen, containing eight towns, packed up and moved in a bloc across the colonial frontier.[68]

Flores de Aldana underwent two *residencias*. His influence at court gained him a brief reinstatement during which he managed to rally the entire colony in a rare show of unanimity against him. The voluminous records of the inquiries revealed few defenders of his actions other than his own minions. On this occasion clergy and laity were in full agreement, since both *encomenderos* and curates had lost many tributaries and parishioners. Flores de Aldana, sought to pin the blame for these losses on the bishop, citing excessive fees collected during a recent episcopal tour of inspection.[69] As for the *cause célèbre* of the Popola and Sahcabchen exodus: that, he insisted, was the fault of the English pirates based in the nearby Laguna de Términos; it was their harassment, not his own, that had forced the two districts to flee.[70]

These ingenuous excuses were contradicted by all the evidence. Much of the considerable fortune the governor had amassed in office was confiscated to repay the fines he had extorted from the Indians and to reimburse the value of the excess *repartimientos* over the limits authorized by the Crown. The trial records end with the sentence, so that we do not know whether this restitution was in fact carried out. At least Flores de Aldana was removed permanently this time, and the new governor was able to persuade many of the Popola-Sahcabchen people to move back to their old villages by assuring them of his benevolence and offering a temporary remission of tribute.[71] Some proportion of the other refugees also returned to their villages, but many did not. Though again we have no figures of the final balance, it is safe to conclude that these and other permanent escapees made a significant contribution to the severe population losses the colony sustained during this period.

POPULATION AND THE TRIBUTE ECONOMY

The conjunction of flight, increased pressure on the Indian population, and heavy mortality was not accidental. They seem to have fed on each other in the latter part of the seventeenth century to produce a crisis in the colonial regime, a crisis that resulted from an increasing disequilibrium between the colony's primitive tribute economy and the human resources on which it depended.

I have suggested earlier that demographic patterns were symptomatic of differences in the colonial regimes. More than a symptom, I would say that they were both a cause and an effect. The particular type of regime established in Yucatan was based on a relative abundance of manpower (that is, a relatively high ratio of Indians to Spaniards) and each helped to sustain the other. Spaniards had less incentive to take charge of production directly; with less drastic disruptions in the Indians' traditional way of life, Indian society was better able to reorganize after the trauma of conquest and begin to rebuild itself.

The early population losses were obviously not irreversible. We have scarcely begun to measure, if such a measure is possible, the devastating social and pyschological effects of the massive mortality the Indians suffered during the first years of contact. There must be a critical mass of population below which any society can no longer function with its traditional allocation of roles. We do not know what that mass may have been among the lowland Maya, nor how close they came to reaching it. Nor do we know what the sudden death of a large proportion of the adult members of a community would do to traditional kinship structures, for example, or how their cognitive system coped with the unaccustomed visitations of epidemic disease that seemed to leave the conquerors largely unscathed. Yet if their view of reality and their social structure had been shattered, the Maya somehow managed to rebuild them both sufficiently to survive and even to replenish their numbers.

Why then did the population suffer a second, more drastic decline in the second half of the seventeenth century? By that time the Maya presumably would have recovered from the initial culture shock and made their major psychological and social adjustments to alien rule. This fifty-year period in the region's history, from around 1650 to the end of the century, still contains many shadowy areas. But enough information is now available so that one can venture a tentative explanation for the decline—an explanation that, in analyzing the dynamic link between demography and the development of the colonial regime, attempts also to account for some of the variations in the two over time and from region to region.

As suggested in chapter 1, the Spanish initially brought to all their New World colonies a common predisposition toward indirect exploitation of a conquered territory through a simple system of tribute (precapitalist in structure but coupled from the beginning with a market economy that operated among the Spanish themselves and in their links to the world market). Also common throughout the colonies was a

80

tendency over time to rely less on tribute in its various forms, in favor of incorporating the Indians directly into the market economy. The rate and degree of this shift depended on the relationship between two interdependent variables: the local supply of manpower and Spanish demand for it.

Spanish demand was in one sense stimulated by the supply of labor, since Spaniards tended to be attracted to the areas of highest Indian population density (which also happened to have the most congenial climate). But they were prepared to shift manpower to some extent to meet needs in other areas. Examples are the early slave raids from the smaller Caribbean islands to Hispaniola and Cuba, the conquest-period shipments from Yucatan to central Mexico and from Nicaragua to Guatemala, and the later mita system of forced labor in the Andes, which drew on a large catchment area for the Potosí mines in present-day Bolivia.[72] The principal variable in stimulating demand was a region's export potential, especially the presence of precious mineral deposits and the attendant economic activities that grew up to support the mining industry. Conversely, the Spanish could respond to significant losses in the labor supply, as I have suggested, by developing new systems of production and labor recruitment, in effect moderating their demands by using the available manpower more efficiently. This and other changes, such as a shift to less labor-intensive enterprises and a slowdown in economic activity, occurred, together or singly, in many colonies after the first frenzy of postconquest expansion. They were, however, adjustments forced on the Spanish because of the decline in the native population and not remedies devised to check the decline by alleviating pressure on the Indians. The Spanish and the Portuguese in America either failed to perceive the link between these demands and depopulation, or they were unable to reconcile the desire for immediate gain with long-term interests.[73] This failure to make more timely modifications in their labor demands must bear part of the blame for what has been called "possibly the greatest demographic disaster in the history of the world."[74]

In Yucatan the ratio between labor supply and demand remained more stable. The poverty of physical resources, the colony's commercial isolation, and the related entrepreneurial sloth of the Spaniards helped to preserve the Maya from the more severe demographic collapse that occured in central Mexico. At the same time, the Maya were saved from the more rapid shift to a market economy that was in part both cause and effect of the collapse in Mexico. For the first century after conquest, the demographic and social strength of the Maya and the tribute economy were all mutually reinforcing. The tribute system was less socially

81

and culturally disruptive than were the more direct methods of tapping the area's resources—the difference, as I have suggested, between a parasite that merely feeds off a host and one that destroys it in the process. However, any class of parasite can prove fatal if it multiplies too fast or if the host's resistance is weakened. In the latter part of the seventeenth century the tribute system nearly proved so for the Maya.

The tribute system, as outlined in royal law and under ordinary circumstances, need not have placed an undue strain on Maya resources. The problem was that it combined inflexibility in the legal demands, which were unresponsive to either individual or collective hardship, with unpredictability in the unsanctioned demands. The Maya had no way of foretelling what, beyond the legal quotas, they might have to contribute in the way of cash, goods, and labor in a given year and thus they had no opportunity to plan for contingencies. A variety of unexpected contributions could be imposed at any time in addition to the usual extras that might not be strictly legal but had nevertheless become customary. Especially capricious and ruinous were the tours of inspection by governors and bishops, as mentioned in chapter 1. The tours had no fixed schedule, and no official quotas regulated the fees, fines, and gratuities collected. The only discernible criterion governing the amount was the degree of rapacity or imprudence of individual officials—whether they were content merely to double or triple their ordinary incomes or sought an even higher return on their investment in colonial service.

The authorized taxes and labor quotas were, on the other hand, all too predictable. Although heavy, they were not necessarily excessive in good years, but failed to make allowances for the all too common bad years. The tithes and *alcabala* levied on *vecinos* were more equitable. Tithes were a tax of 10 percent on agricultural products, and the *alcabala* was an excise tax of 6 percent. If such taxes are considered regressive because they are ungraduated, then the head tax or any fixed rent is manifestly confiscatory when applied to subsistence farmers. In prosperous times the combined head taxes represented one-quarter of the Maya farmer's labor,[75] and they remained fixed and inexorable regardless of crop failure or other calamity, while the tithe was proportionate to the changing fortunes of the producer. Only the worst famines and epidemics prompted the colonial government to grant the survivors tardy and short-term exemptions, which, however, brought no relief from any accumulated tax debts. During the 1769-1774 famine, for example, the Maya were relieved from tribute payment for five years.[76] But crops had either failed entirely or yielded a minimal harvest during nine of the ten years since 1765. The Spaniards acknowledged that the disruptive effects of the migrations and population losses lasted considerably longer,[77] to say nothing of the lingering effects of near starvation on the survivors.

Such special concessions were in fact rare. They were offered primarily to attract the refugees back to their villages (and tax rolls), in the same spirit in which brief tax exemptions were granted to newly reduced Indians from the unconquered zones to make the colonial yoke seem more acceptable. No tax relief at all was granted in individual cases of illness or injury unless they resulted in permanent disability.

The colonial tax and labor systems actually functioned in such a way that the burden on the individual tributary was likely to be increased in times of general calamity, rather than alleviated. All the contributions were imposed as general quotas on the communities. Purportedly calculated according to each community's population, the taxes were based on censuses taken every five years with no readjustments made in the intervals, under the assumption, perhaps, that the number of people removed from the tax rolls by death, old age, or disability would be offset by the number of youths reaching tributary age. As we know, the native population was not stable. And, although some of the decline was due to slow attrition, most came through sudden, massive losses from famines and epidemics. Aside from the temporary relief granted them grudgingly during the most severe general crises, the communities had to wait for the next census for more equitable taxation, with the surviving members liable for the full quotas in the meantime.[78]

Working to the Indians' benefit during the times of population growth, the unresponsive tribute system (tribute in its broadest sense) reinforced any downward population trend. And this is what seems to have occurred in the latter part of the seventeenth century. What may have been a barely perceptible disequilibrium building up in the tribute economy reached a crisis shortly after the middle of the century, when an increasingly heavy burden of *repartimientos* and other exactions followed upon a series of particularly severe epidemics and famines. Population losses were severe and sudden, representing between 1643 and 1666 a sharper and more rapid decline than in the decades following the conquest.[79]

The increase in burdens may have been in part fortuitous, in the shape of a particularly rapacious governor, the aforementioned Flores de Aldana. His *repartimientos* and other impositions on the Indians seem, by common agreement, to have exceeded the normal bounds of official greed to which both Indians and fellow Spaniards had been accustomed. It is likely, however, that the activities of Flores de Aldana and his agents merely accelerated, as they also reflected, a growing disparity between Spanish demands and Indian resources. The essentially static colonial regime may have already reached a point where an ascending curve of demands, due to a gradual rise in the Spanish population, bisected a descending curve of Indian capacity to meet the demands. The lowered capacity resulted from the disastrous combination of yellow fever, smallpox, and famine, which, according to the Franciscan chronicler López de Cogolludo, carried away nearly half the Indian population in the years 1648-1656.[80] Flores de Aldana was as unlucky in his timing as he was greedy. He arrived in 1664 with expectations of making a great fortune in office (expectations that would not perhaps have been wholly unjustified several decades earlier) at a time when the other Spaniards in the colony, their numbers barely checked (and then only temporarily) by the recent calamities, were trying to squeeze more surplus out of a drastically diminished Indian population.

Thus, Indian demographic strength and the tribute system had been mutually sustaining, so long as Indian population recovery during the first half of the seventeenth century had been able to absorb increasing Spanish demands. That same system, without any technological or organizational innovations, contributed to further depopulation once the delicate balance had been upset. The excessive burdens of unregulated *repartimientos* and out-of-date tribute and corvée labor assessments, which did not respond to rapid and massive population losses, interfered with food production and lowered resistance to both famine and disease.

Although heavy mortality was the major factor in the net population decline, increasing evidence also points to mass flights to zones of refuge during this period. This exodus subtracted Indians from the colonial censuses as effectively as death. It probably accounted for a disproportionately large loss of the labor supply: while disease and famine took their highest tolls among the very young, the old, and the sickly, generally only the most able-bodied part of the population had the energy to flee. And every loss through death or flight left that much heavier a burden for the remaining members of each community.

The social costs were high. Mechanisms for mutual aid broke down; community and family ties were strained and often severed, further undermining the survivors' ability to cope with the pressures. Although we lack comparable demographic data for the period after Flores de Aldana's governorship, it appears that recovery did not begin until some time around the turn of the century. Disease and crop failure, disproportionate Spanish demands, mass flights, social disarray at family and community levels: all reinforced each other to sustain a prolonged deficit in the balance of births and deaths.

As for the processes of stabilization and recovery, we need more precise information on their timing in order to supplement the usual biological explanations. No doubt natural selection eventually produced a native population more resistant to the Old World diseases that had caused such devastation in the early years. But both Spaniards and Indians pursued conscious policies of self-preservation also. The crisis was apparently not severe enough to stimulate the Spanish to abandon the tribute system as the main foundation of the colonial regime. Commercial agriculture continued to expand but without any marked acceleration. The bulk of the colony's exports and staple foods continued to be supplied by independent Indian producers until well after the second half of the eighteenth century. Rather than make any radical change in economic organization, the Spanish seem to have sought to temper their demands. Perhaps it was easier to do so in Yucatan, where the nearby zones of refuge demonstrated so directly the link between excessive demands and population losses. Even if the local residents chose to place most of the blame on Flores de Aldana, the mass flights served as a warning to all that some degree of self-restraint was necessary in order to preserve the colony's economic base. *Repartimientos* were moderated,[81] and the fines and confiscations imposed on Flores de Aldana presumably had a sobering effect on his immediate successors. The Crown further lightened the Indians' burden by considerably reducing and restoring to them the municipal revenues that had been diverted into the provincial exchequer earlier in the century. The church made its contribution by regulating all the ad hoc financial arrangements between each parish priest and the local Indian officials. *Limosnas* lost their "voluntary" and therefore their arbitrary character and were brought under diocesan control with a uniform and fixed schedule for per capita *obvenciones* and parish fees.[82]

None of these measures could ward off either epidemics or agricultural crises. But by easing some of the physical and psychological stress of exorbitant and unregulated demands, they could help to lessen the toll of these natural calamities and to hasten recovery in the intervals. The Indians, for their part, had been developing during this same critical period a new institution, the *cofradía* (parish confraternity), which, among its myriad functions, was designed to help cope with the twin evils of Spanish demands and crop failure.

How well the *cofradía* served its many purposes will be left to later chapters that look at colonial Maya history from the inside. We have yet to complete the colonial context, in particular the political, social, and cultural aspects of the relations between Spaniards and the large proportion of Maya who chose to stay under colonial rule and accommodate themselves to it.

· 3 ·

A DIVIDED COLONIAL
WORLD

The physical survival of the Yucatec Maya was ensured by the vigorous demographic recovery that began around the turn of the eighteenth century. By the 1790s they had already surpassed the 240,000 figure derived from the first official colonial census of 1549. Conquest, as it turned out, had not set off an inexorable process of extinction, as occurred in some lowland regions in the Caribbean and South America. Nor have the Maya yet disappeared into a genetic melting pot by another process, that of miscegenation, which has all but eliminated many other groups as distinct ethnic entities. Spanish-Indian and African-Indian mixtures came to comprise an increasingly large proportion of Yucatan's inhabitants, but Indians still accounted for between two-thirds and three-quarters of the population at the end of colonial rule. And although racial distinctions had become somewhat blurred by social and cultural criteria, it is likely that most of those assigned to the category of Indian, and even some of those officially designated as mixed bloods, were pure Maya.

The survival of Maya culture is a considerably more debatable issue, as I have suggested earlier. Insofar as Maya culture was preserved after the conquest, the chief credit must go to the unattractiveness, in Spanish eyes, of the region that had nurtured it. A chain of causal links can be traced back to this basic geographic "fact," coupled with the equally basic demographic fact of a large native population. Flowing immediately from them were the two interrelated and mutually reinforcing phenomena of a relatively low density of Spanish settlement in the region and a relatively low level of economic development. And these in turn fostered a marked degree of physical, social, and cultural distance between conquerors and conquered—a division into two essentially separate worlds articulating at only a few points. It is only within this context of relative isolation that the preservation of Maya cultural integrity can be explained.

POPULATION AND POLITICS: INDIRECT RULE

To say that Spaniards lacked the critical mass in Yucatan to enable them to transform Maya culture more profoundly would be to oversimplify the implications of demographic imbalance. That imbalance, however, is a necessary starting point. Despite the population changes, outlined in the previous chapter, that tended to lessen the disproportion, Indians retained an overwhelming numerical superiority throughout the entire colonial period. Moreover, the disproportion was greatly increased by the Spanish tendency to concentrate in the urban centers and leave the countryside to the Maya.

Responsibility for control of the Maya hinterland was initially invested in the *encomenderos*. Indeed, the entire legal and moral justification for the original *encomienda* system rested on the *encomendero*'s obligation to protect, supervise, and Christianize the Indians entrusted to his care, for which he was to be compensated by the goods and services they would contribute. One hundred and fifty *encomenderos* could not directly govern several hundred thousand Indians, even if it had been their intention to do so, and even if they had not been so busy making forays into unpacified territory and answering alarms raised against pirates on the coast. From the beginning they relied on the Maya's own leaders to maintain order and keep the tribute flowing.

The *encomenderos* seem to have concerned themselves little with the way the Indians managed their own affairs even during the first post-conquest decades. They might visit their districts more or less frequently, depending on distance and the inclination of the particular *encomendero*. But by all accounts they confined themselves to receiving tribute goods, arranging for their transport, negotiating labor allotments, and sometimes organizing the few enterprises, such as indigo production, that required direct Spanish intervention.[1] Only a few took an active interest in converting the Indians: most were indifferent to evangelization, when not actually opposed to it, since the missionaries threatened their unfettered access to Indian resources.[2]

The role of the *encomenderos* in subsequent years of colonial rule is even more shadowy. They could easily have been mere royal pensioners, as they had become in most other colonies, collecting an annuity assigned them by the Crown and having no more influence over the Indians' lives than any other prominent Spaniard. For, by the end of the sixteenth century, tribute had become fixed in practice as well as by law, the local quotas were set by Treasury officials based on the clergy's censuses, and *servicio personal* seems to have been effectively divorced from the *encomiendas*.

I think, however, that this picture of the Yucatan *encomenderos* would be inaccurate. Not a particularly intrusive lot even in the early days, they became almost entirely separated from local governance. Many of them may not even have visited their *encomiendas* after the formal ceremony of "taking possession," in which a representative of the governor presented the *encomendero* to all the local Maya notables to receive their homage.[3] But this ritual was not necessarily merely a quaint anachronism, nor was the title of *amo* (master or lord) accorded him by the Maya officials a wholly empty one. The *encomenderos* earned the great deference and respect with which the Maya always referred to them not merely by virtue of their high rank in colonial society, but also because of the substantive role they played as patron to a collective clientele. They stayed informed of the general welfare of their districts (which, after all, affected their own material interests) via the reports that the Maya leaders presented when they delivered their twice-yearly tribute payments.[4] The *encomendero* was a remote but powerful figure; if he chose to, he could be a useful advocate, offering counsel and, even better, a word with the governor when the Indians approached him with a problem. This paternalistic role is mentioned so casually in the records as to suggest that it was taken for granted. It was also largely keyed to the *encomenderos'* own financial concerns. The most energetic defense of Indian interests was provoked by the establishment of *estancias* in the *encomenderos'* districts, which happened to compete with their own ranching ventures. Major crises, such as famine or large-scale flight, that also directly and seriously threatened their incomes generated the same degree of concern.[5]

In many regions Crown officials, named *corregidores* (or sometimes *alcaldes mayores*), replaced the *encomenderos* as the agents of colonial rule. The Maya of Yucatan were fortunate to be spared the attentions of these officials, who were almost uniformly condemned by contemporaries for their greed and brutality. Their appointment was expressly forbidden in Yucatan,[6] a measure of the continuing political strength of both the *encomenderos* and the clergy in that region. Until a radical reform and expansion of the colonial bureaucracy under the Bourbon monarchy in the late eighteenth century, no administrative structure stood between the individual Indian communities and the governor of the entire province or his immediate assistants in Merida: the Protector de Indios (sometimes called Abogado de Indios or Defensor de Indios), charged with advising the governor of Indian matters, and the Auditor de Guerra, his legal counselor.

The governors of Yucatan tried to circumvent the prohibition against *corregidores* by appointing substitutes under a variety of ingenious titles (among them *juez de milpas, juez de grana, juez de agravios*)—offices that would be prohibited after local protests to the Crown or the Audiencia of Mexico, only to be restored under a new name, then prohibited again, and so on. The governors' stubborn insistence (in one case, to the extreme of being carted off to jail in Mexico City for armed defiance of a royal *visitador*) would appear more than a little quixotic were the issue one of more effective provincial administration, as the governors repeatedly asserted. In fact, the issue was entirely economic. The offices in question were the only available patronage plums to be distributed among relatives and other hangers-on, and they were the sole vehicle for organizing the *repartimientos*, grain requisitions, and other business dealings with the Indians on which the financial gains of the gubernatorial term were almost entirely dependent.[7]

The governors had more success in creating a network of ostensibly military posts, which by all accounts served the same function as the *jueces*. Despite the contention of local critics that they contributed little or nothing to the colony's defense,[8] the structures had become firmly entrenched by the early eighteenth century, with *tenientes del rey* in Campeche, Valladolid, and Bacalar, and *capitanes a guerra* in the largest Indian towns, assisted by *tenientes* or *cabos* in the other major *cabeceras* (parish centers) and lookouts stationed on the north and west coasts. Unsalaried except for a few of the lookouts, all engaged in a variety of commercial operations on their own account and on behalf of their superiors.[9]

In their economic activities, then, all these subordinate officials appointed by the governors of Yucatan, under whatever title, can be considered *corregidores* in disguise. But from the point of view of Indian governance, they were not fully equivalent substitutes. The *jueces* merely visited the countryside, making the rounds at collection time from their base in the capital. The *capitanes* and *tenientes* resided among the Indians, but they had no direct authority over them, except in matters pertaining to defense. They could legally command the local Maya officials to provide transport for military supplies or to supply the labor to man the coastal lookout stations. But they did not collect tribute, apprehend offenders, try cases involving Indians, or supervise the Indian officials charged with these duties. In other words, they lacked the fiscal, administrative, and first-instance judicial authority granted to *corregidores* in other colonies, and to the subdelegates who succeeded both *corregidores* and *capitanes* under the revamped Bourbon administration.[10] It is likely that, had they wished to, they could have exceeded their legal powers and taken charge of local government. The evidence indicates that they did not. Their concern, like that of most other Spaniards in the colony, was to extract goods and services from the Maya. These the Maya's own leaders provided efficiently, rendering superfluous any further exertion by their overlords. It may be that in other colonies *corregidores* totally neglected local administration, confining themselves solely

89

to the same type of coercive, pseudocommercial transactions that characterized Indian-Spanish dealings in Yucatan.[11] In Yucatan, in any case, beyond the material burden that the subprovincial officials placed on the Maya—a burden to which any other Spaniard who had the opportunity added his bit—one can find no sign that they influenced the way in which the Maya conducted their lives.

The principal resident agents of Spanish rule among the Maya—and indeed, for a long time the only ones—were the Catholic clergy. Some of the Franciscan missionaries compared themselves to front-line soldiers.[12] More like garrison troops, they were scattered around the peninsula, each small band of two or three friars surrounded by thousands of conquered Maya. Their intrepidity is all the more striking when one considers that they were also the only Spaniards who regularly sought to exact any behavioral conformity from the Maya besides the fulfillment of labor and tribute quotas.

Of all the colonial institutions established in Yucatan, the Catholic church, through its parish clergy, unquestionably represented the most palpable presence among the Maya, exercising the most direct and powerful influence on their temporal as well as their spiritual lives. This was partly by default, given the exceedingly thin presence of other Spaniards in the Maya hinterland. But it was also because the clergy conceived of evangelization, and their Christian ministry in general, as part of a broader "civilizing" mission that was necessary for the new faith to take firm root. This mission has been called the first example of applied anthropology in the New World.[13] Certainly it was one of the more ambitious programs of social engineering in recorded history.

Religious beliefs and rituals are too intimately and intricately linked to larger sociocultural systems to be neatly separated from them. This insight, which informs the work of any anthropologist—or moral theologian—underlay the church's many-angled attack on traditional Maya patterns of thought and behavior. The effects of these efforts, often unforeseen by the pioneer missionaries and ill-understood by their successors, were correspondingly complex and wide-ranging. Almost every aspect of colonial Maya life discussed in the main body of this study was touched in some degree by the introduction of Christianity, and not merely the particular spheres of cosmology and ritual (analyzed in chapters 10 and 11). Here I shall simply outline the missionaries' goals and their impact on the otherwise largely isolated world of the Maya.

Few Spaniards, lay or ecclesiastic, questioned the propriety of forced Hispanization even if some, over time, grew to doubt its efficacy. They shared with the rest of the European colonizing groups the unswerving conviction of their own cultural superiority. To be fully civilized one must be Christian—Catholic of course—and preferably Spanish. A conviction of cultural superiority may be necessary for the success of any colonizing endeavor. To believe otherwise might weaken the nerve, blur the boundaries between rulers and ruled, and eventually undermine the ties binding colonists to the distant metropolitan center.

What distinguished Spain from other colonial powers was the concerted effort to impose their culture on their colonial subjects by force: to transform the Indians into shorter, darker versions of Spaniards. The French have deemed coercion unnecessary. They have proceeded on the assumption that no rational being would choose other than to adopt French culture once he was exposed to it. To the English, coercion has been pointless. The superior quality of English culture is innate, they believed, as much a product of English blood as of English upbringing, and therefore impossible for any colonial—indeed, anyone unfortunate to be born east of Calais—to acquire in more than a superficial way. As for the Portuguese, they do not seem to have concerned themselves overly one way or the other; they were as willing to take on African and Amerindian ways, if it suited them, as to transmit their own language and institutions.[14]

The Spanish missionaries in the New World thought it not only necessary but possible (in the early years, at least) to transform the Indians into replicas of Spaniards[15]—Spanish peasants, to be more precise, and a highly idealized peasantry at that. If we are to believe contemporary accounts, the Jesuits in Paraguay may have succeeded in molding their Guaraní charges along these faultless lines.[16] Not surprisingly, the peasantry at home fell somewhat short of the standards of perfect piety, docility and submissiveness, sobriety, sexual propriety, thrift, and industry that the missionaries brought to the New World for the Indians' emulation.[17] It was not, of course, a model of Spanish reality at all, but the paternalistic ideal of the good child or servant, an ideal that transcends national boundaries.

For the Spanish clergy in America, the pursuit of this ideal was no more than a corollary to their Christian ministry. Any Catholic priest entrusted with the "care of souls" has the duty to keep watch over the faith and morals of those in his charge. The Spanish missionaries, with the full support of the Crown, interpreted this duty broadly as a mandate to supervise every aspect of the Indians' lives from birth to death and to modify them when necessary in accordance with the church's teachings. Included within their purview were such obvious matters as attendance at mass and catechism classes, as well as many matters not so obvious. They concerned themselves with standards of dress and cleanliness, curing of the sick, patterns of residence, design of houses, inheritance of property, choice of marriage partners, and travel away from home—to give only a partial idea of the clergy's agenda.[18]

This was indeed a weighty responsibility. Regardless of how many generations of baptized forebears the Indians might eventually accumulate, they were always considered neophytes in the Christian faith, neophytes who must be kept under perpetual surveillance lest they slide back into pagan ways.[19] They were not only subject to all the ordinary lapses caused by human frailty, but also apt to deviate from the church's norms in their own peculiarly perverse—that is, non-Spanish—ways.

In their capacity as chief field officers of both church and state, the missionaries played a key role throughout Mexico in consolidating the military conquest. Because of that role, their power was immense. Their mission territories, or *doctrinas* were principalities where their word was law and obedience to it was enforced with corporal punishment. In Yucatan whipping was the standard punishment for any Indian misbehavior short of rebellion. (Since no Indians are on record in colonial Yucatan as having been convicted of murder, it is not certain whether they incurred the death penalty for this crime.) Confinement in the friaries and public display in the stocks were also deemed suitable punishments. The clergy imposed these penalties on their Indian charges with varying degrees of harshness, although they were usually administered by one of the community officials on a priest's orders.[20]

One consequence of Yucatan's economic lag and the correspondingly slow Spanish penetration into the countryside was that the colony retained aspects of a mission territory much longer than the more developed regions. Like the Dominicans in Chiapas, the Franciscans in Yucatan were granted an exclusive concession to the entire area and were able to resist challenges from the secular clergy much more successfully than the missionary orders in central Mexico, who were early given the choice of retiring to their chapter houses or moving north to new mission frontiers. Seculars very slowly made advances in their struggle with the regular clergy in Yucatan.[21] In 1737 the Franciscans still controlled almost half the Indian parishes in Yucatan (twenty-nine out of sixty).[22] By 1766 they had lost nine of these, but the twenty they held until independence were among the choicest benefices in the dioceses, containing altogether 36 percent of the colony's Indian population.[23] Whether in Franciscan *doctrinas* or in the secularized *curatos*, the clergy retained their predominance as Spanish agents in the countryside, with no significant rivals until the advent of the royal subdelegates after 1786.

The clergy's power may have received little challenge from other Spaniards, but they encountered many impediments to their goal of total control over the Maya. Not least of the impediments was their own lack of personnel. They began their labors in 1545 with only four friars. By 1580 their ranks had increased, with various additions and subtractions, to thirty-eight, ministering to twenty-two *doctrinas* throughout the pacified portion of the peninsula, plus four secular *curatos*.[24] This is still an exceedingly small number for such an immense territory; in addition, they were not evenly dispersed but followed, in less extreme form, the patterns of concentration adopted by lay Spaniards. About half the diocesan clergy, regular and secular, at any one time resided in Merida or Campeche—as novices and students; teachers and preachers to the Spanish population; members of the cathedral chapter; and as provincial superiors. Some were merely unemployed and others were absent from their parishes with or without leave. In the countryside the friars always lived in groups of two or three in the parish centers (*cabeceras*), the base from which they rode circuit through the various subordinate towns, called *visitas* in Yucatan. Secular curates tended to follow the same system. Obviously, the goal of close supervision was illusory.

Recent studies of plantation life in the southern United States have suggested that slaves, who lived out their lives within almost constant hailing distance if not within the eyesight of resident owners or overseers, nevertheless managed to maintain a separate, largely unsuspected world of their own, resisting their masters' aim of absolute dominion over their minds and bodies.[25] If that was the case, how much more easily the colonial Maya could subvert the designs of their masters. They were on their home territory, with their own language and their traditional social system (under assault but largely intact at the core), and subject to personal surveillance at most during one day out of seven. The friars' ideal of covering the entire territory once a week could be realized only in the most compact *doctrinas*, if then. At the other extreme were the isolated settlements on the eastern and southern fringes, where a year or so might pass between a priest's visits.[26]

The wonder is that the early friars accomplished as much as they did. Within a short span of years the entire pacified area had been organized into parishes. Every pueblo, even the most remote *visita*, had a Christian church with at least a stone apse and sanctuary. To all appearances Yucatan had already become a wholly Christian territory by the 1560s. But the friars and the Spanish in general lacked the manpower to force more than formal compliance with the norms they introduced. Their superior coercive power proved an effective deterrent to organized resistance or open defiance; it was no proof against the immense inertia of the Maya's passive, perhaps at times uncomprehending, resistance to changing their ways. Any system of control depends on intelligence, and the Spaniards' faltered at the limits of their ability to know what was going on. Aid from within the Maya ranks was not wholly lacking. But it was abundantly clear to the Spanish that what they learned from informers, what they pieced together from unconscious slips by other Maya, and what they observed directly provided only fleeting, imperfect glimpses into a world otherwise totally closed to them.

What they saw in those glimpses was most disheartening. They could ensure attendance at mass and catechism, but were unable to suppress parallel pagan rites.[27] They could enforce their code of dress in public, but not force the Maya to give up their "indecent and scandalous" attire at home: "topless" dress for the women and only a loincloth for the men.[28] All of the Maya were given saints' names at baptism (the Maya patronymics were retained) by which they are known in the documents. These were, for all we might have guessed, the only names they possessed. The only hint to the contrary is an item tucked away in a set of instructions issued by Bishop Juan Gómez de Parada in 1722. Gómez de Parada, an especially zealous prelate, had discovered during his diocesan visitations a practice that was either veiled from or unheeded by his parish clergy, and he admonished them to

> . . . correct the barbarous custom among the Indians of calling themselves by their names from pagan times, entirely forgetting the saints' names given them at baptism, to the extent that we have seen husbands who do not know the Christian names of their own wives.[29]

Lack of information was not the only obstacle to control. The friars received little support from the Spanish laity in any matters not related directly to the latter's material interests or offensive to their basic sensibilities and values. The colonists displayed as much enthusiasm as the clergy, perhaps more, for any expeditions to round up apostate or unpacified Maya, expeditions that swelled the tribute rolls as well as rescued souls from perdition. The friars could also count on a certain amount of cooperation in suppressing idolatry, especially if human sacrifices were involved. When it came to the rest of the clergy's "civilizing" mission, the attitude of both the colonists and the provincial government (however sincere the Crown may have been in its concern) wavered between indifference and opposition.[30]

Over the course of the colonial period, the number of clergy serving Indian parishes increased steadily as the first sprawling *doctrinas* were divided and subdivided, to reach a total of seventy-one by the early nineteenth century. The major Franciscan *doctrinas* had as many as four resident friars and the larger secular parishes had two or three assistants besides the curate himself—altogether almost as many priests as Indian pueblos. This does not mean that the clergy's control over the Indians increased accordingly. It may in fact have diminished for a variety of reasons, the main one being a change in the values and attitudes of the clergy themselves.

Once the clergy were past the first wave of apostolic fervor, their zeal seemed to wane as their numbers grew. Some became disheartened by the slow progress the Maya made toward "civilization." Others, especially the creoles who comprised all of the secular clergy and an increasing proportion of the Franciscans, grew more tolerant of their charges' deficiencies, when they regarded them as deficiencies at all. Although the causes for the change are not fully understood, the change itself is clear. The clergy became less distinguishable from the laity in their attitudes and behavior toward the Maya. This change was especially marked among the secular clergy, although it covered a considerable range determined by individual temperament and character.

The impression left by their own letters and reports, as well as by the voluminous administrative and judicial records of the later Bourbon period, is that the majority of curates had come to regard their benefices as merely a variety of *encomienda*—with some responsibilities attached, but primarily a steady source of income and prestige.[31] The income could be substantial, in local terms. The larger parishes yielded revenues that surpassed the governor's salary and rivaled the bishop's quarter share of diocesan tithes,[32] although without the same scope for extra emoluments. The Franciscans received an estimated 48,000 pesos from *obvenciones* in 1766, only 4,000 pesos less than the entire receipts for the royal Exchequer in Merida.[33] The elevated notion of what constituted an "adequate maintenance" (*cóngrua sustención*) for a curacy helps account for the high number of unemployed clerics in the diocese.[34] Incumbents were able to resist further subdivision of parishes and were even reluctant to hire more assistants, ill paid as they were at ten to fifteen pesos a month plus rations.[35] Clearly it was feast or famine for the colonial clergy.

Once formally appointed to a benefice, curates could not be ousted unless found guilty of gross misconduct. Negligence, a mere sin of omission, was apparently not sufficiently gross. At least there is no record of any curate's removal on that ground, despite ample evidence for conviction in the church's own records.[36] Many curates were residents of their parishes only technically, absent more often than not in Merida; when present, they were concerned mainly with the financial administration of the benefice or their private business ventures. Not a curate (or a Franciscan *doctrinero*, for that matter) lacked some sideline to supplement the ordinary parish income—at the very least a large orchard, a flock of goats, and some cows. Many curates owned *estancias* or haciendas or simply used community lands and labor to raise cotton, maize, and other cash crops.[37] To the extent that these interests predominated, the clergy were correspondingly less inclined to interfere in other local matters.

On the whole the Franciscans appear to have been less venal than the secular clergy. Although the material conditions of the friaries can hardly be described as ascetic, the regulars' vows precluded their amassing personal fortunes to support or bequeath to the hordes of needy relatives who swarmed around the curates. The Franciscans were also more concerned about the achievements of their ministry, taking a corporate pride in the order's role as the first bearer of Christianity to Yucatan. The concern had, however, become a more passive one by the later colonial period, a conviction ranging from resignation to despair that vigilance was largely futile, since the Indians would do and think as they chose regardless of their pastors' efforts.[38]

NATIVE LEADERS AND COLONIAL RULE: A FAILED PARTNERSHIP

Insofar as colonial rule impinged on the Maya world, it did so through the Maya elite, who mediated almost every form of contact between Spaniards and the Maya masses. Their attitudes and motives were therefore crucial in determining the effect on the Maya of the many pressures, direct and indirect, exerted by the colonial regime. The main difficulty the friars encountered in their evangelizing and civilizing mission was that the colony's intelligence operations and day-to-day policing activities were in the hands of a Maya elite whose own commitment to the new ways was grudging or ambivalent at best. Had the leaders themselves been more assimilated into Spanish society and culture, considerably more change, including undirected change, would surely have filtered into the Maya world. That they were not was largely the Spaniards' own choice.

Once the military conquest was complete, all the Maya leaders cooperated with the new rulers. They had no other choice if they wished to remain in power. There was, however, a more positive aspect to this cooperation during the early colonial period that was absent in later, better-documented periods and that contrasts with the usual view of the Maya's implacable hostility, masked, except for rare outbursts of a fury, under a prudent façade of abject docility. We find evidence of a certain creative optimism on the part of many Maya lords, as if they counted on a continuation of the pre-Columbian pattern of assimilation between

96

old and new elites that required only patience and flexibility on their part. Perhaps there was also an element of psychological need, a need to identify with the conqueror, which is said to be common among dominated groups. Whether fueled by calculated opportunism or subconscious need, what we find among the first postconquest generations of the Maya elite, then, is a degree of at least outward enculturation never again to be matched within this group.

By the end of the seventeenth century, only a handful of the Maya elite, if that many, could communicate with Spanish-speaking officials, although others may have known a smattering of Spanish words. It thus comes as a surprise to find that a century earlier the well-known Gaspar Antonio Chi, who served the provincial authorities as official interpreter and even prepared reports on various subjects for the Spanish Crown, was not unique in his day. During the early postconquest decades there were other Maya nobles who, like Chi, were completely *ladino*: that is, they spoke and wrote Spanish "as well as any Spaniard."[39] The friars' evangelization policy was responsible for this. Seeking to reach the Indian masses through their hereditary leaders, they had gathered the sons of the nobility into boarding schools attached to the friaries, where they were taught Spanish and sometimes Latin, as well as Christian doctrine and liturgy.[40] Pedro Sánchez de Aguilar, the creole cleric who wrote the valuable report on native idolatries, *Informe contra idolorum cultores*, in the early seventeenth century and ended up as a canon in the cathedral chapter of Lima, received his first Latin instruction from a Maya schoolmaster, a product of the Franciscan schools.[41]

No education is effective without some cooperation from the pupil, and this the friars must have gained. Many of the Maya elite embraced certain aspects of Spanish culture on their own initiative as well. For example, they built houses in the Spanish style, though some confessed to finding them less comfortable and healthful than their former ones; and they adopted what must have been the even more uncomfortable Spanish style of dress, so unsuitable to that climate, with heavy wool breeches and tunics, capes, cumbersome shoes, and felt hats.[42] They took to horses, swords, and firearms with more understandable enthusiasm, and equally so to European wines and spirits.

With the benefit of hindsight, one perceives these acts as thoroughly pitiful attempts by the Maya to ape the customs of their superiors—a futile and misguided gesture because the Indians mistook the outward trappings for the essence of equality. But here hindsight might prove misleading. A creative synthesis between new and old elites was not necessarily an entirely quixotic expectation at that point. Just such a synthesis was exemplified in the activities of don Pablo Paxbolon, the hereditary lord of the Acalan Maya. He may have been unique in acquiring one Spaniard as son-in-law and another as father-in-law through his second marriage.[43] But in his ability to manipulate the Spanish system, using Spanish backing to extend his own power while aiding in the consolidation of the conquest, he was far from unusual. Other Maya lords took part in, even organized, military expeditions and in many ways acted as partners in colonial rule.[44] If other Maya lords pursued a more distant policy of passive, outward cooperation, that was their personal choice.

The career of one don Fernando Uz at the turn of the seventeenth century illustrates a less flamboyant but nonetheless fruitful kind of partnership. Uz was the *batab*, or hereditary lord, of one of the two towns that had been congregated into the composite town of Tekax, in the province of Mani. He had also been appointed to the local administrative post of Indian *gobernador* in two other major towns of the same region. More importantly, he had served several of the Spanish governors in a variety of prominent positions. For example, he had supervised the construction of the royal road from Merida to Campeche, as well as other public works projects. At age forty-two in 1609, don Fernando appears in the documents as official interpreter and senior aide to the current governor, trusted and relied upon for advice and administrative tasks of considerable responsibility. He lived like a Spaniard, keeping a house in Merida in addition to a country seat. He spoke and wrote Spanish with greater elegance than many Spaniards, as the documents in his own hand and verbatim transcripts of his oral testimony attest.[45]

Uz was clearly no servile, degraded flunky but a man at the top ranks, moving with ease and assurance among the Spanish officials with every appearance of equality. In one sense he achieved a position superior to that of his immediate pre-Columbian ancestors, whose authority, while more autonomous, was much more geographically circumscribed. Spanish centralization had given him wider scope than any Maya ruler had enjoyed during the preceding centuries of political fragmentation in Yucatan.

Uz's career also illustrates the inherent falseness of his position and that of any other ambitious Maya nobleman who may have envisioned a merging of native and Spanish rulership. The Maya nobility continued to be officially recognized in Spanish documents throughout the colonial period as equal in status to the Spanish nobility.[46] That this fiction should have been maintained proves again how little the colonial realities were permitted to obtrude on legalistic principles. Uz possibly represented the last of the truly Hispanized Maya nobility, and the difficulties he encountered suggest why the species became extinct. He was arrested for complicity in the 1610 uprising in Tekax, an internal struggle directed against a local rival of Uz and not against the Spanish.[47] The records of the case, which are incomplete, give no proof of the charge nor do they reveal his fate. What they do reveal is that his main crime in the eyes of his accusers was his "ambitious spirit" and the very success he had achieved.[48] He was an object of envy perhaps, certainly of distrust, because though an Indian he had sought and to a certain extent achieved equality with the Spanish. Indeed, there must have been more than a few Spaniards in the colony whom he outranked in status. He did not, in short, know his place.

During the decades following the conquest, colonial society had been hardening into a system of castes that reduced all social complexities to the simple principle that Spaniards, no matter what their social status, were to be the masters in the larger colonial schema; Indians, regardless of hereditary rank and status within their own society, were to be servants. The blurring of this line of demarcation by people like don Fernando Uz could not be tolerated. Such marginal people can be dangerous not merely in the symbolic sense of taboo that has gained currency in recent anthropological discourse,[49] but also in a very practical sense that may underlie the taboo. These people make others uneasy by challenging an orderly system of classification, a system that, aside from the cognitive satisfaction it brings, serves as a guide to social interaction. The Spaniards who in effect accused Uz of not knowing the place that the colonial regime was in the process of assigning him were perfectly correct, and the unease that such ambiguity aroused was not entirely unjustified. If the Spanish were not prepared to grant full equality to talented Maya nobles like Uz (and Uz's talent was never in question), they were wise to see the risk in granting them the semblance of it. For if such men ceased to think of themselves fully as Indians, yet were not accepted as Spaniards, their equivocal social identity and sense of frustration would simply make them more likely to challenge the system; and their understanding of Spanish ways would make the challenge that much more dangerous. Such figures have been the major protagonists in all the independence movements in Europe's former colonies.

Uz was not the only dangerously talented, uppity, betwixt-and-between Maya to plague the Spanish. A collection of *encomenderos'* reports of 1579-1580, known as the "Relaciones geográficas," contains several splenetic tirades against Indians:

> . . . so favored by the clergy and the royal justices, so shameless and such great knaves that some of them dare to lay hands on

99

Spaniards, and especially the ones who have been reared by the friars, because they think that knowing how to read and write they are equal to Spaniards.[50]

The best-known example comes almost two centuries later in the figure of Jacinto Canek, the leader of the 1761 rebellion that bears his name. Canek was also an educated, Hispanized Maya whom well-intentioned Spaniards had favored. Although apparently an orphan of obscure birth, he was treated like the noble Maya youths in the early postconquest period, taken in and raised by the Franciscans in the order's main friary in Merida.[51]

Canek's abilities and education far exceeded the opportunities open to him and also, it would seem, exceeded his moral fortitude. He became prone to bouts of drunkenness, and the friars, their patience exhausted, eventually cast him out to shift for himself. Perhaps the alcohol was an early symptom of frustration. The descent from a spoiled favorite of the Franciscans, used to a comfortable and secure existence, to a common Indian forced to scrabble for odd jobs either created or strengthened in him a deep bitterness against the Spanish and an identification with his Maya brethren. He hatched a grandiose scheme to expel the Spanish and crown himself "king" in the bargain.[52]

The boundary of caste that had been solidifying in don Fernando Uz's time had become a Berlin Wall by Canek's and his upbringing must have been an extremely rare if not unique case. The Franciscans had long ceased to bother educating the sons of the Maya nobility. Orphans were frequently taken into Spanish homes, but in a thinly disguised form of domestic servitude that left no doubt of their subordinate status.[53] Canek was probably an unusually bright lad whom his indulgent mentors, out of what can only seem misguided affection, prepared for a place that neither he nor any other Indian could occupy in a colonial society.

The retreat from assimilation into the divided world of Spanish masters and Indian servants represented not so much a total reversal of policy as the victory of one strain over another, within a policy that was highly ambivalent from the start. This ambivalence can be seen throughout Mesoamerica and the Andes, where the sophisticated cultures and complex sociopolitical systems of Aztecs, Incas, and their neighbors and vassals inspired some Spaniards to think in terms of at least some degree of amalgamation with the native ruling groups, as both expedient and appropriate. For the Spanish were too aware of social distinctions themselves to lump the haughty, well-educated and often exquisitely refined native nobility together with their humble subjects.

Marriage, the classic means of cementing ruling alliances, was not un-common between conquerors and noble Indian women in either Mexico or Peru, although I know of only one example in Yucatan.[54] The first Franciscan missionaries in Mexico even envisioned a native Catholic priesthood and established their famous school for noble youths at Tlal-telolco, which initially at least had all the marks of a theological semi-nary.

Another current of thought opposed this policy of assimilation, and it eventually prevailed.[55] Indian schools were closed down, and during the entire three centuries of colonial rule the church was to ordain only a handful of Indians throughout the empire, and none of them—to my knowledge—in Yucatan.[56] A native nobility, some with considerable wealth and more than a superficial veneer of Spanish culture, survived well into the eighteenth century in many parts of the Andes and Meso-america.[57] But the Spanish had long ceased to regard them as equals; they were at best agents of colonial rule, not even junior partners.

The prudence of preserving rigid cast boundaries once they exist does not explain how they came to be erected in the first place. Undoubtedly it was dangerous to allow Indians to forget their place, but only because the place assigned to all of them was so unequivocally inferior. The answer to why that should be is not at all obvious. The Spanish of course could no more imagine a society in which opportunities for wealth, high status, and power were accessible to all regardless of birth than could any other Europeans at the time. Such a blurring of distinctions would have been equally inconceivable to the native nobility, who could easily match or surpass the Spanish in their obsession with rank and blood lines. The point is that the Spanish initially acknowledged these distinctions within Indian society and moreover seemed to flirt with the idea of incorporation at the highest ranks. There was nothing in the original encounter, except the Spaniards' repugnance for paganism (which could be easily overcome with Christian baptism), to foretell that the division, which all agreed was proper, would be made purely on the basis of race.

Physical anthropologists tell us that scientifically speaking there is no such thing as race. But for most of recorded history, we must deal with people unaware of this recent finding and for whom race was a palpable reality. It may be that all groups are inherently "racist" in the sense that physical differences are the easiest way to distinguish the "us" from the "them."[58] Another view, not necessarily incompatible, holds that rac-ism is a byproduct of any unequal encounter between two racial groups, as in a colonial situation, in which racial differences become a conveni-

101

ent a posteriori criterion and justification for unequal access to wealth and political power.[59]

One suspects that this is one of those unresolvable, chicken-or-egg questions. All I can suggest from the Yucatan case is that economic considerations gave firm support to the caste system, whatever the wellsprings of the racial criterion that informed it.

The solidification of caste lines in colonial society occurred during a period of vertiginous demographic change, when the first small bands of conquerors were becoming greatly outnumbered by swarms of fortune-seeking newcomers from home, and the original, apparently teeming multitudes of Indians were dying off with a speed that seemed to presage imminent extinction. The concurrence between policy change and demographic change might lead one to conclude that the early experimentation with assimilation was a mere tactical maneuver until the Spanish felt secure enough to relegate Indian rulers firmly to their subordinate place. I am inclined to think it was not an entirely cynical ploy but rather, for some portion of Spaniards at least, a genuine experiment, if only a very cautious one. The experiment was doomed by the fierce competition for limited resources, resources that in the case of Indian labor were rapidly dwindling absolutely as well as proportionately. Had the New World attracted only the original handful of conquerors and had the Indian population remained at least a little more stable, the idea of an amalgamated Iberian-native elite would not necessarily have been a chimera: witness the history of the Portuguese *prazeros*, or frontiersmen, in southeastern Africa or the *bandeirantes* in southern Brazil.[60]

In Spanish America the swelling of the ranks of the conquerors by new arrivals, especially Spanish women, made formal alliance with the native elite less likely. It also created an excess of candidates for the positions of power and wealth, a gap that widened with the natural increase of an exclusively Spanish rather than mestizo caste. The demand for "honorable" employment—that is, nonmanual, white-collar posts in the civil and ecclesiastical bureaucracy—far exceeded the supply, particularly where other economic opportunities such as mining and commerce were limited.[61] Given the apparently universal propensity to take care of "one's own"—one's own family and friends—the caste lines begin to look inevitable. To educate Indian nobles for ecclesiastical benefices, to appoint them to positions of prestige and authority, to include them in any of the material and social rewards of rulership would be to sacrifice the actual or potential interests of all those with superior claims to one's aid and favor through kinship or some other affiliation.

The need to accommodate the bevies of poor relations and other dependents who surrounded *encomenderos,* bishops, governors, and their immediate subordinates eliminated the possibility of continuing to co-opt or assimilate the Paxbolons, the Uzes, and other members of the Maya elite. Indians of whatever rank were to remain firmly and un-equivocally within the Indian universe. They would learn some Spanish ways, but only as outsiders seeking to maneuver through the thicket of Spanish administrative judicial systems in order to defend their com-munities' interests. And because their identity and interests remained firmly embedded within the Maya world, they served as barriers to, rather than conduits of, Spanish cultural influence. The division of colo-nial society into two separate worlds, with all its implications for socio-cultural change among the Maya, was thus a deliberate Spanish choice.

Caste and Culture

If Indians and Spaniards had lived out the colonial period in total iso-lation from each other, the discussion of colonial context could end here. The boundary, however, was not so sharp and clear. First of all, the simple Spanish-Indian dichotomy was complicated by the addition of Africans, and immeasurably complicated by the appearance of mixed bloods in various combinations. Secondly, the geographical division into Spanish city and Maya countryside, though pronounced, was never ab-solute. There were points of contact outside the formal hierarchy of political command. The steady increase of mestizos and *pardos* attests to one kind of encounter between Indians and non-Indians, however fleet-ing. The nature of the interaction and its significance for sociocultural change need to be examined before one moves on to look at the Maya world from within.

From the earliest postconquest days the territorial separation of castes was undermined by the need for Maya labor in the cities. The bulk of it was supplied throughout the colonial period by corvées drawn in rotation from the surrounding districts. As onerous as these labor drafts were to the Maya, they cannot be viewed as an especially effective ve-hicle for enculturation. The sojourns were brief, the tasks themselves were the same ones carried out in the daily round of life in the pueblos, and the draftees were largely segregated from direct contact with non-Indians even in the city. The public works crews worked and lived together in village groups, all of them under Maya supervisors; they might as well have been at home. And the same applied to those work-ing in domestic service. Anyone familiar with the older type of upper-class Merida household knows that except for the owner's living quar-ters, this is a Maya world, steadily replenished by newcomers from the

103

pueblo. And so it was in colonial times, except that the labor drafts were involuntary.[62]

Indians were also drawn into the city's orbit more or less permanently and more or less willingly as *criados*, or personal servants, in Spanish households. *Criados* held an ambiguous status equivalent to the *yanacona* class in Peru: still legally Indian but removed from the sphere of the pueblo, their labor obligations were remitted for full-time service to a particular Spaniard, and their masters were responsible for their tribute payments.[63] As opposed to the revolving crews of *semaneros*, the *criados* held positions of some skill and trust in the domestic establishment; they were the stablehands and gardeners, the cooks and nursemaids, who in the largest households usually worked under an African or mulatto (as often as not a slave) serving as majordomo.[64]

Outside the city walls of the three Spanish centers, satellite barrios grew up that were quite literally half-way houses between Spanish cities and the Maya countryside. Former *criados* and their descendents (called *naborías*) moved out from the cities and were joined by mestizos, mulattoes, and even some Spaniards. Indians sometimes moved in directly from the pueblos, bypassing the intervening stage of *criado*. *Naboría* was another of colonial society's limbo categories, retaining the legal caste identity of Indian and some, but not all, of the Indians' ordinary obligations. In theory they constituted a pool of day laborers for Spaniards in the city, in return for which they were exempt as a group from *servicio personal* and *repartimientos*. Unlike *criados* they were responsible for their own tribute and other head taxes, although these were set at less than half the ordinary rate in the pueblos and this tax advantage was presumably intended as an added enticement.

The *naborías* were, however, scarcely less marginal to the Spanish city than they were to the Maya pueblo.[65] The urban economy was too small to absorb them fully. A very small proportion succeeded in establishing themselves as petty traders, shopkeepers, and artisans. Some supplemented the *semaneros* in the same unskilled service jobs; most were full-time agriculturalists like their country cousins. They worked for *vecinos* as day laborers on nearby estates, raised garden crops and poultry on their household plots, and made milpa on lands rented from non-Indians or owned by the community. Despite their suburban location, the barrios were structurally identical to any rural Indian pueblo. They had their own communally owned lands outside the residential limits, their own municipal government, and their own corporate identity, separate from the *vecinos* who resided within their jurisdiction.[66] Because of their proximity to the urban centers and the concentration of *vecino* residents, contact between Indians and non-Indians was simply more intense than in the ordinary pueblos. It was not a sharp contrast, for the geographical division became undermined in the countryside also, as non-Indians moved out from the cities.

Most of the movement was only temporary. Governors sent out a stream of agents to supervise their business dealings; Spanish merchants and itinerant peddlers of all racial compositions crisscrossed the peninsula; and the urban-dwelling ranchers visited their estates to supervise harvests and the annual cattle round-up, more frequently if the estates were nearby. As the colonial period progressed the number of travelers and also the number of resident *vecinos* increased. Mestizos predominated, followed by *pardos* and a small number of Spaniards. By one calculation, non-Indians accounted for 31.2 percent of the *cabecera* populations in the late eighteenth century, and 14.8 percent in the subordinate *visita* towns.[67] Obviously the segregation policy of the Spanish Crown, which limited the period of time that non-Indians were permitted to sojourn in Indian towns and entirely forbade their permanent settlement there, was a complete fiction in Yucatan.[68]

What does the presence of *vecinos* in such substantial numbers signify? One cannot assume any direct correlation between numbers and cultural change, or, for that matter, between physical propinquity and cultural change. One is struck even in the late colonial period by how socially and culturally self-contained the Maya universe was despite the invasion of their territory by non-Indians. Much of the contact was fleeting and indirect. Just as all of the administrative orders were transmitted through the Maya leaders, so too were the economic transactions, official and unofficial. All the general *repartimientos* were negotiated with the Maya leaders; even the merchants and peddlers worked through one or two Maya agents in each pueblo, and any exchange was supposed to be made only in the presence of and ratified by a Maya official.[69] Weekly labor was all contracted through these same officials. Tenant farmers on the *estancias* made their own arrangements, but except for the larger estates that had resident managers they dealt with the Indian foremen and may scarcely have seen the owner from one year to the next. The agents who descended on the villages in the periodic tours and requisitioning expeditions were analogous to the plagues of locusts that struck the countryside from time to time—as devastating economically as they were culturally insignificant.

Contact with the *vecinos* who were full-time residents in the pueblos was more sustained, although it should be borne in mind that at the same time that the *vecinos* were moving into the pueblos, the Maya themselves were moving out (not entirely coincidentally). By the early eighteenth century, fully one-third of the so-called *indios de pueblo* lived scattered in small settlements on community or *estancia* lands,[70] isolated from the towns except for their weekly or fortnightly attendance at mass.

Within the towns the recorded interaction was confined mainly to economic dealings. *Vecinos* residents bought house plots and parcels of land or rented milpa sites from the Indian town councils.[71] The most influential were able to obtain quotas of draft labor for agricultural work. Some were peddlers, selling the same kinds of goods as the urban–based merchants but on a smaller scale. Otherwise they appear as very shadowy figures. They were in but not of the Maya world, totally excluded from the local political structure and the round of ritual activities that sustained it, and largely excluded from any formal social links.[72]

Parish registers reveal some intermarriage, but caste endogamy was high, and especially so among Indians. In the town of Tekanto during the eighteenth century, for example, the rate of intramarriage was 94 percent for women and 98.9 percent for men.[73] In modern Latin America the ritual kinship system of *compadrazgo* (co-godparenthood) has become a common means of extending social networks and, in particular, of forging links across the hierarchies of class and caste. However, this type of vertical, intercaste integration has been found to correlate closely with the degree of sociocultural and economic mobility in a particular community or region.[74] It is therefore not surprising to find that *compadrazgo* ties between Indians and non–Indians were rare in colonial Yucatan, once the early period of evangelization had passed, when prominent Spaniards commonly served as godparents to the Maya nobility. A thorough sifting of parish registers might reveal more exceptions, especially as the proportion of non–Indians in the total population increased. The examples I have seen occurred mainly in the case of orphans or as adjuncts to the affinal ties already created by intermarriage.[75]

Illicit unions across caste lines were probably considerably more common, although, as I shall show in the following section, they were not necessarily as common as the official statistics on the number of mixed bloods might suggest. And casual encounters—the "ill usage" that Indian women who served in Spanish households or in the travelers' inns were subject to[76]—were vastly different in their sociocultural implications from the more durable unions the church defined as concubinage. Although the bishops viewed concubinage as an all–too–prevalent vice at all levels of colonial society, the incidence of such sustained relationships across caste lines seems to have declined greatly from the early years; or rather, Indian women ceased to be the partners of choice once Spanish, mestizo, and mulatto women became available.[77]

Even if one grants a low level of integration in the shared territories of suburban barrio and rural pueblo, the cultural impact of the *vecinos* still seems uncommensurately weak. These were not large metropolitan complexes, where members of ethnic enclaves might be able to live out physically self-enclosed lives. They were small and medium-sized towns, with only a handful exceeding five thousand inhabitants by the end of the colonial period, and over two-thirds of them containing fewer than one thousand.[78] All had one main plaza and one common place of worship. It would be impossible to escape frequent face-to-face contact of an informal kind that is not likely to appear in the archival records, but a kind that would encourage—indeed, require as a minimum for mutual intelligibility and mutual toleration—some shared codes of behavior, some shared meanings. These did exist. The surprise is that their shape, their flavor, and their origin seem so predominantly Maya with so minor a trans-Atlantic influence.

That Africa should have contributed little to the cultural mix of colonial Yucatan is understandable. The colonists were too poor to be able to import many slaves and it is likely that few of these were *negros bozales* brought directly from Africa. The number of pure Africans in the censuses at any time was very low, for they quickly merged into a mixed population of mulattoes and *zambos*, generally lumped together in the censuses as *pardos*. Spain's cultural influence was naturally more dominant, reaching the Indians directly through the Spaniards themselves (who, besides being the ruling group, represented a much larger migrant strain than the Africans), as well as through what we usually assume to be the Hispanized *castas*, or mixed bloods. Yet that influence also seems disproportionately weak.

Late colonial census figures indicate that non-Indians comprised between 25 and 30 percent of the total population.[79] If the censuses neither grossly overcounted *vecinos* nor grossly undercounted Indians—and there is no reason to think that they did—then these figures raise some question about the relationship between quantitative and qualitative data.

The mass of colonial documentation of many varieties leaves one with the overwhelming impression that Yucatan was, as it still is, much more "Indian" than central Mexico. The weight of attention devoted to Indians in the ecclesiastical and civil administration of Yucatan compared to that of central Mexico is one indication. There is scarcely a file in the local archives or in the Yucatan material in Mexico City or Spain that does not concern itself directly or indirectly with the treatment or behavior of Indians, whether it be *encomiendas*, forced labor, *repartimientos*, Indian *cofradías*, the secularization of *doctrinas*, or boundary settlements. Matters of defense and trade, jurisdictional disputes and finance fueled much paper work there as everywhere in the Spanish empire. But in

Yucatan, Indians are ubiquitous. On the surface nothing could seem more removed from Indian affairs than the early nineteenth-century material on *consolidación* (expropriation of ecclesiastical capital), until one finds that a large part of the funds collected in Yucatan consisted of Indian community reserves as well as Indian *cofradía* property.[80]

Another indication of the dominating Maya presence is that the local Spanish not only harped repeatedly on how vastly outnumbered they were by Indians but also behaved accordingly, for example, in their panic-sticken response to the small and inchoate Canek rebellion of 1761. The two most prominent students of post-conquest demography have stated that one of the major points of contrast between central Mexico and Yucatan is the proportionately far smaller Spanish and African migration, so that "Yucatan remains more Indian in its genetic base."[81] Yet according to their own demographic tables, in the last decades of the eighteenth century non-Indians amounted to roughly equal proportions of the population in both regions—around 28 percent.[82] This is approximately double the ratio in the provinces of Oaxaca and Chiapas,[83] both of which are considered heavily Indian. Possibly they were more so than Yucatan, but not doubly so.

There is a clear discrepancy between these figures and the accumulation of impressions by and from the Spanish rulers, a discrepancy that cannot be explained away by differences in spatial distribution. Spaniards and other *vecinos* remained heavily concentrated in urban centers in Yucatan, but did so also in central Mexico.

Both types of evidence may be thoroughly accurate in their own terms and reconcilable at the same time. The numbers merely need some decoding before they can be translated into social facts. We know that ethnic identities recorded in colonial censuses were mere legal categories based only in part on biological criteria, and highly flexible criteria, at that. Mestizo could signify any genetic mix between pure Spaniard and pure Indian, and in practice the boundaries marking off the supposedly pure groups was far from fixed. The significant inequalities of privileges and obligations attached to the various caste identities created a strong incentive for upward percolation. Differences in wealth, occupation, and way of life, the accident of legitimate or illegitimate birth, and a variety of other nongenetic criteria could determine the difference in the opportunity for light-skinned mestizos and *pardos* to become incorporated into the Spanish caste and for pure Indians and pure Africans to pass into one of the mixed groups.[84]

Two extracts from the parish reports accompanying a 1688 census will serve to underscore the less than rigid criteria for caste designations.

The curate of Valladolid reported the existence of "47 Spanish *solteros* [bachelors], among whom there are 5 or 6 mestizos." From the curate of the parish of Nabalam: "As for Spaniards, mestizos and *pardos*, I have only one in my district. I certify that he passes for a Spaniard [éste se tiene por español] and for that reason I list him as such, not because I judge him to be so on all four sides."[85]

The censuses, then, can provide only an approximation of demographic ratios, an approximation that might vary widely over time and from place to place. The proportionately low rate of Spanish and African migration to Yucatan and the proportionately high number of mestizos and *pardos*—relative to the number of Spaniards and Africans—leads one to the conclusion that these *castas* contained a significantly stronger Indian element in Yucatan: a heavier Indian strain in the genetic mix, and perhaps more pure Indians who had managed to pass into another category.

The genetic composition of *vecino* populations would be impossible to determine precisely, given the number of illegitimate births and foundlings and the unreliability of the racial data that are recorded in the parish registers.[86] Culturally, the boundary between Indians and the vast majority of those who were placed in non-Indian categories was nebulous in the extreme. The legally ambiguous *naborías* are difficult to distinguish from the *indios de pueblo*, and in fact people moved back and forth between the two types of community and the two categories with ease. The *indios hidalgos* were another special subgroup. Descended from the central Mexican auxiliaries who accompanied Montejo's forces, they subsequently merged with the local Maya from whom they were set apart only by their continued exemption from tribute.[87] Most of the mestizos and *pardos* would have been poorly cast in the role of advance guard for Hispanic culture. The local economy was too primitive to absorb more than a small number of them into the market sector as artisans, day laborers, or small-tradesmen. As late as 1811 over 80 percent of the *castas* living outside the urban centers—like the *indios hidalgos* and a large proportion of the suburban *naborías*—followed the traditional Maya subsistence pattern of milpa agriculture on rented pueblo lands, on their own small farms, or as tenants on an hacienda.[88]

By all indications, these groups followed a similar way of life, too, sharing with their Maya neighbors the same farming techniques, housing, and dress, the same diet of maize and beans, and the same language. Most rural *castas* were as monolingual in Yucatec Maya as the Maya themselves. Often they are distinguishable in the documents only by their Spanish surnames.

109

No SIMPLE yardstick exists for measuring cultural influence. The concept of acculturation so often applied in Mesoamerica is obviously too limited to encompass the range and complexity of processes observable in colonial Yucatan (or, I would guess, anywhere else). It ordinarily assumes as inevitable a one-directional process by which the subordinate group's culture is replaced by that of the dominant group, and all that is left to do is measure the rate of replacement. Such a simple formula precludes consideration of what may be a more common consequence of culture contact: what we might call tangential change, stimulated by the dominant culture but ricocheting off in its own direction. It also ignores the possibility that cultural influence may move in the opposite direction. By a variety of fairly simple criteria, one could, in colonial Yucatan, speak as easily of a process of Mayanization as of Hispanization.

In material culture it would be difficult to say who assimilated whom, insofar as assimilation occurred at all. The Spanish brought some of their food crops and domestic animals, but the hostility of the local soil and climate to European crops meant that all the inhabitants depended on the traditional Mesoamerican staple triad of maize, beans, and chiles and a variety of indigenous fruits. Except for some simple metal tools, firearms, and gunpowder, and the reluctant and incomplete adoption by Maya men of the pajama-like trousers and shirt imposed for decency's sake by the friars, one can find little European material impact, and scarcely any influence in the opposite direction. In housing the Spanish made no concessions to Maya styles. The colonial portions of Merida, Valladolid, and Campeche are carbon copies of Puerto Santa María or some other town in southern Andalucia. And in dress, the need to maintain such symbols of European caste must have cost the Spaniards dearly in comfort and in foreign exchange, since wool cloth was among the major imports.

To the extent that language shapes and reflects culture, the Maya more than held their own in the exchange. Despite the considerable isolation between the two groups, they required some shared system of discourse at those points where they did intersect. The verbal language they shared was almost invariably Maya and, moreover, a Maya that did not undergo any basic structural transformation through exposure to Spanish.[89] Yucatec Maya incorporated Spanish vocabulary: nomenclature for specifically Spanish things like cattle and silver coinage, and certain legal administrative terms like *escribano* (notary or scribe) and *testamento* (testament) that referred to the most common areas of official interaction. They also, significantly and predictably, had no word of their own for "Holy Spirit." To the neophyte Mayanist, the Spanish words sprinkled here and there in the colonial Maya texts seem dismayingly sparse. One is more struck by the Maya's frugality, their tendency not to borrow a Spanish word when they could make do with one of their own—for example, *tzimin* (tapir) for horse.[90] And they kept their own suffixes and prefixes, which can effectively disguise the most familiar Spanish word. They took nothing of the structure of the conquerors' language, in contrast to the effect, say, of French on Middle English after the Norman conquest. Other than the adoption of Latin script in place of the Maya hieroglyphs, Spanish would seem to have had considerably less impact on Yucatec Maya than the Nahuatl of previous invaders, although some of the Nahuatl influence that linguists have attributed to earlier contact may have been imported by the Mexicans who arrived with Montejo.[91]

In the late eighteenth century, Spaniards still concerned about their nation's civilizing mission confessed their signal and complete failure after centuries of colonial rule to implant the Spanish language among the Maya.[92] They were not indulging in self-denigratory hyperbole. In a 1755 judicial inquiry conducted throughout the colony, testimony was taken from all the Maya community officials—that is, all the Indians who dealt most frequently and directly with the Spanish in a variety of modes. All without exception required an interpreter.[93] By the late eighteenth century, we find scattered references to *batabs* who were well conversant in Spanish, and to noble Maya youths who were pursuing studies in Merida.[94] But they were referred to precisely because they were exceptional. It should be noted that, although the level of literacy among the Maya nobility had declined greatly since conquest, there still existed an educated cadre in each community who were perfectly literate—in Maya.

Why did the native language exert such a strong hold? Some Spaniards asserted that the Maya clung tenaciously to their language, refusing to learn Spanish out of conscious choice.[95] Perhaps they were correct, and perhaps language was seen by the Maya as a symbol of their identity and resistance to Spanish rule. But it was also generally acknowledged that the Spaniards made no attempt to teach them Spanish.[96] Once the early missionaries abandoned their schools for the nobility, the only education offered to the Indians was in catechism classes, conducted in Maya by a native teacher who also taught some of the young men to read and write, in Maya.[97] The Spaniards' monopoly on the language of rulership may have been a deliberate policy, an instrument of domination and of boundary maintenance. But in part it was also a policy of convenience. Why bother to teach Spanish to hundreds of thousands of Indians when the Spanish, or at least all those locally born, could perfectly well communicate with them in their own language, a language, moreover, that was spoken with little variation all over the Yucatan peninsula? In the sense of language, the Maya lords who may have assumed that the Spanish could be "Mayanized" in the same way as earlier foreign rulers had not been entirely misled.

More than a lingua franca, Maya was the primary language of all the colony's native-born inhabitants of every caste. An anecdote that has achieved the status of folklore in Merida tells of a local physician at the turn of the century, a member of a socially prominent family, whose *third* language was Spanish. Having spoken only Maya as a boy, he was sent to France for his education and only when he returned to Yucatan after receiving his medical degree did he learn Spanish. True or not, the purpose of the story is to illustrate to outsiders the point that in the old days, even (or perhaps especially) among the upper-class Yucatecans of impeccably Spanish blood lines, Maya was the first language. This primacy was a result of child-rearing practices continued from early colonial times. Creole children spent their infancy, literally from birth, and their early childhood in almost the sole company of Maya women, suckled by Maya wet nurses commandeered from the villages, reared by Maya nurses, and surrounded by Maya servants.[98]

Maya was in a very real sense, then, the creoles' mother tongue, the language with which they continued to feel more comfortable as adults and used by preference "not only among the Indians but also at home with their own children, giving as their reason that it is easier to pronounce."[99] They not only preferred to speak Maya but, according to more than one observer, they often acquired a less than perfect command of Spanish.[100]

Many of the *castas* learned no Spanish at all.[101] In the rural areas the priest who was not bilingual could no more deal with his mestizo and *pardo* parishioners than with the Indians. *Castas* might be monolingual, but that need not invariably signify that they were illiterate any more than it did among the Maya. I have found scraps of a correspondence between a creole curate and a mestizo or *pardo* parishioner, written entirely in Maya.[102] The correspondence, really only some brief messages, concerned some minor property transaction and there is no reason to think that it was exceptional other than in having been preserved.

It is difficult to imagine that Spaniards spent their formative years of infancy in the company of Maya servants without acquiring some of their ideas along with their language. Some bishops suspected the worst: that creoles imbibed pagan beliefs from the Maya along with mother's milk.[103] It is not always easy to sort out Maya paganism from the European variety brought over by the Spaniards. But to the extent that creoles along with the other non-Indian castes acknowledged the reality of Maya beliefs and the supernatural powers of Maya shamans, the bishops may have been correct.[104]

I do not mean to rest a case for colonial Maya cultural survival on the Mayanization of the Spanish, which would merely invert the same simplistic model of Hispanization. The Spanish were no more compelled to express Maya thoughts and concepts because they spoke the Maya's language than the Maya were compelled to express Christian beliefs because they used some of the idiom of Christian ritual. The medium is not always the message. I see no evidence that the basic, central features of either Spanish social forms or the systems of meaning invested in them were transformed by contact with the Maya. And, as with the Maya, many of the changes that can be detected were products of the interaction, without therefore moving in the direction of convergence. My purpose is only to underscore, first, that influence in a colonial setting can work both ways and, second, that recording the simple fact of contact is no substitute for analyzing its nature and actual effects.

THIS sketch of cultural exchange is intended to suggest some idea of the processes often obscured by a narrow definition of acculturation. Absorption into the dominant group's culture is only one of the various possibilities. And such absorption should not be viewed as a relentless, inexorable process, responding simply to the intensity and duration of contact, or even to the simple force of pressure. Cultural innovation of any kind implies some measure of choice and therefore requires some incentive or reward. It is the sum of individual decisions to try something new because that something new is seen as enhancing one's chances of success, or diminishing one's chances of failure, in a particular situation. The ultimate choice would be between innovation and death. Usually the alternatives are not presented in such stark terms.

The colonial Maya clearly exercised a degree of choice in their responses to the social and cultural forms introduced by the Spanish, especially when these were presented without any overt compulsion. The high rate of rejection owed less to any streak of conservatism in Maya culture than to the relatively weak pressures for change exerted by the colonial regime. Their resistance also owed much to the absence of positive incentives, to the fact that the Maya had so little to gain from becoming Hispanized.

The rigid caste system of colonial society placed the highest premium on cultural innovations that allowed the Maya to fend off Spanish material demands: it provided precious few rewards for adopting Spanish ways. The caste boundaries and the structural isolation they enforced meant that most Spanish ways were irrelevant to, if not downright incompatible with, success within the Maya world. After these boundaries became solidified, an Indian could move into the Spanish orbit solely as a *criado*, a movement that provided only a minimally secure alternative to going under in the Maya system.[105] He entered the Spanish world at the very bottom and, moreover, knew that he and his offspring would remain there perpetually. Once it became clear that no Indian could aspire to anything more within the Spanish system, only those unable to survive within their own culture were tempted to move out. The social reality supporting cultural conservatism has persisted well beyond the colonial era. Not long ago I asked a Maya villager why he refused to send his children to school to learn Spanish. "Why bother?" he shrugged. "They will still be Indians."

With racial mixture, and sometimes perhaps without, some Indian offspring passed into the mestizo and *pardo* castes, a status that brought relief from the tribute and labor obligations of Indians but not necessarily anything else. The role assigned to all but a small number of the *castas* was the same as the Indians'—to provide the colony's unskilled labor. The place at the top was of course reserved for Spaniards through a variety of formal and informal mechanisms.[106] The undeveloped local economy offered few of the intermediate positions, such as shopkeeper, small-time trader, craftsman, or foreman that would have required and rewarded new skills and attitudes. These low-level occupations and the wage labor that are the peasant's traditional routes into a money economy have been slow to come to Yucatan. The Maya have not been slow to choose these alternatives when available. Their rapid increase in recent years has done more to erode the social and cultural isolation of the Maya than all the centuries of colonial and neocolonial rule together.

The Indians of colonial Spanish America are sometimes seen as having encapsulated themselves from the larger colonial society in order to prevent conquest from being followed by inner distintegration. The encapsulation of the Maya of Yucatan, to which they indeed owed their survival as a distinct social and cultural group, was less a self-designed protective device than a barrier imposed by a rigid caste system resting on a primitive tribute economy.

PART TWO
A FRAGILE SOCIAL ORDER

· 4 ·

THE ELUSIVE SOCIAL
BOND

A strong caste barrier would not in itself guarantee the survival of an identifiable Maya culture and its mutually sustaining social order. A society can be destroyed without being engulfed or its members absorbed: it can disintegrate internally even when the boundaries remain intact. According to some interpretations, the pre-Columbian Maya social system was already a highly problematic affair, with or without Spanish intervention.

Any "lost civilization" will inspire some sense of mystery as one ponders the fate of ancient cities covered over by desert sands or tropical forest. The Maya have a particularly strong claim to the alliterative epithet of "mysterious" that has been applied to them. Even more than the cause of Maya decline, scholars have puzzled over the questions of how this civilization ever existed in the first place, and how, by implication, it could have lasted as long as it did. Most especially they have pondered the question of how it could have existed *where* it did. For the level of social and political organization needed to sustain this civilization is alleged to be incompatible with the physical environment in which it developed.

Part of the puzzle may lie in the particular perspective of scholars from temperate climates whose own discomfort in the region's heat and humidity has been translated into a general theory that tropical lowlands are a hostile environment for any human endeavor. Still, there are aspects of the puzzle that cannot be dismissed so airily and which touch on some basic issues in human history: the nature of the social bond, the foundations of social stratification, and the origins of the state.

The forces that lead people to band together in more than casual, ephemeral groups will probably remain a matter for debate as long as a belief persists in original sin, the selfishness of genes, or any other explanation of behavior based on the primacy of self-interest in human motivation. Despite valiant exertions, no one has come up with any biologically determined need for sustained sociability other than in the mother-infant relationship. The form and function of any enduring group larger than this dyad must, then, be culturally determined, the product of human invention and human choice, regardless of how preordained or imperative the social order may appear to its members.

117

If we assume that people require some incentive for sacrificing their freedom to pursue individual needs and desires—a restraint inherent in any social bond—it is not immediately apparent what this incentive may have been for the lowland Maya. In fact, the search for that incentive or combination of incentives, and with it the explanation for lowland Maya social organization, has been exercising the wits of scholars with varying degrees of intensity ever since it was decided that the "lost cities in the jungle" were an indigenous product and not created by wandering Carthaginians or one of the Lost Tribes of Israel[1] (although there are some who still subscribe to these and other theories of exogenous, not to mention extraterrestrial, origins).

An Unpropitious Environment

The problem posed by the physical environment in the Maya lowlands is not the hot, humid climate, the dense bush, the noxious insects, or any of the other physical discomforts that newcomers have complained about at length from early Spanish missionaries to Yankee explorers. Nor is it the limited capacity of tropical forest agriculture; for archaeologists no longer doubt that the Maya could and did produce enough surplus food to support a complex, urbanized society.[2] The problem lies instead in the "openness" of the environment, in geopolitical terms. The same conditions that made escape from Spanish rule relatively easy made escape from any form of social constraint easy, and they have raised the question of what held pre-Columbian Maya society together in the first place.

The entire peninsula of Yucatan and the adjacent southern lowlands at its base constitute a single geographical unit unbroken by any significant barrier to free movement. The river systems in the south that drain into the Gulf of Mexico and the Bay of Honduras are navigable for long distances and serve mainly as arteries for communication rather than as obstacles. Except for these rivers, the small low range of the Maya Mountains in southern Belize, the rolling hills of the Peten and the Puuc (a ridge cutting diagonally across part of the northern peninsula), and some lakes here and there, the lowlands are devoid of major topographical features. Although local variations in terrain often belie the bird's-eye impression of a smooth, monotonous landscape, climate and vegetation shift almost imperceptibly within the region as a whole, with gradual increases in rainfall and soil depth as one moves south and east. It would be impossible to mistake the arid scrub of the northwest tip for the lush growth of the Peten forest, but equally impossible to say at exactly what point the one begins and the other ends.[3]

Such an open environment has been deemed unfavorable to the development of complex societies, inhibiting the formation of primary states and also discouraging social bonding on a smaller scale. Some degree of geographical circumscription is considered necessary to check a "natural" tendency toward fissioning and to maintain the critical human mass that social stratification requires.[4] Thus highland valleys and basins and lowland river valleys that are surrounded by desert, such as in the Middle East or coastal Peru, have contained complex agrarian societies for thousands of years, while tropical rain forests, savannas, and low-bush country have not. The latter permit the hiving off of splinter groups or factions who can easily move away and settle elsewhere whenever resources become scarce or relations within the original group become irksome. The ability of any members of the group to establish long-term control over others is inhibited, and it is even less likely that one entire group can establish dominance over another. A similar concept of a frontier society has at times been in vogue to explain similar phenomena in historical periods, where social constraints are relatively loose and rogue elements can flourish more easily than in settled areas.

Or so the argument goes. If it is correct, how do we explain the lowland Maya, or for that matter the Khmer of southeast Asia and other agrarian societies, which have produced less spectacular material remains but nevertheless have achieved a relatively high degree of territorial integration and social complexity in similarly open environments?

ECONOMIC EXCHANGE

One favored explanation for the development of complex sociopolitical systems is the exchange of goods, a basic form of human interaction that can stimulate and maintain social bonding at any level of organization. Trade has long been assigned a key role in the pre-Columbian history of Mesoamerica. This emphasis derives in part from the nature of the archaeological record, in which trade tends to leave more abundant and less equivocal evidence than many other kinds of human activity. But trade has also come to be seen as a major driving force for much of the cultural and political integration that the area achieved.

A wealth of archaeological and written evidence attests to the existence of strong networks of long-distance trade that connected the Maya lowlands with highland centers in Guatemala and Mexico from at least early Classic times (ca. A.D. 250) until the Spanish conquest.[5] Without the documentary evidence we might have imagined, against all logic, that the flow of goods was largely one way. In current economic ter-

119

minology, the lowlands were the underdeveloped region, exporting mostly primary products, and these were largely perishable items such as cacao, honey, wax, copal, rubber, tropical bird feathers, jaguar pelts, salt (this last item, if not strictly perishable, was quickly consumed and is therefore untraceable), and, at least in late Postclassic times, slaves.[6] Cotton cloth was the only processed item, in contrast with the predominance of manufactured goods that came in exchange from the highlands, although obsidian, jade, and the small amounts of gold and copper that are found from the most recent period were also imported as raw materials for local manufacture.

It appears that these and other exchanges sustained the whole communications system that linked the different regions of Mesoamerica. Along with the flow of artistic styles and religious cults, trade helped to create a distinctive, pan-Mesoamerican culture underlying—or transcending—the considerable regional diversity.[7] And trade cannot easily be separated from the periodic spread of political influence from the area's dynamic center in highland Mexico, which reached south and east into highland Guatemala and into the lowlands as far as Yucatan.

Evidence has also been building up for a vigorous system of exchange within the Maya lowlands themselves. Cacao may well have been the chief item in earlier times, as it was in the late Postclassic. Although it can be grown almost anywhere in the area, large-scale cultivation of this coveted product—so valuable that cacao beans came to be used as currency—was confined to a thin belt along the Pacific coast and the tropical wetlands of Tabasco, Honduras, and Belize. The Caribbean coasts of Yucatan were also linked to the interior by the exchange of salt and marine products for honey, wax, and other forest products.

A good case can be made for the importance of this trade, along with domination of the long-distance exchanges between highlands and lowlands, in the development of regional centers. Tikal, for example, held a strategic position at the center of the Peten between the riverine systems that penetrated the area from Campeche and Tabasco in the west and Belize in the east.[8] The later rise of the "Putun" Maya has been attributed to their control of new trade routes along the base and around the coasts of the Yucatan peninsula, and this emphasis on the mercantile foundation of "Putun" hegemony has become a cornerstone of Postclassic Maya history.[9]

More recently, Grant Jones has offered a most convincing model for the development of integrated political systems in the central and southern lowlands based on the same type of intraregional and interregional trade.[10] His evidence comes from the area's postcontact history, when the Spanish presence in adjacent areas produced many changes in the economic and political systems within the unpacified zones. What is surprising is how much of the traditional pattern was preserved, even in the responses to the altered conditions. Steel axes and other Spanish tools, introduced via a clandestine trade with the conquered areas to the north, were substituted for the manufactured goods formerly imported from highland Mexico, while within the regional network itself the cacao area of Belize rose in prominence over Spanish-controlled Tabasco and northern Chetumal. And regional predominance passed from the "Putun" (Chontal) Maya of the Acalan district in southwestern Campeche (drastically reduced in numbers after conquest and relocated by the Spanish) to the Itza in the unconquered Peten. The basis of that dominance, significantly, was not control over the production of valued commodities, but control over its distribution through military power and through political and religious influence over the nearby center of production in Belize. When one considers that neither Tikal, Chichen Itza, Coba, Mayapan, nor any of the other major pre-Columbian centers was located in areas producing the chief trade items like cacao and salt, but rather adjacent to them, the implications of Jones's seventeenth-century model for the earlier economic and political history of the area become all the more apparent.

In contrast with long-distance and medium-distance trade, evidence for more localized economic exchange is conspicuously absent. The Maya in the Guatemalan highlands and adjacent piedmont and Pacific coast developed highly integrated networks of local trade, which still exist, based on the diversity of commodities produced in the varying contiguous ecosystems. The units in each local network may not have been as neatly dovetailed as in the "archipelago" system described by John Murra for the Andean region.[11] There, subunits of each community were settled in different ecological niches, geographically separated but closely linked in a system of symbiotic exchange. Still, the fact that in the southern Maya region a distinctive pattern of complementary ecosystems can be correlated with pre-Columbian sociopolitical divisions, and with linguistic boundaries discernible today, suggests that economic exchange was an important integrative mechanism within each of these units—a basic element in the total system of communications.[12]

Southern Guatemala is a world in microcosm, containing the whole range of Mesoamerican landscapes and environments in a confined space. This geographical compression means (and meant in pre-Columbian times) that the products of coast, tropical lowlands, plateau, and cold uplands are all available within the compass of a day's walk. And it is precisely the lack of sharp ecological contrasts that characterizes the lowlands to the north and that is reflected in the region's relative lack of linguistic diversity. The peninsula of Yucatan, with the exception of the "Putun" or Chontal periphery, may well have constituted the largest linguistic unit in Mesoamerica at the time of the conquest. And even before the flood of Yucatec refugees engulfed neighbors to the south, the language map of the central and southern lowlands seems to have been considerably less complex than in the highlands.[13]

The lowlands represent what in economic terms has been called a "redundant" environment. This does not mean complete uniformity. Aside from the gradual shifts in rainfall and general topography mentioned earlier, more localized variations in soil fertility and drainage exist that can be of intense interest to the farmer.[14] But they do not for the most part affect what is produced, only how much. Similarly, very little that one part of the region produces cannot be obtained in another, except for the coastal deposits of salt, fish, and other marine products. Cacao grows best where the soil is richest and the rainfall heaviest. But the same staple crops, forest products, and the few mineral resources that do exist are available everywhere. Limestone is ubiquitous, and deposits of flint or chert used for tools are widely scattered. In other words, the physical environment would seem to have provided very little stimulus for local trade, in contrast with the "symbiotic" links supported by the greater ecological heterogeneity of the highlands.[15]

Yucatan has no indigenous local market system today. Aside from a very unstructured and rudimentary type of barter, in which neighboring families might buy or sell a pig or some other local item, all commerce is transacted via the village stores run by *ladino* (the modern term for non-Indian) shopkeepers or, in many of the remoter hamlets, via itinerant *ladino* traders.[16] The contrast could hardly be greater between this social void (from the Indian standpoint) and the bustling markets of the highlands, markets organized by and for Indians, with *ladinos* participating, when at all, in decidedly secondary roles.

One might presume that some colonial process peculiar to Yucatan wiped out a local market system. It is more likely that there was little or nothing to wipe out. No archaeological evidence for local markets (as opposed to long-distance trading depots) has so far been found.[17] More tellingly, references to them are lacking in the early Spanish descriptions of even large towns. We would not expect anything in Yucatan to compare in size with the great market at Tlaltelolco—the sister city of Tenochtitlan and the commercial hub of the Aztec empire—which excited the wonder and admiration of Bernal Díaz del Castillo and his companions. But the absence of any mention by observers ordinarily so keenly interested in the Indians' material goods suggests that markets were not a prominent feature of local life. The markets they did mention were all in the "Putun" fringe encircling the peninsula. Some of the sites, like Cozumel off the east coast, Nito on the Bay of Honduras, and Xicalango on the Laguna de Términos, have all been identified as port-of-trade enclaves serving long-distance commerce. Others, like Cachi and Chauaca near the north coast, Campeche and Champoton on the Gulf of Mexico, and probably Tzama, Ecab, and other east-coast towns, were also primarily entrepôts, and their markets are likely to have been international bazaars or depots, rather than having served local needs.[18]

Tomás López, the royal *visitador* sent from the Audiencia of Guatemala in 1552, included in the code he issued to regulate Indian affairs in Yucatan an order to establish a *tianguiz* (the Nahuatl word for market) in every town.[19] He probably derived the model as well as the term from his highland experience. The fact that he sought (unsuccessfully, as it turned out) to import this institution into Yucatan barely a decade after the conquest must surely mean that it figured insignificantly, if at all, in the local economy.

The absence, or at least extreme weakness, of local markets and the nature of the long-distance exchanges in which the Maya engaged lead one to question what, if any, role trade could have played in the basic organization of society at the local level. While trade may well have been one of the chief mechanisms for incorporating individual geopolitical units into provincial, regional and even supraregional systems, it cannot easily account for sociopolitical integration *within* the units, nor for the stratified social order that developed among the lowland Maya.

Control of the distribution of goods, which has been offered as one explanation for elite dominance over the Maya masses,[20] requires that the elite should have cornered the supply of some item or items of primary necessity, as opposed to the luxury goods that they consumed themselves. The difficulty is in finding any such item. Basalt *metates* (grinding stones) imported from the highlands are one suggestion.[21] Certainly every Maya family needed a *metate* of some sort to grind corn into meal, and any implement made from basalt or other igneous stone would be far more durable than one made from the local limestone. Basalt *metates* have been found in lowland sites along with cutting blades of the glass-like obsidian, also of highland origin, which is harder and sharper than the local flint. But none of these exotic items has been found in sufficient quantity to constitute a basic commodity of everyday use for the Maya masses.[22] And even if they had been imported in bulk quantities, they would still not qualify as basic necessities, so long as satisfactory substitutes were readily available locally. Flint tools and limestone *metates* are perfectly serviceable, and even if they wear out

123

more quickly, they arc also easy to replace. If there is one thing the lowlands possess in superabundance it is easily quarried limestone, which is relatively soft when first cut from the rock and then rapidly hardens on exposure to air.

There is no reason to suppose that the ordinary Maya farmer did not make do with the local produce in pre-Columbian times as they did after the conquest. Stone implements were not among the items imported from the highlands after the Spanish took over the long-distance trade from the native elites. The metal tools supplied by the new masters gradually replaced the stone implements the Maya had used, but not immediately, and in the case of *metates*, not at all. Yet we hear of no postconquest crisis in the production and processing of the staple food, which would have occurred had the Maya been dependent on imported tools to clear the bush for planting and to grind their corn once it was harvested.

The absence or insignificance of local markets suggests, on the contrary, that for all their basic needs the Maya masses were essentially self-sufficient. Some local barter may have existed, and during the colonial period a small minority of Indians specialized in the manufacture of simple household articles for sale to the Spanish;[23] but colonial evidence indicates that the basic skills of weaving, pottery making, leather working (for deerhide sandals), and simple carpentry were universal among the *macehuales* and that each family supplied its own clothing and household furnishings.[24] A basalt *metate* would be the pre-Hispanic equivalent of a Mercedes-Benz (or, perhaps more aptly, a Cuisinart): a highly desirable item but hardly a necessary one and, like obsidian blades and other imported goods, probably affordable only by the elite households.

Only one item of basic necessity that was not immediately accessible to the Maya farmer comes to mind, and that is salt, considered an important supplement to any largely vegetarian diet. It was available locally; in fact, it was one of the region's major exports, but it occurred principally along the coasts of the Yucatan peninsula. Access to the coastal salt flats was a source of conflict between adjacent provinces and ones further inland during the late Postclassic and probably earlier.[25] But we have no evidence that the rulers in Yucatan sought to monopolize the supply of salt to their own subjects. We are told that the Maya gathered salt as a community enterprise and, aside from whatever tax they may have had to pay to the lords who claimed ownership of the salt deposits, they paid some portion in tribute to their own lords.[26] Thus the direction in which all goods flowed, whether salt or locally produced commodities such as cotton cloth, was from the commoners to the elite, who then controlled the export trade of the surplus. And whatever means of ascendancy the elite possessed that enabled them to extract the surplus, it does not seem to have been through the distribution of locally unobtainable material necessities.

It is of course possible that salt, at least in its usual form, is not a basic necessity after all, and that the dietary requirement of sodium can be met from other sources. In the colonial Peten, unpacified and refugee Maya groups obtained some sea salt in trade from Yucatan, but "in its absence they supplied their own from the ashes of *guano* [a type of palm leaf]."[27] The issue of salt consumption aside, I confess to a certain unease with the idea that the monopoly of any trade item, no matter how essential, could serve as a basis for dominance within a particular group,[28] as opposed to being an effect of that dominance or a means of reinforcing it. The same reservations apply to the control of water supplies for irrigation as the source of political power, a notion that has its own advocates.[29] Neither theory explains how the monopoly was gained in the first place. Presumably it was by force or by common consent. In either case, one must look further for the source of the coercive power or for the quid pro quo on which the consent is based.

Agriculture and Settlement Patterns

Any search for the organizing principles of an agrarian society should begin with its central activity, farming. But a look at agricultural practices in the Maya lowlands merely deepens the puzzle. Rather than explain either the territorial or social integration of the larger geopolitical units, agriculture figures as one more centrifugal force that the open and redundant physical environment exerted on the lowland Maya.

The swidden or milpa system of agriculture is no longer regarded as the sole means of food production employed by the pre-Columbian Maya. Nevertheless, it seems to have been the predominant mode of subsistence in the region during much of the period and, most pertinently, through the late Preclassic (to ca. A.D. 250), when the main outlines of a stratified social order were taking shape.[30] Its basic features remain essentially unmodified to the present. Swidden requires a relatively large amount of land to sustain a family. A field or milpa is first cleared of trees and undergrowth by felling, and then the brush is burned once it has had a chance to dry out. After being planted for several years, principally with the staple crops of maize, beans, and squash, the milpa is allowed to revert to bush or forest again while new fields are cleared in succession until the original site has recovered and can be used again.[31]

The total amount of land required varies according to the type of soil

5. Milpa ready for harvest. The ripened maize is left on doubled-over stalks to be gathered as needed; note the already high weed growth in this second year of the milpa cycle. (Photo by the author)

and the amount of rainfall, as well as the skill and energy of the individual farmer in controlling the weeds that eventually take over. In colonial Yucatan each married man was required to plant sixty *mecates* (a *mecate* is roughly twenty meters by twenty meters) of milpa a year. It was calculated that a milpa would produce for two or three years, but with yields successively declining from the first year's average of one *carga* (equivalent to about six bushels of maize) per *mecate*. The parcel of land then had to lie fallow for at least another eight or twelve years before it could be cultivated again. Thus a total of three hundred *mecates*, or about twelve hectares, was deemed the normal minimum to meet the needs of a nuclear family.[32]

Because of the high acreage requirements, a dispersed pattern of settlement is clearly most convenient to this system of food production. At the same time it is an efficient system in terms of labor and does not require any large-scale cooperative effort. Responding strictly to the needs of milpa agriculture, then, the lowland Maya would have formed no residential groupings above the level of the nuclear family. They would have scattered widely over the land, limited in their spacing only by the occurrence of water sources or the feasibility of small-scale systems of artificial water collection and storage. A settlement pattern exists today in the Chontalpa region of the state of Tabasco that corresponds fairly closely to these criteria.[33] It is a collection of dwellings so lacking in any territorial or social cohesion that it is barely identifiable as a community. This pattern is not common in the Maya lowlands today, nor was it during the area's recorded history, nor by all accounts during much of its prehistory, despite the prevalence and suitability of milpa agriculture.

There is today and has been in the past considerably more clustering of population in Yucatan than can be attributed to a scarcity of water sources. In northern Yucatan, where *cenotes* provide the only natural water supply, almost every contact-period settlement seems to have had a *cenote*, but not every *cenote* by any means had a settlement.[34] In Yucatan as elsewhere, the physical environment merely defines the possibilities and influences the choices but does not by itself dictate how people will dispose themselves over the earth's surface. Whatever may have brought the Maya together into communities and held them there, we must look beyond the influences of their natural setting for the answers.

One explanation that has been offered is a variant on the basic ecological model, in which demographic pressure limits freedom of movement even in an otherwise open environment. According to this argument, population could have increased beyond the carrying capacity of milpa agriculture and forced people to develop techniques of intensive food production that both permit and encourage (1) denser aggregates of population, (2) a higher degree of social cohesion, and (3) a more complex, interdependent, and ultimately more stratified social order.[35] We do know that the Maya developed large nucleated settlements during the Classic period. They do not compare in size with the major highland center of Teotihuacan or the later Aztec capital of Tenochtitlan, and whether they can be considered truly urban or not is a question of interpretation. But there is no longer any doubt that they were residential complexes and not merely ceremonial or administrative centers inhabited primarily by an elite and its personal retainers.[36]

Agricultural terracing, raised fields, and complex hydraulic systems provide substantial evidence that the Maya did not have to rely exclusively on milpa production to feed these urban populations.[37] One could argue that intensified food production, population nucleation, and sociopolitical integration are all adaptations to population growth, and that during the Postclassic period of population decline, the Maya reverted entirely to milpa agriculture and a more dispersed settlement pattern while still retaining some form of community organization. It is generally agreed that intensive agriculture is more efficient in its use of land although less so in its use of labor: that is, the crop yield is higher per acre but lower per man hour. Thus population pressure, or an increase in the ratio of labor to available land, provides the most plausible stimulus for the intensification of agriculture.[38] Without this pressure, it might be difficult to explain why the Maya or anyone else would go to the trouble of building and maintaining terraces, fertilizing the soil, and watering crops, when they could feed themselves with so much less effort under the milpa system.

Population pressure as an all-purpose explanation for every sort of historical development—for prosperity and poverty, for the rise of civilizations and their decline—is seductive in its simplicity. But, like similar notions, what it gains in inclusivity it loses in explanatory power. There is, moreover, a particular difficulty in making population growth the independent variable from which all other changes flow. The notion is a timely one. Population "explosion" has become one of the specters stalking the good life promised by modern technology, and it is difficult to see how earlier societies with less apparent control over their material lives could have controlled their population within the Malthusian limits of the carrying capacity of a particular environment. Yet evidence is mounting that they did—that population growth is not an inexorable force but rather a result of choice, if at times ill-conceived choice, and that preindustrial societies have been able to maintain their numbers around or below the limits placed by available food supplies and to adjust them in response to perceived scarcity or abundance.[39] In that case, then, although population increase can explain agricultural innovation, it will not serve as a universal first cause, since one must still explain why the increase occurred.

It is also difficult to accept demographic pressure as the primary moving force behind the related phenomena of population nucleation and sociopolitical integration. For the Maya lowlands, a general rise in population seems to correlate with increasing size and complexity of communities, as well as with intensified food production, during the Preclassic and Classic periods. But it is not yet clear that the rise preceded, much less that it caused, these related developments, just as we cannot pinpoint the precise link between demographic change and the disintegration of the major urban centers at the end of the Classic period.

Turning to the better known colonial period, we find it no easier to connect overall population density to sociopolitical developments. The biological collapse suffered by all Indian societies in greater or lesser degree is hard to separate from the totality of European impact in accounting for postconquest changes in many aspects of native life. It is particularly difficult to assign the status of primary process to population change, when milpa agriculture persisted and population dispersal proceeded during both the period of severe population decline following the conquest and the later period of recovery.[40] And, as we shall see, the forces affecting social bonds within the colonial community also seemed to operate independently of this variable.

Whatever the carrying capacity of milpa agriculture may be in the Maya lowlands, whatever the maximum population density the system can support given local variations in rainfall and soil depth and fertility, it does not seem to have been reached during the colonial period or in the centuries immediately preceding Spanish conquest. We cannot project on to the lowland Maya, at least at any time between the Classic "collapse" and the early nineteenth century, the kind of competition for land that the central Mexicans experienced under the Aztec empire, and again from the mid-seventeenth century onward with the rapid expansion of Spanish commercial agriculture in the area.

The Maya's incessant warfare during the Postclassic and their vigorous defense of community land titles after the conquest might seem to suggest pressures on agricultural land. However, both the armed clashes and their courtroom substitutes in the colonial period were concerned not so much with land itself as with jurisdiction over a particular territory. Land as mere acreage, whether for agriculture, hunting, or gathering of the myriad forest products on which the Maya farmer also

129

depended, was simply not in short supply despite the high requirements of shifting agriculture. The land squeeze that the communities began to feel toward the end of the colonial period was due primarily, as in central Mexico, to the engulfment of milpa lands by the Spanish estates, and only secondarily to a rise in population.[41]

Perhaps changes in the distribution of populations are the significant variable, more so than changes in absolute numbers. The concentration of all or part of a population of a given region into more compact settlements could produce the same effects in that restricted locale as a general increase in population throughout the region: it could create the same pressure on land and other resources and the same need to utilize them more efficiently. By the same token, the pressure could be reduced by dispersal away from urban centers without any decline in absolute numbers. This is not to say that changes in overall population density did not accompany, follow, or precede shifts in settlement patterns and methods of food production, only that such changes are not required as explanatory devices.

The issue over first causes may ultimately be a metaphysical one, as unresolvable in purely intellectual terms as a debate over free will versus predestination. Man as an active agent in his own destiny will be congruent with one world view, and man as an object of implacable forces beyond his control will suit another better. In the case of the Maya there is not enough firm evidence to make a compelling argument on either side. And even if a plausible case could be made for assigning primacy to cultural decisions as causative agents in population distribution and perhaps even in overall growth and decline, that would not be the end of the matter. We would still be left with the need to explain the basis for these cultural decisions and the integrative forces that encouraged and sustained the fusion into large social groups.

Any increase in population is usually to the advantage of the ruling elite, providing a large labor force and greater military strength in the competition for territorial hegemony. The Maya rulers had every reason to encourage larger urban concentrations to make labor more readily available for the goods, services, and public works they required. Labor, of course, could be and no doubt was recruited on a rotating basis from an entire sustaining area. But, as the colonial Spanish were to find, such a corvée system does not compare in productivity with a permanent, resident work force. As deliberate policies pursued by the official decision makers in society, population growth and nucleation might require no further explanation. However, the implementation of the policy does. To base the social and territorial cohesion achieved by the pre-Columbian Maya on the authority of the elite would be, again, to confuse cause and effect. For what we are seeking in part is the underlying motive for submission to that authority.

The centrifugal pull of milpa agriculture and the economic self-sufficiency and ease of physical movement enjoyed by the lowland Maya masses all require some counterposing force or forces to explain the development of the Maya social order and its maintenance during periods of population decline as well as growth. They also negate any explanation that relies entirely on coercion: escape was too easy. Any system of social control will depend on a mixture of coercion and consent. When, as in Maya society, the benefits seem to be allocated mainly to a small minority, the balance would presumably be heavily weighted toward coercion. Yet the Maya rulers lacked the necessary apparatus to force their will on a totally recalcitrant population. Even the Spanish with their swords, muskets, and horses and their superior military organization were far from achieving a police state. They could not prevent the Maya from fleeing into unpacified areas. On the other hand, they did not need to station troops in every town to compel submission from the remaining population, even if they had had sufficient numbers to do so. They relied instead on the Maya leaders and the system of social control that was already in existence.

Long before conquest the Maya had formed themselves into communities of a size and complexity well beyond what their basic material needs seemed to require or even encourage. They had sacrificed the material convenience of living completely dispersed in individual farming units near their milpas and had gathered in hamlets, villages, towns, and also at times in large urban centers, where the extra labor of intensified food production was required. My premise is that, given a choice, people will seek some advantage in their social arrangements. The Maya masses seem to have had an unusual freedom of choice. They must therefore have received, or at any rate thought that they received, some benefits from membership in larger social groupings. And it is these benefits that students of Maya history have found so elusive.

BONDS OF KINSHIP AND COMMUNITY

The enigma of lowland Maya social organization may lie in our alien definition of need and benefit. We assume that if an individual or family can, from our perspective, satisfy all its material wants without having to exchange goods or cooperate in the development and allocation of scarce resources, then it is self-sufficient. But since social bonding is culturally rather than biologically determined, there can be no objective criterion for mutual need, and the relevant question becomes whether

131

the Maya perceived themselves as self-sufficient. Their social system indicates that they did not. The only explanation of that system consonant with all the admittedly piecemeal evidence of their behavior is that they viewed individual survival as part of a collective endeavor dependent upon mutual assistance and the coordinated activities of the group.

Why the Maya, like many other so-called traditional societies, should have conceived of individual security in collective terms may remain a mystery. It is, however, no less a paradox than the emphasis placed on the autonomy and efficacy of the individual in Western urban industrial societies, where all but the few eccentrics who subject themselves to "wilderness training" would quickly perish if deprived of the goods and services furnished by their fellows. How is it that mutual dependence is most acknowledged where least evident? Perhaps the world is simply too awesome and lonesome a place to confront mentally on one's own, and materially self-sufficient people must invent a fictive interdependence in the absence of the real thing.[42] But aside from whatever emotional comfort the Maya may have derived from sustained interaction with their fellows, they also gained certain material benefits that help to explain their willingness to submit to the social constraints of the community and the state, both before and after the Spanish conquest.

Pre-Columbian Maya society, regardless of the degree of complexity and economic specialization discernible in any one period, remained from beginning to end an agrarian society, based primarily on the labor of a more or less free (from what we can gather) peasantry. Therefore, the search for clues to Maya social bonding must start with the individual farmer, the ordinary *macehual* or commoner, who formed the foundations of the entire social order but whose incentives for doing so seem so feeble. Details about the day-to-day existence and social ties of the *macehuales* are, not surprisingly, much scarcer than information about the elite, their lineage connections, and public activities. Nevertheless, enough evidence exists to form a composite, if spotty, picture of the basic features of *macehual* life during the late Postclassic and colonial periods, features which are likely to have remained stable through internal upheavals and foreign incursions.

THE extended family seems to have been the basic unit of Maya society. In theory the Maya farmer and his wife could satisfy all their own and their children's material needs, according to a strict sexual division of labor. Men were solely responsible for raising the staple crops of maize and beans, and also cotton for clothing. Women, aside from housekeeping chores and food preparation, tended the household garden plot that supplied vegetables and fruit, raised turkeys (and later chickens), and cleaned, spun, and wove the cotton for the family's clothing.[43] While the nuclear family may have been a self-contained unit for the routine business of subsistence, it was not necessarily the most efficient unit, nor did it afford any protection against illness or injury of self or spouse and the other usual vicissitudes of human life, not least of which is old age. The Maya made provision for such contingencies through the co-operation and mutual support of a larger kinship group, the extended family.

The extended family is rarely mentioned as such in any accounts, modern or colonial, of Maya society. It is like an undiscovered planet or star whose existence and movements are inferred from the behavior of known bodies or from debris it has left after ceasing to exist. Aside from such indirect evidence there are also direct glimpses of this kin group in the references to domestic relations, settlement patterns, and property holding contained in the colonial records.[44] As revealed in these records, the extended family was a kin group of patrilaterally related males who, together with their wives and unmarried daughters, functioned as a cooperative economic unit. Ideally the group was three-generational. In practice the network could expand or contract in various combinations according to the vagaries of family history and personal predilection. The standard unit was small—four or five men at the most—perhaps because this was the optimal size for the cooperative labor that linked them together. Fraternal ties could loosen when parents had died or when any one of the brothers had enough grown sons of his own to form a separate mutual support group, even though some degree of reciprocity might be retained. Conversely, uncle-nephew ties could substitute when childlessness or loss of a father disrupted the normal arrangement.[45]

The composition and organization of the extended family and its persistence are attributable in part to its functional link with the most basic business of survival, food production. Although a man can make milpa on his own and raise enough food for himself and his immediate family, it is neither the most efficient nor the favored means of food production. It was customary in colonial times, and remains so today, for a father and sons, a team of brothers, or sometimes an uncle and nephews to share the work on adjoining or communal milpas.[46] Teamwork helps especially in felling and burning the bush, and the group also provides company and a measure of security. Like hunting, which the Maya also prefer to pursue as a small-scale joint endeavor, milpa farming takes a man into the bush for long periods, and it is wise as well as more congenial to have a few companions along in case of injury, sudden illness, or especially snake bite, which the Maya fear even more than the awesome but highly elusive jaguar.

The "milpa gang" of patrilaterally related males served as the typical unit of food production in colonial times and probably long before, whenever and wherever milpa agriculture was practiced. It is also the most likely origin of the Maya system of private land tenure. Early colonial land deeds and testaments refer commonly to "the lands of the Couohs" or of the Pats or other patrilineages.[47] Though individual owners appear in later records, male kin groups continued to function as land-holding units until at least the end of the eighteenth century. Ownership was clearly corporate. Members of the group had no separate title to individual parcels. One case involving a dispute between several brothers and their paternal uncles suggests that a share could be sold if the other members consented,[48] but this case appeared toward the end of the colonial period and could well reflect the influence of Spanish law.

In addition to corporate ownership, land passed exclusively through the male line. Even when Spanish laws undermined traditional patterns of inheritance, the rules regarding land are still discernible in the surviving testaments. Women might inherit beehives, utensils, clothing, and domestic animals, but in the absence of male heirs land was usually passed to the husbands of surviving daughters or nieces.[49]

The patrilineal extended family was also a residential unit. Multiple residences of up to twenty or thirty adults and children were supposed to be common throughout the Maya lowlands.[50] Extended family residence continued in colonial times, although the recorded household sizes are smaller. A census of one of the precincts of Tizimin in 1583, for example, lists fifty-six households, only four of which were composed of nuclear families, and the average number of people for all the households was 9.4.[51]

Sometimes the entire kin group lived in a single large house. More often they shared a residential cluster of dwellings, each one housing a couple with children and perhaps some widowed relative. There has been some confusion about patterns of residence and kinship obligations because of the documentary evidence, which seems to suggest that a couple lived with the wife's family and also with the husband's family. In fact, both types of residence were customary, but at different phases in the nuclear family life cycle. The husband paid a sort of bride price to the wife's parents or kin group, which for colonial *macehuales* took the form of labor for a year or more immediately before or after the marriage,[52] and which contemporary practice has translated into actual goods.[53] Once the bride was paid for, the couple moved to the hus-

134

band's father's house or the paternal residential complex, and the wife and her labor thenceforth belonged to her husband's family.

To what extent the extended family functioned as a single economic unit is uncertain. There can be many degrees of cooperation and mutual assistance, short of pooling all resources in common, that would enhance the well-being of the family members and increase their chances of survival. Women who shared the same household or household cluster presumably also shared some domestic chores, the care of young children, and perhaps even many of the same utensils and furnishings. It is possible that the orchards, gardens, and granaries as well as land were all common property.

In colonial times the extended family functioned more as a cooperative than a collective enterprise, a system of group support with reciprocal rights and obligations but with individual ownership of assets, except for milpa land. It was customary for the men to exchange labor in building and repairing each other's houses, but to maintain separate dwellings. Similarly, while cattle might be herded together, the surviving testaments indicate that the animals were individually owned. It would be misleading, however, to draw too sharp a line between individual and corporate ownership. Even if a shotgun or a horse were not common property, its use might be shared, and a request to borrow an item might be close to an imperative.

Reciprocal aid in necessity was the foundation of colonial Maya family organization, which can be compared to a mutual assurance society. Without this larger support network, no unmarried or widowed person, nor anyone with a disabled or absent spouse, could hope to survive, given the strict division of labor according to sex. The focus of this network of support was the father-son relationship, and its moral underpinning the son's permanent obligation toward the parents—extending even beyond death. To arrange for the proper burial of one's progenitors and to pay periodic homage to one's ancestors are among the most binding obligations in many societies. For the pre-Columbian Maya it is most apparent in the imposing funerary monuments erected to deceased rulers and in the elite tombs crammed with precious artifacts. Offerings provided by *macehual* survivors were far humbler—mainly food in simple vessels to nourish the souls on their journey—but no less obligatory.[54]

In life the filial obligation toward the father, which extended in some degree to uncles and older brothers (and presumably to their spouses), included strict obedience to the father's authority and responsibility for parental support. Children in most premodern agrarian societies are the only form of old-age insurance. The Maya started their contributions at an early age. *Macehual* children began to take part in the tasks of milpa and household almost as soon as they could walk and were performing an adult's share of labor by the time they reached the age of ten or twelve.[55] The reciprocal element in the extended family system eased the burden of filial obligations. All male heirs and their spouses (whose labor had been purchased from *their* parents) were equally responsible for parental support, and the principle of inheritance through the male line was in part a return on their investment.[56] In a shared household or residential cluster they would also receive some help from the elders, as long as they were physically able, aside from the economies of sharing household goods and equipment.

This patrilineal extended family was the preferred residential unit in colonial times in the dispersed hamlets as well as inside the towns and, I would suggest, the basis of similar population clusters that settlement pattern studies have identified as the lowest level of pre-Columbian territorial integration.[57] It seems to have been the smallest subdivision into which Maya society might fragment and still retain some semblance of a Maya social order.

The Lacandones, an isolated group of unconquered Maya in southwestern Chiapas, offer a glimpse of this most basic level of society: a kind of lowland Maya ur-society, stripped of all complex superstructures developed during the millennia of pre-Columbian history, and also largely devoid of any later European accretions. The material culture of the Lacandones is a crude and impoverished version of what we can reconstruct as having existed in late Postclassic Yucatan.[58] Their social organization has been reduced to this lowest common Maya denominator of the small patrilineally related kin group without any discernible structure above it.[59] They live scattered in the bush, sustaining only informal ties with neighboring families, who provide marriage partners and are invited as guests to important ceremonies, but who otherwise pursue an independent existence. Each family has its own deities, whose care is also the exclusive and shared activity of the same male kin group that constitutes the milpa and hunting team. This group, together with wives and children, is the primary unit for survival in an identifiably Maya fashion, ensuring the cooperative effort required to provide the twin necessities of material sustenance and divine protection, now also reduced to the simplest level of family gods. While we may consider the extended family the basic building block of Maya society, only in the case of the Lacandones do we see it functioning in isolation. It has ordinarily been only a component of a larger, territorially-based group—the community.

THE communities may have originally been based on kinship ties like the residential clusters mentioned above. The Yucatec Maya had about 250 patronymics, which may have reflected some kind of lineage division, since the Maya asserted that everyone bearing the same patronymic belonged to the same "family."[60] However, we lack evidence for any functionally significant kinship organization beyond the extended family.

The apparent simplicity of the Maya kinship system as revealed in the colonial records could merely reflect Spanish ignorance or indifference. Their interest in kinship patterns, as in so many other aspects of Maya culture, was confined to possible conflicts with Roman Catholic rules of behavior, in this case those concerning divorce and polygamy. If they inquired very far into the traditional system from which these conflicts arose, they did not bother to record their findings. Some rules about descent and preferred marriage partners can be pieced together from linguistic evidence and parish records, as Philip Thompson has done in his study of the town of Tekanto.[61] But these rules establish only what affinal and lineal ties to expect, and not what rights and obligations went along with them. And it is the content rather than the form of the networks that interests us here.

Only two features of a lineage system are mentioned as operative at the time of conquest. One was a prohibition against marrying someone with the same patronymic, a rule that, according to the colonial parish registers, continued to be honored. The other was a rule that anyone who traveled or moved away from home could count on help from another with the same patronymic even if a total stranger.[62] Such a rule would be meaningless if patronymics represented lineages that shared more or less the same territory. It suggests instead that lineages may once have been coterminous with territorial divisions, but that preconquest migrations had already broken up these geographic concentrations and that the rule of helping strangers with the same surname was only a relic of the older system.[63]

If phratries, moieties, clans, or any equivalent to the Aztec *calpulli* or the Andean *ayllu* existed, the evidence has yet to surface.[64] In its absence we must conclude tentatively that beyond the level of the extended family (which retained its vitality because of its relatively small size and its strong links with the unchanging mode of food production) social grouping had shifted from lineage to locality; to the territorially based community of village or town and the wards or precincts into which they were divided. At both these levels, common residence had replaced common descent as the focus of loyalty and the basis for defining rights and obligations, roles and statuses.

The search for the organizing principles of Maya society merely begins with shared territory. In view of the patterns of settlement prevailing in the Maya lowlands, this principle raises as many questions as it answers. During all of the area's known history, a greater or lesser proportion of the population has lived in residential clusters physically detached from the concentrated nuclei of the towns, yet somehow forming part of the community.[65] The territorial principle cannot account for the links between these satellite clusters and the towns, nor for the existence of the towns themselves. And the elusive key to Maya social organization lies at this level of the territorial hierarchy.

Social cohesion at the level of the community is an issue altogether separate from the integration of communities into provinces or states. The latter depended entirely on relationships between the ruling elites. The trade networks that they controlled (of luxury goods that they consumed), the conquests that they led, and the alliances that they formed were all links that could be made without reference to the ordinary mass of the population. Centralization would require no alteration in local arrangements, nor any forging of bonds between the peasantry and new overlords as long as the stratified community structure was maintained. Such changes at the top might add to the burden on the local *macehuales* if, as occurred after the Spanish conquest, new tribute and labor quotas were superimposed on the demands of the local rulers. But it is the principle of such contributions and the stratified structure they represent that are at issue, not the amount.

The extended family may provide some clues to the organization of the community, in particular the horizontal and vertical bonds that linked periphery to center and peasantry to nobility. It suggests a model based on the same premise that the primary purpose of human bonding is survival. We find that the Maya formed in the extended family larger and more complex permanent groups than were necessary to maintain the species through reproduction and food production, but which nevertheless offered certain life-enhancing and life-preserving benefits. Whether or not the territorial community was originally based on kinship ties, it can be seen as an extended family writ large with similar principles and incentives and a similar structure. That structure was both corporate and hierarchical.

By definition any social group is corporate to some degree; without shared interests and purpose it would remain merely a category of persons. Here I use the term corporate to denote an especially close and all-encompassing identification with the group, which becomes an extension of self. The individual, more than merely affiliated with the group, functions overwhelmingly as a part of it, deriving from corpo-

138

rate membership not only most of his rights and obligations but a permanent and total social identity as well. Corporate is often equated with egalitarian. But the two qualities are not synonymus, and both the Latin root of the word and the imagery that has surrounded it suggest the contrary. The image of the *corpus* in referring to the Christian church and later to the secular "body social" has always had head and members. The Maya apparently saw no contradiction between corporate and hierarchical in their conception of society at any level. The main difference was that in the larger social system the hierarchy of status and authority was (theoretically) determined by birth and therefore fixed, while in the family it shifted over time with seniority.

I do not suggest that the bonds of community were as strong as those of the extended family, only that they were similar in nature. The community was also designed to serve as a joint-stock company: to combine forces to promote the common good, and to spread the burden and risk of individual hardship or calamity more evenly among all its members. Much of the evidence for these community functions comes from the colonial period, when the principles for mutual assistance were severely undermined. Even then, some tangible advantages from a larger network are still discernible in certain provisions made for individual misfortune and in a variety of elite-directed cooperative projects from which the entire community benefited.[66]

Although I have likened the community to a joint-stock company, there is no way to compile a stockholders' report of profits and losses. It is difficult to evaluate the effectiveness of these cooperative efforts, impossible from our own perspective to weigh the advantages gained against the social constraints and tax burdens that represent the *macehaul*'s investment. Even if such a hypothetical balance sheet were to find that in purely material terms the ordinary farmer or his family would have done better on its own, the relevant point is whether the Maya thought so. We must assume that on the whole they did not; but we must also include on the credit side the two cooperative endeavors that were probably seen as yielding the highest returns on the investment in community membership. One was warfare and the other divine worship, activities that must be counted among the strongest social bonds in any society.

WARFARE AND DIVINE MEDIATION

Much historical ink has been spilled on the causes and effects of particular wars, considerably less on the subject of warfare in general, although it has figured prominently in discussions of the origins of the state.[67] So long as it is assumed that pressure for land has been the primary motive for armed struggle, it is difficult to see what contribution warfare can have made to the evolution of complex sociopolitical systems wherever populations were not dense enough to create such pressures. But in fact it has long been recognized that people will fight out of almost any conceivable motive or combination of motives: "For fun and profit, for livestock and land, for glory and freedom, for honors and plunder."[68] Aside from its more obvious purpose of extending domination over neighbors, warfare, it is agreed, can also be an excellent means of gaining ascendancy over one's own fellows. Military leadership is in itself sufficient, without any need to use physical force, or even the threat of it, over subordinates. All that is required is that the subordinates be convinced that the leadership is necessary or beneficial to their own interests.

Whatever the underlying causes of organized aggression may be and whatever the basic stimuli for religious ritual, the Maya, in common with most premodern societies, devoted a major share of their attention to both activities. An earlier, idyllic view of the Classic Maya as the peace-loving flower children of pre-Columbian Mesoamerica has by now been largely discredited. The frequent and widespread military activity that supposedly characterized the Postclassic, especially in the period immediately preceding Spanish conquest, has come to be considered the norm, at least intermittently, for earlier times as well. Social prestige and political authority were associated with leadership in warfare in Classic period art, and it is likely that the military regalia of the Maya lords depicted in sculpture and painting derived from a long tradition of primacy in military affairs.[69] Such a primacy is still evident in the late Postclassic title of War Chief or Captain (*batab*) for the local—that is, subprovincial—territorial rulers.[70]

Evidence of early Classic fortified towns and cities in various parts of the lowlands indicates that the military defense could well have been one stimulus for the development of urban concentrations of varying sizes.[71] As I have argued earlier, general demographic pressure is not necessary to explain such concentrations, since a redistribution of population could produce the same effect. Warfare's contribution to such a decision can be seen elsewhere—for example, in the region of Swat in northern Pakistan. There a relatively sparse population gathered in fortified sites and maintained elaborate irrigation systems. They abandoned both in favor of scattered settlements and extensive cropping techniques (without any decline in overall population) when the establishment of British colonial rule provided security from military raids.[72]

We do not know whether any comparable period of widespread peace ever existed in the Maya lowlands before the Spanish colonial era. The hegemony of some large city states may well have provided periods of security for certain areas. The evidence suggests that these political groupings were highly unstable. But long spells of border skirmishes and a general jockeying for position within and between provinces would have contributed to the cohesion of the individual warring units even while regional integration suffered.

Warfare need not be a simple struggle for land. The issue is as likely to be people as land, for in many societies control over manpower has been the principal source and measure of wealth and power. Wherever people are the scarcer and therefore the more valuable commodity, domination over them will be the primary incentive for territorial expansion, and human captives will be prominent items of plunder in border raids. Certainly land as such did not figure as a motive in the Spanish conquest, and in late Postclassic Yucatan the taking of prisoners for slaves seems to have been a major incentive for much of the military activity rather than simply its byproduct.[73]

A related source of intercommunity and interprovincial strife when the Spanish arrived was personal aggression—insults, blows, homicide—against any member of a neighboring group, and it was the duty of the aggrieved party's ruler to avenge the aggression by punishing the offender's group.[74] The references to this vendetta system suggest one concept of rulership as a formalized but still fairly personal patron–client relationship along feudal or clan chieftain lines, with the territorial lord responsible for protecting his vassals/kinsmen in return for their allegiance and material support.

The military role of the elite could provide a different, and to me more plausible, twist to the economic explanations discussed earlier. The rulers may not have directly controlled the distribution of basic commodities like salt, but through their military leadership they could guarantee their subjects' access to them.

Further reinforcement for the importance of warfare in Maya social organization comes from the central and southern lowlands during the period between first contact with the Spanish in the 1520s and the eventual, though still incomplete, conquest of the region in the late seventeenth century. The Peten region of northern Guatemala and surrounding districts, where many of the major Classic centers were located, seems to have contained far fewer people in Postclassic and colonial times. Yet despite the absence of population pressure on the total available land, the inhabitants lived grouped together in more or less densely aggregated communities with recognizable boundaries, rather than in dispersed settlements with vacant ceremonial centers, or scattered in totally isolated units like the modern-day Lacandones. Whether composed entirely of refugees or unpacified Maya, or a mixture of the two, all the communities had the same basic sociopolitical structure (with *batabs* and high priests and their assistants) and a similar territorial organization.[75] Some of the towns were quite compact, fortified sites and there is some suggestion of more intensive cropping techniques that coexisted with milpa agriculture.[76] One might simply ascribe the patterns to force of habit. But a strong immediate incentive existed for maintaining the habit and for integrating the units into larger political-military systems under the Itza lords and various other "kings" mentioned in the Spanish documents. The incentive can be found in the state of virtually perennial warfare that prevailed throughout the area, warfare against the Spanish but also and mainly with each other.

The Lacandones took part in these clashes. Their current organization in family encampments without larger defensive social pacts is less a reversion to "normal" Maya behavior than an adaptation, and a largely successful one, to the overwhelming power of the Spanish. They eventually relinquished the satisfactions of warfare with their neighbors and large complex settlements because both attracted too much Spanish attention.[77] Moreover, once their principal enemies, the Itza, had been conquered, any continuation of hostilities would have brought Spanish reprisals. Whether the completely atomized and undifferentiated pattern of the contemporary Lacandon was entirely due to colonial conditions or whether it was a further response to harassment from nineteenth-century logging operations, organized warfare came to be more of a hindrance than a help to survival.

RELIGION, if not a stronger force for social integration, is at least a more constant one. Warfare sometimes abates but the supernatural always retains its mystery and power. The processes of secularization that the western world has set into motion had no equivalent among the pre-Columbian Maya, in whose lives religion—as we define it—was all-pervasive. That much the archaeological, pictorial, and written records attest to, even if we are far from having sorted out what all the rich profusion of visual and verbal imagery actually meant to the Maya.

The content of Maya beliefs and rituals aside, it is clear that they served, among other functions, a major role in holding Maya society together at several levels. Certain generalized cults are part of the distinctive cultural configuration that we identify as Maya. The shared attachment to them and the religious pilgrimages they fostered could have been as prominent a vehicle for integration as economic exchange. Indeed, cult and trade may often have served as mutually reinforcing

aspects of a single communications network.[78] At the level of the con-
stituent communities within the larger culture, each town and city seems
to have had its own tutelary deities, which provided a focus for the
community's identity and its own special link with the supernatural.[79]

It has been suggested that the rulers themselves could personify this
link. The institution of "divine kingship" has made appearances at many
other times and in many other places. Maya lords are often difficult to
distinguish from Maya deities in the sculptural and pictorial effigies. It
is more than likely that this merging of identities was intentional and
that the recent discoveries of the dynastic, historical significance of many
glyphs and representations merely add another level of meaning to them
rather than negating the sacred connotations of earlier interpretations.[80]
Some of the portrayals of Classic-period rulers have been interpreted
not merely as symbolizing but as actually embodying the divine within
the human community.[81] Even as mere representatives or mediators,
without claiming divine descent, the elite held a powerful instrument
for legitimizing their temporal authority. Much of this imagery may
have been accessible only to the elite themselves, depicted in murals,
sculpture, codices, and polychrome pottery that the masses seldom saw
and only dimly understood. But we know from better-documented societies with a similar structure that a belief system can have a compelling
verisimilitude for the unsophisticated without their understanding all of
the theological fine points.

One long-standing interpretation of lowland Maya historical development is that the Maya elite were essentially priestly leaders whose
ascendancy had been gained via their specialized knowledge of astronomy. The hypothetical first leaders were those intelligent enough to
note and discern the patterns of astral movements and seasonal variations and to impress their fellow farmers with their ability to predict
recurrences.[82] Although this intellectualist explanation has more recently
been eclipsed by ecological and demographic models, they need not be
mutually exclusive. To reduce the Maya elite's intense (one is tempted
to say obsessive) concern with the measurement of time to a mechanism
for sociopolitical control would be absurd. But that need not negate
political power as one of the consequences of this esoteric knowledge
of calendrics and astronomy, which could serve as a sign of intimacy
with, and control over, supernatural forces. Among those forces, perhaps of most compelling interest to agricultural peoples are the seasonal
alternations of winter and summer, dry and rainy periods. Past experience is not necessarily any guarantee that the days will lengthen again
or that the life-sustaining monsoons will return. Judging both from passages in the pre-Hispanic chronicles and from the colonial records, the

6. Stela 8, Seibal, Peten, Guatemala, dated 869, A.D., portraying a Maya ruler with the head of a deity (God K) held in his right hand; along with military gear, the figure wears jaguar insignia (mitts and sandals) symbolizing rulership. (Photo by Arthur G. Miller)

144

lowland Maya had ample cause for anxiety about the timely arrival of the rains.[83]

It may be that the intense concern with death and rebirth, with the passage of time, and with the recording of the past and prediction of the future, as well as the notion of time as a "burden" that gods bear with man's help, and the idea of the efficacy of sacrificial offerings and a panoply of propitiatory rituals were all confined to the Maya elite,[84] and were so much mumbo-jumbo to a baffled or indifferent peasantry. It is equally possible that the basic structure of symbols and rituals was a comprehensive one in which all levels of society shared to some degree. Since neither interpretation is susceptible to proof at this distance, only the weight of historically documented examples[85] and the greater explanatory power for the particular Maya case favor the latter choice.

To try to separate the sacred from the military, economic, and political function of the Maya elite would be futile; to try to assign them an order of priority would be even more so. They all seem to have been merged together, although we have evidence in the contact period for some specialization within the religious sphere. The role that the Maya lords assumed, as many other territorial rulers have done, was that of patriarch on a large scale, like the head of a Lacandon extended family. They wielded authority and bore responsibility for protecting the welfare of the group, a responsibility that included propitiating the gods on the group's behalf as well as directing the activities necessary for material support.[86]

The origins of the particular population centers in which the Maya congregated may be equally mixed. Paul Wheatley emphasizes the centripetal pull exerted by religion. Developing Fustel de Coulanges's thesis on the origins of cities in the Classical Mediterranean world, he sees urbanization as universally emanating from the evolution of sacred shrines into ceremonial centers. He also sees social and economic differentiation and political power as deriving at least initially from the growth of a specialized priesthood.[87]

The origins of lowland Maya social organization will no doubt continue to be debated. It may turn out that they lie elsewhere—in the highlands, in a very different physical setting—and that much of the stimulus for further development came from the same place, in the form of central Mexican expansion, which brought examples of and incentives for increased complexity and centralization.[88] Even if that were so, we should still need to explain the maintenance of this sociopolitical order. Whatever their origins, the pre-Columbian Maya polities served as foci for military defense and religious ceremonial organized and directed by the ruling elite. This dual function, helping to ensure group survival against aggressive neighbors and against supernatural powers (which could pose an even greater threat to security) is for me the most plausible basis of the social bond that held the Maya together, despite the centrifugal forces that the open and redundant environment exercised.

We should regard social organization as a process rather than an achieved state. The bonds of reciprocity, cooperation, and mutual protection that held the Maya together in more or less bounded, more or less hierarchical, communities were not established at some point and then fixed for all time. This side of Utopia, the identification of society's collective interests—the common good—with the perceived self-interest of its individual members will never be perfect. A dynamic tension will exist between the two, and the balance will be a particularly delicate one in societies like that of the lowland Maya, where the natural setting reinforces any fissioning tendencies.

This setting has remained substantially unmodified throughout the course of Maya history, until the nineteenth-century henequen plantations transformed much of the landscape in the north-central and western portions of the peninsula. Thus the physical ease of fragmentation remained constant. But the cultural forces influencing social and territorial cohesion have ebbed and flowed, creating discernible advances and retreats in the degree of sociopolitical integration. In whatever direction Maya society may have been moving on its own momentum, Spanish conquest and colonization placed considerable strain on what at the best of times would appear to have been a tenuous set of social bonds.

· 5 ·

CREATION OF THE COLONIAL
COMMUNITY

Throughout Mesoamerica and the Andes the Spanish encountered a type of sociopolitical organization similar to that of the lowland Maya, an organization that facilitated the military conquest and also increased the material rewards reaped from it. Instead of small, elusive bands that had to be rounded up and taught—with mixed success—to endure the constraints of "civilized" life in the frontier missions, the dense populations of sedentary agriculturalists in these two core regions were already gathered into stable communities, which in turn were linked into larger political systems. And the peasantry were already used to supporting and obeying a privileged class of rulers along with the functionaries, warriors and craftsmen who served them. The Spanish had only to superimpose themselves at the apex of the pyramid and settle down to enjoy the fruits of conquest.

Or so it may have seemed to the original bands of conquerors. New economic activities, missionary policies, and heavy population losses were all to create disruptions in the indigenous social order far beyond the mere replacement of rulers at the top. Even without these changes, the consolidation of the gains achieved through military conquest required some basic modification of the indigenous system. In particular, the hierarchical organization of provinces and states that had facilitated the imposition of colonial rule was deemed less favorable to its maintenance. The Spanish everywhere in the early postconquest period were aware how tenuous their hold was, vastly outnumbered as they were by a conquered population that was by no means fully reconciled to defeat. In order to consolidate their hold, the Spanish had to divide the larger indigenous political structures, through which any resistance could be organized, into smaller, more easily controllable units.

FRAGMENTATION

The fragmentation of Indian society had less far to go in Yucatan than in central Mexico or Peru, where regional polities had been incorporated into extensive imperial systems. At the time of the conquest, Yucatan was divided into sixteen or more provinces that formed a single cultural and linguistic unit but were politically independent entities.[1]

There no longer existed any supraprovincial organization or capital, although memories of the League of Mayapan, which had united a large part of the region from the late thirteenth century until 1441, were still sharp, and the tradition of Chichen Itza's earlier hegemony was reflected in its status as a pilgrimage center.[2]

Ralph Roys has identified three forms of territorial organization: (1) provinces under the centralized rule of a single lord, a *halach uinic*; (2) confederations dominated by a single lineage; and (3) looser confederations of smaller allied groups that usually cooperated in foreign policy but otherwise maintained their autonomy and equality.[3] This schema fails to do justice to the complex and highly fluid conditions of the conquest period, which a continuum of finer gradations between centralized rule and casual, temporary aggregations might represent more accurately. Some *halach uinics* exercised tighter control over their territories and some may have been simply "first among equals." Some lineages—for example, the Chel of Ahkinchel—were approaching centralized or at least coordinated rule, while the Cupul were as likely to fight each other as to unite against a neighboring province.[4]

Two points about the geopolitical structure are relevant here. One is that the provinces were, for all the flux of political groupings and the varying degrees of cohesion, more than random collections of towns. They all possessed internal ties of some kind and provincial boundaries, which might be readjusted by war or arbitration but which were nonetheless recognized as boundaries. The other point is that these ties were for the most part hierarchical in nature, with a rank ordering of towns at the subprovincial level regardless of how unified or loosely organized the larger entity might be.[5]

In confirming the authority of all the native lords who agreed to accept Spanish sovereignty at all levels of the political hierarchy, the conquerors would seem to be perpetuating and reinforcing the existing territorial and political system in its entirety. Such an effect was only temporary. There is no evidence that the supracommunity organization was actively suppressed. Rather, its dissolution was the inevitable consequence of the administrative structure the Spanish imposed. They erected each community into a completely autonomous administrative unit, the colonial *república de indios*,[6] and by dealing separately and equally with each community and its ruler, by simply ignoring the existing hierarchical structure and chains of command, they allowed them to wither away.[7]

The *encomienda* system gave no support to traditional intercommunity ties. Most of the grants consisted of single towns, and the ones that originally did unite a group of neighboring towns under a single *enco-

mienda were divided up and reshuffled over the years into a patchwork of towns, and even portions of towns, located in various parts of the peninsula.[8] It is hard to believe that such confusion was not deliberate, an attempt to discourage both territorial ambitions by *encomenderos* and Maya territorial cohesion. Yet that does seem to have been the case. As the *encomiendas* became more strictly monetary grants without rights over labor or responsibility for either military control or civil administration, the main concern became the size of the annuity based on the total tributary population included in the grant's components, rather than the *encomiendas'* particular location. Even when several towns remained grouped together and coincided with a preconquest cluster, each dealt with its *encomendero* in the same way as with the civil authorities— as an autonomous unit with its own tribute quota, which was delivered separately.

Aside from any particular colonial policy, the mere imposition of centralized rule could easily by itself, and regardless of Spanish intentions, have resulted in the fragmentation of the larger political units (which seem to have been highly unstable in any case). Just as the supranational integration of the European Economic Community has encouraged latent regional separatism to emerge, the creation of a larger colonial state, and especially the suppression of warfare within its borders, may have encouraged the breakdown of Maya society into the more fundamental unit of the community, because the incentives for banding together in provinces and subprovinces no longer existed. In other words, integration at one level can lead to disintegration at another.

The one exception to the total fragmentation of Maya society into separate and equal communities was the ecclesiastical unit of the parish, the Franciscan *doctrina* and the secularized *curato*. Each parish had a *cabecera*, or principal town, where the *doctrinero*, or curate, resided, and one or more subordinate towns, called *visitas* in Yucatan.[9] Each *visita* had its own church but was administered by the curate riding circuit, or, in some of the large secularized parishes in the later colonial period, by a resident priest assistant to the curate. In organizing their *doctrinas* shortly after the conquest, the Franciscans seem to have respected the native jurisdictional boundaries, as can be seen in a 1582 list of parishes (twenty-three Franciscan and four secular) and their component towns.[10] Some of the parishes were exactly coterminous with smaller preconquest provinces—for example, Sotuta and Ichmul (Cochuah). In the severely depopulated south and east, they tended to incorporate all or most of the peripheral provinces; Champoton, for example, was annexed to Campeche, and northern Cupul was joined with Chikinchel to form

149

Tizimin. The large, densely populated provinces in the north and west, on the other hand, were divided into two, three, or four *doctrinas*, although these generally corresponded to existing subprovincial divisions.

The hierarchical relationships were also preserved within the parishes. The early *cabeceras* were for the most part established in the main indigenous centers, such as Mani, Sotuta, Hocaba, Sisal (Saçi), and Chancenote, which were the residences of the areas' principal Maya lords. Many considerations would combine to favor these choices. They corresponded to the general distribution of population and thus represented the most efficient deployment of the small number of missionaries. Also, the shift in spiritual sovereignty could be most forcefully expressed by physically substituting Christian churches and friaries for the region's main pagan structures (which, moreover, could provide building materials for the new temples).[11] And the friars, like the lay Spaniards, were obviously aware that it was far easier and more prudent to work through the existing native structure of authority than to try to bypass it.

The disintegration of provincial political organization came about as the generation of native lords whose attitudes and habits had been forged before conquest died out. While they lived and while the colonial administrative system was still embryonic, the major territorial rulers continued to exercise authority over their traditional domains and to represent them in external affairs. Records of early postconquest boundary settlements between provinces, and negotiations with the Spanish over such matters as tribute or evangelization, all reveal this hierarchical ordering among the native lords and the continued preeminence of the provincial rulers.[12] One provincial lord in southwest Campeche, don Pablo Paxbolon, managed not only to preserve his territorial domain (although it was in fact relocated to another area), but also to extend his power far back into the interior, incorporating new towns and many fugitive Maya from the north who had never previously been under his rule.[13]

Paxbolon was unusual, combining the expansionist and entrepreneurial spirit of his "Putun" ancestors with a shrewd calculation of how to further his own interests by cooperating with and aiding the Spanish. More commonly, by the time the first colonial generation had succeeded the transitional rulers, their authority was already shrinking to the limited and standard scope of individual *repúblicas de indios*. The successor of a *halach uinic* such as Nachi Cocom might retain the same preconquest title of Lord of Sotuta, but this and similar designations had come to signify authority only over the province's chief town and not, as formerly, over the whole province. Considerable prestige and certain wider powers of suasion continued to accrue to the heirs of the provincial lords for some time.[14] Formally, and largely in practice as well, they had been reduced to a status equal to an ordinary *batab*; that is, they became merely the leader and representative of a single community, albeit a *cabecera* and for a time the largest and most important *cabecera* in the district.

The organization of parish administration helped to preserve some remnant of the old hierarchical structure. Although *visita* towns had their own churches and were therefore ceremonial centers in their own right, they owed certain obligations to the *cabecera* that the latter did not have to reciprocate. The residents of *visitas* had to contribute materials and labor for the construction, enlargement, and repair of the *cabecera* churches. Although one curate attempted to violate this hierarchical principle and commandeer aid from the *cabecera* of his parish to rebuild a *visita* church, he met with firm and apparently successful opposition.[15]

Ordinarily *visita* residents attended mass in their own churches. But on specified holy days the entire population of the parish had to gather in the *cabecera* unless exempt because of age or illness. The particular days so designated varied from parish to parish but usually included the feast of the *cabecera*'s patron saint, Corpus Christi, and Maundy Thursday.[16]

Certain communities retain to this day vestiges of this old relationship even though the subordinate town may by now be a separate parish. This relationship is expressed in the visit by one of the subordinate town's saints to pay homage to a saint of the *cabecera*, or former *cabecera*, on the latter's feast day. Thus, Our Lady of Tetiz, a small town northwest of Merida, is taken out in solemn procession—equipped with a straw hat to shield her from the sun—on a ten-kilometer journey to pay homage to Our Lady of Hunucma, which at the time of the conquest was the principal town in the area and which remained the parish *cabecera* during the entire colonial period.

From the viewpoint of Christian orthodoxy, the two images, both representing the same Queen of Heaven, are of equal status, but in local sociopolitical terms one of them, like the community she represents, takes precedence over the other. Similarly, Christ ought to take precedence over all the saints, including his mother, but not necessarily in the local cosmology. The "Black Christ" of Sitilpech makes an annual pilgrimage, accompanied by the residents of the town, to the shrine of the Virgin of Izamal, which was the colonial *cabecera* of the parish as well as the seat of the patroness of all Yucatan (and a major pre-Columbian shrine). The route follows an ancient *sacbe*, or ceremonial causeway, and traditionally the Christ of Sitilpech breaks his journey to rest at a small chapel erected expressly for that purpose, in front of a sacred (in pre-Columbian cosmology) ceiba tree on the outskirts of Izamal. He then continues on to pay his respects to Our Lady, whose shrine is located in the massive Franciscan church built shortly after the conquest on the base of one of the two principal pyramids in Izamal.[17]

Both Tetiz and Sitilpech have been subordinate in status since at least the beginning of evangelization, and possibly these visits by "subordinate" saints preserve an earlier ritual of obeisance by patron deities, through which regional hierarchical integration was expressed and reinforced. Similar saints' visits have been recorded in the highlands of central Mexico and Chiapas and interpreted as a symbolic expression of former political subordination.[18] The colonial records provide little information on such visits in Yucatan other than that they were made. Like many of the rituals surrounding the fiestas, which will be discussed in later chapters, they were solely Maya activities based on local, probably preconquest, tradition, and the clergy neither organized them nor paid much attention to them as long as proper decorum was preserved in the processions.[19]

If the visits do preserve in ritual form the preconquest regional ties, they represent the last vestige of indigenous political structures above the community level, which in every other way were dismantled under Spanish rule. Even the territorial organization of the parish was on an ever-shrinking scale. The huge early parishes were subdivided again and again, lopping off original *visita* towns to create new clusters with their own *cabeceras*. By the end of colonial rule, the number of Indian parishes had grown from twenty-seven (in 1582) to over seventy, and a number of these consisted of a single town without any *visitas* at all.[20]

As for formal political links, they do not seem to have been preserved either within or without the parish structure. The Maya officials in one town might confer and cooperate with their neighboring counterparts, just as they invited each other as guests to their fiestas and banquets. However, though saints' visits suggest ritual deference, in policy matters the town leaders seem to have acted as independent agents—equally powerful within their own communities, equally powerless outside them, and each answerable separately to the Spanish authorities.

REGIONAL NETWORKS

Regional integration can be and often is achieved in the absence of any formal political apparatus. But local trade, which might have sustained regional networks independently of any administrative structures, as it did in the Mesoamerican highlands, was weak in Yucatan. And the long-distance trade that had supported intercommunity links through the elite traders and consumers was all but wiped out after the conquest. More accurately, it was taken over by the Spanish.

The basic pattern of interregional trade remained unchanged under colonial rule. Yucatan continued to export most of the same raw or only slightly processed materials in exchange for manufactured goods,[21] although the export list was reduced by the royal prohibition against the slave trade and the disappearance of an indigenous market for tropical plumage and jaguar pelts, which were no longer emblems of elite status. The luxury goods imported in return also became European in style if not always in manufacture. Only cacao, for which the Spanish developed a taste bordering on addiction, remained the same. Trade routes remained similar, except that a direct sea link between Campeche and Veracruz was substituted for the overland, riverine, and coastal transport that had connected the peninsula with central Mexico. The principal difference, of course, was that the Maya no longer controlled or even took part in the trade. Even the sailors manning the coastal *bongos* (large dugouts) that carried Yucatecan salt to Tabasco in exchange for cacao were all mestizos or mulattoes.[22]

Information on the native trade that continued between the conquered territory of northern and central Yucatan and the unpacified zones to the south is extremely scanty. We have no way of knowing the volume of this clandestine commerce. No information exists on how it was organized, only that it was part of a general and, by all accounts, fairly extensive system of communication linking both sides of the colonial frontier.[23] What effect it may have had on regional networks within the conquered area is thus impossible to assess, but we can presume that the trade, along with any sociopolitical repercussions it may have had, declined with the expansion of Spanish control over the zones of refuge.

One small remnant of interregional trade persisted into the late eighteenth century, however, and it may provide some clues about the way earlier networks were organized. The trade was carried out by the Chontal Maya of Acalan in southwestern Campeche, descendants of the "Putun" traders who have become so well known in the Mesoamerican literature. The Acalan Maya were able to continue some of their trading ventures across the southern frontier and also with Tabasco for a period after their resettlement at Tixchel, on the Gulf coast south of Champoton. It has been thought that the "Putun" tradition came to an end by the late seventeenth century, destroyed by European pirates, by the increasingly unsettled frontier conditions, and by the disappearance of the Chontal themselves.[24] Swamped by the flood of Yucatec Maya refugees from the north, the Chontal Maya left no recorded trace in the language or surnames of the region.[25] They did, however, leave a trace of the "Putun" commercial tradition in a much reduced trade link between Campeche and Tabasco, via the old inland waterways of the Candelaria and Usumacinta Rivers.

This late colonial trade, while not strictly clandestine, seems to have gone on unnoticed by the Spanish authorities. Its volume posed little threat to Spanish commercial interests and it was conducted (or at least that part of the trade we have any record of) under the very unlikely aegis of local religious confraternities, or *cofradías*.[26] The center of the trade was the town of Chicbul, located between Champoton and the mouth of the Candelaria River, which empties into the Laguna de Términos. The trade routes were the old "Putun" ones and the main product was the traditional cacao from Tabasco. Chicbul itself was almost certainly where the frequently relocated Acalan Chontal ended up, as indicated by the patron saints of the two *cofradías*: the Christ of Tixchel (the former principal town of the Chontal) and the Virgin of Mamentel (a town on a tributary of the Candelaria River by the same name, which had also at some point in the Chontal peregrinations been abandoned). When resettled for the last time in Chicbul, the Chontal had presumably followed the common colonial Maya practice (with possible pre-Columbian antecedents) of bringing their patron saints (deities) with them.

I do not suggest that the *cofradías* dedicated to these saints were a front for mercantile activities that otherwise the Spanish might have discouraged. Such a distinction would have been meaningless to the pre-Columbian "Putun," who had combined commerce with pilgrimage and placed themselves under the protection of the cacao god, Ek Chuah, the patron deity of merchants.[27] Rather, it was a characteristically "Putun" symbiosis between deity/saint and trade, each bringing blessings on the other.

This commercial enterprise helped to make the Chicbul saints among the wealthiest in the diocese of Yucatan,[28] though the town itself was small and isolated from the center of Spanish economic activity. The *cofradía* officers organized twice-yearly expeditions, armed with scapularies and wax images of their local saints to peddle throughout the riverine areas as far as the Usumacinta.[29] I would be surprised to learn that they did not also carry on trade for themselves and as agents for their fellow community leaders, although there is no mention of these private transactions in the *cofradía* accounts, the only known source of information for this commercial network. Cacao was bartered in exchange for scapularies and images and whatever cash or other goods they carried on private account. The highly valued cacao, when brought back for sale in Champoton and Campeche, yielded a handsome profit to pay for the masses, church ornaments, and fiestas in Chicbul.

One wonders what sociological explanation there may be for such a large-scale religious cult. These *cofradía* expeditions are the only colonial analogue to the widespread cults of pre-Columbian times that helped to link the whole area together with their pilgrimages. This was a pilgrimage in reverse, in which *cofradía* officers carried portable images of their saints directly to the devotees (and also scapularies and miniatures for sale to them). It brings to mind the Caste War cult of the Speaking Cross. The *cruzob* practice was to keep the cross shielded from view in a wooden chest inside the *Gloria*, or sanctuary, and bring forth stand-ins for the profane eyes of the ordinary faithful.[30] But I have not read anywhere that these stand-ins were carried around from town to town to collect religious tribute.

Clearly the Chicbul cults and trade were interdependent, and by carrying on the "Putun" link between the peninsula and Tabasco, the Chicbuleños maintained much wider economic and religious horizons than the ordinary Yucatec Maya. One can only surmise that Chontal neighbors in Tabasco continued to pay deference to the old (if relocated) "Putun" capital: a long-distance saint's visit, in reverse.

This vestigial "Putun" tradition may have been unique. We have no indication of any other long-distance commercial venture. I have already discussed the lack of evidence for any system of local trade at the time of conquest that could have supported provincial and subprovincial integration. If any such system ever existed, it also seems to have disappeared. The central Mexican *tianguiz*, or Indian market, that a royal *visitador* tried to introduce into Yucatan in the mid-sixteenth century never caught on.[31] Local trade in colonial times already resembled the system so familiar in the ethnographic accounts of the twentieth century—a trade controlled entirely by non-Indian storekeepers and itinerant peddlars.[32] The peddlars are now losing ground as local transportation facilities improve; where they are still the main source of supply for small villages, they are more likely to transact their business from the back of a truck than the back of a mule. But for almost four centuries they were the principal commercial link for the rural Maya, and in the early colonial period, before permanent stores were established in the larger Indian towns, the only one.

At first either the local *encomendero* or any other Spaniard who happened to visit a town performed this function. Eventually full-time traders with strings of pack animals fanned out from the Spanish centers. When they arrived in an Indian town, they set themselves up in the travelers' hostel maintained in the town hall and proceeded to sell the few outside goods, such as salt or a machete, the Maya needed or wanted.[33]

It would be hard to conceive of a system of economic exchange less conducive to social integration at any level. Not only were the Maya merely passive participants, but they participated purely as individuals and not as a group. The peddlars summoned each "client" one at a time, via their local agents, and dismissed him before doing business with the next. Perhaps it was easier to control the terms of the transaction that way, although a local Indian official was supposed to witness all such exchanges.

The grain and livestock trades were no less socially sterile. The Indians rarely took their produce to the towns. Instead, surplus—and often not so surplus—maize was bought from the individual farmer in the village by city merchants or agents.[34] And except for the *cofradía* estates, the Indians sold their cattle to nearby *estancias* for resale to the urban slaughterhouses. The purchase of a mule or cow was made in the same way, by negotiating privately with the foreman of a neighboring *estancia*. Economic exchanges in colonial Yucatan, controlled by and for non-Indians, were as unrewarding it terms of social communication as they were for the individual Maya's pocket.

The colonial economic system cannot be heavily blamed for the fragmentation of Maya society. The truth is that all but a small minority of the Maya, before or after conquest, were simply outside a market economy with little to sell and little need to buy. In the Maya highlands Indian production, consumption, and trade of goods have all served to link hamlets, villages, local and regional markets, and even the state (and in Guatemala the national) capitals through an Indian network. In Yucatan there does not seem to have existed much in the way of a regional economic network for the Spanish to dismantle.

Despite the lack of political and economic ties, the Yucatec Maya remained a single cultural and linguistic unit and continued to think of themselves as a single people. Colonial rule might in fact have helped to reinforce a sense of a total Maya collectivity by bringing them into prolonged contact with a new set of rulers, immeasurably more alien than any predecessors. The colonial Maya could not escape the consciousness, which the caste barrier enforced and preserved, of belonging to a group distinct from their unassimilated overlords. There were also many informal links that served to sustain a sense of Maya identity and of the group's geographical extension, links that also helped to preserve the region's high degree of linguistic and cultural homogeneity.

The Maya did not remain entirely isolated within their communities. They attended each other's fiestas in the same *comarca*, or vicinity,[35] and beyond that, they moved around over surprisingly long distances. One could doubt the accuracy of the colonial reports if one did not know how far, how quickly, and how willingly the rural Maya travel by foot today, despite an increasing reliance on buses and bicycles. Aside from changes of residence, documents allude to frequent movement back and forth between coast and interior, wax-hunting expeditions that took the Maya far from home for extended periods, and an undetermined but substantial amount of visiting between pueblos.

An informal and largely covert network of information existed among the community leaders. They invited each other to fiesta banquets, and when any crisis arose, such as some objectionable scheme emanating from the colonial authorities in Merida, they exchanged messengers and letters (courtesy of the local *escribanos*, or town clerks, since the vast majority of the other officials could not read or write themselves).[36] They were also able to exchange news in Merida, where all the municipal officers had to come in person at each New Year to present their accounts and the results of their annual elections to the governor for his approval. Tribute payments, due twice a year, were usually delivered to the *encomenderos* (or to the Treasury for Crown *encomiendas*) by a delegation of pueblo officials, who also appeared in person in the Tribunal de Indios or the diocesan chancery whenever they wished to file a grievance or present any kind of petition. These community leaders tended to gather in certain of the taverns or shops in the Indian barrios of Merida outside the city walls. We have no record of what they discussed there, except for the allegation that the Jacinto Canek rebellion of 1761 was hatched in one of these meeting places, where Canek worked.[37]

Community officials also traveled and presumably communicated over wide areas, seeking to track down tax truants who had moved to other towns. Fears of a widespread conspiracy behind the Canek rebellion led the authorities to seek to dissolve even this informal network, which they believed was used to "coordinate treasonous plans." Shortly after the revolt was suppressed, a decree was issued prohibiting Indian officials from collecting taxes outside their own communities, and special agents called *cobradores de indios dispersos* (collectors for dispersed Indians) were commissioned by the Treasury to take over the task.[38]

Ironically, the Spanish themselves, by drafting the Maya into their state militias after independence, helped to translate the very loose and covert network of the colonial Maya into the coordinated resistance that they had so feared. And warfare and religious cult again served as unifying forces for the Maya on a large scale. They produced in the independent *cruzob* "state" engendered by the Caste War a replica of the

157

centralized late Postclassic province, complete with war captains, a supreme ruler similar to a *halach uinic*, a provincial capital centering around a major shrine, and a cult that not only gave supernatural support to their struggle but also defined the boundaries of the polity.[39] The Spanish had managed to destroy the Maya's supracommunity political structures but, it would seem, not the model for it that they had in their minds.

CONGREGATION AND THE *Parcialidades*

The Spanish pursued two different policies that tended toward the same end of simplifying indigenous territorial and political organization. One of them was fragmentation, in which communities at the top of the ranked hierarchy were reduced to equality with their subordinates, in effect dissolving the larger structures. The other was consolidation, in which the hamlet, village, and town levels were all fused together.

Settlement patterns in Yucatan seem to have fluctuated greatly over time along with the degree of sociopolitical integration they reflect. The pattern discernible at the time of conquest befits the interregnum conditions after the fall of Mayapan: decentralized but not totally atomized. There were some regional variations, but most of the peninsula for which we have documentary evidence fell somewhere in the middle between the extreme disintegration represented by the small, scattered, and autonomous settlements of the modern Chontalpa region in Tabasco (mentioned in the previous chapter), and the large, complex, and densely populated cities such as late Classic Tikal and Postclassic Mayapan.

The collection of settlements reported by the Spaniards included many towns with from 500 to 1,000 households (or populations of ca. 2,250 to 4,500, using the conservative conversion factor of 4.5), a much larger number of villages of undetermined size, and a few cities of from 3,000 to 5,000 households (13,500 to 22,500 people), if Spanish estimates are not grossly exaggerated.[40] These cities—for example Chauaca and Campeche—were all in the "Putun" commercial periphery. The Yucatec Maya provincial capitals of the interior were larger than their secondary centers but not by such a wide margin. Small hamlets were very common. Unlike the Chontalpa pattern, however, they do not seem to have existed in isolation but as outlying appendages to villages and towns.

What the Spanish did was to compress this hierarchy from the bottom, as they also did from the top, in the same interest of more effective control of the conquered population. The compression from below was effected through a program of forced resettlement called "congregation," which involved a fusing of settlements at three levels. At one

7. Colonial church and *ayuntamiento*, Chemax, district of Valladolid. (Photo by Arthur G. Miller)

level, scattered satellite hamlets were gathered into their parent towns. At another, two or more towns (as many as eight have been recorded), along with their attendant hamlets, were consolidated into one large unit.[41] And, finally, the internal layouts of all the towns were rearranged from what the Spanish regarded as an amorphous sprawl into the familiar colonial grid pattern. House sites were more uniformly and densely packed around a Christian church with its friary, facing a central square and a town hall (called the *audiencia* or *casa real* or sometimes *ayuntamiento*) either opposite or at right angles. This orderly urban plan, which the Spanish also imposed on their own towns, has remained intact in most of the Maya pueblos in Yucatan to this day.

Urbanism was a characteristic feature of Spanish imperial enterprise, and congregation programs were a major instrument of the colonizing process. Early, fairly haphazard attempts by missionaries to bring together dispersed Indian populations for easier parish administration were followed in some of the highland regions of Mexico and South America by more systematic resettlement schemes, which were conceived by the civil authorities in response to severe population losses among the Indians and to a concurrent increase in Spanish land hunger. By concen-

159

trating the remnant populations of several towns into a single community, their former lands could be freed for distribution to the Spaniards.[42] The congregation program in Yucatan shared features of both types. It came almost as a coda to the military conquest, at a time when population losses had scarcely began to register on the Spanish consciousness. It was as thorough and systematic as later civil congregations elsewhere, but was carried out by the Franciscan missionaries as an accompaniment to evangelization, operating independently of and sometimes in opposition to what the Spanish laity saw as their own material interests.

The Franciscans in Yucatan, like their fellow missionaries in the rest of New Spain, insisted that congregation was a prerequisite for the dual ecclesiastical functions of teaching Christian doctrine and administering the sacraments, and that neither could be performed properly if the Indians were physically out of reach. Moreover, they and their successors invested settlement patterns with a moral and symbolic significance that had at least as much to do with their own need to establish boundaries as it did with the need to supervise Indian behavior. This can be seen in their centuries-long struggle to keep the Maya rounded up in compact towns instead of living in hamlets scattered around the bush, as many of them preferred to do. Settlement formed part of a dyadic code, in which the world was divided into two opposing parts, town and forest. The town represented Christianity, civilization, and indeed all that was human life, in contrast with the forest, where wild beasts lurked and where man risked being overwhelmed morally as well as physically by the untamed forces of nature.[43]

The Spaniards arrived in the New World already possessing a strong urban bias. The Roman emphasis on city life had been strengthened by centuries of reconquest warfare with the Moors, during which fortified towns rather than isolated castles and monasteries provided the main refuge. Even as territory was regained, much of the countryside was left to the conquered Moriscos to cultivate. To own great landed estates was a coveted ideal in the Iberian world; to live on them was another matter altogether. Rural life was brutish, to be left to shepherds and other rustics. The countryside was never idealized in Spanish art or literature, except for the brief Renaissance flirtation with Italianate pastoral poems and novels, which Cervantes parodied in *Don Quixote*.

Such an urban bias could only be reinforced in the New World, where man's dominion over nature seemed considerably more precarious. The tropical lowlands must have been seen as particularly alien and hostile. Some sixteenth-century panegyrists, seeking to present Yucatan and other tropical areas favorably to European eyes, stressed the lushness and variety of local plant life. But there was also a menacing quality to this

160

rampant growth that presses around towns and quickly takes over abandoned fields and houses.[44] Remote archaeological sites not yet manicured for the tourist trade give newcomers to the region the same uneasy sense of nature's energetic reclamation of man's works.

The physical contrast between town and countryside became sharper in America than in the Spanish homeland, and partly by man's design. The "characteristically Spanish" grid pattern of urban layout that is ubiquitous in Spanish American towns dating from the colonial period was not, in fact, common to Spain at all. As George Foster has pointed out, the towns in Spain are "relatively formless."[45] The pattern has usually been seen as a reflection of a new Renaissance ideal of order and symmetry, and in political terms represents the efforts of the Catholic kings and Charles V to impose royal discipline on the turmoil and independence of the medieval Spanish towns. Royal legislation decreed this physical layout in the colonies,[46] but this legislation postdated many of the urban designs, and royal laws were rarely so faithfully honored unless they also suited the colonists. Moreover, the grid pattern was also very common in Anglo-America. It is possible that it responded to a common need for order as well as to a new European aesthetic. To create an urban setting even more controlled than in the homeland was one defense against an unfamiliar and therefore threatening physical environment, and against equivocal feelings about the alien peoples who inhabited it.[47]

Nature continued to be represented as a malignant force in nineteenth-century Latin American literature. And the same opposing imagery of towns versus countryside found in the reports of the colonial friars in Yucatan was elaborated in a lengthy sociopolitical manifesto by the Argentine statesman, Domingo Sarmiento, in which he attributes all that was evil in his country's history to the wilderness of the pampa and its effect on man.[48]

Not all American-born Spaniards, nor even all newly arrived peninsulars, viewed the bush with the same horror and repugnance as the Franciscans. But then theirs was not the responsibility for stamping out paganism. Armed with the general cultural bias in favor of town life, reinforced by the not wholly fanciful conviction that once the Indians were outside the town limits they could and would do as they chose, the friars maintained consistently throughout their ministry in Yucatan that Christianity could prevail only if the Indians were all gathered together under the watchful eye of their pastors.

The Franciscans must have conceived of their program almost immediately after their arrival in late 1544 or early 1545, for a royal decree granting approval was already issued in 1548.[49] But it was only with the on-the-spot support of the royal *visitador*, Tomás López, in 1552 that the plan gained full momentum. The forced resettlement was carried out with an efficiency and ruthlessness that demonstrate the ascendancy the missionaries had already gained among the Indians. When resistance was strong, dwellings, gardens, and orchards were destroyed to discourage the uprooted Maya from returning to their former homes.[50]

Ascendancy over their fellow Spaniards was far less secure, and royal support was needed primarily to overcome opposition from the *encomenderos*. The latter welcomed the first phase of the program, in which the friars somehow managed to round up the large number of Indians who had remained hidden in the bush, and which was as necessary for military security—to say nothing of tribute collection—as it was for preaching the gospel. Their objection was to the resettlement of entire towns and their consolidation into larger centers. The fact that relocated towns retained title to their former lands in Yucatan indicates that the Spanish did not need any artificially created vacant tracts for themselves. This part of the program, in the opinion of the *encomenderos*, cost many lives through disruption in food production and the general hardships of mass relocation, and thus served neither the interest of the Indians nor their own, but only that of the friars.[51] But the argument that congregation in all its phases was necessary for evangelization was unassailable to a monarch whose whole empire rested legally and morally on the salvation of Indian souls, and the friars prevailed, with the firm support of the royal *visitador*.

By 1582, the date of the first full list of postcongregation towns, 26 parishes in the peninsula (excluding Bacalar) served a total of 177 communities, many of them compounds of from 2 to 8 formerly separate towns.[52] There is no comparably precise information for settlement patterns immediately prior to congregation. The 1549 tax list contains only 181 towns.[53] But several were often combined under one *encomienda*, and one would need to add to this list the towns that other documents refer to as having existed separately before the resettlement was carried out. A by-no-means-exhaustive tally of these would bring the 1549 total closer to 400,[54] and this figure probably omits many of the villages that were included under the heading of the dominant town in the cluster. These omissions do not necessarily invalidate the figures of total population based on the 1549 tax list (see table 2.1). They simply preclude any attempt to plot population distributions within each of the territories listed.

The congregation program does not seem to have violated preexisting political boundaries, or the established relationships within them, any more than did the general organization of the parishes. The friars had simply drawn all outlying units into each existing nucleus: hamlets into villages, villages into towns, and subordinate towns into their local centers. They only stopped short of packing *visitas* and *cabecera* into one huge population center in each parish. Nevertheless this process of fusion was as destructive to the preconquest geopolitical hierarchy as was the dissolution of provincial and subprovincial links. For it essentially eliminated the lower levels of hamlet, village, and subordinate town.

Along with this process of fusion or incorporation, the internal structure of the nucleated towns themselves was simplified by the elimination of their political subdivisions. These pre-Hispanic subdivisions, called *cuchteel* or *tzucul* (sometimes *tzucub*), were a kind of precinct or ward, almost a town within a town, headed by an official called *ahcuchcab*, who combined both advisory and executive functions. He represented his district on the town council under the local *batab* and was directly responsible for governing the district and carrying out the *batab*'s orders there.[55] Like the community itself, the wards were primarily, if not exclusively, territorial units. Although they have been compared to Mexican *calpullis* and thought to represent a collection of exogamous patrilineages,[56] any kinship identification or landholding function they may have had was either lost or a well-kept colonial secret.[57] They were, however, more than neighborhoods; they constituted the bottom level of the political system, since the detached hamlets seem to have been only residential designations without any formal status or administrative structure.

Until about the middle of the seventeenth century these wards, or *parcialidades*, as the Spanish called them, continued to be referred to as the standard unit for communal labor service and tribute collection, for calling roll at Sunday mass, and for marching children off to their daily catechism classes.[58] Then they vanished from documentary view. Not only did the Spanish cease to mention them, but the Maya also ceased to identify themselves as members of a particular *parcialidad* or to speak of the patron saints belonging to the *parcialidades*, which formerly had celebrated their own separate fiestas.[59] The *ahcuchcabs* also disappeared, or rather they merged into the colonial *regidores*, or town councillors. The *regidores* performed many of the same functions as the *ahcuchcabs* and may have been their equivalent in most ways, but there is no evidence that they represented or were responsible for particular precincts.[60]

The Spanish documents continued to refer to *parcialidades* but of a markedly different type, and the identity of terms can easily create confusion over the fate of the pre-Columbian ward. The surviving *parcialidad* was originally a separate town that had been moved to a new site during congregation. Some of the relocated towns were almost immediately merged into a single entity. Others, and especially the ones of

163

more or less equal status, kept their own identities, continuing to function as independently as if they had been divided by kilometers of open bush, each with its own patron saint and fiesta, its own *batab* and town council, and its separate tribute quota. They remained residentially separate also, within the boundaries of the same nucleated town, sharing only the same church and possibly, although this is not certain, the same town hall. They even kept title to their former lands, a rule that accounts for the strange shape of many community and parish boundaries.[61] Several towns, such as Nunkini and Halacho, which had been annexed to Calkini, were later allowed to move back to their original sites.[62]

Most of the annexed towns, however, stayed put as part of compound, or rather complex, communities, becoming colonial *parcialidades* and eventually sharing the fate of the pre-Columbian originals. The first step was the loss of autonomy, the formal demotion from the status of administratively independent town to that of *parcialidad*. The four towns joined together at Tizimin, for example, were merged into one *república de indios* by decree of a royal *visitador* in 1583.[63] The process of consolidation was highly uneven, and we rarely have any clue about why autonomy was lost or even exactly when, only that a particular town "disappears" between one document and another of a later date.[64]

The next stage was the erosion of separate identity even as a *parcialidad*, in the same way that the pre-Columbian units disappeared from view. This too proceeded unevenly, for a number of them were still officially recognized at the end of the colonial period. There were also a few annexed towns that even managed to retain their own town councils and *batabs* until the end of the colonial period, insulated from complete absorption by their status as separate *encomiendas* (for example, Dzibikak and Dzibikal at Uman, and Tzeme, which had itself absorbed Kisil, at Hunucma).[65] It is doubtful that they would have long survived the phasing out of the *encomiendas* in 1785,[66] even if the whole apparatus of Indian government had not been dismantled after independence.

As towns within a town, the colonial *parcialidades* were fossil relics of the hierarchical preconquest political organization that the Spanish compressed into the single, homogeneous unit of the *república de indios*. They did not need to abolish the top and bottom tiers of the structure. They simply failed to acknowledge their existence and, by denying them any role in the colonial political system, let them wither away.

A SIMPLIFIED SOCIAL ORDER

So far I have referred only to the effects of Spanish rule on the geopolitical organization of the Maya. The compression and simplification of the hierarchy of territorial units was accompanied by a similar process affecting the social order at the highest and lowest ranks.

The great territorial magnates were not only reduced to community *batabs*. They and the rest of the aristocracy were deprived of the spoils of war and the profits of long-distance trade, and the slaves they had owned were set free to join the ranks of ordinary *macehuales*.[67] The Spanish also siphoned off the major share of the surplus wealth that *macehual* labor produced in the form of tribute goods and labor drafts, which had formerly gone entirely for the support of the native elites. I shall demonstrate later that the leveling process failed to close the gap between nobles and commoners entirely. It was, however, significantly reduced, and the intermediate groups of professional warriors and artisans disappeared altogether. The Maya were homogenized into a collection of farmers, whose differences in wealth, status, and authority were not reflected in any sharp division of labor. Even the *batab* himself, like the other community leaders, had become a milpa farmer writ large who merely commanded more resources, especially human ones, than his *macehual* subjects. Indications of craft specialization are very scarce outside of the main Spanish centers. Pedro Sánchez de Aguilar, born and raised in Yucatan, wrote in the early seventeenth century that "every pueblo has Indian blacksmiths, locksmiths, shoemakers, carpenters, saddlers, tailors, painters, woodcarvers [*entalladores*], stonecutters [*canteros*], and stonemasons [*albañiles*]."[68] An impressive list, but a little difficult to credit even at that relatively early date, and the author must have meant only that certain Indians had particular skills in these crafts. Where, except in the largest towns, would a saddler or tailor or blacksmith have found more than an occasional customer to support his trade? Indians did not go to tailors to have their clothing made, few of them possessed horses or mules then, and only some of the major *cabeceras* had any Spanish residents, who might be potential clients.

A 1766 report on the economic state of the colony provided another weighty list of Maya talents in artisanry, ranging from carving tortoise shell ornaments to fine embroidery. The reporters also rather wistfully acknowledged that these talents were more potential than actual. The Maya, they argued, could supply all kinds of fine manufactures if only a Spanish market existed for them. The export trade, they conceded, was confined to raw or slightly processed materials and the local Spanish population preferred to import most of their manufactured goods from Old Spain and New Spain.[69]

As a matter of fact, some demand for skilled local craftsmanship did exist—a demand created mainly, as in pre-Columbian times, by religious ceremonial. At any rate, it is the buildings and objects associated with divine worship that have survived best from both periods, and church records provide our most detailed sources on colonial crafts.[70] Spaniards took over the prestigious work in precious metals. The production of saints' images, retables, and other fancy woodcarving seems to have been mainly a Spanish preserve also (although not to the total exclusion of the Maya), while the *castas* dominated the other trades from tailoring to ironwork. The only skilled crafts that remained an Indian monopoly throughout the colonial period, and to this day, were stonecutting and stonemasonry.

The Franciscan missionaries had only to look around them for ample evidence of the high level of local skill in stonemasonry, and they set the Maya to work almost immediately on the churches and friaries that blend Spanish design with native techniques. Private construction was confined mainly to the Spanish centers. But church building, with the frequent enlargements, additions and repairs, offered steady employment throughout the colonial period to itinerant teams of master masons and assistants who moved from pueblo to pueblo as the work demanded. Whether the colonial masons came mainly from Oxkutzcab, as they do today, is not known. They were highly paid by colonial standards,[71] and the peninsula is dotted with monuments to their engineering skills and to the sober artistry of the *canteros* who carved the façades, the cornices, the fonts, and other interior stonework. It was the Maya masons who translated the basic Spanish designs into the handsome and soundly built colonial churches that still grace the town plazas of all but recently founded Yucatecan towns; the unskilled work of hauling stone and mortar and much of the actual construction was carried out by the local draft labor under the master mason's direction.[72]

Other traditional crafts were preserved, but rarely if at all as full-time occupations. For some period a surreptitious production of clay and wooden "idols" continued. The Spanish complained that the Maya manufactured new ones as fast as the old ones were destroyed.[73] They give no details about their workmanship but, judging from the quantities discovered, it is likely that they were fairly crude objects that any local potter or woodcarver could produce.

The tendency toward household autarky, already evident in pre-Columbian times, became more pronounced. As I have stated, the colonial Maya were all basically farmers. They continued to produce for themselves, perhaps for some local barter and for the Spanish-controlled regional and export trades, the same simple goods that the ordinary *macehuales* had always produced: mats and baskets, henequen cordage, crude deerhide sandals, pottery (although it is rarely mentioned, and gourds and baskets seem to have been more commonly used for everything but cooking), and, above all, the plain cotton cloth that every Maya woman

could weave on her backstrap loom.[74] They apparently ceased to manufacture any of the fancy cloth of intricate design that is mentioned as
a chief trade good before the conquest and which was probably the
work of highly skilled specialists. The local cotton fiber was considered
of excellent quality, and one plan devised by several colonial officials in
the late eighteenth century (a period rife with abortive schemes for economic development) was to import foot looms and instructors for a
school where Maya girls could learn fine weaving to replace or supplement the coarse cotton cloth in the export trade.[75] The scheme came to
nothing, and weaving continued to be a domestic—indeed, the main
domestic—industry among the Maya.

The economy of the *macehual* was thus as simple as that of his preconquest ancestors. As in many peasant societies, the men fed the family
by their agricultural labor, and the women paid most of the taxes by
spinning and weaving.[76] Some hunting persisted, with Spanish firearms
gradually replacing bows and arrows among the members of society
who could afford them.[77] Vegetables and fruit trees—native and Spanish—were cultivated, and turkeys and chickens were raised for tribute
and eggs (the birds themselves were consumed by the Maya only on
very special occasions). The rest of what the *macehuales* produced was
almost entirely for the Spanish through one or another regime of forced
labor, none of which involved any specialized skills.

The economic base of the colonial Maya elite, which will be discussed
in the next chapter, was slightly more varied, but the major differences
were in scale and in the ability to commandeer the labor of others.
Except for this division between nobles and commoners, it is difficult
to find any signs of socioeconomic differentiation within the Maya
community. There were no shopkeepers, no soldiers, no millers or bak-
ers, no full-time craftsmen of any kind except the small "guild" of masons, and no full-time professionals except the town *escribano*, the choirmaster of the church, and possibly some of the church musicians in the
larger towns. Every other occupation engaged in by the Maya, including service in public office, was a part-time supplement to farming.

Social identities seem to have been defined solely by rank and by
simple rules of descent, with none of the hodgepodge of occupational
affiliations, exchange networks, ethnic identities, and voluntary associations that exist in more complex societies. Caste defined the Maya's
place within the larger social order but provided no basis for group
identity and group cohesion within the racially and culturally uniform
Maya subsystem. We are left with the extended family and the community as the basic social units. Even the religious confraternities, which
in Spanish and Spanish colonial society served to define a variety of

167

intermediate groupings, became among the Maya community-wide organizations with the same membership and structure as the *repúblicas de
indios*.[78]

The *república de indios*, or community, was to be the almost exclusive
focus of colonial Maya social interaction beyond the extended family,
although not necessarily by choice. If the Maya and other colonial Indians encapsulated themselves in these communities, it was largely because the Spanish confined them there, organizing all taxes and labor
service, communal landholding, public worship, and indigenous political authority according to that sole unit.

At first sight the Spanish seem to have made the search for the organizing principles of Maya society easier by eliminating much of the
complexity contained in the pre-Columbian social order. Colonial Maya
society is not only better documented but also more homogeneous and
therefore presumably easier to analyze. We have only to consider these
more or less identical, wholly autonomous communities, composed of
more or less identical (excepting only their division into nobles and
macehuales) patrilineal extended families, with no significant grouping in
between.

This same lack of socioeconomic diversity that appears to simplify
analysis of the community's structure contains a major drawback: it also
makes it difficult to account for the community's existence. The observer's relief at the absence of crosscutting and overlapping social relationships that so muddle the modern urban scene and can even be
found in some peasant societies (the tangled skein of affiliations in Balinese village organization as described by Clifford Geertz comes to mind)[79]
changes to unease with the realization that, as depicted, this neat Maya
scene contains nothing that links the figures in it. The actors stand alone
or move around without reference to each other. The social network is
not so much simplified as eliminated; the community is reduced to a
collection of functionally isolated families who happen to share the same
physical space.

In the previous chapter I mentioned other forms of interdependence
that could have sustained the Maya social order in the pre-Columbian
period in the absence of economic specialization. Let us now turn to
look at how well these social bonds held up under the greatly changed
circumstances of Spanish rule.

· 6 ·

SNAGS AND TEARS IN THE
SOCIAL FABRIC

Whether Maya society could survive within the microcosm of the community—and a simplified microcosm at that—would depend on how well the integrating forces within these individual units could withstand the changed conditions of colonial rule. My thesis is that the Spanish unwittingly undermined the relationships of interdependence within Maya society and distorted the reciprocal arrangements on which social cohesion rested. They did this at two levels of organization: the extended family and the community, which replicated the structure and organizing principles of the family, even though its membership was based on shared territory rather than kinship ties.

THE CORPORATE FAMILY

The Spanish colonial authorities were either ignorant of or chose to ignore the corporate structure of the extended family. In the interests of Christian morality and administrative efficiency, they imposed new rules of behavior on the Maya that upset the balance of rights and obligations within the family, destroying some of its advantages and thus threatening the material security of its members.

The extended family, as discussed in chapter 4, was a three-generational patrilineal descent group that functioned as a single residential and economic unit. Its members shared the same household or household compound. They held joint rights to land and worked the land cooperatively or sometimes in common. And if they did not pool all resources collectively, they depended upon each other heavily for mutual assistance. It is likely that they also shared obligations to the community as a corporate unit.

The Spanish divided the extended family, both physically and fiscally, into conjugal units. The residential division, perhaps the colonial innovation most destructive to the corporate system, was imposed by the Catholic clergy. They insisted that each married couple establish a completely separate household, primarily to discourage what they believed was a strong tendency among the Maya toward incest.[1] This tendency was especially pronounced, so they alleged, between fathers-in-law and daughters-in-law but also existed between fathers and daughters. And

169

for that reason the clergy also sought to encourage early marriage and discourage the practice of "bride-price" service that entailed temporary residence with the wife's family.

The subunits of the patrilineal kin group were presumably permitted to live in contiguous houseplots. But this arrangement, while facilitating a degree of cooperation, lacked the same advantages of a multifamily residence with communal gardens, household equipment, and larder and domestic chores, including child care. The Maya clearly preferred this latter arrangement and reverted to it whenever they had the chance—that is, whenever priestly supervision was distant or lax.[2] They did so, I suggest, because of its mutual economic benefits—with opportunities for incest, whatever its incidence, a decidedly secondary consideration, if not an accidental byproduct or a figment of clerical imagination altogether.

The way that public obligations were levied was equally divisive. The head of the household, and the unit for the tax rolls, was in the early colonial period the *indio casado*, or married man. Tribute and *obvenciones* eventually came to be imposed on all adult *macehuales* regardless of marital status, and also regardless of the physical capacity of the spouse. And in this the Spanish even ignored the much more obvious symbiosis within the nuclear family due to the strict sexual division of labor. They may have seen the tax assessments according to nuclear families or individuals as likely to yield higher returns, or perhaps this system was merely the simplest and most effective way to keep track of the tributary population. Whatever the purpose, it could not fail to weaken the corporate structure of the extended family.

Spanish rules of inheritance conflicted with the reciprocal basis of this corporate structure. The Maya rule of inheritance strictly through the male line was based on the principle that only sons and their wives were responsible for parental support and the production of family assets in general.[3] Daughters formed part of the support system of their husbands' groups, to which they contributed and from which they could expect returns. The Spanish rules made inheritance bilateral and thus distorted the system. According to Spanish law all legitimate children inherited equally.[4] The *mayorazgo*, or entailed estate based on male primogeniture, was an exception to this rule, but an exception that required royal permission, and wealthy Spaniards could more easily avoid dividing estates by filling the religious orders with excess sons and, especially, daughters.[5] The Maya had no such recourse against a law incompatible with their corporate, patrilineal principles.

In colonial Yucatan the church assumed the responsibility of handling all probate questions among the Maya. When attending the dying, the parish clergy were to see that proper testaments were drawn up, including provision for burial expenses and the various pious contributions that every inhabitant of the colonies was obliged to make in his will— including such matters of serious concern to the Maya as the redemption of Jerusalem from the Infidel. They were then to supervise the distribution of property, taking special care to ensure that it was divided equally among all surviving children.[6] The clergy were occasionally accused of irregularities in their duties as witnesses and executors—of forcing Indians to make large bequests for elaborate funerals they could not afford and even of seizing property for themselves, especially if someone died intestate.[7] Whether the allegations of extortion and swindling were true or false, the parish priest was seen to have the right and duty to impose Spanish rules of inheritance on the Maya.

Such interference could affect even the *macehuales*, among whom the disposition of a few shirts and a half dozen beehives could be of as much concern as the allocation of a substantial patrimony of land, orchards, and livestock among the elite. Only a small proportion of Maya testaments has survived, and it is likely that most property passed on without benefit of any written bequests. Nevertheless, the extant record indicates that the principle of exclusively patrilineal inheritance was gradually, though perceptibly, diluted in practice. Late colonial wills still reveal a strong tendency toward inheritance through the male line, especially of land. But a far from negligible amount of property was passing to female kin and to males through the female line even when there were surviving patrilineal heirs.[8]

Neither the extended family nor the patrilineal principle on which it was based was destroyed by Spanish meddling with multiple-family residence and traditional inheritance rules. The role of this family can be seen, for example, in the Maya-Spanish conflict over the definition of orphans, a conflict with more than semantic implications. The Spanish, perhaps inspired by the pre-Columbian rule that orphans belonged to the territorial lord, conducted their own lively trade in orphans, who were sent to the cities (often "sold" by the local priest or the governor, according to some allegations) to be cared for by some Spanish family. This "care" in fact amounted to a form of servitude.[9] Thus the Spanish had every incentive to define the term as broadly as possible, and to them an orphan was anyone who had lost both mother and father. The Maya complained that children were being shipped off who were not orphans at all by their standards, but had kinfolk whose responsibility it was to substitute for the biological parents.[10] Indeed, their kinship terminology does not distinguish clearly between these biological parents and members of the wider network.[11]

171

The extended family also retained the principle of filial responsibility that extended to all senior kin and accounts for the concern over orphans, especially nephews and grandsons. They would be valued for their potential contributions to old-age security. However, the original balance of duties and compensations was upset by Spanish tinkering. The obligation of parental (again, in the wider sense of senior kin) support still fell largely or wholly on the male descendants, direct and collateral. Yet, while they were supposed to cooperate in seeking to maintain or enhance the family's security, and especially that of family elders, they could not expect the same return on their investment—the exclusive right to inherit—nor the economic advantages of shared residence.

Among *macehuales* this could work to the distinct disadvantage of the middle generation. The burden could be especially heavy on the young married couple, as can be seen by tracing the *macehaul* life cycle under the altered conditions imposed by the Spanish. Marriage brought no increase in a *macehual*'s tribute liability. The determining factor was age: women were subject to tribute, *obvenciones*, and other head taxes between the ages of twelve and fifty-five, and men between fourteen and sixty.[12] However, the more onerous burdens of the various labor drafts and *repartimientos* seem to have begun only upon marriage.[13]

In practice then, the heaviest civic responsibilities as fully contributing members coincided with the heaviest family responsibilities—during that period when a young couple owed some undetermined portion of parental support and was obliged to provide full support for their own children not yet old enough to make any significant contribution to the household economy. The load was particularly heavy on women at this time, when pregnancies were frequent but brought no relief from the fixed quotas of cotton cloth they were required to produce on their back-strap looms.

If a couple could survive this stage in the family cycle, their existence usually became more secure. Once one or two sons were old enough to help tend the milpa, a man could count on a life of relative ease in *macehual* terms. His wife, even if not past childbearing, could expect help from older daughters with the spinning and weaving.[14] And any grandparents still alive, if they became too feeble to support themselves at all, also became exempt from their own tax and labor contributions.

In most societies the responsibility for supporting the young and the old falls on the intermediate group, which after all is the strongest physically. The problem with the colonial Maya system is that it combined incompatible features from two different traditions—the indigenous and the Spanish—and therefore distorted this ordinarily logical arrangement. The middle generation acquired total responsibility for its chil-

172

dren while retaining some responsibility toward its elders, who in view of the early age of marriage would usually have been vigorous enough to contribute a full share to the domestic economy in return, had the household not been divided. Once the Maya survived childhood, and barring famine and epidemic disease, they often lived, hale and productive, well into their fifties and sixties.[15] I do not suggest that grandparents and older kin provided no help with child care and other chores and that no mutually beneficial sharing occurred, only that it would have been more difficult—less automatic—than in a single household or compound. The arrangements, in short, had become lopsided.

In addition, it appears that the generations were telescoped during the colonial period, so that the chronological overlap—the simultaneous support by young adults of the very young and the not-so-old—that was the source of the strain in the hybrid colonial system, was increased. A significant drop in the age of marriage occurred from around twenty in preconquest times to around fourteen for men and twelve for women: that is, as soon as they ceased compulsory attendance at *doctrina* or catechism classes and became liable for tribute.[16] The cause of the drop seems, again, to be Spanish pressure. The motives were mixed. Many priests declared that early marriages proved a safeguard against sexual immorality. They urged early marriage and some even resorted to locking up any laggards in the parish friary until they, or their parents, found a suitable mate.[17] As for the financial incentives, there was the direct one of hastening eligibility for the labor drafts and *repartimientos*, and an indirect incentive in the population growth that early marriage was supposed to encourage. The colony's prosperity, and in particular many incomes, were directly related to the tributary head count and the supply of goods and services that it represented.

By insisting on earlier marriages, the Spanish may have helped to increase the rate of fertility among the Maya. They also simultaneously increased the burden on the young family through the imposed household division, and in so doing they may have quite unwittingly lowered the rate of infant survival and inhibited the population recovery they sought.[18]

The persistence of a system that has all the appearances of being dysfunctional would be no rarity in human history. The emotional and moral pressures supporting the sense of filial obligation, with all the supernatural sanctions of the ancestor cult, must have been strong, even when new Spanish regulations undermined the reciprocal basis of the traditional arrangements. Nevertheless, the pattern of out-migration from the colonial communities, which will be discussed in the following chapter, suggests that some extended families may have disintegrated

173

under the new strains. In contrast to the pattern that has become familiar in most peasant societies, the Maya emigrants were not primarily young bachelors and spinsters, forced to seek economic opportunity elsewhere, but the young married couples with one or more small children, precisely those who bore the heaviest burdens in colonial Maya society.[19]

Similar processes with similar effects can be seen on a larger scale within the larger universe of the colonial community, where the element of reciprocity linked rulers to subjects instead of elders to juniors.

ELITES AND *Macehuales*

According to the model outlined earlier for precolonial Maya society, the link between the elite and the *macehuales* was in the services they provided each other in a type of formalized, large-scale patron-client relationship: obedience and material support in return for protection and general supervision of the common good. The legitimacy of the elite's political authority and their wealth derived from what they contributed (or, what amounted to the same, what they were able to convince their subjects that they contributed) to the welfare and security of the corporate group. Any challenge to the specialized roles of the elite would therefore tend to weaken the vertical ties within society and the entire basis of social cohesion.

The elite's loss of control over the trade network, both regional and long-distance, would have been of minor importance. The trade was primarily in sumptuary goods and provided the elite with the trappings but not the substance of power. However, colonial rule also undermined their traditional roles in the more crucial areas of warfare and religion.

The Spanish conquerors established in their American empire a three-hundred-year reign of peace that may have been as damaging to indigenous social and territorial integration as the military security provided by the British was to social cohesion in parts of their later, shorter-lived empire. (I refer to the example, mentioned in chapter 4, of the fortified towns in northern Pakistan that dissolved under British colonial rule when the need for mutual defense ceased.) The *pax hispanica* rendered a native warrior caste totally superfluous. Among the Yucatec Maya, territorial boundaries were guarded just as jealously after conquest as before. Towns and even whole regions were sometimes able to settle their boundary disputes amicably, but when peaceful discussions failed, the Spanish substituted their law courts for the battlefield, the ultimate arbitor in pre-Columbian times.[20] The kind of group vendettas by which an entire polity would take up arms to avenge an insult or injury to one of its members also ceased. Perhaps they continued in some informal, private fashion, but armed strife by entire communities could hardly have escaped the attention of the Spanish, who also prohibited a third important incentive for warfare, the capture of slaves. Raids and local skirmishes for any motive became obsolete, to say nothing of large-scale warfare to further more ambitious territorial designs. Conquest was henceforth to be a Spanish monopoly.

During the early postconquest period, native rulers were occasionally encouraged to organize small armed forces of their own subjects to help repel foreign invaders or to round up fugitives in the unpacified zones. The best known example is the oft-mentioned don Pablo Paxbolon, who devoted many years to "reducing" apostates and unconquered groups in the Montaña region of southern Campeche.[21] Don Juan Chan, *batab* of Chancenote, and his three sons were equally active in the eastern part of the peninsula during the early part of the seventeenth century. Don Fernando Camal of Oxkutzcab organized campaigns from the Sierra region into the central Montaña during the same period. There are also a number of accounts of the aid provided by units of Indian bowmen under their own leaders when corsairs threatened the ports and coasts.[22]

These operations responded primarily to Spanish rather than Maya interests, although one could consider the fugitive-hunting campaigns a type of slave raid, since the fugitives were ordinarily resettled in the territory of the *batab* who had "reduced" them and thus became his subjects, if not his slaves. The expeditions were also usually under the overall leadership of some Spaniard, and in any case declined altogether by the middle of the seventeenth century. The title of "captain" that the governor continued to grant to *batabs* up to the end of the colonial period seems to have become purely honorary, with no military duties attached.[23] It was too dangerous to encourage any military spirit among the Maya. The Spanish preferred to rely on the *castas* instead, and as soon as the number of mestizos and mulattoes was sufficient, they entirely replaced Indians as the rank and file of the colonial militia under Spanish officers.[24]

The introduction of Christianity was a direct attack on the other major elite function, that of intermediary between the community and the supernatural. Christianity's intolerance of any other cult made it the most serious challenge to the Maya lords. They could accept Spanish sovereignty and cooperate with the new rulers in temporal matters without necessarily performing an act of self-immolation, since the Spanish sought to control their political power and channel it to serve Spanish ends rather than eliminate it altogether. Christianity seemed to

175

allow no such accommodation. It was presented as a total system to replace the traditional one entirely, and along with it the indigenous religious experts.

The dilemma that Christianity created for the Maya elite and their responses to it will be discussed in chapters 10 and 11. The elite did not become totally obsolete as divine mediators. They were eventually able to create for themselves a central role in the blend of Maya religion and Christianity that emerged after the initial crisis. Still, the process of adaptation was slow and tortuous; the elite's capacity to interpret and intercede with the supernatural powers was severely strained, and the bonds of reciprocity between them and the masses were weakened accordingly.

In a ledger of elite-*macehual* transactions, the elite's balance of credit fell significantly after the conquest. If they were not exactly bankrupt, they were no longer able to perform all the same services. Yet they still retained many of the old prerogatives that the services had helped to justify. The conventional image of the colonial Indian throughout Spanish America as reduced to a common level of abject poverty and powerlessness has a certain validity within the broad context of colonial society. The Indians occupied the ground floor—or basement, if you will—of the whole colonial social edifice, with the arguable exception of African slaves (arguable, because while all Africans in theory suffered from the stigma of "dishonor" that the Spanish attached to slavery, in practice they often held the more skilled occupations and served Spaniards in positions of trust that placed them in authority over the Indians). Yet this ground floor or basement occupied by the Indians contained its own set of levels, which among the Maya of Yucatan preserved at the very least a distinction between the elite and the masses, or more precisely between nobles and commoners.

From a distant perspective, colonial Maya society may appear flattened out; in fact its shape changed from an elongated diamond to a rather squat pyramid, compressed from above and even more from below. At the top the territorial magnates were reduced to local satraps, only slightly elevated above the lesser nobility. Slaves and personal retainers were entirely eliminated at the bottom, along with a middling level of craft specialists whom the nobility had formerly been able to support. However, the compression of both the geopolitical and the internal social hierarchies left unaltered the basic structure of power and privilege within the individual communities.

Both the composition of the colonial Maya elite and the means by which they managed to preserve, albeit in diluted form, their hereditary privileges, will be discussed in later chapters. My interest here is in the fact of stratification, with the boundary between the mass of Maya commoners and a small, for the most part endogamous, group of families within each community, which perpetuated control over local power and wealth as a group, despite some internal reorderings. These were the *principales*, whom the Spanish sometimes referred to as *nobles* and who were also often explicitly identified in Maya documents as *almehens* (nobles). Their genealogical credentials are for the present of less concern than their privileged position within colonial Maya society.

THE ECONOMIC GULF

The colonial *principales* were able to monopolize whatever material surplus the Maya economy generated that was not siphoned off by the Spanish. Admittedly, that did not leave much by the standards of the colonial overlords. To the Spanish *encomendero*, royal bureaucrat, or merchant, the poverty of the Maya seemed uniform, and such gradations as existed were hardly worthy of note. According to one report, the *batabs* lived much the same as their poorest subjects, distinguished only by the addition of some lard to the usual monotonous diet of maize and beans, and it was rare that an Indian possessed property worth four pesos.[25] The Maya elite may have deliberately cultivated an image of poverty as a useful device in dealing with Spaniards. One Spaniard complained that the Maya leaders deliberately dressed in "patches and rags" when presenting their petitions to the authorities in order to inspire pity and win their cases.[26] Deflecting Spanish greed could have been an equally important motive. Or perhaps some Spaniards simply failed to notice what their own records reveal: that by no means were all the Maya uniformly destitute. Others, such as the parish priests who had more than superficial contact with the Maya, were aware of the differences in wealth, referring to the *indios pudientes* [rich and powerful Indians] in their parishes.[27]

Precisely how much wealth the Maya notables possessed is a well-kept secret, perhaps, as suggested, intentionally so. Unlike the Spaniards or some of the Indian nobility in central Mexico, they never mortgaged their estates to the church, posted bond, or engaged in any kind of transaction that would result in an official evaluation of their property. Nor did their property pass through probate courts. Only a small number of their testaments and bills of sale have been preserved, and they did not usually itemize their movable goods as fully as Spanish testators. In many ways we know more of the riches owned by their pre-Columbian ancestors, many of whose comforts and luxuries were depicted on mural paintings or buried with them in their graves. Nevertheless, the surviving wills and deeds, official inventories carried out during judicial proceedings, and a variety of other colonial documents give us some glimpses of the material benefits that the *principales* enjoyed. These can be most fully appreciated in contrast to the bare-bones existence of the ordinary Maya villager.

Little difference would be found in the style of housing. The *principales* lived in somewhat grander versions of the same pitched-roof, pole-and-thatch houses of the *macehuales*, which are still the standard dwelling of the rural Maya.[28] Either the pre-Columbian structures that archaeologists label "elite residences" served some other purpose, or else stone houses had gone out of fashion by the time of the conquest. The Maya nobles who experimented with Spanish-style masonry dwellings with flat roofs in the early postconquest period are reported to have found them uncomfortable and unhealthy,[29] unaware that Spanish microbes and not architecture were killing them off. In any case, their preference for the airier, less substantial house of Maya design seems to have been a matter of taste rather than economics.

While the design may have been similar, the size and above all the contents of the houses reveal the distinction. The *macehual* and his family crowded into a house of one vault formed by the upright roof posts, in which grain was often stored as well. On the other hand, they did not need much room for the rest of the family possessions. Without exception the Spanish observers stressed the poverty of the furnishings: some sleeping mats and crudely fashioned stools; baskets, gourds, and unglazed clay pots; and the usual tools for preparing the milpa and the maize. When the governor ordered that the property of the ringleaders of the 1610 Tekax uprising be seized, all that could be found worth confiscating in the thirteen households inventoried were the cotton *mantas* the women were weaving, in various stages of completion; a few pieces of extra clothing; and, in one house, some cobbler's tools. Any items too insignificant to list on the exhaustive inventories taken must have been insignificant indeed.[30]

The *macehual* house plot rarely had any accessory buildings. Gardens were small and a mature fruit tree was a prized possession. Many managed to acquire a pig or two, in addition to the usual chickens and turkeys; but cows, and especially horses and mules, were a rarity confined to the truly rich.[31] *Batabs* and *principales* possessed large house plots near the town plaza; a sturdy fence surrounded a spacious house of several vaults with fitted frames, doors, and windows. In addition there were smaller outbuildings and an orchard of avocados, zapotes, citrus and other fruit trees, a large kitchen garden, and sometimes a small stand of henequen plants. The houses themselves contained a range of articles, any one of which was beyond the reach of most *macehuales*: tables and chairs; *ropa blanca* (this can refer to both table linen and bed linen) and cushions or pillows; carved wooden chests with locks containing finely embroidered *huipiles*, petticoats, and shirts; occasionally a cloak of imported woolen fabric, a felt hat, and some items of gold jewelry; a firearm; saddles and harnesses; glazed pottery and metal spoons; a small oil painting or wooden statue of a Christian saint.[32] Heirlooms from another, older tradition are also recorded: idols, passed down through many generations, and "green stones," which I take to be the jade beads (or their equivalent) so treasured by the pre-Columbian Maya.[33]

These items, together with livestock and apiaries, a larger orchard outside of town, milpa land and especially a privately owned *cenote*, and a well-stocked larder with delicacies such as honey, lard, cacao, squash seeds, and spices to liven the diet of corn and beans made up the known wealth of the colonial Maya *principal*. How much he may have stashed away in pieces of eight and gold *escudos* is much more difficult to tell. During the same 1610 uprising, the *gobernador* of Tekax was found to have several leather sacks full of silver pesos in his house.[34] Part of it, perhaps most, was tribute he had collected, and unfortunately the document does not state how much. Nor do we know the amount of the cash endowments, nor the value of the land and cattle that the *principales* commonly donated from their family patrimonies to support the cult of the saints.[35] One *batab* provided his daughter with a dowry of 1,500 pesos in 1689, and another, a decade later, was reported to have left his heirs 2,000 pesos.[36] This would have constituted a more than adequate dowry for a Spanish woman of good family or endowed a perpetual chantry, although it did not exceed the annual income that the best curacies produced in that period.

The Maya openly acknowledged the economic division within their society. For example, in setting the scale of membership fees for parish brotherhoods, *caciques* and *principales* were to pay eight reales (one peso), ordinary *macehuales* four reales, and the poor, defined rather narrowly as "widowers and widows," only two reales.[37] Similar gradations are revealed in a subscription list, dated 1805, from the parish of Uman for the new leper hospital of San Lázaro in Campeche.[38] Compiled by the curate, who is likely to have known the economic strength of his parishioners very well, the list represents in capsule form a local socioeconomic structure that the bulk of colonial evidence would support for the entire colony throughout the period. At the very top came the curate himself with a subscription of six pesos, followed by his coadjutor with three. Since the richest lay Spaniards in the colony had their principal residence in Merida or Campeche, it is not surprising that, except for the local *juez español* (Spanish magistrate) who subscribed one peso, the rest of the *vecinos* of all castes were marked down for either one real (the majority) or a half real. Next came the Indians. But of the total number of adult Indian males,[39] only 13 percent are listed as subscribers—the elite in terms of wealth at least—and of these most pledged only a half real, on a par with the poorer *vecinos*. The fifty-eight who pledged from one to four reales represented *la crème de la crème* of Maya society: 1.2 percent of the total Indian population and 15.8 percent of the elite group.

A major privilege that set the Maya nobility apart from the *macehuales* was the private (ordinarily family rather than individual) ownership of land. (The *macehuales* held usufruct rights to community lands, but not to particular parcels, nor were these rights transferable except to direct descendants.)[40] The type of land the nobility owned is more significant than the amount. Considerably scarcer and therefore of much greater value than land itself were water sources. *Cenotes* and *aguadas* (shallow water holes) and some unspecified amounts of land surrounding them were what the nobility owned, passed on to their heirs, donated to the local saints, and sometimes sold to Spaniards.[41] The economic importance of these water sources lay in the opportunity they provided for producing specialized cash crops on a larger scale than in the village house plots. The most lucrative and common crop was cacao, supplemented by a variety of fruit trees, including Spanish imported citrus, all of which require some hand watering. The small groves that were planted around the privately owned *cenotes* and *aguadas* did not compare with the immense stands of cacao trees in Tabasco and on the Pacific coast. But local scarcity made the cacao and other fruit that much more valuable in Yucatan. The moist, fertile depressions that often surround *cenotes* were called *hoyas* in the Spanish documents. The value placed on these "holes in the ground" would be more than a little puzzling without the rare further explanation of their use for intensive horticulture.[42]

Cenotes or *aguadas* were also a basic prerequisite for raising livestock, whether on a small *sitio* (stock farm), an *estancia*, or a full-scale hacienda. The Maya nobility took to this activity in emulation of the Spanish, although generally on a much smaller scale.[43] They were barred by lack of capital or lack of connections (or both) from the export trade—the colony's main source of wealth. Ranching, therefore, would seem to be an attractive addition to their traditional activities of cacao cultivation, bee keeping, and the commercial production of maize and cotton. They owned or controlled more than sufficient grazing land and water for the cattle; ranching required only a small amount of start-up capital, and, unlike *vecinos*, the Maya were not required to obtain permits for estab-

8. Small *cenote* with fruit trees. (Photo by the author)

lishing a stock ranch. Nevertheless, except for the estates belonging to the local *cofradías*, the Maya *estancias* were almost invariably modest even by local standards. According to a late colonial census, their herds rarely exceeded fifty to one hundred head of cattle, compared to Spanish estates containing from several hundred to several thousand.[44]

Spanish control of the urban supply of meat through the official provisioning system of the municipalities (the *abasto de carnes*) could have proved a deterrent.[45] Or perhaps there was something of a cultural bias against ranching because of its inherent incompatibility with milpa farming. The Maya elite certainly showed themselves to be skilled enough at managing the *cofradía* estates, but these, after all, were for the benefit of the whole community. The unfenced cattle in Yucatan, whether owned by Maya or Spanish, were destructive to milpa crops. Their uncontrolled proliferation was therefore harmful to the community, and to raise large herds for individual gain would have been seen as an antisocial act. Still, though modest in comparison with the majority of Spanish *estancias*, the Indian-owned ranches—even the small *sitios* with a dozen or so head of cattle—were enough to set the owner apart from the mass of ordinary Maya. To the *macehuales* the ownership of one cow, at a price of five to six pesos, represented the equivalent of several years' tribute payments or the purchase price of nearly enough land to sustain a family through the entire cycle of milpa rotation.[46]

Horses, and especially mules, at an average price of fifteen pesos would have been even further beyond the reach of most Maya. Yet one observer estimated that the colony contained over eight thousand Indian muleteers in 1784.[47] A variety of sources agrees that local transport was largely in the hands of the Indians and that the *batabs* and other community officials were the contracting agents, when they did not own the mule trains outright.[48] In some cases they may have supplied the animals on a profit-sharing basis to individual mule drivers. It would have been a reasonably lucrative business even at the low regulated prices; the hire of a pack horse between Merida and Uman, for example, fetched four reales in 1722, compared to one real for an Indian porter for the same trip.[49]

One can easily believe the allegations that Spaniards and other *vecinos* sometimes forced the Indians to carry them and their goods without pay; but one can less easily see how they could have forced the Indians to raise and maintain animals for transport if there were not usually some profit in the enterprise. An additional incentive for the elite, and perhaps the main one, would have been the transport of their own agricultural surpluses directly to the urban and semiurban (very large towns like Tekax, Oxkutzcab, and Tixcacaltuyu) markets, where they could do better than the confiscatory prices offered by the private and official middlemen who scoured the rural areas.

The importance of privately owned land for the production of these surpluses, despite the obvious value of *cenotes*, should not be exaggerated. Even if they had owned no land at all, the nobility had privileged access to the communal lands within the jurisdiction of their towns and villages. The wording of some documents suggests that they regarded themselves in some sense as the actual owners. They do not say in their transactions and petitions that they are acting on behalf of the community, but rather, "We the *batab* and *principales*" donate or sell this parcel of land or claim another tract in dispute with a neighboring community or a Spaniard, land which has "always belonged to us and our ancestors." A fine point of rhetoric, perhaps, but, along with the pre-Columbian names of provinces and towns derived from the patronymics of the rulers,[50] it suggests a blurred line between custodianship and ownership. Whatever the political philosophy, in practice they controlled the common lands through public office. In allocating usufruct rights they could ensure a competitive advantage over the *macehuales*, even if there was no shortage of land, by garnering the best *hoyas* and other choice sites for themselves.

As in any region where land is relatively abundant, wealth will depend mainly on control over manpower, and the loss of that control by the native nobility is considered the main cause of their general economic decline throughout Mesoamerica and the Andes. Certainly the Spanish cornered the bulk of Indian labor, and the total supply declined drastically with the Indian population curve. But in Yucatan the slower and less severe decline, the lower ratio of Spanish to Indians, and the absence of mining and other labor-intensive enterprises all meant that a proportionately larger share of labor remained available to the native nobility than in many other regions. And because the Spanish interfered so little in local affairs, the nobility were able to claim in practice much more of their traditional rights over *macehual* labor than the Spanish rulers either authorized by law or generally seemed to realize.

The only remnant of these rights sanctioned by colonial law was the obligation of each community to furnish servants for the households of the *batabs* and *gobernadores* (when these titles were held separately) and to cultivate a specified amount of milpa for them according to the size of the town. The various legal codes that regulated Indian affairs in the colony admonished the *batabs* and *principales* against using unpaid *macehual* labor for domestic service, agriculture, or transport, in the same adamant terms that they prohibited forced labor drafts for the Spanish— and with equally minimal effect.[51] Considerable labor was required to maintain the households of the *principales*, with their many domestic animals and large gardens to tend, and elaborate rounds of banquets to add to the ordinary time-consuming chores of a *macehual* establishment. The extensive tracts of land the elite continued to own and from which they derived their wealth were far larger than they could cultivate by themselves and thus would have been of little use without some means of obtaining additional labor. This they were able to do largely through the authority conferred by local religious and civil offices. The parish choirmaster (*maestro cantor*) and other members of the local ecclesiastical establishment put the older boys in the catechism classes to work in their houses and fields.[52] Municipal officials had complete control over the community labor drafts (the weekly *tequios*), which they could allocate as they saw fit,[53] and there was nothing to prevent them from channeling part of the labor to their own personal benefit and that of their kinsmen and cronies.

Prohibited by Spanish law, such a practice nevertheless was sanctioned by long tradition within Maya society.[54] The customary recompense of daily rations, the provision of food in times of scarcity, or even the daily wages that at least some *principales* were paying by the end of the colonial period, would not necessarily elicit enthusiastic assent on the part of the *macehuales*. What they suggest is that such labor service existed as part of a web of reciprocal rights and obligations that bound subordinates to their superiors.[55]

Other economic advantages accrued to political power in the communities, probably the least of which were the subsidies authorized for some of the public offices. Only the *escribano* and *maestro cantor* were actually paid a salary from community revenues, usually a combination of maize and cash. The amounts varied slightly according to the size of the town but were most commonly twelve *cargas* of maize plus twelve pesos a year.[56] This was handsome only by *macehual* standards, equivalent to the wages and rations the foreman of a medium-sized *estancia* would receive. It was, however, a minimum income that the *escribanos* supplemented by fees charged for preparing and witnessing contracts, testaments, and any other private documents. The *maestros cantores* did even better; for they received a share of all the parochial fees for baptisms, weddings, funerals, and special masses and another fee for "matrimonial inquiries."[57] In addition to their rotating staff of household servants and the proceeds they received from the communally worked *milpa de cacique*, the *batabs* were paid a commission by the curates for collecting *obvenciones*.[58] Customary "gifts," presented by petitioners and litigants and regarded rather as fees than bribes, also supplemented the incomes of *batabs* and other officials.

Since the elite managed all community finances and tax collection, they could relieve themselves from tax obligations and simply prorate the difference among the *macehuales*. Spaniards never inquired how community quotas were met as long as they were met. Official exemptions were granted sparingly, generally only to *batabs*, members of the town council, and their wives. In practice the *maestros cantores* and the rest of what were called "church servants" could sometimes gain exemptions from tribute as well as *obvenciones*.[59] Even if this privilege was not extended to all the *principales*, taxes were in any case much less onerous than the various labor drafts. Relief from the burdens of *tequios* and *servicio personal* was therefore the unofficial privilege that the Maya officials guarded most jealously for themselves, for their relatives and friends and for former incumbents and *their* relatives and friends—in short, for the entire group of closely linked *principales* in each town.[60]

Differences in wealth certainly existed within the Maya elite. They ranged from fortunes that many a marginal Spaniard (they were not all *encomenderos*, curates, or rich merchants) might envy to the modest capital represented by a herd of pigs and a few score beehives. What distinguished the group as a whole, regardless of such gradations and the ups and downs of individual or family fortunes, was not so much a sumptuous style of life; most lived in a way that all but the most indigent Spaniard would have found beneath his dignity. The distinction lay in the relative ease of life, the absence of physical hardship, and most especially the simple security of existence.

The recurrent famines produced by prolonged drought, sometimes combined with plagues of locusts, provided a dramatic record of the contrasting degrees of security enjoyed by the two ranks of Maya society. It comes as no surprise to learn that the Spanish survived these crises, if not unscathed, at least considerably better than the Maya masses. All but grain profiteers suffered financial losses, as income from tribute and *obvenciones* fell, trade declined, and cattle herds were destroyed.[61] Some, it was reported, faced economic ruin; but none of the lamentations offer a hint that any Spaniards actually died for want of food. Their political power and wealth, no matter how reduced the latter was, enabled them to commandeer much of the local supply of grain that was available, as well as whatever relief shipments were brought in from outside. Starvation was reserved for the poor. Most of the colony's poor were Maya, but not all the Maya were poor. And the famines reveal unmistakably the economic inequalities among them.

The *macehuales*, lacking large grain reserves, cash to buy maize, or property to barter for the maize controlled by the grain merchants, were the first to starve. When the colonial authorities surveyed the effects of

185

the 1769-1774 famine (the best documented though not the most severe of the colonial famines), town after town reported that the only people left were the *batab* and other *principales*. Many of them were forced to sell off much of their property to buy maize from the Spanish when their own stores ran out.[62] At least they survived.

Not all of the *macehuales* perished, obviously, but a simple comparison of population figures before and after the famines conveys a strong enough picture of devastation even without the ghastly details supplied in the Spanish accounts.[63] These speak of corpses strewn along the roads and left to the vultures to dispose of, or gathered up to be dumped, unrecorded, in large pits. Some reported that starving mothers killed and ate their infants, but none of these reports was firsthand.[64]

Epidemics, the other visitation, took comparable tolls, without discriminating so finely between the ranks of *macehual* and *principal*. The diseases brought from the Old World were more respectful of ethnic differences and of the inherited immunity both Spaniards and Africans had developed by long exposure to them. Nevertheless, the consistently better-nourished elite would have had some edge over the *macehuales* as far as resistance goes. And the elite were unquestionably immune from most of the ordinary hardships that were the common lot of the colonial *macehual*.

The life of any peasant farmer and his family is characterized by strenuous labor and material insecurity. As agricultural regions go, Yucatan is not especially well favored. Rain in particular is unreliable, sometimes too heavy in tropical storms, more often too little or too late. On the other hand, the environment is perfectly capable of sustaining human life without herculean effort in "normal" years. The work required for milpa cultivation, although heavy, comes in spurts, and the total expenditure of labor is lower than in most other kinds of nonmechanized agriculture. The Spanish calculated that the colonial Maya swidden farmer could satisfy his and his family's basic subsistence needs with less than three months of labor a year.[65] Where, then, is the hardship of *macehual* life if they could sustain themselves by working only one quarter of the year? If they had only to feed themselves, perhaps their life would have been one of relative ease—by peasant standards. Leaving aside the vagaries of the weather, the epidemics, and the ordinary physical ills that might incapacitate them, the hardships obviously lay in the surplus they were required to produce beyond their own basic subsistence.

Spanish accounts often stress the Maya's shiftlessness and propensity to indolence. One wonders what chance they had to indulge this propensity. An exchequer report in 1766 estimated that the Maya farmer paid as much in taxes as he consumed in food.[66] In fact, the calculation covered only tribute and the other basic head taxes, and not the well-established extras listed in table 1.1. But let us say that tax payments occupied at least another three months of labor and that the women met their tax quotas by weaving *mantas*. That still leaves half the year free. But between *repartimientos*, various sanctioned labor drafts, and all the extra labor exacted unofficially by Spaniards and their own *principales*, it is doubtful that the *macehuales* had much time to spare.

Although hardly sunk in sloth as some Spaniards would have it, the *macehuales* were probably not constantly groaning under an insupportable burden of taxes and labor, either. The principal cause of the hardships was the way the Spanish imposed their demands. Not only did the tax quotas fail to keep up with calamitous population losses, but every unauthorized exemption granted by the clergy or by the Maya leaders themselves meant that the share of taxes and labor service allocated to the nonexempt was increased accordingly.[67] The legal quotas of taxes and labor merely represented the minimum that would be exacted, while the maximum fluctuated in a wholly unpredictable way, dependent on the caprice, financial need, or greed of individual governors, bishops, and their subordinates.[68] If we are to believe the collective wisdom of modern psychology, humans can adapt much more easily to a heavy work load than to the stress of uncertainty about what is or can be expected from them.

The economic gulf between *macehuales* and the elite was no doubt wider in pre-Columbian times—more than a mere margin of security against catastrophe. But the burden of Spanish rule that depressed the whole society did not fall with equal weight on both sectors. The *principales* were exempt in practice from most of the obligations imposed on the Maya, and it was *macehual* labor that supported the old rulers as well as the new.

COLONIAL MIDDLEMEN

The Maya elite's ability to maintain their cushioned economic position rested in large part on their continued monopoly of political power within the circumscribed sphere of the individual communities. How they managed to retain that hold despite the introduction of a new apparatus of local government will be the subject of a later chapter. But there are several points about the nature of native political power and how it was exercised under the system of indirect rule that are relevant here.

From the viewpoint of the Maya masses, the power of their leaders to punish and reward remained virtually limitless, subject only to the

187

constraints imposed by their accountability to the Spanish. They made all the decisions affecting the community as a whole, ranging from the settlement of boundary conflicts with neighboring communities to the choice of activities for the annual fiestas. They adjudicated all disputes within the community and administered criminal justice, except in rare cases involving the death penalty (homicide and rebellion), which were reserved in first instance to the governor in Merida. They also controlled all the public resources of the community, including all labor services as well as the community-owned lands that they parceled out for family milpa sites.

Short of flight, no practical recourse was available for a *macehual* who felt unfairly treated or oppressed by his own leaders. In theory, any Indian could submit an appeal to the Tribunal de Indios in Merida at no cost.[69] But "gratuities" were charged, and literacy and a mastery of Spanish bureaucratic and legal formalities were among the privileges confined to the elite. As we shall see below, on the rare occasions that grievances of *macehuales* against their leaders were brought to the attention of the colonial authorities, the necessary expertise was supplied by a dissident faction or individual from the ranks of the elite.

The political authority of the Maya elite, while absolute from the *macehual* perspective, was subject to many restraints from above, restraints that made that authority more onerous to their subjects than the unlimited power they had exercised as independent rulers. The history of European colonization abounds with examples of the sclerotic effects of indirect rule on native political systems. The foreign presence has often deliberately or inadvertently interfered with what may be considered the natural flow—the internal dynamics—of these systems. It has sometimes temporarily propped up a flagging regime or enabled local strongmen to emerge where none existed before. In the long run and often immediately, the added demands of the colonial masters and their alien norms have as frequently weakened the native leadership they hoped to rely on.[70]

In colonial Yucatan the conquerors and the royal bureaucrats who took over the colony's administration from them had every reason to support the authority of the native leaders, at least at the community level. Yet the Spanish, while seeking to reinforce the authority of these leaders from above, introduced new strains that undermined it from below. The double bind was apparent in the leaders' obligations to meet Spanish demands and execute Spanish laws, which more often than not were incompatible with their traditional obligations to protect the common good of their own subjects. In other words, the ability to fulfill

Spanish requirements depended upon a legitimacy that the requirements helped to erode.

The colonial Maya leaders had the unenviable task of enforcing alien rules that were invariably disagreeable and often incomprehensible to their subordinates. Spanish and Maya norms of behavior coincided in many aspects. Crimes against the person and against property, for example, seem to have been defined similarly in both societies. While the Spanish decried what they saw as an almost universal propensity among the Maya to prevaricate and commit perjury (without acknowledging how well adapted this behavior was to the conditions they themselves had created), a variety of observers stressed the Indians' strong respect for property and their high standards of probity in their dealings with each other and with Spaniards.[71] My point is not so much the acknowledged disparity between Maya and Spanish behavior as the similarity in the way that property rights, and therefore violations of them, were defined.

Rules regarding physical violence also show no major divergence. So far as we know, the Maya code contained no concept of family (as opposed to community) vendetta by which it might be lawful or even required for a kin group to avenge an offense against one of its members, nor any notion of indemnity payments in lieu of vengeance—two concepts that have been a source of much mutual misunderstanding in the administration of European justice in other colonial areas. Thus the Maya officials' responsibility for punishing theft, assault, and related crimes in their communities, whether or not these crimes were as rare as the record suggests, did not conflict with Maya principles.

Spanish and Maya codes differed radically on a number of other issues, and community officials were supposed to enforce the new rules, however meaningless or bothersome. Perhaps the most common divergences were over the questions of marriage and sexual morality. The Catholic church condemned as bigamous, adulterous, or incestuous many types of union that the Maya considered perfectly proper. The Maya permitted divorce, and their definition of consanguinity was totally at odds with canon law. They continued to adhere to a prohibition against marriage between people of the same patronymic, regardless of how distant the biological ties.[72] On the other hand, it has been suggested that cross-cousin marriages were the preferred pattern among the Maya.[73] In these the partners would have different patronymics but, according to canon law, they would also have ties of consanguinity in the second degree and therefore would be prohibited from marrying.[74] The authority granted by the Pope to parish priests in Spanish colonies to dispense marriage impediments for Indians extended only to the third and fourth degrees of affinity and consanguinity.[75] We cannot say how often the Maya were prevented from marrying a preferred partner, if at all. However, the whole process of what were called "matrimonial inquiries," which had to precede any marriage bans, and especially the petitions of dispensation inevitable in small communities where many people were of necessity related to each other, were an expense and a nuisance to the Maya, particularly in view of the fact that they came on top of negotiations that the native marriage brokers undertook in conformity with their own rules.[76]

Perhaps many of the cases of concubinage that the clergy complained of as a sign of moral decay represented marriages that were perfectly valid by Maya standards but could not be solemnized in the Catholic church because of canonical prohibitions. Certainly the Maya officials had to be badgered by the clergy into pursuing people guilty of these so-called illicit unions. They displayed a similar lack of zeal in cases that the Spanish defined as bigamy and adultery, as long as the offenders were openly separated from their spouses, while at the same time proceeding vigorously against adultery committed without benefit of a Maya-style divorce.[77] If the parish clergy are to be believed, the colonial Maya also had fairly relaxed taboos on incest. The practice of father-daughter incest was supposedly common and, even more scandalous, had no shame attached to it. As the Maya—again, reportedly—explained it: "The father planted the seed and he harvests the first fruit."[78] Whether these reports were well founded or the product of collective priestly fantasy is impossible to tell.

Community resistance and the foot dragging of the local officials constantly hampered the clergy's efforts to suppress practices that they considered sinful, superstitious, uncivilized, unhealthy, or merely unseemly. In a host of matters—in curing procedures for the sick, mourning for the dead, standards of dress, and the use of alcohol during religious celebrations, to name but a few—the Maya disagreed profoundly with their new masters about what was acceptable in precept as well as in practice. And the native officials were caught in the classic dilemma of the middleman, risking punishment themselves if they did not chastise behavior that neither they nor the community as a whole viewed with any opprobrium.[79]

The roles of tax collector and straw boss for the Spanish were the most disagreeable to both the Maya leaders and their subjects. The obligation of the *macehuales* to support a ruling class was scarcely a colonial innovation. No one seems to have questioned the principle of tribute and forced labor (bearing in mind that any such protest would have been futile); the issue was rather how much, and how the obligations would be allocated. All the hardships inherent in the colonial tax system and the abuses committed outside the law fell on the *macehuales* via their own leaders. The local officers were held directly liable for the tax quotas of each community. When the population fell below the official assessment, they had to choose between making up the difference out of their own pockets, with attendant financial ruin, and prorating the defaulted taxes (of people who died or fled or simply could not pay) among the remaining tributaries.[80] The same local officials were responsible for filling both the authorized and unauthorized labor drafts from a shrunken pool of unprivileged tributaries, who had to be rounded up for local church repairs or marched off to perform labor service for individual Spaniards with greater frequency because the curate had managed to preempt a portion of the local labor supply, or because the supply had been decimated by famine or epidemic disease. To the Spanish officials and employers, the labor drafts were mere body counts—a specified numbers of workers—and they neither knew nor cared which individuals were included, nor whether they were contributing more than the customary number of weeks of service a year.

Whether or not the *macehuales* actually provided more goods and services under the colonial regime than before, it is safe to say that they received less in return—less from their own rulers and very little at all from the Spanish, whose total contribution to the common good in Maya terms must be counted at close to or below zero. To a certain degree the local clergy, the *encomenderos*, and later the *hacendados* established patron-client relationships with the Maya. The curates all performed a recognizable ritual service that the Maya came to value. Many sought for a variety of reasons to protect their parishioners from the extortions of other Spaniards; some proportion even refrained from undue extortions themselves, and a few were true benefactors. The *encomenderos* and *hacendados* were less of a presence for good or ill but still could be perceived as taking some interest in the welfare of their own tributaries or resident laborers and could sometimes be enlisted in their defense. With these exceptions, and the distant figure of the official Protector de Indios (whose effectiveness was limited even when his zeal was not), the element of reciprocity was missing entirely. Labor for their own elite and for community projects could provide some discernible benefit, but nothing accrued from labor for individual Spaniards or for the state—on roads for Spanish use and on forts to defend Spanish territorial claims.

In assessing the effects of Spanish rule on Maya society, or for that matter the effects of any colonial regime, one has to be careful not to create a precolonial Golden Age of harmony and prosperity that was shattered by the foreign intruders. We can assume that some degree of tension is inherent in any system of domination of the many by the few, and the reciprocal arrangement I have referred to between elites and *macehuales* implies neither an equal exchange of benefits nor the absence of conflict between the two groups. The difference lay largely in degree. There were presumably certain practical if not moral restraints on oppression and exploitation under the pre-Columbian system that the native rulers, dependent on popular acquiescence (if not actual consent) could not disregard with impunity. As middlemen in the colonial system, they could only adjust their own demands to what the community could bear, without possessing any power to moderate Spanish demands, regardless of how damaging these might be to their own position and to the social bonds of community. If the *macehuales* had not received perfect value for value under the old regime, the discrepancies had become glaringly obvious under the new one.

Signs of Social Strain

The Maya community confronted the colonial rulers with what appeared to be a seamless social fabric. It presented an almost somnolent picture of peaceful stoicism that could be roused to energetic defense of its own integrity against other towns or Spanish pressures, but which preserved perfect harmony within its own borders.

From one perspective this picture is fairly accurate. There can be no doubt that the most significant division in colonial society was along caste lines. Foreign domination provided a basis for solidarity among the Maya that transcended or overshadowed any internal fissures that may have existed. Exceptions can be found: Maya informers who without threat of torture were willing to warn the Spanish of some impending danger or to betray some otherwise well concealed wrongdoing.[81] They were, however, exceptions. What is striking is how little the Spanish did learn except by accident—that is, how well the Maya managed to subordinate their own conflicts and animosities to the deeper shared enmity toward the Spanish.[82]

Evidence for internal tensions is very scanty, partly because a united front was the common, though not the invariable, rule and partly because overt manifestations of conflict of any sort among the Maya were rare. It is especially difficult to find signs of hostility directed explicitly against the native leaders. The Spanish were in universal agreement that the *batabs* and other leaders were able to exact the strictest obedience from the *macehuales*. A few speak of the harsh rule of the *batabs* enforced by the whip (a Spanish import, by the way, and we have no information on what if any means of physical coercion were used before the conquest), which inspired the deepest resentment.[83] That may be, but a conscious sense of grievance is not very manifest in the records.

As mentioned in chapter 2, I have found only one case in which *macehual* discontent erupted into a rebellion against their own leaders (if any similar example had occurred, it surely would have received some mention in the records). The rebellion occurred in the town of Tekax in 1610. A group of townsmen, after unsuccessfully appealing to the Spanish governor to remove their appointed *gobernador*, resorted to the more direct expedient of rousing a large part of the town on the occasion of a Carnival festival to overthrow the *gobernador* by force and kill him. They did not succeed. The intended victim was able to take refuge in the Franciscan friary and was rescued from his attackers by a force of Spaniards who galloped in from Mani on receiving word that the friars were under siege. The *gobernador* was eventually replaced but too late to satisfy the ringleaders, who by then had been executed in the main plaza of Merida or sentenced for life to hard labor on the Campeche fortifications.[84]

This was not a simple class war, much less a caste war. The rioters were highly selective. Not only did they respect the two unarmed friars who sought to calm them and another Spaniard who happened to be visiting the town at the time; they also spared the persons and property of all the local notables except the *gobernador* and his closest associates. Two members of his faction were nearly killed and their houses were destroyed. But most of the rage was directed against the *gobernador* himself, whose heart the rioters declared they intended to cut out. They were in the process of scaling the friary walls to carry out their threat when the rescue force arrived.

The rebellion contains some other peculiar features aside from its narrow focus against the *gobernador*. His offenses, as outlined in the list of grievances presented, were in no way exceptional to the time and place. If extra taxes, unpaid labor drafts, and whippings had provided sufficient cause for rebellion, colonial Yucatan would have known no peace. Then there was the ambiguous role of the town's hereditary but non-resident *batab*, the don Fernando Uz whose career was described in chapter 3. Uz, whose antipathy toward the appointed *gobernador* was revealed in the trial, had helped the rebels prepare their prior, unsuccessful petitions for the *gobernador*'s ouster. Things probably went further than he had planned, but it seems that he was at least indirectly responsible for the translation of ordinary *macehual* discontent, which may have been endemic, into this extraordinary and, so far as we know, unique act of open defiance.

For all the signs of *macehual* disaffection, stirred up perhaps but not invented by Uz, the Tekax rebellion falls more properly into the category of elite factionalism than class struggle. The same applies to the references to oppression of the poor contained in the colonial Maya texts called the books of Chilam Balam, books written by and for members of the elite, which express (among many other things) their concern for sorting out legitimate from illegitimate rulers but contain no manifestoes against the social order in general.[85]

Another more successful movement against the *batab* of Tzotzil in the late seventeenth century shares certain parallels with the Tekax case. The defendant was convicted, removed from office, and exiled from the town on the grounds that he had enriched himself at the expense of his subjects, through allowing the Spanish *repartimiento* agents to cheat on the quotas (from which, as it turned out, he had derived no profit himself) and through unpaid *macehual* labor. Again these were common practices. It is clear from the testimony taken in the town (testimony confined to the other *principales*) that the *batab*'s main offense, and the origin of the denunciation against him, was his imposition of a candidate for municipal office who was from another town and thus unacceptable to the local *principales*.[86]

Quarrels and factional strife within the ruling group seem to have been the main source of conflict in colonial Maya society, as it had been in pre-Columbian times. Two explanations for the virtual absence of overt "class" conflict are possible, and by no means mutually exclusive. One is that such *macehual* discontent as existed was unfocused. It was felt as a general sense of alienation, stronger or weaker as the particular conditions of individuals might vary; and it was manifested in a general way by a variety of antisocial acts, such as shirking civic obligations, drunkenness, and running away, that were directed against the system as a whole without distinguishing any particular target. In other words, it may simply not have occurred to the *macehuales* consciously to question the acts of their leaders. If it did, and this is the second possibility, they may have been restrained from manifesting their resistance by the same sense of futility that made rebellions against the Spanish so rare. The risks were high and the chances of success exceedingly slim. Even formal complaints to the Spanish carried risk. Unless the complainants succeeded in having a ruler deposed, he could take revenge on his accusers, as the Tekax petitioners learned.[87] The combination of risk, a habit of deference, and sheer ignorance of bureaucratic procedures help to explain why the petitions that have survived were all evidently inspired and prepared by rival factions within the elite.

Whether consciously or not, the colonial *macehuales* ordinarily eschewed direct protest and resorted instead to more subtle forms that are common to the powerless in many societies and which provide temporary relief without seriously challenging the social order. The Spanish found this behavior easy to overlook, or, when impossible to ignore, convenient to ascribe to the moral perversity of the Maya.

The mock battles and publicly sanctioned drunkenness that the village men engaged in during fiestas served to release tensions and hostilities that would be dangerous if not confined to these ritual occasions. Both practices seem to have originated in pre-Columbian times.[88] Their purpose may have been partly similar, although ritual drunkenness had (and still has to a certain extent) the function of facilitating access to the supernatural by producing an altered state of consciousness. In colonial times fiestas permitted the ordinary rules of decorum and deference to be suspended. They provided the Maya with a temporary license, in what the Spanish regarded as disgusting debaucheries, to express openly whatever personal animosities and factional conflict had been fermenting in the village pot. Teams of young men pelted each other with oranges and other fruit, and during Carnival the line between ritual and real warfare became blurred, as *parcialidades* and villages fielded opposing forces armed with bows and arrows and even firearms.[89] Only once does this more or less sanctioned strife seem to have turned into an assault on established authority—the Tekax rebellion. More commonly, the inebriated *macehuales* challenged the authority of their officials, and even the parish priest, with individual and milder acts of defiance: a refusal to obey orders or an insulting gesture. Such acts must be measured against the extreme deference expected in normal times. A *macehual*'s failure to remove his hat when addressing his superiors was a serious enough sign of disrespect to incur a whipping. These periodic suspensions of the rules do not indicate that society was coming apart. Carnivals and other similar festivals have come to be seen as highly flexible, ambiguous rituals. They can be used not only to challenge, but also, and perhaps more commonly, to reaffirm and reinforce established order through symbolic inversions and by channeling hostility into the safe confines of prescribed ritual.[90] Among the colonial Maya, however, fiesta behavior was not entirely restricted to the chronologically well-defined boundaries of the fiesta. By all accounts one of the more striking contrasts between colonial and preconquest Indian conduct was that the solace of alcohol and the unlicensed behavior associated with it spilled over into the ordinary routine during the rest of the year.

If we are to credit the parish priests, alcoholism was the most pervasive malady of colonial Maya society and the "mother of all other vices" to which the Indians were prone. Brawling, sloth, incest, concubinage, lukewarm devotion to God, disobedience, lying: all of these and a host of other spiritual and social diseases could be laid at the door of drunkenness.[91] Although idolatry was also included in the list, the clergy were not referring primarily to the consumption of *balche*, the fermented honey and bark mixture associated with pagan religious rites, but to the distilled cane liquor introduced by the Spanish, a type of raw white rum that well deserves the name of *aguardiente* (burning water).

Aguardiente had a dual attraction for the Maya. Not only did it induce a temporary state of nirvana in which cares, miseries, and constraints could be forgotten, but it also provided an excuse for ignoring the rules even if they were remembered. One could be punished for drunkenness, but Spanish penal law also allowed one to claim diminished responsibility for any act committed while in that state. According to some of the clergy, the Maya often used drunkenness as a pretext for insolence and insubordination to both their own leaders and their Spanish masters, and could convincingly feign the symptoms whenever convenient. Perhaps, but there is also evidence that leads one to question how often pretense was necessary.

William Taylor, in his recent study of *Drinking, Homicide and Rebellion* in the highlands of colonial Mexico, has argued that the Spanish exaggerated the problem of Indian drunkenness, unable to distinguish between ritual use and social disease.[92] This is no doubt true. However, exaggeration is one thing and invention another, and the evidence on Indian consumption of *aguardiente* in colonial Yucatan indicates that a problem did indeed exist for the Maya as much as for the Spanish.

The Spanish authorities in Yucatan saw drink as cause rather than symptom. They were aware that the pre-Columbian Maya, like the Aztecs and other Indian groups, had been able to control the use of alcohol, confining it to ritual occasions and to the sick and the elderly— that is, to members of society who could be granted special indulgence because they were unable to contribute useful labor anyway, and were certainly unlikely to threaten the political or social order. To acknowledge that Indian drunkenness might be explained in part by the socially and culturally destructive effects of colonial rule would have been highly inconvenient. Besides, the business of supplying drink to the Indians was too lucrative to suppress.

The laws prohibiting the sale of alcoholic beverages to Indians were among the more futile articles in the colonial legal code. Within decades of the conquest, Spanish peddlers were already making a good profit distributing wine to the Maya elite, and when sugar cane production permitted the manufacture of the cheaper and more potent *aguardiente*, the comforts of alcohol became accessible to the Maya masses.[93] More precisely, it became accessible to the men; for intoxication was then, as it is now, an almost exclusively male privilege. *Aguardiente* was one of the very few contributions of European material culture that the Maya had any use for. Why they failed to manufacture their own supply of such a desirable commodity is not clear. Perhaps they never mastered the technique of distilling spirits. In any case, Spanish control of the supply and distribution was merely another source of economic inequality in the colony.

Once the royal *aguardiente* monopoly was established in the colonies in the latter part of the eighteenth century as one of the many devices dreamed up by Charles III's ministers to increase Crown revenues, the incentive for the colonial officials to wink at Indian intemperance was even greater. They must have known that much of the production was ultimately retailed to Indians. Spaniards did not ordinarily drink *aguardiente*, preferring the wine and brandy imported from Europe. Mestizos and mulattoes were the monopoly's other customers, but their numbers could not easily have accounted for a major part of even the legally produced *aguardiente*, much less the reportedly vast amount of clandestine production that escaped confiscation.

Because both the tobacco and *aguardiente* monopolies were extremely unpopular and fairly easy to circumvent, it is impossible to calculate the amount of spirits consumed during this period. Official sales in the province provide only a minimum. This amounted to 147,883 *frascos* in 1780,[94] and a conservative estimate of production from illegal stills would triple the figure. If we assume that mestizos and *pardos* drank at the same rate as Indians, and if we discount the nondrinking females, then we find an average yearly consumption of 7.38 *frascos* of *aguardiente* for each nonwhite male above the age of seven. The *frasco* was a large wine jar, the usual wholesale measure for wines and spirits in the colony, and probably equivalent to the Castillian *cántara* of about sixteen liters.[95] If that is so, then per capita annual consumption was 118.1 liters a year, or 31.2 U.S. gallons. This figure would be raised considerably if we discounted the youngsters between the ages of seven and sixteen (a distinction not made in the census) and the undetermined portion of adult male teetotalers (these did exist), and it would be lowered to 28.7 gallons if we included adult Spanish males. Even taking into account the fact that neither pulque nor mezcal was consumed in Yucatan, a per capita consumption of at least 28.7 gallons of high-proof cane alcohol a year would seem to constitute a social problem of no mean proportions.[96]

Charles Gibson concludes his monumental study of the colonial Aztecs with the statement, "If our sources may be believed, few peoples

197

in the whole of history were more prone to drunkenness than the Indians of the Spanish colony."[97] The Yucatac Maya appear to have been somewhat more abstemious than the Aztecs.[98] Possibly this was because the Maya had another remedy for social dissatisfaction that was more effective than drink and also considerably less risky than open hostility. They could always run away.

Given the "fight-or-flight" choice in any stressful situation, the Maya *macehual* would almost invariably have found avoidance the easier option. This tendency could apply to any type of conflict within the community—personal disputes with neighbors and kinsmen as well as grievances against local officials. Perhaps the picture of the peaceful colonial community is fairly accurate because of the safety valve provided by the easy option of leaving town. One is reminded of the "peaceable kingdoms" of colonial New England in which harmony was achieved by excluding all social misfits.[99] Witchcraft accusations, which, it has been suggested, are a favored means of getting rid of such misfits or dealing with social strains in small unsophisticated communities,[100] held little place in Maya social transactions. Insofar as the notion of *maleficium* existed at all in colonial Yucatan, it seems to have been introduced by the Spanish and it did not take a strong hold among the Maya. The Catholic priests, who were very knowledgeable about and tolerant of their parishioners' magical beliefs, found much "foolish superstition" but little of a socially disruptive kind.[101]

The ease of physical separation whenever social bonds became too onerous meant that such bonds would be more tenuous in the Maya lowlands than in any areas where travel was harder, subsistence more complex, or the spaces already filled by other people. There may have been periods prior to the Spanish conquest when population densities were high enough over large enough areas to leave dissatisfied community members with no choice but to make do where they were. This was certainly not the case in Postclassic Yucatan, and even less so after conquest. Huge, sparsely populated frontier zones and long expanses of bush stretching between many towns and villages gave ample room for the socially alienated.

The Maya community had a built-in line of cleavage between those who had access to power and wealth and those who did not. The Spanish were no more responsible for its existence than they were for the physical setting that made fissioning so easy a response to any internal friction. But they unwittingly did much to encourage fissioning by weakening the delicate ties of reciprocity that underlay the corporate organization of the family and which gave the *macehual* some value in return for his submission to social constraints in the community.

· 7 ·

POPULATION MOVEMENTS:
THE FRAYING EDGES

The colonial Maya changed residence with a facility and across distances that seem more typical of twentieth-century North Americans towing trailer homes along interstate highways than of peasant farmers traveling on foot. Members of premodern agrarian societies in general may have been much more geographically mobile than has ordinarily been assumed, even before the large-scale migrations associated with industrialization. We may then be dealing with degrees rather than contrasts. Even so, the lowland Maya seem to have been uncommonly restless for a people defined as "sedentary."

That the Indians would not always stay put in the towns and villages where the conquerors had found them or later resettled them will come as no surprise to historians of colonial Latin America. The Indians' tendency to wander is usually seen as a direct response to Spanish rule, a failure of Spanish mechanisms of control, and a more or less vexing problem for the colonial authorities. It was also a sign of social dissolution in the Indian community, within the familiar security of which the beleaguered native population had supposedly taken refuge against the pressures of alien domination.

I have earlier argued that social cohesion and the related phenomenon of territorial integration should be seen as processes rather than achieved states. These processes may reach an equilibrium at certain points but are inherently unstable, especially in the open environment of the Maya lowlands. The pattern of population movement during the colonial period suggests that among the Maya a tendency toward physical fragmentation emerges whenever social cohesion weakens at the center: whenever the quid pro quo for the inconvenience of clustering together and serving an elite seems inadequate. The well-documented colonial patterns may help to interpret earlier cycles of consolidation and dissolution that are only hinted at in the archaeological record.

The movement can be gradual and need not result from any massive cataclysm. The term "collapse" is generally used when referring to the end of the Classic period of pre-Columbian history and also the end of the hegemony of Mayapan in the Postclassic. But if the behavior of the colonial Maya is any clue, perhaps the less dramatic metaphor of "crumble" would be more appropriate: people deserting population centers

199

little by little. They sometimes moved long distances, but of equal long-term demographic significance was a slow trickle out to the surrounding countryside—a colonial Maya flight to the suburbs.

We will never know the precise magnitude of the phenomenon. Nevertheless, information pieced together from a variety of sources indicates that a very large proportion—considerably more than a third—of the Indian population in Yucatan at any one time lived permanently separated from their own congregated towns as a result of three related but distinct types of population movement, which I label flight, drift, and dispersal.[1] Flight, as described in chapter 2, refers to the escape of Indians from colonial rule across the frontier into unpacified territory; drift refers to the migrations to other communities within the area under more or less effective Spanish domination; and dispersal indicates the creation of satellite settlements by population spinoff from nucleated or congregated "parent" towns. None of these was an example of mass migration except in the aggregate. Yet, although individually small in scale and uncoordinated, the cumulative effect of these movements on Maya social patterns was profound.

Drift

A large portion, perhaps most, of the Maya who left their communities chose not to escape from colonial domination; they simply moved to another community within the pacified zone. These much more conservative moves within the same shared universe seem so aimless that they warrant the title of "drift." They are among the more mystifying phenomena of colonial Maya history. Why should people have taken the trouble to uproot themselves to move from one community to another, a community that was essentially a carbon copy of the one left behind, offering the same way of life, the same rights, and the same obligations? What was gained, or what did people at least expect to gain from such a move?

The phenomenon of drift is revealed in censuses that distinguish between *naturales*, or people born in the district, and *forasteros* (or sometimes the Maya term *nachilcahob*), meaning outsiders.[2] Also, many of the extant parish registers list the origins of parents, marriage partners, and *padrinos*, or sponsors of baptisms and weddings, so that in many cases it is possible to trace the actual patterns of migration. The proportion of newcomers could vary considerably over time and from parish to parish. In a late seventeenth-century census the figures ranged from zero to 35 percent of the total parish population.[3] A recent study of four parishes (Uman, Conkal, Tixkokob, and Sotuta) in the later colonial period revealed a range from 22.1 percent for Sotuta in the 1720s to 76.6 percent for Uman in the early 1800s.[4] Further work in surviving parish registers and new, as yet undiscovered censuses might reveal that the currently available data are somehow exceptional. Barring that unlikely revelation, we are faced with a rate of internal migration from community to community that is considerably higher than the general norm for colonial Mexico.[5] Despite many gaps in the records, we are able to measure this phenomenon with a degree of sureness that is by no means matched by our ability to explain it.

It is difficult to detect significant patterns in the maze of crisscrossing tracks left by the migrants. One of the main obstacles to finding a satisfactory explanation for the movements is that we tend to see them as a single action, when we really need to break them down into three separate actions, or choices, which sometimes responded to separate sets of motives. These choices are: leaving home, not returning, and resettling elsewhere.

Long-distance migrations did not always or even normally proceed in a steady flow. Their immediate cause was often a particular crisis, such as famine, epidemic disease, or some political upheaval. Any one of these caused people to scatter, and in colonial times could almost empty the affected town from one day to the next.[6] Such wholesale desertions were ordinarily only temporary. People might camp nearby at their milpas or around some *cenote* in the vicinity, where the local priest or one of the Indian officials could round them up at some point and persuade them to return with assurances that food supplies had been obtained, that the epidemic was over, or that amnesty had been declared. Some of the people who left in disgust a second time when, as frequently happened, these assurances proved false, became permanent refugees, as did a portion of those who from the beginning had wandered farther away. The survivors would eventually make their way to another community in the pacified zone or across the frontier to join refugees from earlier crises.

These natural and man-made crises provided motives for leaving home, but the original dislocation does not explain why people failed to return to their native towns and villages once things had returned to normal, nor why they chose to resettle where they did. Some geographical patterns emerge that help to give some purpose to what otherwise might appear to be purely random movement. A two-way flow is discernible between the center (not the geographical center of the peninsula but the economic, political, and demographic hub in the northwest) and the periphery. The flow to the eastern periphery presents a new puzzle, however—an apparent contradiction between the gradual decay of that region and the fact that the towns there at times recorded among the highest proportion of immigrants in the entire colony.[7]

Valladolid and its hinterland, despite having been the granary of pre-conquest Yucatan, suffered an especially severe demographic decline during the course of the colonial period:[8] That is, the decline was both absolute and relative to the districts in the center and northwest (Costa, Beneficios Bajos, Sierra, and Camino Real) that were relatively flourishing but which had the same or at times a lower proportion of *forasteros*. If, as is believed, malaria and yellow fever were introduced from Africa after the conquest, the mortality rate there would have been considerably higher than in the more arid though less fertile zones round Merida. But perhaps the main contribution to the apparent contradiction between population inflow and demographic decline was the proximity of the east coast zone of refuge. A large part of the population that flowed from the interior into the towns along this border flowed out again. These towns became way stations for many migrants who, along with some of the locals, eventually crossed over into the area officially and misleadingly labeled *despoblado* (unpopulated) on the colonial maps.[9] A similar movement occurred all along the southern extension of this colonial frontier from Bacalar to Chicbul.[10] We do not know whether the zones of refuge were the original destination of the migrants, or whether people simply moved to the periphery where Spanish control was more lax and then were lured by the even greater freedom on the other side. In either case, by crossing the frontier the migrants disappeared from the colonial censuses as effectively as if they had died.

The flow in the opposite direction, toward the economic and political center of the colony, presents its own puzzles. Marta Hunt, in her study of seventeenth-century Yucatan, sees a two-way migratory pattern of Spaniards and *castas* moving out from the urban centers and Indians moving in from the countryside. According to her model, the Indians moved in two stages, first from outlying areas to parishes nearer the cities, especially Merida, and next to the suburban barrios.[11] New information has greatly complicated the picture. It reveals a considerable Indian movement out of and away from as well as into and toward the barrios, and also moves that bypassed and leapfrogged the city.[12] Still, there was clearly a buildup of population in the vicinities of Merida and Campeche and along the Camino Real and the Merida-Izamal axis, at the expense of other regions.[13]

The motives for this buildup are less immediately obvious than for the flow toward the periphery. Spaniards with their burdensome demands were concentrated in the northwest and the Maya might therefore be expected to give the area a wide berth. Yet the Spaniards, who exacerbated and sometimes created many of the hardships of village life, could also be perceived as providing some security against them and could thus serve as a magnet as well as a repellant. If an Indian were prepared to abandon his traditional way of life and not merely his native town, he could seek to attach himself to a Spaniard—or even a prosperous mestizo or mulatto—as a *criado*, or personal servant. At the opposite pole from flight, this tactic provided another means of escape from the same burdens of the community that stimulated others to flee across the colonial frontiers.

In becoming a *criado*, an Indian traded the relatively unfettered but precarious existence of a *macehual* for the security of total dependence. His master became legally responsible for his tax obligations as well as his sustenance in return for an exclusive claim to his labor. By custom, if not by law, the master also assumed any debts the *criado* may have contracted previously, and Indians could therefore "sell themselves as *criados*" in order to discharge their debts, or rather, to transfer them.[14] *Servicio personal* in urban households was a prime means of recruitment, because it was much more irksome to both master and draftee than the agricultural corvées. The Spanish always preferred permanent workers, and especially so with domestic servants. It was bad enough to find that the work gang assigned to weed the fields was short of hands one week, infinitely worse to find oneself without tortillas or firewood because there were not enough *semaneros* from Acanceh or Conkal (or whichever town one's allotment came from) to go around. The Maya for their part especially disliked the urban labor service because of the dislocations involved. Since married women were included in the drafts, they also caused highly inconvenient if not painful separations or, more commonly, the temporary displacement of the whole family and what was essentially a double labor duty for the husband: his own and another stint when accompanying his wife.[15] The attractions of leaving home permanently as a *criado* become understandable when the alternative was to trudge to Merida several times a year, with a brood of small children in tow, and with the milpa, the garden, and the weaving—on which one's subsistence and tax payments depended—all neglected in the interim.

Recruitment of *criados* can thus account for much of the migration to the city centers from the general catchment areas for *servicio personal*, but we still need to explain the movement *into* these areas. One major motivation was hunger. During famines Indians flocked to Merida and Campeche and the surrounding areas in search of food supplies.[16] They knew that whatever grain was available tended to be concentrated in the public granaries and private hoards of the cities. Though unable to

203

buy at the inflated prices, they could beg, and they filled the streets and plazas of the Spanish towns in hopes of charity, as they did in central Mexico when famine struck there.[17] We do not know how well they fared in comparison with the ones who chose the more traditional remedy of foraging for wild food in the bush. The relevant point is that many Maya had come to look upon the Spanish as a source of relief, and the ones who did survive in and around the cities must have done so through Spanish aid. It is therefore not surprising that the authorities were not totally successful in persuading them to return to their native villages once the famine had passed. This can be seen clearly in the figures comparing local populations before and after the 1769-1774 famine. The heaviest losses were suffered in eastern Yucatan: Espita, for example, lost 74.8 percent of its Indian population and Chemax, 71.7 percent. In the Campeche-Merida corridor the overall depopulation rate was much lower and decreased even more toward the urban centers, where some actual population gains were recorded. Hecelchakan lost 14.7 percent and Becal 7.3 percent, while the barrio of San Roman of Campeche gained 3.3 percent, and the barrio of Santa Ana of Merida registered a staggering gain of 30.7 percent at a time when the overall *loss* for the entire colony was 34 percent of the Indian population.[18]

The movement away from the colonial center, and in particular away from Spaniards, responded to the same search for relief, whether temporary or long term. The choice between the two movements was presumably dictated by individual calculation of whether survival would be enhanced by greater proximity to or distance from the colonial masters, who came to control an increasing proportion of the region's resources. Either choice, and indeed all the migrations, reflected a less than compelling attachment to the particular community of birth.

The migrations were due largely in first instance to the recurrent crises that cast so many people adrift from their moorings. Joining the refugees in the intervals were an unknown number of other migrants driven away by an accumulation of small miseries. The general burdens of colonial life help to explain why some Indians sought escape either in the cities or across the frontier. They provide no apparent motive for what looks like a patternless drift between communities around the peninsula, in a kind of long-range musical chairs that apparently left them no better off than before. If they chose to stay within the same colonial Maya universe, why move from, say, Yobain to Sotuta, rather than stay in or return to the familiar surroundings and the relatives and friends of one's own community? A sense of place and community ties were clearly not a matter of total indifference to the colonial Maya. Yet they were prepared to sever these ties permanently for no readily discernible improvement in their lot.

We can discount any rule of community exogamy to explain migrations. Even if the Maya had had such a rule, which they did not,[19] they would not need to go clear across the peninsula to find an acceptable marriage partner. We can also eliminate the motive of land hunger. Rural out-migration in modern times, including in Latin America, is often a mechanism for sloughing off excess population. But this does not apply to colonial Yucatan. Migrations went on in times of population decline, especially in times of acute decline from famine and epidemic, as well as in times of population increase; and people were as likely to move to more densely populated parishes as to districts where land was more abundant. The towns of the increasingly land-hungry northwest in the late colonial period made no effort—certainly no successful effort—to close their doors to newcomers.

Migration in colonial Yucatan seems instead to have afforded one means of escaping, if only temporarily and partially, just those pressures of community life that could be intensified by a shortage rather than an excess of people. Spanish demands might become intolerable when community quotas of taxes and labor were arbitrarily raised by venal officials or were not adjusted to a loss in population. Debts accumulated, either in tax arrears or in cash advances or both. For the less adventurous, those unwilling to take off for the unconquered zones of the Peten or to become a *criado*, one solution was to move to another community. First uprooted perhaps by some temporary disaster, they would then find that relocation offered a tempting prospect. In a new community their old debts would be unknown or ignored, and as new contributors to the local tax rolls and labor force they would be welcomed with no questions asked.[20]

The same type of unstructured internal migration took place in highland Peru and Mexico for similar reasons, although in Mexico on a considerably smaller scale.[21] In Peru the incentives for changing residence would seem to be especially strong, since *forasteros* there became permanently exempt from a forced labor system that was possibly the most onerous in the Spanish colonies. In Yucatan they gained no exemption from forced labor or from any of the usual tax obligations. They could thus neither escape from the burdens of colonial domination nor necessarily prevent the accumulation of new debts, but they could, if lucky, wipe away the old ones and start afresh.

If a migrant's *batab* or any other creditor caught up with him, he could be held liable for any debts he had left behind. Judging from the complaints about the rate of uncollected arrears in tribute and *obven-*

205

ciones and defaulted cash advances, and the difficulty of locating tax dodgers and deadbeats, it would seem that they had a good chance of escaping the old debts.[22] Changing residence, then, was the colonial Maya equivalent of declaring bankruptcy, or more aptly, of slipping out of town one step ahead of the bailiff. This explains the fact that when people moved at all they moved to another district altogether, where they could not be easily tracked down.[23]

The reasons for the specific choices of new locations are still elusive. We might find in analyzing the parish registers more closely that there are distinct family or hometown ties: that the Maya followed relatives, friends, or neighbors, as migrants have done the world over, although the migrant kinsmen who are found in the same pueblo are more likely to have transplanted themselves in a body than to have moved as single members in stages.[24] Aside from the very general two-directional movement toward and away from the colony's center, we have yet to find any larger pattern in the drift phenomenon. There seems to have been no incentive for the particular choices of new homes other than distance from creditors and possibly the presence of kinsmen.

DISPERSAL

A more orderly and predictable movement than the exchange of population from town to town, dispersal represented a physical exemplar of the dissolution of social bonds and a serious challenge to the congregation program of the early missionaries.

Despite many complaints from *encomenderos* about the disruptive effects of the congregation program, in one sense it can be seen as a device to strengthen existing social and political ties, at least at the local level, by consolidating the population dispersed in outlying hamlets and bringing small towns together into larger units. Yet the program was a forced nucleation dictated by criteria and motives wholly external to Indian society. The point is not whether congregation was good or bad but whether it would last. It did not. The Spaniards imposed a degree of territorial integration without a corresponding degree of social cohesion to support it. Therefore the territorial integration could not be maintained and a slow process of fragmentation began. The friars, who saw themselves as shepherds watching over their Indian flocks, had a hard time indeed keeping their sheep from straying in body as well as in spirit.

We do not know exactly when the Maya began to reverse the congregation program. Documentation for the immediately succeeding period is scanty. But by the 1580s we find that the process was already underway.[25] Indians were moving out into the bush, recreating hamlet clusters, which eventually became recognized under the label of *ranchos* as settlements administratively dependent on but physically separate from the original town. By the end of the colonial period, some of these *ranchos* had become independent towns, even *cabeceras* of new parishes, and had themselves spawned generations of satellite settlements.[26]

The friars had originally merged approximately 400 separate pueblos into 170 congregated towns, and that number was further reduced by later resettlements of 23 pueblos.[27] By the early nineteenth century the number had grown to 224.[28] The more dramatic change in population distribution was the proliferation of satellite communities. Already around 900 by the 1700s, the number increased to more than 1,500 within the century.[29] The settlements varied greatly in size. The vast majority had fewer than 50 inhabitants, and many of these had only a few families, while several with populations of over 1,000 rivaled the average town.

By the early eighteenth century, satellite settlements already contained about one-third of the Indian population in Yucatan, a proportion that remained constant during the next century,[30] while the absolute numbers more than doubled along with the total Indian population. The wide variation among parishes revealed in the late colonial count (see appendix 1) may have been due primarily to differences in the amount of territory each possessed. For example, the parish of Halacho, where only 13 percent of the population lived outside the towns, simply had much less land and far fewer satellite settlements than nearby Uman, where 69 percent of the population was dispersed.

Colonial dispersal followed two patterns—linear or circular—depending on whether the parent town was on an open, expanding frontier or surrounded by other settled communities. Variations on both patterns have been described in the ethnographic literature for eastern Yucatan. In colonial times towns on the frontiers followed a process very similar to the founding and settlement earlier in this century of the village of Chan Kom, described by Robert Redfield and Alfonso Villa Rojas.[31] The most dynamic colonial frontier was located east and south of Campeche, where towns expanded into the *despoblado* by creating archipelagos of dependent *ranchos*, which in turn became towns and produced their own pioneer *ranchos* still further on.[32]

Much more common was the process described by William Sanders for the Valladolid region, in which the new settlements sprout up in a roughly circular pattern around the parent community.[33] In colonial times they ranged in distance from one-quarter of a league to five leagues (that is, from one to 20 kilometers). The extent of dispersal was limited then by the boundaries of the adjacent towns. In recent times the boundaries of the town *ejidos* (common lands) set the limits. As I have said, there was no empty, unclaimed land in Spanish-controlled Yucatan; all land within the jurisdiction of a *república de indios* not privately owned was in a sense its *ejidos*. People might slip over into the lands owned by the next town to make milpa but not, with rare exceptions, to settle there permanently.[34]

The dispersal process reversed the friars' congregation program, but it disturbed neither the ranked hierarchy of sites they had established (or confirmed) by the organization of parishes, nor the jurisdictional boundaries of the pueblos themselves, except where *ranchos* extended into unclaimed territory along the frontiers. In many cases the original settlement pattern was literally recreated by establishing *ranchos* on the sites of former towns that had been relocated. Except for these towns, which formally reconstituted themselves again at their original locations, we have no way of telling whether the sites simply happened to be the most suitable for settlement, or whether nostalgia and prior claim had some influence on the choice.[35]

Regardless of size or distance, these *ranchos* (as opposed to the towns that moved back to their original sites) remained subordinate to the parent pueblos. Their inhabitants appeared on the town tax rolls and parish records; they were subject to the authority of the *batab* and elected officials, and in every other way were considered full-fledged members of their *república de indios*. If a *rancho* grew large enough, it might petition the colonial authorities for legal incorporation as a separate *república* with its own set of officials confirmed by the Spanish governor, and its own church. Even then the ties with the parent community were not completely severed, for as a *visita* the new town retained a certain dependence on the parish *cabecera*. Other, less flourishing settlements simply remained as totally subordinate appendages or disappeared after a time, their populations absorbed by nucleated towns or new hamlets. Residents of a satellite hamlet might feel a certain civic pride in the growth of their settlement and the attainment of independent status as a new town. But in a sense such success nullified the very advantages that dispersal offered in the first place—relative freedom from the physical and social constraints of nucleated settlement.

Easy access to milpa land was surely a major incentive for the dispersed settlement pattern that reemerged during the colonial period. It has been suggested that the Maya "fled back into the forests" after congregation because of the "difficulty of maintaining large communities with slash-and-burn agriculture."[36] It is important not to confuse preference with necessity. Whatever may be the maximum local population density that milpa agriculture can support in Yucatan, the congregation program did not create anything approaching it. Though fewer in number, the congregated towns were no larger than most of the protohistoric settlements: the program simply redistributed a population that had declined drastically since first contact, and continued to fall. With the exception of some coastal cities that also relied on fishing, the preconquest centers had subsisted primarily on milpa production, supplemented by intensive horticulture in the towns themselves.[37] The congregated populations were also considerably smaller than the later colonial towns that were still supported by the same techniques. Compared to a 1579 census in which no town contained more than two thousand people,[38] by the early nineteenth century, twenty-two towns had between two thousand and four thousand, and eight had been four thousand and fifteen thousand, in addition to the two urban centers of Merida and Campeche (see appendix 1).

The Maya did not flee from the incorporated towns immediately after congregation; they moved out gradually and independently of any general demographic trends. And they left the towns not because they could not subsist in them, but because they could do so more conveniently by dispersing. Even though the towns suffered no real shortage of lands for most of the colonial period, shifting agriculture by its nature rapidly creates a shortage of fallow land close to any population center. If, as the colonial authorities calculated, a nuclear family needs on the average at least twelve hectares of land to support itself over the fifteen-year cycle of rotation, it will not require a very high population density before some squeeze, some inconvenience, is felt. What density will be tolerated above the level of one family per twelve hectares will depend on the strength of the community's integrative forces. When these are weak, dispersal will proceed even when, as happened for a century and a half after conquest, the population is also in sharp decline.

The question of inconvenience, or what William Skinner has called the "friction of distance,"[39] must therefore be viewed as relative. The stronger the social ties that bound a *milpero* to his community, the longer the distance or time he would be willing to travel to his milpa. Distance and time were virtually equivalent throughout the peninsula, since the terrain is fairly uniform and everyone traveled by foot along the trails that still connect towns and villages to outlying milpas. But the critical travel time or distance, the point at which the *milpero* decided to move away from town, cannot be reduced to any general formula.

The move itself may have been a two-stage affair. As in many parts of the lowlands today, the men would build *champas*, or temporary shelters, at distant milpas. They remained there the entire week during the periods of most intensive work—clearing, planting, and weeding—

209

and returned home only for the obligatory Sunday mass. At some point, possibly when they tired of cooking their own food (Maya men are quite capable of making their own tortillas out of the corn meal dough they take with them to the milpas, but they do not like to) and washing their own clothes, they would move the entire household—above all the wife with her *metate* and *comal*—out to the milpa. For some the move was permanent, and the new house site became the nucleus of a new satellite settlement.[40]

The process of dispersal in colonial Yucatan rarely if ever reached the extreme of a single individual or even a single nuclear family living in total isolation. The point at which dispersal ended and aggregation began seems generally to have been a group of several nuclear families or one such family plus several adults, usually brothers or grown sons or other patrilineally related males who cultivated common or adjacent milpas. In other words, the same milpa gang that formed the basic unit of food production was, not surprisingly, the core of a new hamlet.[41]

Despite a very different type of physical environment, the Andean region of South America experienced a roughly similar process of dispersal, which reversed a resettlement program carried out in the 1580s under Viceroy Francisco de Toledo. In the Andes, forced nucleation conflicted not with a rotating field system of maize cultivation, but with a complex socioeconomic structure that had been developed for exploiting the region's diversity of environments—what John Murra has called the "archipelago" system of community organization. The Andean resettlements gathered together groups whose only link was contiguous territory, while separating the component "islands" of the traditional communities.[42] They were therefore much more artificial creations than the congregated towns in Yucatan, where social identity seems to have been much more territorially based and where the compression of subunits into large wholes did not cut across existing sociopolitical boundaries.

The Indians in Peru began to drift back into their traditional settlement patterns, which often resembled the scattered *rancherías* of Mesoamerica, almost as soon as they had been forceably moved, and many of the towns were reduced to "administrative fictions" with few full-time residents.[43] This dispersal can no more be attributed to pressure on land than the similar process in Yucatan. The native population in colonial Peru also suffered a severe decline precisely at the time when people were moving out. It was, instead, a similar reassertion of the prevailing norms for exploiting the environment that motivated the colonial Maya, even if the norms and the environment themselves differed.

In Yucatan the mode of food production merely created a preference

9. Two phases of dispersed settlement: Top, temporary *champa* at a milpa site; the planting of banana trees and palms suggests a move toward long-term residence. Bottom, *rancho*; the wattle-and-daub construction is typical of most Maya houses outside the large towns. (Photos by Arthur G. Miller)

for scattered settlement, which could remain more or less dormant according to the strength of the counterbalancing social forces that held the communities together, or, conversely, according to the burdens and vexations of communal existence. One especially irritating feature of town life for the Indians throughout the Spanish empire was the presence of Spaniards and other non-Indians. There is no evidence that the royal decrees prohibiting *vecinos* from living in Indian pueblos were ever applied in colonial Yucatan. The idea behind the Crown's segregation policy, a benevolent form of apartheid, was to protect the Indians from what was considered morally contaminating contact with mixed bloods (and even the Spanish, whose conduct was seen as a poor advertisement for Christianity) and also from the ill treatment that seemed an inevitable feature of Indian-*vecino* relations.[44]

The Indians' best protection in Yucatan was the Spaniards' own preference for other colonies and for the major towns. Nevertheless, Spaniards, mulattoes, and mestizos eventually spread out, if thinly, into many corners of the colony, and the Maya had every reason to consider these intruders a thorough nuisance.[45] No matter how lowly in station, most non-Indians considered themselves entitled to deference, food, and transport from the Indians. Spaniards invariably succeeded in obtaining them; *castas* did so with varying success, depending on whether they were working for a Spaniard or on their own behalf. It has been suggested that in the Chortí region of Tabasco, where *ladinos* inhabit the core towns and the Indians the hamlets, the Indians have all moved out to escape the *ladinos*.[46] In Yucatan the pattern of dispersal had no strict correlation with the presence of non-Indians. Purely Maya towns spawned as many hamlets as those with a mixed population. And while dispersed settlements generally were first established by Indians, many ended up after a time with non-Indian residents also. Thus escape from them, if that was the motive for dispersing, was at best only a temporary achievement.

The only way to escape the presence of non-Indians entirely was to flee across the frontier. However, some of the other oppressive features of pueblo life could be avoided to some extent by moving to a satellite settlement. As noted earlier, these settlements remained under the jurisdiction of the parent town, subject to the same rules and obligations enforced there. In theory there was no distinction between those who lived in the dependent hamlets and those who lived in the towns. Many censuses did in fact lump them together as if all were physically as well as juridically part of the same community. But the fact of physical separation inevitably diluted the effective authority of both the parish priests and the town officials.

Just how much freedom hamlet residents gained is open to question. The evidence comes mainly from the clergy, and their opinions differ widely. Several are on record as having insisted that hamlet residents fulfilled their Christian duties as well as anyone in the pueblos.[47] One bishop, known for a variety of eccentric notions, actually favored dispersal on the grounds that it would increase agricultural production.[48] In a series of reports in the early 1780s the parish clergy divided fairly equally on the issue among those who expressed no concern about the effects of dispersal, those who complained in mild terms about the inconvenience of ministering to a widely scattered population, and those, particularly the Franciscans, who lamented in great detail and with equal vehemence the moral and spiritual depravity into which dispersed settlement was leading the Maya.[49] Few better examples could be found of the difficulties of reconstructing colonial Maya life through the words of their alien masters.

There can be little doubt that ecclesiastical supervision was considerably less rigorous in the hamlets than in the towns, even when the latter had no resident priest. In the towns the clergy obliged the Maya to break up their large, extended-family residences and to cluster their houses close together and build them with entrances toward the streets, rather than the traditional backyard doorway, which supposedly could more easily conceal sinful behavior within. In the hamlets they were able to regroup under the same roof and build their houses as they chose. Moreover, distance from the parent community was often compounded by a reversion to the more haphazard and loosely scattered precongregation pattern of house sites.[50] Under these circumstances, the hamlet resident appointed as the priest's agent (*fiscal*) had little more chance of monitoring local morals (if in fact he had wanted to) than the priest himself, who at best might visit the settlement during the prescribed semiannual parish tours of inspection.[51]

According to some clergymen, few of the inhabitants learned even the rudiments of Christian doctrine necessary for salvation. Hamlets were often too far for everyone to be obliged to attend weekly mass in the towns. Instead they came in turns, half one Sunday and half the next, when they did not feign illness and stay away for weeks at a time. Such catechism as the children learned was taught by the *fiscal*, who was ordinarily no less ignorant and confused than his pupils. Most died without the last rites, and many infant souls were condemned to limbo because the *fiscales* and midwives were incapable of memorizing the proper formula for valid baptism in such emergencies.

Some curates also saw in each hamlet a miniature Sodom or Gomorrah, where people freely indulged in incest, concubinage, wife-swapping, drunkenness, idolatry, and a variety of other "execrable deeds" to which the Maya were considered prone even when under the watchful eye of their spiritual guardians.[52] How much of this vision derived from what priests learned from the Maya themselves in the obligatory yearly confessions and how much was a product of their own fertile imaginations is hard to say. That vice and sin could go relatively unchecked in the *ranchos* is unquestionable, but evidence for their existence is inevitably less solid. What was so disturbing to the Spanish ecclesiastical mind was precisely the freedom dispersed residence afforded, regardless of what the Indians in fact chose to do with it.

The moral significance that the early missionaries had attached to the division between town and forest continued to inform their successors' attitudes throughout the colonial period. Even Spaniards who recognized a link between local techniques of food production and the Maya's propensity to scatter into the bush still viewed this preference with unease, while acknowledging the practical advantages to the farmer.[53] To some it meant a subversion of good government (*buena policía*); to others, especially among the clergy, the forest represented a threat to Christianity, a place where the Maya could revert to paganism and savagery, conditions which the clergy had come to see as synonymous.[54]

Movement away from the nucleated towns became a serious concern mainly during the eighteenth century. The process had begun much earlier, within decades after congregation, in fact, but both the church and the state had focused their concern on the more threatening problem of flight into the zones of refuge. Toward the end of the seventeenth century, attention shifted to the long pacified areas, where more and more discontented town dwellers who might previously have fled across the colonial frontiers were choosing the modified form of apostasy represented by dispersed settlement. The clergy, however, did not succeed in enlisting the same degree of secular support against dispersal as against flight. The Crown was not prepared to back a new program of congregation when the first one had long since served its purpose of evangelizing the Indians and consolidating the military conquest. Local officials might from time to time favor resettlement on the grounds that dispersed Indians could more easily evade taxes and labor drafts or even, after the Jacinto Canek revolt, that they posed a threat to the colony's security.[55] But their efforts were futile, largely because the majority of Spanish colonists found themselves on the side of the Indians in a rare concurrence of interests. The first *encomenderos* had opposed much of the original congregation program, and their successors, the owners of landed estates (most of whom were *encomenderos* also), helped to subvert it.

The Landed Estate as Satellite Settlement

The early growth of the hacienda (or *estancia* as it was originally called) in Yucatan was part of the process of dispersal into the empty spaces between the congregated towns. In fact, colonial censuses and other documents referring to population distribution often fail to distinguish between residents of independent hamlets and tenants on privately owned estates.[56] To the parish clergy who compiled the censuses, the significant issue was not property ownership but settlement patterns: that is, how many of their parishioners lived in the incorporated pueblos (*bajo de campana*, literally "under the church bell") and how many lived in the surrounding countryside (*fuera de campana*). As frustrating as this lack of clarity is to the historian seeking to trace the growth of the landed estates, it reflects a certain social reality. During most of the colonial period—that is, until the rapid growth of commercial agriculture in the late eighteenth century—the distinction between private estate and hamlet was also relatively meaningless from the point of view of the Indian residents and their parent communities.

The Maya lived on the *estancias* in much the same way as in the *ranchos* or hamlets. They moved there as freely, and they were equally free to move away. For a long time rural labor recruitment in colonial Latin America was thought to be entirely based on overt coercion in one form or another. According to the traditional scenario, the forced labor drafts of the early period gave way to full-time resident labor entrapped into a system of debt peonage from which there was no escape. Charles Gibson and others have begun to salvage some of the "evil reputation" of the colonial hacienda with evidence that debts and peonage were not invariably synonymous.[57] The workers rather than the *hacendados*, it would seem, often held the upper hand in these transactions. They demanded credit as part of the terms of employment and they had the freedom to move on in search of the best terms as long as (admittedly a big qualification) the demand for rural labor exceeded the supply. What coercion existed was largely indirect: in the form of taxation that made Indians dependent on a cash income, and in the physical expansion of the haciendas, which left many Indians and *castas* landless. Even without large cash advances, the hacienda offered a form of security for tax obligations and subsistence that pueblo life could not provide.

In Yucatan the inducements to move on to Spanish estates were far more subtle. Indeed, at first sight they appear nonexistent. No land shortages pushed the Indians there during most of the period, and the *estancias* provided no credit or other financial security for any but a handful of their residents—the salaried cowhands and foremen, who were the only estate residents with the status of *criados* and the only ones whose tax obligations became the responsibility of the owners.

The *criados* were skilled and highly valued employees who were able to demand salary advances as a perquisite of the job. I find no evidence that debts were used to prevent *criados* from moving to another *estancia* (except possibly the money the owners owed *them* in back wages).[58] Owners were more likely to reduce or waive accumulated debts in their wills as a reward for long service.[59] Thus the evidence from Yucatan supports the revised conclusions from other areas that credit was more of an inducement than a form of entrapment. Moreover, it applied to only a small part of the work force.

Most of the residents were not salaried employees. They were the type of tenant farmer (called *lunero* in Yucatan) that is common to the traditional hacienda all over Spanish America under a variety of local titles. What distinguished the system in Yucatan from that of more highly developed agrarian economies was the extremely loose and easy terms for residence on the estates. So long as these were mainly cattle ranches, the demand for resident labor was low, too low for the owners to waste scarce cash in credit advances; and they vehemently resisted all attempts to make them liable for the tribute payment of their *luneros*.[60] Yet the *luneros* were welcomed. They did not interfere with the basic function of the *estancia*. Land was abundant and the burden of protecting milpas from livestock fell on the farmer; once harvested the milpas provided good forage for the cattle. If the tenants were not crucial to the enterprise they could nevertheless be useful. The small amount of maize they cultivated for the owner as part of their residential tax—or rent—fed the ranch hands and the owner's family, and any surplus supplemented the main income from cattle. They could also be called upon to help at branding time, for construction and repairs, and for any other odd jobs that might be required.[61] The rancher could apply for labor drafts from the towns to cultivate his milpas and perform the other unskilled work. But it was much more convenient to have a resident labor force of one's own, without bureaucratic intervention and without competition from other, perhaps more influential claimants.

The *luneros*, for their part, were willing—by most accounts even eager—recruits. We must look elsewhere besides shortages of community lands for the reason. The *estancias*, for one thing, could offer a convenient water supply; more precisely they could offer the new technology of the *noria* (mule-powered water wheel), constructed to water the cattle but also very useful for handwatering household gardens. The *noria*, however, could have been an attraction only for residents who clustered around the *planta*, or core, not to the majority of tenants who lived in scattered settlements. These were like hamlets in every way except that they happened to be located on estate property. And since property boundaries were so vague for much of the period, there had to be some reason why these dispersed residents chose to be affiliated with an *estancia*. The main advantage, perhaps the sole advantage for most tenants, was the patronage of the estate's owner. This was no small attraction. For he could serve as a counterpoise to the authority of the priests and town officials and thus provide an even greater measure of freedom from the burdens and constraints of pueblo life. In effect the tenants exchanged the traditional patron–client relationship with their own leaders (and to a certain extent with the parish priest) for a fairly loose one with the owner, who—until the shift to more intensive exploitation of the estates—demanded considerably less in return for his patronage.

In theory *luneros* remained members of their *república de indios* the same as any hamlet resident. Only the ranch hands as *criados* enjoyed any formal exemptions from forced labor drafts. In practice almost any rancher could provide some immunity against them. The Indians could usually exchange labor on the estate for the invariably more burdensome obligations of the pueblo.[62] The *tequios*, which were a kind of community residence tax, were identical to the labor rent on the estates and obviously their origin: as explained in chapter 1, the term *lunero* is derived from the customary day, *lunes* (Monday), for performing *tequios* in the pueblos. The difference was that the tenant, unlike the hamlet resident, did not have to travel to the pueblo and was also often protected from *servicio personal*, courier service, road building, and all the other forms of compulsory labor that were the pueblo Indian's lot.

The estate owners rarely if ever took the same interest as the clergy in the faith and morals of their Maya "clients." The largest estates eventually constructed their own churches, and some owners tried to have the churches declared *ayudas de parroquia* (a quasi-*visita* status) so that the priest would be obliged to celebrate mass there rather than require attendance in the parent town.[63] Few succeeded but most, with or without an estate church, were prepared to shield their tenants from punishment if they chose to play truant from regular attendance at mass as well as from community labor service.[64] So useful was the estate as a buffer from the authority of clergy and town officials that Indians reportedly connived to create bogus *estancias*. Settlers establishing their own hamlets would seek out a cooperative Spaniard to pose as owner, even supplying him with the money to pay their tribute and other taxes as fictional *criados*.[65] In return the Spaniard acquired a set of clients who cultivated a small amount of milpa for him and could also be called upon when he needed some extra labor.

The exodus of community members, whether through flight, drift, or dispersal, was a source of concern to the Indian officials as well as to the parish clergy. The officials may have cared little about the maintenance of Christian morals, as the clergy alleged, but they did care about the erosion of the community's human resources to meet Spanish assessments and the community's own needs.

Tribute and *obvenciones*, which were paid in small installments over the year, were harder to collect from people dispersed in hamlets and estates.[66] Communal labor obligations were even harder to enforce, and it was well nigh impossible to keep track of Indians who floated from hamlet to hamlet perhaps halfway across the peninsula. Expeditions organized to search for runaways in other districts seem to have met with little success. Refugees across the frontier were of course beyond reach, but drifters to distant parishes were not much easier to find. Some of the clergy asserted that large numbers of Indians were able to disappear from official view by hiding in remote hamlets (always, to be sure, in someone else's parish), able to evade taxes and forced labor altogether. Even if most migrants did not succeed in becoming permanent dropouts, and no evidence has been found in support of these allegations, they would be lost to the tax rolls of their native community.

Because of the competition for manpower, everyone in the colony conspired in one way or another to undermine the congregation program and the integrity of the communities created by the resettlements. In pursuit of their particular interests, the richest and most powerful Spaniards in the province encouraged Indians to transfer from the pool of draft labor to their own private employ in the cities and *estancias*. The parish clergy complained about tax evasion and the risks of bigamous unions that the facility of migration offered (along with the moral and economic drawbacks of dispersed settlement),[67] and the Indian officials, too, complained about the loss of their own community members. Yet both abetted the population drift they deplored by welcoming *forasteros* from other towns and without regard to whether they were tax truants.

CORE AND MARGIN IN MAYA SOCIETY

The colonial Maya were not all equally prone to uproot themselves from their native communities. We have no way of calculating how many of them made this choice. Even if census figures for *forasteros* were complete, they would still not account for escapees to the zones of refuge or for those who may have lived undetected in the bush in the more sparsely settled areas under nominal Spanish control. Whatever the numbers of the uprooted, and these undoubtedly fluctuated considerably with the pressures of Spanish demands and with the occurrence of epidemics, famines, and other crises that drove people from their homes, the choice to leave permanently does not seem to have been entirely random. It is possible to distinguish between a stable core population within Maya society, which remained fixed in place for generation after generation despite temporary displacements during times of crisis, and a more or less fluid group of migrants, who might eventually become incorporated into the core population of a community but who were as likely to move on before that happened.[68]

Not surprisingly, the community elite were part of the core group. What accounts for greater or lesser geographical mobility within the *macehual* population is not so obvious. The structure of colonial Maya society can be discerned from the documentary record only in crude outline. In particular the record gives little sense of the finer gradations that existed among the large and superficially undifferentiated category of *macehuales*, gradations that might help to explain why some more readily abandoned their homes than others. I assume that people did not uproot themselves out of pure wanderlust, that ties of family and community, even if attenuated under postconquest conditions, remained strong enough to make separation a considered, perhaps ordinarily painful, choice determined by some difficulty at home. It would not be necessary that moving elsewhere should actually ease the difficulty, only that people should believe that it would.

It may be that the only differences among *macehuales* were merely accidental or operational and not structural. For all of them, existence was so marginal that any added personal disadvantage could push someone over the line. It is significant in this respect that so many of the migrants were married people with young children rather than unattached young adults,[69] who in the traditional model of rural migration are the ones squeezed out by land shortages; that is, we expect people to leave because they cannot afford to settle down to married life in the villages. The economic opportunity to marry, in the form of enough milpa land to support a family, was accessible to everyone within the village sphere in colonial Yucatan. But it was precisely during this early phase of family formation that life could be most precarious for the Maya *macehual*, because of the postconquest distortion of the reciprocal arrangement of the extended family. Illness, injury, or crop loss could strike anyone at any time. The young couple, on whom the heaviest burdens of family support fell, would have the least cushion against such catastrophe, would be the most likely to fall into debt and tax arrears. And emigration provided one remedy, if only temporary.

Emigration would also presumably free the young couple from labor obligations toward senior kin, completing the process begun by the Spaniards of breaking up the three-generation corporate family. We do not know that the Maya in fact repudiated their filial obligations by changing residence. Family elders may have died already, especially during the famines and epidemics that were the major immediate stimulus for leaving home. I suggest only that the burdens of parental support, until removed by death or migration, could have made life precarious enough for young couples to make permanent migration an attractive choice.

The exact causes of colonial Maya migration may always remain a matter for speculation. Apart from economic stress, personal quarrels and conflicts with local officials could have driven them from their villages too.[70] Such motives would cut across divisions of age and economic condition, although we could expect that those who bore the heaviest share of civic and family burdens might also feel the most disaffected and more often find themselves at odds with their fellows. Older adults, aside from their firmer roots in the community through longer residence, which would make them more reluctant to leave, would also have less cause for estrangement.

Whatever may have distinguished the *macehuales* who chose to abandon their native villages from the ones who remained part of the stable core population, by leaving home they ipso facto entered the category of marginals, where they would remain until or unless they became fully integrated into a new community. We know from parish registers that migrants forged ritual kinship ties of *compadrazgo* with natives as well as other *forasteros* in their new homes. But no analysis has yet been made of the frequency, and in any case it would be impossible to ascertain whether these ties were established fairly quickly or only after long residence. Although other information on how newcomers fared is difficult to come by, the evidence we have on the local political system offers some insight into how the condition of marginality could easily become self-perpetuating.

First of all, positions of responsibility in the colonial Maya communities were reserved for the native born. Many thousands of community officials are named in various kinds of records over the centuries, in the administration of municipalities, parishes, and *cofradías*. Of those whose place of origin can be identified, less than 10 percent fall into the category of *forasteros*.[71] Rather than any formal rule excluding newcomers, it was the local political system with its networks of elite alliances and patronage ties that would work against them. The second relevant political fact is that official positions within the colonial community offered more than prestige; they carried real power that could be used to forge and sustain alliances and systems of clientage. Given the opportunities for preferential treatment, the newcomers were likely to be at a disadvantage: welcomed as additions to the tax rolls and labor supply but placed at the bottom of the heap when it came to the myriad rewards and punishments that were within the power of the community leadership to distribute. They could expect the least convenient house sites, the least attractive tasks in the community *tequios*, the least chance of gaining exemptions from these and other labor drafts, and the least likelihood of obtaining any indulgence for late payment of taxes or for any other infractions of the rules.

A low level of integration into the community network may explain the reports of more than a casual connection between intercommunity migration and settlement in outlying hamlets. Lacking any influence or customary claims to the best and most accessible milpa lands, newcomers would come last in the allocation of sites. They would be pushed to the outskirts of the community's territory—just as they occupied its social periphery—if in fact they had not chosen to settle there from the beginning as a reflection of their own general alienation from community ties.

In a study of Spanish American agrarian structure in the late colonial and early independence periods, Arnold Bauer has divided the rural poor into two groups. He contrasts a stable population consisting of villagers and landless peons more or less permanently attached to the Spanish-owned estates with "an astonishingly large mass of people" who wandered around the countryside in search of food and seasonal labor and sometimes joined the human flotsam of the cities.[72] Yucatan did not reach this advanced degree of rural dislocation, which, as Bauer plausibly argues, was a result of a latifundio system that combined the monopolization of land with a low demand for manpower. The major growth of landed estates in Yucatan coincided with a shift to labor-intensive export agriculture, primarily henequen, so that as Indians were dispossessed of their own land they could be absorbed into the plantation labor force. Indeed, the demand for labor was such that a population of unemployed drifters could not be tolerated by the land-owning oligarchy.[73]

In comparison with more economically advanced regions of the empire, then, rural society in colonial Yucatan seems relatively homogeneous and social dislocation relatively mild despite the amount of physical movement from place to place. If there were any permanently rootless vagrants, they were too few to warrant mention by contemporary observers. Indian migrants remained within the general village system, even if peripheral to local patronage networks. And there was no formalized two-tiered structure within the system as in the Andes, where

221

migrants gained exemption from labor drafts but lost any rights to community lands.[74] Newcomers to a Maya community might find themselves relegated to the least attractive milpa sites but were not denied access to communal resources altogether. In that sense the colonial Maya community was completely open, its membership defined by residence and not by birthplace.

The geographical mobility of the colonial Yucatec Maya calls into question some long-cherished notions about postconquest Indian society. In particular it calls into question Eric Wolf's classic model of the "closed corporate community,"[75] which has exerted such a powerful influence on the way that anthropologists and historians have looked at peasant societies and rural communities. The central idea behind the model, that Indian society under colonial rule separated into cocoon-like entities—communities—as isolated from each other as they were from the dominant Spanish-mestizo society, is certainly valid as far as political ties go. The model is not, however, primarily a political one, but an economic one based on the allocation of scarce resources. The rationale for the isolation is seen as the need to ensure the subsistence of the members of each community through a careful balance between land and population. This balance in turn is supposed to rest—and to have rested—on the mutually reinforced attributes of solidarity and exclusivity, or corporateness and closedness. To incorporate outsiders would undermine the cohesiveness needed to withstand Spanish pressures on communally owned resources. More importantly, it would place an added strain on the resources. In other words, survival required that each community close itself off from the rest of Indian society as well as from the surrounding Spanish world that pressed in on it.

For all its elegance, the model has to be revised to take into account the accumulating evidence on intercommunity migration. In Yucatan in particular, the town boundaries were as permeable as the colonial frontiers and, like them, permeable in both directions. It was not simply a question of sloughing off surplus people to the haciendas and cities in order to maintain a stable ratio between population and land. People moved from one town to another and even, though less frequently, from satellite settlement to nucleated town. The point is that newcomers were not merely tolerated; they were, as I have indicated, cordially welcomed.

This evidence need not totally invalidate the traditional view. It may be possible to separate the "closed" attribute, based on the premise that land was always and everywhere a scarce commodity, from the "corporate" attribute. While population movements obviously eroded the isolation of communities, they need not have destroyed their boundaries or corporate character. Community boundaries, like ethnic boundaries, "may persist despite what may figuratively be called the 'osmosis' of personnel through them."[76]

The large-scale population movements recorded in colonial Yucatan must have represented a serious erosion of corporate identity for the migrants themselves, but not necessarily a breakdown of the corporate community. The integrity of the community could be maintained provided that some portion of the population remained stable. How large and how fluid the marginal population would have to be before it swamped the communities and destroyed their corporate identity is unknown, for that does not seem to have occurred in colonial Yucatan. The fabric of Maya society became somewhat threadbare and frayed at the edges under colonial rule, but it did not entirely unravel.

PART THREE
ADAPTATION AND
SURVIVAL

· 8 ·

MAYA ELITES: THE FIXED
CENTER

The colonial Maya community survived as a viable social entity because of the continuity and cohesion provided by the core population that did not drift or disperse—the ruling elite together with an undetermined number of *macehual* "old-timers." The native elite in particular were the fixed center of each community, stable socially as well as geographically, and as such the linchpin of Maya society. They did not merely represent the community; in many ways they *were* the community: the repositories of its history, the trustees of the corporate patrimony for future generations. They were also the architects of the adaptive strategies required to meet the new conditions of Spanish rule, strategies that allowed the Maya community, and with it Maya culture, to survive the shock of conquest. Since the survival of Maya society and culture in some form depended so heavily on the leadership of the elite, how they themselves managed to survive as a ruling group deserves some scrutiny.

That social ranking persisted among the conquered Maya is unquestionable. There is ample evidence for the existence throughout the colonial period of a native elite in whose hands were concentrated what political power and wealth the Spanish did not appropriate for themselves. What remains at issue is the nature of the social hierarchy and whether it continued to be based on hereditary principles. In other words, can we speak of a colonial Maya nobility or merely some functional equivalent?

The Native Nobility: Mesoamerican Comparisons

The idea that the Maya nobility should have survived the cataclysm of conquest is not wholly inconsistent with current views on the colonial history of other advanced pre-Columbian societies in America. Most students would still agree with Pedro Carrasco that the "most important change" in Mesoamerican society since conquest was the "elimination of the nobility as a separate group with inherited rank, private landholdings, and exclusive right to office."[1] But an earlier view of total social devastation immediately in the wake of Spanish military victories has been modified. The conquerors had neither the means nor the inclination to wipe the sociopolitical slate clean. But if, according to the now-accepted version, the transformation from a complex hierarchy to a simple peasant society was a more protracted and complicated process than originally believed, the end result remained the same and seems to have been accomplished everywhere well before the end of the colonial period.

Not all the native nobility in Mesoamerica and the Andes are seen to have shared identical fates. Two very diverging destinies awaited them, both entailing the disappearance of the native lords qua native lords. A fortunate few managed to preserve high status and wealth, but only by removing themselves in all but the most technical sense from Indian society. The wealthy Peruvian *kurakas* and Mexican *caciques* who prospered under colonial rule, surpassing many Spaniards in the size of their incomes and their sumptuary style of life, derived their wealth originally from their hereditary prerogatives—control over land and especially over labor. The entrepreneurial techniques they adopted to retain and increase their wealth and the ways they chose to display it were Spanish, and these new modalities helped to separate them socially and culturally as well as physically from the indigenous world. They operated instead on the fringes of the Spanish world. They built fine houses in the Spanish style in the cities, managed their estates as absentee landlords like any Spanish *hacendado*, engaged in commerce, sought Spanish titles and honors, and in general emulated the colonial rulers with considerable success if not total acceptance.

The rest of the native nobility, those who remained wholly within Indian society by choice or necessity, found their incomes eroded and their local authority challenged by ambitious *macehuales* with the support of the Spanish, who at the same time were rapidly whittling away at the economic base and political autonomy of the Indian polities. These native lords, then, soon sank into the common mass, distinguishable, if at all, by the scraps of paper some of them retained bearing Spanish confirmation of titles that had lost all meaning. In either case, the Indian nobility ceased to exist; the one group was Indian in name only and the other noble in name only.[2]

Perhaps even this version exaggerates the speed and thoroughness of the nobility's disappearance. Closer inspection might reveal them to be an endangered rather than an extinct species even in late colonial Peru and Mexico, able to preserve some of their former position by strategic adaptation to a radically altered habitat.[3] I am less concerned, however, with questioning the accuracy of the currently accepted view than with its applicability outside the core regions of the two viceroyalties—to areas like Yucatan, where pre-Columbian social organization was similar but where Spanish power, population, and economic activity were all more diluted.

Until recently the fate of the Maya nobility appeared to follow precisely the second alternative presented in the core colonies. The similarity between the "cacique system" described by Ralph Roys for Yucatan and the central Mexican model is not altogether surprising, since he relied heavily on data from that region.[4] The bulk of local evidence supports a very different picture. The early postconquest experiment with assimilation discussed in chapter 3 gave way to a clear separation between native and foreign rulers; and the Maya nobility neither removed themselves from native society nor lost their dominant position within it. The failure to become rich but decultured hangers-on at the periphery of Spanish society may not have been entirely a matter of choice. Even if it should turn out that caste boundaries were no more rigid in Yucatan than elsewhere, the colony's indisputable poverty meant that the native lords lacked the same opportunities for amassing wealth through Spanish-style entrepreneurship that were open to nobles of equivalent rank in Peru and Mexico. In no part of the Spanish empire did noble rank in itself guarantee Indians prosperity and high status within the larger colonial society; in Yucatan it failed to provide even a steppingstone.

From the viewpoint of this larger society, the Maya nobility had all but disappeared by the middle of the seventeenth century. In theory the Spanish continued to acknowledge a division between nobles and commoners among the Indians throughout the empire. Colonial law proclaimed that the descendants of those who had been "natural lords" of the land were to be accorded the same status and prerogatives as the Castilian nobility.[5] In Yucatan these distinctions were exceedingly blurred in practice. Some of the privileges were dictated by economics. For example, the right to bear arms and ride horses was in practice open to anyone who could afford to buy a musket and a horse, regardless of rank. The fact that both items were well out of the reach of most *macehuales* is another matter; differences in wealth were linked to rank within Maya society but did not depend on a patent of nobility issued by the Spanish authorities.

The meaningful noble prerogative of exemption from taxes was also largely divorced from noble rank. That and the use of the title "don" came to be confined to the appointed *batabs* of each town and their retired predecessors. Although these officials may still have been drawn from what the Maya recognized as a noble class, the privileges did not legally accrue to the class as a whole, but only to the particular office.

To enjoy these prerogatives by virtue of noble lineage rather than

229

municipal office required a special act of the colonial authorities. Records of only one such case have survived: the papers that the Xiu family of Mani province compiled in order to substantiate their successive claims.[6] The fact that no other comparable documents are known does not mean that the Xiu were unique. The presumption, however, is that such petitions were rare. Other noble families whose less elaborate dossiers of *mérito y servicios* reached the Spanish Crown in the early colonial period were not concerned with the question of noble status as such, perhaps because it was still taken for granted. They sought more tangible benefits in the form of royal pensions as a reward for specific services to the Crown.[7] The Xiu family's unique role in the Spanish conquest as allies of Montejo may help to explain both their persistence in seeking renewal of their titles and their success in obtaining it.

The appearance in many colonial documents of a group called *indios hidalgos*, which technically means "Indian nobles," could create some confusion over the postconquest history of the local nobility, and in particular could lead to the false conclusion that the official recognition and privileges obtained by the Xiu family were granted fairly extensively. *Indios hidalgos* were not, at least originally, Maya at all. They were descended from the auxiliary troops who had accompanied the Spanish on their second expedition into Yucatan and were granted the rank of hidalgo in perpetuity in recognition of their services in the conquest.[8] Referred to simply as "Mexicans" in later documents, these troops may have been predominantly Tlaxcalans and were certainly all Nahuatl speakers from the central highlands. They soon lost their separate cultural identity. Most blended into the local population, and a smaller proportion into *vecino* society. I suspect that the anomalous cases of acculturated Indians who appear in the later colonial records with Spanish surnames and who seem to operate freely within the Spanish world are from that group.[9]

Regardless of which cultural sphere individual hidalgos leaned toward, as a group they retained their separate legal identity and attendant privileges, including exemption from tribute and labor drafts; and the Spanish always made a careful distinction between hidalgos and *principales*—that is, the local Maya nobility. The quasi assimilation of most hidalgos as a privileged group within Maya society is reminiscent of what we are told in the chronicles of the Toltecs and other pre-Columbian predecessors from the highlands and intermediate areas, from whom the Xiu and other local ruling families claimed descent. However, this latest wave of Mexican invaders settled down in an entirely different context, in which complete assimilation into the local aristocracy was no longer so attractive. On the contrary, the incentives for maintaining a separate identity and thus escaping the burdens imposed by the new rulers were compelling, and they jealously guarded their patents of *hidalguía* (some of them falsified, according to Spanish officials) to prove the distinction.[10] Moreover they never formed part of the local Maya hierarchy in the sense of holding any public office in the communities. They had their own leaders, and functionally they can be considered less a branch of the Indian elite than as an Indian subcategory of *vecinos*.[11]

In contrast with the well-defined and formally acknowledged identity of the hidalgos, the Maya nobility faded into well-nigh total obscurity, reemerging again officially only in the 1780s when the local bishop decided to establish several scholarships earmarked specifically for members of the native nobility. By 1786 three "sons of *caciques*" were already pursuing theological studies at the Colegio of San Pedro in Merida,[12] and though no Indians appeared in the diocesan seminary of San Ildefonso until 1793, at least 11 of the 617 students enrolled there between 1793 and 1822 can be identified as Maya.[13]

Access to this education required considerable personal wealth in addition to scholarship aid, and the education necessary to prepare a young man for admission to one of the colleges would have been beyond the means of most of the *castas* as well as the vast majority of Indians. We know that there were Indians with large enough incomes to take advantage of this opportunity. However, the existence in the late eighteenth century of even a small minority of Maya who combined substantial wealth with the suitable genealogical credentials would not have easily been guessed from other Spanish records. Obviously the Maya nobility had disappeared only from Spanish view.

Other noble families with illustrious pedigrees may have been less assiduous than the Xiu in pressing their claims to formal titles of nobility because they realized how empty they were. If the Maya nobility survived into the late colonial period, this survival owed little if anything to recognition from the colonial government. They maintained their rank and, more important, many of their traditional privileges, not because the Spanish acknowledged the legitimacy of their claims but because the rest of Indian society did.

Structural and Functional Continuities

The chief prerogative the Maya nobility managed to retain, and the cornerstone of all the others, was political power. This power was reduced to the confines of individual communities, but within each community the nobility were able to preserve intact much of the pre-Co-

231

lumbian political system. Shortly after the conquest the Spanish introduced an entirely alien system of local government modeled on the municipal organization of Castile.[14] In other parts of Mesoamerica this system seems to have competed with and eventually replaced the original native structure. The Maya were able to interpret the new municipal offices in such a way that, despite changes in title, they replicated the preconquest chain of command.

Among the Postclassic Maya, the local polities were headed by a *batab* who ruled either independently or under the sway of a provincial *halach uinic*. Each *batab* had been assisted by a group of lesser lords: the *ahkulels*, who were the *batab*'s immediate deputies, and a town council consisting of all the local notables, some of whom (the *ahcuchcabs*) also acted as administrative heads of their wards, or *parcialidades*. There was also a *holpop*, whose place in the scheme is not entirely clear. He was certainly of high rank and had particular responsibility for directing public ceremonial and may have been one of the *ahcuchcabs* who held this title in rotation.[15]

The colonial version of the town council was called the *cabildo* (or *ayuntamiento*), presided over by a *gobernador*. It consisted of two *alcaldes* (sometimes called *justicias*) and almost invariably four *regidores*, regardless of the size of the town. (The standard division of the pre-Hispanic town seems to have been into four wards.)[16] The title *regidor* was used interchangeably with *ahcuchcab* in Maya and early Spanish documents. The *alcaldes'* antecedents are less clear. They seem to have inherited some of the duties of the *ahkulels* as community-wide executive and judicial officers directly under the *gobernador*, but they were considerably higher in rank, and the *ahkulel* may have been closer to the colonial *alguacil mayor*, a kind of head bailiff.

It is futile to try to trace the separate ancestry of each of the colonial offices. The main point is that the *gobernador*, whose prestige and functions were similar to those of the *batab* and who eventually merged with that post, continued to rule through several deputies or assistants, some of whose titles, like that of *procurador*, may have been little understood and put on the books simply to satisfy the Spanish.[17] The colonial *cabildo* was the authorized governing body of the community. However, the entire group of *principales*, from which the formally designated officials were drawn more or less in rotation, was consulted by the *batab* and other incumbent officers in major decisions, and was included as spokesmen on behalf of the community in many documents under the formula: "The *batab*, *justicias*, *regidores* and other [*demás*] *principales*. . . ."[18]

This same pool of *principales* also supplied the officers in the community *cofradías*, or confraternities, and the leading figures in the local ecclesiastical hierarchy that served in the parish churches. At the head of this hierarchy was a *maestro cantor* (choirmaster) and under him were a chief sacristan and his assistants, singers and musicians, catechists, and a host of *fiscales* (a catch-all title, similar to *tupil* or *alguacil* in civil administration), charged with a variety of menial tasks from burying the dead to rounding up the village children for catechism class.[19]

The pre-Columbian temple must have had a similar set of functionaries to assist at religious ceremonies and care for the physical fabric. The key link to the past and the key figure for the Maya in the colonial church was the *maestro cantor*, also called during early colonial times by the preconquest title of *ahcambezah* (sometimes *ahcamzah*), or chief teacher.[20] The full range of activities and responsibilities of the *maestros cantores* will be discussed in chapter 11. Their high social standing (second only to or perhaps equivalent to the *batabs'*), their important role in Christian ritual, and their exclusive control over whatever education the colonial Maya received, all suggest that the office combined attributes of both the pre-Columbian *ahkin* (high priest) and the *ahcambezah*.

The *cofradías* and their officers (*priostes* and *mayordomos*) would seem to have no pre-Columbian equivalents. But in fact they functioned as part of the same community administration rather than as parish brotherhoods on the European model, and thus they can be regarded as a civil-religious extension of the *cabildo*. They overlapped with the *cabildos* in function and in personnel, since the same people served in both either simultaneously or alternatively.[21]

The three groupings into which community leadership was divided (see figure 8.1) were pyramidal hierarchies that interlocked at two distinct levels. At the very top were the *maestro cantor*, the patron of the *cofradía* and the *batab-gobernador*, and with them the *escribano*, or town clerk. All these positions were long term, the *maestro's* for life. The *escribanos*, holding the only other post that required literacy, also had permanent tenure, except that they were usually appointed when quite young and might move up to fill a vacancy in one of the other three offices in the same tier.[22] The move may seem a large leap, but the *escribano* held a position of great responsibility, for he was entrusted with all the community records, including the vitally important land titles.

The offices of *cofradía* patron and *batab*, which, like the lesser offices in the *cofradía* and *cabildo*, were often held concurrently or sometimes alternately by the same person, were also long term, but how long is not certain and may not have been fixed. Many *batabs*, about whom we have more information than about patrons, died in office or retired only

FIGURE 8.1. COMMUNITY POLITICAL STRUCTURE

	República de indios	Cofradía	Church
First-tier elite	Batab/gobernador Escribano	Patrón Escribano de cofradía	Maestro Cantor
Second-tier elite	Alcaldes (2) Regidores (4) Mayordomo Procurador	Priostes (2) Mayordomos (4)	Sacristán Mayor Fiscal Mayor
(Commoners?)	Alguacil Mayor		Cantores Músicos Acólitos
Commoners	Alcalde Mesón Alguaciles Tupiles	Mayoral Vaqueros	Sacristanes Fiscales Cananob

because of advanced age or infirmity. On the basis of a long run of *cabildo* records from the town of Tekanto, Philip Thompson has suggested a term of twenty years, or one *katun* in the old Maya calendar.[23] The *katun* may have been the ideal term, in accordance with pre-Hispanic principles, and the deviations I have found from other communities could represent terms cut short by death or incapacity, or prolonged because of the lack of a genealogically suitable successor.

The next tier was elevated above the common mass but was definitely of second rank within the elite. The church functionaries constituted a completely separate group with its own internal ranking and its own rules for movement through the ranks, which were probably based on seniority. Officers in the interlocking systems of *cofradía* and *cabildo* changed annually, but the same names appear again and again, working their way up one or both hierarchies, in which *regidores* and *alcaldes*, *mayordomos*, and *priostes* were themselves ranked.[24] That the Maya concern with hierarchy was not purely theoretical can be seen in the orderly progression within the system and the distinction preserved between the various levels. It was rare in the known samples, although not unheard of, for anyone to cross the line from petty officialdom to the second tier of elites (for example, from *alguacil* to *regidor*), and also rare to move from the second to the first tier within the elite.

The functional and structural continuities between the pre-Columbian

FIGURE 8.2. EVOLUTION OF POLITICAL STRUCTURE

Pre-Hispanic	Early Colonial (16th Century)	Middle Colonial (17th Century)	Late Colonial (18th Century)
Batab	Batab → Gobernador →	Gobernador/Batab →	Batab
Ahcuchcab	Ahcuchcab → Regidor →	Regidor/Ahcuchcab →	Regidor
Ahkin Ahcambezah	Ahkin Maestro Cantor (Ahcambezah)	Maestro Cantor (Ahcambezah) →	Maestro Cantor

and colonial Maya political systems at the local level do not guarantee any genealogical continuity or even any similarity in the underlying social structure. The colonial regime did little to encourage the long-term maintenance of the traditional Maya ruling class, once their cooperation was no longer required to consolidate the military conquest. The Spanish still needed native leaders, but not necessarily the nobility. The descendants of the old ruling houses gradually lost recognition and status within the larger colonial society; at the same time, their position within Maya society was threatened by the creation of new administrative structures in which offices were gained either by appointment or election rather than through hereditary succession.

Logically these rival structures would shunt aside and eventually replace the rulers and other nobles. The procedures established for filling the new offices seemed to provide an opportunity for the emergence of a new elite from the ranks of the commoners. The *gobernador*, who was head of the *cabildo* and chief executive officer of the *república*, was to be appointed by the province's royal governor; the *cabildo* itself was to be elected, with no officers serving two terms in succession, and the church functionaries from the *maestro cantor* down were appointed by the parish priest.

For a time there seemed to exist two parallel and rival foci of authority: the hereditary *batab* and a clandestine Maya priesthood, on the one hand, matched by the *gobernador* and *maestro cantor* on the other. In practice, considerable overlap existed in personnel;[25] and instead of being eclipsed, the old system eventually merged with the new (see figure 8.2). The merger was complete by the latter part of the seventeenth century. By then, even though alternate titles continued to be used for a time, they referred to the same offices.[26] In order to survive with more than family pride to distinguish them from the mass of conquered Maya, the nobility had to take over the new apparatus of civil and ecclesiastical administration, and this they managed to do even before the merger. The new system permitted or encouraged some realignments within the ranks of the nobility; it did not signal the end of the nobility as a ruling group.

The crucial point is that despite formal appearances, the Maya themselves continued to control their own political system, including access to public office. The *principales* were able to retain control of the *cabildos* by the simple expedient of restricting the vote to outgoing officials. In some documents the *mayordomos* of the *cofradías* were said to be chosen in the same way—that is, elected by the outgoing incumbents; other documents state that they were chosen by the *cabildo*.[27] The formal mechanism did not much matter. The "electorate" for all the offices seems to have comprised the entire group of town notables.

The Spanish governor's confirmation of these yearly elections was, it would appear, a perfunctory matter, a vehicle like the occasional *residencias* taken of Indian officials for the purpose of extracting fees rather than supervising local affairs.[28] The scanty information on the appointment of *gobernadores* (reverting later to the title of *batab*) indicates that this same group of local *principales* also had the main voice, and probably in later years the sole voice, in their selection.[29] They presented by a still imperfectly understood process of selection a candidate on whom the royal governor, knowing little himself of local affairs, would bestow the formal title and appropriate emblem of office—the *bastón de mando*, the staff of command still used in Indian communities in the Maya highlands and in Peru. Both the ritual investiture and the appropriately staggering fee charged would be familiar to the Maya, who formerly took gifts to the *halach uinic* on the occasion of his installing the local *batabs* in office.

Church service, which might seem to offer new avenues to power within colonial Indian society, posed even less of a challenge to the traditional order than the new system of municipal government. The first *maestros cantores* were deliberately chosen from among the nobility, as one might expect, since they alone possessed the necessary prestige and authority over the masses.[30] Once selected and trained, they were able to control their own succession (as well as the choice of their assistants and that of the local *escribanos*) by their monopoly of the knowledge and skills needed for the jobs and their monopoly of local education through which the skills were transmitted.[31] The parish clergy could have widened their choice by taking charge of instruction themselves. By leaving the task to the *maestros*, and the choice of which boys in the catechism classes would receive the special training in music, sacred liturgy, and reading and writing, they effectively left control of church patronage in Maya hands.

In any system of indirect rule the authority of the native leaders rests on two foundations. It must be acceptable both to their colonial overlords and to their own people. The overlords demand submissiveness, and this the Spanish sought to ensure by replacing leaders whose position or actions challenged their own power.[32] Their choice of alternatives was not, however, limitless. Even if they exercised more direct control over local politics than we so far have evidence for in Yucatan, this does not mean that they would seek to create a new native elite or destroy the traditional distinctions of rank within Indian society by backing plebian candidates with dubious credentials. Aside from their own deeply rooted hierarchical values, their main concern was with the performance of community leaders, and the nobility could provide the best performance because of the force of legitimacy behind their authority. As long as the nobility recognized that their own survival required cooperation, the pragmatism of indirect rule on both sides favored continuity.

Hereditary *Señorío* in Theory and Practice

The colonial Maya community in many ways resembles a typical community in any peasant society. In general outlines and even in many details it comes uncannily close to the description in a recent study of a municipality in Aragon, Belmonte de los Caballeros, during roughly the same period—the sixteenth to the nineteenth centuries. Belmonte had its small group of rich and powerful men (*pudientes*) too, who owned most of the land, rotated in the town council, ran the community's religious activities and were consulted as a body—whether holding office at the time or not—on all major decisions. The town council regulated and collected local taxes, administered the municipal patrimony, and could call on fellow townsmen to contribute labor for public works projects.[33] The similarities go only so far. Two fundamental differences can be seen in social relations and in the meanings attached to them. Colonial Maya society retained a concept of lordship that is totally absent in the Aragonese municipality—a degree of authority over subordinates that fell short of absolute only in the limitations imposed from above by the power of the colonial rulers; and an authority that was claimed as an hereditary right.[34]

Some indication of the concept of *señorío*, or lordship, that underlay the socioeconomic status of the Maya elite can be gained from the degree of deference they could command, which ill accords with any standard image of an exclusively peasant society. *Batabs* and *maestros*

237

cantores were addressed as *yum*, meaning lord or master in Yucatec Maya; it was a title reserved for the more exalted figures, human and divine, with whom the colonial Maya had dealings: besides the *batab* and *maestro*, the title was used for the Three Persons of the Trinity, the Spanish governor and bishop, the local *encomendero*, and occasionally the parish priest. The existence of social differences among peasants has become a commonplace by now; still, one would be surprised to find even the wealthiest kulak addressed as "lord." Nor did these honors and the material privileges enjoyed by the elite derive from a special veneration for the aged. Though Maya society valued the old, especially as repositories of oral tradition, community leadership was not a gerontocracy. Indeed, men ordinarily retired from active public life precisely when they reached the category of *anciano* (about fifty-five or sixty) and they sometimes gained the highest offices when barely out of their teens.

The existence of a wealthy and politically dominant elite in colonial Maya society who sometimes bore the same titles and performed many of the same functions as the pre-Columbian nobility is well attested to. But it does not follow that the one descended directly from the other or indeed had any hereditary status at all. Not surprisingly, the documentary evidence is too fragmentary to trace all the postconquest descendants of the old nobility and see how they fared. The early decades of the seventeenth century are an especially shadowy period, after the Spanish (though not the Maya) had lost interest in the nobility's hereditary claims, and before anyone gave much care to preserving parish registers, wills and deeds, election returns, and the other minutiae of local administration that allow one to trace lineage connections and match them with property and political office. There are, however, many bits and pieces of evidence, as well as several large chunks. When assembled they help to establish, first of all, the persistence until at least the early nineteenth century of a formal distinction between the *almehens* (those of noble birth) and the rest of Maya society. Second, it is clear that *almehen* had not been transformed into an honorific title derived from public office; it was inherited. Finally, one can establish a more than casual link between noble lineage and community leadership throughout the colonial period, even in the absence of unbroken genealogical records.

A few fairly long family trees have survived that conveniently set out who begat whom from the time of Mayapan (the Yucatan equivalent of the Mayflower or the Norman Conquest) until well past the Spanish conquest.[35] Other lines of descent, when traceable at all without parish records (which tell us nothing of economic or political status), have to be pieced together from fortuitous scraps. A testator might mention a paternal uncle from whom he himself had inherited some property, the uncle having been referred to as an *almehen* in an earlier document. Or a man designated as an heir in one testament might be linked to a *batab* in the following century, and referred to as an ancestor who had endowed the community *cofradía*; and this *batab*'s son might pop up in another document as the local *escribano* and then appear in a later one as the *maestro cantor* or as father-in-law to a subsequent *batab*.

Most of the thousands of names of officials that are recorded in the colonial documents are just that: mere names with no social identity beyond the particular public office the men were holding and perhaps their age and birthplace. Whenever further information can be found— some biographical scrap to tack on to one of the names—it invariably points to a distinct pattern in recruitment for political leadership. We find either specific mention of noble rank, or kinship ties to someone else of that rank, or membership in a multigenerational family of officeholders—sometimes but not always identified as noble. The absence of the formal designation of *almehen* is no clear indication of commoner status, since it was used erratically, perhaps most often when there was a need for clarity. In fact, its increased use in the late colonial period has been interpreted as a sign of the nobility's declining economic position (and, I might add, declining political power) and their attempt to resist compression into the *macehual* class by emphasizing hereditary distinctions.[36]

A further question is whether this colonial elite, which claimed political leadership as an hereditary prerogative, was in fact descended from the pre-Columbian nobility. Genealogical continuities are by the nature of the evidence bound to be more elusive than the functional ones, although some family lines can be traced for several centuries after conquest. A few, like the Pacab's of the Sierra province, seem to have survived the entire period of colonial rule;[37] and perhaps there were others like the Cocom of Sotuta, whose political dominance stretched back into the mists of the peninsula's pre-Mayapan history (or so they claimed).

It would be futile to look for unbroken lines of succession from father to son through the colonial centuries. By that criterion hereditary rule died out among the Maya within a few generations, if it had in fact ever existed. It was replaced by a looser system that could be defined as hereditary access to rulership and which preserved the basic concept of hereditary rule by adaptation to colonial circumstances.

Hereditary rule among the Indians of Mesoamerica should not, in any case, be interpreted by the standards of modern European monarchies. If we seek a European model, medieval kingship would be more appropriate to what we know of the pre-Columbian political system. Both combined hereditary and elective principles. In both, political power was relatively fluid, diffused through a hierarchy of lesser lordships, who had some say in the choice of the territorial ruler and on whose support, in the absence of well-developed state bureaucracies and standing armies, his actual power depended.[38]

According to the strict rules of male primogeniture that the Spanish introduced to the native lordships, neither the great *tlatoani* of Tenochtitlan nor any of the local lords of Postclassic Mesoamerica (nor of Peru, for that matter) could qualify as hereditary rulers. Although we do not know in detail the rules that guided the transfer of authority, the choice was not automatic. It was restricted only to the particular ruling lineage or lineages—with perhaps a presumption in favor of the elder son, but the choice might fall on a younger son or even a collateral descendant, according to personal ability, experience, and other criteria. Among the Aztecs the choice was made by senior members of the ruling lineage in consultation with a council made up of the leading nobles.[39] A similar procedure was probably followed by the lowland Maya, with some undetermined mix of influence between the ruling dynasty and the lesser nobility. And we can assume that in all cases more informal political maneuvering accompanied or preceded the final selection.

The outlines of the old system are still discernible in the colonial elections to municipal office. These procedures ran so smoothly among the Aztecs, the Spanish noted, because the Indian elite were so accustomed to elections.[40] In Yucatan not only the procedures but also the basic principles were retained. Dynastic affiliation still determined eligibility, but with one major innovation. The pool of eligibles for the top offices was broadened beyond that of a single ruling dynasty to include a larger but still restricted group of "*batab* lineages" distinct from the second tier of nobles. Direct succession within one family was, according to the available evidence, a rare occurrence. During the course of a century several families might dominate the top posts, appearing intermittently or in spurts and sometimes even serving in second-tier posts in the interim.

A small number of *batabs* can be found who had previously served in the lower ranks of *alcalde* or *regidor*. A much more common stepping-stone to any of the first-tier positions (*maestro cantor* and patron as well as *batab*) was a stint as *escribano*, and most common of all was accession without any previous experience whatsoever in public office. The highest officials were often selected at an early age, with little or no apprenticeship and thus no opportunity to achieve any prominence in their own right. Movement across the boundary separating the two tiers was

240

uncommon, and members of the upper tier tended to be drawn from a restricted group of interrelated lineages within the larger rank of *principales*. All these facts suggest that a suitable pedigree was still a major, though not the only, determinant of eligibility to rulership.

The division between *batab* lineages and the lesser nobility must be regarded as a tendency rather than an immutable rule. The tendency, however, might turn out to be even stronger if, as has been suggested, rank could be determined also by descent through the female line;[41] I have based my calculations solely on patrilineal ties.

The theoretical and, to some degree, the historical basis of this division was the pre-Columbian distinction between lords or rulers (whom the Spanish called *señores naturales*) and the lesser nobility, or *principales* (Aztec *pipiltin*). The *batab* system in Yucatan, despite the many permutations I shall discuss, remained truer in spirit to the concept of *señorío* than the hereditary *cacicazgos* (lordships) artificially preserved by the Spanish elsewhere. Election played no part in determining succession to these *cacicazgos* and their legitimacy was further eroded by the failure of *caciques*, partly through choice and partly through Spanish policy, to exercise leadership functions within their domains. In some areas, such as the Chiapas highlands, the concept seems to have disappeared altogether with the elimination of the native rulers by the early part of the seventeenth century.[42]

In Yucatan hereditary *cacicazgos*, as the Spanish defined them, died out fairly early, with the exception of a branch of the Xiu family. This need not have signaled the end either of *señorío* or of the ruling dynasties themselves. Their fate under colonial rule can best be understood against the background of preconquest political arrangements.

The first point to bear in mind is that the Spanish did not break into a static political scene but, as is typical of political arrangements everywhere, a shifting one. In chapter 5 I suggested that provincial political structures in the late Postclassic should be seen as gradations along a continuum from loose confederations to highly centralized polities. The particular point along the continuum that each structure represented depended upon the particular balance achieved at the moment among three groups: a ruling lineage exercising or attempting to establish hegemony over a province; lesser lords with their own hereditary claims to component territories; and what might be called local gentry.

The second relevant point about Postclassic political organization is that, no matter how centralized the rule of the dominant lineages might be, nowhere did it approach absolute power. As in medieval European kingships, it was always shared to some degree with the local lords (*batabs*) and the local gentry (*principales*) under them. Whether it was invariably true that "without their vote nothing could be done,"[43] the *principales* were clearly not mere flunkies doing the *batab*'s bidding. The *ahcuchcabs* had their own power base as representatives of the major territorial divisions, the *parcialidades* (and, we presume, of the chief lineages), within the towns.

Given the degree of military strife that characterized the peninsula's history after the collapse of Mayapan, the balance of power could not have been fixed. It would depend even in periods of relative calm on the political skills and dynastic alliances of rulers and lords. The same variables would also determine the mix of influence when it came to selecting the provincial *halach uinics* and the *batabs*, both subject in theory to the same rule of hereditary-cum-elective succession. The evidence on the succession of *batabs* is equivocal, with some suggestion that they were sometimes subject to confirmation, if not actually appointed by the provincial overlords.[44] This right, like that of the Spanish colonial governor, might cover a wide range of influence from *pro forma* ratification up to and including the imposition of one's own candidate. History provides ample testimony of how hereditary rules can be bent by the realities of power. In most extreme cases, and Postclassic Yucatan is replete with them, the rules are bent by military force.

Colonial rule imposed a certain uniform tranquillity over the peninsula, ending all the miniconquests, overthrows, and other violent rearrangements of power. It did not, however, freeze the status quo, for the fragmentation of the larger polities into independent political units and the creation of rival loci of authority in the municipal *gobernadores* were to bring about a major and permanent shift in the balance of power between local elites and ruling dynasties.

Neither of these two innovations, of which the establishment of local autonomy was the more far-reaching, had an immediate effect on native political organization. The independence of the individual *repúblicas de indios* was at first a legal fiction in the old *halach uinic* provinces, since the ruling lineages retained a fairly firm grip on their districts well into the latter part of the sixteenth century. For example, the head of the small Huit dynasty of Hocaba still had enough power to claim the title of *halach uinic* and to plant four of his close relatives as local *batabs* and a number of others in leading positions around the province.[45]

While eventually reducing the great provincial rulers to the level of mere *batabs* of their own immediate districts, so far as we know the Spanish never interfered with the hereditary succession of any of the *señores naturales* (native lords) from the time of conquest until they fade from view (with the usual exception of the Xiu) in the early seventeenth century. What they did do in Yucatan, as elsewhere, was to divide power between the hereditary lord and the appointed *gobernador* in the new municipal system. The first examples of this split are recorded in 1579, when the title of *gobernador* in two towns, Tixkokob and Mococha, near Merida in the old Cehpech province (Costa district), were reported as being held by someone other than the *batab*, because the latter in both cases was not deemed "*suficiente* [capable]."[46]

This judgment of incapacity conjures up the image of some Maya version of the last Hapsburg king of Spain, the feeble-minded Charles II. It was a good excuse but one that lost much of its plausibility as the practice of separating the two posts increased, barring wholesale mental degeneration among the Maya ruling families. In fact, they were deemed unsuitable for the post of *gobernador* only in their own hereditary territories. Even when the larger political structures decayed, the ruling lineages continued to serve as provincial reservoirs from which the Spanish continued to appoint *gobernadores*—for other towns.

The musical chairs played among the upper nobility of Mani province illustrates what appears to have been a general Spanish policy. By 1610 the Xius had lost the governorship of the Mani capital, but although a relatively small lineage they provided *gobernadores* for a number of surrounding towns (Tekit, Pustunich, Yaxa, Hunacti, Dzan, and Tekax). Similarly, the hereditary *batab* of Tekax had served as *gobernador* of nearby Tekit and later in Oxkutzcab, and when the Xiu *gobernador* of Tekax was replaced shortly thereafter, the choice fell on a Diego Catzim, the young son of the then *gobernador* of Mani but a resident of Tekax.[47] This curious practice, which represented a compromise between indigenous concepts of legitimacy based on hereditary claim (concepts that were in fact shared by the Spanish) and the Spanish desire to curtail the power of the ruling lineages, helped to preserve the hereditary basis of authority through the transition to the later colonial *batab* system.

The great provincial lineages did not so much disappear as become fragmented along with the provincial political structures they had created. As Maya society became more encapsulated in the local communities, so did the upper nobility. They no longer moved around with the same have-pedigree-will-travel facility. It became increasingly common for all the Maya leaders—not only the *principales*, who all along seem to have been local elites, but also the upper tier of *batab* lineages—to be identified with a particular community by birth and by ancestral ties. By the latter part of the eighteenth century, any one of these leaders who could not trace his family roots in the same spot for several generations, if not to "time immemorial," was rare indeed. Most of the recorded exceptions were *batabs*, and one wonders whether these outsiders were chosen because there was no local candidate with suitable genealogical credentials at the time.[48]

Some lineages seem to have preserved kinship ties across community boundaries, but they had ceased to be regional in the same free-floating way, with local power derived from dynastic domination over the entire province. They had instead, when they survived at all, become divided into branches, each one part of a discrete network of community elites on whom had devolved such political power as was left in native society. If the Spanish ceased to draw on a provincial pool of lords to serve as municipal *gobernadores*, it was partly because they wished to discourage intercommunity ties, but also, I suggest, because outsiders regardless of rank became increasingly unacceptable to the local elites.

The shift in power in favor of the local nobility at the expense of the provincial dynasties was a general phenomenon, with certain regional differences that corresponded to variations in preconquest political dynamics. Once the Spanish had succeeded in firmly establishing the office of *gobernador* as the chief executive post in the Maya communities, they seem to have withdrawn from interference in local politics. But regardless of how active a role they played, it is clear that neither the *gobernadores* nor the later *batabs* could gain power, or at least keep it, without the consent of the local *principales*.[49] This does not necessarily signify the total eclipse of the old ruling families. In tracing their fate through the colonial period, it becomes apparent that the longer established and more powerful the dynasty at the time of conquest the greater their chances of longevity afterward. The descendants of the major *halach uinic* lineages—the Cocoms, the Huits, and the Xius—fared relatively well. They could no longer dominate their provinces and impose local rulers at will, but they continued to appear in the records serving in the highest community positions until the end of the colonial period. (The branch of the Xiu family pressing claims for Spanish recognition was not, significantly, the same branch "elected" to public offices, the latter a sign of local acceptance that would have made Spanish recognition superfluous.)[50] No one has bothered to trace these families past independence (or, as far as I know, checked the claim made by a recent state senator named Xiu from Mani district that he is descended from the *halach uinic* ally of the Montejos, Tutul Xiu).

These families had merged into the local nobility but retained some preeminence in the status hierarchy. They became part of the upper tier of the elite, that small group of "*batab* lineages" considered to have a legitimate claim on the highest ranking offices. Other members of the upper tier are harder to trace. Some clearly descended from local lords; others may have descended from either provincial or local dynasties in

244

the female line; or given the elite's preference for endogamy, most likely the lines eventually became thoroughly merged.

Xiu sovereignty had been firmly entrenched since Mayapan and perhaps before. The Cocoms claimed a ruling line back to Chichen Itza.[51] In contrast, the Pech family of Cehpech province, their neighbors, the Chel of Ahkinchel, and the Canul dynasty in Ahcanul had only recently arrived in their provinces during the post-Mayapan turmoil and established hegemony over them within several generations.[52] It could not be sheer coincidence that these descendants of parvenu "adventurers" should just as rapidly have tumbled into the obscurity from which they had risen. By the time of the Spanish conquest, the Pech family had managed to gain lordships in twenty-two of the twenty-five towns comprising the province of Cehpech; in the 1570s they were still ruling all of the eleven towns for which we have information.[53] By the mid-seventeenth century they had all but disappeared from high office, along with the Chels and the Canuls.[54]

All the dynasties in power at the time of the conquest, whether ruling over entire provinces, subprovinces, or only single towns, suffered a severe decline in that all lost their formerly exclusive claim on rulership (although it is not clear that all local lordships had invariably been vested in the same family). Aside from the Spaniards' desire to weaken, although not necessarily destroy, the power of the hereditary ruler, epidemics killed off "many of the *señores naturales*," making it easier for challengers from among the *principales* to gain ascendency.[55] Some lords resisted sending their sons to the friars to be educated, and by their clever ruse of sending their slaves or other substitutes, condemned their own heirs to the loss of their hereditary rights.[56]

These explanations, true enough as far as they go, do not account for the differences in degree of decline among the dynasties. A plague could have carried off most of the Chels and accounted for their poor showing. But the Pech and Canul lineages were exceptionally large, and they did not disappear entirely from public office—only, with rare exceptions, from the very top. What I suggest is an especially strong reaction from the local *principales* against these newcomers, who lacked the legitimacy of more firmly entrenched dynasties in other provinces and who may even have been blamed for introducing the latest set of foreign overlords, the Spanish.[57] Spanish rule gave all local lords and gentry a more or less equal chance at ascendency over the great territorial rulers, an equal opportunity to settle old scores, on a more modest scale but still similar to the reassertion of local autonomy that the Spanish presence stimulated in the former Aztec and Inca empires. Preconquest history helped to determine how they would use the opportunity.[58]

245

LINEAGE, LEGITIMACY, AND SOCIAL MOBILITY

One of the reasons we know as much as we do about the family histories of the colonial Maya elite is their own preoccupation with genealogy. Any aristocracy of blood rather than wealth or other form of achievement ultimately rests on some kind of ideology that equates legitimacy with lineage. If the performance of ancestors is called upon to validate the claims of the living, it is useful to have a record of that performance and the ancestral links. Hence there was a very practical value in the dynastic chronicles and genealogies that the pre-Columbian and early colonial Maya recorded, and in the oral traditions preserved by aged *principales* whose ability to recall who did what and begat whom became more important to the later colonial Maya as literacy became an increasingly rare skill even among the elite.[59]

The idea that legitimate authority was based on descent from a former ruler persisted in Yucatan down to the conquest, despite the turmoil of the immediately preceding centuries when foreign and domestic usurpers frequently rearranged the lines of succession. The same concept of hereditary rule has survived unorthodox transfers of power in many societies, and manipulations of official genealogies to mask these deviations obviously represent a deference to the basic concept.

The Spanish conquest brought an end to the more overt struggles for power among the Maya, while introducing a more general challenge to the principle of hereditary rule in the creation of the rival position of municipal *gobernador*. The kind of conflict within the native ruling class that such a division of authority could create would be largely a matter for speculation if one example had not bubbled to the surface almost by accident in connection with the short-lived but violent disturbance in the town of Tekax in 1610, and thus became incorporated into the Spanish records. The disturbance, as mentioned in earlier chapters, appeared at first to be a straightforward popular uprising against the *gobernador* of Tekax, one don Pedro Xiu. The official inquiry into the affair became complicated by the revelation of a deep antipathy toward Xiu harbored by the hereditary *batab* of Tekax, don Fernando Uz. Don Fernando had hardly been shunted aside into impotent obscurity. He was a trusted advisor to the Spanish governor and had been appointed to a variety of responsible posts in the colonial administration. Nevertheless, he considered Xiu a usurper in Tekax, had openly proclaimed him so, and had publicly insulted and snubbed him on several occasions. Although a final verdict on Uz's complicity in the uprising is missing from the trial record, the Spanish prosecutor found nothing implausible in the idea that an elite dispute over legitimacy lay behind the conflict that had briefly embroiled the entire town in violent strife.[60]

The depth and bitterness of this particular dispute may shed some light on the well-known but not always so well-understood Maya texts known as the books of Chilam Balam. These virtually unclassifiable documents mixing sacred and secular lore and myth, chronicle, and prophecy have roots in the pre-Columbian past, probably deriving from some common text; but the texts we have are colonial documents and as such can provide some clues to the colonial Maya mind. They were not mere relics of the past preserved out of some sense of nostalgia. They were copied and recopied; new bits were added, and perhaps some old ones left out, and other modifications made over time, all according to the tastes and knowledge of the transcribers.[61] And it is thought that many if not all of the colonial communities had their own copies. The colonial Maya or, more specifically, members of the elite, who alone could read or copy them, must have had some use for them. Among other functions, they served to reinforce Maya notions of what constituted legitimate political authority.

The "Chilam Balam of Chumayel," probably the best known of the surviving texts, is replete with references to usurpers: "unrestrained upstarts," "offspring of the harlot" (that is, without legitimate ancestry), and "two-day occupants of the mat [a symbol of chiefly office]."[62] A lengthy section of the book, entitled in one translation "Interrogation of the Chiefs," is a series of riddles based on an esoteric knowledge that was handed down within the "lineage of rulers" and which, like the pea under the princess's mattress, was considered an infallible test of royal or at least noble origins. The chiefs were to be examined to see "whether they are of the lineage of rulers, whether they are of the lineage of chiefs, that they may prove it."[63]

These are the words. If they are not understood by the Chiefs of the town ill-omened is the star adorning the night. Frightful is its house. Sad is the havoc in the courtyards of the nobles.[64]

The purpose of these riddles, then, was to distinguish between the legitimate lords who ruled by virtue of descent and the upstarts. That such a distinction was considered necessary, that upstarts were able to ascend to leadership in pre-Columbian times, is clear from the Chilam Balam chronicles themselves as well as from other sources. Colonial rule created new opportunities for usurpers and for those who may have chosen to regard the current incumbents as parvenus. (The "restoration of legitimate authority" can be used to cover almost any bid for power, given sufficient imagination.)

The colonial Maya elite could no longer organize armed forces to engineer or resist an overthrow. Any member of the nobility who felt dispossessed of his birthright would have had to console himself with the hope that in some future *katun*:

> The unrestrained upstart of the day . . . [shall] be roughly handled,
> his face covered with earth, trampled into the ground and befouled,
> as he is dragged along.[65]

Until the fulfillment of such comforting prophecies, few options were available to dispossessed or disaffected members of the colonial Maya nobility. The Franciscans complained that any *principal* who sought independence could gather a group of followers and establish a separate community.[66] But although secession may have been a common means of resolving elite factionalism in pre-Columbian times, and although territorial fragmentation continued under Spanish rule to provide an escape for town malcontents, it was no longer a very satisfactory one for disgruntled noblemen, as opposed to those of lower social rank. Except in the frontier zones, a satellite settlement could take generations to achieve total independence, and in the meantime the defecting *principal* and his descendants would still be subject to the authority of his rivals in the parent town.[67] The most he could achieve was a little distance and a corresponding loosening of the ties.

Anyone seeking to regain or rise to political prominence would have been better advised to remain in the towns and try to forge alliances among other *principales*. One could curry favor with the Spanish authorities, but that was of little use without the support of the local gentry. The Tekax *principales* backed the incumbent *gobernador* over the hereditary *batab*, who had been a favorite of the Spanish governor, and when it became clear that the *gobernador* could no longer govern effectively they were the ones who chose his successor. The Spanish respected that choice and appear to have followed this practice as common policy, out of a combination of prudence and a kind of laissez-faire torpor that characterized the administrative (though not the economic) activities of the colonial bureaucracy.

Factional struggles within the elite only rarely emerge in the records, not, I suspect, because they were rare but because the elite usually managed to work these matters out among themselves without arousing the attention of the Spanish authorities. They produced only minor tremors for the most part, concerned as they were with establishing or realigning the pecking order within the ruling group but without questioning the basic social inequalities or the principle of hereditary rank that was their sustaining ideology. The only expression of class consciousness we have from the colonial Maya comes from within the upper ranks themselves. The Chilam Balam books condemn the labor exacted by *batabs, maestros cantores*, and other local officials and refer to "blood-sucking insects of the town who drain the poverty of the *macehuales*."[68] Since such services were considered a legitimate perquisite of office, it is likely that these and other vehement indictments were directed against the "upstarts" as ammunition in the intraclass rivalry that figures so prominently in the rest of the book.

There must have been considerable rivalry within the native nobility even after the unsettling period of transition from rule by the hereditary lords to the modified *batab* system of the later colonial period, which retained the principal of hereditary rule but broadened the pool of eligibles. A suitable pedigree would ensure only eligibility for office. Almost invariably there would be more legitimate candidates than posts to fill at any one time, as indeed there would have been under the more restricted pre-Columbian system. Even a partially elective system presupposes a choice.

A system of rotation in the second tier of offices may have been one way of dampening factionalism in colonial as well as pre-Columbian times, if the *regidores*, like the *ahcuchcabs*, continued to represent territorial divisions or at least some kind of stable sociopolitical groupings. Rotation in office among these groups would certainly explain the complex reshuffling of names each year, as people (and the groups they represented) advanced a notch up the rank order—for example, from fourth to third *regidor* and so on, before starting the cycle again—without any discernible change in function.[69] There was also movement back and forth between *cabildo* and *cofradía* offices. It is not clear where this fits into the rotational system, except that the *cofradía* could have functioned as a holding ground because of the Spanish rule against serving two successive years in the *cabildo*. Perhaps *batab* lineages also rotated, but the evidence is inevitably less clear because of the length of the terms involved. In any case rotation does not explain the choice of the particular individuals as representatives of their wards or lineages.

The colonial Maya have left only scattered clues as to what criteria besides lineage they used in selecting community leaders. The political trade-offs that may have been made with relatives, friends, and other supporters in competing for power were kept behind the scenes, although the frequent clustering of office holding from the same lineage suggests that mutual help among kinsmen figured prominently in political success.

The other qualifications for office that are mentioned all have some connection with noble ancestry. We do not know what theories on heredity the Maya held; but the personal qualities of probity, piety, and respect for local traditions, which were given much weight, were certainly easier to display, if not to acquire, through high rank. One's performance in office would be better assured by a family tradition of public service to the community, sustained by the explicit duty to honor the memory and protect the achievements of one's ancestors. Wealth, which the colonial economy provided little opportunity to accumulate by personal effort alone, was crucial. Aside from assuring a place in the network of mutual lending and ceremonial feasting, through which the Maya elite cemented peer relations, wealth was a guarantee of honest and sound management of community property, and necessary for the material support of religious ritual through which piety and devotion to community service were demonstrated.[70]

The colonial Maya sociopolitical hierarchy, then, would seem to be completely self-perpetuating, with inherited rank, wealth and political power all reinforcing each other. Yet the hierarchy was far from static. Many realignments took place not only during the initial phase of post-conquest adjustment but all through the colonial era. The Chulims might be flourishing in one period and the Dzuls in another, duplicating on a greatly reduced scale the hegemony of a rising *halach uinic* lineage, only controlling lesser community offices instead of *batab*-ships throughout a province. Hereditary privilege was only part of the colonial equation; individual abilities played some part also. But in tracing the rise and fall of family fortunes it is hard to escape the conclusion that luck, especially what might be called genetic luck, was a major factor.

A strong male kin group was important at all levels of Maya society. For the *macehuales* it was often a question of mutual help for physical survival. For the nobility the stakes were different. The pooling of resources in cattle raising and in the production, transport, and marketing of agricultural surpluses protected and enhanced the inherited wealth of the group, while reciprocal aid in sponsoring religious fiestas and in mustering electoral support among other *principales* could provide a significant boost to a family's political fortunes. The fictive kinship ties of *compadrazgo* could create a supplementary or alternate network of mutual obligations, but one thing it could not supply was descendants, and the lack of them was the principal cause of the fall of some elite lineages and the rise of others. No dynasty can ever guarantee heirs, even collateral ones. Considering the high mortality rate among the colonial Maya, especially through epidemic disease, which was more indiscriminate in its choice of victims than famine, the degree of longevity that some elite lineages did achieve is surprising.

One lineage's loss was often another's gain. Since the noble families tended to intermarry, the property would then pass through the female line to a son-in-law or a sister's son, often in return for the legatee's assuming the filial obligations of arranging for a funeral (and presumably the other rituals owed to deceased ancestors). Sometimes even these lines of succession failed, and the records reveal poignant cases of old and enfeebled remnants of some ancient lineage, rich in lands but with no kinfolk, who as they neared death were willing to deed their property to someone in exchange for care in their last days or at least a proper burial. Among kinsmen, even distant ones, these transactions were a form of adoption in which the heir was actually called "son."[71] Outside that circle they may have been purely business arrangements without any overtones of filial substitution.

In this way, and also by outright sale, land tended to circulate somewhat, while at the same time the boundary of social rank was preserved. How would *macehuales* acquire the cash to purchase land or to guarantee the expenses of a decent funeral, instead of the unceremonious pauper's burial that was their common lot? Ralph Roys has seen an egalitarian development in colonial land-holding patterns in the town of Ebtun: a "policy of the town tending toward communal land tenure," based on several purchases by the *cabildo* from private owners.[72] Such purchases have been recorded in other towns also, but could as easily represent the community's desire not to have the property fall into the hands of Spaniards or members of another community. Certainly in the region of Ebtun as well as in the rest of the very thinly populated eastern part of the peninsula, communal lands were not in short supply. In any case, the decrease in private land ownership by the Maya was primarily caused by sales to Spaniards rather than to the communities.

Inherited rank and wealth provided some cushion against financial disaster, but not an ironclad protection. Some lineages were less capable, for whatever reason, of weathering the general famines and epidemics that periodically assailed the colony. For example, the Pox family of the Mani district began the colonial period with impressive landholdings extending through several municipalities, and these were even increased through the extinction of related lineages. But as the Pox family itself fell victim to epidemics and other misfortunes and perhaps poor management as well, the survivors sold off what at the time may have been surplus lands at bargain prices.[73]

Others, not coincidentally, were able to improve their positions during the same period of demographic and economic crisis of the seventeenth century. The history of the Ku family of Telchac illustrates in more detail the influence of the various factors mentioned, especially "genetic luck," in the ebb and flow of family fortunes. The antecedents of Francisco Ku, who died circa 1650, are unknown, though not exactly humble, since he himself possessed moderate wealth, including land, and was well connected by marriage with several large property owners. These connections, plus no doubt a measure of financial shrewdness, helped to turn him into a local land baron. Francisco amassed several thousand *mecates* of land plus four large house plots in the town, inherited from six different relatives (in addition to his father), all of whom died without direct or collateral male heirs and whose funeral expenses he paid for: a maternal uncle; the husband of a maternal aunt, whose own son died in a shipwreck; two fathers-in-law (presumably his first wife died); his second wife's paternal uncle; and, finally, his *consuegro* (father of his son-in-law), whose only son died after marrying Ku's daughter.

Thus the patrimonies of five extinct lineages besides his own converged on Ku as sole survivor (without the high natural death rate at this time, one might have suspected foul play). In addition, he purchased land from four other people who died without surviving issue but with whom no affinal or consanguineous ties can be established.[74] And all was passed on intact to his son, Julio Ku, for the rule of patrilateral inheritance was still observed when circumstances permitted.

The highest position Julio Ku had achieved by the time he made out his will in 1685 was *alcalde*. His son's career is unknown, but his grandson, Juan Antonio Ku, had become *batab* and also patron of the local *cofradía* by 1758.[75] Then luck rapidly deserted the family. The 1769-1774 famine, so ruinous to public and private fortunes, struck while don Juan Antonio was still in office. He had to mortgage a substantial portion of his patrimony and sell another part to Spaniards to help settle his official accounts. Worse still, no sons survived him, and his daughters, who left no heirs at all, had sold off the rest of the family lands before the last one died in 1800.[76]

From this and other family histories it would seem that patrilineal kinship ties were crucial to the long-term preservation of the Maya elite. First and foremost was the need to perpetuate the line of descent, but beyond that a large and cohesive kin group could ensure that its status was maintained through mutual political support and economic aid, especially during times of crisis. Even if it had not been contrary to Maya law for an individual to sell off his own share of the lineage's patrimony, the survival of other members who could care for the aged, spread the burden of otherwise ruinous official debts, and cooperate in rebuilding reserves after droughts and other disasters would greatly lessen the need for forced sales.

The link between wealth and community leadership in postconquest

252

Indian society has most generally been seen as a negative one, since the officials were supposed to make good any deficits in the tax quotas assessed collectively on their communities.[77] Keen competition for municipal offices suggests that financial ruin was not always and everywhere the price of public service, although it may have been increasingly so in the viceregal centers, where Spanish interference in local government was more advanced than in Yucatan. There, the economic advantages of office holding generally far outweighed the disadvantages. Since the community leaders retained total control over local finances, the responsibility for external tax liabilities carried some opportunities as well as risk. The Spanish paid little attention to how the quotas were met, how they were apportioned within the community, and what surplus might be extracted for other purposes. *Cabildo* officers could simply lump together the totality of the community's obligations in goods and services, including contributions to their own support, and then mobilize public resources accordingly. The major economic advantage, of course, was control over *macehual* labor, by which they could guarantee a supply for their own agricultural enterprises.

General famines posed the greatest financial threat to the Maya officials, who might have to sell their personal property in order to settle their official accounts. The alienation of much of the land that the Spanish acquired could probably be traced to these hard times when indebted communities and individuals alike sold off parcels for much-needed cash.[78] But they were hard times for all—with the sole exception of the grain profiteers. Other wealthy Indians, and many Spaniards, were reduced to poverty, forced to sell "all they possessed" merely to buy food.[79] Spanish estates were ruined, mortgages were foreclosed, and ecclesiastical endowments were wiped out. The entire colony suffered severe economic stress. It eventually recovered and so, too, did the Maya elite, at least as a group. True, lands once alienated were rarely regained, but as I have repeatedly noted, shortage of land became a problem for the communities and the elite only in the late colonial period. As long as the communities retained a strong economic base and the elite retained political control over the communities, office holding, rather than lead to impoverishment, could help to keep the elite afloat and even to replenish fortunes depleted by periodic crises. Through skill or luck (again, especially "genetic luck") or a combination of the two, some families simply did better than others over the long run.

The fate of the Maya nobility after the Spanish conquest touches on several broad questions that social theorists have pondered inconclusively for societies that are much better documented than colonial Yucatan: How do we define social mobility? And how much mobility can occur before we can say that a society is no longer stratified?

The advantages of inherited wealth and privileged access to public office that the Maya nobility enjoyed, together with the principle of kin group solidarity, would help to explain the relative stability of the social structure. The question is whether the changes in status and the jostling for political power that must have occurred behind the usually decorous façade of municipal elections were confined, as appearances suggest, to the nobility or whether they include challenges from below.

Karen Spalding has argued that colonial rule provided much opportunity for social mobility in Peru. Perhaps it did, although the specific examples she gives represent the traditional ruling group's capture of the new position of power created by the Spaniards, rather than the group being shunted aside by commoners.[80] Without full genealogical records it is impossible to tell how many of the colonial native elite were descendants of the old ruling lineages—a group that could and did include mestizos—how many were members of the lesser nobility but still with some hereditary claim to power, and how many were ambitious commoners. Movement across the boundary separating nobles from commoners may have been more difficult in Yucatan than in areas where many of the old ruling group became detached from local governance, leaving native society acephalous, with a resultant free-for-all among the local gentry and a more propitious environment for competition from commoners. One should not, however, assume that more flexibility in social and political arrangements automatically meant greater opportunities for commoners, rather than a reordering *within* the elite.

A society in which no movement takes place across social boundaries is difficult to imagine. Some noble lineages that fade from the record could have fallen into social obscurity, and one can presume that the Maya aristocrat manqué living in poverty with only his pedigree to distinguish him from the *macehuales* (a pedigree that might become meaningless if not forgotten entirely after a generation or so) was not an unknown occurrence, even if an unrecorded one. Newcomers appear whose lack of antecedents may be less the fault of spotty documentation than the absence of any antecedents they could boast of. Aristocracies have commonly experienced attrition and at the same time permitted a certain amount of replenishment from below in order to survive. In practice, hereditary rank may be hard to distinguish from social class, and class itself may be more or less fixed or fluid. Surely one must look at the meanings that people themselves attach to their social arrangements. If the principle of hereditary rights exclusive to the upper group in society is generally acknowledged, then the boundary remains, even if it allows individuals to pass through it.

Among the Maya it would be difficult to pinpoint the transition from one form of social organization to another. Dynastic changes were not uncommon among the ancient Maya, while in modern Indian communities some gradations in wealth and status can persist within the same families from generation to generation, so that not everyone starts from scratch in the competition. Yet clearly the concept of hereditary privilege that survived the preconquest fluctuations in dynastic fortunes has disappeared. Although inheritance and family ties may provide some initial advantage and some continuity in local leadership, no one commands a station in society by categorical right of birth.

Some time during the four centuries between the Spanish conquest and the "ethnographic present," a change occurred from assigned to achieved status. My contention is that it took place late rather than early, more as a result of changes that marked the end of colonial rule than its beginning. Because of these changes (which I shall discuss in the concluding chapter) the economic and political position of the Maya nobility had already begun to suffer serious erosion during the last decades before independence. What is more surprising is that even at that late date there still existed a class of Indians who were distinguished by relative wealth, noble birth, and official positions of power in their communities.

We do not know how many ambitious *arrivés*, if any, managed to infiltrate the hereditary nobility during the course of the colonial period, nor is it clear how much difference their incorporation would have made to the basic organization of Maya society. For the *principales*, genealogical credentials were clearly a vital issue. For the mass of *macehuales*, the question of who ruled may have been much less important than how they ruled: performance, not pedigree, may have been the crucial factor in guaranteeing the popular assent (or at least acquiescence) on which rested the position of the elite and the social order in general. And performance was judged by services to the community that enhanced the welfare of all its members.

· 9 ·

SURVIVAL AS A CORPORATE
ENTERPRISE

In all groups a tension exists between social imperative and individual interests. It is, we are told, part of the human condition. These centripetal and centrifugal forces are more than figures of speech when applied to the lowland Maya. Unlike many people for whom social ties are not even theoretically a choice, the Maya could readily translate antisocial attitudes into physical separation; the social bond could dissolve literally as well as metaphorically.

Yet despite the new strains that Spanish rule added to this already delicate balance, the community endured, and it endured not merely as a colonial administrative unit, nor merely by virtue of superior Spanish force. The colonial rulers were no more able to keep the Maya locked into the congregated towns than their own leaders were. They did not seek to stop dispersal and drift, but they were not notably successful in preventing flight either. Nevertheless, the mass of the colonial Maya population continued to live as members of some community, even if not always their native one. They did so in part by force of habit, perhaps, but also, I suggest, because the community continued to satisfy some perceived need.

Individual Survival and Mutual Aid

The need for a mutual support system remained as strong under colonial rule as ever. If anything, life was more precarious, with epidemic disease added to the familiar calamities, and the burden of taxation, if not heavier, was at least more unpredictable. By joining forces, the Maya could not necessarily avert either natural calamities or the sometimes equally devastating ones visited on them by the Spanish, although warding off disaster can certainly be considered the primary object of their most intensive combined efforts. The idea was also to spread the risk and burden among all the corporate members in case the preventive measures failed, as they all too frequently did.

The piecemeal migration discussed in chapter 7 would seem to contradict any notion of survival as a collective enterprise, since so many people apparently saw their best chance for survival in abandoning family and community, instead of finding within these two structures the

256

mutual aid in adversity that was in large part their reason for being. If the individual's security was seen as dependent on membership in the group, why did people leave?

Corporate bonds could withstand, even be reinforced by, ordinary adversity. But the mutual support systems of family and community were at best feeble buffers against catastrophe on the scale of severe famine and epidemic, when all or most of the members were struck simultaneously. People did not so much repudiate these systems as find that they had collapsed from under them. Those who could turned to flight as the last resort, either by themselves or in small groups: to escape the epidemic or to seek sustenance when local reserves of food were exhausted.

Such breakdowns in the corporate social order were temporary. Most of the survivors returned, and those who settled elsewhere on either side of the frontier formed or joined another community organized along the same principles. Their bonds of community were not so much destroyed as transferred. Ties with the extended family might be severed; on the other hand, famines and epidemics may have left many of the migrants without a larger kin group to abandon, and these ties could also be transferred or recreated to a certain extent through the ritual kinship system of *compadrazgo*.

The heavy population losses and the mass migrations caused by these catastrophes must have played havoc with traditional kinship ties, which would have to be reconstructed each time out of the bits and pieces of leftover humanity. A patrilineal kin group might be entirely wiped out, and such losses would help to explain, even without the influence of Spanish law, deviations from the Maya rule of patrilateral inheritance. They also help to explain the rapid and thorough adoption of the system of *compadrazgo* introduced by the Spanish, and its peculiar slant in Latin America.

The Spanish introduced the standard Catholic concept of godparenthood. A man and a woman other than the natural parents are chosen to sponsor a child at baptism—the child's spiritual rebirth as a Christian—and assume, in theory, a certain responsibility along with the parents for his Christian education and spiritual welfare. The same person usually, although not necessarily, also serves as sponsor for the child's first communion and confirmation. A spiritual bond of kinship is established that is supposed to be equivalent to the natural one and by canon law even constitutes the same impediment to marriage with anyone in the same degree of affinity or consanguinity. The closeness of the social bond varies greatly, according to the strength of existing ties; in Spain the godparent is usually a relative, in any case.[1]

257

In all the former Spanish colonies, including the Philippines and those in the Americas—but not in Spain—*compadrazgo*, or co-godparenthood, has become a much more elaborate system of fictive kinship, in which different godparents are chosen for many kinds of ritual occasions, some of them with very little apparent spiritual connotation. The Christian sacraments of baptism, first communion, confirmation, and marriage continue to be the principal ones; but a whole range of events has been added, from the appearance of a child's first tooth and a girl's fifteenth birthday or "coming out" party, to wedding anniversaries, roof raising for a house, or even the inauguration of a new truck.[2] None of these events is trivial nor even wholly secular in the eyes of the participants. But the range of possibilities illustrates the point of the *compadrazgo* system, which is to create a multitude of social links between adults, with the occasion itself of secondary importance. Even in the more traditional sponsorship at baptism, the fact that the godparent may be a confirmed atheist does not seem to bother anyone (except sometimes the priest). The emphasis is on the social link between godparent and natural parent, the *compadres*, rather than on the spiritual-cum-social relationship between godparent and godchild, which in the case of houses and trucks is eliminated altogether.

The elaboration of the *compadrazgo* system from the simpler Hispanic model can be explained at least in part during the colonial period by its usefulness in reshuffling and reconstituting networks that were disrupted or destroyed: for the Spanish and Africans by trans-Atlantic migration, for the Indians by high mortality rates and internal migrations.

Both epidemic disease and famine, especially the former, must have left the Maya extended family in a shambles. The economic position of an entire family might influence its ability to survive a famine, but smallpox and other infectious diseases could strike more randomly and leave strange gaps in a family group. In Yucatan both kinds of disaster also broke up families, as members scattered in search of food or in the hope of escaping the disease—thereby, of course, spreading it further.

Hence the attraction of *compadrazgo* for the colonial Indian, a kinship bond that one could create on one's own. The child to be baptized or confirmed and his spiritual sponsorship, the original purpose of the institution, were of decidedly lesser concern in formalizing the bond. Among the Maya, godparents do not seem to have become foster parents to an orphaned godchild. The purpose was to create bonds between the adults to replace or supplement ones that had been or might be severed through sudden death or migration.[3]

The emphasis on the *compadre* link between men rather than women also points to the primacy of the system's social function. Although in theory women are also linked by co-parenthood as *comadres*, the male social network is generally the more important one for the family's welfare, the more essential for economic and social survival. Among the Maya at least nothing else existed on the same scale to supplement the patrilineal kin group, no voluntary associations along occupational or other lines in this simple society. And *compadrazgo* could help to preserve this kin group in principle, by reconstructing it with ritual sanctions when the original one disintegrated.[4]

Migration, therefore, need not have destroyed the extended family any more than it destroyed the corporate community. *Compadrazgo* ties may not have been a wholly satisfactory substitute for a real kin group. Since they were basically horizontal, within the same generation, they could not make up for the lack of male descendants. But they could facilitate integration into a new community and provide some kind of larger support group for the nuclear family.

Maya society was corporate without being collective in the sense of pooling all resources and efforts for the basic support of its members. The day-to-day business of subsistence, including the provision of shelter and clothing as well as food, could be carried on by the nuclear family unit. The material independence of this unit, as I have pointed out earlier, was limited by contingencies to which all humankind is subject. The simplicity of Maya existence, which permitted a high degree of self-sufficiency for the conjugal pair under ideal conditions, also made it highly vulnerable when misfortune struck either of the partners.

One could scarcely survive in the most literal sense within Maya society as an unattached individual, because of the sexual division of labor into producers and processors, a division that is common in many peasant economies but particularly rigid among the Maya. Women simply did not and do not take part in any phase of milpa production even as supplementary labor in weeding and harvesting; men did not grind corn or spin and weave cotton.[5] Nor did any system of wage labor exist by which someone else could be hired to perform these essential tasks. Bachelorhood and spinsterhood were thus exceedingly rare, according to the records,[6] and with good reason. Aside from clerical pressure to marry and marry young, the marriage partnership was a necessity for both male and female if either wanted to eat.

The same censuses that reveal the rarity of the single state also reveal that many other unattached adults did survive: widows and widowers for the most part, and wives abandoned by their husbands. People with physically incapacitated spouses are also recorded, along with people who themselves were chronically ill, crippled, blind, or otherwise disabled, and children orphaned of one or both parents.[7] The fact that they did not perish is indirect but compelling evidence that a wider network of aid beyond the nuclear family functioned within colonial Maya society.

That such a system had to be provided by the Maya themselves is indisputable. They certainly could not count on the Spanish for much help. Neither the state nor the church, through which most public charity was channeled, made any provision for destitute Indians except in the cities, and that was very meager. Out of a total capital fund of approximately half a million pesos that the church in Yucatan possessed in the early nineteenth century,[8] only two ecclesiastical endowments, summing about 5,000 pesos, were set aside for Indians. One was for the distribution of cacao to Indians at the cathedral door each week and the other for the feeding of Indians held in the royal prison in Merida,[9] which, as is still customary in Mexico, provided no food for the inmates.

According to their financial records, none of the religious houses distributed alms or food to the poor of any caste. Some Indians may have benefited from the charity of the colonial bishops, or that portion of the bishops who were said to have distributed much of their incomes in alms. Such largesse, which is only hearsay (the only recorded episcopal donations were adornments and vestments for the cathedral), was confined, like the rest of Spanish charity, to the urban poor.[10]

On the local level, the parish budgets contained no special provisions for poor relief, unless one counts the general custom of feeding and washing the feet of twelve "pobres" (paupers) each year on Holy Thursday in commemoration of the Last Supper. The often vast (by Yucatecan standards) revenues from *obvenciones* and fees were the curate's personal income to spend as he chose, except for the *séptima de fábrica* (one seventh of the total income which was supposed to be used for the upkeep of the church fabric) and the far-from-generous salary (fifteen pesos a month and rations) allotted an assistant curate if the parish had one.[11]

During major famines, some of the parish clergy reported bringing in maize supplies at their own expense to feed starving parishioners.[12] Perhaps others did so and perhaps some also regularly distributed alms to the poor. If so, they did not publicize these worthy deeds. Curates routinely bewailed their personal poverty in letters and reports to the bishop, citing all the other expenses—ranging from support for hosts of indigent relatives to extra adornments for their churches—which made it impossible for them to hire another assistant or contribute more than a small sum to some diocesan or royal fund-raising effort. Their silence on the subject of alms suggests that support of needy parishioners was neither a usual nor an expected part of a curate's responsibilities.[13]

The Roman Catholic doctrine of salvation through good works provided the Spanish with a strong incentive for private acts of charity. No doubt many such acts by laymen and churchmen alike, because they were private, went unrecorded, although, since most Spaniards lived in the cities and had little more than fleeting contact with the mass of the rural Maya, it is doubtful that the latter reaped much benefit.[14] In the absence of any public program of welfare, which the rudimentary colonial bureaucracy would have been ill-equipped to manage even if it had existed, poor relief, like almost all other local affairs, was left to the Maya to arrange in their own way.

The survival of widows, orphans, the old, the chronically ill, and people otherwise physically disabled indicates that the Maya recognized some collective responsibility for the less fortunate members of society. Although we have little direct evidence, it is likely that the extended family was the first resort and the ordinary resource for the needy.

The colonial regime undermined the reciprocal arrangements of the extended family. It also failed to acknowledge the even closer mutual dependence of the husband and wife team (the widowed, for example, gained no exemption from taxes, and although the physically disabled did, their spouses did not). Still, the nuclear family survived, and so apparently did the extended kin group, in varying degrees of approximation of the ideal. The three-generation family continued to be the preferred residential unit, if less frequently under the same roof.[15] Maize production was still commonly a cooperative effort by a small group of patrilineally related males—the milpa gang that often formed the nucleus of an outlying hamlet and that even carried the same structure over into other occupations. Father and sons, uncle and nephews, or some other variation can also frequently be found serving together as foreman and cowhands on the same *estancia*.

The economic arrangements within the *macehual* extended family are obscure. This larger kin group may no longer have functioned, if it ever had, as a collective unit. Some degree of economic cooperation in addition to the sharing or exchange of agricultural labor can be inferred from the preference for residential clustering. House building was a joint project, although there is some suggestion that the construction crews could also include friends and neighbors. All were supplied food and drink and could expect similar aid when their own houses needed repair or replacement.[16]

A form of the corporate extended family has been retained in many parts of rural Yucatan today and can offer clues to the organization of its colonial predecessor. This contemporary family is based on a fluidly defined male kin group, most often father and grown sons. The nuclear families function as separate domestic units, each with its own house, garden, flocks of poultry, and legal rights to *ejido* land invested in the head of the household. But house plots are contiguous, as are the milpas, and the men often work the fields together and invest jointly in larger livestock. There is a sense of commingled interests, which at the very least involves an obligation of mutual aid—the loan of a bicycle, say, or money, which the borrower is expected to repay, but only when able.

This pattern has also been transferred to the new resort areas on the east coast, where men from the interior flock to earn cash as unskilled laborers on construction sites. Like many peasant immigrants to a modern economic setting, they carry their corporate organization with them. Few make a permanent move. Instead, the same milpa team works seasonally on the coast, sometimes leaving one member behind to tend everyone's fields after planting. Whenever possible they work as a team, living together and sharing all expenses while on the job. Although they do not pool their wages, all of the cash reserves of kinsmen are in a sense a common fund that can be tapped when necessary to help pay for a wedding, a curing ceremony, or some other extraordinary expense.

A similar, loosely corporate system was, I suggest, the colonial Maya's usual form of social security, reinforced by the strong belief that the dead would do mischief to surviving kinsmen if the latter had failed in their obligations to them.

The extended family was not an infallible source of aid. Whether by choice or by necessity, many individuals and nuclear families had to manage on their own. What happened to the sick, widowed, orphaned, and others who were in need and also (as could occur) deprived of all close kin, real and fictive? To the old who lacked property with which they could purchase an heir to take care of them? The margin of survival was narrow within Maya society, but the Maya were not bands of hunters whose old and infirm had to be abandoned or killed off for the safety of the group. Those who lacked family support for whatever reason may have gotten by to some extent on the more or less grudging, more or less openhanded charity of their more fortunate neighbors. But there also existed another level of corporate organization beyond the extended family—the community.

CORPORATE RESOURCES: *Cajas de Comunidad* AND *Cofradías*

The colonial Maya community organized a variety of programs and projects to increase the odds for survival of its members. Many of their collective efforts will seem pitifully inadequate, some of them even futile. Their practical value is often difficult to assess or, in the case of corporate intercessions with the supernatural, beyond our capacity to judge at all. Our principal concern is with their social value, that is, with the way in which these efforts sustained and expressed the bonds of community.

The Spanish system of indirect rule in Yucatan, *pace* the rhetoric of royal paternalism, left the responsibility for public welfare, and indeed all matters of local administration, in Maya hands. Local financial organization was given a formal Spanish cast through the creation of a *caja de comunidad* for each town along with the rest of the apparatus of municipal government. The *caja* was supposed to be literally a community "chest," a locked strongbox containing the community's funds, maintained in the town hall under the care of a special fiscal officer, the municipal *mayordomo*. He and the other officers were to keep written records of income and expenditure and render annual account to the provincial governor.[17]

As so often occurred with colonial innovations, the name *caja de comunidad* was misleadingly applied to a Maya institution which bore little resemblance to the Hispanic model. The Maya had their own system of finance, which they continued to follow despite the rules and categories imposed by the Spanish. The *caja* was simply that portion of community resources which was used for local needs, although in raising revenues the Maya themselves made no sharp distinction between the different kinds of taxes that they collected. Instead they treated all as a common fund to be drawn upon as needed—for tribute, church taxes, fiestas, or any other local expenditure.

For the first half century or so after conquest, the colonial authorities seem to have interfered minimally with the fiscal organization of the pueblos, which had probably been little modified from pre-Columbian times. The Maya relied primarily on collective labor to meet their various obligations, assigning community residents to public works projects, to cultivate the *milpa de cacique* for the personal support of the *batab*, and the *milpa de comunidad* for general community expenses (a separation between privy purse and general exchequer for the benefit of the Spanish auditors, and probably only nominal).

In this early period before a formal system of *servicio personal* had been instituted, local officials also contracted directly with individual Spaniards, hiring out workers for construction, transport, and agricultural labor and depositing their wages, which were still often paid in cacao beans, in the local treasury. Men were sent out on hunting and wax-collecting expeditions and women were put to work in the town hall to weave *mantas*, all for the community fund.

A variety of goods, such as cacao beans, salt, and chickens, was also collected from individuals, and like tribute these community contributions came increasingly to be paid in cash as the colonial period progressed. Unlike tribute, however, they were not a fixed head tax. They were ad hoc quotas (called *derramas*), levied in cash or kind to cover particular expenses that were prorated among community members.[18]

During the early 1600s a protracted three-way struggle began among the Maya, the parish clergy (primarily the Franciscans), and the royal officials for control of community revenues. Hard pressed to meet the rising costs of defending the colony against the "Lutheran corsairs" and unable to tamper with tribute, which was set at a fixed rate, the provincial governors realized apparently for the first time what a vast, untapped resource the *cajas de comunidad* represented. The first step in siphoning off local revenues was to transform them into a new head tax that became known as the *comunidades*. (The rate oscillated, from the time the tax was established in 1608, between four and five reales, and was finally confirmed by the Crown at four reales in 1668.) The next move was to eliminate the ecclesiastical competition for these funds, by prohibiting the Indians from paying their contributions to the clergy out of municipal revenues, which had been established practice. These *limosnas* (alms), as their name implied, were henceforth to be truly voluntary and presumably individual contributions. The final step was to appropriate the funds altogether.[19]

The details of the struggle are obscure, the outcome clear: both the friars and the governors won and the Indians lost. The governors diverted the now substantial *comunidades* revenues into the royal Treasury, and at least one governor diverted them into his own pocket. The clergy, unwilling to rely on the uncoerced generosity of the Indians, somehow managed to substitute for the old *limosnas* a new head tax of their own, the *obvenciones*, independent of the *cajas de comunidad* and of civil control.[20] And the Indians were saddled with three head taxes instead of one: *obvenciones* on top of tribute and *comunidades*. Moreover, the clergy regarded *obvenciones* as purely personal income, so that the Indians had to raise additional funds on their own to support all the other religious expenses formerly paid out of municipal revenues, as well as other local expenses no longer covered by the *comunidades*.

Some time in the last decades of the seventeenth century the *comunidades* revenues were restored to the Maya through the combined efforts of the local Protector de Indios and a magistrate from the Audiencia of Mexico, whose vigorous prosecution of a particularly rapacious governor (the Flores de Aldana whose predations were described in chapter 2) seems to have served as a warning to his successors not to loot the *cajas de comunidad*—at least not excessively and not without royal permission.[21] In the meantime the Maya had created an unofficial and therefore less vulnerable substitute for *cajas de comunidad* in the form of confraternities, or *cofradías*.

Anyone familiar with the colonial *cajas de comunidad* in other parts of Mesoamerica will recognize a strong family resemblance between them and the Indian *cofradías*.[22] In Yucatan, at least, the resemblance is not accidental, for there is much indirect evidence that the one descended from the other. Almost all the *cofradías* in Yucatan were either founded or reorganized along the model of the *cajas* during the period when these funds were diverted into the royal Treasury. According to the few surviving account books from the sixteenth century, the municipal revenues were produced and administered in the same way as later *cofradía* income, by officers bearing the same title of *mayordomo*; and the income was spent for similar purposes in roughly the same proportions. Both performed a mixture of civil and religious functions (with a heavy emphasis on the latter) designed to promote the common good and ensure the survival of the community qua community. *Caja de comunidad* and *cofradía*, then, should be viewed merely as different Spanish terms applied to what was essentially the same institution. The shift in labels obscured the continuity of purpose and organization, and in doing so also helped to preserve that continuity in the face of Spanish interference. I am not sure that it was a conscious subterfuge, but it was nonetheless an effective one.

The *cofradías* represent another kind of gap between Spanish terminology and colonial Indian reality, in this case an institution that underwent a profound metamorphosis while preserving the same label. The *cofradías* that the Franciscan friars first established in the late sixteenth century were modeled closely on the contemporary Hispanic version, a combination of religious sodality and burial society, which individuals joined on a voluntary basis and supported with alms and dues.[23] Linked to the rise of craft guilds, the Spanish *cofradías* were primarily urban in character; they served to define social identities in a complex society in addition to promoting personal piety and offering mutual aid in the form of burial insurance and sometimes benefits for the sick, widows, and orphans.[24] As such, they transplanted well to the cities of Spanish and Portuguese America, where they helped to mark social boundaries based on caste as well as occupation.[25] And as such they proved incompatible with the values and structure of Indian peasant society, organized almost exclusively along the lines of kinship and shared territory and with a collective rather than an individual approach to the pursuit of divine blessings.[26]

Throughout Mesoamerica these voluntary associations of pious individuals became transformed into community-wide institutions that replicated the form and function of the *cajas de comunidad*, mobilizing public resources for the spiritual and material welfare of the community. (Gibson calls them "unofficial" *cofradías* to distinguish them from the original type of dues-paying burial society and notes that "their operation lies as close to municipal finance as to normal cofradía business."[27]) In Yucatan the *cofradía* in its modified form *was* the community. Membership in both was coterminous, and although each pueblo might nominally have several *cofradías* dedicated to different saints, they were all integrated into a single *cofradía* organization, with a single set of officers who also served either simultaneously or alternately in the parallel civil posts of the *cabildo*.

The *cofradías* were among the more ingenious adaptations the Maya made to the harsh realities of the colonial regime. Much of the community's public revenues was generated and allocated under their aegis, but unlike the *cajas de comunidad* they remained virtually immune from the royal officials. Even if they had not been "spiritual property" (*bienes espirituales*) and therefore, according to Spanish law, under the church's jurisdiction, the governors and other officials were scarcely aware that they existed; for no one bothered to apply for the royal license that technically all ecclesiastical foundations required.[28]

The church, to be sure, could be as rapacious as the state in dealing with the Indians. However, for most of the *cofradías'* history—until they began to accumulate sizable amounts of property—they managed to escape the notice or at least the attention of bishops as well as royal officials. *Cofradía* property could not so easily be kept hidden from the parish clergy. But it was in the latter's interests to leave the Maya a more or less free hand, since a considerable portion of the revenues went in any case into the curate's pocket, either directly as fiesta fees or indirectly by subsidizing the costs of divine worship.[29]

The *cofradías* generated income in a variety of ways, most of them reminiscent of the original *caja de comunidad*. In the early stages of their transformation from Spanish-type sodalities or brotherhoods charging annual dues, they relied on the traditional system of collective labor. Part of the community labor tax was assigned to *cofradía* milpas, and the maize, beans, cotton, and other crops produced there continued to be the major source of income for some of the *cofradías*. Others raised funds through *derramas*, or individual assessments of cacao beans or Spanish coin, and even through the *repartimiento* system; the cash advanced in the *repartimiento* was put into the *cofradía* coffers instead of being distributed to the individuals who produced the cloth and bees-

266

wax.[30] Since this system was also used to raise money for tribute and other taxes, it provides another link between the *cofradía* and the rest of public finance.

Many of the *cofradías* ventured into a very untraditional but profitable enterprise that they had learned from the Spanish—cattle ranching. A local *principal* would donate a *cenote*, others some cash or a few head of cattle to launch the operation. Unpaid communal labor was still used to construct corrals and ranch buildings and to grow the staple crops that supplemented the sale of beef cattle, horses, and mules. Otherwise the *haciendas de cofradía*, as they came to be called, were indistinguishable from the privately owned Spanish estates. Like the Spanish estates, they eventually acquired their own resident population of *luneros*, who worked exclusively on the haciendas as their community *tequios*. Even the salaried ranch hands were treated like any Spanish-employed *criados* whose masters (in this case the *cofradía* officers) paid their tribute and made other advances on their wages.[31]

The *cofradía* officers were astute and careful administrators. I have no account books from Spanish haciendas in Yucatan to compare with the ones that have been preserved for the *cofradías*. It is likely that the *cofradía* estates were as well run and certainly more honestly run, since the *mayordomos* were answerable to their own communities (or at least their fellow elite) and to the saints, whereas the managers of Spanish estates rendered account only to absentee owners living in the cities.

We have records pertaining to 137 haciendas of various sizes belonging to 108 of the 203 pueblos existing in Yucatan in the mid-eighteenth century. Some prospered quite spectacularly by local standards, rivaling all but the largest Spanish estates. In eastern Yucatan most of the *cofradía* estates were small and concentrated more on apiculture, perhaps because the local Spanish market for cattle was so small. In the far south the Spanish population was even smaller, but there were few private *estancias* to compete with, and the local *cofradías* supplied beef to the military posts in Bacalar and Peten Itza, and all the mules and horses that were virtually the only export item the Peten produced.[32]

The *cofradías* in southern Campeche were the most prosperous, combining cattle ranching with interregional trade in cacao. Their *mayordomos* traveled widely through the Usumacinta valley and into Tabasco with portable images and scapularies of the saints, and the cacao they collected and bought with the alms given in cash was then brought back to sell in the port of Campeche.[33]

Except for the cattle ranches, obviously a postconquest innovation, both the *cofradías* and their progenitors, the *cajas de comunidad*, were indigenous institutions. Their ostensible organization and purpose satisfied Spanish notions of how and why things should be done, but these were essentially administrative formulae under which community resources could be mobilized for community needs—as defined by the Maya, and in their own way. Certainly the distinction between the two colonial institutions is far from clear, if indeed there was one in Maya eyes. And the *cofradías* may have continued to substitute for the *cajas de comunidad* even after these revenues were restored to the Indians. The four-real head tax was still supposed to be levied but must have been a fiction tacitly accepted by the royal governors, who reviewed the accounts each year along with the *cabildo* election returns. Expenditure conveniently equaled income almost invariably. Only 4,086 pesos of surplus had accumulated in the royal Treasury for all the community accounts combined, from the inception of the system in the sixteenth century until 1777, although the annual yield was estimated at 28,030 pesos in 1766, according to the tribute rolls.[34]

What did the Maya officials do with that income? The *cofradía* had already absorbed many of the local expenses, and in addition to the cash head tax the community milpas were still supposedly being cultivated. Treasury officials suspected malfeasance. The more likely explanation is that the head tax was never collected, at least in its entirety, and instead *derramas* continued to be levied as they were needed to defray whatever expenses were not covered by revenues from the *cofradías* and the community milpas. The royal governors apparently did not inquire very closely into either income or expenditure so long as they received their customary gratuities for their annual audit of the books.

By far the major part of recorded expenditure from all sources of revenue was devoted to the cult of the saints.[35] Although the Maya's negotiations with their saints formed part of their total strategy for survival, indeed its chief element, I shall concentrate in this chapter on the more secular aspects of their program, with the caveat that the Maya themselves made no sharp distinction between sacred and secular in either theory or practice.

Epidemics and famines presented the most serious challenge to the community's corporate organization and to the survival of its members. Sometimes the strain was intolerable. When able, people scattered to seek deliverance on their own, and the community ceased to exist for all practical purposes for the duration of the crisis.[36] This does not mean that the Maya made no cooperative efforts to deal with these calamities or that the efforts were totally ineffectual, although they were nearly so in the case of epidemics.

The Maya had no hospitals nor any desire for them, having come to the not wholly unfounded conclusion from their observations that these

European institutions were for dying.[37] They preferred to recover or die, as the case might be, at home. Professional healing was a private arrangement with a local shaman who provided a combination of "spells" and herbal remedies that the patient or his relatives paid for in cash or goods.[38] The communities or *cofradías* were supposed to provide some care for the sick, although this was primarily spiritual and primarily when people were beyond any material aid. A part-time staff of *fiscales* had the responsibility to seek out the sick, ensure that they were being cared for, and help those *in extremis* to "die properly" (*morir bien*), calling in the priest when the last rites were needed.[39] The fact that the same *fiscales* also doubled as the parish gravediggers suggests that their efforts were seen more as a contribution to the whole death ritual than as an aid to recovery. It is unlikely that they were able to provide for either the spiritual or physical needs of the sick during any serious epidemic. When these occurred, the communities were hard pressed to dispose of the dead as fast as they succumbed, and in the worst visitations the dogs and vultures took over even that task.

No one knew how to prevent or cure the diseases that took such heavy tolls among native Americans. The remedies, private and public, that the Maya applied were as beneficial as anything available and probably a lesser impediment to recovery than many that were current in Western medicine. The lower mortality rate among the Spanish was due to better nourishment and especially to their greater natural immunity to the diseases they had imported, and not, one imagines, to such therapeutic techniques as bloodletting or to potions concocted of ground boar's tooth.[40]

Nor were the Maya (or anyone else) able to avert the more familiar calamities of crop failure caused by the droughts, tropical storms, and plagues of locusts with which their ancestors had always had to contend. They had somewhat better success in mitigating the effects through community organized famine relief, despite the Spaniards' propensity to look upon any Maya reserves as a resource to be tapped for themselves. No record exists of whether the Maya communities had communal granaries before the development of the *cofradías* into community funds during the mid-seventeenth century. It is likely that they did, and that this function was transferred to the *cofradías* like so many others formerly under the expropriated *cajas de comunidad*, and for the same reason—the lower risk of interference from the provincial authorities. In all but name, the *cofradías* served as famine stores: their reserves of maize and beans, produced by communal labor and ordinarily intended for sale in order to support the local fiestas and other religious rituals, were distributed among the community in time of need.

269

The *cofradía* estates also provided cattle. This new resource to help stabilize the food supply was nonperishable (at least while on the hoof) and in good years multiplied with very little labor. Beef cattle eventually became the *cofradías'* main source of income and also their main source of famine relief. Although considered the property of the saints and therefore normally sacrosanct, the *cofradía* cattle could be used to feed the community in bad years because, as the Maya explained, most of the cattle would starve anyway during a prolonged drought. The herds could be rebuilt again so long as a few head survived, but if the whole community perished there would be no one left to worship the saints.[41] When the clergy objected to what they considered illegal seizures of church property, the *cofradía* officers simply attributed the losses to cattle rustling, which they maintained was impossible to prevent when people were starving. One doubts that they made much of an effort, since they and the other community leaders also maintained that famine relief was a legitimate if secondary goal of the *cofradías* and one of the original purposes for which the haciendas had been established. However inadequate the herds were to sustain life through repeated crop failures, the Maya believed that without them the recurring famines that so depleted their numbers would have been even more devastating.

Aside from these attempts to meet general emergencies that affected the community as a whole, the Maya made some provision for chronically needy individuals. It would seem that these individuals did not have to rely entirely on the spontaneous help of neighbors and friends, for the communities possessed a formal if rudimentary system of public assistance, which, like most of the Maya's corporate projects, was based on communal labor. The weekly *tequios* that the able-bodied males contributed were divided into four tasks in rotation: one Monday a month was devoted to cultivating the *batab*'s milpa, one to the community milpa, one to public works projects, and one to "milpas and other ministrations for the old, the disabled, and widows."[42]

The Maya also provided some kind of tax relief for these and other individuals who were in need but who were nevertheless unable to gain exemptions from the Spanish authorities.[43] The community fiscal system was organized in such a way as to permit flexibility. In raising revenues the Maya officials tended to treat all community obligations in common, whether ultimately to be allocated for tribute quotas, church taxes, special fees and fines imposed by bishops and governors, or for their own local needs. Over time individual or family contributions in goods or cash, as opposed to the production of goods by communal labor, may have accounted for an increasing proportion of revenue. Even then, so long as the Maya officials remained in charge of tax collection, tax obligations never became a wholly individual liability, since the community retained responsibility for those who could not pay their share.[44]

The Maya officials had in practice absolute discretionary power in apportioning the tax burden. While this power could be used to provide exemptions for the privileged members of the community, it could also be used to grant tax relief for those in need. The old, the infirm, widows, and anyone else the Maya considered legitimately unable to pay taxes could be relieved in whole or in part, even when they were officially included in the tax rolls. The rule of striking all men over the age of sixty and women over the age of fifty-five from the tax rolls was not always honored by the Spanish; the definition of *impedidos* (disabled) depended entirely on the will of the priest, *encomendero*, or royal official; and no allowance was made for people with disabled spouses or for temporary or less than total incapacity. One dispute, for example, centered around two old sisters with cataracts whose curate maintained that they were not so blind that they could not continue to weave mantas.[45]

It should be emphasized that the principle underlying tax relief, public assistance, and the social order in general was corporate without being egalitarian. Aid was limited in scope and intention, designed to alleviate only the neediest cases rather than equalize economic differences. The use of the term *pobre* (poor) by both the Maya and the Spanish when speaking of people who were granted any special concession can be misleading. If "poor" means someone living at the margin of subsistence, with few possessions and little chance of accumulating any, then most of the people in any peasant society would qualify. Obviously the Maya defined poverty more narrowly, referring to a specific and small category of publicly acknowledged paupers, below the ordinary mass of *macehuales* and far below the upper category of *pudientes*. To be a pauper—to have, that is, a legitimate claim on assistance from the rest of the community—one had to be destitute: both unable to sustain oneself and lacking the primary support group of the family, which was expected to take care of its own.

Thus the tax system was far from perfectly equitable. There is no evidence that any of the contributions levied by the community for any purpose were set at a graduated rate, other than the tripartite division into the rich, the ordinary, and the poor. Still, their system was an improvement over the rigid fiscal policy of the Spanish. Much financial hardship no doubt escaped the strict definition of pauperism. But the unpaid tax debt that so many people left behind when they died or moved away indicates that deferrals were frequently granted, in addition to the exemptions given to the official "poor."

271

All the defaulted taxes and the portion of the official quota represented by the exemptions were prorated among the rest of the community. During times of plague and famine when the weakened remnant populations had no hope of paying off the accumulated load of tax arrears by *derramas*, the Maya had to resort to selling off a portion of the corporate patrimony, the community-owned lands, to raise the necessary cash. A drastic step but one that underlies the corporate nature of the tax burden.

ELITES AND COMMUNITY DEFENSE: LAND AND LITIGATION

If survival was a joint enterprise in which the whole community participated, the particular strategies pursued were devised and directed by the elite. They were the ones who organized all the corporate projects, from fiestas to famine relief, and the programs to aid needy individuals; they were the ones who defended the community's interests, its resources, and its members against external threats.

Unlike their predecessors, the colonial elite could no longer take up arms to protect their territories, nor could they make raids on a neighboring province to avenge insults to their subjects, which had been one of the chief responsibilities of the pre-Columbian lords. But the colonial system still left them with a crucial role in defending the territorial integrity of their communities and the rights of their subjects.

The Maya did not bury their differences in order to unite against the Spaniards during the conquest, and old rivalries persisted, especially along the former provincial borders, for example those between Sotuta and its Cupul and Xiu neighbors on either side.[46]

The colonial boundary disputes were confined to minor border skirmishing—forays to support claims on disputed territory by clearing milpas there, and retaliatory raids from the other side to destroy the milpas and chase out the intruders. Anything more serious would have brought heavy penalties from the Spanish, and in fact the Maya leaders were forced to take most of their battles to the law courts.[47] The Spanish generally respected the Maya's jurisdictional boundaries as the basis for the colonial units of administration, and when the Maya could not agree on the boundaries among themselves, the Spanish officials did their best to arbitrate impartially. The role of the Maya elite was as repository of the communities' collective memory and historical rights. They were the ones who made and preserved the record of these rights in the sacred *títulos* (land titles): the collection of maps, testaments, deeds, border agreements, and every other scrap of paper referring to land that each community guarded so assiduously. As the most stable members of the stable core population of each community, they were also the ones who preserved its oral traditions. And they were the formal spokesmen, marshaling the evidence, preparing the petitions and traveling to Merida to press the community's claims before the Protector de Indios and the governor.

As the colonial period advanced, boundary disputes with other pueblos became insignificant compared to the task of protecting community territory from Spanish encroachment. In order to understand the corporate organization of the community as well as the struggle to retain its most vital corporate resource, a few points about their systems of land ownership and land use need to be mentioned.[48]

Most of the land within the jurisdictional boundaries of a particular community was owned in common. Even the nobility, to whom private ownership was customarily restricted, did much of their farming, and the macehuales did all of theirs, on lands belonging to the community. There were no permanent boundaries within the commonly owned lands because of the nature of swidden agriculture. The right of usufruct allocated to each family lasted only the life of the milpa, which would yield maize for only two or three years at a time and then reverted to the community to be reassigned after the appropriate period of fallow.

The responsibility for allocating milpa sites belonged to an alcalde col (col = milpa in Yucatec Maya), which may have been a title held by one of the two ordinary alcaldes elected each year rather than a separate office.[49] Land was plentiful enough during most of the colonial period so that in theory every farmer could freely choose his own parcel of fallow bush for a milpa without bumping into a neighbor. But competition and disputes were likely to arise over the best sites. To a casual observer the uniformity of Yucatecan geography might suggest that one milpa site is as good as another. Not to the Maya. Subtle variations in moisture, soil depth, and evenness of terrain are of intense interest to the milpero, and three conditions above all make a parcel of bush more or less attractive: proximity to town (for some a negative factor—the farther away the better), proximity to a water supply, and length of time the land has lain fallow. High bush that has not been cultivated for many years is and was especially coveted, for it is easier to clear and produces a higher crop yield. Thus, to avoid a free-for-all, the distribution of these temporary land rights had to be controlled. The allocation of this most vital resource was an important source of elite power in general, and we can surmise that it helped to support the clientage networks through which particular political arrangements were made and unmade in each community.

The value of community lands was not confined to the production of

273

basic food crops. Most of the Maya's other needs were met from the publicly owned but privately exploited resources these lands yielded: firewood, all materials for building and for household furnishings (including clay deposits for pottery), wild fruit and game, and fodder for cattle, mules, and horses.

Even when land was owned privately, the concept of ownership differed markedly from that held by the Spanish, and therein lay a major source of the conflicts that arose between the two groups. In contrast to their deep concern over precise jurisdictional boundaries between communities, the Maya were by our standards extraordinarily casual (in their formal documents at least) about delineating boundaries of the individual parcels of land that were owned by elite families and the parcels that were sold by them or by the communities to Spaniards.[50] This vagueness was certainly not due to any ignorance of the terrain. One piece of bush may look like the next to an outsider, but the Maya knew the exact location of every small savanna, every rock outcrop, ceiba tree, and *cenote* in the district, and each little section of bush had its own name. If in their documents and discussions about land they tended to emphasize some particular feature of the landscape instead of amounts or extents of land, it was because actual acreage was relatively unimportant, not because they were incapable of measuring it or fixing precise boundaries.

The Maya may not have originally had any system of private land ownership in the sense of exclusive right. One owned what was worth owning, which was not the land itself but any improvements to it. These became private property for the duration of their "useful life." The rights to a milpa could be sold, a recently cleared site (*milpa en roza*) being worth one real a *mecate*, and a milpa in the second year of the planting cycle (*milpa en caña*) being worth one-half real. What the buyer was paying for was the labor of preparation, and not the land itself.[51]

Houses, fruit trees, and henequen plants were also classified as improvements to the land. They belonged to whoever had built them or planted them, and even if it turned out that they were located on someone else's house plot, the owner of the house plot acquired possession only if he paid compensation to the person who had built the house or cultivated the tree.[52] The house plots themselves were considered more or less permanent improvements, and the families acquired outright title to them by virtue of squatter's rights or by some more formal procedure that has not been recorded. They could be inherited and they reverted to the community only if the whole family moved away.[53]

Aside from improvements to the land, the other real property worth owning was an *hoya*, an *aguada*, or a *cenote*—most commonly a *cenote* in northern Yucatan to which most of the colonial documentation refers. The ownership of a *cenote* included rights, although perhaps not exclusive ones, to some undetermined portion of land surrounding it—undetermined but not necessarily indeterminate.[54] Maybe the extent of each particular parcel was common knowledge; maybe a more or less standard amount of land, also common knowledge, was always attached to *cenote* ownership. Or it could be that acreage was simply not an issue, that no one owned tracts of land, and that when referring to the "lands" of the Couoh or the Pacab lineage, for example, the Maya meant only some preferential claim to use the land around privately owned *cenotes* to make milpa. Whatever rules about amounts of land may have been current among the early colonial Maya, they omitted to mention them in their testaments and in the bills of sale they made out to each other and to Spanish buyers. That omission was to create serious problems for their descendants.

By the late colonial period the Maya had become considerably more specific about titles to ordinary milpa land. Whether they were merely writing down what had always been tacitly understood, or whether later deeds and testaments reflect an actual change in the concept of rights over land cannot be determined. In either case they would have been influenced by Spanish example and the necessity of protecting their claims to this increasingly valuable resource. At least in the densely populated west, especially around Merida, where competition over land arose earliest, they carefully recorded exact quantities of privately owned land even in transactions among themselves.[55]

For most of the colonial period the Spanish found little difficulty in acquiring as much land as they wanted. In the immediate postconquest years sharp population losses, the dislocations of conquest itself, and the resettlements carried out under the congregation program left much supposedly unclaimed land that could be obtained directly by royal grant. Some of it belonged to communities that had ceased to exist. If some remnant population that had been relocated in another town still technically held title to lands granted by the Crown, they were unlikely to make any effective opposition even if they were notified of the grants.[56] As the territorial boundaries of the communities became more firmly reestablished, *tierras baldías* (unclaimed lands) were no longer so easily available. Nevertheless, the Spanish could still purchase titles easily enough from individuals and from the communities themselves.[57]

One gets the impression that many of the sales were as much a favor to the Indians, who needed the cash, as any pressing need for land on the part of the buyer. Both private owners and communities could fall

275

heavily into debt during famines and epidemics. Usually the individual owner or the town *principales* went in search of a buyer, who more often than not simply held the parcel for resale or to stock it with cattle at some later date. I do not suggest that the Spanish became uncharacteristically indifferent to acquiring land when they happened to settle in Yucatan, only that for long the supply more than equalled the demand. If they bought more than they could use at the time it was because the predilection for landowning was so deeply rooted in Spanish culture and because the prices were so low in what was essentially a buyer's market that they could afford to invest in some parcel of bush and let it sit indefinitely.[58]

Nor do I suggest that, on the other hand, the Maya were indifferent to even the partial loss of their lands, private or communal, no matter how plentiful. The sales were often an act of desperation resorted to in times of crisis: a clear-cut choice (for both individuals or lineages and communities) between partial divestment and total ruin. Community leaders were the trustees in charge of protecting the communal patrimony, but like other trustees they sometimes had to sell off some of the corporate assets to keep the entire operation from going under.

Most of these sales were not strictly legal, for they lacked the formal approval of the Protector de Indios, which was required for the alienation of any community-owned lands. There is no record that the Protector was even notified of them. However, the main contention that developed beween the Maya and the Spanish was not over the legality of the transfers themselves but over what was included in them.

The early deeds were exceedingly brief documents. They would mention a section of territory called a *chakan* (translated as *sitio, paraje* or *asiento*—place or site), deriving its name from the *cenote* with which it was associated. No indications were given of its size, and certainly no detailed property boundaries. It is impossible to tell from these deeds exactly what the Indians thought they were selling or what the Spaniards thought they were buying. The Spaniards themselves were little more precise, concerned about the legality of their titles and little if at all about what the titles included. They took advantage of the wholesale *composiciones de tierras* offered by the Crown, by which any dubious land titles could be validated for a fee (a common technique used to raise revenues and reconcile the gap between royal law and colonial practice in many areas of life). These certificates, however, merely confirmed the original deed, no matter how illegal, without providing any more details on the property's extent. And when property was resold to another Spaniard, the new deeds were almost as vague, merely designating the general location. A deed of sale issued in 1720 for the "*paraje* with its *cenote* named Pibixa" and recorded in the Merida notarial archives is not an untypical example. Its boundaries were listed as "to the north the cattle ranch Calactun, to the south milpa fields of the pueblo of Hocaba, and other boundaries."[59]

For a long time it hardly mattered what either the original sales or the later transfers included. No fences or even boundary markers were put up, and both sides shared use of the same lands. The shared use created its own set of conflicts independent of the issue of ownership, and these arose from the inherently incompatible mixture of stock raising and milpa farming. The Spanish could interfere seriously with Maya food production even without acquiring outright title to large tracts of land. Wherever they settled in the New World, the Spanish brought along with their cattle the pastoralist values of Castilian society. Ranching, the economic base of the Castilian reconquest, took precedence in social prestige and political power over farming (which was often left in the hands of the Moriscos), and the interests of stockmen prevailed over those of the conquered farmer on both sides of the Atlantic.

The hardy Spanish breed of cattle did very well in America, proliferating rapidly everywhere but in deserts and mountains and almost invariably at the expense of native fauna, including humans. Andean Indians were skilled herders, but they generally grazed their llamas in the high *puna* where the animals did not compete with farming for the same space. In Mesoamerica, Indians had no experience with large domestic animals. Cattle caused much damage to maize crops in central Mexico and indirectly contributed to the high mortality rate in the early postconquest period, until the Indians learned to keep them out. The encircling rows of organ cactus, so characteristic a feature of the landscape in the central and northern plateaus, provide an excellent defense for permanent fields. The Maya lowlands were much less crowded but the shifting fields of swidden agriculture cannot so easily be protected against marauding cattle. In keeping with pastoralist values and the primitive style of ranching, cattle were to be fenced out, not in. And although there is a technique of clearing a milpa so that the felled trees and brush form an interlocking barrier, a local cattle rancher has confirmed what I have heard repeatedly from milpa farmers, which is that this barrier will not keep out a determined cow or bull, much less a small herd.

In colonial Yucatan, then, cattle roamed free throughout the unfenced land surrounding the *planta*, or ranch headquarters, except when they were brought in to be watered, and they understandably found the growing corn in the scattered Indian milpas more succulent fare than the scrubby vegetation of the fallow bush. Most of the communities themselves owned one or more cattle ranches—the *cofradía* estates and small stock farms and *estancias* belonging to individual Maya. According to the Maya, however, they were careful to control both the size and the movement of their herds in order to protect their own crops, precautions that the Spanish ranchers and their employees did not bother to take.[60]

Long before the Maya communities experienced any shortages of land (at least as early as 1603), they were complaining about cattle invading their milpas.[61] And for most of the colonial period their struggles with the Spanish estate owners continued to focus mainly on crop damage rather than on property boundaries. The *república* officers, whose task it was to defend community resources, were kept busy marching off to *estancia* headquarters to protest to the foremen, buttonholing the owners on their rare visits and, when these tactics failed, traveling to Merida to lodge formal complaints with the provincial authorities.

Colonial legislation gave precedence to the rights of the Indian farmers. In addition to the requirement that approval be obtained from the Protector de Indios for all sales of land to Spaniards, once the land had been bought the owners still had to obtain a permit to stock the site with cattle, and these permits required the consent of the community officials in whose territory the property was located. In theory, then, the Maya could have prevented this plague of cattle invasions, which was at the very least a nuisance and could threaten their food supply. As with so much colonial legislation, local economic interests prevailed over paternalist royal policy, sometimes with the connivance of the Crown itself. The royal *composiciones de tierras* validated illegal land titles (*componer* = to fix or repair), while bribes to local officials secured permits to stock cattle. The Maya too could be tempted to give their consent by offers of cash from the prospective rancher to help out with their often precarious community finances or, in lieu of cash, some cattle to start their own *cofradía* estate.[62] Once the permit was obtained there was no control over the expansion of the herds, even though each permit specified the maximum number of cattle for the particular property. Since the boundaries between *estancia* land and community land were so ill-defined, the only limit on pasturage was the competition with the ill-protected milpas of the Maya.

One of the colony's most forceful champions of Indian welfare, Bishop Juan Gómez de Parada, presented the problem of cattle depredations to the Crown in 1722. There were, he wrote, too many *estancias* and they were often too close to the Indian towns and villages. He described how time after time during his episcopal tour of inspection he had seen free-roaming cattle trample crops close to the towns and invade gardens inside the town limits. In several places the Indians had even had to drive cattle away from the town hall, where they—no respectors of episcopal prerogatives—had started to eat the fodder gathered for the bishop's own mules.[63]

The bishop recommended that all *estancias* established within one league of any pueblo be destroyed; presumably he meant that the cattle should be sold or moved and the *planta* be abandoned. As it turned out, the famine of 1723-1726, possibly the worst in the colony's history, resolved the problem temporarily, killing off a large portion of the cattle and taking a heavy toll among the Maya as well. Within several decades both populations had more than recovered and were in serious competition again. By then a royal decree of 1731, which by prohibiting the granting of any new permits to stock cattle had sought to compromise with Bishop Parada's more drastic proposal, had been shelved.[64]

In these clashes over cattle the question of property limits lay dormant. No one seems to have disputed the right to make milpa or to graze cattle on the same land. The conflict was over who had the responsibility for keeping the two activities operationally separate: whether the Maya were supposed to fence their milpas and bear the liability, or whether the rancher should pay damages if his cowhands failed to keep the herds under control; whether *vacas milperas* (cows who displayed a stubborn predilection for milpas under cultivation) could be destroyed by the farmers, and if so, who kept the meat and hides; whether the farmers were obliged to avoid recognized routes of access in choosing their milpa sites; and a variety of other ancillary issues. In all these disputes the Maya were on the defensive but by no means totally defenseless. The community leaders' incessant needling on the spot, their persistence in filing complaints with the Protector de Indios, and their more direct methods of dealing with rogue cattle were sufficiently irritating to ranchers to serve as a partial check on cattle encroachments. However, these tactics eventually became irksome enough to stimulate the ranchers to encroach in a more serious way on Maya lands.

The question of ownership developed slowly and began in earnest only in the last decades of the eighteenth century, because of certain demographic and economic changes that combined to transform the issue of land rights into one of land ownership.[65] The first push came from the Spanish side, although stimulated in part by pressure from the Maya in the form of more extensive milpa farming and more frequent clashes over cattle invasions. Primarily the Spanish needed more land to expand production, and they decided both to fix the previously blurry boundaries of their increasingly valuable land and to assert exclusive rights to it.

After years, sometimes more than a century, of more or less peaceful coexistence, the Maya suddenly found themselves denied access to land they had been using undisturbed (except by cattle invasions) and most of which they considered their own. Their Spanish neighbors, usually new owners who had recently purchased or inherited the estates, put up boundary markers and ordered their *criados* to keep anyone not resident on the hacienda from trespassing. Not only milpa lands, but also hunting grounds, stands of palm for roof thatch, and rights to all the other forest products on which the Maya depended were at stake.[66]

Some degree of discrepancy between the conflicting property claims may have been due to a genuine misunderstanding of what the original deed had signified to the other party. The Maya asserted that their ancestors had never intended to sell whole sections of land outright; they had sold only the *cenotes* and the rights to pasture their cattle. Perhaps they did transfer some land outright, but it is difficult to imagine that they would ever have knowingly alienated such large chunks of their territory, as the Spanish later claimed, no matter how desperate they had been for cash. The sums they had received were absurdly low and represented only a small fraction of the value of the disputed land, even at the bargain prices current when it was originally sold. Aware of this, some of the communities offered to return the original sale price in order to settle the issue. The estate owners understandably would have none of that and argued that the offers were only a clever attempt to renege on an agreement that the Maya might now regret but that had been perfectly valid.

The Maya interpretation of the original deeds of sale would have placed an effective curb on any future development of commercial agriculture. It is not surprising, then, that the communities were forced to accept some version of the Spanish claims, although not necessarily to their full extent. Whatever part honest error or confusion played in the initial confrontations, it cannot account for the continued attempts to expand hacienda borders once the Maya had grasped the concept of exclusive ownership and hence the crucial importance of delineating—and recording—boundaries precisely.

The first line of defense of community lands was entirely in the hands of the local Maya elite. The Protector de Indios in Merida, even when well intentioned, had no records of land titles or any firsthand information about local developments; and the curates rarely intervened on behalf of their parishioners. When they were not *hacendados* themselves, their kinsmen were. The colonial clashes over territory were a far less showy affair than in pre-Columbian times. The Maya had to substitute lawsuits for military defense. Instead of the gorgeous costumes of the

Mesoamerican war captains, designed to inspire awe and fear in the enemy troops, the colonial Maya leaders—if we are to believe their Spanish opponents in the law courts—deliberately put on their most tattered clothes when appearing in Merida to plead their cases, in order to arouse the pity of the judges.[67] However, the struggle was no less crucial to the group's survival, and although the balance of power lay clearly on the *hacendados'* side, it was restrained by the legalistic ethos of the Spanish colonial regime. The crasser forms of land grabbing awaited emancipation from Spanish rule; so long as that rule lasted, justice must at least appear to be served. Whatever successes the Maya scored would depend on the adroitness with which the *batabs* and other community spokesmen mastered the intricacies of Spanish law and the popular Spanish pastime of litigation.

If the Maya were not "by nature prone to litigation," as their adversaries asserted, they learned quickly. They especially learned the importance of keeping detailed records of property limits, since their folk archives, the elderly *principales* who kept the oral traditions of rights dating back to the "ancients" (that is, before the conquest) or "time immemorial," were not always considered sufficient evidence. Once the *repúblicas* began to keep careful records and a careful eye on the boundary markers to make sure they tallied with the documents, the Spanish had to change their tactics. One enterprising landowner even tried to steal the land titles belonging to the town of Telchac. He apparently borrowed them under the pretext of checking some boundary question and then claimed that he had bought them along with a goodly portion of the community's lands from the *batab*, who had in the meantime conveniently died. The new *batab* and his colleagues won the case, and fairly quickly: the stratagem lacked finesse.[68]

Stealing community land titles was a little blatant for even the most indulgent colonial judge to stomach (although apparently not for their less squeamish successors in the republican law courts). The *hacendados* generally resorted to somewhat more subtle tactics. They sometimes used or leased lands belonging to the community and then claimed title on the basis of "possession." Another maneuver was to destroy old boundary markers or, even better, move them. Either side could call for an official boundary survey (*mensura*) by a supposedly neutral party appointed by the court. Armed with their respective land titles, the opposing contingents—the *batab* with his *cabildo*, and the owner or his manager with a crew of *criados*—would accompany the surveyor, asserting claims and counterclaims as they covered the terrain, and arguing for the relatively new or old appearance of the boundary markers encountered. The surveyor adjudicated on the spot, with an official in-

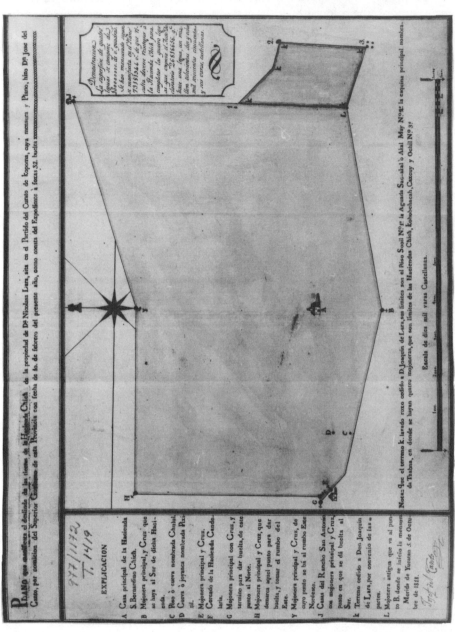

10. Map of hacienda San Bernardino Chich, 1818, submitted in a lawsuit (AGN, Tierras 1419) with the *rancho* San Antonio Buluch (marked "J" in upper right corner); the *rancho*'s lands are included in the 4 square leagues (64 square kilometers) claimed by the owner. (Photo courtesy of Archivo General de la Nación)

terpreter and an *escribano* on hand to record the proceedings. If, as sometimes happened, the surveyor was a close associate of the owner, the decisions were very simple. And if either party, as often happened, was dissatisfied with the survey, the next step was to seek to have it overruled or a new one ordered.

Maya and Spanish litigants were equally adept at applying the basic dictum in all law cases: whenever the case appears to be going in favor of the other party, obstruct the proceedings. It is hard to find final judgments in the judicial records except in criminal cases, and not because the documents have mysteriously disappeared. Spanish legal procedures could have served as a model for Dickens's *Jardyce vs. Jardyce* in *Bleak House*. They seem designed to prolong lawsuits indefinitely, allowing objections, motions, interrogatories and appeals to continue as long as the judge's patience held out. Since judges' incomes depended on court costs, their patience was well-nigh boundless. As for the parties to the suit, the fact that Indians were exempt from court costs or legal fees (a special head tax of one-half real supported the Tribunal de Indios) helped to balance the inequalities of wealth. The trips to Merida and the unofficial "gifts" they usually had to distribute to the governor, his legal advisor, the Protector de Indios, and other officers of the court were a heavy expense to them but no more ruinous, perhaps less so, than the fees and costs charged to non-Indians. The truly disadvantaged were the *castas*, who were often as poor as the Indians but were subject to the same legal expenses as the Spanish. They had no chance in a legal battle with either side and did not participate in the assault on Indian lands in even a modest way except as employees of the large estates. Some owned small properties either purchased from Indians or inherited from some Indian ancestor, but they apparently kept within what the communities considered legal boundaries.[69]

The skill and tenacity of the Maya leaders in their legal battles with the Spanish is best revealed in the splenetic outbursts from their exasperated opponents that sprinkle the judicial records. The following sample comes from the curate of the Sagrario in Merida complaining to the governor about the Indians of Halacho and Becal who had been disputing the property limits he claimed for his nearby hacienda:

> The captiousness, malice, and dishonesty of the Indians are well recognized in the sacred laws that govern us. If royal officials do not stand firm against their feigned humility and other tricks, we Spaniards will never be able to enjoy peaceful possession of our property, especially since they are led by the detestable propositions that they are in their own homeland, that all belongs to them, and other insolent notions.[70]

The curate went on to offer a counter proposition: that the Indians had no legal claim to any land whatsoever, since it all belonged to the Crown by right of conquest. However attractive this argument was, the *hacendados* were obliged to continue whittling away at the community land titles rather than dismiss them outright. The conflict over Indian land gained momentum at the end of the eighteenth century. Given the distribution of power in the colony, the efforts of the Maya leaders were at best a holding action. But in retarding the process of engulfment, the elite made a vital and tangible contribution to community welfare.

The elite's responsibility to defend the community against predatory Spaniards extended beyond the question of land to include all corporate property. They were the ones who kept the inventories of church ornaments and protested if the curate took the church bell with him to his next parish or sold off a set of silk vestments.[71] They managed the *cofradías* and fought a long battle in the last decades of colonial rule against the expropriation of *cofradía* property and income.[72] They kept the written accounts and receipts that proved that the quotas for taxes, *servicio personal*, and *repartimiento* had been met and that extra fees and fines levied on the community had been paid. They petitioned the authorities for deferrals or exemptions when the quotas could not be met; and they occasionally obtained a refund of illegal payments by presenting their records to a sympathetic royal *visitador*.

The batabs and other officers were also responsible for protecting the personal rights of community members. While often forced to be the conduit for Spanish abuses and extortions, they could at other times serve as a buffer, filing protests, giving testimony in official inquiries, and representing individuals in the Indian court. The ability to compile precise and detailed evidence about some incident of physical violence or damage to a milpa, and to ensure, moreover, that the testimony of all the witnesses tallied, would not necessarily guarantee a redress of the grievance, much less prevent a future occurrence. But it did help in countering the usual defense plea made by Spaniards in seeking to dismiss the charge, which was that the Indians were given to vague and unfounded accusations out of malice or caprice.

The community leaders could not always protect their people or even themselves from abuse. They were, however, the only reliable advocates the *macehuales* had, since the clergy were so often in either collusion or competition with the Spanish laity in exploiting them. When curates and bishops protested to the Crown about royal officials' ill treatment of the Indians and royal officials repaid the compliment (if they had not in fact initiated the round of accusations), these charges, however sincerely motivated, were also invariably maneuvers in the incessant rivalries that church and state engaged in at all levels.[73] If the original issue (or pretext) of Indian rights did not become totally eclipsed by tooth-and-nail conflict over jurisdiction, the proceedings might eventually produce some decree from the Audiencia of Mexico or the Council of the Indies designed to correct the abuse. These pieces of high-minded legislation, with which the Crown sought to "unburden the royal conscience," fill volumes of the colonial records, sometimes as verbatim reissues of the same unheeded decrees. They had to be executed by the same people whose actions had led to their promulgation in the first place (or their successors), and as often as not they conflicted with other legislation that subordinated Indian rights to the Crown's own financial interests.

Spanish colonial rule was too inconsistent, too self-contradictory, to be a perfect instrument of either benevolent paternalism or oppressive exploitation. Paternalism became increasingly diluted with administrative distance from the center, but enough deference for the sanctity of royal law remained at even the provincial level to provide some protection to the Indians, so long as their spokesmen could gain a hearing.

Advocacy with the Spanish overlords played a relatively minor part in the elites' efforts to promote the common good and protect the security of the community and its members. Even if the law courts had provided a more reliable remedy against the evils of colonial rule, these evils were themselves an insignificant part of the general problem of human existence, which was of cosmic dimensions and depended on supernatural forces over which the Spanish had no more control than the Maya—perhaps less. The major effort in the colonial Maya's collective enterprise of survival, like that of their preconquest ancestors, was directed toward the realm of the sacred.

· 10 ·

THE COSMIC ORDER
IN CRISIS

In the Maya scheme of things, man's existence depended on a host of sacred beings who controlled the universe and everything in it. The Maya cosmos was neutral. Its sacred forces or beings—let us call them gods—were neither good nor evil, merely capricious; and their whims could be manipulated because they in turn were dependent on human attention for their welfare, if not their very existence. Mesoamerican gods were like extremely powerful infants (indeed the Olmec "Were-Jaguar" god is often portrayed as an infant, though a rather disconcerting one with large fangs)[1] likely to go into terrible tantrums and eventually expire if neglected. They had to be housed and cared for, diverted with music, dance, and colorful paintings and—most especially—fed.[2]

Religion is a highly complex expression of human fears, needs, and desires; and Maya religion no doubt operated at many levels—personal and public, intellectual and emotional, as well as spiritual. I assume that it satisfied the need for meaning, helping to explain why things are the way they are, and provided some comfort for the fact that they are no better. I am concerned here with Maya religion mainly as a social activity designed to keep the cosmos in operation and thereby ensure the continued survival of its human component.

The introduction of Christianity into Yucatan produced a far more serious crisis in the Maya world than the devastation of military warfare and political domination. We have no way of comparing the magnitude of material losses with anything the Maya had suffered in the past. Nothing in the Mesoamerican history of conquests could have prepared them for the Spaniards' determination to obliterate their entire religious system. Acknowledging the political sovereignty of the Spanish king and acknowledging the spiritual sovereignty of the Christian God must have appeared at first as familiar and related acts of vassalage from a defeated people; the symbol of conquest in the Mesoamerican tradition, after all, was a burning temple. The very different meaning that the new conquerors attached to "spiritual" submission would not have been at all clear during the military campaigns. The Montejos (father, son, and nephew), who directed the conquest of Yucatan, proceeded with either more prudence or less zeal than Hernán Cortés in his sweep through Mesoamerica to the Aztec capital, which he punctuated with dramatic scenes of idol smashing. Neither they nor the few clergymen who accompanied them gave much attention, if any, to evangelization. Some of the allied Maya leaders were baptized—at their own request, we are told. What the ceremony signified to them is impossible to say. Only with the arrival of the first group of Franciscan friars in 1545 (or possibly early 1546) to launch the missionary effort in earnest did the intentions of the conquerors become apparent.[3]

It must have been a profound shock to the Maya when they realized that the Christian God was not merely to take precedence over their own gods but to replace them altogether. There is no evidence that the Maya totally rejected this new deity in the sense of refusing to acknowledge His divinity. Their initial acceptance of Christianity; the very early amalgamations of pagan and Christian rituals (including all-too-realistic reenactments of the crucifixion); the docility with which they received missionaries and later the parish priests, who traveled and lived alone, unarmed and unprotected among them, making a thorough nuisance of themselves (yet producing only one martyr in Yucatan during the entire colonial period, and only a rumored one at that):[4] all these responses could well have derived from a prudent recognition of the Spaniards' superior military power. They could also derive from Maya recognition of the sacred power that the Catholic priests represented. And the two explanations are wholly compatible. The Spaniards' military success could be seen as a sign of divine favor, and it would have been rash, perhaps impossible for the pantheistic Maya, to deny the possibility that the Spanish god was a force to be reckoned with.

To accept this new personage as a sacred being, even as an especially powerful one, was not the same as accepting Him as the *only* sacred being in the cosmos. And it was the Judaeo-Christian God's intolerance of rivals that created the crisis in the Maya's corporate relationship with the supernatural. The friars could forbid the new catechumens to worship their deities, but convincing them that such worship was unnecessary or futile was another matter. The Maya believed that a sacred umbilical cord, through which nourishment flowed in both directions linked heaven and earth.[5] It is not clear whether gods or men would perish first if the life-sustaining cord were cut, as the ban on pagan rituals threatened to do. Regardless of the exact sequence, the existence of the world and everything in it was placed in peril.

IDOLATRY VERSUS SUPERSTITION

The Maya, in common with most people, divided their dealings with the supernatural into public and private spheres. Within the private domestic sphere, involving the everyday concerns of the Maya farmer and his family, Christianity seems to have produced little conflict between behavior and belief and only minor changes in either. The modern ethnographic literature contains descriptions of many domestic rituals, especially those surrounding childbirth, illness and death, which could have been copied almost verbatim from colonial documents.[6] The search for animal tracks around a house at the time of a child's birth to determine the identity of his particular guardian spirit; the use of grains of maize for divination and curing, and the characteristically Yucatecan *zaztun*, or crystal, through which the shaman sees hidden causes and events; the ceremony of *kex*, or "exchange," by which food is offered to the spirits of death as ransom for the recovery of a sick person; the placing of work tools appropriate to the sex of the individual (spinning and weaving tools for women, machete and digging stick for men) on the mat of a deceased family member: these are among a variety of rites that, along with their underlying concepts, have been reported in similar form through the past several centuries.

Some of the elements in this private sphere can be traced back to the pre-Columbian period, and fuller documentation would doubtless reveal many others. It is in fact highly likely that this decidedly folk level of religion has functioned with scant modification from very early times, long before the arrival of the Spanish and probably long before the arrival of earlier invaders who came from central Mexico with their religious cults. It would seem that this humble domain of belief was no more affected by foreign conquest or changing elite fashions than the way of life with which it enmeshed.

This continuity in lifeways and beliefs can be seen most strongly in the all-important task of food production, with its locus in the milpa. A few Christian elements have crept into the complex of ceremonies linked to clearing, planting, and harvesting. The Holy Trinity (*Dios Yumbil, Dios Mehenbil, Dios Espiritu Santo*) is often invoked in the prayers, along with indigenous sacred beings. Among these are the four *pauahtuns* (possibly manifestations of the *chaacs*, or rain spirits), which although they bear ancient Maya associations with the four cardinal directions and their identifying colors and are embedded in an equally (if not more) ancient complex of symbols centered on rain, have also acquired the names of Christian saints.[7] These elements do not seem to be more than minor accretions. The traditional methods of subsistence, and the beliefs and rituals associated with them, have remained virtually unchallenged. I once asked a Maya farmer why, if he was a Christian, he made offerings to the *chaacs*. He answered, with the air of one stating the obvious, "Because I make milpa."

288

Apart from its close ties to the Maya's immediate physical environment, and to an unchanging agricultural system and associated way of life, the stability of this substratum of traditional Maya religion is mainly due to its lowly and private nature. The Catholic priests in Yucatan, as in other parts of Spanish America, made a convenient distinction between this level—which they labeled superstition—and idolatry.

Superstitious beliefs and practices, confined to the individual and his kinfolk and to the forest, milpa, and household, were particularly difficult to detect. Some scholars have seen in the Catholic clergy's greater tolerance for these practices an ill-disguised confession of failure to eradicate pagan ways. But because the rites were domestic and addressed themselves to the humbler spirits in the indigenous cosmology, the clergy also came to regard them as less dangerous. They were only venial sins, arising from ignorance rather than perversity, and they usually elicited no more than an admonition or mild penance when detected. The rites were performed by minor religious practitioners, the village shamans, whom the clergy sometimes called witches (*brujos*) or sorcerers (*hechiceros*) but whom they nevertheless tolerated as long as they did not seem to be creating any mischief. Some of the more "enlightened" curates in the later colonial period, influenced by general intellectual trends among the educated elite in Europe and America, even came to be skeptical of the shamans' supernatural powers and to regard anyone who claimed control over the spirit world as a charlatan rather than a witch.[8]

Superstition might be foolish and futile and even wicked at times. It did not pose the same threat to Christianity as idolatry, nor the same threat to the social and political order on which Christianity rested. The shaman's power, though far from negligible, operated within a very circumscribed sphere. It was the upper level of the Maya priesthood, the deities they served and the public rituals they and the civil-religious leaders performed—that is, the state religion—with which the friars were in competition and which they sought to replace.

This state religion, which might more aptly be seen as a Weberian "community cult," was linked to the private sphere through the family-owned idols that the Spaniards found in such bewildering and frustrating profusion. References to these idols and to household shrines and the proliferation of these shrines in the late Postclassic site of Mayapan have led some scholars to see a fragmentation of Maya religion in this period into almost purely family devotions.[9] But the existence of household icons and shrines does not signify a breakdown of public worship among the Maya any more than it does among Roman Catholic and Orthodox Christians. Spanish accounts and court records make clear that Maya obsequies to their family idols, whether these represented

289

lineage gods or community gods—or both—did not replace but were performed in parallel with the public cults; sometimes the family idols were trotted out to be included in the public ceremonies.[10] Although the Spanish were not always precise in their own verbal distinctions, referring at times to "idolatries" as any kind of ritual involving idols, in practice they focused their evangelical fervor on the public rites that by tradition were performed in temples and plazas and which represented the Maya's collective bond with the supernatural.

We need not question the evangelical sincerity of the missionaries in order to recognize the social and political, and even the military, needs that were served by forced conversion. If the religious underpinnings of the old system had to be destroyed in order to consolidate and preserve the new, that did not negate the moral imperative of preaching the gospel. Nor need we attribute purely political motives to the Maya elite who resisted the change, simply because their own power and prestige were so firmly linked to the idolatry the conquerors wished to eradicate.

Unless we assume that the Maya leaders had been engaged in an elaborate and conscious fraud, they believed that the sacrifices and rogations they made were necessary to ensure the common good as well as to support their own authority.[11] I assume that their subjects shared this belief with more or less conviction, even if they were not initiated into the complex calendrical and astronomical computations and the other esoteric lore with which the specialists sought to understand and control the supernatural forces and, above all, keep the cosmic order from coming apart. Hence the dilemma of external conversion: to worship their deities provoked punishment from the Spaniards; not to worship them courted perhaps less immediate but more terrifying consequences.

This dilemma produced a split within the public or corporate sphere of religion between open observance of Christian ritual and clandestine adherence to the old religion. The Christian ritual took over the towns, just as the churches took over the temple sites, and the friars replaced the *ahkins*, the Maya high priests. The Maya ritual remained as a parallel system driven underground—often literally, into sacred caves. There, in the bush, or in the houses of the *principales*, the idols were hidden and when possible worshiped and fed with copal incense, maize gruel, and the blood of sacrificial victims, including humans.[12]

These furtive rites were not a satisfactory substitute for the old religion. By their nature they could not be public in the same way. In the more remote towns, all or a large part of the community could still participate. Wherever a friar was in residence the rites had to be highly secret, sometimes attended by only the *batab*, the *ahkin*, and a few close kinsmen. Even then word sometimes leaked out (thereby entering the historical record) and the cost was high. Investigations were made, the idols smashed, and the idolators severely punished. The lightest sentence was a hundred lashes, and the interrogation techniques the friars had brought with them from Spain were none too gentle. The church's laws forbade any procedure that involved "effusion of blood" or "loss of life or limb." The water torture and stretching inflicted on the Indians were designed to stay within those limits, but the friars were heavy-handed, perhaps accustomed to the larger, more robust physical specimens the Holy Office dealt with in Spain. Witnesses sometimes died or were crippled or "displayed their cowardice" by committing suicide before the questioning could be completed.[13]

The famous (or infamous) and well-documented idolatry trials conducted under the supervision of Fray Diego de Landa while he was Franciscan Provincial in 1562 revealed a disheartening gap between the Maya's public acceptance of Christianity and their private activities. A substantial portion of the Maya elite of Mani, Sotuta, Hocaba, and the other districts investigated—almost the entire core area of the colony except the territory between Campeche and Merida—were found to have been engaging in sacrificial rituals devoted to their pagan gods. The less densely populated and more supervised areas to the east and south were reported somewhat later to be even more flagrant in their idolatries. They still openly worshiped their gods with the whole community in attendance, and they threatened to provide the church with a new set of martyrs when the clergy attempted to interfere.[14] But these territories were not yet considered very secure in the faith. What especially dismayed the friars in the 1562 investigations was the evidence of widespread apostasy within the regions where Christianity had seemed to take root so well. They were also deeply horrified. Some of the more gruesome (to Western eyes) rites had been practiced inside the churches and had incorporated Christian elements in what seemed a demonic parody, notably the crucifixion of children. All had gone on right under their noses, and not by ignorant commoners either but by *maestros cantores* and other church assistants, by the native rulers, and by other members of the most illustrious lineages, all of them educated by the friars.[15]

The trials created a double furor in the colony, first over the shocking finds and next over the harsh methods the inquisitors had used to elicit confessions. Many of them were later retracted under the milder rule of the first resident bishop, Fray Francisco de Toral. The original confessions are, however, too circumstantial, too detailed, and too much in agreement with other evidence to be dismissed as fabrications simply because they were obtained under torture.

Rigged trials are not unknown in the colonial records, but they are easy to spot. The testimonies are monotonously repetitious, all in the same stilted language; and there are no messy details, even confirming ones, to interfere with the neatly concocted and smoothly flowing narrative. The testimony in unrehearsed trials is colloquial, almost conversational in style, as spotty and confused as human memory usually is, with conflicting details and loose ends. If the original testimonies in these idolatry trials were invented, the friars went to unequalled lengths to create an air of verisimilitude, even to coordinating evidence from different trials by different judges in neighboring districts to dovetail into a plausible, if disjointed, picture. Independent documentation, including somewhat later reports in a less hysterical atmosphere by a variety of officials less single-minded in their pursuit of idolatry, lends further credence to the trial. All together the evidence leads to the conclusion that for at least the first decades after conquest, the old gods were alive and well behind the public façade of Christianity.

The Christian forms of public worship eventually won out over the rival pagan tradition. One could argue that the steady decline in the number of cases of idolatry reported after the purge of the 1560s meant only that the Maya had become more circumspect or the clergy more relaxed in their vigilance. The clergy did become increasingly tolerant, but they could afford to be. If idolatry had not been entirely extirpated it had ceased to pose a serious threat to the new state religion. Christianity had taken over the towns, and the Maya, who formerly had infused their whole environment with their own symbols and rituals, were left with the ones associated with the forest: the milpa ceremonies for rain and good harvests, hunting rituals, and the rituals related to caves, cenotes, wild beehives, and ceiba trees; or at best some furtive offerings in long-abandoned temples.[16] We would know from current practice that these ceremonies persisted even if we did not also have the colonial accounts by a few zealous priests who, like modern narcotics agents, were tipped off by informers or followed the whiffs of copal incense to the scene.

The boundary between idolatry and superstition became largely obscured. Banished entirely to the milpas and forest, the clandestine rites ceased to be a regular community activity and became instead a more or less secret offering made by individuals or families in some out-of-the-way sacred spot. The one quasi-communal rite of which we have any record was the Cha-Chaac ceremony to avert drought. A few images preserved as family heirlooms might be taken from their hiding places and brought to a milpa, where a small group of men—certainly no substantial portion of the community—would gather to make their offerings.[17] One gets the impression that in the intervals between these emergencies, so long as the rains came more or less on schedule, the milpa gods or spirits received only the private ministrations of each farmer. This does not mean that the Maya abandoned their corporate efforts to maintain the cosmic order, only that the community as a whole, and particularly the civil-religious elite, were channeling their efforts through a new set of sacred beings and sacred rituals. These were the Christian saints and the Christian liturgy. And if they were not an entirely new set, they at least had new names and new houses.

SPANISH AND MAYA MICROCOSMS

The colonial clergy had a conveniently simple explanation for the apparent oscillations in Maya behavior. According to them the Maya had freely accepted the Christian gospel of salvation, presenting themselves for baptism as they became persuaded of its redemptive power. No one had threatened them with any but other-worldly sanctions if they chose not to undergo this rite of initiation into the Body of Christ (technically this official version is on the whole true).[18] Many of them had then succumbed to Satan's temptations and committed apostasy—that is, defected from their voluntarily professed beliefs. But they recanted when their idolatry was discovered and they returned chastened to the fold, convinced of the essential truth of Christian doctrine. For the more pessimistic among the clergy, the Maya's lack of spiritual fortitude left them perpetually exposed to the danger of apostasy. The zones of refuge served as a constant lure and source of "infection," and the residents in the more isolated hamlets also tended to slide back into old ways. Not all the clergy shared so bleak a view. There were some who thought that in general, and especially in the towns, the Maya had managed to become as good Christians as any ignorant and brutish group of peasants could be.[19]

The main trouble with this explanation is that Christianity and paganism are offered as mutually exclusive alternatives from which the Maya had to choose and between which they might switch back and forth as the forces of light and darkness struggled for their souls. Certainly the friars saw and presented the two systems in that light, but it is far from certain that the Maya perceived them in the same way.

Much of the comparative study of religion is based on the same either/ or dichotomy, although the theological categories and value judgments have been replaced by intellectual ones. According to the standard typology derived from Max Weber, traditional (or primitive or magical) religions are contrasted with universal (or "rational") ones such as Islam, Christianity, and Buddhism. When dealing with religious change, this typology easily feeds into an evolutionary model (or perhaps the model itself is the implicit source of the typology) in which rationalized religions arise in a few favored spots and spread at the expense of less enlightened, more primitive ones. The model is not very different from the one presented by the missionaries. One has only to substitute the terms "weak," "incoherent," and "primitive" for "false" and "evil," and "rational" and "sophisticated" for "true" and "good." Neither model is particularly helpful in explaining how or why universal religions replace primitive ones except when implanted by superior physical force, and that sidesteps the issue of whether forced conversion brings about any actual changes in belief.

Robin Horton, in a series of articles based on evidence from sub-Saharan Africa, has developed a model of voluntary conversion from traditional (read primitive) belief systems to a universal religion that, while stimulated by outside contacts, does not depend on the introduction, peaceful or forced, of an alien religious system. The central hypothesis is that all traditional religions contain some latent notion of a universal supreme being. Horton argues that traditional religions (particularistic, segmental, local) are satisfactory explanations of, and modes of dealing with, the microcosmic world of geographically and culturally isolated groups. When the boundaries of that microcosm dissolve or significantly weaken through trade, conquest, or other sustained contact with the outside, the need to deal with this wider reality will stimulate the emergence of a latent concept of a universal supreme being whose power encompasses the world as a whole—that is, the macrocosm. Thus the monotheistic message of Islam and Christianity has been less important in stimulating both conversion and the rise of universalistic sects than the gradual incorporation of the sub-Saharan peoples into a wider political and economic sphere.[20]

For colonial Mesoamerica it would be more useful to abandon altogether the Weberian typology and the evolutionary schema it feeds into. Neither Spanish Catholicism nor Mesoamerican paganism fits neatly into either the universal or the traditional category (nor, I would suggest, do Islam and the French and Portuguese brands of Christianity that were introduced into Africa; only the "disenchanted" Protestantism that served as Weber's touchstone seems to correspond to the pure "universal" type). Both conceived of the divinity as at the same time unified and multiple, a conception that may be more common to religious thought than generally acknowledged. The complex Mesoamerican iconography and the multiplicity of gods have tended to obscure the fact that these were refractions or manifestations of sacred power emanating from a

294

single source, whether called Hunabku, Itzamna, Ometeotl, or Tezcatlipoca.[21] Faced with this apparent contradiction, Spanish friars postulated a possible descent from some past monotheism;[22] modern scholars have suggested an ascent *toward* monotheism. Both have failed to see that the one could encompass the many and that the imported and indigenous religions possessed certain structural similarities based on this same concept.

Some of the early Spanish missionaries, influenced by the reformist Erasmian Humanism of the early sixteenth century, attempted to purge their religion of medieval accretions, which might more properly be called incorporations, and to present to the Amerindian neophytes a pristine form of Christianity (whatever that may be). The version that was transplanted to America fell far short of this ideal. For the mass of the Spanish laity, and the majority of the clergy as well, the uncompromising monotheism of the Old and New Testaments had become tempered in their Mediterranean version of popular Catholicism by the incorporation of a rich variety of sacred beings. Angels, saints, the Prince of Darkness and his minions, and a host of lesser spirits accompanied and aided or sometimes sought to foil the will of the supreme godhead. For most of the Spanish culture-bearers, the Christian cosmos was as densely populated as that of the Maya.[23]

Both Spanish Christianity and Mesoamerican paganism, then, represented richly complex, multilayered systems instead of any one pure type. Only if we recognize that they confronted each other as total systems and interacted at a variety of levels can we begin to make some sense of postconquest religious change, not as a shift from one type to another (the standard model of conversion), nor even necessarily from one level to another (the modified "emergence" model) nor as the superimposition of Christianity on a pagan base (a common syncretistic model applied to Latin America), but as a set of horizontal, mutual exchanges across comparable levels.

In distinguishing among these levels, Horton's microcosm-macrocosm concept serves as a useful ordering principle. To be sure, microcosm and macrocosm are but opposite ends of a continuum. We could find almost an infinity of gradations corresponding to levels of contact with the world "out there": gradations among people, among spheres of activity, among sacred beings, and among religious modes related to them. The more isolated the group and the more private the activity, the more particularistic the religious expression is likely to be. But for the present analysis the gradations can be divided into three broad categories.

Starting with the universal level, I find that Horton defines his upper tier rather narrowly as monotheism or monolatry (the worship of one god while acknowledging the existence of others). A more general, and therefore for our purposes more useful, distinction would be between lesser, localized members of the cosmos and an all-encompassing concept of the divinity, whether seen as single or multiple, or both. Accompanying this concept would be a greater elaboration of a transcendental theology addressing itself to the larger question of where we come from, why we are here, and where we are going when we leave: in other words, questions transcending the immediate concerns of human existence emphasized in the more pragmatic goals of geographically bounded spheres.

Horton's lower, microcosmic tier needs to be divided in two. At the bottom we find what I have identified as the private sphere in Maya religion. Defined by the Spanish clergy as superstition and corresponding to what later taxonomies have come to call magic, this level involves the manipulation of highly discrete and localized supernatural forces for the benefit of the individual and his family. I have created a new middle-level niche for corporate or parochial cults with their patron deities or saints; they are still microcosmic because they are tied to a particular group but are less particularistic than the magical. Although these corporate cults might shade into semiprivate devotions to family patrons, I place them in the public, collective sphere of religious activity referred to earlier in the chapter.

Like many other sixteenth-century Christians, a substantial portion of Spaniards shared with the Maya a belief in magic as a means of controlling one's immediate environment and personal welfare. Considering the private, everyday concerns of this belief, it is not surprising that it has been the least affected by political change or the erosion of cultural boundaries, whether in Spain or Yucatan—or, for that matter, in Ireland, France, or Java. I have suggested that the magical sphere of Maya religion survived Spanish conquest and colonization largely intact. As long as we look only for cultural loss or attrition or the assimilation of Christian elements—that is, vertical influences from orthodox, universalistic Christianity—this appears to be the case. However, we should not ignore the possibility of horizontal enrichment from the Spaniards' own magical world or even a reciprocal movement. Maya magic and orthodox Christianity did not on the whole impinge on each other, but that does not preclude the possibility of mutual influence at more compatible levels.

From the perspective of a twentieth-century urban dweller, the magical beliefs held by the Maya and the Spanish in Yucatan seem like minor variations on the same theme. It would require a far more de-

tailed comparison than is warranted here, and perhaps much more information than is now available on the preconquest versions of both
traditions, to be able to judge how much the similarities are structural
and coincidental and how much they derive from mutual influence. The
main point is that Spanish religion did not all float like a layer of oil on
the surface of Maya magic but had its own magical layer that could
blend with the Maya's.

The Spaniards' own magical beliefs help to account for the ambivalence behind the church's stance on Maya "superstitions." These were
not condemned as doctrinal errors, nor even, despite the official label
of superstition, always dismissed as fabrications or delusions. How could
they be, when so many of the clergy themselves saw the world teeming
with demons, imps, and other disembodied spirits and shared the same
belief in the power of spells and incantations?[24] No distinction seems to
have been made in practice between the indigenous and the imported
versions of magic. The church in Yucatan as elsewhere was far more
concerned with heterodoxy, whether idolatry or Lutheranism, which
challenged its ideological and ritual supremacy. When it did bother with
magic, the issue in question was whether a particular person had sought
to call upon supernatural forces and to what end. The ethnic identity of
the practitioner and his or her familiar spirits were largely irrelevant
except in a jurisdictional sense, since Spaniards and *castas* were subject
to the Inquisition, while the episcopal courts handled Indian cases.

These cases reveal that Maya and Spanish magic did not operate as
separate and equal systems but commingled in a two-way exchange in
which the Maya system seems to have been dominant. It was almost as
if the political and economic prostration of the Indians was partially
compensated for by their superior supernatural powers. Spaniards (including some of the wealthiest and most influential colonists) as well as
castas acknowledged these powers, feared them, and sought their help
in need: to exorcise a bewitched cow, remove the curse from a field,
relieve an ailment, or cure infertility.[25] The Indian shamans were the
experts from whom an enterprising mestizo or mulatto might learn some
very useful and marketable skills, though it seems that the magical powers were not always transferable. One unfortunate mulatto ran afoul of
the Inquisition because he had bragged to his fellow inmates in the Merida
prison that an Indian sorcerer had taught him how to turn himself into
a bird and fly.[26] The judges did not take the boast seriously—after all,
the man had not managed to fly out of the prison yard. But neither did
they find it totally absurd. By the late colonial period the Inquisition
had become defunct in all but name. Yet parish clergy still expressed
only hesitant doubts about witchcraft accusations on the grounds of

insufficient proof. And as late as 1813 one curate reported with half-hearted skepticism a girl's claim that in the guise of a bird she accompanied sorcerers on their nocturnal flights through the countryside, commenting that she had "probably dreamed" these occurrences.[27]

Spaniards and Africans brought their magical beliefs with them to America, but in leaving behind their own microcosms, they had to leave behind the supernatural beings and forces associated with them. The broadening of their geographical and cultural horizons did not preclude their having to deal with their immediate surroundings when they found themselves in the alien microcosms belonging to the Maya and other Indians. This was a different spirit world inhabited by another set of beings and forces, tied to the particular place, and with which anyone living in that place would have to reckon. And just as they had to rely on the Indians' knowledge of the physical environment—which plants were edible, which snakes venomous, and what signs presaged the coming of the rains—they must have felt that the Indians understood and could control the local spirits better than outsiders.

Wherever a large African population has replaced the Amerindian, as in parts of Brazil and the Caribbean, they have been able to transplant or reconstruct their own spirit world in the new setting with their own shamanistic specialists. There the same ambivalent attitude that Spaniards displayed toward Indian magic was transferred to Africans.[28] I have known European ex-*colons* in the West Indies who have lost their own rural traditions but not all the beliefs associated with them and who are not above employing the services of an obeah man or woman. They perceive the country folk, though also descended from transplanted stock themselves, as being more in tune with the land and the place, and therefore with the sources of any obscure powers that might be there to tap. In Yucatan both the Europeans and the Africans deferred to the Maya's superior knowledge of that particular microcosm and its spirits. Even those who chose to ignore these spirits in practice and rely exclusively on the Christian god or the saints to intervene in their daily lives did not therefore deny their reality. And some who had doubts still turned to Maya magic in a kind of Pascalian hedging of bets, just in case there might be something to it.

Beyond the level of magical beliefs and practices, Maya and Spanish religions appear to diverge sharply. According to the standard models of conversion, the choice between traditional polytheism and universal monotheism is clear, even if not always conscious. The two are antithetical. Thus the choice faced by the Maya would be modified by the superior military power of the Spanish but it would still be well defined: either accept the new religion as a replacement for their traditional beliefs, or retain these beliefs intact, plus whatever rituals could be carried on sub rosa, while submitting only nominally to Christianity's external forms.

A long-standing axiom in Mesoamerican studies is that this choice is precisely what the Indians could not or would not make. Scores of accounts with hundreds of photographs of village fiestas have been published to illustrate the colorful ways in which the Indians have blended the two traditions,[29] all the more quaint because almost, but not quite, familiar to the Western eye. It is possible to see this blend as a confused jumble created by accident and ignorance—as the incorporation of whatever ill-understood Christian elements happened to strike the Indians' fancy. Since Christianity and pre-Columbian paganism are incompatible, so the argument goes, confusion must lie at the heart of any amalgamation between the two. Some confusion no doubt did exist, but much of it may disappear if we cease to see polytheism and monotheism as mutually exclusive alternatives. They can represent, as I have suggested earlier, simply two different levels—the parochial and the universal—within the public sphere of religion, which can coexist with each other as well as with the magical level.

The parochial tier, though still microcosmic and particularistic, has wider horizons than the individual or family and the immediate surroundings. It concerns the welfare and identity of the community, be that hamlet, village, province, or city-state, and the community's corporate relationship with the supernatural. And that welfare and identity are the responsibility of one or more particular sacred beings. The Mesoamerican pantheon was inhabited by a host of deities, with multiple attributes, human and anthropomorphic, and shifting identities, represented in rich, many-layered clusters of visual and verbal imagery. The symbolic system, still only partially decoded, that linked this kaleidoscopic profusion of sacred beings into an all-encompassing conception of the divinity need not concern us here, only their role as tutelary gods on which group loyalties were focused.

Each collection of deities was discrete, corresponding to particular geopolitical units and ruling lineages, in addition to the special patrons of occupational groups such as merchants. The nature and astral deities, like the gods of maize, of rain, of the sun and the moon, that regulated and sustained the farmer's central concern—his maize crop—were pan-Mesoamerican. Indeed, their equivalents can be found in any peasant society. But the peasant does not conceive of them as any more universal than the particular ancestral and territorial gods that watch over his own community and with whom some of them may in fact have been associated in the Mesoamerican system as variants or local manifestations.

It was at this parochial or corporate level of religion that the Maya and Spanish systems competed most directly. This middle tier of the Spanish cosmos was no more a void than the humbler domain of "ghosties, ghoulies, and things that go bump in the night," from which, in the old Scottish Book of Common Prayer, the Good Lord is asked to deliver us. The Christian God reigned supreme but He had not absorbed all lesser beings. And the Christian saints transported across the Atlantic were in their own way as much tutelary deities as the collections of gods that watched over the Maya communities. Each neighborhood, town, and region in Spain had its own patron saint or saints; and the territorial hierarchy culminates in the guardian spirit for the entire Christian nation, Santiago Matamoros (Saint James the Moor Killer).

Some of the patrons are historically associated with the locale, like Saint Isidore, the seventh-century bishop of Seville. The universality of other saints was subordinated to their roles as local manifestations of the sacred and as repositories of local welfare and local pride.[30] Although in theory Mary is the same Mother of God regardless of what physical image represents her, in the popular mind the Virgin of Macarena, say, is the rival of the Virgin of Triana, who resides across the river in Seville. Each set of devotees takes corporate pride in extolling the superior beauty, greater pathos of expression, and richer adornments of their own Queen of Heaven, and the rivalry has been known to erupt into physical violence during Holy Week, when the jewel-bedecked images are taken out in candlelit processions through the city streets and partisan fervor reaches its height.

The social as well as the geopolitical map of sixteenth-century Spain could be drawn by plotting out the spaces allocated to their sacred sponsors. Each craft speciality or other occupational group also had its own patron saint—for example, Saint Joseph for carpenters and Our Lady of Carmen for fishermen. These had no place in the largely undifferentiated peasant society of the postconquest Maya. But the saints rapidly became the focus of corporate identity for the territorial groups—the *parcialidades*, the pueblos, and the quasi pueblos or large haciendas.

CHRIST, KUKULCAN, AND THE MACROCOSM

In this scheme of consonances at the magical and parochial levels, the third or universal level of religious expression appears to be left dangling. Without any equivalent of the Christian Almighty in the indigenous system, there is no possibility of amalgamation. The Maya would have to make a leap of faith in accepting this alien concept, or fail to make it. Or at best, according to Horton's modified model of conversion, the arrival of the Spanish and the incorporation of the Maya into a wider universe would stimulate the emergence of such a concept already there in latent form.

Whether the Indians "really" became Christians is one of the more intriguing questions in Latin American history, or so I must assume since I am so frequently asked; and it is a perplexing one, starting with the distinct lack of agreement among Christian theologians over the exact definition of "Christian." When asked, I take it to mean whether the Indians genuinely came to believe in "One God, Father Almighty, Maker of Heaven and earth . . ." and so on down the articles of faith in the Nicene Creed. The answer is elusive even for contemporary Maya whom one knows personally, and all the more so for their colonial ancestors, who so rarely speak for themselves. Judging from the words and actions of the colonial Maya, reaching us mainly through the alien perspective of their conquerors and thus subject to double distortion (first the Spaniards' and then our own), the missionaries do not seem to have succeeded in converting more than a handful of their catechumens. The same evidence also points to a more novel proposition: that Maya cosmology became less, not more, universalistic after the conquest.

I have earlier suggested that the pre-Hispanic Maya in common with the rest of Mesoamerica already possessed a concept of the all-encompassing divinity of whom the lesser deities were refractions or manifestations. This does not mean that either Hunabku or Itzamna was the exact equivalent of Jehovah. Whether conceived of as an extremely remote being who directed the cosmos only through his multiple manifestations or more in the way of an abstract principle, a creative force, or prime mover,[31] the Maya supreme godhead does not seem to have intervened directly in human affairs. Nor did he figure prominently, in his unitary aspect, in Maya ritual. More to the point is that the Maya, or rather the educated elite, were far from living totally enclosed in a microcosmic world, either mentally or physically. They possessed the leisure and inclination for metaphysical speculation and a consciousness of wider horizons beyond their own locale through their activities in warfare, long-distance trade and diplomacy. Their transcribed writings reveal a concern with the transcendental, in particular a highly elaborated eschatology, that goes far beyond the manipulative pragmatism usually associated with traditional religions.[32]

In assessing the impact of Christianity we have to distinguish between the ordinary Maya villager and the cosmopolitan elite, who were already conscious of and involved in events beyond the boundaries of their own group, who held a more abstract and formalized idea of the divine, and for whom Christianity therefore presented a different challenge. This is not to say that the elite's response would be uniform either. Some of them led resistance movements during and directly following the military conquest that were aimed explicitly against Christianity; others seem to have "converted" with a certain alacrity and even proselytized actively among their followers.[33] Though contrasting, these responses may have been equivalent, the reverse sides of the same intellectual coin. The Maya elites, as distinct from the peasantry, may have found enough theological congruence between Christianity and their own religion to facilitate either an informed acceptance or an equally informed rejection of what they perceived as analogous but rival doctrines. The Christian idea of the Trinity, of a god who is One God but at the same time Three Persons, would be no more incomprehensible, I should think, to the sophisticated ruling groups among the Maya, whose gods had multiple (although usually four) identities, than it is to the Christians who routinely repeat their belief in this divine mystery when they recite the Creed.

Whatever other affinities may have existed between the formal theologies elaborated by the two cults, the Christian doctrine of exclusivity gained few if any adherents among Maya priests and rulers. Their inclination to incorporate new elements rather than substitute new for old can be seen clearly on the east coast of Yucatan, an area where Christianity was adopted—or rather adapted—with little coercion, or even supervision, from the Spanish. Archaeological data from the region have provided some glimpses of the kind of syncretic practices that, when recorded in documents at all, generally come filtered through Spanish observations and assumptions.

The east-coast Maya were brought under Spanish rule with scarcely a battle and then quickly left to their own devices. Their spiritual conquest was, if anything, more relaxed and perfunctory than their military conquest. Cortés was the first to preach the gospel, during his brief stopover on the island of Cozumel in 1519, and perhaps the only ardent proselytizer the area was ever to see. Certainly neither Montejo nor his chaplain showed much interest in converting the inhabitants when the 1527 expedition passed through, and the Franciscans who arrived in the colony in the 1540s could spare no friars for what was by then a thinly populated region isolated from the main colonial centers to the west. It received little attention from either church or state, and only occasional visitors. Even when a resident curate was appointed in 1582, he could not, from his offshore base on Cozumel, have kept very close watch over a parish scattered along more than one hundred kilometers of coast.[34]

Not surprisingly, pagan practices continued barely checked. The *encomendero* was absent and in any case inimical to ecclesiastical incursions, and the few clergymen who did visit the area were totally dependent on the good will of the native rulers. What is surprising is that these same Maya who withdrew food supplies and threatened worse to any priest attempting to interfere with their idolatries were at the same time cordially welcoming other clergymen who stuck to purely Christian business; so generous was their support that an enterprising Portuguese sailor thought it worth his while to sojourn these posing as a priest. They docilely lined up for masses, baptisms, and weddings in fairly substantial Christian churches that must have been built with very little clerical supervision.

Recent excavations in one of these churches, at the coastal site of Tzama (present-day Tancah), unearthed a pagan cache offering under the base of the altar and two pre-Columbian-style burials (flexed position, one with a jade bead in the mouth) under the floor of the nave.[35] Equally significant are the seventeen other burials in the sample, all in standard Christian fashion and all or most presumably interred when no Spaniard was around—unless everyone happened to die during the rare priestly visits. Perhaps they did, but then we have the cross that Cortés erected in one of the main temples of Cozumel, which later visitors found in place alongside the restored traditional deities. Did the Maya hastily reerect the cross every time they spotted a Spanish sail on the horizon? A somewhat less strained explanation for all the assembled evidence is that the Maya were receptive to the new cult, but on their own terms, which meant incorporating it into the existing system.

Neither the written reports nor the archaeological evidence makes clear exactly what frame of reference the new symbols and rituals were incorporated into. The cross among the Maya seems to have signified the sacred "First Tree of the World," which linked heaven and earth.[36] We also know that the east coast was a center for the cult of Kukulcan, himself an alien deity (Quetzalcoatl) imported from the highlands and blended into the local tradition. The particular focus of the local cult was Quetzalcoatl in the form of Venus as morning star, representing the risen god. Having their own god who died, descended into the underworld, and rose again (as in the cycle of Venus) and who was expected to come again to reclaim his earthly kingdom, the Maya could well have found the teachings on Christ a variation on a familiar theme.[37]

The east coast was part of Yucatan's "Putun" periphery, which on the whole displayed a much more open and flexible attitude toward the

Spanish and their new cult than the more geographically and culturally isolated provinces in the interior. As principal links in a pan-Mesoamerican system of commercial exchange, the "Putun" rulers were particularly involved with the wider world beyond their immediate territory. We have no idea how prominent the idea of a supreme being or beings was in "Putun" cosmology. But their cosmopolitan perspective, reflected in their devotion to the "international" cult of Quetzalcoatl, suggests that the receptive responses to Christianity of the east coast Maya were based on some concept more overarching in scope than the rulers' own ancestral and territorial deities.

One might expect the Spanish conquest to stimulate further elaboration of a universal concept of the divine and to help spread the concept to more isolated regions and to the lower levels of Maya society, even without missionary efforts on behalf of Christianity. The Spanish, after all, were much more foreign to the Maya than their former trading partners and the earlier invaders from the highlands. The Spaniards' arrival thus represented a more drastic erosion of cultural boundaries, a forced awareness of a world far wider than Mesoamerica. This does not seem to have happened. The cause lies partly with the quality of religious instruction. The early missionaries, handicapped by lack of personnel and by ignorance of the language, had to rely on native interpreters and catechists. Even when a Catholic priest was in residence he would have found it difficult to monitor either covert resistance to the gospel message or unwitting distortions in its transmission. And only a small proportion of congregated towns had resident priests.[38]

If evangelization is measured in terms of architecture, liturgy and administrative organization, the friars' achievement is most impressive. Within a few decades of their arrival, the entire population under Spanish military control had been congregated into towns and the towns organized into parishes. Grandiose stone churches and friaries had been constructed in the major centers, and even the most remote villages had their stone chapels with pole-and-thatch naves to house the congregations. The vast majority of adults had been baptized; catechism classes were held regularly; and the ordinary parish routine of infant baptism, Christian marriage and burial, and yearly confession and communion was well underway through the tireless activity of the circuit-riding friars. There are signs, however, that even two and half centuries later the less tangible goal of implanting orthodox Christian doctrine had eluded them.

As the numbers of clergy in the colony increased, the level of enthusiasm declined. Most of them were creoles and therefore bilingual from infancy, yet by their own admission the vast majority of curates continued to leave the catechism completely to the Maya *maestros cantores* and counted these successful if the catechumens learned to repeat from memory the "Four Prayers" (the Creed, Hail Mary, Our Father, and Salve regina) by the time they were ready for first communion.[39] The more conscientious priests reexamined the adult parishioners before admitting them to the sacraments for their annual Easter Duty and sent those with faulty memory back to remedial catechism class on Sunday afternoons. Even so, the bishops who bothered to examine candidates for confirmation during their diocesan tours found the majority grossly ignorant of even these rudiments. And the few clergymen who ventured to inquire whether the rote learning had inculcated any understanding of Christian precepts came to the painful conclusion that the gospel seed had borne little fruit among the Maya.

It must be admitted that the ground was not fertile. It is doubtful that the ordinary Maya peasant had ever possessed more than a hazy notion of Itzamna or Kukulcan or the complex cosmologies in which they were embedded. If the vast majority of colonial Maya found the concept of a distant, all-encompassing god who meted out rewards and punishments in the hereafter meaningless or irrelevant, it was surely as much the fault of the content of the message as of the manner of instruction. The concerns of the Maya peasant, Spanish conquest notwithstanding, were still confined to the welfare of his family and his village, his hunting grounds and beehives, and above all his milpa; and his negotiations were directed to the less awesome beings who were in charge of them. If anything, religious universalism suffered a decline after the conquest.

If rationalization of the sacred is tied to the breakdown of cultural and geographical isolation, then the process must be reversible, ebbing and flowing according to circumstances. By thinking of the magical, the parochial, and the universal as levels or spheres rather than stages of development, we can consider the possibility of shifts in emphasis in both directions. The Spanish conquest may have provided an initial stimulus toward increased universality, but before long Maya society became more self-contained, more microcosmic in outlook than before.

The colonial Maya texts called the books of Chilam Balam, which blended Christian concepts and biblical lore into the esoteric learning of traditional Maya cosmology, demonstrate that at least for some period after conquest a corps of priestly intellectuals survived for whom Christianity was not an entirely mystifying ragbag of curious notions. Though the meaning of the books is often obscure because of our ignorance of much of the complex Maya symbolic system, enough can be puzzled out to suggest a response to Christian dogma at a highly sophisticated level of interpretation. As I have already suggested, an association of

Christ with Kukulcan is not necessarily whimsical. The church's teachings on Christ's death, rebirth, and prophesied second coming, as mentioned earlier, had more than faint echoes in the pre-Columbian beliefs about Kukulcan. It has been argued that the Maya associated the Virgin with the moon goddess Ixchel because of the Virgin's common depiction on a crescent moon. That may be so. But the moon goddess was also the consort of the creating sun god. And there is no Christian imagery, only meaning, to associate Mary, as she is associated in the "Chilam Balam of Chumayel," with the Maya "Cord from Heaven"— the divine umbilical cord that signifies the link between the natural and sacred worlds, between man and God (or the gods).[40]

The priestly corps eventually died out, and along with it the theological sophistication that informed the Chilam Balam texts. It is unlikely that the later colonial scribes added anything of substance to the early postconquest versions of the cosmological sections or even understood much of what they copied. Christianity did not replace Maya paganism at the upper levels of theology, nor did it even blend with it; they both lost out to the syncretic parochialism of the cult of the tutelary deity-saints, as the Maya elites became reduced to purely local and subordinate status and their horizons shrank to the size of their *macehual* subjects. The functions that had previously taken them beyond their cultural boundaries—warfare, diplomacy and long-distance trade—were taken over by the conquerors. After the region was pacified, the Spanish for the most part withdrew to the cities, and the Maya from top to bottom of the sociopolitical hierarchy turned inward, encapsulated in their microcosmic boundaries, which they were able to rebuild and even to strengthen after the first shock of conquest.

The increased parochialism of the colonial Maya outlook did not depend on a hermetic seal around each township or parish. Changes of residence from one community to another, temporary migrations to the coastal salt flats, even movement across the colonial frontier either by flight into the unpacified zones or forced repatriation from them, were all within the same self-contained universe of the lowland Maya. Except for references to a few men recruited as seamen in the early postconquest period, no Maya seem to have traveled outside that universe. The Spanish not only took over the long-distance trade but also employed only *castas* to man the *bongos* (large canoes) and other craft that plied the coast and gulf.

The old pilgrimage centers of the east coast of Yucatan died out along with the trade routes to which they had been linked. During the late Postclassic period these shrines, especially the ones on Cozumel, had brought devotees from Campeche, Xicalango, Tabasco, and perhaps more distant parts of Mesoamerica, as well as people from the interior of the peninsula. It would be futile to try to decide whether they came primarily to exchange goods or to make offerings and consult the island's sacred oracles. The two activities mingled, as did the diverse populations of visitors to this cosmopolitan spot. The Spanish asserted that Cozumel retained its importance for decades after the conquest, as the Maya equivalent of Jerusalem or Rome.[41] But its decline to a sparsely populated, rarely visited backwater had already started before the final military campaigns were over. The area was eventually abandoned to the pirates and smugglers who carried on the "Putun" tradition in their own way.[42] It had long been a victim and a symptom of the lowland Maya's isolation within their own cultural and geographical boundaries.

Two pilgrimage traditions developed in colonial Yucatan, but both were entirely Spanish in organization and largely Spanish in participation. One centered on a shrine to the Virgin in the small inland village of Hool, south of Campeche.[43] Why this particular image of Our Lady was singled out from all the others located in Indian villages throughout the peninsula is a mystery. For some as yet obscure reason our Lady of Hool became the object of intense devotion to the Spanish population of Campeche, and the three-day sojourn in the little *visita* town to celebrate the festival of Candlemas in her honor was one of the major events in the Campeche social calendar.

The fiesta at Hool exposed the local residents, all of them Maya, to a brief glimpse of the non-Indian world. But they were kept at a distance from what was essentially a Spanish show. The Spaniards brought their own servants, most of their own food, and their own musicians and acolytes, so that even the local *maestro cantor* and his staff were shunted aside for the occasion. Indians were excluded from the high mass in the small church and were provided instead with a less elaborate one later in the day.

The second and more important pilgrimage was to the shrine of Our Lady of Izamal, the patroness of Yucatan and the regional equivalent to the miraculous image venerated at Guadalupe outside Mexico City. There is no known direct link at this site with any pre-Columbian female deity like the Virgin of Guadalupe's predecessor, the earth goddess Tonantzin, who helps to account for the spread of the new cult among the recently converted Aztecs. Izamal had been a major site in early Classic Yucatan, associated with the creator god Itzamna and with the sun god in his manifestation of Kinich Kakmo, as well as with a variety of founder deities. Something of its history and religious significance was still preserved in the conquest-period oral traditions.[44] But it did not figure nearly as prominently as Chichen Itza as a shrine and pilgrimage center,

307

and we have no explanation for why the Franciscans chose the site for their magnificent church and convent, aside from the existence of the enormous temple mounds (the largest in total mass in the Maya area) and the great quantity of building stone already available there. For whatever reason, the shrine became the religious center of Spanish colonial Yucatan.

The principal festival at Izamal was the December 8 feast of the Immaculate Conception, the commercial as well as the social event of the year. It was the province's only trade fair and drew crowds from all the Spanish centers for a week of devotion, business, and gaming. According to the Franciscans, it also drew many Indians from far and wide.[45] In fact, most of them seem to have come from the immediate vicinity, where devotion to the cult of Our Lady of Izamal was intense, but it remained a local cult. Although Our Lady of Izamal is mentioned in the various versions of the Chilam Balam books, even today Izamal is not an important shrine to the Maya beyond the neighboring parishes. Every town has and had its own cult to the Virgin and its own round of celebrations for her major feast days. Pilgrimages, if they can be so called, were confined to reciprocal visits within circumscribed areas—towns in the same or adjacent parishes—to help celebrate patron saints' fiestas.

Presumably the perceptual boundaries of the *macehuales* had always been so circumscribed, and the elite's horizons contracted to the same dimensions after conquest. For them as well as the *macehuales* there was little to heighten awareness of the world outside. Even the intermittent presence of the Spaniards, once the Maya had incorporated their demands into their scheme of reality, came to lose its strangeness and be counted among the other common and explicable woes to which human existence was subject. For most Maya the postconquest disintegration of interprovincial and intercommunity ties within Yucatan meant that the social world was confined even more closely to the community in which they had been born or to another barely distinguishable one to which they might migrate.

Colonial Maya religion reflects this increased isolation. The idea of an all-encompassing godhead was not necessarily totally lost. It could have survived and become merged into the remote figure of the Christian *Dios*. But even if deferred to in theory, this vaguely defined and omnipotent being held no prominent place in either the ritual or what we can recover of the cosmology of the colonial Maya.

The implantation of a universalistic religion among any peasant population would seem to be a futile exercise. They may be willing to pay more or less formal homage to the abstract entity of whose divinity the saints or lesser gods are supposed to be mere reflections. But it would be difficult to find a peasant group, whether nominally followers of the Buddha, Shiva, Christ, or Mohammad, who have totally and permanently forsaken the more accessible sacred beings of the locale or group, so long at least as they remain peasants—that is, bound by their microcosmic worlds.

Old Gods in New Guises

The colonial Maya continued to concentrate their collective attention on the middle range of the cosmos, on the tutelary beings identified with their own communities. Within this public sphere no shift in emphasis toward universality can be discerned. On the contrary, universality withdrew further into the background once it lost its only class of adherents within Maya society.

The evangelistic zeal of the friars, backed by the military power of the conquerors, ensured that the parochial level of religion would eventually be expressed exclusively within the framework of Christianity. The outward transformation was accomplished rapidly. Within a decade or so after the friars' arrival the pagan temples, except the ones already long abandoned to the bush, had been destroyed and their stones incorporated into the fabric of the Christian churches erected on their platforms. The old idols had also been destroyed or hidden away. Their place had been taken by effigies of Christian saints adorned with European finery and served by foreign priests with a whole new array of vestments, ritual objects, and sacred symbols. Even if the indigenous long-distance trade had not been destroyed, the new temples had no place for the jade masks, jaguar-pelt draperies or the iridescent plumage of the quetzal bird. Moreover, the ceremonial round that focused on the new temples, the various feasts and rites that marked the passage of time were not only new; they also moved to the different rhythm of the Christian calendar.

The pagan cults that had persisted as a clandestine rival were no match for the officially sanctioned cult, for the more stealthy and exclusive the ritual, the less it fulfilled its purpose. Hidden worship can sustain a personal relationship with a supreme deity; secret gifts to the corporate gods that no one else knows about or shares in, although possibly satisfying to the individual, cannot express and sustain an entire community's links with the sacred. The Maya's corporate relationship with the supernatural was triadic, consisting of deities, elite mediators, and the rest of the community. With the third element removed by the vigilance of the friars, the mediators would become superfluous. They might as well cease their intercessions—and, incidentally, renounce their claim to legitimacy—unless they could transfer them elsewhere.

The ancient calendar round that the gods sustained may have been forgotten; the gods themselves were not. They were transformed into the particular collections of Catholic saints assigned to each town or village according to the whim or special devotion of the friars who established its church. It is unlikely that the neophytes had any say over whether they would be placed under the special protection of Saints Cosme and Damian or Saint Bernardino de Sena; or whether the Virgin Mary in their community should have the title of the Immaculate Conception (a special favorite of the Franciscans, which accounts for nearly half the Our Lady cults in the original foundations) rather than the Assumption (the next in popularity), the Rosary, the Visitation, or some other Marian advocation.[46] It did not really matter, except in establishing which annual feast days the community would henceforth celebrate in honor of its protectors.

Much of the rich lore of Christian hagiography was lost in the transfer to Yucatan. Whatever information may have been transmitted to the Maya about the life histories, the personalities, the special powers, and other idiosyncrasies of their designated patrons, it seems to have had little impact. There is no evidence that Saint Anthony's power to trace lost objects or cure sore throats was ever appealed to, or that Saints Michael, Peter, and Gregory were distinguished in any way other than as patrons of different Maya communities. And their importance, like that of the various local images of the Virgin, was measured purely in terms of the intervillage hierarchy.

The physical images of these saints were as foreign to the Maya as the names and particular miraculous traditions they bore. Few if any were produced in the peninsula, even after Spanish craftsmen had begun to settle there and teach their skills to the Maya. Carved and painted in pure European style, the images were imported from Guatemala and Mexico, to be deposited in the village churches ready made for local veneration. Although through the centuries silver halos, silk robes and canopies, and other locally made adornments were added, and arms were replaced and faces retouched, none of the later embellishments reveals any influence of local styles or visual symbolism.[47]

Some formal deference was paid to a God, who had no Maya name (only the Spanish term *Dios*) and who was invoked either alone or as the Trinity at the beginning of prayers and the most solemn documents, but was otherwise ignored. We can only guess what this God meant to them: The ultimate source from which the other sacred beings derived their powers? The Creator who had withdrawn after setting things in motion? The Maya equivalent of the Athenians' "Unknown God," included as an insurance policy? Some mysterious Spanish divinity who had to be taken into account, just as the people who represented him could not be ignored? Whatever his nature, he did not intervene directly in their lives, and their attention was focused on those who did—the local Virgin and the patron saints, who were with few exceptions male. The Virgin was called *colebil* in Maya, meaning "lady or mistress of servants [or serfs] or slaves."[48] The other saints were referred to as *bolonpixan*, which the Spanish translators rendered as blessed (*bienaventurado*), but which literally means "nine-souled." Nine was a sacred Maya number, and this designation may refer to the nine states of transformation through which the souls passed to achieve their immortality.[49]

Nuances aside, the Virgin and the patron saint were viewed as the proprietors as well as the protectors of the community, rather like lord and lady of the manor, whose manor house was the church. The other holy images that resided there, though also venerated, were accorded a slightly lower rank.

Included in these collections of community guardians was any special image of Christ that the local church might have acquired. Each one was regarded as a separate entity, whether as Christ the King, Jesus the Nazarene, Christ of the Transfiguration, or the Infant Jesus (*Niño Dios*); and none of them was equated with the second person of the Trinity (called *Dios Mehenbil*), or for that matter with the figure on the crucifix placed above the main altar in every church. None of these separate Christ entities seems to have held any special status above the "other" saints. Each was alloted his particular feast day in the Christian calendar, in addition to the separate ritual observed everywhere for the "Dead God" on Good Friday, when the Descent from the Cross was reenacted in each church and a life-sized Christ figure placed on a catafalque before the main altar. The clergy believed the Maya entered into this sacred drama with great devotion, and no doubt they did. However, there is no indication that they regarded the death and resurrection of this particular sacred being in accordance with Christian doctrine as *the* central events that had permanently transformed the cosmic order.[50]

Good Friday and Holy Week in general were secondary festivals in the yearly calendar of the Yucatec Maya, in sharp contrast with Hispanic custom and even the postconquest traditions that have developed in highland regions of Mesoamerica. Holy Week fell somewhere on the scale between Christmas, a decidedly minor feast, and All Souls' Day—the Day of the Dead on which the ancestors were especially honored—and well below the feasts of the patron and the Virgin.

As alien as the Iberian saints were originally—in name, in physical

appearance, and in the whole devotional apparatus surrounding them—
the Maya were able to merge them with their traditional gods. We have
no reliable guide to which particular gods might have merged with
which saints, or even whether there was a one-to-one correlation.
Whatever ordered complexity the popular cosmology of the colonial
Maya may have had, we must be content with lumping the saints together into more or less undifferentiated assemblages and concentrate
on their collective role as community guardians, rather than on any
specialized attributes and powers that might have been assigned to them
within that category.

Some have seen in the Christianized religion of postconquest Mesoamerica simply a cover for the old gods, who as "idols behind altars"
have remained hidden in the saints' shrines or at least in the minds of
the Indians.[51] The evidence suggests a more subtle and complex process
of gradual fusion, at least among the Yucatec Maya.

Few areas under Spanish rule had the freedom enjoyed by the east
coast Maya to work out on their own terms a satisfactory combination
of the new cult with their pagan practices. In more closely supervised
areas those who were prepared to accept the Christian God, even as
supreme being, had no easier a time than those who rejected him. The
sticking point was his jealous nature, the idea that all divinity was concentrated in this one remote figure to the exclusion of all the more
familiar and more intimate deities that permeated the Maya's world. We
can only guess at the disorientation and anxiety the Maya must have
suffered as the first shock of conquest became deepened by the friars'
assault on their deities, indeed on their whole world order. One assumes
that their earliest reactions were what has been termed "culture shock,"
or loss of "plausibility structure," or what Anthony Wallace has described in the psychological terms of personal loss as "Disaster Syn-
drome": the destruction of one's familiar world first brings about disorientation and numbness, followed by a denial of the loss, then severe
anxiety, and finally anomie or despair, unless the world can be pieced
together again, albeit with an altered configuration.[52]

The creative process of reconstruction, adaptation, and fusion that the
Maya pursued in order to adjust their "reality" to the new circumstances created by evangelization is almost as obscure as the earliest
responses, since only a few clues surface now and then from the records.
The early adaptation of certain ritual elements from Christianity is well
documented, such as the famous cases of human sacrifice in the Sotuta
region in which the Maya priests added crucifixion to their standard
repertoire and performed these and other sacrifices inside the Christian
churches.[53] Idols were still being discovered through the first half of the

seventeenth century, and according to the Spanish, as soon as they were smashed, the Maya would fashion new ones of clay or wood "overnight" and simply place them in a different cave. There they would continue to nourish them with copal incense, the ritual drink *balche*, maize, and offerings of turkey and deer (apparently the menu had ceased to include human hearts).[54] These might seem to indicate that Christianity and paganism were still perceived and practiced as two entirely separate, parallel cults. In fact, the fusion was already well underway, in the caves as well as in the churches.

Rather than simply addressing their community gods through Christian stand-ins, the Maya had given them a dual identity, smuggling idols into churches and also giving saints' names to the idols that they were at the same time worshiping in the caves, where they had no need for pretense.[55] Indeed, the Catholic clergy found these syncretic mutations, whenever they learned of them, even more offensive than unadulterated paganism. The "chameleon" nature of Maya gods has made the task of sorting out the pre-Columbian pantheon a frustrating puzzle. It may also have facilitated the process of fusion in this early stage of dual identity. The addition of one more guise to the multiple permutations each diety already possessed would hardly have fazed the Maya theologians.[56]

What I suggest is a gradual shift in emphasis from the old, risky, and increasingly dysfunctional (because necessarily secret) idolatry, which itself was becoming infused with Christian elements, to the less obviously syncretic worship of saint-deities in the churches. The shift would have received a major push from Fray Diego de Landa's vigorous campaign against paganism in the 1560s, which included the wholesale destruction of Maya codices as well as the more easily reproduced idols. The loss of the major part of these "books of the devil," the gradual extinction of a priestly class who could interpret them, and the general decline in literacy after the conquest (including a total loss of the ability to decipher the pre-Columbian glyphs) all facilitated innovation and adaptation, as oral tradition began to replace written texts in the transmission of sacred lore. The Chilam Balam books, and perhaps other colonial texts, preserved in Latin script some of the ancient cosmology, and the colonial *maestros cantores*, the *escribanos*, and some other members of the elite were able to read the words. But the ability to understand their full meaning got lost somewhere along the way.

The gradual extension of the colonial frontier also helped to isolate more and more of the pacified Maya from the "contaminating" contacts they maintained with their unconquered brethren even before the last pagan stronghold at Lake Peten Itza was taken in 1697. The clergy believed that this isolation was a major cause of the decline in idolatry in the older territories. I am inclined to think that the main cause was the high psychic as well as social costs of the conscious subterfuges. In any case, by the middle of the seventeenth century the traditional idolatries had been firmly relegated to secondary status, although not totally eclipsed.

By the end of the colonial period the saints had lost whatever surrogate status they may have had. Even when free to reinstate the old gods and rituals, such as during the rebellion led by Jacinto Canek in 1761, the Maya did not do so, presumably because the old gods no longer had a separate identity. Indeed, the only insignia left for the supernatural and supreme political authority that Canek claimed for himself were the crown and blue mantle of the local Virgin in the church of Cisteil, both of which he donned for his royal investiture.[57]

Jacinto Canek, the anonymous "authors" of the books of Chilam Balam, and the Caste War Maya of the nineteenth century all expressed strong nativistic sentiments. All wished to restore the remembered cultural and political autonomy of preconquest times by expelling or annihilating the foreign rulers. But as creatures themselves of a centuries-long interchange with the Spanish, and as so often occurs in such nationalistic movements, the Maya were necessarily selective in their repudiation of the alien cultural tradition. They drew ideological support and symbolic elements from Christianity for their opposition to Spanish rule (a rule that did not end for the Maya with formal separation from Spain). Canek sought to reestablish links with the native past by taking the Peten Itza ruler's name of Can Ek, to which he added the name of Chichan (little) Montezuma (it is more likely that Canek learned the name of the last Aztec ruler from his reading in the Franciscan convent library where he was educated than that it was known in local Maya tradition). But in assuming the regalia of the Cisteil Virgin Mary, he acknowledged the special status and power of the Christian saint (regardless of gender). And prominent among the grievances he listed in a speech made to rally supporters was the neglect that *visita* towns like Cisteil suffered from the clergy, who left them for weeks without hearing mass.[58]

Just as the Virgin of Guadalupe had become a totem for the Indians of the Hidalgo revolt of 1810 that turned into a war against whites, the Maya rebels of the Yucatan Caste War took the local saints as their patrons and literally captured the holy images. In retreat they sought to keep these powerful images from falling into the hands of *ladino* pursuers, and they pressed into service any Catholic priests they were able to take prisoner to honor the saints with masses and fiestas. In their

314

manifestoes they depicted themselves as the true Christians, and the Spanish as impious hypocrites or, perhaps worse, unbelievers.[59]

The Caste War Maya gave no hint that they regarded Christianity as a new element in their own traditions. The Chilam Balam books, in which some have seen the origins of their ideology, sometimes distinguish the two and sometimes blend them. What they invariably make clear is a distinction between Christianity and Spanish rule. The material consequences of Spanish conquest are eloquently bemoaned; but in a number of passages reminiscent of Old Testament appeals to Yahweh, it is the Christian *Dios* who is invoked as the scourge of the oppressors and the power that will deliver the Maya from injustice.[60] The Bible could be as subversive a document among the Maya as among the plantation slaves in the Old South.

That people can share the same symbols without attributing the same meanings to them has become a truism, but no less cautionary for its wide acceptance. The "Speaking Cross" of the Caste War Maya is a prime example of the divergence between form and meaning. The form is probably taken from Christian rather than pre-Columbian iconography. Although the latter included some cross motifs, they do not figure prominently.[61] The cross was an ubiquitous symbol and object of veneration throughout the colonial Maya environment, placed at the four pathways entering each town, atop boundary markers, and on the doorways of the houses.[62] In the colonial churches, as in all Catholic churches, a crucifix was the central symbol, placed above the altar and the object of all genuflections as well as the symbolic focal point of the Mass. In Maya conception the cross and crucified Christ figure would have become blended together into one entity, the cross losing the Christian significance of the instrument of God's self-sacrifice and becoming the God himself. The *cruzob* crosses I have encountered are all simple crosses without any human figure attached, but all are clothed in *huipiles* draped over the "arms." My own ethnocentric bewilderment has been met with equal bewilderment or rather indignation from the crosses' custodians that I could imagine anyone's displaying *unclothed* crosses: it would be "indecent." The crosses have become the corporate deity-saints that the rebels and *cruzob* descendants no longer had access to, joined by more elaborate human images whenever available. The "speaking" element can be traced easily to the oracular deities of some pre-Columbian temples who communicated to their devotees through an intercessor or, depending on one's interpretation, through whom the human agent communicated.[63]

Whether the contemporary *cruzob* cult is simply a local variant of Christianity, as a Maryknoll missionary has asserted to me, is a theo-

11. Cross with *huipil*. (Photo by Arthur G. Miller)

logical question beyond my competence to judge. The *cruzob* priests themselves acknowledged the Maryknoller as a fellow clergyman of the same communion, granting him the right to celebrate mass in their *Gloria*, or inner sanctum, and they retain many of the visible trappings of the more orthodox Catholicism their forefathers had assimilated before the "schism."

However nativistic in purpose, none of the manifestations of anti-Spanish sentiment have been anti-Christian. Nor could they be, since within less than a century after conquest, the Maya had fully incorporated Christian saints, perhaps some vaguely articulated notion of the Christian God, and many Christian symbols and rituals into their own system.

A pre-Caste War glimpse of unconstrained Maya behavior was provided by the short-lived reforms promulgated by the Liberal Cortes (parliament) of Cadiz, in force in Yucatan during 1813 and 1814. Many curates interpreted this behavior as implacably hostile to Christianity; on closer inspection it turns out to have been hostile only to the curates. Taking advantage of their newly proclaimed freedom as "equal citizens," the Maya refused to pay their ecclesiastical head taxes and provide the clergy with any labor. Some also stopped coming to mass once the penalty of whipping was abolished, but most continued to attend regularly and to organize their fiestas with the same enthusiasm as before. No idolatries came out from hiding, and any neglect of Christian duties can be better accounted for by anticlerical euphoria, fanned by some Liberal *vecinos*, than by any resurgence of a long-suppressed pagan tradition.[64]

Some might argue that a rival system of corporate worship persists in the milpa ceremonies that are still performed and in the offerings still made in the ruins of ancient temples that have been preserved in out-of-the-way places. It was still possible to see the remnants of copal and maize offerings and candle stubs at some of the pre-Columbian sites on the east coast before the opening of a road made the area a tourist mecca. In 1959, after sealed inner chambers of the grotto of Balamcanche near Chichen Itza were discovered containing large caches of pre-Columbian offerings (from around A.D. 900), a local *h'men* (shaman) and his assistants conducted a ceremony to appease the sacred residents for this unauthorized trespass.[65]

The offerings made in abandoned pre-Columbian sites are, like the milpa ceremonies, all more or less private rites conducted for the benefit of individuals—in the case of Balamcanche, for the archaeologists who otherwise would have suffered the curse of the grotto's offended spirits. They do not mediate for the community as a whole. Although derived from the pre-Columbian past, all of these rites are legacies of what I have termed the magical level of Maya religion, the domain not of the major deities to whom the temples and the Balamcanche offerings were originally dedicated but of the *aluxes*, the *chaacs*, the *balams*, and other local spirits whose propitiation and manipulation have always been the business of the *h'menob*. The major deities, the territorial and ancestral gods of the corporate level, have been transferred to a Christian framework.

No sharp division need exist between the magical level and the Christianized corporate level. It is only from an external perspective that the Maya appear to shift between paganism and Christianity, as they move back and forth between house and church, village and milpa. After the initial conflicts and confusion produced by evangelization, the Maya were able to reintegrate both levels into a single system with no more internal contradictions than most systems of meaning and probably no more many-layered and fragmented than the earlier adaptations to foreign cults. The new system was a creative synthesis that drew mainly on the indigenous tradition for its ideational structure and combined Christianity with paganism in varying strengths to devise new forms.[66]

Conceptual coherence at the corporate, parochial level was achieved by merging the tutelary deities with the saints. The restoration of ritual unity was, however, a more difficult undertaking. As explained earlier, in the Maya scheme of things the maintenance of man's bond with the sacred at the corporate level was a public, collective enterprise. This concept favored the eventual triumph of the Christian forms of worship over the pagan rites that could be performed and witnessed by only a handful of courageous diehards. The split between the two competing rituals remained for some time, although the dual identities of the deity-saints provided a bridge, because the authorized Christian forms were not totally satisfactory either—socially or spiritually. The crisis in their world-maintenance activity could not be overcome entirely so long as the Christian forms remained alien rites that the Maya could not participate in actively and direct to their own purposes.

An early attempt to capture the apparatus of Christian worship was made in 1610 by two Indians who, proclaiming themselves "pope" and "bishop," proceeded to offer their own masses in the local church (with the addition of a few idols), to administer other Christian sacraments, and to ordain their own Maya clergy to assist them.[67] The political issue underlying the doctrinal split between Maya and Spaniard was especially clear here. The Spanish were determined to control all access to the sacred, and any appropriation of Christian symbols and liturgy represented as serious a challenge to their monopoly as pagan idolatries.[68] The clergy's indignation is thus explicable, but the fact remains that these and similar acts of appropriation represent in their own way an acceptance of Christianity. They find echoes in the Tzeltal Maya revolt of 1712 in Chiapas, in which native *fiscales* (the local equivalent of *maestros cantores*) simply constituted themselves as a Catholic priesthood in the service not of any overtly pagan deity, but of their own miraculous image of the Virgin.[69] In both cases the Indians were seeking to assert control over the new cult rather than reject it.

In Yucatan, Maya leaders less "audacious" than the self-proclaimed prelates were in the same period beginning to develop a more subtle and therefore more effective way of restoring unity to their collective religious enterprise. The purpose was the same, to Mayanize the Christian framework of public worship, but the means they chose were the officially sanctioned religious *cofradías* dedicated to the community saints.

Fusing the two strands of public worship required the emergence of a more flexible postconquest generation of Maya lords who could shift their attention from the older rituals to this neo-Christian cult. Perhaps the transition could be made in one lifetime: that is, if the don Francisco de Montejo Xiu, *batab* of Mani, who promoted idolatry so energetically in the early 1560s, was the same don Francisco de Montejo Xiu who some decades later so generously endowed a *cofradía* in honor of the local saints.[70]

· 11 ·

MAINTAINING THE COSMOS

The syncretic religion that the colonial Maya created by joining the two strands of public worship took most of its outward form from Spanish Catholicism. Pre-Columbian songs and dances were incorporated into the Christian round of fiestas, and the great wooden drum, the *tunkul*, was still being used to accompany the dances, as well as summon people to mass, throughout the colonial period.[1] These and other indigenous elements that have been mentioned in the documents are but isolated motifs woven into the overwhelmingly Hispano-Christian fabric of public ceremonial. Alien symbols and rituals had taken possession of the sacred.

The substance of postconquest religion resides in the meaning that the Maya invested in these forms, whether pagan survivals, Christian imports, or some colonial innovation. Such meaning is often elusive even when the actors are alive and can be directly observed and pestered with questions about what they make of what they are doing. The colonial Maya have left some evidence, mostly indirect, to suggest that to them the cult of the saints signified essentially the same corporate bond with the supernatural that their ancestors had sustained and which the militant Christianity of the conquerors had threatened to sever—that same symbiotic relationship between gods and men through which the survival of both parties and that of the universe was assured.

Were the holy images themselves worshiped as gods? I am not sure that the colonial Maya could have answered that question unequivocally, any more than the pilgrims who file past Our Lady of Montserrat to kiss her feet have a clear opinion on whether that image is, or merely symbolizes, the Mother of Christ. The infusion of divine essence into material substance is obviously a delicate and subtle question; the line between idolatry and more "acceptable" forms of worship is a fine one, and one that the Roman Catholic doctrine of transubstantiation appears to transgress in the minds of many Protestants. The pre-Columbian Maya are regarded as idolators; yet they periodically renewed the old idols with fresh images without changing the gods they represented. The Lacandon Maya still discard "dead" incense burners representing their deities, retiring them to special burial grounds and transferring their obsequies to new ones,[2] just as the Hindus do with some of their images after their term of service is over. The most we can say for the colonial Maya is that the wooden polychrome figures of saints were treated *as if* they personified the sacred entities they represented. The question of how symbolic this personification was thought to be must remain open.

THE CARE AND FEEDING OF SAINTS

The saints were endowed with very human attributes. They were not unfailingly benevolent. Like the pre-Columbian gods, they were capricious, morally neutral beings whose well-being and good will required careful attention to their physical comfort as well as deference to their high status. Their linen had to be washed and their worn garments replaced; it was thought that the Virgin would be displeased if her dress were allowed to become shabby.[3]

The fiestas were designed as much to entertain as to honor the saints. After high mass they were taken out in procession accompanied by their "servants" (the officers of the *cofradía* and *república*) and the band of musicians they had hired. Homage was paid by community members and invited guests, who might include saints from subordinate villages, and then the images were installed under a temporary arbor or pavilion to witness the festivities. Bishops repeatedly objected to these "profane amusements": the bullfights, mock battles, dances, theatrical performances, banquets, and fireworks displays on which the *cofradías* expended so large a part of their income.[4] The bishops would undoubtedly have found them even more lamentable had they suspected that the Maya invested these amusements with more than profane value.

Food played a major role in all the colonial Maya's solemn observances. Communal banquets accompanied all the fiestas, the wakes and other observances for the dead, the rain-making *Cha-Chaac* ceremonies and more apparently secular occasions such as weddings and roof raisings. Commensality clearly serves social purposes. Shared meals establish the boundaries of a group, express its collective identity, and sustain its internal cohesion. Ceremonial meals can also define divisions within the group; seating arrangements, the manner and order of serving, and other details of etiquette are capable of denoting the nicest gradations of rank. Maya feasting certainly fulfilled these functions.

Fiestas also provided an opportunity for people who existed on the simplest fare (and even that not always abundant) to relish delicacies they could not ordinarily afford. Even the *principales* subsisted mainly on maize and beans. Domestic fowl were kept primarily for their eggs, with the meat usually reserved for the sick. Game was a rare treat; pigs were raised for sale to *vecinos*, and cattle served as a form of capital

321

investment, used for food only in times of emergency when famine threatened the whole community with starvation. But all rules of frugality were suspended at fiesta time. Savory dishes of turkey, pork, and beef were served, cooked with plenty of lard (which is more of a treat to the Maya than the meat itself) and expensive condiments.[5] *Balche* and *aguardiente* would flow, and even the poorest man might enjoy the unwonted luxury of passing out on a full stomach.

Fiesta banquets could not have had much nutritional importance in the overall diet of the Maya. They were too infrequent and the normal fare of maize, beans, and chile, if abundant enough, is perfectly adequate and well balanced. On the other hand, it would be misleading to see these banquets as purely social and gustatory events. There was something special that set him apart from ordinary meals, even beyond their relative sumptuousness. This can still be seen in the excitement a Maya villager today will display when talking about the forthcoming pig roast on the patron saint's day, in contrast with the more muted enthusiasm reserved for a similar spread that the municipal *alcalde* may offer on a national (and therefore to the Maya largely meaningless) holiday. Feasting is a common enough element in religious celebrations. What I refer to here is a particular significance attached to fiesta banquets which, if scarcely unique to the Maya, is nevertheless very much their own and not discernible in Spanish religious festivals, then or now.

The fiesta meals of the colonial Maya should be seen as a kind of communion, an offering of food to the divinities made and shared by the community through their civil-religious leaders. These offerings constituted the principal source of legitimacy for the ruling group, as they had done in the past. The bread and circuses the leaders provided were of a special kind—food and entertainment for the saints. The people partook of them, but the primary benefit was the link they sustained with the sacred and the divine favor they elicited.

The propitiatory role of food carried over to the rituals associated with the dead. We cannot be sure where the dead stood in relation to the corporate patrons of the community. It is believed that the ancestors of pre-Columbian ruling lineages became deified as guardians for the entire polity;[6] and among the colonial Maya "our ancestors" were invoked as a general collectivity that retained an interest and stake in the community's welfare.[7] As well they might, since their own well-being was regarded as dependent on the actions of the living. Whether the dead became corporate deities or merely joined the cosmos as minor spirits, they had to be dealt with in much the same way.

Like any members of the spirit world, the souls of the dead could be helpful, or harmful, to the living, depending on how well they were provided for during the journey to their final resting place and after they reached it. The modern Maya have retained the pre-Columbian custom of burying food with their departed kinsmen.[8] Presumably they did the same in colonial times, although no one else was around to record the practice: the *maestros cantores* and their assistants presided over the burials of all but the wealthiest Indians, who alone could afford the curates' fees for an elaborate funeral.[9] We do, however, have reports that when someone died his soul was lured to follow the body to the burial place by scattering maize in the path of the corpse, all the way from *rancho* to pueblo if necessary.[10] And the family provided food and drink for the rest of the journey at a series of communal *velorios* (vigils) held in the home of the deceased at specified intervals after burial.

The merger between the Catholic concept of the restless souls in purgatory and Maya notions of the afterlife is revealed in the observance of the Day of the Dead (All Souls' Day) when prayers are offered for the souls still waiting in purgatory. For the colonial Maya it was the occasion for the *cofradías* to stage one of the year's most splendid masses honoring all the community's forebears and, most especially, their own elite ancestors who had founded the *cofradías*. The church was filled with votive candles and the smoke of incense that had replaced copal as a nourishing essence for sacred beings; and maize and other food offerings were placed on the tombs.[11] (Once the practice of burying the dead under the church floors ceased, in the early nineteenth century, the tradition evolved into the family picnics at the cemetery that so bemuse visitors to modern Mexico.)

The colonial Maya have left no document in which they expressly state that the communal feasts they organized were offerings to the saints, who would, by partaking of the food's essence, sanctify it for the other commensals and in return for this nourishment ensure the continuing supply of maize and other food for all concerned. The fact that such a mutually sustaining relationship, common to many belief systems in other parts of the world, formed the core of pre-Columbian Maya ritual is no guarantee that it survived under the altered guise of Christianity; nor is the fact that maize cakes, chickens, and *balche* continued to be offered under these same terms to the *chaacs* in the milpa ceremonies and to other supernatural beings in the position to grant or withhold sustenance.[12] Yet no other explanation serves as well for the configuration of rituals surrounding the fiesta banquets, served in the presence of the saint being honored, offered first to the saint and consisting, as the *pièce de résistance*, of food expressly belonging to the saint—the meat from one or more bulls raised on the saint's own *estancia* and slaughtered during the fiesta bullfight (surely a form of sacrifice to the saint).[13]

The Maya expressed the dual sacred quality of food—as something the divine powers give and receive—in their use of the Spanish term *gracia* as a synonym for the all-important, and sacred, maize.[14] One could argue that the Maya made a distinction between the saints and the other spirits they had to propitiate, that unlike them the saints required only prayers or other devotional acts. That would not account for the reports of food offerings, nor for the fact that the same term, *matan*, referred both to communal religious feasts and to the offerings in cash or kind to support divine worship.

A stripped-down version of the pre-Columbian *matan* is preserved by the Lacandones, a splinter group of refugee Yucatec Maya who live in the adjacent Chiapas lowlands. The Lacandon "community" has been reduced to the extended patrilineal family, and it is the head of the family who makes the offerings to the gods, placing morsels of food (even an occasional cigar) in the mouths of the family idols before he eats; he then distributes the rest to the other males who have been assisting, and finally to the women.[15] He performs this ritual not simply as a prelude to a particular meal, just as the *matan* of the Yucatecan fiesta is not a mere thanksgiving; he feeds the gods so that they in turn can continue to provide food for himself and his family.

The Yucatec Maya distinguish themselves, as Christians, from the "gentile" Lacandones, with whom steady contact has nevertheless been maintained since the conquest. But to the Lacandones the distinction is minor: the Maya of Yucatan, they say, simply have "different saints."[16]

THE COLLECTIVE PURCHASE OF SURVIVAL

The cult of the saints was the colonial Maya's chief corporate enterprise, the one to which they devoted most of their collective energies and material resources. The major part of all the surplus goods and labor they contributed under various headings was destined in one way or another for support of the saints, their churches, and their ministers. The exact proportions are hard to measure, especially in the early part of the colonial period when ecclesiastical *limosnas* were totally unregulated and a matter for negotiation between each friar and the community officials. There is enough evidence to show that the Franciscan standard of asceticism applied neither to their churches nor to their own maintenance. The Maya provided silk vestments and altar clothes, silver vessels and carved retables for the one, and impressive living quarters, a large domestic staff, and a well-stocked larder for the other.[17] The friars did not share the simple diet of their parishioners. Along with the staples of maize and beans, they demanded chickens, turkeys, lard, suckling pigs, and, during Lent and Advent, fish and iguanas (iguana is considered a delicacy by the Maya and, according to colonial diocesan rules, could be eaten without breaking the Lenten fast).

In time the ad hoc arrangements between friars and Maya officials became fixed in each town by custom. The quantities of food and other items extracted—say, one chicken and a half pound of wax from each of the five hundred tributaries in the town on every major feast day—far exceeded what the Franciscans could consume themselves, even if they had been so many Friar Tucks and had also kept the churches ablaze with candles day and night. The *limosnas* had become like tribute: the surplus food and wax, the cloth not used in the liturgy and friaries (and, we presume, *all* the petticoats and *huipiles*) were sold for cash to support other parish expenses and the main Franciscan convent in Merida.

Encomenderos and royal officials complained frequently to the Crown about these unregulated contributions. From the inquiries they made (the Franciscans could not be persuaded to open their books) they were convinced that altogether the *limosnas* far exceeded the sum of the civil contributions made by the Maya, and the attempts to regulate *limosnas* (and not incidentally to divert municipal revenues into the provincial exchequer) merely increased the total cost to the Indians.[18] The fact that all ecclesiastical exactions combined, including special fees for catechism, baptisms, and other services, equaled or surpassed the taxes levied by the state (see table 1.1) was a matter of Spanish policy over which the Indians had no control. Yet if we look at the public revenues they managed themselves, the predominance of religious over civil expenditure is even more marked, and there is no reason to think that this order of priorities was imposed by the Spanish.

We must distinguish, as the Maya themselves did, between personal support for the clergy, for which the Maya had no more enthusiasm than any Spanish peasant,[19] and the cult of the saints, to which they were genuinely devoted. It could be argued that the *cofradías* which maintained the cult, were created and run by the clergy for their own benefit. Certainly it was to their advantage to encourage the Maya's devotion to their saints. Aside from the extra fees they received for the masses, sermons, processions, and other services during fiestas, the more money the *cofradías* spent on candles and incense, on adornments for the images, and on refurbishing the church, the less the curate would have to spend from his income for these expenses.

Some curates demanded additional perquisites from the *cofradías*, such as one or two head of cattle a year for themselves, as a kind of extra tithe on the production of the *cofradía* estates.[20] Extortions on a larger scale have been recorded but do not seem to have been common.[21] Perhaps the curates preferred not to provoke protests to the bishops and awkward inquiries into general parish accounting. There was also the risk of killing the proverbial source of the golden egg.[22] But, however lucrative the *cofradías* may have been to the parish clergy (and we should not exaggerate their income from fiesta fees; half of the fee for a sung mass went to the *maestro cantor* and his staff),[23] they were essentially Maya institutions managed by them for their own purposes, many of which served to generate no income at all for the clergy and the rest only incidentally. Clerical supervision over the *cofradías* was in general fairly perfunctory. The officers administered the property and lands and all the income and expenditures themselves. Insofar as formal records were kept at all, the clergy merely copied the amounts presented by the Maya, or they countersigned the entries. Many did not bother to do even that or to concern themselves about accumulated surpluses or deficits, unless prodded by the bishops.[24]

Expenditure varied greatly according to the wealth of the particular *cofradía*, ranging in the extant account books from twelve pesos a year to one hundred and fifty pesos or so from a medium-sized *estancia*.[25] The major cash expense was the yearly round of fiestas, especially the "profane amusements" that the bishops found so objectionable as inappropriate to the spiritual nature of the occasion. Fiesta fireworks accounted for most of the gunpowder consumed in the colony and were considered at times a threat to its security, because of the shortages they created for military ordnance.[26] Many of the other main ingredients of the fiesta, such as beeswax for the vast quantities of candles and most of the banquet ingredients, came from the *cofradía* estates or private contributions. They were not entered into the accounts and it is therefore impossible to calculate either total *cofradía* income or the total costs of the fiestas.

The *cofradías* spent as lavishly for their celebrations as their means allowed, and sometimes they went beyond their means, incurring deficits when droughts reduced agricultural production and the size of the herds. Surpluses did not accumulate for long but were spent on bedecking the churches and saints with silken draperies, fringes, and tassels and silver ornaments of various kinds. (Yucatan was too poor to afford the gold that emblazoned the central Mexican churches.) These and other less costly items needed for displaying proper care of the saints must have represented a large proportion of the Maya's surplus resources. The proportion would be even larger if we counted the salary for the *maestro cantor*; the subsidies provided for the host of sacristans and other church servants; and labor and materials for the temporary structures erected for the fiestas, for the *cofradía* estates (corrals, wells, watering troughs), and for the ordinary rounds of cleaning and repairs that kept the churches in fit condition for the saints. None of these costs were entered into any account books. The churches alone represented an enormous investment. The stone and other material that the community supplied were never counted as construction costs, nor was the bulk of the labor, only the hardware that had to be purchased and the wages paid to the occasional master mason or cabinetmaker imported to do any fine carving on façades and retables. And yet enlargements and reconstructions went on all during the colonial period.[27]

The massive churches that still loom over the pueblos symbolize the preeminence of the sacred over the secular in colonial Maya society. They dwarf the puny *audiencias* (town halls), the seat of secular power. Their grand scale, like their general design, was no doubt dictated by the clergy. *Encomenderos* in the sixteenth century complained of the size and sumptuous style of the churches, blaming the severe population losses in part on the friars' heavy demand for labor.[28] Yet whatever the *macehuales* thought of the demands (and we need not assume unalloyed enthusiasm for pre-Columbian temple construction), their leaders do not seem to have objected to the ambitious programs of church building, nor to the enlargements and renovations that were carried out in the later colonial period. The only recorded complaints concerned the pace and the timing: when curates tried to force the Indians to double their customary weekly stint of *tequios* or to continue building at the ordinary rate during the planting and harvesting seasons.[29] The Maya elite at least came to regard the churches and all they contained, including the saints, with pride and a sense of proprietorship. This attitude was on the whole useful to the parish clergy, although community leaders also kept a very close eye on their investment and would denounce a curate for selling off any item in the church inventory.

Most of the colonial Maya lived a threadbare existence with little above the bare necessities of life in good years and no cushion against lean ones. Their expenditure of cash, goods, and labor in honor of the saints must seem extravagant, not to say wildly improvident. The money spent on a silver crown for the Virgin could have paid half the annual assessment for a town's tribute;[30] the cost of such ephemera as candles and fireworks for the year's fiestas could represent everybody's wages for *servicio personal*. The Maya certainly were not constantly on the verge of starvation, but for subsistence farmers existence can never be secure. If existence depended in large part on propitiating the divine powers that controlled the universe and the fate of the community in particular, then such expenditure was a sound investment. The fiestas and adorn-

327

ments for the saints were the main installments in the purchase of survival.

Anyone tempted to mutter caveat emptor should consider that, within the terms of their belief system, the Maya got their money's worth. The universe did continue to hold together in a more or less orderly fashion, and so did the community; and world order and social order were mutually sustaining. In a secular age the slogan "The family that prays together stays together" offers an ominous prognosis for the future of the family. For the colonial Maya, who had not yet lost a sense of the sacred, prayer in its widest sense could still be a powerful social bond.

For reasons that may remain stubbornly obscure, the Maya saw survival as a collective enterprise. The saints on whom survival depended were community guardians, not universal deities whom an individual might approach on his own. The direct, personal relationship with a supreme god or his mediators that Christianity stresses in common with other "world" religions seems to have remained as alien as the concept of universality itself. Any communal expression of religion is likely to be better documented than private devotions. But there is evidence that the Maya placed little reliance on such private relationships to help them either in this world or the next.

The Christian concept of personal salvation did not take strong root among the Maya. They went to yearly confession but only because they were obliged to, according to the clergy, and did not seem to grasp the transcendental import of the sacrament. The curates complained that though their Indian parishioners believed in life after death, it held no prospect of eternal reward or punishment for the person's earthly life.[31] The souls of the dead were subject to good and bad fates (given the Maya's life of unremitting toil, reports that they defined "heaven" as a place where no one worked are highly plausible), but the individual's fate was determined by the collective obsequies performed by others after his death rather than his own actions while alive. It was the survivors' obligation and in their interests to see that the disembodied spirits of the dead went to their place of repose without delay; for restless spirits—in purgatory, so to speak—could bring misfortune on the living. The family held immediate responsibility for the well-being of its deceased kinfolk, who at some undetermined point became assimilated into the general category of ancestors to whom the entire community as well as the family paid homage on the Day of the Dead.

The individual's well-being in this world was also dependent on collective action. Whatever private dealings the Maya had with the sacred were conducted through the lesser spirits. The major spirits were corporate divinities who had to be petitioned through the corporate group, and the individual's personal responsibility was to contribute to the group's rogations according to his role in the community. The practice of making personal vows (*promesas*) to the saints and dedicating household shrines to them is of more recent vintage in the Yucatecan villages. There is no evidence for such vows among the colonial Maya nor among the contemporary *cruzob* Maya, who for all their Caste War innovations have remained in many ways closer in spirit and practice to what we know of colonial Maya life than the more orthodox Christian villagers. Even among the latter, *promesas* are still not as common as in the larger towns, and although the intention is usually some personal matter such as recovery from illness, the means—communal rosaries and prayer feasts—are not.[32]

The evolution of the colonial *cofradías* underscores the inappropriateness of private negotiations with the sacred from the Maya's point of view. The original *cofradías* were distilled versions of the institution that has figured so prominently in Spanish popular devotion, especially in the cities: voluntary associations dedicated to a particular saint, supported by yearly dues that paid for special masses, rosaries, and other pious observances, as well as for funerals and memorial services for the brothers (and sisters) who died in good standing.[33] On paper at least, they were a model of pure Christian spirituality, pursuing the aim of personal redemption and purged of all the obviously profane and pagan elements that popular devotion had introduced into the Old World.

Popular devotion has a way of obtruding itself in all its local richness in defiance of the theological and liturgical purists. Like many other Spanish institutions, the *cofradías* produced some strange though healthy fruit when grafted onto Indian root stock. The early documents that have survived show a decline in dues-paying membership. This did not signify a decline in devotion to the saints, only a shift to a more suitable means of expressing it. As outlined in chapter 9, the Maya transformed the *cofradía* from a particular group of devotees pursuing personal salvation through individual contributions into public institutions supported by the entire community and dedicated to promoting the general welfare of the community through general obsequies to its sacred guardians. Such a thorough and widespread transformation suggests that the Hispanic model introduced by the friars violated basic Maya theological and social principles. Or, rather than a specifically Hispanic model, the original *cofradías* represented an urban religious mode, at the same time universalist and individualistic, which the mendicant orders in both Europe and America have sought to promote at the expense of the localized, collective mode of peasant society.[34]

329

The logic, within Maya terms, of concentrating the major part of their corporate resources on what we would call religious ritual has already been discussed. Whatever their more transcendental efficacy may have been, these rituals were a crucial underpinning to their social system. Whether man invents a cosmic order to sustain the social order, or vice versa, I shall leave to the metaphysicians to debate. Here the social instrumentality of Maya efforts to maintain the cosmos is offered merely as a consequence of, rather than any explanation for, this collective activity.

The cult of the saints was the shared experience that most clearly defined group boundaries in Maya society and the roles and statuses of members within the group. Most especially it defined the boundaries of the community, translating the geographical fact of shared territory into the social fact of community. The church itself was the physical token of community status, its presence or absence marking the difference between autonomy and dependence for any population cluster, regardless of size. The church housed the community's collection of divine guardians, who might be similar in name and appearance to those belonging to adjacent groups, but were not shared by them.

The geographical boundaries of the community possessed more than administrative significance to the Maya. When the bishops sought to change boundaries and shift outlying hamlets from one jurisdiction to another in order to make parishes more uniform in population, the hamlet residents as well as their *república* officials resisted. One might imagine that such changes would be a matter of indifference to the dispersed population, since tribute and labor obligations were the same from pueblo to pueblo. Closer proximity to the new parent town, which the clergy cited as the principal advantage of the proposed boundary changes, could have been regarded as a drawback by the hamlet residents, but hardly enough of one to account for the strength of their opposition. Maya calculations of who belonged where were not based on physical distance and certainly not on the bishops' criterion of equalizing parish incomes. People belonged to the pueblo where their local saints were honored, where they were accustomed to attending mass and fiestas, and where they buried their dead (and where some of them continued to bury their dead in defiance of the bishops' orders), regardless of whether it was twice as far away as another "ceremonial center."[35]

What gave life to the community as a social organism was the shared effort of sustaining their relationship with the saints. The saints did not bestow their benefits gratuitously. One shared in them only because one had contributed to the collective effort of obtaining them. The cult of the saints was thus more than a mere emblem of group identity. Active participation in the common endeavor gave subjective reality to the territorial boundaries separating one Maya group from another. It also distinguished the Maya from any non-Indians who might share the same territory. Whether resident *vecinos* were thought to share incidentally in the rewards, they were not expected to, nor did they, with rare exceptions, contribute to the care of the saints. That was the exclusive responsibility of the exclusively Maya *cofradías*. The occasional unsolicited contributions from *vecinos*, even the hired services of the local priest, made non-Indians no less marginal to the basic endeavor than the Maya were to the *vecino* cults of Our Lady of Hool and Our Lady of Izamal.

The reciprocal nature of the relationship with the saints helps to account for the territorial limitations of the saints' advocacy. They were tied to the locale not because they were associated with a particular terrain or feature of the landscape like the lesser spirits, but because their supporters were organized by territory rather than lineage, occupation, or some other principle. They were portable only when the entire community moved, as in the congregation program when any resettled town that had already been evangelized brought its saints with it to the new church.[36]

The family or individual who migrated independently simply switched saints along with the change in community affiliation. Fiestas did not ordinarily attract former community members, nor were the friars successful in extending the cults of what they considered particularly efficacious images beyond the images' own territories, even though they tried to encourage regional sales of scapularies and pilgrimages to the Virgin of Motul and other saints besides the Virgin of Izamal.[37] The jurisdiction of the saints was as limited as the horizons of their Maya devotees, and for the same reason. The lack of supracommunity ties meant that members of one group could not make an organized cooperative investment in the support of any other advocate, and without any such investment they could expect no returns. An individual could in theory cross the boundaries, making a private contribution for a private rogation, except that, as already explained, the colonial Maya placed little confidence in such personal transactions even with their own patrons. The widespread cult of the Virgin of Mamental (Chicbul) in southwestern Campeche and adjacent areas of Tabasco was exceptional, as were the region's inhabitants. These descendants of the preconquest "Putun" merchant princes seem to have defied the general Yucatecan norm of total fragmentation and maintained an intraregional commercial and devotional network.[38]

Saints and fiestas provided the one formal intercommunity link that remained in Yucatan from the preconquest systems of alliances and ov-

331

erlordships. Visits to neighboring fiestas were common, especially within the same parish. They did not, however, blur community boundaries. The guests came as ambassadors from one polity to another, sometimes accompanying their own patron saints. They would reciprocate with invitations to their own fiestas but without sharing in the maintenance of each others' saints.

The symbiotic relationship between community and patron saints could not prevent dispersal and permanent migration but it could help to neutralize their effects, drawing *forasteros* and scattered hamlet residents into this cooperative activity. Fiestas were the one occasion in which the entire population was certain to gather in the center, where all members could see themselves as a community and reaffirm social bonds outside the family circle. In theory, they all assembled for the obligatory weekly mass, but residents of distant hamlets rotated attendance, sending half of their population one week and half the other. Children, the old, and anyone else with a halfway plausible excuse for not making the trip into town stayed at home. Weddings, baptisms, and funerals and reverence for the deceased ancestors buried in the church brought dispersed families to the center, but as separate families, except for the community-wide rites for the dead on All Souls' Day. This and other fiestas brought them all in to stay with friends or relatives or camp around the plaza for the duration of the celebrations.

No one willingly missed his village fiestas, no matter how far from home. Men might be gone for months on a distant wax-collecting expedition, but if anyone failed to show up for a major fiesta it was assumed that he was injured or gravely ill, if not already dead, or had permanently decamped to the unpacified zones. Contemporary Maya sojourners will still make every effort to be on hand for their fiestas, regardless of the cost. I recall the terrible dilemma faced by one worker on an archaeological dig. Should he quit early so that he could attend the week-long celebrations, or stay on and earn more money toward the next year's fiesta, of which he was to be one of the sponsors? He stayed on, as much out of loyalty to the project director as for the extra wages, but a prolonged migraine headache was the price.

The Maya were and are drawn from their *ranchos* and from temporary migrations for the show itself: the ear-splitting rounds of fireworks and the bullfights, real or mock (when they cannot afford to purchase a bull); the music that provides an unrelenting accompaniment to all the festivities (musicians are and were well paid by local standards,[39] but they work hard for their fees); the feasting and drinking; the processions and solemn liturgies with colored streamers, masses of flowers and candles, and the saints in their best finery. Fiestas are a time of plenty and pageantry in otherwise drab, pinched lives, and even if designed to entertain the saints the celebrations cannot fail to please the human participants. But the Maya did not and do not come solely to be entertained. These ephemeral delights betokened the general benefits that the saints were expected to provide and in which all could share because all had shared in their purchase. Even the most marginal *macehual* had all through the year been making his own small contribution either through fiesta preparations, repairs to the church and other *cofradía* projects, or through the chores and taxes that maintained the whole apparatus of community governance, which in turn organized the cult of the saints.

Dispersal attenuated the social bonds of community. Physical distance itself did not break them. This happened only when a satellite settlement was able to attain independent status with its own church and saints and thus to effect a switch of allegiance. The later colonial haciendas sought to acquire *de facto* autonomy, establish greater control over their resident laborers and wean them away from attachment to the pueblo and the rival authority of curates and *república* officials. Only the largest haciendas, such as Chencoyi or Uayalceh, which could provide churches with their own patron saints and annual fiestas, were entirely successful.[40]

WORLD ORDER AND SOCIAL ORDER

The cult of the saints was the main horizontal bond that linked *macehual* to *macehual*, helping to overcome the physical distances that separated dispersed portions of the community. It was also the main vertical bond between *macehuales* and *principales*, helping to overcome the inherent divisiveness of unequal rank and privilege.

Direct access to the corporate divinities had traditionally been reserved exclusively to the Maya nobility. The Classic period rulers were closely identified with the deities, claiming descent from them, achieving apotheosis at their own death, and representing the sacred in society during their own lifetimes.[41] Although the emperor of the Aztecs clearly fits this same model, we do not know whether a full-blown concept of divine kingship persisted into the Postclassic period in Yucatan. Nevertheless, a strong link between deities and rulers can be seen in the rituals that have been recorded. The Maya conception of the past as something both irrevocably lost and infinitely repeatable may help to elucidate that link and also one aspect of the relationship between lineage and legitimacy that has already been discussed.

Hereditary rulership and the emphasis on the length of a dynasty's genealogy can be seen as hardheadedly pragmatic in cosmic terms, apart from their usefulness in ensuring orderly transfers of power. People often look to the past as a guarantee of the future. For a ruler, a long pedigree—that is, a good ancestral track record in administration and military deeds—can provide some promise of future performance. But in addition, a genealogical link with the past creates a metaphysical link with the divine powers that once created and continue to sustain the cosmos, and thus helps to ensure success in the ruler's crucial mediatory role. The more remote the past, the closer to the "beginning of things" before the two worlds of gods and men were split apart.[42] Whether or not the Postclassic Maya rulers still claimed descent from the gods, they could claim through their ancestral ties a closer proximity to and therefore greater efficacy with them in the rituals designed to keep the world going in endless cycles of renewal. Translated into the less abstract and more immediately practical terms of reference of the Maya farmer, this meant that the ruler could ensure the reappearance of the sun each day after its passage through the underworld and the renewal (usually) of the rains each season for the life-supporting maize. These and other tangible benefits that the rulers continued to offer as intermediaries between the sacred and the body politic would provide as firm a foundation as any for a stratified social order.

How could that social order be sustained, when an alien regime had taken possession of the sacred, at least in its public arena? By fusing the ancient corporate deities with the Christian saints, the Maya could redefine Christian notions of the sacred on their own terms. But that would still leave the elite without any significant ritual function to justify their existence. The introduction of Christianity certainly created a stumbling block for postconquest Maya leaders, but not an insurmountable obstacle. The Mayanization of Christianity extended beyond the sphere of belief to include ecclesiastical administration and sacred ritual as well.

The Maya nobility never wholly regained their religious ascendancy in the neo-Christian cult. The colonial church had no place for them or for any other Indians in its hierarchy. The Indians' status as perpetual neophytes meant that their doctrinal lapses and aberrations were treated with greater indulgence, subject to the milder authority of the bishops rather than the Inquisition (caste distinctions were not always disadvantageous to the colonial Indian). It also meant that they could not be trusted to undertake the duties of the priesthood, and the Spanish creoles and peninsulars retained a near monopoly on the Catholic priesthood throughout the colonial period and beyond. A small proportion of mestizos and even a few candidates with some African mixture managed to infiltrate the clerical ranks (over the protests of the creole elite), but no Indians.[43]

Christianity in fact relegated the Maya nobility to the religious side-lines only in a formal sense. The Spanish clergy were, in theory, the only mediators between the Maya and the supernatural. In the church militant they were the sole officers, with the bishop as the distant com-mander-in-chief who put in very occasional appearances to review the troops, and all the Maya of whatever status served as the rank and file. The captains were few in number, however, and everyone knows, in any case, that it is the noncommissioned officers who really run things; in the colonial church of Yucatan these were all Maya.

The sergeant-major of parish administration was the *maestro cantor* of each church. From the beginning of evangelization the Franciscans had had to rely on native assistants to help preach the gospel and supervise the material and spiritual affairs of the newly created parishes. In each friary they established a small boarding school, taking in youths from noble families and teaching them Christian doctrine and liturgy, reading and writing, and also music. These young men would then accompany the friars as personal interpreters (*naguatlatos*) or be sent out on their own as catechists. The schools were later abandoned, but in the mean-time a self-perpetuating cadre of Maya assistants had been created, headed by the *maestro cantores*, who trained their own successors.[44] Fray Diego de Landa summed up the friars' reliance on the *maestros* and other *prin-cipales*, "on whom everything depends, because of the confidence placed in them, having been made almost the friars' colleagues in preaching and instructing the Indians in the things of our Holy Faith."[45] The *maes-tros* in fact always remained subordinate to the friars and curates; but because of the shortage of ordained clergy, they were given very wide powers and much independence, in effect serving as deputy curates.

The range of functions and the importance the *maestros cantores* were to assume within the church and within Maya society are most inade-quately conveyed by the English rendering of *maestro cantor* as "choir-master." They were the parish secretaries, keeping notes for entry into the registries of births, marriages, and deaths, and often recording the entries themselves.[46] They supervised the catechism and selected and taught the youngsters who would receive special training in vocal and instrumental music, in liturgy, and in reading and writing; and they thus controlled who would become church functionaries, *escribanos*, and their own successors in the post of *maestro cantor*.[47] They examined and coached the candidates for the sacraments of adult baptism (in the early period), confession and communion, confirmation, marriage, and ex-treme unction. They made the matrimonial inquiries concerning the prospective marriage partners to avoid bigamy and unions within the prohibited degrees of kinship. They were responsible for all the music, vestments, and sacred vessels; they organized the liturgy and led the daily recital of the rosary in the churches and a modified Sunday and holy-day liturgy if a priest was not present. They buried the dead and baptized the newborn when the curate was absent or could not be bothered.[48] In short, they did everything but perform the sacraments reserved to an ordained presbyter (eucharist, extreme unction, and confession) or a consecrated bishop (confirmation). The face that Christianity presented in day-to-day contact with the faithful was a Maya face.

The increase in the number of parish clergy during the course of the colonial period would in theory have greatly cramped the style of the *maestros cantores*. Depending on the distance from the *cabecera*, the *visita* towns could usually count on seeing a priest at least every few weeks. Certainly long gone were the days when outlying areas were left on their own for six months at a time. But the early wave of missionary zeal had played itself out also, and the numerical increase was offset by an increase in indolence.

Some of the later parish clergy, particularly the Franciscans, continued to be conscientious pastors. Not content to confine themselves to a starring role in the liturgy, they took what must have been to the Maya an irritatingly active interest in parish affairs. These were exceptions. The detailed diocesan records of the late colonial period, even discounting general fulminations from bishops about the laxity of the local clergy, lead to the unavoidable conclusion that the vast majority of the secular clergy had come to view an Indian parish as a lucrative but tedious sinecure, which was left in the hands of the *maestros cantores* even when the curate was technically in residence.[49]

The clergy could be confident that although the Indians' grasp of Christian dogma might be feeble, their devotion to the saints was unshakable. The cult of the saints permitted the rest of the Maya elite, besides the *maestro cantor* with his large staff of assistants, to participate in the direction of the community's religious affairs, to recreate for themselves a prominent role in propitiating the corporate deities under the aegis of the Christian church. The structure of local ecclesiastical organization can be seen in figure 11.1.

Responsibility for the cult was formally vested in the patron, *priostes*, and *mayordomos* of the *cofradías*, although the line between civil and religious authority in the community was far from distinct, and the existence of a separate *cofradía* structure responded more to Spanish than to Maya notions of administrative organization. Any of the community leaders, regardless of whether they were serving in a *cabildo* or *cofradía* office at the time, could give precise information about the history and management of the local *cofradía*. They all knew who had originally

FIGURE 11.1. COMMUNITY RELIGIOUS ORGANIZATION

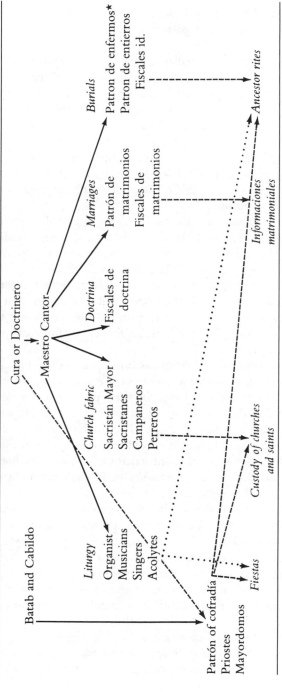

* Includes care of the dying (Last Rites)
→ Appointive authority
-→ Administrative authority
··→ Participation

donated the land, how many head of cattle had been counted at the previous branding, and what particular celebrations and activities the *cofradía* supported.[50]

No matter how much surveillance the parish priest might exercise over the finances of the *cofradía*, and I have suggested that it was fitful at best, the Maya leaders regarded themselves rather than the Catholic clergy as the guardians of the saints and all that belonged to them. The clergy could not be trusted with this responsibility. Curates came and went; they did not have the same stake in the community as the elite. And even if they had stayed permanently, they remained outsiders who never became integrated into Maya society, never shared the same values, and were therefore incapable of understanding the true significance of the saints in the world order.

The care of the saints was too crucial to the survival of the community to leave in the hands of the *dzuls*. It was also too crucial to the survival of the elite's place in society. The reciprocity that underlay the Maya social order was tripartite. The elite received deference and obedience and material support from the *macehuales*, both for themselves and for the public expenses of the community. They in turn were to protect the welfare of the community primarily by procuring the good will of the saints, and the flow of benefits from the saints completed the three-way exchange.

If the line between civil and religious functions in the political system was blurred, the distinction between ranks was not. Only the elite were the servants of the saints, in charge of their persons and property.[51] I have mentioned that all the community leaders were well informed about the *cofradías*' history and management. The *macehuales*, whether or not they cared to know the names of the founders or the price of the virgin's new cape, had no access to this information, which was kept in the *cofradía* books guarded by the *principales* or in the oral traditions they transmitted among themselves.

The *principales* were servants of the saints in a more literal sense. Even the menial tasks of caring for the saints' person were too sacred and prestigious to assign to *macehuales*. The *mayordomos*, who rotated in weekly teams in domestic service of the saints, had the privilege of dressing the images, keeping their garments and furnishings clean and in good repair, and tending the altars, especially the candles, while the lower-ranking sacristans were in charge of the general cleaning and upkeep of the rest of the church.[52]

The material support of the saints was the sole right and responsibility of the elite. This did not mean that they provided the adornments and fiesta fireworks out of their own pockets. Some private donations were

338

made and most of the *cofradía* estates had been established by *batabs* and other members of the nobility with endowments of land, cattle, and beehives. Most of the cult expenses were in fact met from the community's public resources. The *macehuales* were obliged to provide all the labor and materials for the fiesta arbors, enclosures, and platforms as well as much of the food for the banquets, either through labor on the *cofradía* milpas or through individual assessments.[53] The elite mobilized and channeled all the surplus wealth of the community, and in so doing could represent themselves as the source of all the material goods they offered on the community's behalf. The idea that the state is the personal patrimony of the leader and that public benefactions paid for by public taxes are somehow his own personal gift was no doubt as rooted in Maya political culture as it was among the Spanish.[54] It remains pervasive in Mexico, as witness the innumerable plaques affixed to everything from bridges to public drinking fountains proclaiming that the President "gives" this particular benefit "to the people" of whatever town or district in question. The colonial *macehuales* have left no record of their views on the matter. Insofar as they remained more or less docile members of the social order, we have to assume that in some degree they shared their leaders' interpretation of its workings.

The elite's vital role as intermediaries, channeling gifts between saints and community in both directions, is impossible to dismiss as an imaginary or trivial claim, unless we dismiss their public ritual as an elaborate and costly farce that the entire population engaged in solely to entertain themselves. Social behavior invariably has some social meaning; public ritual satisfies the senses but it also expresses the shared values of the group and the way it organizes itself.

As a social text the public rituals of the Maya, which revolved almost exclusively around homage to the saints, are incompletely recorded, but enough bits and pieces can be assembled to reveal the basic grammar of social relations.[55] The annual fiestas were the most ambitious and public of all the rituals the Maya staged—the showpieces of the cult of the saints that all the other activities during the year led up to. They help to explain how Maya society held together, for they literally brought everyone together. The exchange of gifts between community and tutelary saints, represented in the commensality of the fiesta banquets, also served to sustain social differentiation, defining as well as expressing the roles and statuses of the community members.

Preconquest religious organization and ritual provide some clues for understanding the mediatory role or roles performed by the leaders. There was no clear separation between church and state in preconquest Maya society, but a distinction existed within the ruling caste, at least in late Postclassic times, between (1) the *halach uinic*, the *batab*, and other leaders who combined civil and religious roles, and (2) the full-time religious specialists—the *ahkin* (chief priest), the *ahcambezah* (chief teacher), and the rest of the temple staff. The former were responsible for the security and welfare of the polity and directed all its affairs, spiritual as well as temporal, to that end. The latter were the theological and liturgical experts, the keepers of the sacred lore of cosmology and ritual.[56] There appears to be an overlap, but in fact a well defined division in sacred functions can be discerned. The *batab* and his group provided for the material support of the deities, while the *ahkin* maintained direct contact with the deities and conveyed the offerings supplied by the *batab*. In other words, divine mediation was a two-step process requiring the services of both priest and ruler.

A major duty of the pre-Columbian lords was to sustain the gods— literally with food. Feeding the gods was, as noted earlier, the chief element in the Maya liturgy, and the division of labor between procurement for and delivery to the deities can be seen clearly in the rituals reported in the early postconquest idolatry trials conducted by Fray Diego de Landa.[57] The general responsibility for providing the banquet belonged to the *halach uinic* or the *batab* and their colleagues. They decided whether a feast should be given; they set the time and place, and provided the ingredients—the copal, the *balche* and the maize, and the animals and the human beings who were to be sacrificed and offered to the gods. The last item could require complex negotiations after the conquest. If no suitable victims (usually orphans) could be found locally, they had to be obtained by trade, or sometimes by stealthier means, from neighboring provinces, since the supply of prisoners of war had been cut off. The role of the *ahkins* was crucial, for they conveyed the offerings to the idols, smeared their faces with blood, and deposited the bodies in the sacred *cenotes*. But it was the ruler in his role as donor, or his deputies, who performed the first stage of the sacrifice, cutting out the hearts and handing them to the *ahkin* to present to the image of the god.[58]

These furtive offerings made to idols smuggled into the church at midnight were a poor substitute for the pageantry of the old temple rites, and as I have explained, their secrecy obscured their function as links between community and deity, and hence both their social and spiritual value. Nevertheless, this stripped-down version contained the essential core of the ritual, which was retained under the new and more satisfactory—because it was more public—guise of the cult of the saints. Feeding the gods remained the central element in the syncretic rites of the fiestas and even in the liturgy of the mass, both of which culminated in the ritual sharing of food and drink between deity and worshipers; and the same division of labor remained.

The *maestros cantores* were the first bridge between the old and new religious forms, leading a dual existence as deputy curates in the Christian structure and also participating in the proscribed rituals—at least one of them as the principal *ahkin*.[59] We know only of the ones who were detected by the Spanish and have no reason to believe that they were exceptional cases. The friars were particularly distressed to learn of what seemed to them a cynical betrayal of the confidence they had placed in the *maestros*. They could not see the unresolved metaphysical conflict that lay at the heart of the "apostasy."

The *maestros cantores*, if not all originally "converted" *ahkins*, had, as nobles, close ties with the Maya priesthood, and they also continued to be the repositories of whatever indigenous sacred lore survived. The versions of the Chilam Balam books and other holy texts that have survived must all have been the work of colonial *maestros* or their proteges, the *escribanos*. Who else could both read the ancient glyphic texts and transcribe them into Latin script? Aside from having monopolized the necessary skills, they are the most likely source of the incorporation into the texts of Old and New Testament references, which they learned from the friars. The Maya laity, even some *batabs* we are told, were hard put to repeat the Hail Mary and Our Father without some prompting.[60]

Under Christianity the *ahkin/maestro cantor* had to share priestly functions with the Catholic clergy. The Spanish priests thought they were the only mediators between the divinity and the community once the clandestine idolatries were suppressed; they were mistaken. To be sure, they played the leading part in the liturgy of the mass but not the only part, nor was the mass the only or even necessarily the most important element in the whole cult of the saints or the fiesta in particular. It is hard to say whether, given the choice, the colonial Maya would have dispensed altogether with the Catholic priests. They certainly acknowledged the priests' sacred powers, which helped to guarantee the efficacy of the rogations to the saints. A fiesta without a mass was simply not a proper fiesta, and during the Caste War the rebels forced captured priests to say mass for them. However, the *maestros cantores* who joined the rebels—liturgical specialists themselves who had officiated alone at rosaries, vigils, and other litanies—soon took over the priestly role entirely.[61] Their successors among the *cruzob* Maya, who have continued the cult of the saints (transformed now mainly into "Holy Crosses," with a Maya-Christian liturgy) recognize the Catholic clergy as fellow priests of equal but not superior status. The local Yucatecan clergy, in contrast to some of the North American missionaries, have not been willing to repay the compliment.

The *cruzob* Maya have obviously carried syncretism a bit far for local tastes. However, one reason the colonial Maya were able to fit the Catholic priests into their ritual schema and preserve or recreate much of their traditional relationship with the supernatural was the considerable tolerance the local clergy displayed toward the new syncretic forms. It might be more accurate to say that they were unaware that the forms were in fact syncretic. It was not only the general indolence and indifference of the postconquest generations of clergy that facilitated the Mayanization of the Christian framework of corporate worship. The later generations were increasingly creole. Born in Yucatan, raised by Maya servants from infancy, speaking Maya as their first language and accustomed to local ways, the creole clergy became partly Mayanized themselves.[62]

It is not clear whether in later colonial times the local clergy knew anything at all about the pre-Columbian origins of the *tunkul* (ceremonial drum), of the fiesta dances[63] that the peninsular ecclesiastics found "indecent," or of the food offerings and other pagan practices that had been incorporated into the neo-Christian cult. Some of the bishops, coming with fresh eyes to the local scene, were horrified in their diocesan tours by these practices and the sight of many of the village churches: the "ridiculously dressed effigies," the "indecorous" mural paintings, and the other signs of Indian munificence and taste.[64] To them the creole clergy were not trustworthy either: "Since they suck no other milk but that of Indian women, they are very partial to [*amantíssimos a*] the local rites."[65]

In the colonial fiestas the *maestro cantor*, together with the Catholic priest, continued to serve as the direct link with the deity.[66] Both held the place of honor not only in the masses and processions but also at the banquets, dramatic performances, and other amusements that the parish clergy clearly found less distasteful than the bishops. Nor did the clergy seem to object seriously to the Maya's "superstitious" practice of offering food to the saints during their fiesta celebrations.[67] Unfortunately they do not specify who made the offerings, so that we do not know if the *maestros cantores* made the presentation in person according to the pre-Columbian formula or if the *batab* and *cofradía* officers had taken over that task, with perhaps the *maestro* and the priest (the latter unwittingly) having consecrated all the gifts merely by their participation in the mass and fiesta in general.

The gifts themselves were still provided by the civil-religious leaders. They could no longer summon divine aid with human sacrifices, but otherwise their traditional role in the two-step mediatory process was even more well defined than that of the *maestros cantores*, for they did not have to share the function of donors with any outsiders. They were the impresarios, who planned and organized the fiestas and obtained the food, drink, and entertainment and the priestly presence that was required to complete the transaction. Both the *maestro* and the Catholic priest, the only servants of the saints who were paid a fixed salary, also received fees for their services in the fiesta. They were in that sense part of the staff, like the musicians who were also indispensable to the success of the fiesta, although of much lower rank.[68] As possessors of an essential expertise, the priest and *maestro* were greatly honored, but they definitely were hired help. Their fees were paid by the patron of the *cofradía* and the other community officials; it was the latter who presided over the fiesta as hosts for the saints and the community, sustaining the world order and the social order in the triadic, reciprocal relationship.

Convites AND *Cargos*

The horizontal and vertical integration of the community and the definition of the boundary between *principales* and *macehuales* are the most obvious contributions that the cult of the saints made to the social order. But something else was going on at the fiestas and it had to do with the finer gradations of rank among the *principales* themselves.

The colonial Maya elite, if we are to believe the Spanish accounts, spent much of their time and their own money, along with a substantial portion of public revenues, on banqueting. They treated each other and themselves to *convites*, or banquets, for every conceivable occasion, domestic and official: baptisms and weddings, even burials; elections and installations of public officials and plenary sessions of the *cofradía* and *cabildo*, including the occasion of the *cofradía*'s yearly cattle branding; religious festivals from Shrove Tuesday to the Day of the Dead, and especially during the novenas of the major feast days for the patron saint and the Virgin.[69]

Shortly after the conquest a royal *visitador* tried to ban *convites* as a serious nuisance. Not only did they encourage drunkenness (which the Maya considered an essential feature of the feast rather than a byproduct) and waste, leaving the Indians financially "ruined"; they also provoked discord, because the people who were not invited felt insulted.[70] The attempt to abolish *convites* was futile. The Maya valued them too highly precisely for the reasons the *visitador* found them objectionable.

Convites defined social boundaries, especially the boundaries between elite and *macehuales*, since the latter hovered too close to the subsistence

343

level to take part in this round of mutual feasting. Even at the fiesta banquets the choicest delicacies were often reserved for the community officials and other *principales*, while the simpler fare was distributed to the rest of the community.[71] Exclusion from the banquet table signified unequivocal relegation to *macehual* status, which condemned one to the leftovers in food and no power at all. Within the elite group a rank order was also maintained, which included the visitors from other communities. The curates extended invitations to other priests in the vicinity, we are told, and the *batabs* and the *regidores* invited their counterparts from neighboring towns.[72] *Cofradía* officers, *maestro cantor*, sacristans and members of the choir, dancers, musicians, and "players" (*comediantes*) all had their place, too. If a complete guest list and diagram of the seating arrangements were available, it would no doubt save much of the labor required in piecing together scraps of information about the social structure by showing us at a glance precisely where everyone stood (or sat) in the hierarchy.

Banquets were obviously a clear representation of social stratification in the Maya community. There is some indication that they had a dynamic function also: that feasting and sponsorship of other rituals in honor of the saints did not simply express but also helped to establish the pecking order of power and prestige among the elite. Although the structure of colonial Maya society was well defined and stable, the relative positions of lineages and individuals were far from immutable. The boundary between *macehuales* and *principales* might allow passage through it while remaining firm. And within the rank of *principal*, only eligibility to public offices, and not the offices themselves, was hereditary. These official positions with all the perquisites of prestige, authority, and control over public resources were far fewer in number than the people who were qualified to hold them. We know the procedure for filling the positions—election by the community notables[73]—but not how or why the particular choices were made. Yet some fairly orderly system for allocating power must have been at work to keep factionalism within its usually discreet bounds.

Colonial Maya politics are like a jigsaw puzzle in which most of the pieces are missing. But if we lay them out on the board and add a few related pieces from preceding and succeeding periods, we can get some hint of the general outlines. Rotation in office was part of the system, possibly among *batab* lineages and certainly among the second tier of *cabildo* and *cofradía* positions. The *cabildo* positions were very finely graded (perhaps the *cofradía* offices were, too, but we have less information about them), from the most junior *regidor* through the higher ranking of the two *alcaldes*. Rotation was not a simple circular movement but rather a spiral or zigzag in which people normally reentered at a higher level. Detailed *cabildo* records from the town of Tekanto covering well over a century have enabled Philip Thompson to trace certain patterns in the movement, which he sees as a device to alternate power among four political groups.[74] His calculations, based on the careers of scores of individuals, suggest a highly complex system whereby each group was able through its representatives to move up the political ladder and have its chance to fill the higher posts of *alcalde* before starting again at the bottom.

Thompson makes a convincing case for this pattern as a set of guidelines rather than an absolute rule, with deviations attributable to political deals and trade-offs among the groups. It bears much resemblance to, and indeed is partly derived from, Michael Coe's model of pre-Columbian political organization based on a four-year cycle in the ritual calendar and on the traditional Maya division of the towns into four wards or *parcialidades*.[75] According to Coe, the four wards corresponded to the four "year-bearer" days which, in rotation, began the Maya solar year. The rotation of the four days, each with its guardian spirit, its own presiding deity, and its own color and cardinal direction, had a very elaborate ritual conducted during the period that marked the transition from old to new year. The rituals (called *uayeb* rites) have been described in considerable detail in Fray Diego de Landa's early postconquest account.[76] Although their political function is mainly a matter of inference, Coe argues convincingly that the *uayeb* rites were part of a system of rotating office holding through the person of a *principal* chosen each year to preside over the transfer from one year and one "year-bearer" to the next.[77]

Linguistic evidence lends further support to the argument, through the root word *cuch*, which signifies both a burden or load and office (or trust or charge). *Cuchteel* is one of the Yucatec terms for ward, the head of which was the *ahcuchcab*—the bearer of the burden—and that meaning is linked in turn to the year-bearer day, *cuch-haab*.[78] (Any public official would doubtless appreciate the symbolism that equates office holding with bearing a burden on one's back.) Taken together, these and other related Maya terms suggest that when its turn came, each ward through its leader (the *ahcuchcab*) assisted the annual deity associated with the initial day of the new year to bear the year through its full cycle—that is, to keep time and the world going on behalf of the whole community.[79]

The lineal descent from pre-Columbian *ahcuchcab* to colonial *regidor* has been mentioned in an earlier chapter. An even richer pattern of associations can be found between the *uayeb* rites and the rituals of the

12. Fiesta sponsors preparing for Dance of the Pig's Head. (Photo by Arthur
G. Miller)

colonial fiestas, which represent the essential but heretofore missing link
(missing, that is, in the scholarly literature) between the pre-Columbian
and the modern Maya politico-religious systems. Pre-Columbian
processions accompanied by the lord, priests, and nobles conducting the
deities to various points in the town; decorative arbors erected for the
festivities; ritual dances and food offerings made by the *principales* to the
deity; and a banquet presented to the rest of the elite in the house of the
presiding *principal*: these descriptions of the *uayeb* rites read like the stage
directions for the colonial fiestas in honor of the saints. One of the
colonial rituals, which has survived to the present, gives an especially
strong hint of *uayeb* rite origins. At the fiesta's end a dance was performed in which a decorated head of a pig slaughtered for the feast
(surely the transmogrified deer head of pre-Columbian offerings) was
carried around and then presented to the person who was to be in charge
of the next year's ceremonies as a token of the "burden" he was assuming.[80]

What is missing from the colonial documents is any mention of a
direct connection between an individual's fiesta sponsorship and the system of rotating office-holding, although we know that public officials
were responsible for organizing the fiestas. The *cofradías* in some ways
merely complicate the picture, as if the office of *ahcuchcab* had become

346

split into that of *mayordomo (cofradía)*, with more direct responsibility for ritual, and that of *regidor (cabildo)*, with more purely civil duties. Yet the line between the two is far from clear. The structure of the *cofradía* replicated that of the *cabildo* exactly and there was much overlap in function and in personnel. Unfortunately there are no long runs of both *cabildo* and *cofradía* records for the same town, which could reveal if the *cofradía* served as a steppingstone to the *cabildo* or a holding ground for those waiting to come back into the *cabildo* at a higher level, or indeed if there was any regular pattern of movement between the two at all.[81]

The lack of information on these and other inner workings of colonial Maya politics should not surprise us. The postconquest generations of Spaniards developed the view, so convenient to a colonial regime, of the conquered race as rather simple-minded children motivated largely by impulse, with a capacity for cunning but not for anything so sophisticated as an organized political system. With an obtuseness bred from condescension, they had no reason to inquire what the Maya were up to. The Maya had no reason to enlighten them, either, and have left few of their own documents to enlighten us.

One thing stands clear out of this obscurity, and that is the continued association of political authority with religious ritual. Less certain but highly likely is the instrumental role of fiestas and feasts in the dynamics of local politics. They served, in other words, not merely as a sign of status and power but also as a means of acquiring them. It is difficult to accept that the Maya elite's persistent addiction to *convites* over the strenuous objections of the Spanish authorities was only a token of their irrepressible conviviality. Wealth was considered an important qualification for office because of the public trust involved in administering community finances. Perhaps it could also earn political advancement in a more direct fashion, through the rounds of *convites* that featured so prominently in the lives of the *principales*. The sharing of food and especially of drink, regarded as so frivolous and wasteful by the Spanish, were, I suggest, the Maya's chief way of creating and consolidating political alliances beyond the circle of the extended family.[82]

Private *convites* would be a useful mechanism for parlaying personal wealth into political power. Fiestas, including the central element of the public banquet, would be another. Most if not all the support came from public sources. But the officeholders had the ultimate financial responsibility as guarantors. Even if they did not ordinarily have to make some contribution of their own, and it is most likely that they did, they would still have to make up the deficit if for any reason public funds were insufficient. Aside from the fact that the ability to meet these expenses if necessary (or be able to call upon a group of kinsmen and supporters for credit) was thus a prerequisite for public office, the offer to undertake the obligation was in essence the offer of a gift to the community. Such a gift, which in gratifying the saints also guaranteed the flow of future benefits, would demonstrate one's willingness to serve the community's collective interests.[83]

The link between the cult of the saints and community leadership has persisted throughout the Maya area down to the present. A system of fiesta sponsorship called the *cuch* or *cargo* (from the Spanish translation that has the same dual meaning of burden and office) occurs with many local variations, achieving its most elaborate and closely scrutinized form in the highland Maya communities of Guatemala and especially Chiapas.[84] The *cargo* is a ritual office in which a man undertakes to organize and subsidize all or part of a religious fiesta and other annual devotions dedicated to one or another of the saints in the local pantheon. The year's service, which can be highly costly in time and money, repays the donor in status. In fact, in many pueblos the hierarchy of *cargo* offices through which an individual can work his way has become synonymous with community leadership.

Because of the distinctively Maya flavor of the system under the veneer of Christian terminology and symbolism, the *cargo* has been offered as that elusive key to the mystery of pre-Columbian social organization which Mayanists spend so much time pondering.[85] Some scholars have questioned whether social processes in the twentieth-century Maya highlands can shed any light on what was going on in the very different physical and social environment of the lowlands more than a millennium earlier.[86] Such a vast leap across time and space is in fact unnecessary; there are a few steppingstones in the colonial records from Yucatan. They at least help to tie an ancient *cargo* system hinted at in the descriptions of the *uayeb* rites of the Postclassic (with no doubt remoter origins) to the modern one; they also show that a number of important changes have occurred along the way.

Perhaps the least of the changes is the introduction of Christianity. Most of the formal elements of the contemporary *cargo* system are colonial adaptations of earlier practices. Its underlying rationale, in which prestige and authority are based on material support of the corporate deity-saints, also has deep roots in the Maya past and is so common as to be symptomatic of traditional political culture around the world.

What has changed drastically is the social structure on which the *cargo* rests and hence, it would follow, the way it functions. Maya society has ceased to be a stratified one in which a small elite, whether a strictly hereditary nobility or not, monopolizes power and wealth. It has become, if not egalitarian, at least a society in which socioeconomic differentiation is slight and status is achieved rather than inherited. It is also a society in which sacred and secular power have been divorced and the latter transferred out of the hands of the Maya to government-appointed *ladinos*. Ritual functions are still tied to community leadership but it is a leadership of prestige and status only. The Maya religious hierarchy that coexists along with the local *ladino* administration may retain some of the trappings of civil governance inherited from their colonial predecessors (such as the titles of *alcalde* and *regidor* and the staff of office) but little of the substance.

In view of these contrasts, the result (in Yucatan at any rate) of changes that occurred in the late colonial and postindependence periods, the modern *cargo* system cannot be an infallible guide to either colonial or pre-Columbian social organization.

Let us take the question of economic differentiation. Nowadays one of the chief functions of the *cargo* system is supposedly to prevent the formation of an elite by encouraging the translation of any accumulated wealth into status through fiesta sponsorship. Some have questioned this leveling function: on closer inspection, it turns out that not every-one starts out equally in the bid for status; some families through in-herited reserves and mutual lending networks predominate in the higher *cargo* positions and rich families remain rich, expensive *cargos* notwith-standing.[87]

A recent, even more iconoclastic interpretation of the modern Chia-pas *cargo* hierarchy is that it is neither inimical nor even incidental to economic inequality, but rather the product of a class system that emerged in the late nineteenth century in response to the expansion of Spanish-controlled commercial agriculture in the region.[88] If, as is asserted, a small group now dominates society, reinforcing its wealth and power through control of the *cargo* hierarchy, then the only thing new about the system, the only fundamental departure from a social structure that can be traced back for millennia (in the Maya lowlands at least), is a shift from an hereditary elite to one that is *wholly* based on wealth and the political manipulation of sacred ritual.

Let us grant for the sake of argument that the modern *cargo* system does impoverish its participants. If so, that is not a function included in the original design. No hereditary ruling group devises a system the purpose of which is to destroy its economic base; or if it does, it does not last very long as an hereditary elite. The support of public worship among the pre-Columbian and colonial Maya was a duty of the ruling group but it was not intended to, nor did it, bring financial ruin on the sponsors, any more than patronage of Chartres cathedral emptied the treasury of the Capetian monarchy or the endowment of philanthropic foundations has beggared the Fords or Mellons. Elites throughout the ages have found it prudent to give away part of their wealth in order to keep the rest.

The key element in both the colonial and pre-Columbian civil-religious hierarchies in Yucatan that is missing in the modern age is political power. The colonial elite dipped into their pockets—though not to the bottom—to support public worship. Sponsorship helped them to gain or at least validate political power, including control over public resources. This control enabled them in turn to subsidize the major cost of worship and to enhance their personal wealth, thereby completing the cycle. Public office in general carried some risk of financial loss, through responsibility for the community's collective tax assessment and for its collective cult of the saints, since these liabilities and obligations did not cease when plague, famine, or some other calamity diminished public revenues. According to the Maya's own account, the *principales* developed the *cofradías* as public corporations primarily because of the ruinous personal cost they sustained in supporting the fiestas during the period when the *cajas de comunidad* were appropriated by the royal Treasury.[89]

Financial sacrifice, then, was a sign of dysfunction in the system in colonial times. Detailed records of *cofradías* in Michoacan in central Mexico reveal the system's breakdown in the late colonial period when the economic base of the Indian communities was declining. As in Yucatan, the chief *cofradía* officers also took responsibility for the expenses of the cult when funds were insufficient, although they were not required to pay all the expenses personally; minor officers and the rest of the community were obliged to supply them with goods and labor. Even so, the native economy had become virtually destroyed by the late eighteenth century, and some officers fell so deeply into debt that they had to "enslave themselves" to haciendas as peons.[90] The original purpose of the religious *cargo*, however, would seem to have been elite maintenance and not self-immolation. The system became unstuck when the leaders, whose position continued to depend on ritual functions, could no longer command public resources to support them.

The modern *cargo* system can also be a misleading guide to the vexing question of social integration in the past: how did the pre-Columbian Maya manage to integrate a largely self-sufficient and territorially fragmented peasantry into a more or less cohesive polity with a definable center? In contemporary Chiapas, we are told, this is achieved mainly by the rotation of ritual offices among a large part of the population, including those normally living in outlying hamlets; and it has been suggested that the ancient Maya used a similar mechanism to unite component groups of a larger community, whether scattered hamlets or *parcialidades* of a town center.[91] The problem with this model is that it assumes that the common people had any access to political power or ritual functions in pre-Columbian times. It is of course possible that *macehuales* played a more active and prominent role in public ritual and governance before the conquest than afterward, but all the available evidence points to a movement in the opposite direction. The evidence from colonial Yucatan also suggests that political power was not only exercised in, but also derived entirely from, the nucleated towns. The hamlets, by definition marginal in every way, had no elite population and no separate power base. With one exception (the *batab* of one community who spent part of his childhood on a *rancho*), high-ranking officials seem to have been townsmen from birth.[92] And yet hamlet residents, without any apparent direct political representation, retained some affiliation to the towns, visited them more or less regularly, and contributed their labor and taxes, however grudgingly, to the common pool.

Rotation of ritual functions and civic leadership among a large part of the population, or at least potential access to these positions, may be an excellent means of integrating component groups of a polity.[93] It is not, however, the only way. In fact, it is fairly rare and bears more resemblance to the democratic federal ideal of the modern North American political system than anything likely to have been dreamed up by the hierarchically minded pre-Hispanic Maya. Traditional Maya society was integrated vertically through reciprocity, in a stratified system in which an hereditary elite monopolized the substance and emblems of power and the masses took no active part in either choosing the leaders or in shaping their decisions.

This reciprocal relationship was unquestionably lopsided in colonial Maya society. Although the *principales* had responsibility for protecting the community's collective interests, and so far as we can tell served as diligent and honest stewards of the community's resources, they certainly served their own interests in the bargain and allocated to themselves most of the tangible rewards these resources produced, including the food and drink offered to the sacred guardians. But to work as a social bond, reciprocity does not require that the distribution of benefits be equitable, only that the rank and file derive from their share enough incentive to stay and obey. If my reading of the Maya's conception of the world order is correct, the benefits the *macehuales* derived from their contribution to the collective enterprises organized and directed by the elite were far from trivial. For they included life and all that was needed to sustain it.

351

PART FOUR
NEO-COLONIAL SOCIETY

· 12 ·

THE SECOND CONQUEST

For the Maya of Yucatan a long, relatively quiescent period followed the first postconquest decades of adjustment to the imposition of Spanish rule and to the massive population losses that accompanied early contact. Some further, mutual adaptations were made during the next two centuries and their cumulative effect was far from negligible. Yet for fundamental changes in the colonial regime that was established in the wake of conquest, and in the native society that had developed in response to that regime, we must look to the late colonial period. Starting approximately in the last quarter of the eighteenth century, Indian society came under a renewed assault, a second conquest that in many ways was to prove as devastating as the original conquest of the sixteenth century.

The major impetus for this second conquest came from outside the colony, from a series of innovations generally referred to as the Bourbon reforms, which originated in Spain and were applied with varying effects throughout the colonies. Their purpose was to restore and even to strengthen royal power and the ties of empire that had weakened during Spain's long decline under the increasingly ineffectual Hapsburg monarchy. Adopting new means and infused with new ideas derived from the European Enlightenment, the Bourbon reforms marked a radical break with the past despite their basically conservative aim and the inevitable gap between promise and performance.[1]

Historians have made much of the effect of the Bourbon reforms on the Spanish American creoles, whose comfortable accommodations with the theoretically more restrictive but in practice more flaccid regime of the later Hapsburgs came under a variety of attacks.[2] The effect on the Indians has largely been overlooked.[3] Yet for them the break with the past was as radical as for any other group, perhaps more so. It signaled the end of the colonial period proper and the beginning of a "neo-colonial" era, during which their assimilation into the larger society dominated by the creole descendants of the conquerors was greatly accelerated. The neo-colonial era spanned the divide of formal independence from Spain, with policies first tentatively pursued by royal ministers and applied in more extreme form by the newly independent governments. On the surface of things nothing could seem in sharper contrast with the royal absolutism of the Bourbon monarchs than the

355

Liberal reaction of their republican successors. But underlying this apparent opposition was a common thread of state activism and a certain leveling thrust to that activism directed especially against corporate privilege, which the Crown perceived as an obstacle to centralized royal power, the Liberals perceived as an obstacle to individual freedom and equality and both saw as an obstacle to material progress and the solvency of the state. As juridically defined corporate entities set apart from the rest of society, with certain legally defined privileges and large amounts of corporately owned property, the Indian communities, like the church, were to be special targets of the Bourbon reformers and their Liberal heirs in this neo-colonial period.[4]

From Indirect to Direct Rule

In regions where the Indians had little or no autonomy to lose, the consequences of the centralizing policies of the Bourbon monarchs may have been minimal or even beneficial, to the extent that more effective royal government meant stricter enforcement of the laws protecting Indians from Spanish greed and ill treatment.[5] In Yucatan the Maya had retained something better than royal protection: a considerable degree of de facto independence under the system of indirect rule.

The administrative structure of the colony was as primitive as its economy. The province still resembled a mission territory well into the latter part of the eighteenth century, with the Spanish population for the most part huddled in the few urban centers and responsibility for the Indian hinterland shared by *encomenderos* and *doctrineros*. This responsibility was, however, largely nominal, for the real job of governing the Indians was left in the hands of their own leaders.[6] There is no sign that the local Spaniards were dissatisfied with this arrangement. Although their grip on the province had certainly become secure enough for them to have subverted the Maya's system of internal government without endangering the security of the colony, they apparently saw no reason to dismantle a system that kept the Indians under control with little bother or expense on their part.

The attack on the political autonomy of the Indian communities came from Spain, and it came in the form of a general reorganization of the colonial bureaucracy under the rubric of the intendancy system, introduced throughout the empire in various stages and reaching Yucatan along with the rest of New Spain in late 1786.[7] In Yucatan the new system brought no structural change at the top. The governors merely added "intendant" to their list of other titles without any increase in the scope of their powers (although there was a considerable increase in the probity and efficiency with which those powers were exercised). For the Indians the most significant innovation was the creation of a set of local officials called subdelegates, each in charge of a *partido*, or district (the province was divided into eleven *partidos*), and each assisted by *jueces españoles* (a kind of justice of the peace), in all the seventy parish *cabeceras* that were not administrative seats of a district.

In many parts of the empire the subdelegates were merely recycled *corregidores* or *alcaldes mayores* with no significant change in role and sometimes no change in personnel either.[8] In Yucatan they were new in fact as well as in name. As I discussed in chapter 3, the Crown, had expressly forbidden the appointment of *corregidores* in Yucatan. The *capitanes a guerra* and other subordinate officials that the governors used as surrogate *corregidores* seem to have confined themselves to the military matters that were their legitimate purview and to the business affairs they conducted on their own and their superiors' behalf.[9] Under the intendancy system the subdelegates were granted all the formal administrative authority that the former officials lacked, and they set about using that authority with full encouragement, if not to say prodding from the governors.

The apparatus of local Indian government that had first been established in the ordinances of royal *visitadores* shortly after the conquest remained intact. The difference was that for the first time the Indian officials were answerable not to a distant governor in Merida, but to agents of the Crown resident in their own pueblos, who not only transmitted the orders emanating from Merida (or Mexico City or Madrid, as the case might be), but also saw conscientiously to their enforcement.

The implications of that innovation were many and subtle, for they reached far beyond any formal circumscription of the authority of the native leaders. The Maya officials continued to be responsible for the maintenance of law and order within their communities, punishing offenders and adjudicating disputes, while referring any conflicts involving non-Indians to the governor in the Tribunal de Indios. Under the new system they had to go through one and sometimes two intermediaries (a local *juez español* as well as a subdelegate) to reach the provincial authorities.[10] But considerably more significant was the fact that these intermediaries began to intervene directly in cases involving only Indians, cases that previously would have been settled internally without any recourse to the Spanish, indeed for the most part without their knowing anything about it.

The subdelegates need not have sought actively to invade the judicial jurisdiction of the *batabs*. Rather, their presence and the new administrative system in general encouraged the Maya themselves to take their squabbles outside the community in defiance of the traditional structure of authority. Starting in the early 1790s, and with increasing frequency thereafter, petitions appear from community members appealing decisions and actions of the *república* officers. They also began regularly to take private disputes with other Maya and grievances against *vecinos* directly to the subdelegates, bypassing their own leaders altogether.[11]

Such acts were rare before this period. The ordinary Maya would have found it extremely difficult to deal directly with the distant and rather awesome authorities in Merida, even if it had occurred to them to do so and had the governor been willing to listen. They lacked the legal expertise to negotiate the intricate procedures of the higher court. Now all they had to do was walk to the center of town—or, if they lived in a *visita*, to the parish *cabecera*—and present their case orally to the *juez español*, who could then draw up a petition for them and forward it to the subdelegate. The risk of reprisal for what would have been considered a serious act of insubordination in the past became minimized by the presence of these resident colonial officers, who could have the *batab* himself whipped if he sought to punish the petitioner. I find no evidence of increased ill will toward the community leaders, no intensification of social conflict, no deliberate attempt to challenge the established order. Recourse to the Spanish officials was a pragmatic response to a changing reality that the Maya rank and file could not fail to recognize. The almost absolute control over the lives of the community members that the leaders had formerly exercised was disappearing. They could still distribute some rewards and punishments but increasingly only as constables for the local Spanish officials rather than as rulers in their own right.

Colonial legislation by itself would reveal little of these changes. Without the records of actual administrative practice, one might even suppose that local government gained in autonomy in this period with the phasing out of the private *encomiendas* beginning in 1785. The decline in autonomy was real, but it came not so much from the formal authority granted the subdelegates and *jueces españoles* as from their simple presence on the spot—in contrast to the remote, town-dwelling *encomenderos*. Most especially it came from a new spirit infusing colonial government at all levels, a spirit that violated all the tacit assumptions by which colonial affairs had been managed for centuries. No matter how strictly regulated these affairs may have been in theory, in practice colonial governance had been largely a laissez-faire market system at least in the more remote provinces, permitting the Spanish to buy off the Crown by such devices as *composiciones de tierras* and the Indians to buy off Spanish interference with similar fees, fines, and "gifts."[12]

Possibly because of the scarcity of other economic opportunities in Yucatan, the tax commissions paid to subdelegates attracted candidates of high caliber.[13] These in turn were accountable to governors who were notably more conscientious (or officious, depending on one's point of view) than their predecessors. The complacency of the earlier governors, and sometimes their outright collusion, had left the Indians prey to the extortions of *capitanes a guerra* and other agents, who had compensated, and perhaps more than compensated, for the lack of any legal remuneration with *repartimiento* commissions and their own unauthorized demands. The Maya gained some relief from these and other extortions. The hated *repartimientos* were abolished in fact as well as in law.[14] The clergy, some of whom were implacably hostile to the subdelegates as rivals for local hegemony, could find no grounds for impugning their financial probity: "despotism" aplenty but no illegal exactions of cash, goods, or labor.[15] The price of this relief, however, was the loss of the autonomy that the corrupt and slovenly administration of the old regime had helped to preserve.

Along with inroads on their judicial authority, the Maya leaders were entirely deprived of their control over public revenues on which much of their political as well as their economic power had been based. Tribute and also the *holpatan* tax (both of which the *batabs* and their assistants had collected even in the Crown *encomiendas*) were made the sole responsibility of the local royal officials, collected by the *jueces españoles* and transmitted by the subdelegates to the Treasury offices in Merida and Campeche without any intervention from the Maya leaders.[16] In some of the parishes (I have no record of what proportion) the clergy also commissioned the *jueces españoles* to collect their *obvenciones* on the side. The royal officials may have been more efficient or ruthless than the *batabs*, who had performed this service for centuries, but they were not always as honest, and several curates found the experiment a failure.[17]

Infinitely more serious was the loss of control over the Indian communities' own public revenues. The *cajas de comunidad* had been restored to the *repúblicas* some time before the end of the seventeenth century, after having been diverted into the provincial Treasury for about fifty years. They were taken over by the Treasury again in 1777, even before the introduction of the intendancy system, and this time by order of the Crown.[18]

In theory this order was intended simply as a change in administration. The four-real head tax and the other income-forming community revenues were placed under the direct supervision of the Treasury officials. The proclaimed purpose was laudable: to manage the revenues on behalf of the communities in order to protect them from the negligence, dissipation, and possibly even graft they had supposedly suffered while administered by the Maya officials, who had never provided a satisfactory reckoning in all the years they had handled these funds. They had presented some token accounts each year (with expenditures almost invariably equaling income) for review by the governors, who apparently gave them as little scrutiny as they gave to the annual election returns presented for approval at the same time.

After 1777 the Maya officials continued to collect the tax themselves. The difference was that they were obliged to deliver the entire proceeds to the Treasury officers, except for small, fixed amounts authorized for the routine administration of the community. These expenditures, prescribed in advance for each *república* according to its size, were limited to such recurring expenses as stamped paper for official business, the annual fee paid to the governor for confirming elections, and the salaries for the *maestro cantor* and *escribano*. After 1786 the subdelegates were placed in charge of reviewing the accounts and transmitting the balances to the Treasury offices, where they were to be credited to each community's account.[19]

The Treasury officials were justly pleased with the rapid growth of these revenues. Under the relatively efficient and honest management of the reformed Bourbon bureaucracy, the *bienes de comunidad* (the combined account of all community funds) accumulated a surplus of over half a million pesos in less than forty years, compared to a balance of only 4,086 pesos during the entire period up to 1777 (see table 12.1). The annual gross yield from the tax had of course been rising during this period along with the substantial increase in the Indian population. Nevertheless, the sum was impressive by any standard and for Yucatan it represented a "king's ransom" in more than a figurative sense. All but a small cash reserve of 8,065 pesos left in 1813 had in fact been used since the 1780s to help rescue the sinking royal Treasury from bankruptcy, either as loans on which the interest was never paid or as "emergency deposits" (plus another 32,000 pesos granted as an outright "donation for the war").[20] When in 1804 the Crown decreed the desamortization of all corporately owned funds to help stave off insolvency, over half the *bienes de comunidad* account from Yucatan had already been raided. Even so, the sum transferred to the new "Consolidation Account" (*Caja de Consolidación*) in Mexico City exceeded the total obtained from the capital endowments owned by the church, a substantial portion of which was also Indian property belonging to the community *cofradías*.[21]

As impressive as the fund was from the point of view of the Excheq-

TABLE 12.1. *Bienes de Comunidad* IN ROYAL TREASURY, 1777–1813
(IN PESOS)

Year	Amount
1777[a]	4,086
1781	27,000
1785	51,799
1798	110,000
1805	354,817[b]
1813	516,757[c]

Sources: AA, Oficios y decretos 4, Abogado de indios to Governor, 25 Sept. 1781; AGI, Mexico 3123, Relación . . . Real Caja, 1785; Mexico 3139, Governor to Miguel Cayetano Soler, 24 Feb. 1799; AGN, Consolidación 10, Exp. sobre bienes de comunidad, Yucatan, 1805–1806; AGI, Mexico 3138, Oficiales reales to Governor, 22 April 1813.

Note: This and the following tables in this chapter first appeared in Farriss, "Propiedades territoriales."

[a] Before being placed under direct royal administration.

[b] Includes 36,563 pesos of accumulated *réditos* on 81,250 pesos deposited in the royal Renta de Tabacos since 1786.

[c] Includes 55,627 pesos of accumulated *réditos*; 172,193 pesos in the Caja de Consolidación; 253,000 pesos on loan to the local Treasury; 11,000 pesos on loan to the Monte Pío de Oficinas (royal officials' pension fund); 15,652 pesos on loan to individuals; and 8,065 pesos in cash. Other sums removed from the fund and not included in this account are: 32,000 pesos "gift" to the Crown for the war; 1,000 pesos for an orphanage and 50,000 pesos for the leper hospital of San Lázaro, both in Campeche; and 58,000 pesos on loan to the Treasury from the accumulated surplus of the *holpatan* tax, to a total of 666,757 pesos accumulated surplus from the Indian communities.

uer, for the Indians the new system was a decidedly retrograde step even if the surpluses had not been siphoned off. Certainly the Maya officials had produced scarcely any surplus, but then it had undoubtedly not been their intention, nor was it in their communities' interest to do so. As I have argued earlier, they probably had not collected the full four-real tax. Despite the Treasury officials' allegation that the Maya had mismanaged or perhaps even embezzled these revenues, it is more likely that they had simply adjusted the amount they collected to the communities' total needs and balanced that against the income obtained from other sources, such as the *cofradías*, the community milpas, and the rent paid by landless *castas* for milpa rights on community lands.

Under the new system, only a small part of local revenues was spent on local needs and these were now to be defined by outsiders. The Treasury officials' zeal to accumulate surpluses transcended the boundary between frugality and stinginess. In 1817, for example, the officers of the town of Espita requested permission to spend forty pesos on new furniture for the town hall. Espita, which was the largest town in the district of Tizimin, yielded at that time an annual municipal revenue of at least six hundred pesos. But the Treasury officials found this request "excessive" and authorized only twenty-five pesos, and this only because of the subdelegate's report that the *cabildo* had had to borrow a table and chairs from the curate in order to hold recent elections.[22]

The most serious drawback to this forced program of thrift from the Maya's point of view was that they were not permitted to pay for fiestas or any other expenses relating to the cult of the saints out of their municipal taxes. By itself this prohibition would probably have produced no great hardship. The *cofradías* had assumed the full burden of these expenses during the time that the revenues had been expropriated previously and presumably they could have done so again, except that the *cofradías* themselves were coming under attack from another quarter. As ecclesiastical institutions the *cofradías* were safe from the civil authorities (at least until the church's own property became the target of confiscations). They were not, as it turned out, safe from the church itself, which was pursuing its own policy of fiscal centralization in this period. It cannot be entirely coincidental that in 1780, after many years of intermittent and cursory attention to *cofradía* finances, similar to the governor's review of municipal accounts, the bishop suddenly decided to take over all the Indian *cofradías*. His idea was to sell off the estates and invest the proceeds in *censos* (a kind of mortgage on real property yielding a standard annuity of five percent) in order, he explained, to "preserve these pious foundations and avoid the losses to which they are otherwise exposed."[23]

At best the plan was ill-conceived. Only two-thirds of the estates (78 out of 117) were in fact auctioned off before the civil authorities intervened to halt the sale (see table 12.2). Ironically, or perhaps predictably, the 39 estates retained by the Maya were the only ones still producing income by the end of the colonial period. Many of the *censos* fell into arrears and in some cases both the accumulated interest and the principal were lost (a common enough occurrence with ecclesiastical *censos* in the diocese and one that the bishop might have foreseen). In fact, less than half the interest owing for the years 1787-1796 was actually collected (see table 12.3). The bishop could not have foreseen the ultimate irony, which was that *all* ecclesiastical capital, including what was left of the *cofradía* capital (but not the unsold estates), would be expropriated in turn by the royal Treasury in exchange for government bonds, to disappear along with the insolvent Spanish Crown and the *bienes de comunidad* when independence was declared in 1821.[24]

The Maya, in any case, had seen little of the income from any of the *cofradías*. The unsold estates had been effectively expropriated by placing

TABLE 12.2. *Cofradía* ESTATES IN YUCATAN, 1770-1787

District	1770	1780[a]	Sold (1780-1781)	Sale Price (1787)[b]
Merida	4	4	3	1,320 pesos
Camino Real	27	27	11	20,710
Campeche	5	5	2	2,505
Costa	42	38	28	22,316
Sierra	23	23	20	23,723
Beneficios Bajos	16	15	12	12,308
Bencficios Altos	2	1	-0-	-0-
Tizimin	10	2	2	415
Valladolid	8	2	-0-	-0-

Sources: AGI, Mexico 3066, Informaciones haciendas de cofradía, 1782, cuads. 1, 5-10, 12, 16-18; AA, Visitas pastorales, 3-6, Parish reports, 1782-1784; Oficios y decretos 3, Haciendas de cofradía vendidas y su importe impuesto, 1782-1786; Libro de cofradías, 1787-1796; Cofradías e imposiciones 1, 1704-1818; Obras pías, 1760-1842.

[a] Number of *cofradía* estates in operation. There is record of only one sold in this period (belonging to the town of Uayma, Valladolid district); the rest had been ruined in the severe drought of 1769-1774 and permanently abandoned.

[b] These figures represent the amount of the *censo* capital of only seventy of the *estancias*. The eight missing *estancias* were large, and judging from the value of comparable nearby *estancias*, all of which sold for 2,000-6,000 pesos each, they could raise the figure by at least another 20,000 pesos. The actual sale price is unknown in many cases but there is evidence that part of the principal belonging to many of the *cofradías* had already been lost by 1787. The total amount of the combined sale prices was estimated by local sources at "over 100,000 pesos" (AA, Oficios y decretos 4, Testimonio Tesorero Real Caja, 3 April 1782).

TABLE 12.3. INCOME FROM *Cofradía* CAPITAL IN YUCATAN, 1787-1796
(IN PESOS)

Interest (*réditos*) owed on principal[a]	41,441
Interest collected	19,381
Expenses paid for fiestas[b]	8,739
Administrative costs[c]	1,551
Cash balance (*alcance en la caja*)	8,691
Unaccounted for in the records	400
Uncollected interest	22,060

Sources: AA, Oficios y decretos 3, Haciendas de cofradía vendidas y su importe impuesto, 1782-1786; Libro de cofradías, 1787-1796; Cofradías e imposiciones 1, 1704-1818.

[a] *Réditos* at 5 percent on principal of 82,882 pesos (not including the 415 pesos from the Valladolid district, since no information is available on collection or disbursement of this income).

[b] Fees and other expenses for *festividades* paid to the parish clergy.

[c] Fees to Administrador General de Cofradías, at 8 percent of *réditos* collected.

them under the management of Spanish patrons. And, taking his cue from the Treasury officials again, the bishop had drastically curtailed all *cofradía* income in order to allow the balance to accumulate in diocesan coffers,[25] in the same way that the *bienes de comunidad* were accumulating (although with more efficient management) in the royal Treasury.

The almost simultaneous takeover of the *cajas de comunidad* and the *cofradías* was a serious blow to the communities and particularly to their most important corporate enterprise, the cult of the saints. Royal officials alleged that the Maya "squandered" much of the municipal revenues when they were under local control on "drunkenness . . . and festivities, sacred and profane."[26] I have no doubt that this allegation was well founded. There is plenty of independent corroboration that fiesta entertainment, especially alcoholic beverages, accounted for a substantial part of the public and private expenditure of the Maya. But I also do not doubt that this is precisely what they wanted to spend their money on—and still do.

Although some Maya leaders issued dire warnings to their curates that if the *cofradías* were sold the communities would cease their attentions to the saints, religious devotion would end in general, and the churches would have to close for want of worshipers,[27] they could not afford to carry out their threat and abandon their saints. Yet they could count on no support for religious ritual from the *cajas de comunidad*, and at best on a minimal amount from the *cofradías*. Defaults on the invested principal and malfeasance in the management of unsold estates were the norm, and even when income was collected, the bishop limited expenditures to the clergy's fees for masses and a small amount of candles for the saints' principal fiestas.[28] If they were to maintain the full round of fiestas, with the traditional complement of fireworks, music, and all the other "amusements" that were as essential to the enterprise as the mass itself, and if they were to keep the saints decently dressed and their churches properly adorned, they would have to pay for it themselves.

The expropriations of the *cajas de comunidad* and *cofradías* were officially justified on the same paternalistic principle that the Indians could not be trusted to judge their own best interests, a principle on which the royal officials and the ecclesiastical hierarchy were in complete agreement despite the many jurisdictional battles they engaged in. It inspired a profusion of proposals from both groups for the use of the confiscated funds, all designed to improve the lot of the Indians according to the particular lights of the proponent. Some of the schemes were disingenuous in the extreme. A school to train Indians for work in textile factories, endowments for university chairs in canon law and moral theology, and the construction of better accommodations for travelers in the villages are among the projects that would seem to serve Spanish rather than Indian interests.[29] Whatever their purpose, most, in any case, came to nothing. The diocesan chancery kept the *cofradía* surplus, and the Treasury officials vetoed all the more grandiose proposals for the *bienes de comunidad*. The idea was that the reserves should be allowed to accumulate to the point where they yielded enough income to "alleviate the miseries of the Indians" by providing aid in times of emergency, by supporting paupers, and even eventually paying the Indians' tribute.[30] These long-term goals, worthy as they were, were never realized either. Instead, the fund was used to alleviate the Crown's financial needs and, like the *cofradía* capital, it disappeared permanently at the end of colonial rule.

What made the centralizing tendencies of both church and state more insidious in effect than a simple appropriation of Indian revenues was the combination of a new bureaucratic efficiency with the old paternalistic principle, which had after all informed royal and ecclesiastical policy from the beginning of colonial rule. The Maya were accustomed to coping with extortions and appropriations by the Spanish. Left to their own devices, they might well have contrived, as they had done in the past, some alternative means that would perhaps stretch their resources further but still enable them to meet community needs. The fact is that the Spanish were no longer content to grab the money and run. They sought to protect the Indians from their own waywardness and incompetence. And these agents of benevolent despotism, backed by a greatly enlarged and rejuvenated apparatus of royal government, were able to achieve a degree of control over the Indians that the sixteenth-century friars would have envied.

Any attempt by the Maya to develop a new communal enterprise to remedy the financial crisis was exposed to the same risk of expropriation, now that they were subject to the meddlesome vigilance of zealous Crown officers stationed in their own communities. When the local subdelegate informed the governor of a new *estancia* that the town of Izamal had established as a substitute for their two expropriated *cofradía* estates, the governor decreed that it was legally a part of the *bienes de comunidad* and therefore to be administered also by the Treasury in order to "protect the Indians, who as minors are very vulnerable to fraud." Above all, they were to be prevented from spending this or any other community revenues "on the drunken revels and other vices to which they are inclined."[31] So much for that alternative source of fiesta support.

From the Maya's point of view fiestas, including the drunken revels with their sacred connotations, were far more conducive to the common good than any of the ingenious projects dreamed up by more or less well-meaning Spanish bureaucrats.[32] Indeed, from any disinterested point of view some of the schemes, as already noted, benefited only Spaniards. Others, though clearly worthy in intent, may have been of dubious value (such as the governor's bounty program for controlling locusts) or at least of dubious value to Indians (such as the hiring of *vecino* schoolmasters in all the villages).[33] But a few of the projects must have produced some material benefits. The construction of cemeteries, for example, to provide for burial outside pueblo limits instead of under church floors, was a long overdue sanitary measure that may well have mitigated the death toll during epidemics (far more effective, I should think, than the physicians dispatched from Merida and also paid for from municipal taxes). On the other hand, the public granaries that the governor ordered to be built in all the pueblos were merely state-controlled substitutes for a famine-relief program that the Maya had already organized themselves through the *cofradías* and which had been destroyed by Spanish interference.[34]

All of the projects, whether of material value or not, were wholly negative in their sociopolitical effects. Even if they had corresponded to Maya ideas of what was needed, which they rarely did, all were proposed by Spaniards, carried out under their direction, and paid for by funds collected and allocated by them, leaving the Maya nothing but the passive role of beneficiary—or victim, as the case might be. The harmful consequences of the new Bourbon policies were therefore not merely or even mainly in the added material burden placed on the Maya, but in the helplessness and dependence they produced by attacking the organization and the resources the Maya possessed for self-directed action.

THE EXPANDING HACIENDA

The Maya were engaged during this period in another, in many ways fiercer, struggle against Spanish encroachment—a struggle over land. Whatever flexibility or capacity for creative adaptation to Spanish demands the Maya possessed depended ultimately on this basic resource. Without their own land, political autonomy was meaningless.

The alienation of Indian lands proceeded much more slowly in Yucatan than in central Mexico. It began in earnest only in the late eighteenth century, coinciding with the main thrust of the Bourbon administrative and fiscal reforms. The sudden increase in the number and volume of lawsuits over land at this time could possibly be due in part to the general paper explosion produced by the later Bourbon bureaucracy, which has left the shelves of all colonial archives sagging with documents. However, many of the private hacienda *títulos* have been preserved by current owners more or less intact from the original grant or purchase, and they too begin to bulge with petitions and counterpetitions in this period. And it is readily apparent through boundary maps and survey records that the spate of litigation coincided with, indeed, was stimulated by, a territorial explosion: the sudden expansion of the haciendas from the small nuclei of the original deeds.[35]

The metamorphosis from the modest cattle *estancias* of the early colonial period into the vast henequen plantations that came to dominate the social, political, and economic life of Yucatan—as well as its landscape—was completed in the last decades of the nineteenth century. It began in earnest a century earlier under the reign of Charles III, whose ministers initiated the shift to the laissez-faire economic policies that characterized the neo-colonial era.

Yucatan was among the first colonies to benefit from the commercial reforms introduced in the latter part of the eighteenth century to stimulate trade between Spain and America. The old restrictions of the Hapsburg system that had reinforced the isolation and economic backwardness of peripheral regions like Yucatan, had become discredited; they merely encouraged contraband, which brought no revenues to the Crown and, moreover, weakened the economic foundation of empire. Freedom of trade was introduced into Spain and the Caribbean islands in 1765, and extended to Yucatan in 1770 and to the rest of the empire in 1778, except for Mexico and Venezuela, which were finally included in 1789. In the intervening decade, colonial trade had already expanded by an estimated 700 percent.[36]

Freedom of trade, or *comercio libre* as it was called, did not eliminate the prohibition against trade with foreigners, although trade with neutral-flag carriers was temporarily permitted during the Napoleonic wars. The changes were still significant. Vessels could sail directly between all major ports within the empire and Spain without convoy or special license, and the former stultifying welter of import and export taxes was simplified and reduced. Yucatan was unable to take full advantage of *comercio libre* immediately, since it came at the beginning of the severe drought of 1769-1774 when the colony could not even feed itself. But recovery was well underway by 1780 and agricultural production, along with local and foreign trade, increased dramatically in the following decades.

Some measure of these increases can be derived from the official figures on ecclesiastical tithes (table 12.4), which gauge production in the Spanish sector, since Indians were exempt from this tax, and from the

TABLE 12.4. TITHE INCOME, DIOCESE OF YUCATAN, 1635–1815

Year[a]	Tithes
1635	11,223
1713	17,892
1738	15,864
1757	17,406
1764	16,992
1774 (famine year)	11,475
1775	12,546
1777	25,857
1784	33,507[b]
1787	35,550
1794	35,032
1809	47,673
1815	44,608

Sources: AGI, Contaduría 919, no. 1, Tanteo de la real caja, Merida, 1636; AA, Real cedulario 26, Royal cédulas to Bishop of Yucatan, 6 July 1714 and 12 May 1739; AGN, Real Hacienda 9, Libro de cargo y data, 1759; AGI, Mexico 3121, Libro de cargo y data, 1765; AGN, AHH 2134, Libro de Cargo y data, 1778 (reporting tithes for 1774, 1775, and 1777); AGI, Mexico 3123, Tanteo de la real caja, 1785, and Libro de cargo y data, 1788; AGN, Clero regular y secular 70, exp. 11, Autos de los expolios . . . obispo Fray Luis de Piña y Mazo, 1795–1807; AA, Oficios y decretos 6, Recibo de la cuarta episcopal, 18 July 1809; AA, Estadística 1, Manifiesto de lo que tiene que haber . . . , 17 January 1817.

Note: Includes Tabasco and, after 1697, the Peten, which, however, produced only a negligible amount of tithes.

[a] The year of production, entered in Treasury accounts in following year.

[b] Tithe collection was farmed out from 1779 onwards in Yucatan, according to AGN, Diezmos 4, Certificacíon del escribano de diezmos, 24 March 1794.

figures on customs duties collected in the main port of Campeche (table 12.5). Both show a sharp recovery after the 1769-1774 drought, surpassing the prefamine levels within a few years and continuing to rise at a rapid rate thereafter. The income in tithes in the diocese grew by 279 percent between 1775 and 1794; in the two decades from 1778 to 1798 customs dues almost exactly quadrupled.

These figures give only a very rough estimate of the total increase in production and trade, which may have been considerably higher. Tithes were still being farmed out instead of collected directly and bids lagged behind changes in production. The Campeche revenues reflect only legal trade through that port. Sisal, Dzilam, and other smaller ports were beginning to take over some of the trade with nearby Caribbean and Gulf ports, and smuggling remained active along Yucatan's poorly guarded coasts. Customs duties may have been lowered, but tax-free trade still held an allure.

TABLE 12.5. TRADE VIA THE PORT OF CAMPECHE, 1700-1798

Year	Import and Export Duties (in pesos)
1700-1717	7,614[a]
(annual average)	
1760	5,117
1761	5,664
1767	5,664
1773	6,230[b]
1774	5,973
1775	3,679
1776	4,462
1777	5,324
1778	7,914
1779	8,257
1780	15,163
1781	12,324
1784	24,163[c]
1798	31,794

Sources: AGI, Mexico 886, Consulta Council of the Indies, 17 Sept. 1717. The remaining figures are taken from the Libros de cargo y data (referring to revenues collected the previous year) of the Real caja, Campeche, in: AGI, Mexico 3132 (1761, 1762, 1768); Mexico 3133 (1774-1777); Mexico 3134 (1778-1782); Mexico 3135 (1785); Mexico 3137 (1799).

[a] To nearest peso. Totals are for *almojarifazgos* and do not include the special taxes levied on salt and dyewood.

[b] Height of the 1769-1774 famine; most of the duties represent food imports.

[c] The rates and bases for duties were modified in 1770, 1782, 1796, and thereafter with increasing and bewildering frequency, the confusion enhanced by a welter of particular exemptions and confiscations (*comisos*). The volume of trade continued to increase, according to the Treasury officials, despite the unsettled international conditions, but the totals of revenues collected are necessarily only an approximate reflection of changes in volume.

Not only did the value of trade increase; there was also a shift in the export emphasis. New Spain's market for Yucatecan. *mantas*, the rough cotton cloth woven by the Indian women for tribute and *repartimiento*, had been declining because of competition from the small textile factories in central Mexico. Different goods bought by new trading partners more than compensated for this. The booming port and shipyards of Havana and the island's equally booming sugar industry provided rival outlets for Yucatecan cordage and rigging from henequen fiber; for salt, salted meat, lard, maize, and beans for marine provisions and local consumption; and for hides and dyewood for reexport.[37]

Whether Yucatan's total exports tripled or quadrupled or rose even more after the relaxation of trade restrictions, the growth was impressive by any standards.[38] Despite continued complaints of local poverty and the disruption caused by various wars in the last two decades of the colonial period, Yucatan was rapidly being converted from a thoroughly primitive colony, which had lived off and exported little besides tribute goods extracted from the Indians, into a still relatively backward but increasingly prosperous region supported by Spanish agriculture—still based of course on Indian labor.

Reinforcing all the statistical evidence from tithes and external trade is the fact that both the *encomienda* and the *repartimiento* could be abolished in this period with scarcely a murmur from colonists and provincial officials. For centuries, local Spaniards had insisted vehemently that the colony could not survive without tribute in various forms (including *repartimiento*). Official *repartimientos* ended in 1783 with so little stir that I find only a few passing references in 1784 to the fact that the Indians had recently been relieved of this burden.[39] The private *encomienda* was to be phased out after 1785 with the death of the current incumbents. Conflict was confined, significantly, to the ancillary issue of whether estate owners would be held responsible for the tribute payments of their resident Indian laborers.[40]

Another cumulative change that was accelerating during this period was the rise in the number of *vecinos*, which greatly outstripped even the substantial growth rate of the Indians during the eighteenth century. Increasing from a possible 10 percent of the total population at the turn of the century to 28.8 percent in 1780,[41] *vecinos* still tended to concentrate in the major towns, stimulating a demand for commercial agriculture and an increase in the market sector of the economy in general. Local trade was further stimulated by the rapid growth of local military forces, heavily subsidized from Mexico City. The large new military post at Laguna de Términos and the garrisons at Campeche and Bacalar were all wholly supplied with foodstuffs from Yucatan.[42]

Larger local markets and increased access to foreign ones (which I see as the more significant factor in the sudden spurt of growth) provided the incentive for the transformation in agrarian structures. The transition from an Indian–based agricultural system to a Spanish one involved two interrelated changes: expansion in size and a shift in land use from a rudimentary style of ranching to the production of cash crops. In other words, the old *estancias* were fast developing into full-fledged haciendas. The staple crops of maize and beans and cattle fodder replaced open ranges, and there was a further move, which gained momentum during the early nineteenth century, away from beef and maize and to the more labor-intensive crops of cotton and sugar and then henequen.[43] Henequen came eventually to monopolize such an extensive part of the peninsula that Yucatan became and remains a net importer of foodstuffs.

To develop their haciendas the Spanish needed more land. Since there was no unclaimed land in the core region, it had to be obtained from the Indians, and the Indians were no longer prepared to part with their land without a struggle. Sales of private and community lands to pay off tax debts during times of crisis had been common in the seventeenth and early eighteenth centuries and occurred as late as the 1769-1774 famine. But what may have seemed a prudent measure at one time became a cause for deep regret as the need for land became far more desperate than the need for cash.

The difference was partly demographic. The Maya, who had been dying off with ups and downs since the conquest—or actually since first contact with the Spanish—seem to have reached their low point some time around the end of the seventeenth century. To say that within less than a century their numbers had then more than doubled gives no real sense of the sudden pressure suffered in the few decades following the devastating famine of 1769-1774.[44] The surviving Indian population of less than 130,000 rose to 175,000 by 1780 and to almost 254,000 by 1794.[45] The Maya began to feel cramped for space in the 1780s, probably for the first time in colonial history. The growing numbers of mouths to feed on the Indian side, particularly after recovery from the recent famine, and the growing market for cash crops on the Spanish side placed both in competition for the same resource. It was not simply that a larger number of Maya had to make do with the same amount of land. They were also losing land to the Spanish, and the most massive single loss was through the appropriation and sale of *cofradía* estates in 1780.

The sale of these estates was a tremendous boon to the Spanish. It came precisely at a time when land was becoming both more profitable and harder to obtain. Lack of capital presented no obstacle to the buyers. Rather than sold for cash, the expropriated estates were simply exchanged in full for mortgages without even a down payment.[46] The bishop may not have intended the auction as a special favor to the *hacendados* and would-be *hacendados* in the colony, but the timing and the terms could not have been more helpful.

The Maya, understandably, were deeply dismayed.[47] When word of the intended sale filtered out (they were never notified of the decision, but were simply ordered to hand over all the *cofradía* account books, land titles, and other documents without any explanation), deputations filed into Merida in hopes of dissuading the bishop, only to be turned away from the chancery with the threat of imprisonment if they should try to oppose the transfer. Some of the officers hid the *cofradía* deeds and books, presumably believing that this would prevent the sale. In several other pueblos the *principales* pooled resources in order to buy the *cofradía* estates themselves. Only one pueblo (Muna in the Sierra district) was successful and then only through the intervention of the Protector de Indios, who filed suit against the diocesan chancery when it accepted a new bid from a Spanish buyer after having closed the sale in favor of the local *batab*. In other instances the chancery simply refused to accept bids from Indians.[48]

Most of the community leaders did not bother to protest or take any action at all, having heard from neighboring officials of their futile efforts. The only effective opposition came from the governor, who took up the Indians' cause as part of his running battle with the bishop. He was able to obtain a restraining order from the Audiencia of Mexico that saved over a third of the estates from the auction block, but not the larger ones, and all but seven of the seventy-eight sold were located in the most heavily populated core region, principally the Costa and Sierra districts (see table 12.2).

The *cofradía* land was ultimately far more important than the cattle both to the Maya and to the Spanish buyers. In their protests against the sale were included the first complaints from Maya communities that they did not have enough land left for their milpas.[49] Such severe shortages were still rare. The Maya were worried mostly about long-term consequences, which, as it turned out, they greatly underrated. They feared that since they could no longer control the herds and limit their size, the cattle would overrun their milpas or even their gardens (the *cofradía* estates tended to be located closer to the towns than the private estates).[50] What most of them could not yet foresee was that a revolution in land use would deprive them altogether of much of the milpa land they had formerly shared with the *cofradía* cattle.

Maya milpa farming and Spanish stock raising had coexisted with varying degrees of irritation on both sides since the beginning of the colonial period. The vague delineation of property lines that permitted this coexistence had also applied to the *cofradía estancias*. To the Maya these *estancias* consisted only of the central core, or *planta* (with its water wheel, buildings and corrals), plus grazing rights for the cattle on community lands. The *cofradía* estates thus had no fixed boundaries, nor do the documents concerning the sales specify either boundaries or the total acreage being transferred. Indeed, the official line at first was that only the cattle and *plantas* were to be sold, and not the land.[51] It was not until later that the Maya realized how large an additional chunk of community land had been lost along with the property they had specifically donated to the saints.[52] No records have been found of how the new owners or their successors established their inflated claims. Presumably this was done in the same way that other estates in this period were spreading out from their original vaguely defined nuclei: by simply placing markers wherever they believed or wanted their boundaries to be.[53] As the owners began to expand cattle production, raise fodder to help maintain the larger herds, and add cash crops to supplement stock raising, they were no longer prepared to share the land with the Indians.

The struggle over land proceeded unevenly, appearing first and most intensely in the Merida-Campeche corridor, where urban markets, proximity to the export trade, and the highest population densities of both Indians and *vecinos* all combined to heighten pressure on the land from both sides. The struggle then spread to the rich agricultural lands of the Sierra district and to the more arid but also densely populated Costa district along the northern band from Merida east through Izamal toward Valladolid. In this entire core region, which also included the northern and western parts of the Sotuta district, Indian communities were being squeezed by the expanding haciendas.

Some of the haciendas were already huge expanses by the end of the colonial period, built up from a number of smaller, scattered *estancias* and swallowing up whatever Indian lands lay in between. Among the largest were Tabi, with two thousand head of cattle in 1811; Mukuyche (with nineteen hundred); Uayalceh (with twelve hundred); Ticopo (twelve hundred); and Xcanchakan (thirteen hundred)—all in the Sierra district.[54] And besides these large herds (large by Yucatecan standards, at any rate), all the major haciendas were engaged in large-scale cereal production.[55]

No one has attempted so far as I know to establish how much land in total the haciendas engulfed during the last decades of colonial rule. In the records I have consulted from this period, Spanish estates were pushing out their boundaries to cover double or triple the acreage that the Indians asserted was the original size, and sometimes more. In extreme cases, such as that of San Bernardino Chich, an hacienda near Abala in the Sierra, a new owner might suddenly lay claim to a goodly portion of the whole parish.[56] Whatever the exact quantity lost, most of the communities in the core region were suffering serious pressures on land before independence.[57] They were forced either to rent milpa lands when they could from the same haciendas that had formerly rented from *them* or, more commonly, to shed their excess population into the permanent hacienda labor force.[58]

Even the unsold *cofradía* estates contributed to the land shortages. Under the administration of Spanish patrons they, too, were expanding agricultural and ranching production at the same rate as the private estates and also at the expense of community milpa lands.[59]

The competition over land never approached the same level in the eastern part of the peninsula. The districts of Valladolid, Tizimin, and Tihosuco actually suffered a population decline during this period, and in every way the region lagged behind the northwest and Campeche. Only two *cofradía* estates were sold there. Without urban markets or easy access to the export trade, the few local Spaniards had little incentive to buy them or to expand their own small and widely scattered cattle ranches, and the cotton produced in the Tizimin district continued to be grown largely in milpa style on what was essentially unclaimed land.

The contrast with the rapid and early growth of the landed estates in central Mexico could not be more striking. William Taylor has attributed the difference to the stronger organization of the Indian communities in the heavily Indian areas of Oaxaca and Yucatan, which enabled the Indians to mobilize more effective resistance.[60] Without strong community leadership the Maya were certainly almost totally helpless, as can be seen in a dispute between the *rancho* of San Antonio Buluch and the hacienda San Bernardino Chich.[61] In 1792 the hacienda's new owner laid claim to the *rancho* along with a modest four-league chunk of land surrounding it, a total of sixty-four square kilometers (see the owner's map of the hacienda reproduced in chapter 9.) Because of a long-standing boundary disagreement among the pueblos of Abala, Uman, and Dzibikal, no *república* could claim undisputed jurisdiction over the territory, so that the *rancho* residents were forced to deal with the hacienda on their own. They had no group of *principales* armed with carefully preserved land titles and the authority and expertise to represent them in the labyrinth of Spanish judicial procedure. Not only did they lose all the land; they were even unable to save their own house sites or to retain possession of milpa rights while the case was being decided, a tactic that experienced *república* officers used with much skill (when it looked as if they might lose, they simply delayed proceedings and kept on farming in the meantime).

For all their expertise and resourcefulness, however, the Maya elites could do no more than retard the process of alienation. The same conditions that had preserved their political autonomy were also the only effective protection for their territorial integrity: the relative sparseness of Spanish settlement and the colony's backward economy. These conditions remained particularly pronounced in eastern Yucatan, which has also produced the main published source on Indian lands for the whole colony—the land titles for the small town of Ebtun near Valladolid.[62] There the Maya retained a vigorous community organization, but they were also still able to concentrate on boundary disputes with neighboring pueblos, even after independence, because they had not yet encountered serious pressure from the Spanish.

The Maya retained their land only so long as the Spanish were not seriously interested in obtaining it. Whenever the Spanish became determined to expand their estates—when the potential profits gave them sufficient incentive—they succeeded, and the best that even the most cohesive communities could do was to fight a rearguard action. The Maya could not count on the reformed Bourbon bureaucracy to step in and assume the protective role that general economic backwardness and Spanish indolence had played in the past. To be sure, the large-scale alienation of community lands that quickened so notably in pace during the last decades before independence would have proceeded even more rapidly had the governors and subordinate officials been as lazy and corrupt as their predecessors. Still, although few if any seem to have profited personally at the Indians' expense, their own values and attitudes, their identification and often close personal ties with the rest of the Spaniards in the colony, and the general structure of power in colonial society limited their capacity to protect the Indians. Land-grabbing *hacendados* and royal officials were all inevitably members of the same small social circle when not actually *compadres*, cousins, or in-laws. And even the most scrupulous official could not fail to note the contradiction between the Crown's benevolent legislation and the economic interests of the colony *and* of the royal Exchequer, both of which demanded the growth of commercial agriculture.

THE NEO-COLONIAL COMMUNITY

The late colonial Bourbon reforms and the economic changes associated with them represented a break with the past that for the Maya was fully as radical as the sixteenth-century conquest, although far less abrupt and dramatic. The full implications would become apparent only over the longer term. For the Bourbon reforms were merely the opening round in the new assault on the traditional Maya social order, which was left to the Liberal legislation of independent Mexico to complete.

A dress rehearsal was provided during the brief life of the constitution promulgated by the Spanish Cortes in 1812 and repudiated by Ferdinand VII and the Conservative reaction that accompanied his restoration in 1814.[63] Guided by the same high-minded and often muddle-headed principles that influenced various Liberal reforms in republican Mexico, the Cortes attacked many of the privileges and social divisions that char-acterized the *ancien régime* at home and in the colonies. One target was the system of caste. Indians were to be granted the full citizenship so long denied them with all the attendant rights and obligations. Their organization into *repúblicas de indios* separate from the rest of society violated the Liberal ideals of liberty and equality; the *repúblicas* were therefore abolished in favor of municipalities to be governed by "con-stitutional" town councils that would be elected by all the local residents regardless of caste.[64] The effect of this innovation, however well inten-tioned, was to destroy the last vestige of Indian political autonomy. Whether elected under the short-lived 1812 constitution or simply ap-pointed by state and federal politicians, as occurred after independence, non-Indians took over the integrated local administration completely. A few Maya names appear in the town councils elected in 1813. Most of the councillors were *vecinos*, as were all of the *alcaldes constitucionales* and their secretaries, despite the overwhelming numerical superiority of Indians in the electorate.[65] The Indians lost all voice in local affairs and with it any formal mechanism for protecting their interests. The town governments were clearly run by and for the *vecinos*, or rather non-Indians, since everyone was designated *vecino* and acquired the title of "don" for the duration of the reforms. The new officials, for example, immediately began to sell off community lands, now deemed to belong to the whole municipality, in order to "raise revenues."[66] Only the timely restoration of the reactionary Ferdinand saved the Indian communities from these technically legal seizures.

The 1812 reforms gave the Maya a heady taste of freedom that dis-tracted them from the drawbacks of political integration with *vecinos*, many of whom appeared in the guise of allies against former oppressors and were thus able to gain Indian political support.[67] The total package of treats offered the Maya, for which the loss of autonomy may have seemed a small price at the time, included the abolition of the onerous burdens of tribute and *servicio personal* along with the penalty of whip-ping.[68] Indians were granted the same legal freedom as any *vecino* to reside anywhere—even in their own milpas if they chose.

In particular, the Maya were freed from the centuries-long authority of their parish priests. This was achieved mainly through the local ef-forts of a small but politically active group of Liberal creoles in Merida who came to be known as the Sanjuanistas and managed to persuade the governor to declare that the Indians were to be exempt from eccle-siastical *obvenciones*, forced labor service for the clergy, and all other special contributions not specifically mentioned in the general decrees emanating from Spain.[69] Encouraged by the more or less sincere championship of the Sanjuanistas (a championship flavored with more than a dash of anticlericalism) and "seduced by bad Christians" residing in the pueblos, the "ungrateful" Maya also refused to pay the tithes and parish fees that *vecinos* were subject to, and to serve the clergy in any capacity even for pay.[70] While the churches, which the Maya considered their property, were well cared for, many curates suffered the indignity of having to provide and even cook their own food. Attendance at mass fell off and the boycott of catechism classes was unanimous. The stream of protests that poured into the bishop's chancery from the outraged parish clergy attests to the enthusiasm with which the Maya responded to their new rights.[71]

The freedom and equality granted to the Indians by independent Mexico were considerably more spurious. In Yucatan, as in many other states of the republic, tribute, *obvenciones*, and *servicio personal* were retained, although often under different names, and a more recent form of servitude, debt peonage, acquired a sanction in law that it had never been accorded under colonial rule.[72] At the same time, the *repúblicas de indios* were permanently abolished. And as with the Bourbon attacks on political autonomy, it was left to the financially strapped independent governments to carry the despoliation of community property to extreme lengths under the Liberal guise of freeing corporately owned property for individual ownership. The state legislature of Yucatan confiscated the remaining *cofradía* estates in 1832, and in 1843 the rest of community lands outside a perimeter of one square league around each town (measured from the main plaza) were put up for sale to amortize the state debt.[73] There was no Tribunal de Indios to appeal to; for this and a variety of other protective measures and institutions that had been restored in 1814 along with tribute and forced labor were abolished also. In other words, all the most repugnant features of the old regime were kept while the few compensating benefits it had provided were eliminated. The discrimination of the colonial caste system lingered on. Other criteria besides formal caste distinctions could be used to deny political rights to Indians, and the same poverty and illiteracy that made them legally ineligible to vote would in any case have rendered that vote meaningless.

Outwardly, Maya society would have appeared little altered by these changes, except for physical encirclement by the expanding haciendas. In its internal structure we can already see the outlines of the modern Maya community, which is often regarded as the result of the original conquest but which actually began to emerge in the neo-colonial era ushered in by the Bourbons. Under attack were the two central principles of reciprocity and corporateness around which Maya society had for so long been organized. Both of them were to survive, but badly eroded and radically altered in nature.

Reciprocity had served to justify the hereditary privileges of the nobility and hold the social order together through an (admittedly unequal) exchange of services between nobles and commoners. Neither the imposition of Spanish rule nor the ability of ambitious and talented commoners to rise in rank destroyed the Maya nobility. This required the collapse of the whole stratified social structure on which hereditary privilege was based. And while the conquest began the leveling process, the main impetus came from the innovations first tentatively introduced by the Bourbon reformers. Whatever the composition of that elite may have been by then—how many deviations in practice from the hereditary principle—the issue was becoming increasingly irrelevant. The power and wealth that had for long been reserved to those of noble rank (whether legitimate or spurious) were rapidly disappearing.

The elimination of the *repúblicas de indios* was the most serious blow. As long as they existed, crippled though they were by the late Bourbon intrusions, their formal structure helped to sustain the hierarchical organization of Maya society and the ties of reciprocity that gave it legitimacy. The *república* officers (still being chosen from the same pool of elite families whose inherited rank and wealth made them eligible for leadership by Maya standards) were not entirely reduced to a constabulary force for the local agents of the Crown. They retained considerable freedom of action, independent of and sometimes even in defiance of the subdelegates, especially when the communities confronted the Spanish over land boundaries and other issues of collective concern. They were still officially recognized as the spokesmen for their communities, and even the most self-serving among the Maya leaders could serve their communities and defend their integrity in a way that the best-intentioned Spaniard could not duplicate.

Shorn of much of their political authority and then denied all official status once the *repúblicas* were abolished, the Maya elite were left with only the ritual functions that had survived the earlier and much more obvious challenge of Christian evangelization. No *ladino* officials, colonial or republican, could replace the Maya's own leaders in their central role as mediators between the community and the supernatural (the curates themselves were only adjuncts, and dispensable ones, as the *cruzob* Maya were to demonstrate when they established their own clergy during the Caste War). But these sacred functions were becoming increasingly difficult to fulfill in the traditional way, because the necessary economic base was being destroyed—both the private wealth of the elite

378

and the public resources they had drawn on to support the cult of the saints.

The loss of the community's public revenues, which had largely financed the elaborate rituals that were the main source of elite legitimacy, created a dilemma and a financial crisis for the whole community, but in an especially acute form for the elite. The cult of the saints was too essential to the welfare of the community and to the maintenance of the social order to be abandoned. No other mechanism existed for establishing and confirming status within Maya society and it is therefore not surprising that the ceremonial role of community leadership should have persisted to the present day. Nevertheless, the cost of preserving the ritual function was high, once it was divorced from secular authority and had to be supported from private contributions alone. The *cargo*, which is still the sign of and justification for high status (if not the only means of achieving it), truly became a burden, especially in view of the elite's deteriorating economic position. The continued sales of private land despite its increasing scarcity both signaled and contributed to that deterioration in the late colonial period. The records also reveal a shift away from corporate family ownership, which had helped to protect the wealth of the noble lineages, toward individual ownership and toward bilateral, equal inheritance, through which dwindling family patrimonies were partitioned into smaller and smaller shares.[74]

The expansion of Spanish commercial agriculture impoverished all of Indian society. It compressed the already slim margin of subsistence of *macehuales* and transformed many of them into landless peons. The elite, however, had the most to lose. They were losing their lands to the haciendas, which took over the production of foodstuffs for the local market; deprived of their political power, they also lost the ability to command *macehual* labor, without which extra land was of little profit, in any case. To work one's own milpa was, to be sure, preferable to peonage on an hacienda, but it was hardly the basis for a class of *indios pudientes*, which was fast disappearing by the end of colonial rule.

Economic gradations within Indian society, although never totally erased, became much more subtle. Perhaps some deference to lineage distinctions survived for a time in an informal way, but eventually the old boundary between nobles and commoners disappeared. The terms *almehen* and *principal* fell into disuse and *macehual* became synonymous with Indian in general, a purely ethnic category distinguishing the more or less uniform mass of Maya from the *dzuls*.[75]

Like social stratification and hereditary rank, the corporate foundations of Maya society fared badly under the centralizing policies of the Bourbons. The colonial fiscal system had already begun to weaken these foundations by gradually transforming the various kinds of tribute from quotas of goods produced by communal labor to monetary head taxes. So long as the *república* officers remained in charge of tribute and all the other community obligations, they retained much of their corporate character, even if technically levied on the individual. However, the transfer of fiscal control to royal officials under the intendancy system accelerated the shift from a corporate to an individual assessment. Moreover, once private *encomiendas* were abolished and all tribute was paid to the Crown, the link between a person's tax liability and his community was severed; community quotas were eliminated and tribute was made a direct obligation of the individual.[76]

The corrosive effects of the new administrative system are revealed clearly in the judicial sphere, in the private petitions and appeals submitted to the subdelegates and governors in the last decades of colonial rule.[77] Before then each community had with few exceptions spoken with a single voice. The *macehuales* had been mere names in the parish registers and even the leaders had acted as one in dealing with the Spanish. The private petitions appearing in this period do not necessarily signify any increase in internal dissension. Corporateness does not preclude conflict, whether within the Maya communities or within the monastic communities of medieval Europe; it merely defines the terms of conflict and how it will be handled. Signs of strain existed in colonial Maya society long before the Bourbon reforms. But they had either been resolved internally or driven people away. There was no possibility of defying the community's corporate structure and its leadership from within.

The cohesion of the Maya community required, as a counterweight to the socially divisive forces, the merging of the individual's interests with those of the community. It was sustained not merely by the concept of collective survival but also and mainly by the various cooperative activities by which the communities sought to ensure that survival and through which the concept was given actual social expression. The centralizing policies of the state and the church interfered with these efforts by depriving the communities of the material support for their communal enterprises and by allocating much of the responsibility for community welfare to the state. Whether the state's measures did more to alleviate certain specific emergencies such as famine and epidemic is open to question. There can be no doubt that in undermining the community's mutual support system, which had been organized and directed by the elite, and in emphasizing the individual's rights and obligations in relation to the central authority of the state, the Bourbons weakened both the vertical and horizontal ties that bound the members of the community together.

What, then, remained of the social bond of community? We know that the Maya community survived, in some form, the innovations of Bourbon reformers and the more extreme measures of the nineteenth-century Liberals. The decline of the elite's position brought its own compensations, removing the grosser distinctions of wealth and power and thereby blurring the major cleavage within Maya society.[78] But an increase in equality does not necessarily bring any increase in cohesiveness and may in fact decrease the interdependence on which the organic unity of a group rests. I would argue that the neo-colonial community's survival depended more on external factors. The delicate balance between centrifugal and centripetal forces in Maya society was maintained because both were weakened simultaneously. Community became less a matter of choice than of necessity for the Maya. As their population increased and their lands dwindled, they no longer had room to leave.

Survival remained a corporate endeavor for the Maya because ownership of the essential material resource of land remained corporate and because a united corporate defense of that resource in the unequal struggle with the *hacendados* had a better chance than any individual effort, just as the collective propitiation of the cosmic forces through the cult of the saints had a better chance than any individual petition.

The external pressure exerted by the haciendas, which continued to expand at an increasing pace during the nineteenth century, more than offset any weakening at the center. The cult of the saints and the other integrating forces in colonial Maya society had not held the community together nearly so tightly. In the south and east, where isolation from Spanish centers helped to preserve both the political and economic independence of the communities, satellite settlements were still reaching out into unpopulated regions well into the nineteenth century and resumed expansion in these peripheral areas once the disruptions of the Caste War ended.[79] To the north and west, the core of the colonial province, the creation of new Indian communities reached its peak in the mid-eighteenth century and then tapered off. It is no coincidence that few of the place names in what is now the state of Yucatan and in northern Campeche postdate independence despite a considerable increase in population.

The expanding haciendas checked the fissioning process much more effectively than any internal forces of cohesion. They also inhibited the drift from one community to another, since each had to protect the scarce resource of land from outsiders. There was no more room for marginals in Maya society, only a stable core, with the excess from any population growth to be sloughed off to the haciendas, just as in modern Mexico corporate Indian structures are preserved, and the pressure on resources eased, by migration to the cities or across the Rio Grande.

Eric Wolf's classic model of the Mesoamerican "closed corporate community" comes in for vindication here. For only the timing of the model is off for Yucatan. Wolf sees the closed corporate configuration as a "creature of the Spanish conquest."[80] As I pointed out earlier, the corporate organization of colonial Maya society, which derived from pre-Columbian antecedents, did not depend on a scarcity of resources nor on closed community boundaries to protect them. The functional link between "closed" and "corporate" becomes discernible only in this neo-colonial period. The corporate structure is preserved, although altered in its foundation; the closed boundaries, which now underlie and reinforce the corporate structure, are a "creature," not of the sixteenth-century conquest but of the second one carried out by the Bourbons and their Liberal successors.

No account of neo-colonial Maya society can ignore the alternative institution of the hacienda, which influenced much of the internal structure of the community as well as shaped its geographical boundaries. Originally a mere social and administrative appendage of the community, the hacienda came to compete with it for land and people and, in the end, became a kind of community in itself for an increasing number of Maya. In the haciendas the Maya were to experience the complete loss of control over their own lives that the pueblo Maya suffered only in part through the Bourbon and Liberal reforms. In a continuum of autonomy to dependence, running from the preconquest Maya polities through the colonial communities and then the neo-colonial communities, the haciendas represent the extreme end of the scale.

For most of the colonial period, movement to the haciendas or their precursors, the *estancias*, was part of the voluntary process of dispersal out of the congregated towns. Even more than the Indian hamlets, the Spanish-owned *estancias* offered an escape from the various labor conscriptions to which the town dwellers were subject and from the authority of curates and *república* officers.[81] At the time, however, the move did not appear to be either a sharp or an irrevocable break with ordinary community life.

By the late eighteenth century, Spanish estates were no longer such attractive places to live. With the shift from ranching to cereal production, the conditions of residence became harsher; yet at the same time the Maya's freedom of movement had been curtailed. When the *cofradía* estates were sold off in 1780, the new owners assumed that they had purchased the resident *luneros* along with the livestock, the land, and the buildings, and the *luneros* for their part objected to the sales on the grounds that they did not want to "serve Spanish masters."[82]

No law yet existed to keep *luneros* on the estates. *Criados* ran up debts from advances on their wages and from the tribute payments their employers made on their behalf. But even if such debts had been a mild form of peonage, they would have applied only to the small proportion of salaried workers. Yet some kind of unofficial pressure must have existed, since many *luneros* took advantage of their new status as free citizens under the 1812 constitution to escape from what the Maya were beginning to view as "enslavement." Most scattered into the bush, but some moved back to what had by then become the comparatively tolerable burdens of town life.[83] However, the freedom to move off the haciendas was being limited steadily by the loss of community lands to support them.

As their labor needs increased, the haciendas and plantations had little trouble recruiting the necessary manpower: the surplus population had nowhere else to go. At least they had nowhere nearby; for the peonage laws enacted by the state governments after independence were designed more to keep the Maya from moving into the still relatively open regions to the east and south than to keep them from returning to the hemmed-in pueblos in the developed northwest.[84] For the milpa farmer, much of Yucatan had ceased to be an open environment.

The movement of Indians to haciendas in the late colonial period is impossible to trace with any exactitude. While demographic data become almost oppressively abundant, the censuses are not always clear about place of residence. A figure of 35 percent of the rural Indian population living on Spanish-owned estates in the early nineteenth century would have to be considered an outside limit, since the parish censuses on which it is based include many settlements of equivocal status.[85] The proportion of Indians living outside the congregated towns in the various kinds of satellite settlements had not increased greatly since the early eighteenth century, although in absolute numbers the size of the estate population had grown substantially along with the total Indian population.[86] However, the significance of the population movements cannot be measured solely in terms of numbers. Like the transfers of land, the transfers of population had acquired new and very different meanings. In a sense not previously experienced, the communities were losing both people and land to the rival institution of the hacienda. The losses became massive and they also become complete. Unlike the more relaxed regime of the cattle *estancias*, under the new hacienda system there were to be no divided allegiances and obligations for the *luneros* and no shared rights to the use of land for the pueblos.

The *hacendados* welcomed new residents more than ever but under much less congenial terms than the *estancias* had offered. Full-time work on the new labor-intensive cash crops was increasingly substituted for milpa tenant farming, and hacienda Indians were no longer free to settle anywhere they chose. The disciplined work force needed to run the large haciendas, and especially the more complex operations of sugar mills and henequen-processing plants, could not be sprawled in little settlements throughout the property. Instead they were concentrated around the main house and buildings, in as orderly and nucleated a fashion as any sixteenth-century missionary could have wished.[87] Harvest of profits clearly replaced harvest of souls as the motivating force behind this secular congregation program. Yet in physical layout the hacienda settlements became copies of the old incorporated towns, surpassing many of them in size and population density.[88]

Because of this physical resemblance one might imagine that the neocolonial haciendas were simply re-creations of the Maya community under another name. They had roughly the same ethnic mix—mostly Maya with a smattering of *vecinos*—and they succeeded in duplicating the outward forms of pueblo life. All but the smallest estates had their own chapels, patron saints, and fiestas, complete with fireworks and processions, by the time of independence. Indeed, the major haciendas had become *visita* towns in all but name, with episcopal licenses that granted them quasi-*visita* status under the label of *ayuda de parroquia* and signaled their complete social autonomy from the "parent town." The estate residents were permitted to attend mass and be married, baptized, and buried in the hacienda churches. Encouraged by the *hacendados*, they severed remaining ties, paying their municipal head tax (most of which was destined for royal coffers anyway) but refusing to contribute labor for the community milpa, for church repairs, or for the other public works drafts to which all Indians except *criados* and residents of suburban barrios were legally subject.[89] Although the estate residents lacked any administrative structure of their own, the *repúblicas de indios* had lost much of their autonomy, and once they were abolished the pueblo Maya had no formal system of self-government, either.

The hacienda, however, was only a deformed imitation of a pueblo, lacking the internal organization that the communities were able to retain even after the loss of official status as *repúblicas*. Any hacienda large enough to achieve a quasi-pueblo status was also dominated completely by the owner and his resident *vecino* staff. The churches themselves were all dwarfed in size by the owner's house, and the whole settlement came to be dominated by the great chimney stack of the sugar mill or the henequen shredding plant. Equally significant, the hacienda Maya had

13. Henequen plantation, dating from the latter part of the nineteenth century and still in operation. The flatcars (right foreground) convey the henequen to the original steam-powered shredding mill, its chimney stack almost obscured by the clock tower. (Photo by Arthur G. Miller)

no *cofradías*, no corporate structures of any kind, no leaders of their own except the foremen and *fiscales* appointed by the owners to enforce hacienda discipline.

The *hacendados* had assumed the mantle of the *encomenderos* in the colony, and even the same title of *amo* (master); but they achieved a degree of control over the lives of their subjects that even the early postconquest *encomenderos* would have envied. They owned the land, after all, and with it, the means of subsistence. Also, they had no feisty, zealous missionaries to compete with for hegemony, only a complacent creole clergy residing in the town centers. Nor did they need to rely on a native leadership, for even the largest haciendas were much smaller units, in territory and population, than the original *encomienda* grants and thus easily managed by a resident majordomo.

On the haciendas the role of the Maya elite was assumed by the Spanish owner through the agency of the *vecino* majordomo, who directed all the affairs, civil and religious, of the estate. Responsibility for the welfare of the residents belonged entirely to the owner. They were de-

385

pendent on him for food or for the land to produce it themselves, for famine relief in time of shortages, for the administration of justice, for protection from other Spaniards, and for all the other services that the community leaders had formerly provided. The Spanish *amo* even provided the gifts that the group offered to its sacred guardians: the masses, the church adornments, and the fiestas for the patron saints of the hacienda. One *hacendado* (and perhaps others) actually created a *cofradía* on his estate—with himself as patron—which consisted of a separate herd of cattle that he used to defray fiesta expenses.[90] Survival was no longer a collective enterprise in Maya hands.

IN 1847 the Maya of eastern Yucatan rose up in arms against the whites. The time had come to fulfill the prophecies foretelling that the Spanish, like the Itza and other foreign oppressors before them, would be driven out. It is no accident that the impetus for the revolt, its sustained leadership, and the bulk of the fighting forces came from the Maya heartland in the districts of Valladolid, Tihosuco, and Sotuta. These were the same former provinces of Cupul, Cochuah, and Sotuta that had united with an identical purpose in the Great Revolt three centuries earlier (301 years almost to the day), and were the locus of the much more circumscribed Canek revolt of 1761. These were also the districts were the social, economic, and political structure of the Maya community had best survived the pressures of colonial rule. More accurately, it was where those pressures were weakest: where the Spanish and *casta* populations were least heavily concentrated and commercial agriculture was least developed, although cattle ranching was beginning to expand into the Valladolid area, and sugar plantations were spreading into southern Sotuta and Tihosuco.

Fueled by centuries of resentment, the Caste War was, in an immediate sense, an attempt to preserve community autonomy against these latest encroachments, and recent land grabbers were particular targets of the rebels' wrath. At the same time, the revolt was possible only because community autonomy was still a de facto reality in most of the eastern part of the peninsula. The three original leaders were all *batabs*—of Chichimila, Tepich, and Tihosuco.[91] Emboldened by service in the whites' factional struggles, these and other *batabs* drew upon the traditional structure of local authority to mobilize men and material for the war. Supra-community organization on a large scale remained an elusive goal, but the *batabs* managed somehow to keep the revolt alive until a "mini-empire," as one white chronicler called the rebel state,[92] was forged around the Maya-Christian cult of the Speaking Cross. Although the *cruzob* state was destroyed with the capture of its capital (Chan Santa

14. Church destroyed during Caste War, Tihosuco (Photo by Arthur G. Miller)

Cruz, or Little Holy Cross) at the beginning of this century, the *cruzob* Maya preserved the cult and smaller-scale versions of the state in their isolated retreats. In that sense their struggle had been a success, for they had preserved their community organization against white pressures. Without any shortages of land or other economic incentives to hold them together, they retained strong social cohesion and a firm structure of authority based on military defense and divine mediation: the same leadership roles portrayed so prominently in pre-Hispanic Maya iconography and the same collective strategies for survival that had underlain social solidarity long before the Spanish arrived on the scene.

For many of the Maya—for the substantial portion in western Yucatan who had become incorporated into the expanding orbit of the haciendas—the Caste War came too late. Only a small number of them joined the rebels. It has been suggested that the rest remained apart from the struggle because they "had transferred their loyalty."[93] Rather than actually transferring their loyalty, I would argue that the hacienda Maya had been reduced, if not to the paternalist ideal of passive docility that the Franciscan friars had sought to achieve, then something close to it. Acephalous coresidents of a shared territory, dependent on the will of the Spanish *amo*, they no longer constituted a community. They had lost the capacity for self-directed collective action that the village Maya retained through the organization of the community, and which neither the first nor the second conquest had succeeded in destroying.

EPILOGUE

Between the world of the Maya as it was when the Spanish first encountered them and when they departed as colonial masters three centuries later the differences are vast. They emerge sharply from the impressions recorded by two of the peninsula's most famous visitors whose travel accounts bracket the colonial period. The first is Bernal Díaz del Castillo, who took part in the earliest Spanish expeditions to the peninsula in the years 1516 to 1519; the second is John Lloyd Stephens, who explored Yucatan in the 1840s, barely two decades after independence.[1]

There seems little to connect the Indians described by Stephens with the by then remote pre-Columbian past that he was seeking to rediscover, and of which Bernal Díaz gives us a glimpse at its tail end. The temples had been abandoned or demolished, their stones incorporated into Christian churches, and blood sacrifices replaced by the Christian sacrifice of the mass. Instead of high priests and powerful rulers magnificently arrayed in plumes, jade, and jaguar pelts, Stephens found an undifferentiated mass of humble peasants all clad in the simple colonial uniform of white cotton shirts and trousers and all "trained to the most abject submission."[2]

Stephens missed much. Within a few years thousands of these "docile" Indians were again in arms against the white men. Unsuccessful in its ultimate aim of driving the heirs of the Spanish conquerors back into the sea that had carried them to Yucatan, the Caste War reveals the continued vitality of Maya culture. Not only were the Maya capable of organized resistance but they had also preserved a collective memory of their past and their own distinctive interpretation of reality, from which would emerge a new and vigorous religious cult.

Clearly much was destroyed or altered. Only the most narrowly Eurocentrist vision could contemplate the remnants of pre-Columbian Maya civilization without a sense of loss. Some might argue that this civilization was already in such a shambles by the late Postclassic period that there was little left to destroy. But one has only to look at the mural paintings dating from this period for a hint of what still remained when the Spanish arrived and for a measure of what was subsequently lost.[3] Nothing remotely comparable in artistic skill or iconological sophistication had been produced in the Maya lowlands since the conquest.

Without doubt Maya culture was greatly simplified. Much of the complexity, the richness, and the grandeur was stripped away, along with much of the wealth and political power of the urban elite that had

389

sustained them. But the culture need not be any less Maya for being humbler in style and simpler in conception, unless one assumes that folk culture is invariably an impoverished derivation of elite culture and, once cut off from this source, can have no independent existence. The vitality of postconquest Maya culture would seem to bely this argument. One of the humbler denizens of Mayapan, abandoned in the early fifteenth century, would have found much that was familiar in colonial Yucatan and, equally significant, he would have encountered few changes that could not be made comprehensible within his own frame of reference.

In any case, Spanish colonial rule represented only the first phase of a more extended process of change and assimilation. Conquest did not entirely destroy the protective barrier of isolation behind which the cultural development of the Maya had proceeded on its own autonomous course. From the perspective of the "ethnographic present" it all looks the same, telescoped into the general heading of "culture contact," or whatever it is that has made the Maya of, say, 1930 different from the Maya of 1510. But it is important to distinguish the phases and, in particular, to separate two kinds of influences that are often lumped together. One is Westernization, or the impact of Europe on the non-Western world (culturally non-Western even if not always geographically non-Western); and the other is the complex of forces that for want of a better name we call modernization.

The two sets of influences have since the mid-nineteenth century been inseparable, if not synonymous. Modernization was an integral part of the imperial package that northern European nations, preeminently Great Britain, brought to Africa and to large parts of Asia; and it is easy to forget that by then the Iberian empires in the New World had already come and gone except for a few remnants in the Spanish Caribbean. What sets Latin America apart and lends so much comparative value to its history is the chronological separation between the two influences; this enables us to sort them out analytically and assess the particular impact of each. In other words, the West encountered America before becoming modern itself.

For Spanish America the Bourbon reforms herald the transition from one phase, one set of influences, to the other. The reforms were in turn the particular Spanish response to a general intellectual movement in the West, the European Enlightenment, in which new ideas on nature, on human nature, and on knowledge itself radically altered the ways that men looked at the world around them. Out of these ideas would flow so many of the changes, planned and unplanned—the official policies, the accumulation of technological innovations, and the social transformations that accompanied them—which we think of as both signaling and creating the modern era. However much the exact causal chain may be debated, and even the nature of the changes themselves, there seems to be fairly general agreement that something profoundly significant happened, and that much of the ideational support for the change can be traced to the varied yet interrelated ideas gathered under the heading of the Enlightenment.

The student of Latin American history can legitimately skirt the thicket of controversy over origins and causes. The wellsprings of modernization clearly lie elsewhere and, though it is worth pondering why that should be, the fact remains that Latin America, along with the rest of the so-called "Third World," has been handed a decidedly secondary, although not entirely passive, role in this historical process.

For Spain and its empire, for Yucatan in particular, there can be no doubt about the shift from one phase to another. Yucatan made no dramatic leap into the modern era at the turn of the nineteenth century. In many ways, to associate Yucatan with anything "modern" even today might seem a contradiction in terms. Nevertheless, the Bourbon reforms, though they were tentative in concept and faltering in application, broke down barriers that had isolated Yucatan from the larger imperial system, and they also integrated the Maya more fully into the local colonial regime. In so doing they initiated the Maya's confrontation with the modern world, so different in concept and reality from the semimedieval world of the sixteenth-century Spanish.

From the evidence in the case of Yucatan, modernization emerges as the much more devastating influence. If, as I have argued at the beginning of this study, sociocultural disintegration and absorption depend primarily on the level of structural integration into the Western-controlled global system of economic exchange, Westernization and modernization can be seen as stages in the same, still unfolding process initiated by conquest. The pressures have increased greatly in the more recent stage, only temporarily checked during the upheavals of independence and revolution. Through all the political turmoil, the intrusive role of a centralizing state (*pace* whatever federalist rhetoric might be in vogue at the time) has expanded hand-in-hand with the economic ties that have linked Yucatan and the Maya ever more intimately with the larger system as both producers and consumers.

The effects on semi-isolated subsistence farmers are so familiar as to have become commonplace. Drawn into national political struggles by those seeking a popular base of support, they lose the last vestiges of autonomy while gaining more or less token concessions in the form of a village water pump or perhaps even some land, whose distribution and allocation are controlled from state and national capitals. New desires, new "needs," are stimulated, which cannot be satisfied by the accustomed way of life. The women, while continuing to wear the traditional *huipil* (somewhat modified by Spanish colonial notions of modesty), will want a treadle "Singer" so that they can replace the old hand-stitched borders with fancier machine embroidery, and the cloth and thread themselves will be purchased with cash. An automobile does not yet figure even in the fantasies of most Maya men, but the new macadam roads make a bicycle a universal aspiration and bus fares an essential item in all family budgets. One man I know rides the bus part of the way to a distant milpa, some ten kilometers away. As is also well-nigh universal, the growth in material wants outstrips the opportunities to earn the necessary cash. But these have increased greatly in recent years as Mexico's tourist and petroleum booms reach into remote areas of the peninsula. The newly perceived needs and the new income-producing means have together done more to erode the cultural autonomy of the Maya than all the efforts of missionaries and Liberal reformers combined. The process is in no way abstract or mysterious; it is merely the sum of small decisions—individual deviations from inherited norms all reinforcing each other to create new patterns and finally new norms.

This outline of cultural change does not imply a strict chronological boundary prior to which all contact produced only superficial results. Rather, it points to the importance of integration into an alien economic system as a major, perhaps the major, catalyst for change. Without it contact alone will not effect radical transformations in the basic orientations toward reality that we define as culture. Nor does the emphasis on economic integration, with attendant alterations in patterns of behavior, minimize the importance of mental constructs. The catalyst will stimulate change and influence its nature, but the final product also depends on the original ingredients.

To assign to modern influences the credit, or blame, for the major changes that have occurred within Maya culture since conquest would seem to ignore the enormous contrast between the subjective realities of the Maya and their conquerors (not to mention the objective reality of colonial domination in which they confronted each other). Even if the contrast with modern Western culture were not much more extreme, the point of the argument is that the circumstance of political domination is not in itself a compelling force for change. The Spanish could require the Maya to adopt certain alien modes of behavior but could not prevent them from investing this behavior with their own sets of meanings and thereby fitting them into their own world view. For at the same time the primitive colonial regime—persisting with only slight modification until the last decades before independence—left intact most of the basic economic and social institutions that sustained this world view. The Maya were forced to make some alterations in their shared map of reality, but not to scrap it altogether.

Yucatan's postconquest history in all its aspects could be seen as a simple case of retarded development. The temptation is to start with the better-known sequence already plotted out for the dynamic center of the region, central Mexico, and merely transpose it to the margins with an appropriate chronological adjustment. The line of development in Yucatan looks conveniently familiar, only lagging behind a half century or more. The military conquest itself started later and was more prolonged. Population decline and recovery, the transition from a tribute to a market economy, the emergence of large cereal-producing haciendas from simple cattle ranches, the consequent pressure on Indian lands and the absorption of a large part of the Indian population as landless peons on the great estates, the economic and political decline of the native elite, the blurring of distinctions between nobles and commoners and the relegation of the elite to an almost purely ceremonial role: these are all central Mexican replays, in slow motion. All we need to do is establish the extent of the time lag. Or so it would seem.

The idea of identical but delayed processes is tempting but risk-laden. For the difference in pace responds to a difference in structures and may alter the processes themselves. Politically there have been various fluctuations in the degree of centralized control in Mesoamerica, but central Mexico has always been the dominant region, with all the implications for historical development that such dominance carries. In the economic sphere we have certainly been amply warned of the dangers in assuming that stages repeat themselves exactly in different locales. The one aspect of dependency theory that all economists seem to agree on, however variously they may view the prospects for development, is that time lags between regions both reflect and produce structural differences. If Latin America has been one of the world economy's peripheries since the sixteenth century, Yucatan has been a periphery of a periphery (if not fourth in line during the colonial period, linked to northern Europe via central Mexico and the secondary metropolis of Spain). Yucatan is no more likely to duplicate the exact processes of change charted by central Mexico than central Mexico is likely to follow the same path as England. Even now Yucatan has yet to reproduce either the social complexity or the economic diversity already evident in the highlands during the colonial period. When the hacienda did finally emerge, it was never tied to a strong local market; the hacienda itself was a relatively brief episode in Yucatan's transition from the semiautarky imposed by the Hapsburg commercial system to the export monoculture of the henequen plantation.

The reshaping of Indian society and culture under Spanish rule is subject to the same rules of analysis. It is possible, indeed likely, that there too what appears to be a simple delay may be a different process at work. Surely the different tempos embody qualitative differences as well. The sudden collapse of the centralized state systems of the Inca and Aztec empires, with the elimination of the central political and religious figures, contrasts with the gradual fragmentation of much smaller polities in Yucatan. And the mining booms that followed shortly afterward in Mexico and Peru, stimulating a massive influx of Spaniards and a heavy demand for labor, contrast with Yucatan's prolonged reliance on the indigenous economic system. The trauma of conquest was clearly of a different order of magnitude in Yucatan: instead of one massive earthquake, the region was subjected to an extended series of smaller tremors.

In comparing the "spiritual conquests" of Mexico and Peru, one can see that chronological differences have resulted in different effects. The missionary effort began considerably later in the Andes, after the first wave of fervor was spent and when the more flexible Erasmian humanism of the earlier sixteenth century was giving way to the Tridentine rigidities of the Counter-Reformation. Moreover, the long delay between military conquest and evangelization precluded a clean, clear break with pre-Columbian religion, at least on the subimperial level. For these reasons, it has been suggested, conversion was more superficial among the Incas, producing less of an amalgam than a very thin veneer of Christianity over a solid pagan base.[4]

In Yucatan the break with the pre-Columbian past was even less drastic and abrupt than the Andes in many aspects of native life—political, economic, and social, as well as religious. Many of the changes in the Indians' objective reality that were compressed into the decades after conquest in Mexico and Peru were stretched out over centuries in Yucatan, and the difference in tempo affected the Maya's responses to these innovations. They were given more breathing space, more time to adapt to changing circumstances on their own terms and within their own basic cultural framework. The elapsed time would not preclude internal sociocultural change, only allow for more conservative change, the kind that tinkers with the system while preserving its basic design.

Adaptability is a prerequisite for cultural survival under all but the most static conditions. Change is thus a quasi universal in all societies, even the ones that seem most "uncontaminated" by outside influences. The difference for colonized groups is that change will proceed along more or less indigenous lines according to the speed and thoroughness of the colonizing enterprise. Added to their own strengths—numerical and social—of a relatively dense population and a settled agrarian way of life that was adaptable to the demands of their new rulers, the Maya had the good fortune to inhabit a region that held little potential for commercial profit by Spanish standards and hence little attraction for Spanish settlers. To this combination of blessings the Maya owed the continued integrity of their social order and the preservation of a separate, identifiably Maya culture through all the changes induced by colonial rule.

I suspect that in the Andes the pagan religious base persisting under a Christian veneer was in fact much modified after the conquest, but not necessarily in the direction of Christianity. And in Yucatan the Maya did not become any less Maya as they adjusted to conquest and colonial rule—developing strategies designed to deal with Spanish innovations but tailored to their own values and principles. They simply became colonial Maya.

APPENDIX 1
POPULATION OF YUCATAN,
1806[a]

Partido	Parish	Vecinos	Indians	Dispersed Indians[b]	Total Population
Campeche	Campeche (casco)	7,896	0	0	7,896
	San Francisco Extramuros	7,337	2,597	?	9,934
Champoton–	Champoton	1,109	801	?	1,910
Sahcabchen	Seiba	1,525	1,925	?	3,450
	Lerma	1,005	4,066	?	5,071
	Chicbul	152	550	?	702
Pich	Pich	385	1,453	437	1,838
Carmen	Presidio del Carmen	2,850	509	?	3,359
Merida	Merida (Sagrario)	11,948	0	0	11,948
	Jesús (mulattoes)	6,051	0	0	6,051
	San Cristóbal	419	5,286	3,338	5,705
	Santiago	481	3,819	1,394	4,300
Camino Real	Calkini	1,039	8,022	?	9,061
Alto	Becal	501	4,770	124	5,271
	Hecelchakan	1,415	7,022	3,658	8,437
	Hopelchen	1,450	5,083	1,446	6,533
Camino Real	Halacho	380	2,578	337	2,958
Bajo	Hunucma	1,868	5,171	1,559	7,039
	Kopoma	846	4,242	1,993	5,088
	Maxcanu	1,933	3,732	2,416	5,665
	Uman	2,589	5,345	3,705	7,934
Costa	Cacalchen	463	1,055	315	1,518
	Cansahcab	638	2,236	1,056	2,874
	Conkal	1,402	4,661	?	6,063
	Izamal	1,823	2,910	306	4,733
	Mococha	632	3,179	879	3,811
	Motul	1,766	5,749	1,500	7,515
	Nolo	17	3,569	1,106	3,586
	Tekanto	513	2,876	595	3,389
	Telchac	925	2,863	869	3,788
	Temax	2,178	6,162	3,700	8,340
	Teya	203	1,857	606	2,060
	Tixkokob	1,056	3,099	1,571	4,155
	Dzindzantun	1,691	2,161	284	3,852
Sierra Alta	Mani	1,829	4,863	949	6,692
	Oxkutzcab	4,222	12,706	6,141	16,928

Partido	Parish	Vecinos	Indians	Dispersed Indians[b]	Total Population
	Tekax	6,381	15,186	3,796	21,567
	Ticul	5,127	11,122	1,714	16,249
Sierra Baja	Abala	462	3,377	3,212	3,839
	Acanceh	222	2,133	1,283	2,355
	Mama	1,363	5,299	2,489	6,662
	Muna	2,132	4,279	3,209	6,411
	Sacalum	342	4,358	?	4,700
	Teabo	891	5,018	692	5,909
	Tecoh	798	5,433	3,819	6,231
Beneficios	Chikindzonot	156	2,954	320	3,110
Altos	Chunhuhub	117	2,135	0	2,252
	Ichmul	1,331	8,196	360	9,527
	Peto	1,365	3,798	1,915	5,163
	Sacalaca	450	1,273	91	1,723
	Tahdziu	408	3,112	8	3,520
	Tihosuco	710	6,646	391	7,356
Beneficios	Hocaba	1,537	3,630	666	5,167
Bajos	Hoctun	791	2,442	1,165	3,233
	Homun	253	2,043	861	2,296
	Sotuta	974	3,584	?	4,558
	Tixcacaltuyu	703	6,468	0	7,171
	Yaxcaba	1,134	6,468	3,993	7,602
Tizimin	Calotmul	490	1,381	?	1,871
	Chancenote	734	2,127	956	2,861
	Espita	1,042	4,054	2,426	5,096
	Kikil	1,187	1,016	687	2,203
	Nabalam	222	836	248	1,058
	Tizimin	778	1,393	988	2,171
	Xcan	28	1,865	810	1,893
Valladolid	Chemax	153	3,894	2,105	4,047
	Chichimila	14	2,344	93	2,358
	Sisal	20	2,693	554	2,713
	Tekuch	42	1,040	112	1,082
	Tixcacalcupul	80	1,555	477	1,635
	Uayma	790	4,076	270	4,866
	Valladolid	8,625	4,540	1,580	13,165
	Dzonotpip	1,438	4,240	1,134	5,678
	Totals	115,827	272,925[c]	82,268	388,752

Sources: AA, Estadística 1 & 2, Estados que manifiestan . . . , 1806 (exceptions: Carmen, Chicbul, and Calotmul, 1802; Kopoma and Homun, 1803; Hoctun, 1804; Telchac and Uayma, 1807; Tahdziu, 1808; Sotuta, 1810). Parish censuses for this period are missing for Campeche, Champoton, Seiba, Lerma, Calkini, and Sacalum and the figures for these parishes are taken from AEY, Censos y padrones 1, nos. 2, 4, 7, 10, and 11, 1811.

[a] For 57 parishes; dates for the remaining 16 parishes range from 1802 to 1811.

[b] Residing in *ranchos, sitios, estancias*, and haciendas; included also in total Indian population.

[c] For purposes of calculating the proportion of dispersed Indians, the number is reduced to 229,213 (omitting parishes for which the breakdown is unavailable).

APPENDIX 2
SOURCES AND METHODS

Official Spanish documents compiled by the agents of both church and state are the major sources of information on the colonial Maya. And a voluminous mass they are. The Spanish satisfied the bureaucrat's penchant for record keeping—on the subjects that interested them—in often mind-boggling detail. Given their concern with fiscal matters (especially head taxes), with caste distinctions, and with keeping track of people in all categories to ensure compliance with a variety of church laws, it is not surprising that the parish registers and the censuses compiled from them are especially rich in information. Historical demographers feel they are fortunate when they find a reliable census from a premodern society. The Spanish could be counted on occasionally to list everyone not only by name, sex, and age, but also by kinship affiliation, household grouping, occupation, racial category, and social rank.

The Spanish legalistic mentality ensured that judicial records of all kinds would predominate in sheer bulk and as the chief source of data on all aspects of colonial life. Even ordinary administrative procedures, such as *residencias* and *visitas*, took the form of a full judicial inquiry, as did most conflicts over policy issues and the application of royal legislation. The judicial system was ponderously thorough. Depositions and counterdepositions were taken down more or less verbatim from all witnesses and any conceivably interested party, and the process was repeated with new interrogatories in seemingly endless rounds. Usually the names, ages, residences, and statuses of the witnesses were recorded, and often information on their particular experience and qualifications was noted as a basis for judging their competence and reliability. Thus, in addition to the evidence in the depositions themselves, the judicial records contain miniature biographies of a wide range of the colonial inhabitants.

The Maya are well represented in civil suits, undeterred by the heavy expense of litigation that burdened non-Indians; their legal fees were paid from the one-real head tax that supported their own tribunal. Criminal cases involving Indians that were serious enough to reach the royal courts—that is, conspiracies and rebellions—are rare, but they make up in length and detail what they lack in frequency. More common are the idolatry trials, ostensibly handled only by episcopal courts if the defendants were Indians but with much overlapping jurisdiction in practice.

As rich as they are, the official Spanish records have their limitations.

They are, for one thing, highly uneven in coverage, heavily concentrated in the early postconquest period (through the mid-1580s) and even more so from the middle of the eighteenth century to independence. This seems to be only in part a question of preservation; for in the intervening period of Hapsburg decline, colonial administration was relatively slack and produced far less in the way of letters and reports and the detailed inquiries on which they were based.

Here the clergy have helped to fill the gap somewhat, with several chronicles based partly on civil and ecclesiastical records that have since disappeared and partly on their own and their fellow clergymen's experiences and observations. Among the Franciscans, Diego López de Cogolludo, writing in the 1650s, is the best known, but Bernardo de Lizana (ca. 1629) is also extremely informative (and was in fact one of Cogolludo's chief sources), as is the 1588 account of the *visita* of Fray Alonso Ponce, attributed to Antonio de Ciudad Real. For the secular clergy, Pedro Sánchez de Aguilar, a native-born Yucatecan, has provided an invaluable synopsis of diocesan records on idolatry cases from the late sixteenth and early seventeenth centuries (cases pursued by the author as *Provisor*) along with many observations from his childhood and parish ministry. Francisco de Cárdenas Valencia, writing in 1639, provides far fewer details on Maya life, even though he was another long-time curate among the Indians.

Aside from gaps, the Spanish documentation has other, more serious limitations as a source for colonial Maya history, limitations that arise from the colonial situation in which it was produced. The Spanish could not oversee all the Indians' actions, still less their thoughts. They did not trouble to note what did not interest them nor what they took for granted; and much of what they did record is distorted by their own culturally alien lens. In other words, the Spanish observed only part of what the Indians were up to, and understood even less.

As a partial remedy, the Spanish have provided us with what one might call hybrid, Maya-Spanish documents—recorded by the Spanish but derived entirely either from Maya written texts or from their oral traditions. The two best-known examples date from the early postconquest period and are especially valuable for late pre-Hispanic politics and religion. Diego de Landa's account, compiled from native informants (the final version apparently composed sometime in the late 1560s), has become the basic handbook on the pre-Hispanic lowland Maya. I have cited in this study the scrupulously accurate and copiously annotated translation by Alfred Tozzer, rather than the less reliable published Spanish versions. The "Relaciones Geográficas," compiled in 1579-1581 by *encomenderos* in answer to a royal questionnaire, drew heavily on native informants also (many of the accounts were in fact prepared by the interpreter, Gaspar Antonio Chi). They have been published in an extremely faulty version, which I have checked against the originals in the Archivo General de Indias. Aside from sections in Lizana, also taken from native sources (and reproduced by Cogolludo), there are a number of unpublished documents in which the Spanish merely reported, at second hand, Maya versions of their past or present. Much of the testimony in judicial records falls into this category (for instance, the trials resulting from the Tekax riot of 1610 and the Canek revolt of 1761), concerning, as it does, events and backgrounds to events about which the Spanish had no direct knowledge. An especially useful example for this study are the 1782 inquiries concerning the sale of *cofradía* estates, in which the local Maya officials traced the history of the *cofradías* back to their original donations, based on their own oral traditions and written records, information to which the Spanish otherwise had no access.

Even these documents do not entirely satisfy the urge to penetrate the colonial façade and find an "untainted" Maya perspective. Inequalities of power and diverging interests inevitably influenced what information the Maya chose to give to their colonial masters, no matter how faithfully the words were recorded.

Fortunately, the colonial Maya have left some records of their own. The incidence of literacy declined from preconquest times, when the entire nobility and not only the priests were reportedly able at least to read the hieroglyphic texts. Nevertheless, a small cadre in each community (the *maestros cantores*, the *escribanos*, and some portion of the *batabs* and other officials) preserved the ability to read and write in the Latin script taught by the missionaries. Most of the surviving documents they produced are official records, such as boundary settlements, testaments and deeds of sale, *cofradía* records, lists of officeholders, and petitions and legal briefs submitted to the Spanish authorities. Many of them thus respond partly to Spanish concerns. But there is a small corpus of documents that the Maya quite deliberately, and for the most part successfully, guarded from Spanish eyes. The most important and complex of these are the texts known under the collective title of the "Books of Chilam Balam" (from the name of the prophet and reputed author). Their most likely origin is a pre-Hispanic hieroglyphic text or texts, transcribed shortly after conquest and then copied repeatedly over the course of the colonial period with embellishments, modifications, and possibly deletions, few of which can be dated with any accuracy. Comparisons among the roughly ten extant versions, which by internal evidence date from the late eighteenth or early nineteenth century, suggest that they were all at one point based on at least a common model, and it is likely that the elite in every town preserved their own copy or copies. (For a listing of the extant and allegedly extant versions, see the *Handbook of Middle American Indians* 15: 379-381).

Students of pre-Hispanic Maya history have long wrestled with these sometimes baffling mixtures of chronicle, prophecy, myth, and calendrical, astrological, and ritual lore and with the problems posed by the cyclical, past-as-prophecy approach to chronology—as if events in, say, the 1480s, the 1680s, and the 1980s in our calendar were all telescoped. Whatever they tell about pre-Hispanic history and symbolic systems, the Chilam Balam books, as they survive today, are preeminently colonial documents, not only copied repeatedly but also repeatedly read and consulted in the gatherings of *principales* (*juntas* and *convites*) that made the Spanish so uneasy. They thus provide unique insights into what the colonial Maya elite thought worth preserving from their past and what they were thinking and talking about in their present—most especially on the subjects of cosmology and the nature and practice of legitimate authority.

The other extant Maya documents fall more neatly into the categories of either chronicle or ritual (examples of both are the Chronicle of Calkini and the *Cantares* of Dzitbalche), all also recorded after conquest with more or less extensive colonial modifications but based originally on pre-Hispanic texts. For these and other published Maya documents, I have used the versions edited and translated by Ralph Roys and by Alfredo Barrera Vázquez in preference, where a choice exists, over other versions, which either fail to provide the original Maya text or offer less reliable translations, or both.

All the Maya documents were prepared by or by order of the community leaders, and most of the Maya testimony in Spanish documents came from the same group, so that these records necessarily reflect the native elite's concerns and points of view. Moreover, there are many aspects of Maya life and thought that are inadequately or misleadingly covered or simply ignored in any of the written records. Such gaps are not unique to the history of non-Western societies under colonial rule. They are in some degree common to the history of peasants, the urban poor, indeed all except the highly articulate elite in any society: all whose voice is largely mute in the written record and yet who have values, ideas, and attitudes that are not necessarily mere impoverished versions of those held by the politically powerful. All historians of these groups and, one might argue, all historians who seek to recover the systems of meaning that informed social behavior in the past, must turn to more or less unorthodox types of evidence to supplement standard documentary sources.

ONE type of evidence I have turned to is material remains. In that regard the historian of colonial Yucatan is blessed by the region's seemingly incorrigible backwardness. Colonial structures abound: urban houses, haciendas, government buildings, and, above all, churches, often with their decaying colonial saints and fixtures untouched. Town layouts remain unmodified and so do the styles of domestic interiors; Maya houses have remained unchanged, perhaps for millennia. Ruins of abandoned colonial sites dot the landscape, not nearly as ubiquitous as pre-Columbian sites but numerous enough to tempt the frustrated archival researcher into some historical archaeology. A summer's excavation of an early colonial church, at the site of Tancah on the peninsula's east coast, yielded evidence of religious syncretism that would simply have been unobtainable from the written sources, although these sources were necessary to evaluate and interpret the archaeological data. From the historian's viewpoint, archaeology seems to require an immense investment of time and money out of all proportion to the amount of information it yields. The difficulties of correlating the documentary evidence, usually at a macrolevel, with the microlevel evidence of an excavation are also great; and archaeology has its own unresolved methodological problems in inferring behavior—to say nothing of cognitive systems—from the material detritus the behavior leaves behind. Nevertheless, the information is often unique in quality and much more could and should be done with colonial sites.

The principal method I have used in seeking to fill gaps in the contemporary records, and to decode what information they do provide, is that of comparison, principally comparison across time. The rationale behind this method is that regularities exist in social and ideational configurations and that, given certain basic similarities between two systems, inferences can be made from the more fully known to the less fully known. Few would claim any predictive value for this method, but it can suggest possibilities and also warn against assumptions and conclusions that have been invalidated for other times and places.

Comparison over space, or cross-cultural comparison, tends to be used with caution. The need to define precisely and appropriately the units of comparison is well recognized, and the risk of being found, after all, to have compared apples and oranges is ever present. The same risk attends comparison over time. It is one that historians employ more frequently, although usually less explicitly and therefore usually with less rigor. Anyone who "understands" French history better because of his experience of contemporary France is relying on cross-temporal comparison; so too is anyone who draws on Confucian thought to interpret modern China. Yet here the danger of falling into that most heinous methodological sin, the failure to control variables, is as great as in cross-cultural comparison. Perhaps it is greater because, although trained to sniff out particular anachronisms, historians are likely to assume a general cultural continuity—a kind of *genius loci* conferred by the physical location. Such continuities may persist through centuries of technological and social change, but they need to be established.

Comparison across time has proved indispensable to this study. Without archaeological and epigraphic evidence from pre-Columbian times, supplemented with oral traditions recorded shortly after conquest, and without the rich ethnographic literature on Yucatan, much of colonial Maya history would be unrecoverable. Some of the evidence would, I think, be misinterpreted. Some of it is so allusive that it would, unaided, defy any explanation at all; and many of the bits and pieces would simply be passed over, unrecognized as usable evidence.

One guideline for comparison across time, largely self-evident but worth mentioning, has to do with context: the fuller the context, the sounder the inferences; that is, the more information available about different periods, the more confidently one can fill in pieces of fact and interpretation from one to the other. This prescription would seem to enclose a paradox, to the effect that comparison is least reliable as an explanatory tool when it is most needed. To a certain extent this is so. In anthropology the technique known as "upstreaming," or moving back in time, has fallen into some disrepute because it has so often been used to project an "ethnographic present" into some misty past that has yielded few if any records of its own. In other words, the present is used as a substitute for rather than a supplement to historical documentation. I myself would not attempt comparison without a fairly rich body of data to support links over time—preferably (to display an historian's bias) written data, but not excluding oral traditions and visual and material evidence.

Such caution will strike researchers working in less richly endowed regions as unduly restrictive. Scholars studying North American Indians and sub-Saharan Africa in particular have developed a variety of ingenious methods for reconstructing the past without benefit of written records or, in the case of Africa, much in the way of recovered archaeological material. One of these methods, a sophisticated variant of upstreaming called the "age-area" method, seeks to relate relative chronology to present-day spatial distribution. Most simply stated, the idea is that the more broadly distributed a particular cultural trait or complex is within a general geographical area, the more remote its origins can be presumed to be. This proposition is certainly plausible. Still, for my own use I would want to see it tested first elsewhere against historical evidence.

This brings me to my second, more specific guideline: the need to establish by way of historical evidence (rather than assume or infer) the degree of stability in the central elements of any sociocultural system on which other parts depend. These are the basic variables, and to the extent that they are enduring, more or less continuity can be inferred in the corollary elements. My choice of a comparative laboratory has been a fortunate one, as excolonial areas go. It offers a considerable and well-documented degree of stability in some of the more obviously central or basic features of the cultural configuration. The Maya's relationship with their physical environment, in particular their mode of subsistence, is one such feature; their organization into corporate patrilineal kin groups is another; and their contractual relationship with supernatural beings who are offered gifts of food in return for specific favors, still another. These and other traits that could be mentioned have persisted from pre-Columbian times through colonial rule, and in large parts of the peninsula up to the present.

While it is relatively easy, given sufficient documentation, to trace specific elements in a sociocultural system and to measure continuities and changes in these elements over time, such sleuth work is unprofitable if we do not know how the elements relate to each other and to the system as a whole. For in these relationships lies much of the explanation of how and why continuity is maintained and changes occur. I would go further and suggest that the elements are defined by the relationships and therefore cannot even be identified, much less understood, in isolation. Neither, needless to say, can any processes of change they might undergo be explained in isolation. This raises the question about how to deal with change in social and ideational forms, when these are conceived of as components in systems that are interconnected internally as well as with each other: how does one reconcile the linear, dynamic approach of history with the systemic, holistic approach of anthropology? Even if we can devise satisfactory explanatory models showing how systems can undergo change while remaining more or less integrated, the models offer no prescription for the practical task of how to depict a structure in motion. Carlyle has said, "Narrative is linear; action is solid." Structure is more solid still.

Obviously we have to freeze the movement in order to explore the structure, to see how the parts fit into the system and how it works as a system. This is far simpler in precept than in practice. At best the movement can be slowed down. The nature of historical as opposed to ethnographic research is such that no one moment will disgorge all the

405

necessary evidence. Then how do we turn dissociated historical information into associated ethnographic fact? Bits and pieces from more or less distantly separated moments will have to be assembled with the hope that, if not concurrent, they are at least congruent. Serious incongruencies can be avoided in the same way as in any well-controlled comparison—with a careful eye to context.

I am less confident that the exercise itself, no matter how carefully performed, is not in some fundamental way incompatible with historical explanation. It may give a false impression of stability or equilibrium that, while not necessarily precluding the possibility of change, masks its frequently incremental nature. An historian is unlikely to ignore change altogether. The greater risk is that change will be misrepresented, compressed into sudden spurts in between the analyses of structures. This study may have sacrificed some of the sense of gradual change occurring throughout the colonial period by concentrating on the early postconquest period and the late eighteenth century. Intervening adjustments and modifications are noted, but the colonial systems and subsystems are not consistently analyzed as in a state of perpetual motion. These are periods of accelerated change, without a doubt, and no blame attaches to focusing on those points in any narrative when the action seems particularly intense—so long as the shift from static image to high speed is not too abrupt.

To do full justice to the accumulation of smaller, less perceptible changes would have greatly extended an already far-from-skimpy manuscript. But the issue is not simply one of length nor one of balance between structure and process. There is an inherent methodological problem in combining the two, a problem that may not have a satisfactory solution. Neither structure nor process can be explained without reference to the other; yet analysis of the one necessarily involves some distortion of the other. Given the impossibility of achieving a perfect "moving picture," one can only hope that historians will find the tempo too slow and anthropologists find it too fast—in equal measure.

NOTES

In citing works in the notes, short titles have generally been used. Manuscript repositories and works frequently cited have been identified by the following abbreviations:

AA   Archivo del Arzobispado (Secretaría), Merida
AC   Archivo del Obispado, Campeche
AEY   Archivo del Estado de Yucatan, Merida
AGA   Archivo General del Arzobispado, Merida
AGI   Archivo Gencral de Indias, Seville
AGN   Archivo General de la Nación, Mexico, D. F.
AHH   Archivo Histórico de Hacienda (in AGN)
ANM   Archivo de Notarías, Merida
BL   British Library, London
BN   Biblioteca Nacional, Mexico, D. F.
DHY   *Documentos para la historia de Yucatan.* 3 vols. France V. Scholes et al., eds. Merida: 1936-1938
IJ   Institute of Jamaica, Kingston
IY   Instituto Yucateco de Antropología e Historia, Merida
RY   "Relaciones de Yucatan." In *Colección de documentos inéditos relativos al descubrimiento, conquista y organización de las antiguas posesiones de Ultramar.* 25 vols. Madrid: 1885-1932, vols. 11 and 13
TUL   Tulane University Library, Latin American Library, New Orleans

INTRODUCTION

1. Carneiro, "A Theory of the Origin of the State," is the classic statement of this theory.

2. See Michael Coe, "Social Typology and the Tropical Forest Environment."

3. These are discussed in chapter 4. They include the theory of "secondary state formation" in response to expansionary pressures from primary states evolving in the more favorable environment of central Mexico (see Sanders and Price, *Mesoamerica*); various demographic models based on the idea that population pressure can limit movement in an otherwise open environment (see, for example, Adams, *Origins of Maya Civilization*); and the notion of elite control of scarce goods (see especially the various formulations by Rathje, for example, "Origin and Development").

4. Wolf, "Closed Corporate Peasant Communities."

5. See, for example, Frank, *Capitalism and Underdevelopment*, 123-142, and Foster, "What is Folk Culture?" offering different perspectives on this same basic contention.

6. For criticisms of this assumption, which often underlies attempts to apply modern ethnographic models to the pre-Columbian past, see Barbara Price,

"Burden of the Cargo," Grant Jones, "Southern Lowland Maya Political Organization," and, especially, Kubler, "La evidencia intrínseca," which presents the most thorough and explicit statement of the argument in favor of total disjunction between the pre-Hispanic and colonial periods.

7. Peter Berger has chosen the conquest of the Incas to illustrate what he means by cultural devastation in its most extreme form: "When the conquering Spaniards destroyed this plausibility structure [Inca society] the reality of the world based on it disintegrated with terrifying rapidity" (*The Sacred Canopy*, 45). Similarly, George Kubler offers the conquest of Mexico as the paradigm of historical crisis and the *locus classicus* of cultural destruction and replacement (*The Shape of Time*, 57-79, 111-112).

8. Berger's and Kubler's models are both based on the destruction of the state structure and the high culture it represented and sustained (see also Kubler, "On the Colonial Extinction"). By implication, then, they might agree with those of the "continuity" school who see modern Indian culture as an ossified folk remnant of pre-Columbian culture: see, for example, Redfield, *Folk Culture of Yucatan*, 1-18, 338-368, and "The Folk Society," which define folk culture by the absence of urban (Spanish, then modern) influence.

PROLOGUE

1. Chamberlain, *Conquest and Colonization of Yucatan*, provides an impeccably documented summary of the main events from discovery to the establishment of royal government in 1551.

2. The journey, which actually lasted from October 1524 to April 1526, is recounted in Cortés, *Cartas de relación* (fifth letter), 185-208; and Díaz del Castillo, *Verdadera historia de la conquista* 2: 188-217.

3. J. Eric Thompson, *Maya History*, 7. The basic study of the late Postclassic "Putun" and their commercial and political networks is Scholes and Roys, *Maya-Chontal*, 15-87. See also Chapman, "Port of Trade Enclaves"; J. Eric Thompson, *Maya History*, 3-47, 124-158; Sabloff and Rathje, "Rise of a Maya Merchant Class"; and Miller, *On the Edge of the Sea*, chapter 4.

4. Cortés, *Cartas*, 185-186, 206.

5. On the postconquest decline and eventual abandonment of the east coast, see Roys, Scholes, and Adams, "Report and Census," and Miller and Farriss, "Religious Syncretism," 224-229. On southwestern Campeche, see Scholes and Roys, *Maya-Chontal*, 159-167, 299-315. On the effects of pirate raids, see, for example, AGI, Justicia 1029, Probanza sobre los daños . . . corsarios luteranos, 1565; Patronato 75, no. 1, ramo 1, Probanza Diego Sarmiento de Figueroa, 4 April 1578; Mexico 359, Governor to Crown, 28 Nov. 1565, 2 April 1579 and 15 Nov. 1600; Mexico 360, Governor to Crown, 10 July 1638; and a number of *expedientes* from the 1670s and 1680s in AGI, Escribanía de cámara 307-A and 307-B.

6. Two Dominicans in the southern Peten in 1555 (Villagutierre Sotomayor, *Historia*, 49-54) and a Franciscan in Tayasal in 1628 (López de Cogolludo, *Historia de Yucatan* [hereafter cited as Cogolludo], Lib. 10, cap. 2). Five others were

killed while they were accompanying Spanish military expeditions, which appear to have supplied the provocation: one in Saclum in 1624 (Cogolludo, Lib. 10, cap. 3) and four in or near Tayasal in 1696 (Villagutierre Sotomayor, 284-294, 314-315, 352, 375). An unverified martyrdom is reported by Sánchez de Aguilar, *Informe*, 120-121, who alleged that the Indians of Cozumel had deliberately drowned their curate in a boating "accident."

7. AGI, Mexico 359, 367, 369, and 3048, and Indiferente 1387 contain many letters and reports, 1564-1585, referring to the sporadic missionary activity on Cozumel and the east coast, some of them published or summarized in Roys, Scholes, and Adams, "Report and Census"; Miller and Farriss, "Religious Syncretism"; Scholes and Adams, *Don Diego Quijada* 2: 79-83; and DHY 2: 70-94. See, especially, Mexico 369, Relación del viaje de Fray Gregorio de Fuente-ovejuna y Fray Hernando de Sopuerta, 15 Aug. 1573. Missionary activity, sometimes in conjunction with military *entradas*, was more intense along the southern frontier. Scholes and Thompson, "Francisco Pérez Probanza," summarizes information on the Bacalar-Tipu region, 1618-1655. See also Cogolludo, Lib. 8, caps. 5-10, 12-13 (including Tayasal), Lib. 11, caps. 12-17; AGI, Mexico 360, Governor to Crown, 10 July and 30 Nov. 1638; and Mexico 369, Bishop to Crown, 1 June 1606, and Memorial Bishop of Yucatan, 1643. Scholes and Roys, *Maya-Chontal*, 251-290, contains material on the Montaña and Tichel-Popola-Sahcabchen regions to the 1660s. Villagutierre, *Historia*, 119-128, 156-158, 200-208, 233-243, 252-257, 262-264, 303-311, summarizes activities converging on Tayasal, 1575-1700. On the Montaña region, 1604-1624, see also Cogolludo, Lib. 8, cap. 9, Lib. 10, caps. 2-3 (including Tayasal); Cárdenas Valencia, *Relación historial*, 74; AGI, Mexico 359, Cuaderno de documentos, 1604, Governor to Crown, 21 June and 19 Sept. 1608, and Certificate Francisco de Sanabria, 22 June 1608; Mexico 369, Governor to Crown, 22 Dec. 1604, Bishop to Crown, 29 Sept. 1604 and 12 Dec. 1605; Mexico 294, Testimonio del requerimiento, 1604, and Testimonio de varias cartas, 1604-1605; Escribanía de cámara 308-A, no. 1, pieza 3, Probanza Fray Gerónimo de Porraz, 1624.

8. For raids into the *despoblado* of the east coast, see Cogolludo, Lib. 7, caps. 13 and 15 (1592 and 1596), and Lib. 8, cap. 8 (1602); AGI, Patronato 56, no. 2, ramo 4, Probanza Juan de Contreras, 1596; Mexico 294, Probanzas Andrés Fernández de Castro, n.d. (1601), and Antonio de Arroyo, 1604; Mexico 130, Información . . . Br. Juan Alonso de Lara, 1611; Mexico 140, Probanza Capt. D. Juan Chan, 1622; and Escribanía de cámara 308-A, no. 1, pieza 6, Testimonio de información a favor de la religión franciscana, 1644.

9. Cogolludo, Lib. 8, cap. 9. See also Grant Jones, "Agriculture and Trade," and, among the many references in the contemporary documents to the "comercio oculto," AGI, Mexico 359, Franciscan Provincial to Audiencia of Mexico, 5 May 1606.

10. On *sublevaciones* in the central Montaña region in the period 1614-1624 (including the Saclum massacre of 1624), see Cogolludo, Lib. 10, cap. 3; AGI, Escribanía de cámara 305-B, ramo 6, Antonio de Salas to Governor, 16 Oct. 1624, and ramo 7, Méritos y servicios Diego de Vargas Mayorga, 12 Nov. 1624;

Mexico 359, Royal cédula to Governor, 18 Nov. 1624; and Escribanía de cámara 308-A, no. 1, pieza 3, Probanza Fr. Gerónimo de Porraz, 1624. Documentation on the heightened unrest in the 1660s and 1670s is voluminous, most of it contained in the *residencia* of Governor Rodrigo Flores de Aldana: see especially AGI, Escribanía de cámara 317-A, cuad. 4, Autos contra Antonio González, 1670; Escribanía de cámara 317-5, cuad. 8, Autos hechos por Pedro García Ricalde, 1668; and Escribanía de cámara 317-C, Papeles y recaudos presentados por . . . Flores de Aldana, 1664-1674. Franciscan reports are in AGI, Escribanía de cámara 308-A, no. 1, piezas 13-15, 1664-1680; and BN, Archivo Franciscano 55, nos. 1142 and 1143, letters from Fray Cristóbal Sánchez to the Provincial, 1672-1673.

11. The actual battle for the Itza stronghold in Tayasal, recounted in Villagutierre, *Historia*, 366-373, was brief, culminating a two-year campaign of encirclement and intense diplomatic pressure.

12. See Eugenio Martínez, *Defensa de Tabasco*, 72-158, on expeditions against the English, 1680-1717. On the construction of the fort, 1718-1765, see AGN, Real caja 54, Informe Antonio Bonilla, 29 April 1772.

13. Raids by and against both pagan and apostate Maya were reported into the nineteenth century: AGI, Mexico 1018, Sobre conversiones del Itza y Peten, 1703-1704; Mexico 898, Josef de Zaldívar to Crown, 14 Dec. 1742; AGN, Historia 534, no. 4, Sobre aprehensión de indios caribes en los ríos de Usumacinta, 1784; AA, Asuntos pendientes 2, Expedte. sobre . . . la misión de Chichanha, 1782; Oficios y decretos 3, Franciscan Provincial to Bishop, 9 Sept. 1786; Oficios y decretos 4, Joseph Nicolás de Lara to Bishop 19 Feb. 1782, and Juan José Arias Roxo to Bishop, 10 April 1785; Documentos del Petén Itzá, Exp. sobre residencia de un religioso en el pueblo de San Antonio, 1799; Domingo Faxardo to Provisor, 21 Oct. 1800, and Faxardo to Bishop, 14 May 1813.

14. Reed, *Caste War of Yucatan*, is an excellent summary account of the war and the *cruzob* Maya up to 1915. González Navarro, *Raza y tierra*, links the war to the socioeconomic background of nineteenth-century Yucatan.

15. The earliest extant accounts are probably two almost parallel texts written by members of the Pech lineage of Ceh Pech province in the mid-sixteenth century: "Chronicle of Chac-Xuleb-Chen [Chicxulub]," Maya text and English translation, in Brinton, *Maya Chronicles*, 187-259, and Martínez Hernández, *Crónica de Yaxkukul*, Maya text and Spanish translation. Barrera Vázquez, *Códice de Calkini*, Maya facsimile and Spanish translation, written in the latter part of the century, is a history of the Ah Canul province, including an account of the conquest period, 25-31, 41-57. Gaspar Antonio Chi, of the Xiu lineage of Mani province, has accounts of the conquest in RY 1: 42-45, and AGI, Mexico 104, Probanza de Gaspar Antonio Chi, 1580. See also AGI, Guatemala 111, Probanza de don Francisco, cacique of Xicalango, 1552; and the Acalan Chontal account, composed c. 1610 from oral traditions or earlier documents, in Scholes and Roys, *Maya-Chontal*, 367-382. It should be noted that all these accounts were written by Maya lords (or their descendants) who had allied themselves early with the Montejos and were concerned to record (and sometimes exaggerate)

410

the friendly reception they gave the Spanish, in contrast with the Chilam Balam books, cited below, which were intended solely for a Maya audience and reflect purely Maya concerns.

16. From internal evidence the extant texts of the Chilam Balam books seem to date from the seventeenth century. They were copied and recopied later but without major modification. They thus represent mid-colonial perceptions of the pre-Columbian and the conquest pasts. In addition to the straightforward historical accounts of the conquest, in, for example, Roys, *Book of Chilam Balam of Chumayel* (hereafter cited as Roys, *Chumayel*), 119-120, 145-146, the sections known as *katun* prophecies contain many references, some of them explicit, more commonly veiled in the characteristically metaphorical language of Maya sacred texts, to the conquest and the afflictions and miseries that followed: Roys, *Chumayel*, 144-163; *Codex Pérez*, 157-171. Roys, "Maya Katun Prophecies," contains a composite translation of the Series I prophecies from the Chilam Balam books of Tizimin, Mani, Chumayel, and Kaua, with notes and commentary.

17. León-Portilla, *Visión de los vencidos*, contains Spanish translations from a variety of Nahuatl sources, prose and verse, many of them previously unpublished. Not surprisingly, the Tlaxcalan version, excerpted here, is closer in its pragmatic tone and self-serving interpretations to the accounts produced by the Spaniards' Maya allies, cited in note 15. Wachtel, *Vision of the Vanquished*, 13-32, compares Maya, highland Mexican, and Andean perceptions of the Spaniards and the conquest, based on these same texts. It may not be fortuitous that the Peruvian and highland Mesoamerican "Dances of the Conquest" (analyzed in Wachtel, 33-58) have no counterpart among the lowland Maya. Perhaps, having assimilated the fact of conquest into their cyclical conception of time, the lowland Maya have had no need to reenact it in search of psychic resolution.

18. Willey, "External Influences," summarizes the archaeological literature on the entire Maya lowlands from 1940 to 1975. Many references to foreign intrusions (usually lumped together under the label "Itza") into the northern lowlands are contained in the oral traditions recorded in Landa, *Relación*, 16-17, 20-26, 32-35; RY, for example, 1: 121-122, 161, 213, 254-255, and 2: 159-161; Sánchez de Aguilar, *Informe*, 140; and a fragment from the "Valladolid Lawsuit" (1618), in Brinton, *Maya Chronicles*, 114-116, in addition to the chronicles and *katun* prophecies of the books of Chilam Balam. For recent attempts to sort out the obscure chronology of these references and correlate them with archaeological evidence, see J. Eric Thompson, *Maya History*, 5-25; Ball, "A Coordinate Approach"; Miller, "Captains of the Itza," and "The Little Descent."

19. Barrera Vázquez, *Códice de Calkini*, and Landa, *Relación*, 32-39. See also Roys, "Literary Sources for the History of Mayapan."

20. See the chronicles and oral traditions (recorded by the Spanish) cited in notes 16 and 18.

21. RY 2: 221-222, Relación of Giraldo Díaz del Alpuche, who married doña Isabel, daughter of an unnamed brother of Moctezuma in charge of the invading force. The Mexican garrison apparently remained at Xicalango (RY 1: 352,

364), where Diáz del Alpuche presumably learned the story and teamed up with doña Isabel in 1537 en route to Campeche from Tabasco on Montejo's second *entrada*.

22. Ciudad Real, *Relación* 2: 400-401, 413. A 1605 document mentions that there were "criollos mexicanos" in Merida who could still speak Nahuatl (AGI, Mexico 369, Memoriales de los indios de los pueblos de Usumacinta), but by the eighteenth century only the patents of *hidalguía* distinguished them from the Maya: AGI, Mexico 898, Diego de Anguas to Crown, 12 July 1735. See also the parish censuses, 1784-1785, in AA, Visitas pastorales 5, for Sisal de Valladolid, and Visitas pastorales 6, from Chunhuhub, and the material cited in chapter 3, note 87.

23. In addition to the native chronicles of the conquest already cited, Spanish accounts of the initial contact with both groups also attest to the differing reactions. See Henry Wagner, *Discovery of Yucatan* and *Discovery of New Spain*, for texts (in translation) relating the early voyages of exploration. For a comparative view, see Díaz del Castillo, *Verdadera Historia*, who participated in all the voyages (except the Grijalva voyage of 1518, according to Wagner) as well as the conquest of Mexico. On Maya reactions to the first Montejo *entrada* in 1527, see Oviedo y Valdés, *Historia*, Lib. 32, caps. 2-3; and, among the various conquerors' accounts, the Probanza of Blas González, 1567, in AGI, Patronato 68, no. 1, ramo 2.

24. The Xiu later claimed (RY 1: 44-45) that they had submitted to the Spanish because of prophecies of their arrival (without any suggestion that the Spaniards themselves might be gods), but their cooperation seems rather to have been stimulated by the recent flare-up of their old conflict with the Cocom of Sotuta province: RY 1: 288-289; Landa, *Relación*, 54; AGI, Mexico 104, Probanza Gaspar Antonio Chi, 1580, all recounting the Cocom massacre of Xiu nobles on a pilgrimage to Chichen Itza. A later, more self-serving Xiu version of the incident, with the victims portrayed as peace emissaries of the Spanish, is given in *Codex Pérez*, 187-188; Cárdenas Valencia, *Relación*, 100-101; and Cogolludo, Lib. 3, cap. 6.

25. See Scholes and Roys, *Maya-Chontal*, 88-128, on the Acalan Chontal. For the east coast, see Oviedo y Valdés, *Historia*, Lib. 32, cap. 2; AGI, Patronato 68, no. 1, ramo 2, Probanza Blas González, 1567; RY 2: 110-111. Roys, *Political Geography*, summarizes the background of the Canul (pp. 11-13), the Pech (p. 41), the Xiu (pp. 61-64), and the Chel (p. 81) dynasties, which will be dealt with at greater length in chapter 8.

26. "Valladolid Lawsuit," in Brinton, *Maya Chronicles*, 114-116; and Landa, *Relación*, 23, note 126 (quoting from Torquemada on the Cocom). Corroborative evidence is equivocal but the Cupul are elsewhere identified with early invaders from the east (RY 2: 161-162), and the Cocom claimed to be a more ancient lineage than the Xiu "foreigners": RY 1: 161, 288; Landa, *Relación*, 26, 31, 40.

27. Tozzer, *Chichen Itza*, is a detailed treatment of "Toltec" influence at Chichen Itza. For other discussions of "Mexican" cultic influence, see Andrews, *Balan-*

kanche; Miller, *On the Edge of the Sea*; and Pollock et al., *Mayapan*, especially pp. 136-139, 428-431. The frequent assertions that idolatry and human sacrifice were unknown in Yucatan until introduced by Kukulcan (RY 1: 52, 78-79, 121-122, 215, 225-226, 242-243, 270-271) presumably refer to new cults and a greater emphasis on human sacrifice.

28. The Chilam Balam books contain many expressions of disapproval directed against the Itza ("insolent," "impudent," "rogues," "rascals," "vulgar foreigners," "lewd," and "dissolute"), who were held responsible for the decline in Maya learning and religion. See the *tun* prophecies in Roys, "The Prophecies for the Maya Tuns," especially 173; and *Codex Pérez*, 98-116, especially 104-105, 108. A major complaint was the introduction of sexual licence— a cult of eroticism that may have included homosexuality (*crimen nefando*): Roys, *Chumayel*, 151; RY 1: 149, 216, 256.

29. AGI, Patronato 80, no. 1, ramo 1, Instrucción dada por el Adelantado n.d. (1534), in Probanza of Alonso Sánchez de Aguilar. See also AGI, Justicia 300, Residencia Adelantado Francisco Montejo, 1549, for much detailed testimony on the Montejos' policies.

30. Juan de Caraveo (probanza in AGI, Indiferente 1294, no. 11, 1533) accompanied the first *entrada*. Francisco Hernández, who accompanied the second, distinguished himself principally for his role in supervising the branding of slaves, for which services he was awarded an *encomienda* by Montejo (AGI, Justicia 300, Residencia Montejo, 1549; Mexico 364, Cabildo Merida to Crown, 14 July 1543). A third cleric, Francisco Niño de Villagómez (probanza in Indiferente 1209, 1547), did not arrive until the very end of the conquest.

31. Cogolludo, Lib. 2, cap. 5, Lib. 5, caps. 1 and 5, Lib. 8. As a Franciscan, Cogolludo was hardly an unbiased source, but he was generally favorable to Montejo. The evidence for the dating of this and an earlier abortive mission to Champoton in c. 1534 is analyzed in Gómez Canedo, "Fray Lorenzo de Bienvenida."

32. AGI, Justicia 300, Residencia Montejo, 1549. Justicia 244, no. 3, contains a summary of the 29 charges brought in the *residencia*. See also AGI, Justicia 126, Juan Ote Durán con el Adelantado, 1537. The colonists' main grievance was in fact the suppression of the slave trade: AGI, Mexico 364, Cabildo Merida to Crown, 14 June 1543; RY 1: 229, 234.

33. *Cartas de Indias*, 70-80, Fray Lorenzo de Bienvenida to Crown, 10 Feb. 1548, quoting Montejo, "No querrán ir los amigos, si no les damos licencia de hacer esclavos."

34. See León-Portilla, *Tiempo y realidad*, for a discussion of the ancient Maya's conception of time.

35. Although the ancient *tzolkin*, or ritual calendar of 260 days, may have died out among the Yucatec Maya (see Redfield and Villa Rojas, *Chan Kom*, 367), awareness of the prophecies of Chilam Balam, with the notion of recurring events, was still widespread in the mid-nineteenth century: Sierra O'Reilly, *Indios de Yucatan* 1: 87.

Chapter 1, A Colonial Regime

1. See Foster, *Culture and Conquest*, 12-20, on the selection processes resulting in a fairly uniform "conquest culture."

2. Díaz del Castillo, *Verdadera historia* 2: 366.

3. The Crown continued to pay travel expenses and other subsidies for frontier missions throughout the colonial period. Although no longer technically missions, the parishes in the Peten in the early nineteenth century were still partially supported from the royal exchequer: AA, Oficios y decretos 7, Domingo Faxardo to Bishop, 22 Aug. 1811.

4. The returned emigrant, or *indiano*, became a synonym for new wealth and a stock satirical figure in the picaresque literature of the period. See, for example, the *perulero* (*indiano* from Peru) Marquina in Alonso de Castillo Solórzano's *La garduña de Sevilla* (1642).

5. Domínguez Ortiz, *Sociedad española*, 1: 223-226, 275-280. That even mechanical trades were socially disqualifying can be seen in many kinds of colonial records, for example, the applications for ecclesiastical benefices, in AA, Concursos a curatos.

6. Landa, *Relación*, 186-205; Fray Lorenzo de Bienvenida to Crown, 10 Feb. 1548, in *Cartas de Indias*, 70-80; and most of the reports in RY contain lengthy and, on the whole, enthusiastic descriptions of the local flora and fauna, while emphasizing the lack of precious metals.

7. For a comparison, see Toussaint, *Colonial Art in Mexico*, in which Yucatan is typically and symptomatically represented by only two out of 391 illustrations (figures 6 and 121, the former nunnery and the Montejo house). Much of downtown Merida is still of colonial construction and is extensively illustrated in the *Artes de Mexico* series, "Merida de Yucatan."

8. Testaments and property inventories can be found in the Merida notarial archives (ANM) and in the diocesan records on probate, pious endowments and liens or mortgages of ecclesiastical capital (AA, especially the sections Obras pías, Cofradías e imposiciones, Asuntos de monjas, Capellanías, and Asuntos terminados, which contains many foreclosure proceedings). Both archives contain predominantly eighteenth-century material but copies of earlier records are often included. Sixteenth-century material is very scarce, but see Bishop of Yucatan to Crown, 7 Sept. 1596, in DHY 2: 108-111, describing the material wealth of the local colonists in comparison with those in Peru and arguing that the colony was too poor to support a nunnery.

9. AGI, Escribanía de cámara 1006-A, Probanza Francisco de Montejo, 1552.

10. Miranda, *Función económica del encomendero*, shows how *encomienda* tribute and labor were used to finance this transition in the immediate postconquest period in central Mexico, even before the northern mining boom. On early silver mining, see Bakewell, *Silver Mining and Society*; on *obrajes* (textile factories), see Bazant, "Evolución de la industria textil." For Peru, Lockhart, *Spanish Peru*, has much information on early economic activities; and Wiedner, "Forced Labor in Colonial Peru," treats Indian labor in mines and *obrajes*.

11. This chronology, first proposed by Chevalier, *La formation des grands do-*

mains, although based primarily on northern Mexico, is supported by Gibson, *Aztecs under Spanish Rule*, 257-334, for the central plateau; Torre Villar, "Algunos aspectos de las cofradías," for Michoacán; and Brading, "Estructura de la producción agrícola," for the Bajío. Although Indian communities managed to retain some land even into the twentieth century, the main point is the contrast with the much slower pace of absorption in southern Mesoamerica, noted by Taylor, *Landlord and Peasant in Colonial Oaxaca*, and "Landed Society in New Spain."

12. Marta Hunt, "Colonial Yucatan," 375-442, traces the expansion of stock raising in the seventeenth century.

13. On the economy of the Laguna de Términos region, see the visitation report by Joseph Manuel de Nájera, 1755, in AA, Visitas pastorales 1; and report from the Governor of the Presidio del Carmen, 31 Dec. 1792, in AGN, Indiferente de guerra 160. For the Peten, see the report by Juan José Rojo, 2 Dec. 1786, in AA, Oficios y decretos 3.

14. Prices of land and cattle and horses can be derived from deeds and evaluations recorded in ANM, and a virtually unbroken run of cattle prices can be obtained from the various *libros de cofradía* in AA, containing overlapping yearly accounts from 1703 to 1819. Philip Thompson, "Tekanto," chapter 3, contains a series of price tables based on *cabildo* records from the town of Tekanto, 1720-1820. Land and cattle prices are extremely scarce before the mid-seventeenth century and are contained mainly in the estate *títulos* listed in note 18. However, price series for maize, honey, beeswax, and other commodities from the records on ecclesiastical *limosnas* and *obvenciones* (see notes 43 and 44) from the late sixteenth to the early nineteenth century confirm the same trends for livestock: sharp short-term fluctuations responding to climatic conditions but long-term stability. The "normal" price for cows and bulls remained steady at five pesos from the mid-seventeenth century, rising only in the early nineteenth century to six or seven pesos. Horses sold for six to eight pesos. Brood mares, selling at ten to twelve pesos, and *burros hechores*, selling at thirty-five to fifty pesos, were necessary only for raising mules, which sold at about fifteen pesos. Land prices varied according to time and place, but an unimproved parcel suitable for a *sitio* could be purchased from Indian communities and individuals for from ten to thirty pesos, depending on how desperate the seller was for cash. See, for example, TUL, Documentos de Tabi 1: 61-61v, Carta de venta, 16 March 1594; Títulos de Chactun, carta de venta, 24 Dec. 1700.

15. Chevalier, *Formation*, 203 (citing Diego de Basalenque, *Historia de la provincia de San Nicolás Tolentino de Michoacán* [1673], Lib. 2, cap. 10).

16. AEY, Censos y padrones 1, exp. 4, contains a census of rural estates, including livestock counts. The five largest in the colony, all in the Sierra district, were Tabi (2,000 head), Mukuyche (1,900), Xcanchakan (1,300), Uayelceh (1,200), and Ticopo (1,200).

17. Detailed inventories of rural estates are fairly common from the eighteenth century: in the notarial archives, in probate and foreclosure cases in the diocesan archives, and in civil property suits referred on appeal to the Audiencia

of Mexico (few of the local records have survived). As a small sample, see ANM, vol. 3, 1720-1722, Carta de venta de la estancia Kiva, 3 May 1720; vol. 23, 1770, Inventario de la estancia Kaxtamay, 11 May 1769; AA, Capellanías 1, Concurso a los bienes del Br. Esteban Pérez, 1773; Obras pías, 1760-1862, Embargo de la estancia Chacsinkin, 1789; Asuntos de monjas 2, Testamentaría del Capt. D. Juan Francisco Quijano, 1792-1795; AGN, Tierras 1255, no. 1, Inventario de bienes de Juan de la Barrera, 1783-1789.

18. The discussion of landed estates in this and later sections has also been based on extant collections of estate *títulos* (all the legal documents referring to land ownership): Hacienda Tabi (jurisdiction of Mani), in TUL; Hacienda Chichi (Merida), in IY; Sitio Suitunchen (Merida), IY and AGN, Tierras 1061, no. 1; Sitio Yaxché (Hecelchakan), IY; Hacienda San Bernardino Chich (Abala), AEY, Tierras 1, no. 20, and AGN, Tierras 1419, no. 2; Hacienda Uayelceh (Tecoh), courtesy of D. Alonso Peón Bolio; Hacienda Chactun (Becal), courtesy of Da. Sara Arrigunaga de Mancera; Hacienda Poxila (Uman), courtesy of D. Julio Laviada; Hacienda Kisil (Uman), courtesy of D. Fernando Zapata Espinosa; and Sitio Zahe, courtesy of D. Alvaro Domínguez Peón. Two other sets of *títulos*, for Hacienda Canicab (Seyé) and Hacienda Cucá (Tixpeual), are summarized in Chardon, *Geographic Aspects of Plantation Agriculture*, 82-88, 173-176.

19. Marta Hunt, "Colonial Yucatan," 587-589, and "Processes of Development," 51, 54-57, sees the emergence of the "full-fledged" great estate as the dominant force within the local economy by the end of the seventeenth century and a lag of from 50 to 100 years behind central Mexico. Patch, "Formación de estancias y haciendas," and "A Colonial Regime," 124, 210-216, suggests a transition in the latter part of the eighteenth century, and I would agree: see Farriss, "Propiedades territoriales."

20. AGI, Mexico 3052, Relación . . . pósito de Campeche, 3 Jan. to 24 May 1763, and Cabildo Campeche to Crown, 22 Oct. 1763. See also the governor's district-by-district report on agricultural production, in AGI, Mexico 3061, Demostración del número de poblaciones, 15 April 1781; and compare with the Guadalajara region, where independent Indian producers accounted for only 12-13 percent of the maize supplied to the urban market in the period 1750-1770: Van Young, "Urban Market and Hinterland," 629.

21. See appendix 1, "Population of Yucatan, 1806," and chapter 7, note 56, on hacienda populations.

22. Among the many laments about the colony's commercial isolation and/or lack of mineral wealth, see AGI, Mexico 364, Cabildo Merida to Crown, 14 June 1563; Mexico 360, Governor to Crown, 12 Aug. 1635; Mexico 1007, Parecer Junta de guerra, 10 Feb. 1661; Mexico 897, Tesorero interino of Campeche to Governor, 11 Sept. 1703; Tesorero to Crown, 30 Aug. 1705; Mexico 3100, Tesorero Campeche to Crown, 6 Dec. 1756; AGN, Intendentes 52, Governor to Viceroy, 20 Jan. 1798. The detailed annual shipping and customs records forwarded by the treasury officials in Campeche corroborate the lamentations about the low level of trade: AGI, Contaduria 911-919, 1540-1760; Mexico 3132-3138, 1761-1815.

23. AGI, Patronato 80, no. 3, ramo 4, Probanza Marcos de Ayala, 1578, who claimed to have introduced silkworm cultivation as well as the commercial exploitation of dyewood and indigo. The indigo industry, which seems to have flourished in the 1570s (AGI, Mexico 359, Governor to Crown, 26 March 1575; Mexico 101, Memorial Defensor de naturales, 20 Feb. 1576; RY 1: 55, 62, 2: 35, 69-70; DHY 2: 45-53, 68-69), continued for at least a short period after its prohibition in 1581 ("Visita García de Palacio, 1583") and then ceased to be mentioned.

24. MacLeod, *Spanish Central America*, 170-175, describes a similarly abortive attempt to introduce cochineal into Guatemala and suggests elsewhere ("Forms and Types of Work," 86-87) that ignorance of the complex skills involved in cochineal production may have been an obstacle. But in Yucatan the promotor "brought Indians from New Spain who taught the Indians [in Yucatan] how to cultivate cochineal": Cogolludo, Lib. 9, cap. 2.

25. For efforts to break England's virtual monopoly of dyewood in the area, see AGI, Mexico 1007, Exp. sobre el estanco de palo, 1657-1679; Mexico 3100, Autos sobre . . . palo de tinta, 1753-1754; Mexico 3065, Exp. sobre corte de palo, 1785.

26. Pares, *War and Trade in the West Indies*, 547.

27. BN, Archivo Franciscano 55, no. 1150, Discurso sobre la constitución de las provincias de Yucatan y Campeche, 12 July 1766 (published as DHY 3). This astute and detailed report on the local economy, commissioned by *Visitador* José de Gálvez, is an extended inquiry into the causes of contraband; it led to the liberalization of trade restrictions for the colony in 1770.

28. IJ, Description of the Bay of Honduras and the Black River . . . , n.d. (c. 1790), mentions the Baymen's "advantageous trade with the Spaniards." The shipping news published in Jamaican newspapers lists vessels clearing for and arriving from the "Bay of Honduras" and also has some information on ships trading directly between England and Belize: IJ, *Weekly Jamaica Courant*, 1718-1730; *Jamaica Gazette*, 1745-1775; *Jamaica Mercury and Kingston Weekly Advertiser*, 1779-1780; *Royal Gazette*, 1790-1802. The Baymen numbered about five hundred in 1740, according to Pares, *War and Trade*, 102.

29. MacLeod, *Spanish Central America*, 349-351, 356-360, 366, 371-373.

30. AGI, Mexico 898, Oficiales reales to Crown, 20 Oct. 1745. On smuggling with official connivance via *vigía* stations on the north and east coasts (including Bacalar), see AGI, Mexico 2053, Governor and Contador real to Crown, 1 July 1767; Mexico 3057, Governor and Contador real to Crown, 18 Oct. 1775; AA, Oficios y decretos 3, Curate of Valladolid to Bishop, 22 Nov. 1785. For Laguna de Términos and complicity of the local military authorities, see Priestley, *José de Gálvez*, 137-138, 159-161.

31. MacLeod, *Spanish Central America*, 373, 384-385, has suggested that in the late seventeenth and early eighteenth centuries smuggling rivaled, if it did not actually exceed, Central America's legal trade. He may well be right and Guatemala, at least, may be a special case. Guatemala produced the one item besides silver that the English, Dutch, and French coveted from the Spanish Caribbean:

Guatemalan indigo, which was considered to be of the best quality (Pares, *War and Trade*, 101).

32. Although some of the imports from the "Spanish coast" were items (such as mules, horses, cattle, hides, cotton, and sarsaparilla) that Yucatan produced, they were not exclusive to Yucatan, and the specific places of origin mentioned are all on the coast of Tierra Firme and Central America, including the aptly named Puerto Caballos: IJ, Council of Trade, 17 Dec. 1707; Correspondence of William Parke, agent, and Messrs. John and Thomas Eyre (London merchants), 1706-1708; *Royal Gazette, Postscript*, 17 Nov. 1792.

33. See table 12.5 for trade figures.

34. For material on trade with Caribbean ports, especially Havana, see the Libros de cargo y data, port of Campeche, 1774-1815, in AGI, Mexico 3135-3138; Mexico 3052, Exp. sobre que se permita a los habitantes de Yucatan, 1771; AGN, Intendentes 58, Governor to Viceroy, 23 Dec. 1801; AGI, Mexico 1975, Diputados del comercio de Campeche to Crown, 23 April 1808. AA, Asuntos terminados 8, Testamento José Antonio Martínez, 14 Dec. 1796, describes one local merchant's operations in Veracruz, Havana, and New Orleans.

35. AGI, Mexico 1007, Junta de guerra, 10 Feb. 1661; AA, Oficios y decretos 4, Bishop Piña y Mazo to a "pariente" in Spain, n.d. (c. 1783); AGI, Mexico 3100, Juan de Isla to Joseph Banfi, 6 Aug. 1753.

36. The local economy's dependence on the export of these two items lasted from the time of conquest until the late eighteenth century: *Cartas de Indias*, 70-80, Bienvenida to Crown, 10 Feb. 1548; Ordenanzas of Visitador Tomás López Medel, 1552, in Cogolludo, Lib. 5, caps. 16-19; RY 1: 70, 152, 184; Ciudad Real, *Relación* 2: 391-392; AGI, Mexico 897, Tesorero Campeche to Crown, 30 Aug. 1705; Mexico 1039, Governor to Crown, 21 July 1724; BN, Archivo Franciscano 55, no. 1150, Discurso, 1766; AGN, Real caja 54, Governor to Viceroy, 16 Oct. 1771.

37. "Visita García de Palacio, 1583"; AGI, Mexico 359, Lic. Bustamante Andrade to Crown, 11 April 1587. The Indians seem to have retained some rights to gather salt for their own use despite Spanish attempts to monopolize extraction for the local market as well as the export trade: RY 1: 92, 100, 196, 2: 73, 193; AGI, Mexico 3139, Royal cédula to Governor, 22 July 1677; AA, Oficios y decretos 4, Abogado de indios to Crown, 25 Sept. 1781, Bishop to Audiencia of Mexico, 4 Aug. 1782.

38. See BN, Archivo Franciscano 55, no. 1150, Discurso, 1766, and AGI, Mexico 3139, Contador real Merida to Viceroy, 23 Feb. 1787, on the Indians' economic activities. The clergy provided much detailed information on wax hunting and the extraction of other forest products, activities they believed encouraged idolatry and apostasy: see bishops' reports in AGI, Mexico 369, 1643, and Mexico 1039, 6 April 1722; and AA, Visitas pastorales 1, Autos de visita, 1764. On hunting and the export of deerhides, see AGN, Real caja 54, Governor to Viceroy, 27 Sept. 1771. On weaving, see AGN, Historia 498, Expediente sobre el establecimiento de escuelas en Yucatan, 1790-1805, Parecer Defensor de naturales, 20 Dec. 1791; AGI, Mexico 3168, Informe Bartolomé del Granado

Baeza, 1 April 1813 (an incomplete version of this valuable report is published in the *Boletin del Archivo General de la Nación* 12 [1941]: 223-236).

39. The royal *cédula* abolishing the *encomienda*, 16 Dec. 1785, was promulgated in Yucatan in April of the following year. For these and related documents, see "Incorporación a la real corona." On the *encomienda* in Yucatan, see the two complementary studies by García Bernal, *Yucatán*, and *Sociedad de Yucatán*.

40. AGI, Guatemala 128, Tasaciones de los naturales de las provincias de Guatemala, Nicaragua, Yucatan y Comayagua, 1548-1551, ff307-369v, Yucatan, 1549.

41. García Bernal, *Yucatán*, 378-394, summarizes the legislation on tribute in Yucatan through the seventeenth century. The transition to a fully monetary head tax was gradual and not completed until the transfer of all *encomiendas* to the Crown: AGI, Mexico 3139, Reglamento provisional para el cobro de tributo, 28 July 1786.

42. García Bernal, *Yucatán*, 282-297, 399-420. The average *encomienda* income fell from 1,390 pesos in 1607 to 659 pesos in 1666, taxed at 15 percent and rising to 31 percent by 1688 (pp. 418-419).

43. For details on these negotiations, see "Visita García de Palacio, 1583"; AGI, Mexico 3167, Franciscans to Council of the Indies, 3 May 1586; BN, Archivo Franciscano 55, no. 1142, Información hecha por Fr. Leonardo de Correa, 1636; AGI, Mexico 369, Información sobre limosnas, 1643; AGI, Escribanía de cámara 308-A, pieza 16, Información ante el Marqués de Santo Floro, 1643; Sánchez de Aguilar, *Informe*, 81-84 (who maintained the fiction that these were "voluntary contributions").

44. The struggle to regulate *limosnas* began in the sixteenth century (see, for example, AGI, Indiferente 2987, Ordenanzas Visitador Diego García de Palacio, 1584), persisted throughout the seventeenth century (see the series of royal *cédulas* from 1627 to 1665 compiled in AA, Oficios y decretos 2, Varios reales cédulas a favor de los indios; AA, Real cedulario no. 5, Actas del Capítulo provincial franciscano, May 1657; AGI, Escribanía de cámara 308-A, pieza 15, Información sobre la orden de San Francisco, 1680; Mexico 1035, Memorial Franciscan Comisario general, 28 July 1702) until finally taken up by several reforming bishops in the early eighteenth century (see AGI, Mexico 1037, Autos sobre las doctrinas, 1711, and the material cited in note 45).

45. The *arancel* prepared by the bishop in IY, Constituciones sinodales, 1722, ff217-225v, was enforced immediately among the secular clergy but among the Franciscans only after another decade of resistance: AGI, Mexico 3168, Bishop to Crown, 26 Sept. 1726, and 28 July 1737. See also Exp. sobre el sínodo de Yucatan, 1725-1738, in Mexico 1040 (which contains another copy of the minutes and acts of the synod).

46. A detailed description of the Tribunal (established in 1591), its history, personnel, and functions is in AGI, Mexico 3056, Governor to Crown, 8 Nov. 1767.

47. AGI, Mexico 897, Francisco de Aróstegui and Félix de Sosa Aragón to

Crown, 5 July 1723. For evidence on unauthorized fees and gratuities exacted by the governor and other civil officials, see Scholes and Adams, *Don Diego Quijada* 2: 379-391, Sentencia against Quijada, 3 Oct. 1570; AGI, Mexico 359, Franciscan Provincial and Definidores to Crown, 22 June 1629; Mexico 158, Razón de lo que obró en su gobierno . . . (report by Luis Ramírez), 1665; Mexico 1036, Autos sobre repartimientos, 1711; Mexico 3056, Protector de indios to Crown, 11 May 1770. Information on the clergy's unofficial exactions is contained in IY, Constituciones sinodales, 1722, and the documents cited in note 44.

48. Mentioned in AGI, Mexico 359, Franciscans to Crown, 22 June 1629, and Escribanía de cámara 315-A, Pesquisa y sumaria secreta, 1670.

49. González Cicero, *Perspectiva religiosa en Yucatan*, 184-190. See also Scholes and Adams, *Don Diego Quijada* 2: 79-93, Alcalde mayor to Crown, 20 May 1564; AGI, Mexico 369, Bishop to Crown, n. d. (c. 1567).

50. The most notorious and most fully documented example was Governor Rodrigo Flores de Aldana: AGI, Escribanía de cámara 318-A and 318-B, Visita que hizo en los pueblos de esta gobernación, 1659-1665. See also Escribanía de cámara 315-A, pieza 4, Cargos y descargos . . . residencia de D. Rodrigo Flores de Aldana, 1670, cargo 4. The governor made his own investigation of the bishop's *visita*: Escribanía de cámara 315-B, pieza 16, Demanda del Obispo Fr. Luis de Cifuentes, 1670; and Escribanía de cámara 317-C, Papeles y recaudos presentados por . . . Flores de Aldana, 1670. On other *visitas* made by governors or their agents, see AGI, Mexico 3048, Franciscans to Crown, 20 May 1572; Mexico 3167, Memorial Franciscan Provincial, 3 May 1586; Mexico 1039, Testimonio de la visita ejecutada . . . , cuads. 4 and 5, 1722 and 1723. On bishops' *visitas*, besides the material cited in note 49, see AGI, Mexico 359, Governor to Crown, 15 Nov. 1600, 30 April and 14 May 1601; Mexico 360, Governor to Crown, 10 May 1648 (plus three *cuadernos* of supporting material); Escribanía de cámara 308-A, Testimonio de los trasuntos de los indios de 52 pueblos, 1680; Mexico 1036, Testimonio de los doctrineros sobre excesivos derechos, 1711.

51. AGI, Mexico 3139, Resumen de los productos de las encomiendas, 28 July 1786. The subsidy to the Concepcionists had been paid since 1610 (Mexico 3167, Consulta Consejo de Indias, 11 Aug. 1639) and to the Jesuits since 1627 (Mexico 3052, Royal cédula to Governor, 7 May 1627).

52. AA, Capellanías 1, Testamento Juan Antonio Garrido, 24 Aug. 1781. Other AA sections, especially Asuntos terminados, contain testaments (or sometimes merely extracts of pious bequests) with similar clauses drawn up throughout the diocese. See also Marta Hunt, "Colonial Yucatan," 524-525, for another example, from ANM. Cogolludo, Lib. 6, cap. 9, mentioned deathbed restitutions made by a governor to the Indians, "a certain sign that one has not carried on business with a clear conscience."

53. Juan and Ulloa, *Noticias secretas*, 239-250.

54. See García Bernal, *Sociedad*, 126-133, on *repartimientos* in Yucatan. For a similar system in Oaxaca and in Chiapas, see Hamnett, *Politics and Trade in Southern Mexico*; Wasserstrom, *Ethnic Relations in Central Chiapas*, chapter 3; and

Gosner, "Soldiers of the Virgin," chapter 2. Goods were sometimes advanced along with cash, but the main purpose, as in Yucatan, was to force Indian production of exportable goods (cochineal and *mantas* in Oaxaca; cacao and *mantas* in Chiapas).

55. Again, the *juicio de residencia* of Governor Flores de Aldana provides the most detailed information. See especially AGI, Escribanía de cámara 318-A, Averiguación que . . . Fr. Luis de Cifuentes . . . , 1669. Cogolludo, Lib. 7, caps. 8 and 15, Lib. 10, caps 8-13, relates earlier denunciations and the ineffectual attempts of the Crown from 1580 to his own time (1650s) to control these abuses. Subsequent inquiries are essentially variations on the same theme: Mexico 1035, Memoriales sobre abusos de repartimientos de patíes y cera, 1700; Mexico 1036, Autos sobre repartimientos, 1711; Mexico 1020, Exp. sobre repartimientos y servicio personal, 1722-1724 (entire *legajo*); AA, Oficios y decretos 4, Abogado de indios to Crown, 12 Aug. 1782.

56. AGI, Mexico 1037, Defensor de naturales to Crown, 15 Sept. 1711, Mexico 1020, Cabildo Merida to Bishop, 16 Nov. 1723; Mexico 1021, Governor to Crown, 12 Feb. 1724; Mexico 1039, Governor to Crown, 21 July 1724. See also a 1755 inquiry conducted by the governor to prove that *repartimientos* were useful to the Indians (Mexico 3048, Testimonio . . . sobre el repartimiento de patíes y cera).

57. Marta Hunt, "Colonial Yucatan," 513-536, has much information on the activities of peddlers in the countryside.

58. "Visita García de Palacio, 1583"; AGI, Mexico 3048, Autos sobre venta de vinos a los indios, 1609; Mexico 1037, Defensor de naturales to Crown, 15 Sept. 1711; Mexico 1039, Governor to Crown, 2 July 1723. See also the series of parish reports, 1782-1784, in AA, Visitas pastorales 3-6.

59. Spanish items commonly listed were machetes, shotguns, images of saints, silver spoons, and gold jewelry (including rosaries); see, for example, Roys, *Titles of Ebtun*, 294-297, 326-329, 340-341; AEY, Tierras 1, no. 14, Testamento Antonio Tamay, 17 Oct. 1764; Marta Hunt, "Colonial Yucatan," 483; and Philip Thompson, "Tekanto," 112-115, summarizing the contents of the set of Maya wills in the Tekanto *cabildo* records, 1720-1820.

60. See chapter 6 for a discussion of the economic base of the Maya elite.

61. AGI, Mexico 1039, Governor to Crown, 2 July 1723. See also Cogolludo, Lib. 10, cap. 13.

62. AGI, Mexico 158, Auto Audiencia de Mexico, 23 July 1660; Testimonio de las sentencias dadas . . . , 11 Nov. 1667; AA, Oficios y decretos 4, Representación Abogado de Indios, 25 Sept. 1781; AGI, Mexico 3103, Certificado Mayordomo del pósito, Merida, 4 Oct. 1784. See also Cogolludo, Lib. 7, caps. 8 and 15, and AGI Mexico 359, Franciscan Provincial and Definidores to Crown, 10 Feb. 1629, on the activities of governors' commercial agents.

63. Cogolludo, Lib. 6, cap. 9 (1571-1572 famine), and Lib. 12, cap. 21 (1650-1651 famine). Much information on private and official grain requisitions is contained in the reports on the 1769-1774 famine in AGI, Mexico 3057 (for example, Testimonio del informe hecho por el Ilustre Ayuntamiento sobre la

mortandad de tributarios, 1775). See also Patch, "Colonial Regime," 314-318, summarizing the records of one commissioner's foray in 1773. On the 1880-1804 famine, see AA, Oficios y decretos 5, Governor to curas, 17 Dec. 1803, and Governor to Bishop, 31 Dec. 1803 and 13 April 1804.

64. Vicens Vives, *Economic History of Spain*, 346-347. Lynch, *Spain under the Habsburgs* 2: 146, gives more weight to heavy taxation.

65. Colonial land tenure and land acquisitions are dealt with in chapters 9 and 12.

66. Chamberlain, *Pre-Conquest Tribute*.

67. See AGI, Mexico 158, Representación Abogado de indios to Audiencia de Mexico, 1663, and Abogado de indios to Crown, 28 July 1668, for descriptions of the various community service obligations. On service in the *casas reales, correos*, state public works, and transport, see AGI, Mexico 1039, Governor to Crown, 2 July 1723; Mexico 1021, Governor to Crown, 12 Feb. 1724; Mexico 1040, Governor to Crown, 19 March 1734, and Cuaderno de autos sobre servicio de correos, 1737. No one seems to have questioned the obligation to provide transport for curates traveling outside the *cabeceras*, only the amount of food: AGI, Mexico 1037, Testimonio de autos . . . entrega de las doctrinas, 1711; Mexico 1039, Testimonio de la visita . . . de Hunucma . . . a Valladolid, 1722.

68. Scholes and Adams, *Don Diego Quijada* 2: 101-102, Royal cédula to Audiencia de los Confines, 13 Dec. 1551; Ordenanzas Visitador López, 1552; AGI, Indiferente 2987, Ordenanzas Visitador García de Palacio, 1584.

69. On the controversy over Indian *tamemes*, see Scholes and Adams, *Don Diego Quijada* 2: 107-160; AGI, Justicia 1016, ramo 6, piezas 1 and 2, Francisco de Palominos con los encomenderos de Yucatan, 1573-1579.

70. Scholes and Adams, *Don Diego Quijada* 2: 102-108, Traslado del concierto . . . , 27 Oct. 1553; AGI, Mexico 1020, Governor to Audiencia of Mexico, 16 Sept. 1722. In the pueblos, *semaneros* received only 3 reales: AGI, Mexico 3168, Arancel Diocesano, 1737.

71. AGI, Mexico 3048, Representación Fr. Francisco de la Torre et al., 20 May 1572; Mexico 1020, Certificado Escribano mayor de gobierno, 27 July 1722; Mexico 1039, Testimonio . . . vejaciones a los indios, 1722, and Bishop to Crown, 6 April 1722; AA, Asuntos terminados 5, Cuentas del Colegio de San Ildefonso, 1786. For evidence that some of the same abuses occurred in labor service for the Church, see AGI, Mexico 1039, Testimonio . . . indios que trabajaban en la fábrica de la catedral, 1724.

72. AGI, Mexico 1020, Governor to Audiencia, 16 Sept. 1722.

73. AGI, Mexico 1039, Bishop to Crown, 6 April 1722; Governor to Crown, 2 July 1723; AGN, Historia 498, Parecer Defensor de naturales, 20 Dec. 1791, in Exp. sobre establecimiento de escuelas, 1790-1805.

74. AGI, Mexico 1039, Governor to Crown, 2 July 1723; Mexico 886, Consulta Council of the Indies, 10 July 1729; Mexico 3168, Bishop to Crown, 28 July 1737; BN, Archivo Franciscano 55, no. 1150, Discurso, 1766; AA, Oficios y decretos 4, Bishop to Minister of the Indies, July 1784; AGI, Mexico 3168,

Manuel Pacheco to Diputación Provincial, 10 Dec. 1813. For comparative evidence on this common view of the colonized, see Alatas, *Myth of the Lazy Native.*

75. The idea of a cultural conflict between rural peasant attitudes to work and the demands of industrial production is derived mainly from E. P. Thompson, "Time, Work-Discipline and Industrial Capitalism," and Gutman, "Work, Culture, and Society." For similar interpretations applied to commercial agriculture in Anglo- and Latin America, see Genovese, *Roll, Jordan, Roll*, 285-324, and Bauer, "Rural Workers," 48-59. Rodgers, "Traditions, Modernity, and the American Industrial Worker," argues against Gutman's cultural interpretation and attributes absenteeism, high turnover, and other signs of maladjustment to the unstable conditions of employment in industry.

76. The most detailed account of the henequen economy, including labor recruitment, is González Navarro, *Raza Tierra*. I refer not to the harsh conditions on the henequen plantations, which provided some of the best—or worst—evidence for Turner's exposé of Porfirian Mexico, *Barbarous Mexico*, but to the continuation of a state-supported system of compulsory labor.

77. AGI, Mexico 886, Consulta Council of the Indies, 7 March 1722; Mexico 1039, Bishop to Crown, 6 April 1722. This is one of the allegations that neither the governor nor the *cabildos* attempted to refute. For standard *jornales*, see AA, Asuntos terminados 5, Cuentas del Colegio de San Ildefonso, 1786; and Cuentas de Fábrica 1, containing various accounts for church construction, 1784-1816.

78. Bauer, "Rural Workers," 53. See also Klein, "The State and the Labor Market."

79. AGI, Mexico 1020, Cabildo Valladolid to Crown, 27 June 1723. For similar sentiments, see Cabildo Merida to Audiencia of Mexico, 18 Sept. 1722.

80. See AGI, Mexico 886, Consulta Council of the Indies, 10 July 1729, summarizing royal policy from 1662; Mexico 3052, Royal cédula to Bishop, 1 July 1731; and Mexico 3168, Royal cédula to Bishop and Governor, 5 July 1761.

81. This is a notion that persisted throughout the colonial period, and beyond. See, in addition to the references in note 74, RY 2: 192-193, 211-212; Cogolludo, Lib. 10, cap. 13; Sierra O'Reilly, *Indios de Yucatan* 1: 81.

82. The various testimonies and letters of the 1722-1724 controversy in AGI, Mexico 1020 and 1039, deal primarily with household labor. According to Sánchez de Aguilar, *Informe* (1613), 170, "about 1,000 Indians [approximately 2 percent of the colony's tributary population] arrive each Wednesday in Merida for service in the households of *encomenderos* and other *vecinos*."

83. AGI, Mexico 1039, Governor to Crown, 2 July 1723.

84. AA, Real cedulario 5, Actas del Capítulo franciscano, 6 May 1657; AGI, Mexico 1035, Bishop to Crown, 3 April 1702; IY, Constituciones sinodales, 1722; AA, Visitas pastorales 1, Mama, 1768.

85. AGI, Mexico 3168, Bishop to Crown, 28 July 1737.

86. BN, Archivo Franciscano 55, no. 1150, Discurso, 1766. Complaints about forced labor in the *salinas* are recorded: AGI, Indiferente 1373, Memorial Bishop of Yucatan, n. d. (c. 1580); Mexico 360, Governor to Crown, 12 Aug. 1635;

AA, Oficios y decretos 4, Representación Abogado de indios, 25 Sept. 1781, Bishop to Audiencia, 14 Aug. 1782, and Cabildo Merida to Bishop, 8 Sept. 1795. But they do not compare in number or vehemence with the complaints about labor for transport, household service, logging, fishing, and cotton production.

87. On cotton (mainly in eastern Yucatan), see AGI, Mexico 369, Royal cédula to Bishop, 10 Aug. 1664; Mexico 886, Consulta Council of the Indies, 7 March 1722; AA, Oficios y decretos, Razón de los agravios, 22 Nov. 1785; Visitas pastorales 5, Parish reports Chikindzonot, Nabalam, Tihosuco, Ichmul, Tizimin, 1784. On sugar and tobacco (mainly in Campeche and the Sierra districts), see AA, Oficios y decretos 4, Bishop to a "pariente" in Spain, n. d. (1783), and Report to Crown, 23 April 1784; AGI, Mexico 3139, Síndico general to Cabildo Campeche, 9 Aug. 1787; AGN, Intendentes 80, Informe . . . Estanco de Tabacos, 1796; AEY, Ayuntamientos 1, no. 5, Representación Justicias de Dzitbalche, n. d. (1811). See also the district-by-district report on agricultural production in AGI, Mexico 3061, Demostración del número de poblaciones, 15 April 1781.

88. Among the more detailed discussions of conditions of residence on the Spanish estates are AGI, Mexico 1037, Governor to Crown, 15 Sept. 1711; Mexico 3168, Bishop to Crown, 28 July 1737; and Mexico 3139, Contador real to Crown, 28 Feb. 1787.

89. For a discussion of the various types of dispersed settlements, including haciendas, see chapter 7.

CHAPTER 2, INDIAN REACTIONS

1. For recent summaries of the literature, see Denevan, *Native Population*, 1-12, and Borah, "Historical Demography."

2. The high figure is from Borah and Cook, *Aboriginal Population*, and the low figure from Rosenblat, *Población de América*. These and other estimates are reviewed by Denevan, *Native Population*, 77-83. See also Sanders, "Population of the Central Mexican Symbiotic Region," whose calculations yield a total of around 12.5 million for the same area.

3. Lange, "Una reevaluación de la población." Preconquest population estimates for Yucatan, summarized by Cook and Borah, *Essays* 2: 22-24, fall into two main groups. The low figures, given, for example, by Roys, "Lowland Maya Native Society," 661 (300,000), and Sanders, "Cultural Ecology of the Maya Lowlands," 94 (535,000 to 592,000), are derived from the first colonial census of 1549, with relatively conservative additions for contact-period losses and missing regions. The highest figures, including Lange's and an estimate of eight million offered by Helmuth Wagner, "Subsistence Potential and Population Density," are based on calculations of the area's maximum carrying capacity, and they are linked to the issue of agricultural systems and subsistence base, which will be discussed in chapter 4.

4. Cook and Borah, *Essays* 2: 38. Their entire study (2: 1-179) extends to 1960. García Bernal, *Yucatan*, 7-166, covers only the Hapsburg period, up to

1700. Another detailed analysis for the period 1500-1650 is Solano y Pérez-Lila, "La población indígena." All the figures quoted from Cook and Borah and García Bernal in table 2.1, as well as those I derive directly from manuscript sources, should be considered approximations. Aside from inaccuracies in the original counts themselves, these with few exceptions included only tribute-paying Indians or, in the ecclesiastical censuses, what were called *almas de confesión*, and therefore some conversion factor must be used to derive the estimate for total population. For my eighteenth-century estimates based on civil censuses (that is, all but 1736) I have used the factor of 3.7 and for the 1809 count the factor 4, because of the presumably larger number of children in the rapidly growing population.

A conversion factor for the ecclesiastical censuses is more conjectural. Unlike eligibility for tribute and other head taxes, which was set at age 12 for girls and age 14 for boys in Yucatan, there was no fixed age for the group *almas de confesion*," that is, those admitted to first communion and confession. Seven was considered the ideal age (the supposed age of reason in canonical terms) but in practice it varied according to the criteria applied by each parish priest for deciding when a child was adequately *instruído* and according, no doubt, to the quality of instruction and the aptitude of the child. Thus, no standard factor will be strictly correct for all parishes even at the same date. However, Cook and Borah (*Essays* 2: 52-55) have compiled evidence suggesting that the age tended to be close to tributary age and from that they have convincingly derived a conversion factor of 1.67. This evidence is reinforced for the later colonial period by individual parish censuses (AA, Estadistica 1 and 2, 1802-1806), which provide detailed breakdowns according to age and to category. The resulting estimates are generally consonant both with contemporary reports of population trends and with civil tributary lists. For that reason I find the Cook and Borah and García Bernal estimates for ecclesiastical censuses (1609, 1639, 1700, 1736) more acceptable than those offered by Gerhard, *Southeast Frontier*, 62. Gerhard has used a factor of 1.25 for the 1609 and 1639 (but not, inexplicably, for the 1700) censuses, apparently based on a misleading statement in Cárdenas Valencia, *Relación*, 99, which I suggest refers to seven as an ideal rather than actual age for the *alma de confesión* category. For the 1736 census, Gerhard (pp. 62-63) seems to have taken the term "indios" to mean heads of families, whereas the bishop in his report (AGI, Mexico 3168, Bishop to Crown, 28 July 1737) makes clear that his count includes all adult Indians of both sexes, except *reservados*.

No conversion factor has been applied to arrive at the figure I give for 1806. This is derived from parish censuses that were supposed to be listing total population (see appendix 1), and I have conservatively treated the approximately 10 percent of censuses for which there is some doubt about whether all *niños y párvulos* were included as total population as well. This may mean some under-counting for the entire population but would not affect the ratios of Indians to non-Indians, since within each parish the same criterion was applied to all castes.

5. According to Cook and Borah, *Indian Population of Central Mexico*, 48, table 6, the Indian population declined from 6,300,000 in 1548 to 1,891,267 in 1580

and to 1,069,255 in 1608. These figures are more widely accepted than their estimate of 25 million for 1519 and 16,871,405 for 1532.

6. Robinson and McGovern, "Migración regional," compiles birth, marriage, and death figures for Indians for the parish of Uman during the eighteenth century; Marta Hunt, "Colonial Yucatan," 238, 241-242, gives Spanish births and deaths in Merida during the seventeenth century.

7. Cook and Borah, *Essays* 2: 113, fix 1736 as the low point. García Bernal, *Yucatán*, 126-143, makes a good case for recovery beginning around 1700. Losses from the 1726-1727 famine, compounded by epidemic, have been estimated at 17,000 (Molina Solís, *Historia de Yucatán* 3: 178-181, and García Bernal, *Sociedad*, 25). This famine was recalled as severe and possibly as catastrophic as the prolonged famine of 1769-1774 (AGI, Mexico 3057, Testimonio del informe . . . sobre la mortandad de tributarios, 1775; Sierra O'Reilly, *Indios de Yucatan* 1: 16, 74).

8. Wrigley, *Population and History*, 62-70.

9. AGI, Mexico 3057, Estado general de todos los indios tributarios, 10 Feb. 1774, registers losses of 41 percent between 1765 and 1773, including *huídos*, and the total may have reached 50 percent by the final tally. Cogolludo, Lib. 7, cap. 6, estimated that almost half the Indians had died during the series of famines and epidemics that scourged the peninsula from 1648 to 1656.

10. Scanty rains, swarming insects, thirst, and hunger figure prominently in the *tun* prophecies: Roys, "Prophecies," 166-178. Among the *katuns*, 10 Ahau was particularly noted for drought, bringing such severe heat that the "rocks shall crack" (Roys, *Chumayel*, 159), and such mortality that the "vultures shall enter the houses" (Barrera Vázquez and Rendón, *Libro de los libros*, 224-225). Landa, *Relación*, 54-56, records the first "colonial" famine, a five-year period of drought and locusts (1535-1540) between the first and second *entradas*.

11. AA, Oficios y decretos 5, Governor to curas, 17 Dec. 1803; Cabildo Merida to Bishop, 31 July 1804.

12. AGN, Intendentes 75, Autos sobre escasez de maíz en Yucatan, 1795; AA, Oficios y decretos 5 and 6, contain a voluminous correspondence from the governor on efforts to alleviate the famines of 1803-1804 and 1809-1810, including grain shipments from Havana, Veracruz, New Orleans, and Charleston. Cogolludo, Lib. 6, cap. 9, refers to the difficulties of procuring supplies from outside, which he characterized as "too little, too late and too expensive." For the complex negotiations to overcome import restrictions during the 1769-1774 famine (*pace* the introduction of *comercio libre* in 1770), see AGI, Mexico 3054, Governor to Julián de Arriaga, 27 April to 28 Sept. 1771; AGN, Real caja 54, Governor to Viceroy, 19 Jan. to 27 Sept. 1771, and Governor Presidio del Carmen to Viceroy, 21 Dec. 1772.

13. All attempts at famine relief and measures against profiteers (*logreros*) were concentrated on the cities to the neglect of, and often at the expense of, the countryside: see, for example, Cogolludo, Lib. 10, cap. 12; the citations on grain imports in note 12 and on local grain requisitions in chapter 1, note 63;

AGI, Mexico 3054, Autos de la Junta celebrada, 1767-1769. Mexico 3057, cuads. 1, 2, and 3, 1775, contain additional material on private and public relief efforts.

14. AGI, Mexico 1035, Auto Franciscan Definitorio, 16 June 1700: "Pues importa más que no se pierda un indio que cuanto tiene el mundo." Somewhat more moderate but similar sentiments are found throughout the documentation on famines. See, for example, AGI, Mexico 3057, Encomenderos of Yucatan to Treasury officials, 11 Sept. 1770.

15. AA, Oficios y decretos 5, Governor to Bishop, 13 April 1804. Most documents simply refer generally to "roots and wild fruit."

16. Roys, *Ethno-Botany of the Maya*, 226.

17. See AGI, Mexico 360, Governor to Crown, 2 Dec. 1631, 5 Nov. 1653, 20 Nov. 1659, and Memorias de los indios que se redujeron, 1653; Cogolludo, Lib. 12, cap. 23. For similarly premature efforts, see AGI, Mexico 1035, Informe Guardián Oxcutzcab, 30 Nov. 1699 (epidemic); AGI, Mexico 3057, cuad. 1, Autos formados sobre la falta de tributarios, 1775; and AA, Visitas pastorales 3, Parish report Ticul, 1782, and Visitas Pastorales 6, Parish report Conkal, 1785, both relating the general roundup made in 1772.

18. MacLeod, *Spanish Central America*, 49-63, 73-79, 92-94, 104-106; Denevan, *Native Population*, 35-41; Radell, "Indian Slave Trade."

19. According to Cook and Borah, *Essays* 2: 82, free Negroes and mulattoes were still paying tribute in the 1640s. Perhaps a legal obligation existed, but in practice it must have been largely a dead letter by that date. By their calculations the tribute records show only 160 free Negroes and mulattoes. Yet the governor had already reported the presence of 2,000 in the colony in 1618: AGI, Escribanía de cámara 305-A, Auto Governor, 5 Feb. 1618.

20. AGI, Mexico 3048, Governor to Crown, 12 May 1586.

21. See García Bernal, *Yucatán*, 153, on Spanish population in 1676, and p. 101, for a male tributary count of ca. 33,585 in 1666.

22. Cook and Borah, *Essays* 2: 83. This estimate may be high. It probably grossly undercounts the number of *negros* and *pardos* at 350, in view of the 2,000 figure provided by the governor in 1618 (see note 19). On the other hand, it also includes 10,320 *naborías*, who were tribute-paying Indians and should not be included among the *vecino* population.

23. One indication and cause of the *vecino* growth rate is the sharp rise in Spanish births between 1640 and 1700; Marta Hunt, "Colonial Yucatan," 242, figure 3.

24. AGI, Mexico 3061, Demostración del número de poblaciones, 15 April 1781.

25. A set of censuses for 1802-1806, in AA, Estadística. See appendix 1 for a summary by parish and caste.

26. AGI, Mexico 3061, Demostración, 15 April 1781: a total of 16,810 Spaniards.

27. Some of the parish *matrículas* of 1688, in AGI, Contaduría 920, provide a breakdown by caste. Censuses of Franciscan parishes (AGI, Mexico 1035, Matrícula de los vecinos españoles, mestizos y mulatos, 1700, and Matrícula de los

427

indios tributarios, 28 June 1700) show *vecinos*, mostly mestizos, accounting for only 2.6 percent of the rural population in 1700. Information on population distribution for the late eighteenth century is contained in AGN, Historia 498, Exp. formado sobre el establecimiento de escuelas en Yucatan, 1790-1805, and summarized in Cook and Borah, *Essays* 2: 87-91.

28. RY 2: 20-22, 82-84, 131-132, 157-158, 178-179; AGI, Indiferente 1209, Probanza Francisco Niño de Villagómez, 1547; Patronato 80, no. 1, ramo 1, Probanza Hernando de Aguilar, 31 Jan. 1789; and no. 3, ramo 5, Probanza Juan de Montejo 1591; Sánchez de Aguilar, *Informe*, 135-136 (one of the victims was Aguilar's grandfather); Martínez Hernández, *Crónica de Yaxkukul*, 20.

29. AGI, Mexico 359, Información . . . sobre el peligro que tienen con los franceses, 6 Nov. 1565; Mexico 3048, Governor to Crown, 12 May 1586; Escribanía de cámara 305-A, Fiscal contra D. Diego García de Montalvo, 1618-1619, a lengthy case with much detail on matters of defense; Mexico 1007, Consulta Council of the Indies, 22 April 1668; AGN, Real caja 54, Governor to Viceroy, 29 Jan. 1771.

30. AGI, Mexico 3050, Testimonio de autos sobre la sublevación, Dec. 1761, concerning the Canek revolt.

31. This was still the mode of dealing with Indian insurrections and coastal attacks during the 1760s: AGI, Mexico 3050, Testimonio de autos sobre la sublevación, 1761; Mexico 3017, Cabildo Campeche to Crown, 15 Jan. 1763.

32. Reed, *Caste War of Yucatan*, covers the struggle, including the cult of the Speaking Cross, through 1915. For a contemporary analysis of the rebel's attitudes and motives, as well as the historical antecedents of the war, see Sierra O'Reilly, *Indios de Yucatán*.

33. Cogolludo, Lib. 12, cap. 14.

34. AGI, Mexico 3050, Autos sobre la sublevación, 1761.

35. Sierra O'Reilly, *Indios de Yucatán* 1: 87. Sierra O'Reilly, born in 1814, refers to his own late colonial childhood and, although he elsewhere dismisses the Chilam Balam stories as "ridiculous humbug" (1: 32), they left a strong impression on him and on the locally born Spanish population as a whole.

36. Huerta and Palacios, *Rebeliones indígenas*, 29-68, 94-99, 114-135, 174-190.

37. The Bacalar-Tipu apostasy of 1636, taken from Cogolludo, Lib. 11, cap. 12.

38. The Campeche "rebellion" of 1584-1585, taken from Cogolludo, Lib. 7, cap. 11.

39. There were actually two so-called "uprisings" in the Campeche district, one in 1584 supposedly led by the *cacique* of Campeche and the other in 1585, led by D. Andrés Cocom from Sotuta, who had managed to escape while being sent into exile in San Juan de Ulua for idolatry: Sánchez de Aguilar, *Informe*, 137-138; Cogolludo, Lib. 7, cap. 11; AGI, Patronato 58, no. 1, ramo 1, Probanza Juan Vázquez de Andrada, 1598. AGI, Mexico 3048, Governor to Crown, 12 May 1586, relates the Campeche "uprisings" and other suspected movements in Hocaba and around Merida. See also Patronato 75, no. 2, ramo 1, Probanza

Diego Sarmiento de Figueroa, 4 April 1578 (alleged conspiracy in Tekuch); and Mexico 3048, Diligencias que se hicieron, 1607 (alleged conspiracy in Sotuta).

40. In the absence of any local records on the case, later accounts tended to question whether the rebellion was anything more than a minor altercation, inflated by Spanish hysteria and racial hatred: Sierra O'Reilly, *Indios de Yucatán* 1: 20-33; Molina Solís, *Historia de Yucatán* 3: 237-244; and Ancona, *Historia de Yucatán* 2: 438-451. The most reliable published account is Ríos, "La rebelión de Canek," based on an unidentified but obviously accurate summary of the case located in AGN. The complete judicial records are in AGI, Mexico 3050, Testimonio de autos sobre la sublevación que hicieron varios pueblos de esta provincia en el de Cisteil . . . , 1761, and Autos criminales seguidos de oficio de la Real Justicia . . . , 1761.

41. E. P. Thompson, "Moral Economy of the English Crowd," deals with food prices and food riots in eighteenth-century England. Scott, *Moral Economy of the Peasants*, applies the concept to landlord-tenant relations in southeast Asia.

42. On central Mexico and Oaxaca, see Taylor, *Drinking, Homicide and Rebellion*, 112-151; on Guatemala, see MacLeod, *Spanish Central America*, 344-345, and "Ethnic Relations."

43. AGI, Escribanía de cámara 305-A, no. 2, Autos en la causa criminal contra varios indios del pueblo de Tekax, 1610.

44. Villagutierre Sotomayor, *Historia*, 262-264, 303-311, recounts Avendaño's diplomatic mission to Tayasal in 1695.

45. According to the Indians' own testimony in the Canek rebellion (AGI, Mexico 3050, Testimonio de autos, 1761), of the rebel force of 1,200 at Cisteil, 200 were "fusileros," and one of the first steps taken to contain the rebellion was a general confiscation of the "muchas escopetas" belonging to the Indians (Mexico 3050, Ayuntamiento of Merida to Crown, 12 Jan. 1763).

46. AGI, Escribanía de cámara 305-A, Autos Tekax, 1610, Testimonio de Juan Bote.

47. AGI, Mexico 3050, Testimonio de autos, 1761.

48. AGI, Escribanía de cámara 305-A, Autos Tekax, 1610; Mexico 3050, Autos criminales, 1761. The same sentences of drawing and quartering for leaders and 100-200 lashes and exile with forced labor for the moderately culpable were meted out in roughly the same proportions after the 1712 Tzeltal revolt in Chiapas (Gosner, "Soldiers of the Virgin," chapter 4). Harsh, "exemplary" punishment for ringleaders (real or alleged), combined with amnesty for the majority, was common colonial policy, according to Taylor, *Drinking, Homicide and Rebellion*, 120-122.

49. On postconquest political fragmentation, see chapter 5.

50. See Reed, *Caste War*, 24-34, 54-95, on the *ladino* political conflicts prior to and during the first years of the Caste War.

51. AGI, Mexico 3017, Cabildo of Campeche to Crown, 29 Dec. 1761; Mexico 3050, Cabildo of Merida to Crown, 12 Jan. 1762, and Joseph de Alcocer and Juan de Mendicuti to Crown, 30 Aug. 1762.

52. The idea that the Maya, by prearranged signal, would set fire to the

Spaniards' houses as a means of drawing them out unarmed for easier dispatch seems to have been a recurrent fear, for precisely the same plan was attributed to the Campeche conspirators in 1585: AGI, Mexico 3048, Governor to Crown, 12 May 1586.

53. These were, of course, common strategies of local leaders in any peasant society and not confined to colonial regimes: see, for example, Adas, "From Avoidance to Confrontation."

54. Leaving aside how closely controlled slaves were within the system—a point on which Genovese among others has challenged earlier views—the chances of permanent escape were very low: see Genovese, *Roll, Jordan, Roll*, 648-657, and compare with the accounts of runaway slave communities in the Portuguese, Spanish, French, and Dutch colonies, in Richard Price, *Maroon Societies*.

55. Cárdenas Valencia, *Relación*, 113; BN, Archivo Franciscano 55, no. 1150, Discurso, 1766: "Tienen por caudal una libertad ociosa y por ajuar el que no puede incomodarles para llevarlo a costilla siempre que proyectan mudar su mal llamado domicilio."

56. See, for example, Grant Jones, "Levels of Settlement Alliance," on the San Pedro Maya.

57. RY 1: 297, 2: 85. Both the chronicles and the *katun* prophecies of the Chilam Balam books refer to depopulations and resettlements, most often linked with Katun 8 Ahau: See Roys, *Chumayel*, 135-162, and Roys, "Maya Katun Prophecies," 19-29, 25-26. Oral traditions also recorded the en masse abandonment of Mayapan: Landa, *Relación*, 37; RY 1: 254, 286.

58. J. Eric Thompson, "A Proposal for Constituting a Maya Subgroup," is a valiant attempt, but see, on the mixing of ethno-linguistic groups and the gradual extension of Yucatec Maya: AGI, Mexico 369, Report Bishop of Yucatan, 1599; Cogolludo, Lib. 12, caps. 3-7; AA, Oficios y decretos 3, Descripción que hace . . . vicario del Peten, n.d. (1785); Oficios y decretos 4, Bishop to José de Gálvez, July 1784.

59. Spanish reports on settlements of *indios huídos y gentiles* are cited in the prologue, notes 7, 10 and 13. See also, on zones of refuge on the east coast, RY 2: 30-31; Ciudad Real, *Relación* 2: 407-408; Sánchez de Aguilar, *Informe*, 39-40, 120, 164-165; AGI, Mexico 361, Documentos sobre la pérdida del galeón Santiago, 1649; Mexico 1017, Cabildo of Merida to Crown, 7 Oct. 1719, in Exp. sobre desalojo de ingleses, 1702-1760; AA, Visitas pastorales 6, Parish report Tihosuco, 1784.

60. Grant Jones, "Agriculture and Trade," and "The Last Maya Frontiers."

61. In addition to the material on famines and epidemics in note 17, see Cogolludo, Lib. 10, cap. 27; AGI, Mexico 898, Oficiales reales to Crown, 20 Oct. 1745; Mexico 3057, Encomenderos of Yucatan, 11 Sept. 1770, and Autos formados sobre la falta de tributarios, 1775; AA, Cuentas de fábrica, Report cura Chancenote, 1813. On flight after rebellions, see AGI, Escribanía de cámara 305-A, Autos Tekax, 1610; Mexico 3050, Testimonio de Autos and Autos criminales, 1761.

62. The motives attributed in the earlier colonial period were generally either

escape from *vejaciones* or a desire to return to paganism or both: see, for example, DHY 2: 81, Memorial Bishop, 1582; Mexico 359, Governor to Crown, 28 April 1584. By the end of the period, propensity to idolatry had supposedly given way to the more purely profane motives: "por flojos, por ignorantes de la doctrina, por adeudados, o por otros delitos o motivos que les hacen perseguidos en sus curatos y pesada la sociedad de sus pueblos." (AA, Documentos del Petén Itzá, Fr. Francisco Sánchez to Provincial, 16 Oct. 1799).

63. See the reports on the whereabouts of men who abandoned their families, in the episcopal visitations: for example, AA, Visitas Pastorales 1 (Valladolid, 1755, and Bolonchenticul, 1768), 3 (Chicbul, 1781, and Mani, 1782), and 5 (Sotuta, 1784).

64. AGI, Mexico 369, Governor to Crown, 22 Dec. 1604, estimated 30,000 in the Montaña region; Escribanía de Cámara 317-A, Royal cédula to Governor, 1 Aug. 1633, in Causa criminal, cuad. 1, 1670, referred to a recent exodus of 6,000 refugees from the Costa district alone; and Mexico 361, Defensor de indios to Crown, 19 July 1664, alleged a recent loss of 12,000. The figures of 9,423 Indians "reduced" in 1643, and 22,000 in 1652, given by Cogolludo, Lib. 12, caps. 1 and 23, refer in part and perhaps mainly to Indians living in other districts within the pacified area.

65. AA, Visitas pastorales 5, Parish report, Nabalam, 1784. The Indians of Bacalar gained relief from extra *tequios* by making the same threat: AGN, Historia 534, Governor of Presidio of Bacalar to Governor of Yucatan, 31 Aug. 1785.

66. For a sample of the long list of accusations and counteraccusations (involving *vejaciones* of various kinds), see RY 2: 30-31; AGI, Mexico 101, Memorial Defensor de naturales, 20 Feb. 1576; Mexico 3048, Auto Governor, 13 June 1609; Mexico 1037, Royal cédula to Governor, 17 March 1627, and Encomenderos to Bishop, 27 April 1711, in Autos sobre doctrinas de Maxcanu, 1711; Mexico 349, Franciscan Provincial and Definitorio to Crown, 10 Feb. 1629; Mexico 369, Memorial Bishop of Yucatan, 1643; Mexico 158, Juan Ayala Dávila to Council of the Indies, 27 Oct. 1666; Mexico 1036, Autos sobre repartimientos, 1711; Mexico 1039, Bishop to Crown, 6 April 1722; AA, Oficios y decretos 4, Bishop to Crown, 23 April 1783.

67. See Marta Hunt, "Colonial Yucatan," 146-151, 247-262, 315-322, on marriage alliances between local *encomendero* families and peninsular officials.

68. AGI, Mexico 369, Bishop to Crown, 31 Oct. 1668. A considerable portion of the voluminous documentation from Flores de Aldana's *residencia*, which fills nine *legajos* (AGI, Escribanía de cámara 315-A to 318-B), concerns this exodus and flight from other towns in the southern Campeche region. See especially Escribanía de cámara 315-A, Cargos de residencia . . . , 1670 (cargos 2 and 3); Pieza 5, Cuaderno de la residencia en la villa de Campeche, 1670; Pieza 6, Pesquisa secreta, 1670; Pieza 7, Cargos de Campeche, 1670; and Pieza 8, Ratificaciones de los indios, 1670; Escribanía de cámara 317-A, Causa criminal, cuad. 4, Autos contra Antonio González, 1668; Escribanía de cámara 317-B, Causa criminal, cuad. 8, Autos fechos por Pedro García Ricalde, 1668. For

information on the flight of Indians from other districts throughout the peninsula, see especially Escribanía de cámara 317-A, Causa criminal, cuad. 1, Autos
sobre agravios, molestias y malos tratamientos, 1670; Escribanía de cámara 318-
A, Averiguación que . . . Fr. Luis de Cifuentes Sotomayor, obispo, 1669.

69. AGI, Escribanía de cámara 315-A, Pieza 4, Cargos y descargos, 1670
(cargo 6); and Escribanía de cámara 315-B, Pieza 16, Demanda del Obispo Fr.
Luis de Cifuentes, 1670.

70. AGI, Escribanía de cámara, 315-A, Cargos de residencia y descargos, 1670
(cargo 3); Escribanía de cámara 317-A, Causa criminal, cuad. 7, Autos y testimonios presentados . . . por D. Rodrigo Flores, 1668; Escribanía de cámara
317-C, Causa criminal, Papeles y recaudos presentados, 1670.

71. See the material on the reductions cited in the prologue, note 10, and in
Escribanía de cámara 319-B, Residencia tomada al Dr. D. Frutos Delgado, 1672-
1675.

72. Kubler, "The Quechua in the Colonial World," 371-372, who also suggests that flight into the unpacified *montaña* to escape the *mita* and other burdens
was a major cause of Indian population decline in the Andes (pp. 334-339, 347).

73. One of the more extreme cases involves Portuguese dealings with the
Indians in early colonial Brazil, described in detail in Hemming, *Red Gold*. See
also Sánchez Albornoz, *El indio en el alto Peru*, 1-6, on the Spaniards' lack of
simple prudence in Peru, recognized by Viceroy La Palata: "Si cada uno tira de
la manta del indio para cubrirse sólo la harán pedazos y quedarán todos desnu-
dos" (p. 10).

74. Denevan, *Native Population*, 7.

75. See chapter 6, note 66, for calculations of labor required for taxes and
subsistence.

76. AGI, Mexico 3057, Acuerdo Audiencia of Mexico, 27 July 1775, and
Conde de Miraflores et al. to Governor, n. d. (1775).

77. AGI, Mexico 3057, Respuesta Fiscal, 31 Aug. 1777. A decade later many
were lamenting that the province had still not recovered from the "mortandad
de los años de la necesidad": see, for example, AA, Oficios y decretos 4, Bishop
to Crown, 14 Feb. 1784, 29 May 1785; Visitas pastorales 5, Parish report, Nabalam, 1784; Visitas pastorales 6, Parish report, Conkal, 1785.

78. On the failure to discount *huídos y muertos* from the tribute quotas, see,
for example, AGI, Mexico 359, Bishop to Crown, 18 July 1566; and Mexico
898, Oficiales reales to Crown, 2 Oct. 1745.

79. García Bernal, *Yucatán*, 94-109, makes a good case for this sharp drop,
which is also supported by reports of especially heavy losses through mortality
and flight during this period.

80. Cogolludo, Lib. 7, cap. 6.

81. AGI, Escribanía de cámara 319-B, Residencia Frutos Delgado, 1672-1675.
See also Mexico 1035, Memoriales de abusos de repartimientos, 1700; Mexico
1036, Autos sobre repartimientos, 1711; and Mexico 886, Consulta Council of
the Indies, 7 March 1722. These later denunciations attacked the system qua
system as fundamentally abusive, and not the particular actions of the officials.

82. See chapter 1, notes 44 and 45. On the expropriation of *comunidades*, see AGI, Mexico 158, Abogado de indios to Crown, 28 July 1668, and below, chapter 9.

CHAPTER 3, A DIVIDED COLONIAL WORLD

1. References to early *encomendero* activity in the countryside, scattered among the accounts of the conquest period, all emphasize the priority placed on tribute collection and labor drafts; see, for example, Martínez Hernández, *Crónica de Yaxkukul*, 9-11; AGI, Residencia Adelantado Montejo, 1549; and Fr. Lorenzo de Bienvenida to Crown, 10 Feb. 1548, in *Cartas de Indias*, 70-80. For more detailed information, see Cogolludo, Lib. 7, cap. 4; AGN, Inquisición 6, no. 4, Proceso contra Francisco Hernández, 1558-1562; "Visita García de Palacio, 1583"; AGN, Tierras 2688, no. 43, Pesquisa secreta contra Da. Isabel Escobedo, 1583; Tierras 2726, no. 6, Autos de visita del pueblo de Espita, 1583; the *encomenderos'* own reports in RY; and the lengthy lawsuit between the *encomenderos* and the Defensor de indios over *servicio personal*, in AGI, Justicia 1016, ramo 6, 1573-1579.

2. Occasionally *encomenderos* went beyond complaints about the friars' ambitious building projects, excessive *limosnas*, and congregation program and actually opposed evangelization: see Landa, *Relación*, 70; report by Pe. Cristóbal Asencio, 1570, in Roys, Scholes, and Adams, "Report and Census," 24-29; and AGN, Inquisición 32, no. 11, Proceso contra Francisco Hernández, 1561.

3. For a detailed description of such a ceremony, see AGI, Mexico 3048, Toma de posesión de la encomienda de Juan Rosado de Contreras, Hecelchakan, 8 Sept. 1625.

4. This is clear from the *encomenderos'* testimony in AGI, Escribanía de cámara, 315-A, Pesquisa y sumaria secreta . . . Flores de Aldana, 1670; and Mexico 1035, Memoriales sobre abusos de repartimientos, 1700. Unlike the procedure in other colonies, in Yucatan the Indians continued to pay their tribute directly to the *encomenderos*, not via the Treasury officials, who received, again directly from the Indian officials, only that portion of tribute the *encomenderos* owed in royal taxes; see, for example, AGI, Mexico 3132, Libro de cargo y data, Real caja, Campeche, 1761; AGN, AHH 2132, Libro Real común de cargo y data de Real Hacienda, Merida, 1677.

5. See AGI, Mexico 248, Juan de Ayala Dávila to Council of the Indies, 27 Oct. 1666; Escribanía de cámara 315-A, Pesquisa y sumaria secreta, 1670; Mexico 3054, Autos de la junta celebrada en Merida, 1767-1769; Mexico 3057, Conde de Miraflores et al. to Governor, n.d. (1775), and cuad. 1, Autos formados sobre la falta de tributarios, 1775 (prepared by the *encomenderos*). On opposition to *estancias*, see AGN, Tierras 483, no. 2, Cristóbal Carrillo de Albornoz, encomendero de Cuzama, contra José de la Peña, 1728-29; and Marta Hunt, "Colonial Yucatan," 404-409. For other evidence on the *encomenderos'* protective role, see AGI, Escribanía de cámara 305-A, Autos Tekax, 1610; Mexico 3050, Autos criminales, 1761; and Mexico 3053, Causa de remoción Bernardo Echeverría, 1767.

6. Royal cédula of 11 Nov. 1580, quoted in Cogolludo, Lib. 7, cap. 8. See also DHY 2: 51-54, Governor to Crown, 25 March 1582.

7. Cogolludo, Lib. 7, caps. 8 and 15, Lib. 10, caps. 8-13, narrates the struggle from 1580 to the mid-seventeenth century, including the imprisonment of Governor Juan de Vargas in 1631. See also AGI, Mexico 359, Franciscan Provincial and Definidores to Crown, 10 Feb. 1629.

8. AGI, Mexico 369, Royal cédula to Bishop, 10 Aug. 1664; Mexico 886, Consulta Council of the Indies, 7 March 1722.

9. The sources cited in chapter 1, note 55, contain much material on the economic activities of the *capitanes a guerra, tenientes*, and *vigías*. See also AGI, Mexico 1020, Governor to Audiencia, 16 Sept. 1722; Mexico 1039, Governor to Crown, 2 July 1723; Mexico 1021, cuad. 5, Testimonio de declaraciones por los indios, 1723; AA, Visitas pastorales 5, Chancenote and Calotmul, 1784; and Visitas pastorales 6, Oxkutzcab, 1782. By the early eighteenth century *capitanes a guerra* were stationed in Tizimin, Chancenote, Tihosuco, Sotuta, Oxkutzcab, Sahcabchen, Hunucma, and Dzidzontun. *Vigías* were appointed at Chuburna, Chicxulub, Ixil, Telchac, Santa Clara, Dzilam, Río Lagartos, El Cuyo, and Tihosuco (Bahía de la Ascención), but only those in Ixil, Chuburna, and Tihosuco were assigned salaries from the royal treasury (AGI, Mexico 898, Oficiales reales to Crown, 20 Oct. 1745).

10. The system of local administration in force prior to the introduction of subdelegates is described in detail in AGI, Mexico 3139, Reglamento provisional para el cobro de tributos, 28 June 1786. The role of subdelegates and other aspects of late colonial administration are discussed in chapter 12. The *capitanes a guerra* did play a role in local civil administration but only in relation to *vecinos*—for example, in the collection of the *alcabala* (from which Indians were exempt): see Marta Hunt, "Colonial Yucatan," 476-545.

11. Although the emphasis on economic activities in the studies of *corregidores* and *alcaldes mayores* may reflect their own priorities, the fact remains that unlike local officials in Yucatan they were empowered to collect tribute, hear judicial cases, maintain good order, and generally supervise pueblo administration, including the election of Indian officials; see *Recopilación de leyes de los reynos de las Indias*, Lib. 5, tit. 2, leyes 10, 21, 25-27; Gibson, *Aztecs under Spanish Rule*, 82, 90-93; Kubler, "Quechua in the Colonial World," 367-370.

12. AGI, Escribanía de cámara 305-A, Fr. Juan de Coronel to Teniente general, 25 Feb. 1610, in Autos Tekax, 1610. The military analogy was particularly apt in this case, since Coronel and his companion, although not personally under attack, had rescued the local *gobernador* and held off a mob of more than five hundred besieging the *convento*. Similar imagery can be found in the various accounts of Franciscan missionary work compiled by the order from 1605 to 1689 in a *pleito* with the secular clergy, AGI, Escribanía de cámara 305-A, no. 1, piezas 1, 2, 3, 6, 14, and 15.

13. Sanchiz Ochoa, "Cambio cultural dirigido en el siglo XVI."

14. Although the idea that the Portuguese were singularly lacking in racial prejudice has been debunked (see, especially, Boxer, *Race Relations in the Portu-*

guese Colonial Empire), there is substantial evidence for a comparatively relaxed attitude toward assimilation into local ways and groups. On the *prazeros* in East Africa, see Isaacman, *Mozambique*; on the Brazilian backlands, see Morse, *The Bandeirantes*.

15. There is some question about whether the early missionaries (or at least the Franciscans) sought to Hispanize the Indians or merely Christianize them; see Ricard, *La conquista espiritual*, 138-153, 112-113, 495-500; and Baudot, *Utopie e histoire au Mexique*, especially 77-113. The issue of conscious intention is largely irrelevant, however, since even the most "indigenist" friars failed to realize how profoundly Hispanic (and therefore alien to Mesoamerica) their model of a good Christian was. Hispanization was, therefore, a necessary if unwitting part of the millenarian vision. For a clearer treatment of the issue, see Phelan, *The Hispanization of the Philippines*.

16. Many of these accounts are summarized in Hernández, *Misiones del Paraguay*. For a succinct statement of the same paternalist ideal, applied to estate workers, slave and "free," see Chevalier, *Instrucciones a los hermanos jesuítas*, 49-84.

17. Weisser, *Peasants of the Montes*, and Bennassar, *Spanish Character*, provide enough evidence from criminal and Inquisition records to suggest that the sixteenth- and seventeenth-century Spanish peasants, so idealized in the Golden Age literature, were after all made of the same human stuff as the equally exaggerated antihero, the urban *pícaro*.

18. While a large proportion of the reports and letters from bishops, provincials, and parish clergy throughout the colonial period deal with these and related subjects, for a systematic codification see IY, Constituciones sinodales, 1722, "Instrucciones a los curas de indios." The *ordenanzas* issued by *Visitador* Tomás López Medel in 1552 and published in Cogolludo, Lib. 5, caps. 16-19, for the "spiritual and temporal government" of the Indians, were clearly influenced, if not in fact dictated by, the local Franciscans.

19. See, for example, AGI, Mexico 3168, Manuel Pacheco to Diputación provincial, 10 Dec. 1813, who, after listing the various vices to which the Indians were particularly prone, declared that they would always be "gente neófita." By the time of the Third Mexican Provincial Council in 1585, the clergy were already equivocal about whether the problem lay in fact that Christianity was still new or in the inherent incapacity of the Indians; see Llaguno, *La personalidad jurídica del indio*, 117, 121-135, 151-154, 272-277. In Yucatan, the image of Christianity as a young, tender plant among the Indians persisted well into the seventeenth century; see Cogolludo, Lib. 4, cap. 18; AGI, Mexico 1007, Consulta Council of the Indies, 6 Oct. 1664. It eventually gave way to a conviction of innate incapacity: see, for example, IY, Constituciones sinodales, 1722, "Instrucciones a los curas de indios." The Indians of Yucatan, according to the bishop, "son los más bárbaros que hayamos conocido y en quienes menos señales hayamos visto de cristianos y reconocido más y mayores impedimientos para poderlo ser." Later explanations veered between blaming the clergy's negligence for the Indians' "barbarity and idiocy" (AA, Visitas pastorales, 4 and 5, Autos

de visita, Becal, 1782, and Uayma, 1784) or the Indians' "limited intelligence" (AGI, Mexico 3168, Informe Bartolomé del Granado Baeza, cura of Yaxcaba, 1813), or their ineradicable preference for "drunkenness, idleness, and vice" (Mexico 3168, Manuel Pacheco to Diputación provincial, 10 Dec. 1813).

20. The clergy's right to apply corporal punishment occasionally surfaced as one of the more heated issues in the three-way power struggle between Franciscans, bishops, and governors in the early colonial period; see, for example, the documents on the idolatry trials carried out by Diego de Landa, in Scholes and Adams, *Don Diego Quijada*; AGI, Mexico 3167, Franciscans of Yucatan to Council of the Indies, 3 May 1586; Mexico 369, Bishop to Crown, 1 April 1598; and Sánchez de Aguilar, *Informe*, which was an extended brief in the early seventeenth-century conflict over punishment in idolatry cases (see also this chapter, note 30). By the eighteenth century the issue had been reduced to whether the clergy inflicted "excessive" or unjustified floggings; see, for example, AGI, Mexico 1036, Testimonio de informaciones sobre las graves vejaciones . . . Partido de Ticul, 1712; and AA, Visitas pastorales 3, Auto visita, Ticul, 1778 (admonishing the cura not to administer whippings personally and to limit the number of lashes to eight for minor infractions of the rules). Even ecclesiastics who had a reputation for benevolence believed that the Indians' adherence to Christian norms was entirely dependent on corporal punishment: AGI, Mexico 359, Bishop Toral to Crown, 18 July 1566; AA, Visitas pastorales 5, Parish report, Espita, 1784; AGI, Mexico 3168, Informe Bartolomé del Granado Baeza, 1 April 1813.

21. These struggles spanned much of the colonial period: see, for example, AGI, Escribanía de cámara 308-A, no. 1, El Deán y cabildo y clerecía de Yucatan con la religión de San Francisco, 1680-1702, concerning the secularization of six *doctrinas* carried out in 1681 but with thirty *cuadernos* of material dating to 1605. The secularization of another six *doctrinas* in 1754 culminated a struggle lasting from 1702 and filling four *legajos* (AGI, Mexico 1035-1038, Expedientes sobre doctrinas de Yucatan, 1702-1739). The latter conflict included an armed battle between clerics and friars at the wall of the episcopal palace, described in Mexico 1036, Auto Bishop, 8 March 1712.

22. AGI, Mexico 3168, Bishop to Crown, 28 July 1737.

23. AA, Estadística, Parish censuses, 1798-1828. In 1806 the twenty Franciscan *doctrinas* contained 96,305 Indians out of a diocesan total of 272,925 in seventy-one parishes (excluding Tabasco).

24. DHY 2: 48-50, Informe Franciscan Provincial, 1580, giving the figure of thirty-eight friars and eighteen *doctrinas*. However, the Memoria de los conventos, vicarías y pueblos, 1582 (DHY 2: 55-65), lists twenty-three Franciscan *doctrinas*, while the Tasas de los indios tributarios, 3 May 1586 (AGI, Mexico 3168), lists twenty-two with forty-eight "sacerdotes señalados" and 78,099 tributaries (see also DHY 2: 77-79, 80, 682).

25. Genovese, *Roll, Jordan Roll*; Faust, "Culture, Conflict, and Community."

26. See Miller and Farriss, "Religious Syncretism"; AA, Real cedulario 5,

Información sobre que no se doctrinan bien los indios . . . , 1601; AGI, Mexico 369, Bishop to Crown, 1 June 1606, and 24 Feb. 1643.

27. Postconquest pagan "survivals" are discussed in chapter 10.

28. This was a common complaint in the parish reports submitted to Bishop Luis de Piña y Mazo, 1782-1784, in AA, Visitas pastorales 3-6.

29. IY, Constituciones sinodales, 1722, "Instrucciones a los curas de indios."

30. *Encomenderos* as well as the Alcalde Mayor cooperated in the idolatry trials of the 1560s: Scholes and Adams, *Don Diego Quijada*. Governors and *encomenderos* continued to express some concern about the persistence of idolatries: RY 2: 190, 213; AGI, Mexico 359, Governor to Crown, 11 March 1584, 28 April 1584, 9 Oct. 1601. But see the opposition to the clergy's temporal power in idolatry cases: AGI, Mexico 359, Bishop to Audiencia, 2 May 1606, and Bishop to Crown, 6 May 1606; Sánchez de Aguilar, *Informe*, 165 (on the attitudes of *encomenderos*). After the early seventeenth century the civil documentation ceases to be concerned with idolatry except when connected with overt (real or suspected) resistance to Spanish rule. On secular opposition to the friars' congregation program, see chapter 5.

31. The major sources on parish administration in the late colonial period are the detailed and probing visitations of Bishop Luis de Piña y Mazo, 1782-1785, in AA, Visitas pastorales 3-6; the judicial cases and correspondence in Asuntos terminados 2-10, 1774-1819, in Oficios y decretos 2-8, 1762-1814.

32. The governor's salary in 1766 was 4,000 pesos (AGN, AHH 2132, Libro de cargo y data, Merida, 1766); the bishop's share of the 1757 tithe revenue was 4,351 pesos (AGN, Real Hacienda 9, Libro de cargo y data 1759). Based on the number of tributaries, the *obvenciones* income in 1755 from the six largest curacies ranged from 3,150 to 6,804 pesos, not counting parish fees (BL, Add. Mss. 17569, Report on visita pastoral, 1755). By the 1800s the bishop's tithe income had grown to 11,918 pesos (AA, Oficios y decretos 6, Recibo de la quarta episcopal, 18 July 1809), but parish income had increased accordingly, with six parishes yielding over 12,000 pesos (AA, Cuentas de fabríca, 1794-1816).

33. AGI, Mexico 3101, Royal cédula to Bishop, 6 Feb. 1768; AGN, AHN 2132, Libro de cargo y data, Merida, 1766.

34. Forty-six out of the 72 clerics in the diocese in 1643 were unemployed (AGI, Mexico 369, Memoria de la clerecía, 8 March 1643). In 1811, 120 were "sin destino," compared to 97 curates and chaplains (including Tabasco) and 194 assistants: AA, Estadística, Estado que manifiesta al número de sacerdotes, 7 Aug. 1811.

35. AA, Estadística, Relación jurada qu hacen los curas, 1774. The sections Arreglos parroquiales and Asuntos terminados contain much material on the issue of *cóngrua sustención*, on resistance to parish subdivisions, and on the appointment of assistant curates.

36. Again, the most detailed evidence comes from the latter part of the eighteenth century. During the visitation of 1755, the bishop found *all* the Franciscans negligent but apparently removed none (BL, Add. Mss. 17569, Bishop to

Crown, 26 Oct. 1755). Between 1777 and 1784, the curates of the following parishes were found to be seriously negligent in the performance of their pastoral duties: Uman and Sahcabchen (AA, Visitas pastorales 2, 1777 and 1778), Usumacinta and Campeche, 1781 (Visitas pastorales 3), Ticul, Becal, Hopelchen, and Tecoh, 1782 (Visitas pastorales 4), Uman, 1783, and Ichmul, Sotuta, Valladolid, Tikuch, 1784 (Visitas pastorales 5), Chunhuhub and Uayma, 1784 (Visitas pastorales 6). The curates of Tecoh and Chunhuhub were suspended but without losing their benefices (AA, Oficios y decretos 4, Bishop to Crown, 23 April 1783; Causa seguida al cura de Chunhuhub, 1791). The curate of Hopelchen, brought to trial on, among other charges, chronic drunkenness and gambling and physical assaults on parishioners, was permitted to exchange benefices with the curate of Valladolid (AA, Arreglos parroquiales 1, Autos sobre permuta de curatos, 1783). Only the curate of Uman seems to have overstepped the accepted limits by the scale and boldness of his "trafficking," forced labor systems, excessive whippings, extortions and fraud, as well as negligence, and was relieved of his benefice (AGI, Mexico 3064, Causa contra Br. Luis de Echarzarreta, 1783; and correspondence on the case, 1782-1787, scattered in AA, Oficios y decretos 3 and 4). The bishop sought to have the Franciscan provincial remove nine friars serving in three different *doctrinas* on the grounds of "neglect of parish duties, dishonest friendships, ill treatment of the Indians, excessive use of *aguardiente*, and notorious incompetence," but he seems to have been unsuccessful; see AA, Oficios y decretos 4, Bishop to Provincial, 1781, and a lengthy ensuing correspondence through 1784.

37. Complaints about unpaid forced labor in curates' agricultural operations were the most common after complaints about excessive *limosnas* or *obvenciones*. See, in addition to the material in note 36, AGI, Mexico 1039 (1722, 1723, 1724); Mexico 3168 (1737 and 1748); AA, Visitas pastorales 1, 1755; and numerous reports in the sections Asuntos terminados, Asuntos pendientes, Oficios y decretos and Arreglos parroquiales, from 1755-1820; and in the various Reales cedularios and Libros de mandatos, 1628-1812, all in AA.

38. See the parish reports from the Franciscan doctrineros, in AA, Visitas pastorales 3-6, 1782-1784, especially Ticul, Mani, Teabo, and Tixcacalcupul.

39. AGI, Escribanía de cámara 305-A, Autos Tekax, f367v, Certificate of Escribano, referring to D. Fernando Uz, 23 March 1610. The same phrase is used to describe Gaspar Antonio Chi: Sánchez de Aguilar, *Informe*, 144, RY 1: 98, describes D. Francisco Cocom, son of Nachi Cocom, as "hombre muy hábil y ladino" and also mentions "many Indians who are *ladinos*" in the Valladolid area (RY 2: 175). Lizana, *Historia de Yucatan*, 46v, tells of Diego Na, *cacique* of Campeche, the first Indian baptized by the friars, who after he became "ladino y latino y naguatlato [interpreter]," wrote a chronicle in Spanish of the conquest and evangelization of Campeche.

40. On the early Franciscan boarding schools, see Lizana, *Historia de Yucatan*, 47v-48, 50-50v, 52, 56, 61v, 78v-79. The friars may not have taught all the pupils Spanish, as distinct from reading and writing in "Spanish [Latin] characters" in the Maya language. But many learned Spanish to serve as *naguatlatos*

for the friars who were unable to preach in Maya: Ciudad Real, *Relación* 2: 472. See also Sánchez de Aguilar, *Informe*, 72-73; and the *naguatlatos* mentioned in "Visita García de Palacio, 1583," and in the testimony of the Landa idolatry trials in the early 1560s, in Scholes and Adams, *Don Diego Quijada*.

41. Sánchez de Aguilar, *Informe*, 144-145, referring to the same Gaspar Antonio Chi trained by Fr. Diego de Landa and also apparently conversant in Nahuatl (RY 1: 264).

42. RY 1: 83, 139, 2: 29. Don Fernando Uz, in his trial in 1610 (see below) is also described as wearing a Spanish hat, cape, and breeches: AGI, Escribanía de cámara 305-A, Autos Tekax, 1610.

43. Scholes and Roys, *Maya-Chontal*, 11, 248-249.

44. Paxbolon's career is dealt with in Scholes and Roys, *Maya-Chontal*, 175-178, 185-250, 254-264. For information on the military activities of other Indian leaders, primarily in the later sixteenth century, see AGI, Mexico 140, Probanza D. Juan Chan, 1601; Mexico 294, Probanza Andrés de Arroyo, 1604, Escribanía de cámara 305-B, ramo 6, Probanza Antonio de Salas, 1624; Patronato 56, no. 4, ramo 2, Probanza Juan de Contreras Durán, 1610; Patronato 80, no. 1, ramo 1, Probanza Alonso Sánchez de Aguilar, 1617.

45. Most of the evidence from and about Uz is appended to the lengthy trial of the Tekax rebels (AGI, Escribanía de cámara 305-A, Autos Tekax, 1610, ff 367v-389, 420-463v), but other information is scattered throughout the records of the main trial.

46. See, for example, AA, Oficios y decretos 2, Royal cédula circular, 11 Sept. 1766.

47. The Tekax uprising is discussed in more detail in chapter 6.

48. AGI, Escribanía de cámara 305-A, Autos Tekax, 1610. In his two main briefs of 24 and 27 March 1610, the prosecutor asserted that Uz had been a favorite of *Visitador* García de Palacio and of various governors, who protected him, and he argued that Uz should be given exemplary punishment "por ser indio muy ladino, de depravada intención y costumbres, inquieto y ambicioso."

49. Douglas, *Purity and Danger*.

50. RY 2: 191. Although progressively incoherent as it continues, this and a similar passage (2: 212-213) express clearly both the sense of rage and its source.

51. On the revolt and Canek's background, see chapter 2, note 40.

52. Twenty-five years later one of the Franciscans, who perhaps had known Canek personally, cited his case to argue the dangers of Hispanization: "For we have seen that it is precisely the ones [Indians] who by intercourse with the Spaniards have become civilized and learned the Spanish language who have given the most trouble" (AA, Visitas pastorales 6, Parish report, Mococha, 1785, Fr. Lázaro Calderón).

53. On the quasi-slave trade in orphans carried on by both clergy and laity, see, for example, AGI, Mexico 3048, Franciscans to Crown, 20 May 1572; "Visita García de Palacio, 1583"; AA, Visita pastoral 1, Interrogatorio, 1755, and 1764, question 25; Oficios y decretos 5, Exp. sobre extracción de huérfanos, 1804-1805.

54. RY 2: 221-222: Giraldo Díaz de Alpuche, conquistador and *encomendero*, who in fact married not a Maya but an Aztec princess (purportedly a niece of Moctezuma) living in Xicalango. The daughter of don Pablo Paxbolon married a Spaniard but he was not a conquistador, and the daughter of a Spaniard whom Paxbolon himself married after his first wife died may have been a mestiza (Scholes and Roys, *Maya-Chontal*, 248-249, 351).

55. The definitive shift in policy about creating a native priesthood seems to have occurred between the founding of the Colegio in 1536 and the First Mexican Provincial Council in 1555: Llaguno, Personalidad jurídica, 20-21, 32, 169-170; Ricard, *Conquista espiritual*, 398, 404-419.

56. Ricard, *Conquista espiritual*, 419, suggests that a few Indians were ordained in Mexico later in the colonial period, although he gives no examples. According to Figuera, *Formación del clero indígena*, 312-360, some mestizos but no Indians, were ordained in the viceroyalty of Peru, although see Tibesar, "The Lima Pastors." In Yucatan, sons of Indian nobility began to be enrolled in the diocesan seminary in the 1780s: AA, Oficios y decretos 4, Bishop to Minister of the Indies, 13 Nov. 1786; Oficios y decretos 5, Lista de los estudiantes . . . Colegio de San Pedro, 16 Dec. 1806 (5 Maya out of 62 students). In the Colegio de San Ildefonso, 11 out of 617 of the students accepted from 1793 to 1822 were Indians (AA, Expedientes de hábitos, becas y órdenes). I have found no record of Indian ordinations in the sections Informaciones de órdenes and Dimisorias para órdenes, but the documentation is disordered and not necessarily complete.

57. See chapter 8 on the colonial Indian nobility.

58. The literature on race relations, because of its restricted focus on European "racism" in a colonial or neo-colonial setting, is as unilluminating as it is voluminous. A more useful approach, acknowledging the phenomenon as both ubiquitous *and* culturally specific, is Barth, *Ethnic Groups and Boundariess*, 9-38.

59. See, for example , Memmi, *Dominated Man*.

60. See note 15.

61. Marta Hunt, "Colonial Yucatan," chapter 3, discusses the fierce competition for the colony's limited spoils between old-timers and newcomers, with some accommodation through intermarriage.

62. Information on the tasks and working conditions of *servicio personal* in the cities is scattered in many sources: for example, RY 2: 244-263, Alcalde Mayor to Crown, 6 Oct. 1561; AGI, Mexico 3048, Franciscans to Crown, 20 May 1572; AGI, Mexico 1039, Bishop to Crown, 6 April 1722; Mexico 1020, Escribano mayor de gobierno, 27 July 1722, and Procurador Cabildo of Merida to Crown, 8 March 1723. For the later colonial period, episcopal visitations or urban benefices are the chief source: for example, AA, Visitas pastorales 1, Valladolid, 1755, and Campeche, 1757; Visitas pastorales 3, Campeche 1781; Visitas pastorales 6, San Cristóbal, 1785, and Campeche, 1787. See also AGN, Historia 498, no. 7, Exp. sobre el establecimiento de escuelas en Yucatan, 1790-1805, Parecer Defensor de naturales, 20 Dec. 1791.

63. The legal status of the urban *criados* was somewhat obscure, for even the church authorities could not agree on whether they should belong to the Indian

parishes or the *vecino* parishes, and be taxed accordingly; see AA, Asuntos pendientes 2, Exp. sobre derechos parroquiales, 1783.

64. Spanish testaments (in ANM and AA, sections Obras Pías, Cofradías e imposiciones, Asuntos de monjas, Capellanías and Asuntos terminados) are the best available source on *criados*, slaves, and domestic arrangements in general, but see also the testimony of a number of *encomenderos' criados* (AGI, Escribanía de cámara 305-A, Exp. sobre que los encomenderos se aperciban de armas . . . , 1619), who were Spanish-speaking. Another valuable source is a thirty-page fragment of an account book for the not wholly atypical household of the curate of Campeche, covering the years 1746-1762, AC (shelved among the Libros de cofradía).

65. The term *naboría* (or sometimes *laborío*) was originally synonymous with *criado* (RY 2: 40), but separate barrios of *naborías* had already begun to form outside the city walls (*extramuros*) within several decades of the conquest (DHY 2: 55, 63, and 65, Memoria de los conventos, vicarías y pueblos . . . , 1582; Ciudad Real, *Relación* 2: 400-401). Marta Hunt, "Colonial Yucatan," 206-237, discusses the growth of the barrios during the seventeenth century. On the rate of taxation, see AA, Estadística, Relación jurada que hacen los curas, 1774; and AGI, Mexico 3123, Tanteo y corete de la Real caja, Merida, 1785, Ramo Tributo ("según tasa desde immemorial tiempo"). The differences in status and function between *criados*, *naborías*, and *indios de pueblo* are discussed in AA, Asuntos pendientes 2, Representación Diego Hore, 1808.

66. The political administration of barrios and the economic activities of the residents are outlined in AGI, Escribanía de cámara 315-A, Pesquisa y sumaria secreta, 1670, ff210-232v, Testimony of *caciques*, *alcaldes*, and *justicias* of San Cristóbal, Santiago, and Santa Ana; AA, Visitas pastorales 1, Valladolid, 1755, Testimony of *caciques* and *justicias* of San Marcos and Laboríos; AGI, Mexico 3139, Contador real to Viceroy, 28 Feb. 1787; and AA, Asuntos pendientes 2, Representación Diego Hore, 1808. See also AEY, Censos y padrones 1, nos. 1 and 2, Censuses of Merida, 1809, and Campeche, 1810, which list the occupations of barrio residents.

67. Cook and Borah, *Essays* 2: 86.

68. Various *ordenanzas* on the administration of Indian pueblos (those of *Visitador* López, 1552, in Cogolludo, Lib. 5, caps. 16-19; *Visitador* García de Palacio, 1584, in AGI, Indiferente 2987; and Governor Juan de Esquivel, 1666, in Mexico 361) reiterated these general prohibitions in specific terms for Yucatan and incidentally provided much information on *vecino* sojourners and residents (see especially, nos. 13-15 and 21 of Esquivel's *ordenanzas*). One governor made the curiously candid admission that he allowed some *encomenderos* to reside in their districts temporarily "so that they could thereby recoup their diminished fortunes" (Mexico 359, Governor to Crown, 1 June 1598).

69. AGI, Indiferente 2987, Ordenanzas García de Palacio, 1584; and Mexico 3048, Auto Governor, 13 June 1604. Even if this rule was not strictly enforced, both the official *repartimientos* and the private transactions were mediated through

either the Indian officials or local Indian agents: see chapter 1, notes 55, 58, and 63.

70. AGI, Mexico 1037, Governor to Crown, 15 Sept. 1711: 33,774 (35.5 percent) of a total of 95,017 Indians age 14 years and up. The movement to *ranchos* and *estancias* is discussed in chapter 7.

71. Rental of milpa lands to *vecinos* appears in the late colonial municipal accounts incorporated into the Expediente sobre cajas de comunidad de Yucatan, 1805-1806, in AGN, Consolidación 10. Philip Thompson, "Tekanto," 118-120, 123-124, tables 3.3 and 3.5; records eighteenth-century land deeds, including sales to *vecinos*. A handful of the many local property disputes that must have arisen in the pueblos during the colonial period has been preserved in AEY, Tierras 1, nos. 1, 5, 6, 11, and 12, all dating from the late eighteenth and early nineteenth centuries.

72. From the Maya's own perspective, *vecino* residents appear in figure even less prominently in their lives than transients. The only local *vecinos* who receive more than a very rare mention in Indian testimonies, petitions, or local records (except for land deeds) are the curates and occasionally the *capitanes a guerra* (and later the subdelegates).

73. Philip Thompson, "Tekanto," p. 253, table 4.7. The endogamy rate for the entire community was 86.5 percent. However, a comparison of parish registers suggests a considerably higher rate in the suburban barrios than in the pueblos.

74. Mintz and Wolf, "An Analysis of Ritual Co-Parenthood," 190-196.

75. All extant parish registers for the entire archdiocese of Yucatan (excluding Campeche) have been deposited in AGA (separate from the administrative records in AA). The majority date from the eighteenth century, with a small number from the seventeenth, and only the Sagrario in Merida contains entries from the sixteenth century. In the diocese of Campeche the registers remain scattered in the individual parishes. AC contains only the registers from the Sagrario (formerly the parish of San Francisco de Campeche) and some of the suburban parishes (formerly *ayudas de parroquia*): San Román, Lerma, Santa Ana, and Guadalupe. As for the rural parishes, I have verified the existence of colonial-period registers only in Becal and Hecelchakan. My observations on *compadrazgo* are based on a sampling of baptismal records from Santiago (Merida), Mochocha, Hocaba, Maxcanu, and San Román (Campeche).

76. See RY 2: 260-261, Alcalde Mayor to Crown, 6 Oct. 1561; AGI, Mexico 3048, Representación Franciscans of Yucatan, 20 May 1572; Mexico 361, Ordenanzas Governor Esquivel, 1666; Mexico 1039, Bishop to Crown, 6 April 1722. But see one *encomendero*'s assertion (RY 2: 190-191) that Indian women "go in search of Spanish men."

77. All of the *amancebamientos* denounced or investigated during episcopal visitations (see AA, Visitas pastorales) were among *vecinos*. Although the curates complained in their parish reports that the practice was very common among Indians, they presumably handled the cases themselves without episcopal intervention.

78. AA, Estadística, Parish censuses, 1802-1806.

79. Cook and Borah, *Essays* 2: 84, 93-94, based on a variety of censuses and contemporary estimates from 1789 to 1814. Two additional sources support their conclusions: AGI, Mexico 3061, Demostración del número de poblaciones, 15 April 1781, yields a figure of 28.8 percent out of a total population of 210,472; AA, Estadística, Parish censuses, 1802-1806, yield a figure of 29.8 percent out of a total population of 388,752.

80. AGN, Consolidación 4, Cuentas de la Caja de consolidación, Merida, 1806-1809. The alienation of Indian *cofradía* property and *cajas de comunidad* is discussed in chapter 12.

81. Cook and Borah, *Essays* 2: 178-179.

82. According to the population figures in Cook and Borah, *Essays* 2: 214, table 2.4, 28.4 percent for the central Mexican plateau and coasts (excluding Oaxaca).

83. The figure for Oaxaca is 11.7 percent (Cook and Borah, Essays 2: 214, table 2.4); for Chiapas 15.4 percent according to a 1778 census published by Trens, *Historia de Chiapas*, 181-193.

84. Many authors have noted the incidence of "passing" from the *casta* to creole category (see especially Chance, *Race and Class in Colonial Oaxaca*, 128-133, 157-158, 172-181), but not from Indian or African to mestizo or mulatto. Yet, given the blurring of phenotypes at all caste boundaries, the latter type of movement was equally probable.

85. AGI, Contaduría 920, no. 1, Matrícula de los pueblos con certificaciones de sus curas y vicarios, 1688.

86. Episcopal fulminations about sloppy record keeping run throughout the Visitas pastorales section in AA. On the added problems of fraud, see IY, Constituciones sinodales, 1722; and AA, Visitas pastorales 3, Edict Bishop, 2 Jan. 1782, in *visita* of the Cathedral and Sagrario.

87. There has been some confusion in the literature (and in the later colonial documents) about the origin and status of the *indios hidalgos*. Mexicans were the original *naborías*, settling in their own barrios outside the Spanish centers (Santiago and San Cristóbal in Merida, San Román in Campeche, San Marcos in Valladolid, and Santa María in Izamal): DHY 2: 55, 60, 63, 65, Memoria de los conventos, vicarías y pueblos; Ciudad Real, *Relación* 2: 400-401, 413, 433. For that reason the later *naborías* were sometimes identified as descendants of the Mexicans and their lower tax rate was attributed to their services during the conquest; see, for example, Cogolludo, Lib. 7, cap. 4; AA, Oficios y decretos 3, Bishop to Audiencia of Mexico, 22 Nov. 1786. The most reliable sources on the status and origin of the *hidalgos*, based on their own *títulos* are: AGI, Mexico 898, Contador real to Crown, 12 July 1735; Mexico 3139, Contador real to Viceroy, 28 Feb. 1787. See also the prologue, note 22.

88. AEY, Censos y padrones 1, nos. 3-11, cover the rural *partidos*. The occupational category of *labrador* could include everything from *jornalero* to *hacendado*, but it is clear from a variety of other evidence, including the more detailed information in an earlier Franciscan census of *vecinos* (AGI, Mexico 1035, Ma-

trícula de los vecinos españoles, mestizos y mulatos, 1700), that most of the non-Indian *labradores* were *milperos* who, like the Maya, supplemented subsistence agriculture with hunting.

89. Published works from the colonial period in and on Yucatec Maya have been catalogued by Tozzer, *A Maya Grammar*, part 3. There are enough documents written by the Maya themselves (published and unpublished) to correct for any distortions the Spanish clergy may have introduced in their grammars, dictionaries, catechisms, and sermons. My impression of minimal structural change has been supported by a far more knowledgable opinion (Alfredo Barrera Vázquez, personal communication), but I know of no systematic study of the subject.

90. In addition to Spanish incorporations, the Maya vocabulary suffered considerable impoverishment during the course of the colonial period, as can be seen in thir documents and by comparing the sixteenth-century *Diccionario Motul* with the nineteenth-century *Diccionario de la lengua maya*, edited by Juan Pío Pérez.

91. Campbell, Justeson, and Norman, "Foreign Influence on Lowland Mayan Language and Script," assign this influence primarily to the Postclassic, on the basis of glottochronology. It would be difficult with this technique to distinguish loan words arriving in 1450 from those arriving in 1550 (John Fought, personal communication).

92. BN, Archivo Franciscano 55, no. 1150, Discurso, 1766; AA, Oficios y decretos 4, Bishop to José de Gálvez, July 1784. The parish reports in Visitas pastorales 3-6, 1782-1784; and the subdelegates' reports to the governor, 1790-1791, in AGN, Historia 498, Exp. sobre establecimiento de escuelas en Yucatan, 1790-1805, contain similar statements.

93. AGI, Mexico 3048, Testimonio de autos sobre repartimientos, 1755.

94. AA, Oficios y decretos 4, Bishop to José de Gálvez, 13 Nov. 1786; AGI, Mexico 3139, Contador real to Viceroy, 28 Feb. 1787; AGN, Exp. sobre establecimiento de escuelas, 1790-1805, Report from Subdelegate of Campeche, 1791.

95. AA, Vistas pastorales 3, Parish report, Ticul, 1782; Visitas pastorales 5, Parish report, Tixcacaltuyu, 1784.

96. AGN, Historica 498, Exp. sobre establecimiento de escuelas, 1790-1805, contains detailed information on language and primary education in the colony, especially the subdelegates' reports, 1790-1791, and the various *respuestas* of the Asesor general, the Defensor de indios, and the Procurador de indios, 1791-1792. From the clergy's side AGI, Mexico 886, Bishop to Crown, 4 Sept. 1701; IY, Constituciones sinodales, 1722; AA, Visitas pastorales 3-6, Autos de visita and parish reports, 1782-1784.

97. In addition to the material cited above, note 96 (including testimony from *batabs* and *maestros cantores* in the *visitas pastorales*) see chapter 8 on the role of the *maestros cantores*.

98. Various complaints about, and edicts against, the sometimes forceable recruitment of Maya *chichiguas* (wet nurses) and the upper-class custom of leaving children to be brought up entirely by Maya servants were apparently to

little avail; see "Visita García de Palacio, 1583"; AGI, Mexico 361, Ordenanzas Governor Esquivel, 1666, no. 25; IY, Constituciones sinodales, 1722; AA, Visitas pastorales 4 and 5, Parish reports, Teabo (1782), and Yaxcaba (1784).

99. AA, Visitas pastorales 5, Parish report, Espita, 1784. For similar statements, all made by creoles themselves, see the subdelegates' reports, 1790-1791, in AGN, Historia 498, Exp. sobre establecimiento de escuelas, 1790-1805; and AGI, Mexico 3168, Informe Bartolomé del Granado Baeza, 1 April 1813.

100. IY, Constituciones sinodales, 1722; AA, Visitas pastorales 5, Parish report, Ichmul, 1784.

101. See the parish reports in AA, Visitas pastorales 3 (Saclum, 1782), 4 (Becal, 1784), 5 (Xcan, Yaxcaba, Tixcalcaltuyu, Tahdziu, Espita, 1784), and 6 (Uayma, 1784, and Teya, 1785); and the subdelegates' reports in AGN, Historia 498, Exp. . . . escuelas, 1790-1805, according to which even some of the *vecino* schoolmasters did not know Spanish well.

102. AEY, Tierras 1, no. 5, Autos sobre propiedad de un solar, Suma, 1755-1791. See also AEY, Tierras 1, no. 7, Autos sobre la estancia San Antonio, 1789.

103. AGI, Mexico 886, Bishop to Crown, 4 Sept. 1701; IY, Constituciones sinodales, 1722; Mexico 3168, Bishop to Crown, 28 July 1737.

104. See chapter 10 for a discussion of Maya and Spanish religion and possible interchange.

105. As the proverbial exceptions, two brothers in the mid-seventeenth century seem to have been at least partially assimilated into Spanish society and moderately prosperous as *estancia* owners: Marta Hunt, "Colonial Yucatan," 386, 463, 632 note 18.

106. It may be that in Yucatan light-skinned *castas* were able to move into the creole category, as occurred in other colonies, but provision of scholarships, dowries, chantries, and other financial boosts remained tied to Spanish descent, and the relative paucity of economic opportunites would have inhibited mobility in general.

CHAPTER 4, THE ELUSIVE SOCIAL BOND

1. Early colonial speculations, with theological overtones, on the origins of the Indians (see Huddleston, *Origins of the American Indians*) gave way, especially in Yucatan, to debate over who had built the abandoned cities. Lizana, *Historia de Yucatan*, 4, is considered an early proponent (1633) of the Carthaginian thesis, but see AGI, Indiferente 1528, Relación de la gobernación de Yucatan, n. d. (ca. 1580), reporting the discovery of some impressive ruins near Mani (probably Uxmal): "Se cree que la gente que estos edificios hicieron eran de razón y cristianos y algunos curiosos dicen que fueron cartagineses y poblaron en muchas partes." Stephens's arguments that the ruins were an indigenous creation (*Incidents of Travel in Yucatan*) were refuted by local creoles, who understandably found it difficult to accept any link between the subjugated Maya and the remains of a sophisticated civilization, except perhaps as a "raza esclava" who had

labored for some earlier group of foreign conquerors: Sierra O'Reilly, *Indios de Yucatan* 1: 32-34.

2. Meggers, "Environmental Limitations on Cultural Evolution," is an extreme version of the idea, which underlay much earlier discussion of Maya prehistory, that tropical agriculture cannot support a population dense enough for advanced culture. But see note 37, this chapter, for contrary evidence from the Maya lowlands.

3. Recent emphasis in the literature has been on topographic and meteorological variations from zone to zone (summarized in Hammond and Ashmore, "Lowland Maya Settlement," 19-28), which tended to be slighted in the past. But they are subtle variations and do not invalidate the notion of a relatively (in Mesoamerican terms) open and homogeneous environment.

4. For the concept of environmental circumscription, see Carneiro, "A Theory of the Origin of the State," which acknowledges that lowland Maya civilization is an exception, possibly explainable by the existence of population pressure even in an unbounded environment. Sanders and Price, *Mesoamerica*, apply a similar model of geographical circumscription and critical social mass to the basin of Mexico, explaining Maya sociopolitical development as a reaction to expansionary pressure from central Mexico (based on Fried, *The Evolution of Political Society*; see also Barbara Price, "Secondary State Formation").

5. J. Eric Thompson, *Maya History*, 124-158, "Trade Relations between the Maya Lowlands and Highlands," is still a useful survey despite much new material on specific items and routes of exchange. See also Lee and Navarrete, *Mesoamerican Communication Routes*, and the material cited in the prologue, note 3, on the Postclassic "Putun" trading network.

6. Roys, *Indian Background of Colonial Yucatan*, 53-56, and Cardos de M., *Comercio de los mayas antiguos*, summarize much of the documentay evidence on Postclassic trade. See also Anthony Andrews, "The Salt Trade of the Maya."

7. Nicholson, "The Mixteca-Puebla Concept," and Donald Robertson, "The Tulum Murals," refer to a specific stylistic horizon in the Postclassic, but many basic elements of a Mesoamerican cultural configuration are discernible from Olmec times: Michael Coe, *America's First Civilization*.

8. Christopher Jones, "Tikal as a Trading Center."

9. On the shift from riverine to circum-peninsular trade routes and the rise of the "Putun," see J. Eric Thompson, *Maya History*, 3-47, "Putun (Chontal Maya) Expansion," and Christopher Jones, "Tikal as a Trading Center."

10. Grant Jones, "Agriculture and Trade." For additional material on seventeenth-century developments in the southern border zones, see the prologue, notes 7 and 10.

11. Murra, "El control vertical de un máximo de pisos ecológicos."

12. Morris, "Ethno-linguistic Systems." See also Miles, "Summary of Pre-Conquest Ethnology," and MacBryde, *Cultural and Historical Geography*.

13. Exactly what the linguistic boundaries were in this region at the time of the conquest is not known, much less in more remote periods, but see J. Eric Thompson, "A Proposal for Constituting a Maya Subgroup," and, for colonial

evidence, in addition to the documents cited in chapter 2, note 58, see Hellmuth, "Progreso y notas sobre la investigación etnohistórica."

14. Sanders, "Environmental Heterogeneity," and many of the articles in Harrison and Turner, *Pre-Hispanic Maya Agriculture,* provide data on micro–ecological variations.

15. This dual model has been most explicitly formulated by Sanders, "Central Mexican Symbiotic Region," and "Cultural Ecology of the Maya Lowlands," 233-234, but see also Michael Coe, "Social Typology." Sanders has more recently suggested ("Cultural Ecology of the Lowland Maya," 348-353) that population pressure could stimulate some local economic specialization based on variations in agricultural productivity, but without abandoning his original conclusion that local trade and markets were extremely weak in the lowlands.

16. Except for the peddlers' substitution of trucks for pack mules and the villagers' easier access to stores in the district centers (for example, Valladolid), I see little change from the pattern described by Redfield and Villa Rojas (*Chan Kom,* 58-60) for the 1930s.

17. In the southern lowlands, one late Classic structure at Tikal has been tentatively identified as a "market place" (William Coe, *Tikal,* 73; Christopher Jones, "Tikal as a Trading Center"); and another suggested at Quirigua (Sharer, Jones, and Ashmore, *Quirigua Reports 2*). There are, however, no clear criteria for establishing such identities nor, without documentary evidence, for distinguishing between local markets and trading depots.

18. On Postclassic trading depots around the rim of the peninsula, see Chapman, "Port of Trade Enclaves"; Sabloff and Freidel, "Model of a Pre-Columbian Trading Center" (among the various recent publications on Cozumel); Roys and Scholes, *Maya-Chontal,* 33-36, 82-86; Oviedo y Valdés, *Historia,* Lib. 32, caps. 5, 6, and 8. Landa, *Relación,* 96, refers to markets, but without making clear whether they are for local exchange or long-distance trade.

19. Ordenanzas Tomás López, 1552, in Cogolludo, Lib. 5, caps. 16-19.

20. Rathje, "Origin and Development," "Praise the Gods and Pass the Metates," "Classic Maya Development and Denouement," and "Tikal Connection," all develop this theme.

21. See note 20.

22. Sharer, "The Maya Collapse Revisited," 533-534; Ball, "Rise of the Northern Maya Chiefdoms," 110-112; Sanders, "Cultural Ecology of the Lowland Maya," 352-354.

23. We have no figures for the number of craft specialists in the early colonial period, but in the beginning of the nineteenth century *fabricantes* and *artesanos* accounted for about 2 percent of the Indian population outside the Spanish urban centers: AEY, Censos y padrones 9, cenus for all the *partidos,* 1811.

24. Aside from Roys's compilations of sixteenth-century documentary material (*Indian Background,* chapters 7 and 8), many references to the domestic economy of the Maya are scattered among the later colonial records: see especially Sánchez de Aguilar, *Informe,* 148-150; BN, Archivo Franciscano 55, no. 1150, Discurso, 1766; AA, Oficios y decretos 4, Bishop to José de Gálvez, July

1784; and Anonymous report to Bishop, n. d. (ca. 1792); AGI, Mexico 3139, Diego de Lanz to Viceroy, 28 Feb. 1787; AGN, Historia 498, Expedte. sobre el establecimiento de escuelas, 1790-1805, Subdelegates' reports and *pareceres* of Defensor, Abogado, and Procurador de indios, 1790-1791; AGI, Mexico 3168, Informe Bartolomé del Granado Baeza, 1 April 1813.

25. Landa, *Relación*, 40; RY 2: 90. According to RY 1: 124, 2: 73, the coastal provinces lost control over the adjacent salt flats after conquest.

26. Landa, *Relación*, 26, 87, 230.

27. AA, Oficios y decretos 3, Descripción que hace el vicario del Peten de los indios monteses, n. d. (1785). Puleston, "Terracing, Raised Fields, and Tree-cropping," 228-229, mentions the same practice among "old *chicleros*" in the Peten.

28. See Gilman, "Development of Social Stratification," 4-5, for similar reservations about the "commodity-exchange theory of elite origins" (including control of salt) as applied to Bronze Age Europe.

29. For the application of Wittfogel's hydraulic agriculture model to central Mexican sociopolitical development, see Sanders and Price, *Mesoamerica*, 175-188; Barbara Price, "Shifts in Production and Organization," 214-215, 219.

30. Recent research on pre-Columbian agriculture in the lowlands, much of it summarized in Harrison and Turner, *Pre-Hispanic Maya Agriculture*, has provided a useful corrective to earlier notions of the Maya's total dependence on swidden agriculture. The evidence for alternative crops and techniques in some appropriate areas during some periods does not, however, mean that the Maya could not and did not depend primarily on swidden-produced maize, although this is the impression perhaps unintentionally produced by revisionist enthusiasm (for criticism, see Sanders, "Jolly Green Giant," and, for reply, Turner and Harrison, "Comment"). In colonial Yucatan a variety of intensively cultivated garden and orchard crops and forest products was produced and consumed (almost identical to the list compiled by Hellmuth, in "Choltí-Lacandon [Chiapas] and Petén-Ytzá Agriculture," 428-432, except that fish and seafood were confined to coastal dwellers and Spaniards), along with new Spanish foodstuffs (for example, rice, sugar cane, citrus, beef, and pork). But all of these items, new and old, served only as supplements. Maize, "produced mainly in the milpas, although the *solares* produce much corn also," continued to be "the principal and sole sustenance for the entire population" (AGI, Mexico 3054, Governor to Julián de Arriaga, 11 Aug. 1767). By the end of the period this population had reached localized densities comparable to the highest estimates for the Classic Peten. The approximately 16 sq. km. of Merida and *extramuros*, with a population of 25,000 to 30,000 in the late eighteenth century (AGN, Historia 523, Estado general de la problación, 20 May 1791), compares with a population estimated variously at 39,000 (Haviland, "A New Population Estimate") and 20,000 (Sanders, "Cultural Ecology of the Lowland Maya," 355-357) for 64 sq. km. of central Tikal. Campeche contained a nucleated population of approximately 18,000 and Tekax 14,500 *bajo de campana* (see appendix 1) in the early nineteenth century. Local transportation had improved since pre-Columbian times,

but not dramatically (porters continued to supplement mules, and wheeled vehicles were not used); and presumably metal tools increased the yield per man hour (but not necessarily per unit of land). None of this evidence proves that swidden, supplemented by house plot gardening, provided the subsistence base for the pre-Hispanic Peten or elsewhere. It merely suggests that it *could* have done so, since it produced enough maize to feed equivalent population densities in colonial times and also to supply a substantial surplus for export once trade restrictions were lifted.

31. Swidden techniques, which do not seem to have changed throughout the colonial period nor, in essentials, up to the present, are described in RY 1: 263, 305, 2: 192-193; Ciudad Real, *Relación* 2: 390; BN, Archivo Franciscano 55, no. 1150, Discurso, 1766; AGI, Mexico 3168, Parecer Manuel Pacheco to Diputación Provincial, 1 March 1814. Particularly detailed information on milpa preparation, grain storage, and other related matters can be found in Mexico 3048, Instrucciones Governor Diego de Cárdenas, 15 Sept. 1621.

32. On the sixty-*mecate* requirement, see AGI, Indiferente 2987, Ordenanzas García de Palacio, 1584, no. 6; AGI, Mexico 1039, Governor to Crown, 2 July 1723; AA, Oficios y decretos 4, Representación Abogado de indios, 25 Sept. 1781. On the average yield per *mecate*, see AGI, Mexico 3054, Governor to Julián de Arriaga, 11 Aug. 1686. On declining yields and fallow periods, see AGI, Mexico 3048, Instrucciones Governor Cárdenas, 15 Sept. 1631; and Mexico 3168, Parecer Manuel Pacheco to Diputación Provincial, 1 March 1814. The amount of required acreage would of course vary according to local soil conditions and would be considerably reduced in the more fertile central and southern lowlands, without, however, negating the general convenience of dispersed settlements.

33. Sanders, "Settlement Patterns," 69.

34. Although not all contact-period settlements are still occupied, Roys's exhaustive investigations have located a substantial number of the sites abandoned since conquest: see his *Political Geography* and "Conquest Sites."

35. Population pressure has become a favored causal agent in pre-Columbian history, accounting for both the rise of Maya civilization (see Adams, *Origins of Maya Civilization*, especially contributions by R.E.W. Adams, William Sanders, Joseph Ball, and summary by Gordon Willey) and, to a more limited extent, its decline (see Culbert, *The Maya Collapse*, especially Willey and Shimkin, "The Maya Collapse," 486-488, 490-491, 497).

36. No longer questioning the existence of residential concentrations, the discussion of lowland Maya settlement patterns now focuses on the actual size and density of specific sites, the hierarchical relationships among them, the degree of nucleation in general, and the political, economic, and ecological implications of demographic concentrations. See Ashmore, *Lowland Maya Settlement Patterns*, for articles summarizing recent research, as well as discussions of the major methodological and theoretical issues.

37. Siemens and Puleston, "Ridged Fields and Associated Features"; Turner, "Prehistoric Intensive Agriculture"; and Matheny, "Maya Lowland Hydraulic

Systems." See also Harrison and Turner, *Pre-Hispanic Maya Agriculture*, especially Turner and Harrison, "Implications from Agriculture for Maya Prehistory."

38. Boserup, *Conditions of Agricultural Growth*, has been the most influential exponent of this argument, reversing the traditional idea that agricultural innovation precedes and stimulates population increase.

39. See Wrigley, *Population and History*, especially chapter 3. Abernathy, *Population Pressure and Cultural Adjustment*, also argues for homeostatic processes, which can be upset under particular, culturally defined conditions. For the opposite, inexorable "demographic stress" model, see Mark Cohen, *Food Crisis In Prehistory*. For arguments against the validity of the Malthusian model in pre-Columbian Mesoamerica, see Cowgill, "On Causes and Consequences of Ancient and Modern Population Changes," "Teotihuacan, Internal Militarist Competition," 55-58, and his review of Adams, *Origins of Maya Civilization*, in *American Scientist* 67 (1979): 366-367.

40. On colonial population dispersal, see Farriss, "Nucleation versus Dispersal," chapter 7.

41. For a discussion of boundary conflicts, see chapter 9; for late colonial hacienda expansion, see chapter 12.

42. Durkheim, *Division of Labor*, has pointed out the distinction between these two types of social link, the one based on functional interdependence ("organic solidarity") and the other on a kind of moral compact among homogeneous segments ("mechanical solidarity"), but without delving into the purpose or motive behind the latter.

43. See note 24, this chapter, on *macehual* domestic economy.

44. The principal source of Indian property holding and inheritance, and therefore a major key to kinship organization, is wills. They refer predominately to the elite but not exclusively, since the clergy sought to ensure that all Indians, regardless of status and wealth, executed testaments (see IY, Constituciones sinodales, 1722, Instrucciones a los curas de indios). Four collections of Indian testaments have survived that I know of: TUL, Libro de Cacalchen, 1-33, contains thirty-seven wills dated 1646-1679; a similar series of thirty-six wills, 1748-1760, from an unidentified Franciscan *doctrina* in northern Yucatan, misfiled in AA, Documentos del Petén Itzá; the *cabildo* papers of the town of Ebtun, published by Roys, *Titles of Ebtun*, containing a number of wills mainly from the eighteenth and early nineteenth centuries; and a similar set of *cabildo* papers with many wills, mainly from 1720-1820, for the town of Tekanto, in ANM, and analyzed in detail by Philip Thompson, in "Tekanto," chapter 3. Other Indian testaments can be found scattered in ANM and also inserted in many of the lawsuits over land and in most of the estate titles listed in chapter 1, note 18. Another major source for family structure is the house-by-house censuses listed in note 51.

45. The same terms were employed for father/father's brother and for son/ brother's son (see Beltrán de Santa Rosa María, *Arte del idioma maya*, 223, and Philip Thompson, "Tekanto," 67-74, tables 2.1 to 2.5, for kinship terminol-

ogy). Thompson, "Tekanto," 105; Roys, "Personal Names of the Maya," 37-38; and Haviland, "Rules of Descent," all note linguistic evidence for bilateral descent, although they acknowledge the primacy of patrilineal organization. The function of matrilineages, if they did exist, remains obscure.

46. See, for example, AEY, Tierras 1, no. 18, Don Manuel Barnet con los indios Ciau, 1804. This communal work pattern accounts for the residential groupings of patrilateral kin in the dispersed *ranchos*: AA, Visitas pastorales 5, Padrón curato Sisal de Valladolid, 1784; Arreglos parroquiales 1, disputes over Xuxcab, 1784, Santa Rosa, 1789, and Xunabchen, 1804; AEY, Tierras 1, no. 8A, Diligencias practicadas sobre nulidad de la venta del paraje Petcah, 1804; AA, Asuntos terminados 10, Exp. sobre Oxnachboc, 1810.

47. Documentos sobre demarcación de tierras, Tinum, 16 March 1569, in Títulos de Tabi; land titles of Uman, 1557, in Títulos de Kisil; border survey, province of Sotuta, 1545, in "Documentos de las Tierras de Sotuta," published by Roys, in *Titles of Ebtun*, 424-429. Similar designations can still be found in legal documents several centuries later: see, for example, AEY, Tierras 1, no. 18, Escritura de venta, 22 Sept. 1796, giving as the boundaries of a property, "to the east a paraje named Panaba belonging to D. Ignacio Cocom, to the west another named Payum belonging to the Indians Chi, to the north another named Takuch belonging to the Indians Cime. . . ."

48. AEY, Tierras 1, no. 8A, Diligencias practicadas sobre nulidad de la venta del paraje llamado Petcah, 1804.

49. Landa, *Relación*, 99, states that "If they were all daughters, the cousins or nearest relations received the inheritance." But, if Haviland's analysis of dynastic succession in Classic period Tikal ("Dynastic Genealogies from Tikal") is correct, the practice seen in colonial testaments of inheritance by sons-in-law when direct male heirs were lacking may have been an ancient formula and not a colonial innovation at all.

50. Fr. Lorenzo de Bienvenida to Crown, 10 Feb. 1548, in *Cartas de Indias*, 74; Ordenanzas Tomás López, 1552, in Cogolludo, Lib. 5, caps. 16-19; Scholes and Roys, *Maya-Chontal*, 43; Hellmuth, "Choltí-Lacandon (Chiapas) and Petén-Ytzá Agriculture," 438-440. See also the early colonial censuses listed in note 51.

51. "Visita García de Palacio, 1583." For other early colonial house-by-house censuses, see Roys, Scholes, and Adams, "Report and Census," 14-22; and "Census and Inspection of the Town of Pencuyut, 1783"; AGN, Tierras 2726, no. 6, Autos de visita del pueblo de Espita, 1583; Scholes and Roys, *Maya-Chontal*, 470-481, "Matrícula of Tixchel, 1569." For an analysis of extended family organization in a central Mexican district, ca. 1540, see Carrasco, "Joint Family in Ancient Mexico."

52. Ordenanzas Tomás López, 1552, Cogolludo, Lib. 5, caps, 16-19; AA, Visitas pastorales 5, Parish report, Chunhuhub, 1784: "Si son de primeras nupcias, ha de estar corriente en la casa de la novia el indio mozuelo haciendo servicio y amansándose los dos (como ellos dicen) para casarse." See also AGI,

Mexico 3168, Informe Bartolomé del Granado Baeza, 1 April 1813; and Landa, *Relación*, 41, 101.

53. Redfield, *Folk Culture of Yucatan*, 204, 213-216.

54. Ruz Lhuillier, *Costumbres funerarias*, 79-167, summarizes data on types of burials and burial offerings from 115 excavated sites.

55. AGN, Historia 498, Exp. sobre el establecimiento de escuelas en Yucatan, 1790-1805, Parecer Defensor de naturales, 20 Dec. 1791, and Governor to Audiencia of Mexico, 20 Nov. 1795, both of them describing the children's contribution to the household economy as an explanation for parental resistance to schools.

56. Distinctions among heirs were sometimes made in the colonial testaments (see note 44) and may respond to the rule mentioned by Landa, *Relacion*, 99, that brothers inherited equally, "except that the ones who had aided the most notably in increasing the property, they gave the equivalent."

57. The scattered groups of from five to twelve dwellings that Willey and Bullard ("Prehistoric Settlement Patterns," 368) label "clusters," appear to be similar to the *rancherías* and small *ranchos* of colonial documents (see note 46).

58. Tozzer, *Comparative Study*, 1, 4, 36-38, views the Lacandones as a branch of the Yucatec Maya, like the Peten Itza, and therefore presumably an immigrant group. J. Eric Thompson, "Proposal for Constituting a Maya Subgroup," 16-19, argues that they are a separate indigenous group. The most likely explanation for both the strong similarities and the minor differences between modern Lacandones and Yucatec Maya is the heavy postconquest flow of Yucatec refugees from the north, who merged with and eventually engulfed the local population: see chapter 2, note 58. Hellmuth, "Progreso y notas," sees the modern Lacandones as an entirely Yucatec migrant population from postconquest times.

59. On Lacandon social organization, agriculture and material culture, and family-oriented religious rituals, see Tozzer, *Comparative Study*, 38-39, 44-46, 51-73, 80-81, 104-150.

60. Landa, *Relación*, 99. See Roys, "Personal Names of the Maya," 42-44, for a list of known patronymics from colonial records.

61. Philip Thompson, "Tekanto," chapter 2. See also Eggan, "The Maya Kinship System," on cross-cousin marriage, and Haviland, "Rules of Descent," on ambilineal versus patrilineal descent.

62. Landa, *Relación*, 99.

63. We have only indirect evidence from pre-Columbian times of the type of piecemeal migrations so characteristic of the colonial Maya (see chapter 7), in the references to the scattering of populations during times of upheaval: see, for example, Roys, "Maya Katun Prophecies," 19-20, 25-26, and *Chumayel*, 136-141. But such movements are much less likely to have been preserved in the collective memory than the migrations of entire groups (such as that of the "Itza" from northern Yucatan to the Peten), which have been recorded in the chronicles and oral traditions; see RY 1: 297, 2: 85, for migrations of single communities. The wide distribution of patronymics already discernible in the

early colonial censuses (see note 51; Roys has unfortunately lumped together the censuses of 1583 and 1688 in his tabulation, in *Political Geography*, 9, table 1) can be attributed in part to the dislocations that occurred during the conquest, but surely only in part.

64. Becker, "Moieties in Ancient Mesoamerica," suggests that the theme of duality in Mesoamerican symbolic systems could have been linked to a political moiety structure in central Mexico and, by extension, the Maya lowlands. The idea is not implausible, but we still lack concrete evidence.

65. The prevalence of this pattern of nucleated core and dispersed periphery seems to be generally accepted despite disagreement about the kind of socio-political organization the pattern signifies; see, for example, Sanders, "Classic Maya Settlement Patterns," and Freidel, "The Political Economics of Residential Dispersion."

66. See chapter 9 for a discussion of these cooperative efforts on the family and community levels.

67. See, among some of the recent general discussions, Webb, "The Flag Follows Trade"; Carneiro, "Political Expansion"; and Lewis, "Warfare and the Origin of the State."

68. Lewis, "Warfare and the Origin of the State," 208. Historically documented examples of warfare during periods of low and even declining population densities are numerous. Cowgill, "Teotihuacan, Internal Militarist Competition," sees warfare as an explanation for sociopolitical disintegration—that is, the Maya "collapse"—rather than integration, but presents a good case for the motive of territorial hegemony operating independently of poulation pressure on land (but cf. Webster, "Warfare and the Evolution of Maya Civilization," and Ball, "The Rise of the Northern Maya Chiefdoms," 122-132).

69. Stelae reliefs of Maya rulers in battle garb have been reproduced in many publications. For a comprehensive coverage, see Graham and Van Euw, *Corpus of Maya Hieroglyphic Inscriptions*. For mural evidence, see Ruppert, Thompson, and Proskouriakoff, *Bonampak*, 41-64, and figure 28.

70. Although the *batab* (often translated as *caudillo* or *capitán*: see, for example, RY 1: 210, 222, 2: 182) seems to have had an actual battle chief (*nacom*) serving under him, it is clear that one of his major functions was military leadership and a principal attribute of his sovereignty was the authority to call on his subjects to follow him in war; Landa, *Relación*, 122-123; RY 1: 78, 89, 116, 137-138, 148, 149, 176, 187, 226, 270, 288, 2: 66, 185.

71. Webster, *Defensive Earthworks at Becan*; Kurjack and Andrews, "Early Boundary Maintenance." Fortifications at Tikal (Puleston and Callender, "Defensive Earthworks at Tikal") may date from the early Classic (Puleston, personal communication cited in Webster, "Warfare and the Evolution of Maya Civilization," 337). See also Matheny, "Maya Lowland Hydraulic Systems," on a moat and fortification system at Edzna, in southwestern Campeche.

72. Heston and Kessinger, "Toward a Paradigm for Peasant Economies," 9-10; Stein, *Innermost Asia* 1: 12. Blanton, *Monte Alban*, offers a similar explanation for the nucleated settlement at Monte Alban, which grew up apparently without

the stimulus of general population pressure and was abandoned when no longer needed as a counterweight to the power of Teotihuacan.

73. On the taking of prisoners for slaves as a major motive for warfare, see Fr. Lorenzo de Bienvenida to Crown, 10 Feb. 1548, in *Cartas de Indias*, 70-80; Landa, *Relación*, 123; RY 1: 81, 89, 96, 130, 149, 257, 2: 161, 186, 209.

74. RY 2: 66, 186, 209.

75. For data on the social, political, and territorial organization encountered by Spanish soldiers and friars in the southern unpacified zones, see the material cited in the prologue, notes 6, 7, and 10; Grant Jones, "Southern Lowland Maya Political Organization"; Hellmuth, "Some Notes on the Ytza," Progreso y notas," and "Choltí-Lacandon (Chiapas) and Petén-Ytzá Agriculture"; J. Eric Thompson, "Proposal for Constituting a Maya Subgroup," 26-27, 34-36.

76. Grant Jones, "Agriculture and Trade"; Hellmuth, "Choltí-Lacandon (Chiapas)."

77. The eighteenth- and nineteenth-century Spanish accounts of encounters with the *indios gentiles* in the region, cited in the prologue, note 13, indicate the adaptive value of small, dispersed settlement. See also J. Eric Thompson, "Proposal for Constituting a Maya Subgroup," 19.

78. The association between trade and pilgrimage is well documented for the island of Cozumel in the late Postclassic: Landa, *Relación*, 109, 184; RY 2: 54; Cogolludo, Lib. 4, caps. 7 and 9; AGI, Mexico 359, Governor to Crown, 11 March 1584. See also Miller, "The Maya and the Sea," and *On the Edge of the Sea*, chapter 4, on the east-coast sites of Tancah and Tulum. Freidel's suggestion that pilgrimage fairs ("Political Economics of Residential Dispersion," 378-382) were the principal integrative institution among the Classic Maya is, therefore, not implausible, although shrine centers without formalized trading fairs are also possible. And it should be noted that in many cases the major economic underpinning of cults and pilgrimages is not trade but "tribute" or offerings made to the sacred shrine, a part of which may be redistributed to the donors (see, for example, Appadurai and Breckenridge, "The South Indian Temple") or the offerings may be exchanged for other divine "favors" (see, for medieval Europe, Sumption, *Pilgrimage*, and Geary, "Ninth-Century Relic Trade"). Conquest-period pilgrimages to Chichen Itza and Izamal, whatever their economic role in earlier times had been, indicate that among the Maya shrines could attract devotees independently of trading functions.

79. See Miller, *On the Edge of the Sea*, chapter 4, on tutelary deities in eastern Yucatan. The local gods referred to in the Postclassic, which were probably deified lineage ancestors, may have been a late, alien innovation, but the idea of ancestor worship among ruling lineages in the Classic period has also been proposed (see this chapter, note 81), and it is possible that the "emblem glyphs" denoting particular sites (Berlin, "El glifo 'emblema' en las inscripciones mayas," and Marcus, *Emblem and State*) represent tutelary gods.

80. Among the major contributions to the new interpretations are Proskouriakoff, "Historical Implications of a Pattern of Dates," and "Historical Data in the Inscriptions"; Coggins, "Painting and Drawing Styles"; Christopher Jones,

"Inauguration Dates"; Kelley, "Glyphic Evidence for a Dynastic Sequence"; and a number of the contributions in Merle Greene Robertson, *Primera Mesa Redonda de Palenque*, and *Art, Iconography and Dynastic History*. See also the dynastic emphasis in Kubler, *Studies in Classic Maya Iconography*, especially 10-28.

81. See Schele, "Accession Iconography of Chan-Bahlum," and J. Eric Thompson, "Maya Rulers of the Classic Period." This notion goes further than the earlier and perhaps still more generally accepted idea of the deification of rulers after or upon death and a general ancestor cult fostered by ruling lineages; see Ruz Lhuillier, *Costumbres funerarias*, 188-192; J. Eric Thompson, *Maya History and Religion*, 314-319; Michael Coe, "Death and the Ancient Maya."

82. J. Eric Thompson, *Rise and Fall of Maya Civilization*, 81, 264.

83. On preconquest and colonial droughts, see chapter 2, note 10, and table 2.2.

84. Chapter 10 deals with Maya cosmology.

85. If not proven, this is at least the principle informing studies of other societies in which the rulers' links with the sacred are seen as the basis of secular power: for example, Tambiah, *World Conqueror and World Renouncer*; Geertz, *Negara*; Beidelman, "Swazi Royal Ritual."

86. See chapters 9 and 11 on the protective and mediatory roles of the Maya elite.

87. Wheatley, *Pivot of the Four Quarters*, 225, 267, 302-311.

88. See Sanders and Price, *Mesoamerica*, and Barbara Price, "Secondary State Formation."

CHAPTER 5, CREATION OF THE COLONIAL COMMUNITY

1. This delineation, following Roys, *Political Geography*, is somewhat arbitrary for the southern portion of the peninsula. The Chontal-speaking Champoton province is included, but Acalan is not (see Roys and Scholes, *Maya-Chontal*); and Chetumal is defined as a province on the basis of no more evidence than for the center region, which is omitted (see Grant Jones, "Last Maya Frontiers").

2. On memories of Mayapan, see Roys, "Literary Sources," and Documentos sobre demarcación de tierras, Tinum, 16 March 1569, in TUL, Documentos de Tabi. On pilgrimages to Chichen Itza, see AGI, Mexico 104, Probanza Gaspar Antonio Chi; Landa, *Relación*, 54, 109, 180-182, 184; RY 2: 24-26; Scholes and Adams, *Don Diego Quijada* 1: 135-162, Información hecha en el pueblo de Homun, Sept. 1562.

3. Roys, *Political Geography*, 6.

4. On the Chel, see Landa, *Relación*, 40, 52-53; RY 1: 193-194, 68-269; Roys, *Political Geography*, 79-91. On the Cupul, RY 2: 5, 23, 43, 53-54, 86, 129, 150, 161; Roys, *Political Geography*, 113-134. See also AGI, Patronato 65, no. 2, ramo 1, Probanza Francisco de Montejo (hijo), 1563, and for a further discussion of late Postclassic political organization, see chapter 8.

5. Maya *sacbes* (causeways) provide archaeological evidence of earlier hierar-

chical links of the same type revealed in the documentary records: Kurjack and Garza T., "Pre-Columbian Community Form," 300-302.

6. Gibson, *Aztecs under Spanish Rule*, 32-57, 166-172, describes for the valley of Mexico the fragmentation of political units and the development of the Spanish-style *cabildo* government, which was introduced into Yucatan by *Visitador* Tomás López (see Ordenanzas López, 1552, in Cogolludo, Lib. 5, caps. 16-19; and Martínez Hernández, *Crónica de Yaxkukul*, 10, 21). The new political system did not expressly forbid but simply ignored supra-community structures.

7. These separate and equal dealings can be seen in a variety of early postconquest sources on Indian government and tribute collection, in addition to the López Ordenanzas of 1552; see "Visita García de Palacio, 1583"; AGN, Tierras 2726, no. 6, Autos de visita del pueblo de Espita, 1583; and AGI, Indiferente 2987, Ordenanzas García de Palacio, 1584.

8. García Bernal, *Yucatán*, 479-548, lists known *encomienda* grants, 1549-1700.

9. See Gibson, *Aztecs under Spanish Rule*, 102-119, 372-376, on the *cabecera-sujeto* organization of central Mexican parishes.

10. DHY 2: 55-65, Memoria de los conventos, vicarías y pueblos, 1582.

11. This is the major theme of Roys, "Conquest Sites."

12. On boundary adjudications, see Documentos de tierras de Sotuta, 1545, in Roys, *Titles of Ebtun*, 424-427; Land Treaty of Mani, 1557, in Roys, *Indian Background*, 185-190, Land titles of Uman, 1557, in Títulos de Kisil. On territorial ranking in dealings with Spaniards, see, for example, Lizana, *Historia de Yucatan*, 55-56; and the various native accounts of the conquest and early postconquest history (for example, Martínez Hernández, *Crónica de Yaxkukul*) cited in the prologue, note 15.

13. Scholes and Roys, *Maya-Chontal*, 175-178, 185-250, 254-264.

14. The Landa idolatry trials, in Scholes and Adams, *Don Diego Quijada*, contain much information on the continued power of the Cocom, Xiu, and Huit rulers during the transitional decade of the 1560s (see especially 1: 71-129, 135-162). On the Chan family in the former Tases province, see AGI, Mexico 140, Probanza D. Juan Chan, 1601; on the Xiu family, AGI, Escribanía de cámara 305-A, Autos criminals, Tekax, 1610. Roys, *Indian Background*, 129-171, summarizes the colonial history of the Xiu, based on the Xiu family papers, located in the Peabody Museum, Harvard University.

15. AGN, Historia 498, Exp. sobre el establecimiento de escuelas en Yucatan, 1709-1805, Pleito . . . partido de la costa, 1790. I have found references to a royal *cédula* relieving *visita* residents of the obligation to contribute labor and materials to *cabecera* churches (for example, AA, Oficios y decretos 6, cura of Nabalam to Bishop, 26 June 1807), but the practice continued nonetheless (see, for example, AA, Libro de cuentas de fábrica, Seybacabecera, 1798-1827).

16. Días de provincia are listed for most parishes in AA, Visitas pastorales 3-6, Parish reports, 1782-1784. There is also evidence that *visitas* may have been obliged to help support the fiestas of *cabecera* patrons: AA, Real cedulario 5, Actas del capítulo provincial, May 1657.

17. Lizana, *Historia de Yucatán*, 10–31v, is the main source on Izamal's sacred structures, rituals and deity-saints, pre-Hispanic and Christian.

18. Harvey, "Religious Networks on Central Mexico," 137; Vogt, "Some Aspects of Zinacantan Settlement Patterns," 162-163. Conversely, local autonomy can be asserted by refusing to send saints to the *cabecera*: Wasserstrom, "Exchange of Saints."

19. See, for example, AA, Arreglos parroquiales 1, Expedte. sobre erección en ayuda de parroquia, 1792; and AA, Oficios 5, Cura of Abala to Bishop, 26 April 1806.

20. AA, Estadística, Parish censuses, 1798-1821. The censuses for 1821 are incomplete, but at least two new parishes had been added to the seventy-one in existence in 1802-1806. AGI, Guadalajara 323-A, Estadística del Reino de Nueva España, 1810-1811, lists eighty-five for Yucatan, including Tabasco, which had ten parishes. Single-pueblo parishes were: Muna, Saclum, Abala, Maxcanu, Halacho, Chicbul, Espita, Chemax, Xcan, and Chichanha (actually a *misión viva* rather than a true parish).

21. RY, vols. 1 and 2, and BN, Archivo franciscano 55, no. 1150, Discurso sobre la Constitución de Yucatan, 12 July 1766, contain much information on Yucatan's exports. The only change was the virtual disappearance of the early colonial (and preconquest) trade with Guatemala and Honduras. See chapter 1 for a discussion of the colony's export trade in general.

22. The customs records from Campeche (AGI, Contaduría 911-919, 1540-1760; and Mexico 3132-3138, 1761-1815) contain information on the vessels, masters, crew, and cargo of the coastal shipping between Tabasco and Yucatan.

23. See Scholes and Roys, *Maya-Chontal*, 245-247; Cogolludo, Lib. 8, cap. 9; AGI, Mexico 359, Franciscan Provincial to Audiencia of Mexico, 5 May 1606. Much of the trade seems to have been carried on as an adjunct to or under the guise of wax-hunting expeditions into the interior: see AGI, Mexico 369, Bishop to Crown, 24 Feb. 1643.

24. Scholes and Roys, *Maya-Chontal*, 299-315.

25. Chontal surnames accounted for about 11 percent of the total in the district in 1688: Scholes and Roys, *Maya-Chontal*, 314. I have no comparable lists for the late eighteenth century, but all of the *cofradía* officers and civil officials listed in the entire area, including the Usumacinta districts, had Yucatec Maya surnames: AA, Libro de cofradía, Chicbul, 1758-1810; Visitas pastorales 1, Usumacinta, Laguna de Términos, Seyba, Sahcabchen, and Chicbul, 1755; Visitas pastorales 3, Ríos de Usumacinta, Sahcabchen, and Chicbul, 1781.

26. AA, Libro de cofradía, Chicbul, 1758-1810 (entitled "Admon. dineros SSma. Virgen de Mamentel de 1758 a 1759"), so far as is known, the sole source on this trade.

27. J. Eric Thompson, *Maya History*, 9, 45, 306-308.

28. The economic organization of the Yucatecan *cofradías*, based ordinarily on cattle ranching, is discussed in Farriss, "Propiedades territoriales," 164-185, and chapter 9. Nuestra señora de Mamentel and el Cristo de Tichel also had a combined hacienda, but most of the cash income, which fluctuated between 175 and

250 pesos a year, came from the cacao trade. The Mamentel *cofradía* also had 950 pesos invested in *censos* before 1780 (the ony case I have found in Yucatan). By way of comparison, the *cofradía* of Tipikal had a cash income of 25-50 pesos a year, 1739-1786; Hocaba, 100-115 pesos, 1730-1765; and Euan, 78-110 pesos, 1747-1771: AA, Libros de cofradía, nos. 14, 15 and 16.

29. For descriptions of canoe routes through the region, from Tabasco to Campeche, see AGI, Patronato 58, no. 1, ramo 1, Probanza Jorge Hernández, 1585; and Mexico 889, Francisco Gómez de la Madriz to Crown, 2 May 1701.

30. Reed, *Caste War*, 139; Villa Rojas, *Maya of East Central Quintana Roo*, 98. The same practice continued in Chancah, Chumpom, and Tixcacalguardia into at least the early 1970s.

31. Ordenanzas Tomás López, 1552, in Cogolludo, Lib. 5, caps, 16-19.

32. See Redfield and Villa Rojas, *Chan Kom*, 58-60.

33. For descriptions of the activities of peddlers and commercial transactions in Indian pueblos (excluding the official *repartimientos*), see "Visita García de Palacio, 1583"; AGI, Indiferente 2987, Ordenanzas García de Palacio, 1584; Mexico 3048, Autos sobre venta de vino, 1609; Mexico 361, Ordenanzas Governor Esquivel, 1666; Mexico 1035, Autos que remite el governador, 9 Aug. 1700; Mexico 1020, Cabildo de Merida to Bishop, 16 Nov. 1723; AA, Visitas pastorales 1, Valladolid, 1755, Testimony of D. Juan Pacheco et al.

34. See chapter 1, note 63.

35. See Cogolludo, Lib. 4, cap. 18. Fiestas are discussed in chapter 11.

36. The most explicit accounts of this information system are in the two lengthy rebellion trials: AGI, Escribanía de cámara 305-A, Autos Tekax, 1610; Mexico 3050, Testimonio de autos . . . Canek, 1761, and Autos criminales . . . pueblo de Cisteil, 1761. Other judicial inquiries (for example, Mexico 3066, Informaciones instruídas . . . cofradías, 1782, cuads. 5-10, 16-18; and Escribanía de cámara 315-A, Pesquisa y sumaria secreta, 1670) provide further evidence that pueblo officials systematically exchanged information and views on issues of common concern.

37. AGI, Mexico 3050, Autos criminales, 1761.

38. This new rule, apparently decreed by the governor some time in 1762, is mentioned in AA, Real cedulario no. 27, Royal cédula to Bishop, 11 March 1764; and BN, Archivo franciscano 55, no. 1150, Discurso sobre la constitución de Yucatan, 1766.

39. Reed, *Caste War*, 159-228, provides the most vivid account of the Santa Cruz polity in its heyday and decline, but see also Grant Jones, "Revolution and Continuity in Santa Cruz Society," and Dumond, "Independent Maya."

40. Cook and Borah, *Essays* 2: 22-40, discusses the major published documentation on population and settlement at the time of conquest. Unedited sources, like the *residencia* of Adelantado Francisco de Montejo, 1549 (AGI, Justicia 300), and the *probanzas* of conquistadores (scattered mainly in the Patronato section of AGI), provide additional, albeit still impressionistic, evidence. See also Kurjack, *Prehistoric Lowland Maya*, 10-17, for a discussion of sixteenth-century settlement patterns.

41. Compare the town lists in AGI, Guatemala 128, Tasaciones de los pueblos de Guatemala, Nicaragua, Yucatan y Comayagua, 1548-1551, with Memoria de los conventos, vicarías y pueblos, 1582, in DHY 2: 55-65. For information on the congregation program and preceding settlement patterns, see also Roys, *Political Geography*; RY 1 and 2, passim; Cogolludo, Lib. 4, cap 20, Lib. 5, caps. 5 and 7, Lib. 6, cap. 8, and Lib. 8, cap. 6; and Ordenanzas Tomás López, 1552, in Cogolludo, Lib. 5, caps. 16-19. Lizana, *Historia de Yucatan,* pp. 47, 58v-59, 83v-84, deals with the earliest "reductions" of dispersed populations. Gerhard, *Southeast Frontier*, 54-146, provides much information on settlement and political boundaries throughout the colonial period, and excellent maps.

42. See Ricard, *Conquista espiritual*, 265-276; Kubler, *Mexican Architecture* 1: 86-91; and Llaguno, *Personalidad del indio*, 27, 35, 52, 135, 178, 191, 201, 286, on the early missionary efforts in central Mexico. See Cline, "Civil Congregation"; Gibson, *Aztecs under Spanish Rule*, 282-285; Spalding, "Indian Rural Society," 79-81, on later, civil congregations. Villamarín and Villamarín, "Chibcha Settlement," discusses ongoing congregation efforts throughout the colonial period in the Sabana de Bogota, with an early phase, similar to that of Yucatan, pursued at one point (in 1560) by an *oidor-visitador* (p. 40) who appears to be the same Tomás López who enforced the program in Yucatan during his 1552 *visita*.

43. This imagery is expressed most vehemently in many of the parish reports submitted to the bishop in the 1780s. See especially AA, Visitas pastorales 3 (Mani and Ticul, 1782), 5 (Tizimin, 1784), and 6 (Conkal, 1784). But it appears throughout the colonial period, including in reports from civil officials: see, for example, AGI, Mexico 359, Governor to Crown, 28 April, 1584; Franciscans to Audiencia 5 May 1606, and Bishop to Audiencia of Mexico, 2 May 1606; Mexico 369, Bishop to Crown, 10 Dec. 1604, 12 July 1607, 12 Dec. 1607, and 14 Sept. 1665; IY, Constituciones sinodales, 1722; AGI, Mexico 3139, Contador real to Viceroy, 28 Feb. 1787. Sánchez de Aguilar, *Informe*, frequently equates the *monte* with idolatry in his lengthy indictment, and the rhetoric of the various accusations and counteraccusations between civil and ecclesiastical officials about responsibility for Indian flight (see chapter 2, note 66) lays heavy stress on the moral dangers posed by the *monte*. Rosaldo, "Rhetoric of Control," attributes a similar polarity in Spanish views of the Philippine Ilongot and the equation of environmental and moral disorder to a more straightforward concern with sociopolitical control

44. Spanish colonial documents and chronicles rarely refer to the physical dangers of the bush. Its menacing quality is primarily metaphysical, the fact that the vegetation is uncontrolled and also that it hides things from view; see, especially, AGI, Mexico 369, Bishop to Crown, 12 July 1607; Sánchez de Aguilar, *Informe*, 37-38; AA, Visitas pastorales 5, Parish report, Calotmul, 1784.

45. Foster, *Culture and Conquest*, 34, 38-49. See also Kubler, *Mexican Architecture* 1: 91-100, for comparisons between Spanish and Spanish colonial urban planning.

46. See Nuttall, "Royal Ordinances," and Kubler, *Mexican Architecture* 1: 90.

47. The cognitive and psychological unease that the wilderness and its inhab-

itants inspired has been a prominent theme in colonial North American history since Pearce's pioneering study, *Savages of America*. On the need to set symbolic and physical boundaries, see Hiemert, "Puritanism, the Wilderness, and the Frontier"; Plumstead, *The Wall and the Garden*; and Zuckerman, "Pilgrims in the Wilderness."

48. Sarmiento, *Civilización y barbarie*. The morally destructive power of another type of wilderness, the tropical jungle, is the subject of the well-known Colombian novel, *La vorágine*, or *The Vortex* (1924), by José Eustasio Rivera.

49. Mentioned in Sánchez de Aguilar, *Informe*, 173.

50. The evidence for these draconian measures comes primarily from the *encomenderos'* reports in RY (see, especially, 1: 42, 47, 2: 69, 132, 187, 209). But the techniques were common enough elsewhere and the heavy-handedness of the friars well enough documented in other matters (such as the idolatry trials), when they believed the Indians' spiritual welfare was at stake. The native chronicles mention the resettlement only in such laconic statements as: "The scattered divisions of the town under their local chieftains were gathered together" (Roys, *Chumayel*, 149-150; see also Martínez Hernández, *Crónica de Yaxkukul*, 10).

51. RY 1: 42, 47, 49, 182-183, 252-253, 2: 69, 75, 80, 122-123, 132, 201-202, 209. For evidence of active *encomendero* opposition, see Royal cédulas, 9 Jan. and 5 Feb. 1560, quoted in Cogolludo, Lib. 6, cap. 8; and AGN, Inquisición 6, no. 4, Proceso contra Francisco Hernández, 1558-1562.

52. DHY 2: 55-65, Memoria de los conventos, vicarías y pueblos, 1582. This is the number of physically separate communities, excluding the barrios of Merida, Campeche, and Valladolid and counting as one all the pueblos congregated in one site ("en el mismo asiento").

53. AGI, Guatemala 128, Tasaciones de los pueblos de Guatemala, Nicaragua Yucatan y Comayagua, 1548-1551.

54. The additional settlement names are derived from Roys, *Political Geography*; DHY 1: 55-65, Memoria de los conventos, vicarías y pueblos, 1582; documents compiled by the Franciscans on early *doctrina* foundations, in AGI, Escribanía de cámara 308-A, no. 1, El Deán y cabildo de Merida con los franciscanos, 1680, piezas 1 and 2; the idolatry trials of the early 1560s, in AGI, Justicia 245 and 249, Residencia de Diego Quijada, 1565 (partially published in Scholes and Adams, *Don Diego Quijada*); and a variety of other early postconquest documents.

55. The main sources on pre-Columbian wards and *ahcuchcabs* are the definitions in the early dictionaries (see Philip Thompson, "Tekanto," 315-318, table 5.8) and RY 1: 137-138, 2: 85-86, 103-104, 182-183, 211. But much can be inferred from the functions of early colonial *ahcuchcabs*: see, for example, "Visita García de Palacio, 1583"; AGI, Escribanía de cámara 305-A, Autos Tekax, 1610.

56. Villa Rojas, "Notas sobre la tenencia de la tierra," 29-34; Michael Coe, "A Model of Ancient Community Structure," 106.

57. For evidence on patronymic distribution across *parcialidad* boundaries, see Roys, *Political Geography*, 7, 74-75; and AGI, Escribanía de camara 305-A, Autos Tekax, 1610. Spores, *Mixtec Kings*, 91-92, finds no evidence of any kinship

or landholding aspects to the Mixtec barrios, which also seemed to function as purely residential administrative units.

58. AGI, Escribanía de cámara 305-A, Autos Tekax, 1610, has much detail on the administrative functions of *parcialidades* and *ahcuchcabs*. See also Cárdenas Valencia, *Relación historial*, 112-113, and Cogolludo, Lib. 4, cap. 17.

59. Every mention I have seen of a *parcialidad* made after the mid-seventeenth century can be traced to a formerly separate town, except one, a reference to San Felipe and Santiago Yotholin, in TUL, Documentos de Tabi, Mensura de tierras, 20 May 1718.

60. *Ahcuchcab* and *regidor* were interchangeable terms at first (see, for example, "Visita García de Palacio, 1583"). They then seemed to split into two separate offices (see, for example, AGI, Escribanía de cámara 305-A, Autos Tekax, 1610; Mexico 3048, Toma de posesión, Hecelchakan, 3 Sept. 1625; Mexico 140, Petition from town of Sicpach, 12 June 1627), merged again as *ahcuchcabs-regidores* (see, for example, AGI, Mexico 886, Consulta Council of the Indies, 7 March 1722), and then universally as *regidoresob* in the Maya documents. See chapter 8 for a comparison of pre-Columbian and colonial offices.

61. On title to former lands, see Royal cédula, 9 Jan. 1560, quoted in Cogolludo, Lib. 6, cap. 8. Nohcahcab, a town resettled at the site of Becal, sold its former lands in 1700, which became the hacienda of Chactun Nohcahcab (Títulos de Chactun). The lands of Kinlakam, moved to Calkini, became a *cofradía* hacienda belonging to the dominant town (AGI, Mexico 3066, Informaciones instruídas . . . cofradías, 1782, cuad. 1, oral traditions reported by the curate of Calkini, 1782). But Kisil, congregated with Tzeme and then relocated along with Tzeme at Kinchil, lost its separate identity early, and its lands were simply granted in *merced* to a Spaniard in 1603 (Títulos de Kisil).

62. Nunkini, Cuzama (which had been annexed to Homun), and Tabi (annexed to Tibolon) had moved back by the 1650s (Cogolludo, Lib. 4, caps 19 and 20), and Halacho some time between then and 1755 (BL, Add. Mss. 17569, Visita Pastoral, 1755), by which time Polyuc, formerly annexed to Chunhuhub, also appeared as a separate *visita* town.

63. "Visita García de Palacio, 1583," Ordenanza, 13 Dec. 1583, although Cogolludo, Lib. 4, cap. 20, was still referring to these *parcialidades* as separate "pueblos" in the 1650s.

64. The loss of separate status can be traced through the general judicial inquiries, which almost invariably list most of the town officers as well as the name of the town, and sometimes specify whether the town is a *parcialidad*. Especially detailed lists are: AGI, Escribanía de cámara 318-A and 318-B, Visita que hizo D. Diego Flores de Aldana a los pueblos de indios, piezas 1-143, 1666; Mexico 1035, Memoriales de abusos de repartimientos, 1700; Mexico 3048, Testimonio de autos sobre repartimientos, 1755; and Mexico 3066, Informaciones instruídas . . . cofradías, 1782, cuad. 5-10, 16-18. I have found no comparable general inquiry in the early nineteenth century, but see AA, Estadística, parish censuses, 1798-1828, many of which list the separate towns and *parcialidades*.

65. See AGI, Mexico 3066, Informaciones instruídas, 1782; and AA, Visitas

pastorales 3-6, 1782-1785. Other examples are San Pedro and San Juan de Mama, Yaxa at Oxkutzcab (but with only a *teniente de batab*), Santa Barbara and San Mateo Nohcacab, Nohcahcab at Becal, Tzabcanul at Espita, and Chibzul at Chichimila (but with only a *teniente de batab*: see AA, Arreglos parroquiales 1, Exp. sobre permuta de curatos de Chichimila y Muna, 1782).

66. AGI, Mexico 3139, Reglamento provisional para el cobro de tributos, 28 June 1786: "There are towns with two and three caciques and the same number of cabildos with their justicias because they used to belong to two, three or more *encomenderos*, and this has been a source of confusion and disturbances. Therefore, it would be wise to reduce the pueblos of this type to one sole cacique, two *alcaldes* and the corresponding number of *regidores*." However, Espita, for example, still had two *cabildos* in 1817 (AEY, Ayuntamientos 1, no. 28, Petition from las repúblicas de este pueblo de Espita y su parcialidad Tzabcanul, 29 May 1817), and there may have been others that retained this modified compound structure.

67. The *ordenanzas* of the *visitadores* López (1552, in Cogolludo, Lib. 5, caps. 16-19) and García de Palacio (1584, in AGI, Indiferente 2987) make clear that the Spanish did not succeed in eliminating slavery or personal servitude among the Indians immediately. But if some form of master-servant relationship persisted between Maya nobles and individual *macehuales* past the sixteenth century, it escaped the notice of the Spanish.

68. Sánchez de Aguilar, *Informe*, 148.

69. BN, Archivo franciscano 55, no. 1150, Discurso sobre la constitución de Yucatan, 12 July 1766.

70. The detailed records of church construction and adornment, with the names of craftsmen, wages and rations (or payment by the piece for some jobs), and descriptions of materials and procedures, are all from the late colonial period. See AA, Libro de cuentas de fábrica de Ichmul, 1700-1818; a number of account books for church construction in the *legajo* Cuentas de fábrica, especially Chancenote, 1796-1819, San Sebastián, 1796-1815, and Seye, 1811-1812. But see also, on skilled crafts and craftsmen, AA, Libro de cuentas de cofradías del pueblo de Hool, 1741-1799; and Libro de cofradía de Xbalantun (Tipikal) 1736-1787. ANE has much scattered information from the late seventeenth century onwards, and see also Marta Hunt, "Colonial Yucatan," 83-91.

71. Maya masons and *canteros* were paid, in addition to four reales a day in cash, very choice rations of meat, eggs, lard, and spices on top of the usual staples of maize and beans paid to all *jornaleros*. *Semaneros* at best earned four reales a week and often only a ration of maize and beans with no cash wages. A Spanish master carpenter (with "don" preceding his name) was paid one peso a day without rations. Some were paid by the job: Bernardino Canul received 55 pesos for carving the high altar of the Cathedral (AA, Cabildo, Cuentas del coro desta santa iglesia catedral, 1816-1817), and three master carpenters from Xcan received 25 pesos for the *cabecera*'s *coro* (AA, Cuentas de fábrica, Libro 2 de la fábrica de Chancenote, 1796-1819). If a mason worked full time he could

earn as much as a Spanish *teniente de cura* (at a standard salary of 10 to 15 pesos a month) with considerably better rations.

72. On church-building procedures, see in addition to note 70, AGI, Mexico 1039, Declaraciones en atención a pagarse los indios que trabajaban en la fábrica de la catedral, 1724; Mexico 3168, Bishop to Crown, 28 July 1737; AA, Oficios y decretos 4, Bishop to Crown, 14 Feb. 1784. There is also evidence that the barrios and towns near Merida had resident *canteros* skilled enough to supply "worked stone" to the city: AA, Asuntos terminados 9, Razón de las varas cuadradas de piedra de cantería, 30 Dec. 1804.

73. AGI, Mexico 3048, Governor to Crown, 16 April 1585; Mexico 359, Bustamante Andrada to Crown, 4 April 1587.

74. On weaving and other household crafts, see BN, Archivo franciscano 55, no. 1150, Discurso sobre la constitución de Yucatan, 1766; AGN, Real Caja 54, Governor to Viceroy, 16 Oct. 1771; Historia 498, Exp. sobre establecimiento de escuelas en Yucatan, 1790-1805, Parecer Defensor de Naturales, 20 Dec. 1791; AGI, Mexico 3168, Informe Bartolomé del Granado Baeza, 1 April 1813. As for pottery, clay pots of various kinds were early tribute items, but the only two references I have seen to pottery produced for sale are a complaint from the *batab* of Uayma that some Spaniard had appropriated the clay pit ("mina de barro") they depended on for some income (AGI, Mexico 3066, Informaciones instruídas . . . cofradías, 1782, cuad. 8) and a note to an 1811 census explaining that the potters in the pueblo of Tepakam who manufactured clay pitchers were also milpa farmers (AEY, Censos 1, no 4, Estado general de la población de este partido del Camino Real Alto, 13 March 1811).

75. AA, Oficios y decretos 4, Representación Abogado de indios, 25 Sept. 1781; and Informe Tesorero Real, 3 April 1782.

76. Similar to nineteenth-century Irish peasant society, except that the taxes paid by the women's weaving and spinning was in the form of land rents: Lees, "Mid-Victorian Migration," 28. *Visitador* López's order that *macehual* men should learn to weave in order to help their wives in producing *mantas* for tribute (Ordenanzas Tomás López, 1552, in Cogolludo, Lib. 5, caps. 16-19) clearly went unheeded.

77. Some income was derived from the sale of the deer hides for export (AGN, Real caja 54, Governor to Viceroy, 27 Sept. 1771), but this must have been a very minor item in the Indians' domestic economy and in the export trade.

78. See chapter 9 for a comparison of Spanish and Maya *cofradías*.

79. Geertz, "Form and Variation in Balinese Village Structure."

CHAPTER 6, SNAGS AND TEARS

1. The original order in the Ordenanzas of Tomás López, 1552 (Cogolludo, Lib. 5, caps. 16-19), which were essentially a Franciscan program, was repeated during the course of the colonial period: see, for example, AGI, Mexico 361, Ordenanzas Governor Esquivel, 1666, no. 10: "In order to avoid other sins and offenses against Our Lord, the pueblo officials are to take care that husband and

wife live in a house of their own and not mixed together with others no matter how closely related." On the Maya's alleged tendency toward incest, caused by multiple-family residence, see AGI, Mexico 369, Bishop to Crown, 14 Sept. 1665; IY, Constituciones sinodales, 1722; AGI, Mexico 3168, Bishop to Crown, 28 July 1737 and 8 July 1769, Informe Bartolomé del Granado Baeza, 1 April 1813, and Manuel Pacheco to Diputación Provincial, 10 Dec. 1813; AA, Papeles de los señores Gala, Guerra, Carrillo y Piña, Memorial Fr. Joseph Baraona, 21 May 1770; and a number of parish reports, in AA, Visitas pastorales 3-6, especially Teabo and Mani, 1782, Telchac, 1784, and Conkal, 1785.

2. This was especially so in the dispersed *ranchos*, but see also the house-by-house census for the town of Bolonpoxche, parish of Uman (AA, Estadística, Matrícula de los vecinos e indios, 1815), in which all the dispersed Indian households were composed of three or more adults, and of those *bajo de campana* (in the congregated towns) 39.7 percent contained three or more (27.6 percent contained four or more). This is a substantial proportion, but a considerable decline from the 1583 figures for Tizimin ("Visita García de Palacio, 1583"), in which all but 7 percent of the households were multiple-family residential units.

3. See Landa, *Relación*, 99, on inheritance rules and chapter 4, note 44, on colonial Maya testaments.

4. Actually, a testator could dispose of up to one-fifth of the property as he saw fit, either increasing the portion of one or more of the children, allocating all or part to other relatives or to servants, or, very commonly, devoting this portion to the "benefit of the soul" of the testator, in masses, chantries, or other pious works. The point is that the bulk of the estate was divided equally, regardless of sex or seniority, and that no legitimate child could be disinherited.

5. The religious of both sexes renounced all inheritance claims upon taking vows, and while the dowry required on entering a nunnery might be equivalent to a marriage portion, in the wealthier families it would still be considerably smaller than the full share of inheritance otherwise due at the parents' death. In Yucatan a generous marriage dowry among Spaniards was 1,000-2,000 pesos (see AA, Obras pías, Autos sobre obra pía de Juan Muñoz Bermon, 1692; Asuntos terminados 7, Autos de la obra pía de Alonso Ulibarri, 1722-1795). The dowry required for the nunnery was 2,000 pesos, which is all some families could scrape together but still a very small portion of some of the estates, according to records of litigation on payment of the principal and/or *réditos* on the dowries (see AA, Asuntos de Monjas 1 and 2).

6. AGI, Mexico 369, Avisos Bishop Toral, n.d. (ca. 1565); Mexico 1037, Royal cédula to Governor of Yucatan, 20 June 1628; IY, Constituciones sinodales, 1722, Instrucciones a los curas de indios. In two collections of Indian wills (TUL, Libro de Cacalchen, 1646-1649, and AA, Documentos del Petén Itzá, unlabeled cuaderno, 1748-1760), the local Franciscan *doctrineros* countersigned each testament to the effect that its clauses had been complied with. The 1628 *cédula* mentioned reports that most Indians in Yucatan died intestate. The Franciscans may have been particularly zealous in the matter of Indian inheritance, but the set of wills for Tekanto (in ANM; see Philip Thompson, "Tekanto,"

chapter 3), which was also a Franciscan *doctrina*, indicates that they did not uniformly enforce a Spanish system of partible inheritance, even when testaments were made.

7. AGI, Mexico 1037, Royal cédula to Governor, 20 June 1628; AA, Real cedulario 5, Royal cédula to Bishop, 8 oct. 1631; AGI, Mexico 1035, Franciscan Comisario general to Council of the Indies, 14 Feb. 1704; Mexico 3064, Autos contra el cura de Uman, 1783. This did not, however, appear in a list of the eleven most common ways that *curas* illegally enriched themselves at the Indians' expense (AA, Visitas pastorales 1, Auto general de visita, 1755), nor in the colonial documentation in general, and I suspect that the practice was unusual.

8. The Cacalchen and "Petcn Itza" collections cited in note 6 contain many examples of mixed inheritance (although none of land). In a published example, c. 1811 (Roys, *Titles of Ebtun*, 326-329), Antonio Dzul left money, silver spoons, beehives, wax, and honey in almost equal amounts to two sons and a daughter. On land inheritance, Philip Thompson, "Tekanto," 167-168, table 3.24, calculates the bequests at a ratio of more than four to one in favor of sons for the period 1720-1820, but without making any chronological distinction within that period. The Pox family papers, in TUL, Documentos de Tabi, 1 ff1-32v, 45v-57 (1569-1778), demonstrate the shift from the total exclusion of women, through daughters inheriting some property (but not milpa land), to land passing through the female line from mother to daughter.

9. General and particular complaints about the "gathering up" of orphans are recorded in: AGI, Mexico 3048, Franciscans to Crown, 20 May 1572; IY, Constituciones sinodales, 1722; AA, Visitas pastorales, 1, Interrogatorio for visitas of 1755 and 1764, question no. 25; Visitas pastorales 3, Visita Campeche, 1781; AGI, Mexico 3103, Certificate of Escribano mayor de gobierno, 1 Oct. 1784 (citing the "placement" of Indian orphans as one of the governor's "good works"); AA, Oficios y decretos 3, Governor to Br. Nicolás Solís, 17 Feb. 1787; AGN, Clero 152, no. 15, Queja contra el Visitador eclesiástico, 1788; AGI, Mexico 3072, Autos contra Fr. Josef Perdomo, 1790-1792; AA, Decretos 1, Royal cédula to governor, 30 Jan. 1792; and the documents cited in note 10. For a continuation of the practice after independence, see González Navarro, *Raza y tierra*, 57-58. Although there is evidence from Spanish wills that some of the orphans were in fact well provided for by their masters (see, for example, AGI, Mexico 886, Testament of Diego Rodríguez de Olmo, 23 Jan. 1699; AEY, Tierras 1, no. 12, Testament of Pbro. José Tadeo de Quijano y Zetina, 20 June 1809), so too often were African and mulatto slaves.

10. "Visita García de Palacio, 1583"; AGI, Mexico 1039, Testimonio de personas puestas en prisión, 30 Aug. 1772; AA, Oficios y decretos 5, Expedte. sobre extracción de huérfanos, 1804-1805.

11. See chapter 4, note 45.

12. The only two exceptions I have seen were Campeche, where a curate said he waited until Indians married before charging them *obvenciones* (AA, Visitas pastorales 1, Visita Campeche, 1757), and Tabasco, where Indian women re-

mained exempt from tribute until marriage (AGI, Mexico 3168, Bishop to Crown, 8 July 1769).

13. AA, Visitas pastorales 4, Parish report Maxcanu, 1782. I have nowhere seen this exemption codified, but references to *semaneras* and *semaneros* as invariably married indicates that it was a general rule, at least for *servicio personal*: see, for example, AGI, Mexico 1039, Bishop to Crown, 6 April 1722, and Governor to Crown, 2 July 1723; AA, Papeles de los señores Gala, Guerra, Carrillo y Piña, Memorial Fr. Joseph Baraona to Bishop, 21 May 1770; AGN, Historia 498, Expedte. . . . escuelas, 1790-1805. On *repartimientos* confined to *casados y viudos*, see AA, Visitas pastorales 4, Parish report Becal, 1782.

14. AGN, Historia 498, Expedte. . . . escuelas, 1790-1805; and AGI, Mexico 3168, Informe Bartolomé del Granado Baeza, 1 April 1813, contain material on children's labor contributions.

15. The impression of physical vigor comes mainly from the elite class of pueblo officials, who continued to serve in these fairly demanding posts until their mid-fifties or so (see, for example, AGI, Mexico 3066, Informaciones instruídas . . . cofradías, 1782, cuad. 6-10, which give the ages of witnesses). The early nineteenth-century parish censuses that give a breakdown according to age (AA, Estadística, parishes of Hunucma, Motul, Tekanto, Chichimila, Espita, and Tizimin, 1802-1815) show a remarkably uniform proportion of all Indians, *casados y viudos*, over the age of fifty in the range of 18-19 percent.

16. First reported by Landa, *Relación*, 100, but see also AGN, Historia 498, Expedte. . . . escuelas, 1790-1805, Parecer Defensor de naturales, 20 Dec. 1791.

17. AA, Visitas pastorales 5, Información secreta, visita Uman, 1782; AGI, Mexico 3064, Autos contra el cura de Uman, 1783; Mexico 3072, Autos contra Fr. Josef Perdomo, 1790-1792. The Defensor de naturales in 1791 (see note 16) indicated that forcing the Indians to continue attending *doctrina* until they married produced the same effect, but the *cura* of Maxcanu complained that dislike of *servicio personal* made them resist pressure for early marriage (AA, Visitas pastorales 4, Parish report Maxcanu, 1782).

18. The link between colonial pressures and Indian population change in general is discussed in chapter 2. Except for one *cura*, who alleged that the heavy burden of weaving for *repartimiento* and the physical punishments administered caused many Indian women to miscarry (AA, Visitas pastorales 4, Parish report Becal, 1782), I have seen no evidence that the Spanish made any causal connection between their own demands and the rates of fertility and mortality, as distinct from population loss through flight.

19. The lists of *huídos* contained in AGI, Escribanía de cámara 318-A, Averiguación . . . Fr. Luis de Cifuentes Sotomayor, 1669, specify the fugitives' marital status and children. Supporting evidence for this mobility comes from the variety of *naturalidades* and places of baptism within the same family, as indicated in marriage registers. Gosner, "Uman Parish," 5, table 1, has tabulated these for Uman in the latter part of the eighteenth century. The Spanish also acknowledged repeatedly that *repartimientos* and *servicio personal*, from which the

unmarried were exempt, along with *accumulated* tax debts, were the major motives for flight.

20. Early postconquest boundary settlements are recorded in Documentos de tierras de Sotuta, 1545, in Roys, *Titles of Ebtun*, 424-427; Land Treaty of Maní, 1557, in Roys, *Indian Background*, 185-190; Land titles of Uman, 1557, in Títulos de Kisil. Martinez Hernández, *Crónica de Yaxkukul*, 33-37, contains a boundary survey of 1544, submitted in a lawsuit with the town of Mococha in 1793, and Barrera Vázquez, *Códice de Calkini*, 47-113, records boundary negotiations and settlements made in 1579 and 1595, but with pre-Columbian antecedents. For later surveys and conflicts, see Roys, *Titles of Ebtun*, 71-119, for 1600-1776, mainly between the old Cupul and Sotuta provinces; AEY, Tierras 1, no. 20, Títulos de San Bernardino Chich, containing a boundary dispute between Uman and Abala, 1719-1764; Títulos de Chactun, incorporating land titles of Maxcanu, with boundary settlements between Maxcanu, Becal, Halacho, and Calkini, 1623-1689. A number of examples of a different kind of boundary dispute, concerning jurisdiction over dispersed settlements, can be found for the later eighteenth century in AA (Arreglos parroquiales and Asuntos terminados); they were settled by the ecclesiastical courts because they involved parish boundaries and church affiliations.

21. Scholes and Roys, *Maya-Chontal*, 186-236.

22. See chapter 3, note 44.

23. Why some *batabs* bore this title and others did not (see, for example, the list of witnesses and their titles in AGI, Mexico 3048, Testimonios de autos sobre repartimientos, 1755) is not clear.

24. The only mention of local Maya recruited for military activities after the early seventeenth century was an *entrada* in 1668 to the frontier region south of Champoton, in which almost all the Indians ran away en route (AGI, Escribanía de cámara 317-B, cuad. 8, Autos hechos . . . sobre la reducción de los indios de Sahcabchen, 1668). The "Mexican" *naborías* (later called *indios hidalgos*), on the other hand, were all organized into militia units under their own "captains," distinct from the *batabs*, and retained military functions and military *fuero* until the end of the colonial period; see AGI, Mexico 360, Governor to Crown, 3 May 1648; BN, Archivo franciscano 55, no. 1150, Discurso sobre la constitución de Yucatan, 1766; AA, Visitas pastorales 6, Visita Temax, 1785; AEY, Censos y padrones 1, censuses for the *partidos*, 1811, with data on *fuero militar*.

25. BN, Archivo franciscano 55, no. 1150, Discurso, 1766. Cárdenas Valencia, *Relación historial*, 113, presents a similar picture, allowing that the "richest Indian" might be worth 4½ pesos.

26. AA, Asuntos terminados 3, Francisco Bravo to Bishop, 30 March 1818.

27. See, for example, AA, Estadística, Relación jurada que hacen los curas, 1774; and a similar set of reports for 1814. See also, Mexico 3168, Informe Bartolomé del Granado Baeza, 1 April 1813.

28. Wauchope, *Modern Maya Houses*, compares modern style and construction with pictorial and archaeological evidence on ancient dwellings.

29. RY 1: 87.

30. AGI, Escribanía de cámara 305-A, Autos criminales, Tekax, 1610. On the meagerness of *macehual* possessions, see also Cárdenas Valencia, *Relación historial*, 113; AGI, Mexico 3168, Bishop to Crown, 28 July 1737; BN, Archivo franciscano 55, no. 1150, Discurso, 1766.

31. The Tekax inventories are the most detailed record of colonial *macehual* property, but the Cacalchen, Tekanto, "Petén Itzá," and Ebtun collections of wills (see chapter 4, note 44) provide a range within the obviously very small minority who had anything at all to pass on to their heirs, with the lower echelon of this "propertied" group represented by several dozen beehives, some fine shirts, and several head of cattle. Overlapping this group and descending to the bottom of the scale is an 1807 census of a *rancho* in the parish of Uayma (AA, Estadística), containing thirteen nuclear families, one of which possessed two horses, four head of cattle, two pigs, twelve chickens and fifty beehives, while the rest possessed fairly even combinations of one to three pigs, five to twelve chickens, and two to eight turkeys.

32. In addition to the testaments cited in chapter 4, note 44, two detailed inventories of elite households, both belonging to *gobernadores*, are contained in AGI, Escribanía de cámara 305-A, Autos Tekax, 1610, and Escribanía de cámara 318-A, pieza 9, Querella de los indios principales del pueblo de Tzotzil, 1670.

33. AEY, Tierras 1, no. 14, Testamento Antonio Tamay, 17 Oct. 1764. Sánchez de Aguilar, *Informe*, 166, reported offerings of "*cuzcas*, which are their emeralds," that the Maya continued to make in temples along the north coast. On "heirloom" idols, see AGI, Mexico 369, Bishop to Crown, 11 Jan. 1686.

34. AGI, Escribanía de cámara 305-A, Autos Tekax, 1610.

35. Oral histories of the *cofradía* estates, including the original endowments and the names (and sometimes genealogies) of the donors, are recorded in AGI, Mexico 3066, Informaciones instruídas . . . cofradías, 1782, cuad. 5-10. For similar reports based on written records, see Mexico 3066, Testimonio de real provisión, 1782; and AA, Visitas pastorales 3, Mani, 1782. Several of the libros de cofradía (AA and AC) also mention endowments, and AA, Asuntos terminados 9, Autos de cofradía, Cuzama, 1696-1800, contains a copy of an original deed of endowment of several tracts of land, 23 Sept. 1696. An unusually detailed record of such an endowment appears in an undated preface to AA, Libro de cofradía, Euan, 1737-1786: an *estancia* donated ca. 1726 by the *batab* of the pueblo, containing thirty-seven head of cattle, twenty-two horses, and ninety-eight beehives.

36. According to Marta Hunt, "Colonial Yucatan," 642 note 17.

37. See the constitutions for the *cofradía* of Dzan (1607), copied in AA, Visitas pastorales 3, Visita Mani, 1782; and the Cofradía de Ánimas, San Román (1685), in AC, Libro de cofradías, San Román.

38. AA, Asuntos terminados 9, Padrón de los que se han suscrito, 2 June 1805.

39. AA, Estadística, Estado que manifiesta el número de personas, Uman, 28 July 1802, provides a breakdown according to sex, caste, and age group.

40. AGN, Consolidación 10, Exp. sobre bienes de comunidad de Yucatan,

1805, Reglamento para la administración de bienes de comunidad, 12 July 1797. See also AGI, Mexico 361, Ordenanzas Governor Esquivel, 1666, no. 11.

41. See note 35 on donations to *cofradías*, and chapter 4, note 44, on Indian testaments. Most of the hacienda *títulos* consulted (listed in chapter 1, note 18) contain deeds of sale by Indians as well as by communities, as do the notarial records (ANM), usually accompanied by more or less accurate contemporary Spanish translations. For further discussion of land ownership and land transfers, see chapter 9.

42. See, for example, Sánchez de Aguilar, *Informe*, 148; Cogolludo, Lib. 4, cap. 3. AA, Visitas pastorales 6, Parish report Tixacacalcupul, 1784, mentions a *capellanía* founded by an Indian "sobre una hoya de cacao." Orchards were a major component of elite wealth (see Sánchez de Aguilar, *Informe*, 182), and the high value placed on fruit trees can be seen in the family disputes over them, recorded in TUL, Documentos de Tabi 1: ff 49-50, 1686; and AEY, Tierras 1, no. 4, Diligencias promovidas por Domingo Ku, 1791.

43. Early seventeenth-century references to the Indian elite engaged in livestock production mention goats and sheep (Sánchez de Aguilar, *Informe*, 150; AA, Visitas pastorales 3, Visita Mani, 1782, refers to the donation of an "estancia cabría" by the *batab* in 1601 to found the local *cofradía*). The Cacalchen collection of wills, 1646-1679 (TUL, Libro de Cacalchen, 1-34) and the inventory of a *batab*'s property, in AGI, Escribanía 318-A, Querella de los indios principales, 1670, as well as the material on *cofradía* endowments (note 35) indicate that the shift to cattle, horses, and mules had been made before the end of the century.

44. AEY, Censos y padrones 1, no. 3, Relación de estancias, haciendas y ranchos, 1811, for the *partidos* of Tizimin, Valladolid, Costa, Sierra Baja, Sierra Alta, and Camino Real (the *partidos* of Bolonchencauich and Champoton are also included but list no estates privately owned by Indians), giving owners' names and the number of cattle and horses for each estate. An exception was Buenaventura Xul, whose *estancia* Xkulum in the parish of Mama contained 261 head of cattle.

45. See Patch, "Colonial Regime," 327, and "Haciendas and Markets," 9-14, on the monopoly maintained by the major creole ranchers. The *cofradía* estates were permitted to sell meat in Merida, but presumably individual Indian ranchers were not.

46. The usual price of uncultivated bush in eighteenth-century Tekanto (Philip Thompson, "Tekanto," 118, table 3.3) was 2½ pesos for one hundred *mecates* and was probably lower in less densely populated areas. Three hundred *mecates* were calculated as the average requirement for a nuclear family (see chapter 4, note 32).

47. AA, Oficios y decretos 4, Bishop to José de Gálvez, July 1784.

48. AGI, Mexico 361, Ordenanzas Governor Esquivel, 1666, no. 19; Mexico 1039, Governor to Crown, 2 July 1723; Mexico 1029, Cabildo of Merida to Bishop, 16 Nov. 1723; Mexico 3052, Autos sobre el pósito de Campeche, 1765; AA, Oficios y decretos 4, Bishop to José de Gálvez, July 1784; AGI, Mexico

3103, Representación Antonio de Argaiz, 28 Sept. 1784. In late colonial times funds from the *bienes de comunidad*, no longer controlled by the Indian officials, were loaned to *arrieros* to buy mules on time payments: AGN, Consolidación 10, Exp. sobre bienes de comunidad, 1805, Governor to Junta de real hacienda, 23 Nov. 1805; AEY, Ayuntamiento 1, no. 5, Expedte. sobre arrieros de Dzitbalche, Feb. 1811.

49. AGI, Mexico 1039, Testimonio de la regulación de precios, 1722.

50. The practice continued after conquest with several newly formed towns— for example, Chancenote (AGI, Mexico 140, Probanza D. Juan Chan, 1601) and Dzonotchuil, in Tizimin, under the Chuil family ("Visita García de Palacio, 1583"). New satellite *ranchos* and *sitios* were usually referred to as belonging to the particular parent pueblo, but in a census of Uman parish (AA, Visitas pastorales 5, 1784) they were designated as belonging collectively to "los principales del pueblo."

51. On authorized and unauthorized labor for *batabs* and *principales*, see Ordenanzas López, 1552 (Cogolludo, Lib. 5, caps. 16-19), "Visita García de Palacio, 1583"; AGI, Indiferente 2987, Ordenanzas García de Palacio, 1584; Sánchez de Aguilar, *Informe*, 183-184; AGI, Mexico 361, Ordenanzas Esquivel, 1666. For complaints about unauthorized labor (lodged, it should be noted, by fellow *principales*), see notes 52 and 86.

52. That this was both a common and a generally accepted practice is suggested by the fact that *maestros cantores* and sacristans in one pueblo went on strike to protest the new curate's prohibition; see AGI, Mexico 3053, Autos de la causa de remoción, Becal, 1767. See also AA, Visitas pastorales 2, Sahcabchen, 1778; and the complaint in Roys, *Chumayel*, 20, against labor service to the "batabob," "camzahob" and "fiscalob" (mistranslated on p. 79 as "public prosecutors" but in fact assistants to the *maestros*).

53. Among many documents describing the organization of *tequios* and other labor drafts and the control exercised in recruitment and allocation by the *república* officials, see especially IY, Constituciones sinodales, 1772, Instrucciones a los curas de indios; AGI, Mexico 1039, Testimonio de la visita . . . Costa, 1723, and Testimonio de la visita . . . Camino Real, 1723; AA, Visitas pastorales 1, Visita Valladolid, 1755, testimonies of *batabs* and *justicias*, San Marcos and Tixhualahtun; visita Mama, 1768, testimonios of *caciques* et al. of Mama and Tekit; Visitas pastorales 6, visita and parish report Chunhuhub, 1783; AEY, Ayuntamiento 1, no. 5, Los Alcaldes de Dzitbalche to Defensor de naturales, 1811.

54. Chamberlain, *Pre-conquest Tribute and Service System*.

55. AGI, Mexico 3168, Informe Bartolomé del Granado Baeza, 1 April 1813.

56. AGN, Historia 498, Exp. sobre establecimiento de escuelas, 1790-1805, reports from subdelegates, 1790; and Consolidación 10, Exp. sobre bienes de comunidad, 1805. Earlier lists of stipends are recorded in "Visita García de Palacio, 1583"; and AEY, Ayuntamiento 1, no. 1, Cabildo records, Tekanto, 1683-1704. One well-informed source reported that *cantores*, sacristans, organists, *fiscales*, *mayordomos*, and also "*república* officials" received salaries from the

bienes de comunidad (AGI, Mexico 158, Abogado de los naturales to Audiencia of Mexico, 1663), but he may have been referring to fees and services rather than fixed stipends.

57. These fees, referred to in a variety of documents, are specified in some of the *cofradía* accounts (see, for example, AC, Libro de cofradía, Pociaxum, 1710-1748), and Visitas pastorales (see, for example, AA, Visitas pastorales, 1, Bolonchenticul, 1757, and Visitas pastorales 2, Mama, Tekax, and Oxkutzcab, 1773). See also Asuntos terminados 10, Petition Maestro de capilla de Halacho, April 1815.

58. AA, Visitas pastorales 1, Valladolid, 1755, and Campeche, 1757, report that the *maestros cantores* sometimes collected the *obvenciones* (for a fee of 4 reales for every 57 pesos collected) but the more usual agents were the *batabs*.

59. The clergy consistently sought exemptions from tribute and other civil taxes for their church staff as a recruiting device, with little success in law and uneven success in practice: AGI, Indiferente 1373, Memorial Bishop to Council of the Indies, n.d. (1580s); "Visita García de Palacio, 1583"; AGI, Mexico 158, Abogado de los naturales to Audiencia of Mexico, 1663; Mexico 3139 Exp. formado a instancia de los indios cantores y maestros de capilla, 1792.

60. AGI, Mexico 361, Ordenanzas Governor Esquivel, 1666. For disputes over the exemption of "church servants" from labor drafts, see AA, Real cedulario 5, Actas del capítulo provincial, May 1657; AGI, Mexico 1035, Bishop to Crown, 3 April 1702; Mexico 1039, Juzgado de indios to Bishop, 1722, and Governor to Crown, 2 July 1723; AA, Asuntos terminados 9, Cacique and justicias of Santa Ana to Subdelegado, 1803; Oficios y decretos 6, Cura of Uman to Bishop, 12 Nov. 1807.

61. On the economic losses, see Farriss, "Propiedades territoriales," 188-189; AGI, Mexico 898, Oficiales reales to Crown, 20 Oct. 1745; Mexico 3054, Governor to Julián de Arriaga, 11 Aug. 1767; AGN, Real caja 54, a series of letters from the Governor to the Viceroy, 1771-1772; AA, Estadística, Relación jurada que hacen los curas, 1774; AGI, Mexico 3057, Petition encomenderos to Real hacienda, 11 Sept. 1770, Encomenderos to Governor, 1775, Informe hecho por el Ilustre Ayuntamiento de Merida, 1775, and Governor to Crown, 26 Oct. 1775.

62. AGI, Mexico 3057, Autos formados sobre la falta de tributarios, 1775, cuads. 1 and 2, testimonies of *curas*, *capitanes a guerra*, *caciques*, and *justicias*.

63. AGI, Mexico 3957, Estado general de todos los indios tributarios, 10 Feb. 1774, lists 58,879 tributaries (that is, Indian men from 14 to 60 years of age) in 1765 and 34,776 in 1773, a loss of 41 percent.

64. AGI, Mexico 3057, Autos formados sobre la falta de tributarios, 1775, cuad. 1.

65. AGI, Mexico 3168, Bishop to Crown, 28 July 1737: "Para mantenerse [el indio] le sobra con trabajar tres meses al año." Morley, *Ancient Maya*, 139-140, cites Carnegie Institution studies for the Chichen Itza area, which yielded an estimate of forty-eight days for bare subsistence and seventy-six days as a norm.

66. BN, Archivo Franciscano 55, no. 1150, Discurso, 1766: "Importa tanto

lo que contribuye como lo que come." It was calculated that an adult Indian male consumed 4 *almudes* of maize a week. The yearly total of 17 *cargas* 4 *almudes* (24 *almudes* = 1 *carga*), if sold at the normal price in that period of 2 reales a *carga*, would yield 34 reales 4 granos, compared to 31 reales for the basic head taxes.

67. This was the major thrust of the arguments against "excessive" labor exemptions, outlined in the documents cited in note 60.

68. See chapter 1, notes 44, 47-50, 55, 62, and 63, for material on unregulated *limosnas, derramas*, fees, fines, gratuities, *repartimientos*, and requisitions.

69. See AGI, Justicia 1016, no. 6, ramo 1, Residencia Francisco Palomino, Defensor de naturales, 1573-1580; Mexico 158, Testimonio de Luis Tello, Abogado de naturales, 1663; Mexico 3056, Governor to Crown, 8 Nov. 1767, and Protector de indios to Crown, 11 May 1770, for material on the history and operation of the Tribunal.

70. See Brown, "From Anarchy to Satrapy," and, among the many studies on the effects of colonial rule on African political systems, see Fallers, *Bantu Bureaucracy*.

71. Lizana, *Historia de Yucatan*, 40v; AA, Papeles de los señores Gala, Guerra, Carrillo y Piña, Informe Fr. Joseph Baraona to Bishop, 21 May 1770; AGI, Mexico 3168, Informe Bartolomé del Granado Baeza, 1 April 1813. The parish reports, 1782-1784, in AA, Visitas pastorales 3-6, list perjury among the most common Indian "vices," but none mentions theft or cheating. References to the contrast between Maya and Spanish standards of probity are also scattered in the *cofradía* records in AA.

72. Later colonial parish registers (in AGA) and surviving house-by-house censuses (AA, Estadística, 1798-1821) all attest to the extreme rarity of marriages between people of the same patronymic. Miles, "Sixteenth-Century Pokom-Maya," 760-764, discusses a similar conflict over definitions of consanguinity between canon law and highland Maya kinship rules.

73. Eggan, "The Maya Kinship System."

74. The church's definitions of consanguineous and affinal impediments have remained basically unmodified since well before the Council of Trent. For an explanation of the various degrees and impediments, see *Código de derecho canónico*, Lib. 2, canons 96 and 97, Lib. 3, canons 1076 and 1077.

75. Colonial marriage procedures for Indians, including dispensations, inquiries, and bans for the diocese of Yucatan are discussed in IY, Constituciones sinodales, 1722, Instrucciones a los curas de indios. See also Ordenanzas Tomás Lopez, 1552, in Cogolludo, Lib. 5, caps. 16-19; AGI, Mexico 369, Avisos Bishop Toral para los padres curas y vicarios . . . , n.d. (c. 1565); AA, Visitas pastorales 3 (Seyba, 1781, Ticul 1782), 4 (Becal, 1782), and 5 (Xcan, 1784).

76. On marriage brokers, see Landa, *Relación*, 101; AA, Real cedulario 5, Actas del definitorio franciscano, May 1657; IY, Constituciones sinodales, 1722, Instrucciones a los curas de indios. According to the *ordenanzas* of García de Palacio, 1584, (AGI, Indiferente 2987), marriage arrangements also required the approval of *batabs* and *principales* in return for fees or "gifts."

77. See, for example, "Visita García de Palacio, 1583." In another case (AA, Visitas pastorales 5, Sisal de Valladolid, 1784) the *batab* denounced to the bishop two adulterous servants of the *cura*, who created "scandal" in the town under the *cura*'s protection.

78. AA, Visitas pastorales 4, Parish report Teabo, 1782. See also the material cited in note 1.

79. See IY, Constituciones sinodales, 1722; and AGI, Indiferente 2987, Ordenanzas García de Palacio, 1584, the latter specifying penalties of fines, whippings, removal from office, and exile for failure to enforce the regulations. Among the numerous complaints about the complicity of *batabs* and other officials in the misdeeds of their subjects, see AGI, Mexico 359, Governor to Crown, 11 March 1584; Mexico 3167, Franciscans to Council to the Indies, 3 May 1586; Sánchez de Aguilar, *Informe*, 72, 180; AGI, Mexico 369, Bishop to Crown, 24 Feb. 1643, and 11 Jan. 1686; AA, Papeles de los señores Gala, Guerra, Carrillo y Piña, Informe Fr. Joseph Baraona to Bishop, 21 May 1770; Asuntos pendientes 3, Francisco Bravo to Bishop, 30 March 1818. Among the recorded cases of *batabs* removed from office for complicity and failure to enforce Spanish rules, see AGI, Mexico 369, Bishop to Crown, 11 Jan. 1686; and Mexico 3053, Causa remoción, cura of Becal, 1767.

80. AGI, Mexico 1035, Governor to Crown, 20 Aug. 1700; Mexico 1039, Testimonio de la visita . . . Costa, 1722, and Testimonio de la visita . . . Camino real, 1723; Mexico 898, Oficiales reales to Crown, 20 Oct. 1745; AA, Visitas pastorales 1 (Bolonchenticul, 1768), 4 (Becal, 1782), 5 (Tixcacaltuyu), and 6 (Tixcacalcupul, 1784, concerning the Bula de la Santa Cruzada); Asuntos pendientes 3, Queja de Pedro Ceh, 1811.

81. In addition to the well-known examples of the 1548 arson plot in Oxkutzcab (Lizana, *Historia de Yucatan*, 52v-55) and the discovery of the idolatries of Mani (Cogolludo, Lib. 6, cap. 1), an idolatry case in Chemax (AGI, Mexico 249, Residencia Diego Quijada, 1565, Información hecha en Valladolid) and the Jacinto Canek rebellion (Mexico 3050, Testimonio de autos sobre la sublevación, 1761, Tiburcio de Cosgaya to Governor, 20 Nov. 1761) were also reported by Indians. See also note 86 for denunciations against *batabs*.

82. Later idolatry cases on record were all discovered by clerical snooping or by accident. The curate of Yaxcaba explained that it was impossible to eradicate "misas milperas" because the Indians "will not denounce each other" (AGI, Mexico 3168, Informe Bartolomé del Granado Baeza, 1 April 1813).

83. See the *descargos* presented by the Defensores de naturales in AGI, Escribanía 305-A, Autos Tekax, 1610; and Escribanía 318-A, Visita que hizo . . . Flores de Aldana, 1666.

84. AGI, Escribanía 305-A, Autos Tekax, 1610.

85. Roys, *Chumayel*, contains only one section clearly referring to oppression of the "macehualob" by the native leaders (p. 20, translated on p. 79), but many referring to legitimate rulers versus "upstarts" (pp. 75, 83-84, 89, 91, 92-93, 103, 105-106, 112, 124, 149).

86. AGI, Escribanía 318-A, pieza 9, Querella de los indios principales del

pueblo de Tzotzil, 1670. The *visita* by governor Flores de Aldana and subsequent investigations provided an opportunity for a rash of similar cases, all promoted by local *principales*; see Escribanía 318-A and 318-B, Visita que hizo . . . Flores de Aldana, 1666, piezas 1-143; Escribanía 318-A, cuad. 13, Averguación . . . Fr. Luis de Cifuentes Sotomayor, 1669; Escribanía 317-A, cuad. 2, Autos por donde consta los repartimientos, 1670.

87. AGI, Escribanía 305-A, Autos Tekax, 1610.

88. Pre-Columbian ritual drunkenness associated with religious celebration is well attested to. The evidence on mock battles is much less clear, but Landa, *Relación*, 94, 144, 158, mentions warlike dances and dances of warriors that were the possible predecessors of the colonial mock battles described as pre-Columbian in origin by Ciudad Real, *Relación* 2: 411-412.

89. The Carnival street fights with oranges and stones that are referred to as a common occurrence in AGI, Escribanía 305-A, Autos Tekax, 1610, seem to fall halfway between the very ritualized mock battles described by Ciudad Real, *Relación* (1588) 2: 406, 411-412, 463, and the more serious conflicts (again referred to as a common occurrence) that the governor legislated against in AGI, Mexico 361, Ordenanzas Governor Esquivel, 1666, no. 7. See Bricker, *Ritual Humor*, 84-126, on warfare as the dominant theme in the Carnival of Chamula in highland Chiapas, and 124-125, on mock battles (using lumps of horse dung), which formerly engaged one barrio against another.

90. Among a variety of recent works on the ambivalent sociopolitical role of ritual license and disorder, see Burke, *Popular Culture*, 199-204; Davis, *Society and Culture*, 97-123; Gluckman, *Rituals of Rebellion*; and Abner Cohen, "Drama and Politics," and "A Polyethnic London Carnival," using the model of collective "joking relationship."

91. Most of the parish reports in AA, Visitas pastorales 4-6, 1782-1784, expatiate in more or less detail on the prevalence of drunkenness among the Indians and the particular evils of *aguardiente*. See especially Becal, Bolonchenticul, and Pich, 1782; Xcan, Chancenote, Nabalam, Telchac, Sisal de Valladolid, Tixcacaltuyu, Chunhuhub, aand Tixcacalcupul, 1784. Ritual drinking and feasting in relation to religious fiestas will be discussed in chapter 11.

92. Taylor, *Drinking, Homicide and Rebellion*, 68-72. I would agree with Taylor that alcohol intake is not a simple measure of psychic and social stress, much less a cause, as the Spanish authorities chose to believe. I also find evidence from colonial Yucatan that drinking was primarily a social activity for colonial Indians. But I would assign more significance than Taylor does to the partial desacralization of drinking, its extension to a common, every-day activity for any kind and size of gathering, and its new association with *unsanctioned* antisocial behavior (particularly on the part of *macehaules*).

93. "Visita García de Palacio, 1583." See also AGI, Escribanía 305-A, Autos Tekax, 1610; Mexico 3048, Autos sobre venta de vino a los indios, 1609, and Auto Governor, 4 Jan. 1622; Mexico 361, Ordenanzas Governor Esquivel, 1666, no. 4. The first complaint I have seen about local *aguardiente*, as opposed to imported wine, is AGI, Mexico 1035, Fr. Joseph de Frías to Provincial, 15 June

1700; and this becomes the major concern throughout the rest of the colonial period; see, in addition to note 91, AGI, Mexico 1037, Defensor de los naturales to Crown, 15 Sept. 1711; AA, Papeles de los señores Gala, Guerra, Carrillo y Piña, Informe Fr. Joseph Baraona, 21 May 1770.

94. AGI, Mexico 3061, Demostración del número de poblaciones, 15 April 1781, contains figures for *estanco* sales as well as for the population for 1780. The number of nonwhite males age seven and up was 60,130, and the total number including Spaniards was 65,358. The contention that Spaniards were not major consumers is supported by the fact that a relatively small amount was sold retail in Merida: only 8,700 *frascos* for the last six months of 1784 (AGI, Mexico 3123, Cuentas del estanco de aguardiente, Merida, 1785).

95. I have not been able to find any precise measurement for a *frasco* in colonial Yucatan, only that it was a large jar interchangeable with a "barrel" (see, for example, AA, Cuentas de fábrica, Libro de fábrica, Chancenote, 1796-1819; and AGN, AHH 78, no. 5, Libro común de cargo de Real hacienda, Campeche, 1799). On the *cántara*, the standard wholesale measure for wines and spirits in Castile throughout this period, see Hamilton, *American Treasure*, 159-160, 171.

96. I thought it would be useful to compare Yucatan with another, supposedly drink-prone peasant society under foreign rule, Ireland, but the manufacture of poteen was so widespread as to make any excise figures meaningless (Connell, *Irish Peasant Society*, 1-50). Figures for annual consumption in pretemperance England in the 1820s of 23.1 gallons (imperial) of beer and 1.13 gallons of spirits (Brian Harrison, *Drink and the Victorians*, 69), seem low but are calculated for the entire population of both sexes and all ages. See note 98 for Mexico City. Kula, *Economic Theory of the Feudal System*, with which a number of scholars have found parallels in Latin America, cites no figures for per capita alcohol consumption in Poland but shows a dramatic increase in the proportion of the landed aristocracy's income that derived from sale of alcohol to the peasantry and suggests that this became a major means of siphoning off peasant wealth (see pp. 75, 134-137).

97. Gibson, *Aztecs under Spanish Rule*, 409.

98. Scardaville, "Alcohol Abuse and Tavern Reform," note 7, estimates a per capita consumption of *aguardiente* in Mexico City ranging from 2.5 to 4 gallons a year between 1797 and 1804, based presumably on official sales and calculated for the entire population above the age of fifteen (p.645 note 11). If calculated on the same basis as my figures for Yucatan of three times the legal consumption (judging from the evidence provided in the article for heavy bootlegging activity) and discounting one half of the population as female, a figure of 15 to 24 gallons results. This is still lower than Yucatan but supplemented by 187 gallons of pulque per capita a year.

99. See Zuckerman, *Peaceable Kingdoms*.

100. Evans-Pritchard, *Witchcraft, Oracles and Magic*, and Kluckhohn, *Navaho Witchcraft*, are two classic treatments of the subject. See also, for a modern Mesoamerican case study, Selby, *Zapotec Deviance*.

101. AA, Papeles de los señores Gala, Guerra, Carrillo y Piña, Informe Fr.

Joseph Baraona, 21 May 1770, suggests that the Maya picked up the idea from the Spanish, who frequently leveled witchcraft accusations against them. See also, Cuentas de Fábrica, Libro de fábrica, Chancenote, 1796-1819, Cura of Chancenote to Bishop, 1813; and AGI, Mexico 3168, Informe Bartolomé del Granado Baeza, 1 April 1813 (cura of Yaxcaba).

CHAPTER 7, POPULATION MOVEMENTS

1. I have here expanded and revised an earlier discussion of population movements in Farriss, "Nucleation versus Dispersal."

2. AGI, Contaduría 920, Matrícula de los pueblos, 1688 (secular *curatos*); Mexico 1039, Testimonio de las certificaciones dadas, 1721 (Franciscan *doctrinas*); Mexico 3047, Estado general de todos los indios tributarios, 10 Feb. 1774. See also Mexico 1037, Auto Governor, 6 March 1710.

3. AGI, Contaduría 920, Matrículas de los pueblos, 1688 (which also sometimes list the place of origin of the *forasteros*).

4. Robinson, "Indian Migration," 11, table 2. See also Gosner, "Uman Parish," 5, table 1. A census for the year 1783 (AGI, Mexico 3139, Estado del numero de mantas . . ., 14 July 1786) yields the following proportions of male tributaries who were *forasteros*: Partido de Campeche, 37.2 percent (out of a total of 10,230); Merida, 48.3 percent (total of 7,467); Valladolid, 46 percent (total of 6,171); Costa, 42.6 percent (total of 6,263); Beneficios, 21.1 percent (total of 8,948); Sierra, 39 percent (total of 10,585).

5. Robinson, "Indian Migration," 7: "The usual figures for exogamous marriages in colonial Mexico range between 15-20 percent."

6. On wholesale flight due to epidemic, famine, political upheaval, and *vejaciones*, see, in addition to chapter 2, notes 17, 61, and 68, AA, Estadística, Relación jurada que hacen los curas, 1774; Cuentas del curato de Mama, 1795-1800, and Cuentas del curato de Chancenote, 1796-1816.

7. See note 2.

8. On the early decline and depopulation of the east coast region, see Roys, Scholes, and Adams, "Report and Census," and Miller and Farriss, "Religious Syncretism," 224-229. On the isolation and economic decay of Valladolid and eastern Yucatan in general, see AGI, Mexico 3061, Demostración del número de poblaciones, 15 April 1781, containing reports on the economy of each district; AA, Oficios y decretos 4, Bishop to José de Gálvez, July 1784, and 11 Dec. 1785; Asuntos pendientes 2, Juan Esteban Rejón to Provisor, 1795; Cofradías e imposiciones, Descripción en que manifiesta el estado de las fincas, 1800. Alcabala revenues in Valladolid in 1766 totaled 122 pesos 6 reales, and in Merida, 2,620 pesos (AGN, AHH 2132, Libro Manual de cargo y data, 1766). For comparisons of Indian population changes among the colony's parishes, 1582-1813, see Cook and Borah, *Essays* 2: 108-111, table 1.14.

9. AGI, Mexico 3168, Bishop to Crown, 28 July 1737; AA, Visitas pastorales 5, Parish report, Nabalam, 1784; AGN, Historia 534, Governor of Presidio to Governor of Yucatan, 31 Aug. 1785.

10. On the role of border towns as both magnets and siphons for refugees

from the north, see Cogolludo, Lib. 4, cap. 20; AA. Arreglos parroquiales 1, Autos sobre permuta de curatos de Valladolid y Hopelchen, 1783; Visitas pastorales 3 (Chicbul, 1781) and 5 (Ichmul, 1784); Oficios y descretos 4, Visitador del Peten to Bishop, 19 Feb. 1782; Documentos del Peten, Fr. Francisco Sánchez to Provincial, 16 Oct. 1799; Oficios y descretos 5, Governor to Bishop, 20 March 1805.

11. Marta Hunt, "Colonial Yucatan," 225-227, 237.

12. Robinson, "Indian Migration," 18-20. See also AGI, Mexico 3139, Reglamento provisional para el cobro de tributos, 28 June 1786, which discusses the migration of barrio residents to the "internal pueblos of the province."

13. Cook and Borah, *Essays* 2: 108-111, table 1.14. For additional census data, see AA, Estadística, Relación jurada que hacen los curas, 1774; AGI, Mexico 3061, Demostración del numero de poblaciones, 15 April 1781; AA, Visitas pastorales 3-6, parish reports, 1782-1784; Estadística, Parish censuses, 1802-1806 (summarized in appendix 1); and AEY, Censos y padrones 1, nos. 2-11, 1811.

14. AA, Visitas pastorales 4, Parish reports, Teabo and Pich, 1784. The motive for advancing cash and goods (mainly *aguardiente*) to Indians seems to have been mainly to force production of *repartimiento* goods rather than recruit *criados*; see AGI, Mexico 361, Ordenanzas Esquivel, 1666, no. 33; Mexico 1037, Defensor and Procurador de indios to Crown, 15 Sept. 1711; AA, Visitas pastorales 1, Valladolid, Testimony of D. Juan Cipriano Pacheco; Visitas pastorales 4, Parish report, Oxkutzcab, 1782; and the material cited on the sale of wine and *aguardiente* in chapter 6, notes 91 and 93.

15. AGI, Mexico 1039, Bishop to Crown, 6 April 1722, Governor to Crown, 2 July 1723; AA, Papeles de los señores Gala, Guerra, Carrillo y Piña, Informe Fr. Joseph Baraona, 21 May 1770; AGN, Historia 498, Expediente . . . escuelas en Yucatan, 1790-1805, Parecer Defensor de Naturales, 20 Dec. 1791. See also on urban *servicio personal*, chapter 3, note 62.

16. AGI, Mexico 3057, cuads. 1 and 2, Autos formados sobre la falta de tributarios, 1775, and cuad. 3, Testimonio del informe sobre la mortandad de tributarios; AA, Oficios y decretos 5, Governor to Bishop, 12 Sept. 1804; Oficios y decretos 7, Governor to Bishop, 20 July 1810.

17. Florescano, *Precios de maiz*, 147-148, 155-158.

18. For population figures, see AGI, Mexico 3057, Estado general de todos los tributarios, 18 Feb. 1774. On difficulties in getting the refugees to return to their villages, see the material in note 16 above.

19. *Encomenderos* and curates were accused of trying to discourage marriage outside the community for fear of losing tributaries, but there is no suggestion that they were thwarting a general rule: AGI, Indiferente 1373, Bishop to Council of the Indies, n.d. (ca. 1580); Indiferente 2987, Ordenanzas García de Palacio, 1584; AA, Oficios y decretos 5, Exp. sobre esponsales, Cuzama, 1805.

20. For complaints about the problem of debts left by *huídos* and the difficulty of tracking them down, see AGI, Mexico 1035, Governor to Crown, 20 Aug. 1700; Mexico 1039, Bishop to Crown, 6 April 1722; Mexico 1020, Governor to Audiencia, 1 Feb. 1723; Mexico 898, Oficiales reales to Crown, 20 Oct. 1745;

AA, Visitas pastorales 1-6 (many complaints lodged by curates and *república* officials, 1755-1785); Estadística, Relación jurada que hacen los curas, 1774, and Parish report, Muna, 15 Oct. 1800; Asuntos pendientes 3, Cura of Homun to Bishop, 30 March 1818.

21. Gibson, *Aztecs under Spanish Rule*, 149-150. On Indian migrations in Peru and Alto Peru, see Spalding, "Indian Rural Society," 90-95; Klein, "The State and the Labor Market"; and, especially, Sánchez Albornoz, *El indio en el Alto Perú*, amplifying and supporting the earlier argument by Rowe, "Incas under Spanish Colonial Administration," 175, 180-181, linking labor recruitment on the haciendas to the mita exemption for *forasteros*. See also Mörner, *Pérfil de la sociedad rural*, 49-55.

22. Royal policy regarding these migrations was inconsistent and equivocal. During the sixteenth and seventeenth centuries local officials sought to prevent changes of residence and to oblige Indian leaders to track down *forasteros*, with, however, very limited success, while the Crown upheld the Indians' right to live where they chose so long as they paid their taxes: AGI, Mexico 359, Governor to Crown, 28 April 1584; Mexico 361, Auto Governor, 7 Sept. 1663, and Ordenanzas Governor Esquivel, 1666; Cogolludo, Lib. 10, cap. 7; AGI, Escribanía 318-A and 318-B, Visita que hizo . . . Flores de Aldana, 1666, 143 piezas; Royal cédula, 14 July 1693, cited in García Bernal, *Yucatan*, 399. Although the Crown reversed its stand in 1731 (AGI, Mexico 3052, Royal cédula to Governor and Bishop, 1 July 1731, inserted in cédula 5 July 1761), local civil officials had become increasingly tolerant of *forasteros*, opposing repatriation unless the migrants owed substantial debts or sought to evade community obligations by virtue of *forastero* status: AGI, Mexico 1037, Auto Governor, 6 March 1710; Mexico 1035, Governor to Audiencia, 1 Feb. 1723; AA, Oficios y decretos 3, Exp. sobre indios huídos de Sahcabchen y Champton, 1782.

23. Robinson, "Indian Migrations," 11. See also AGI, Mexico 3168, Bishop to Crown, 28 July 1737 (the Indians "flee to *curatos* 30 to 40 leagues away"); and BN, Archivo Franciscano 55, No. 1150, Discurso sobre la constitución de Yucatan, 1766. Places of origin for the *forasteros* are recorded in some of the *matrículas* of 1688, AGI, Contaduría 920.

24. Robinson, "Indian Migrations," 20, gives several examples of these family groups in Tixkokob. Lists of *huídos* (for example, AGI, Escribanía 318-A, Averiguación . . . Fr. Luis de Cifuentes, 1669), as well as the evidence from the parish registers (in AGA) for the migration of parents *and* children through more than one change of residence, suggest that the norm was for family groups to move together, except in the less common cases in which men chose to desert wives and children.

25. Objections to these early clandestine settlements are recorded in AGI, Mexico 359, Governor to Crown, 28 April 1584, and Franciscan Provincial to Audiencia, 5 May 1606; Indiferente 2987, Ordenanzas García de Palacio, 1584, no. 17; Mexico 369, Bishop to Crown, 10 Dec. 1604, 12 July and 12 Dec. 1607. See also Mexico 361, Governor to Crown, 27 Oct. 1663, arguing that a new congregation was needed.

26. A fairly well–documented example was Xcupilcacab, first listed as a *rancho* with 108 Indians (AA, Estadística, Relación jurada, Hopelchen, 1774), then with 168 Indians (AA, Visitas pastorales 4, Parish census, Hopelchen, 1782), elevated to the status of *visita* town with 888 Indians and 48 *pardos* (AA, Estadística, Parish census, Hopelchen, 5 March 1806), and by 1811 already having spun off four satellite *ranchos* of its own (AEY, Censos y padrones, 1, no. 4, Relación de las haciendas y ranchos, Camino Real Alto, 1811). For the history of former *rancho* Abala, which became *cabecera* of its own parish, see AEY, Tierras 1, no. 20, Pleito entre el rancho San Antonio Buluch . . . , 1764-1825; on Pocboch, see AA, Visitas pastorales 5, Parish report, Calotmul, 1784; on Pich, AA, Arreglos parroquiales 1, Traslación y erección de cabecera de curato, 1779-1780. For other examples, compare the pueblo lists in AGI, Contaduría 920, Matrículas, 1688 (secular *curatos*); Mexico 1035, Matrícula y razón individual, 28 June 1700 (Franciscan *doctrinas*); BL, Add. Mss. 17569, Visita pastoral (report), 1755-1757; AA, Visitas pastorales 3-6, Parish censuses, 1782-1784; AGI, Mexico 3139, Pueblos anexos a cada curato, 14 June 1786; AA, Estadística, Parish censuses, 1798-1828.

27. Compare DHY 2: 55-65, Memoria de los conventos, vicarías y pueblos, 1582, with the lists of *cabeceras* and *visitas* in Cogolludo, Lib. 4, caps. 19 and 20 (1650s).

28. AA, Estadística, Parish censuses, 1802-1806. This figure applies only to geographically separate entities and thus excludes the satellite barrios of Merida, Campeche, and Valladolid and counts as one all divisions of congregated towns (*parcialidades*), even when they retained separate administrative structures. Secular records in the seventeenth century will tend to list a misleadingly large number of towns (for example, AGI, Mexico 158, Abogado de indios to Crown, 28 July 1668, giving the figure of 270 "pueblos"), referring not to separate geographic entities, but to administrative units. On the other hand, the late colonial figure would equal or exceed the early postconquest count of four hundred towns, if we included the haciendas with populations large enough to have gained administrative autonomy if they had not been privately owned.

29. AGI, Mexico 1037, Governor to Crown, 15 Sept. 1711. Early nineteenth-century figures are derived primarily from AA, Estadística, Parish censuses, 1802-1828; and AEY, Censos y padrones 1, Relaciones de haciendas, estancias y ranchos, 1811.

30. AGI, Mexico 1038, Governor to Crown, 15 Sept. 1711: 33,774 out of a total Indian population of fourteen years and over (35.5 percent) resident in "las estancias, milpas, sitios y ranchos." The previous Governor reported that half the Indian population was dispersed but provided no figures (Mexico 1035, Governor to Crown, 15 June 1700). The parish censuses of 1802-1806, summarized in appendix 1, yield a figure of 35.9 percent living in all dispersed settlements. See note 56 for a discussion of data on population distribution.

31. Redfield and Villa Rojas, *Chan Kom*, 22-30.

32. See, for example, AA, Arreglos parroquiales 1, Traslación y erección de cabecera de curato del pueblo de Pich, 1779-1789. Other expanding parishes

were Hopelchen, Bolonchenticul, Seyba, Sahcabchen, and Chicbul (from which Sabancuy was formed and eventually became a separate parish).

33. Sanders, "Cultural Ecology," 103-108, and "Settlement Patterns," 76-80.

34. The only case I have found specific reference to is a *rancho* in the parish of Uayma, settled by a group from the barrio of San Juan, Valladolid (AA, Oficios y decretos 6, Cura of Uayma to Bishop, 20 Nov. 1807). But there are other general references to people from other parishes setting up similar clandestine *ranchos*, motivated in that sparsely populated region by an attempt to escape community obligations rather than by land hunger.

35. Most of the sites recorded in the early postconquest documents (see chapter 5, note 41) which seem to disappear—with or without a record of their relocation to a congregated town—and of which Roys in his *Political Geography* finds no record until the late nineteenth century, can be found as *ranchos* or *estancias* in the late colonial censuses. An example with explanatory documentation is Cumpich, listed in the 1549 *tasación* (AGI, Guatemala 128) as Yxconpiche, and "disappearing" until 1861 (Roys, *Political Geography*, 24) but actually resettled from Hecelchakan as a *rancho* some time in the 1780s on a site that the Indians remembered as a former town; see AA, Asuntos terminados 9, Causa entre don Juan Zervera y los indios del rancho Cumpich, 1804.

36. Sanders, "Cultural Ecology," 93.

37. Information on late preconquest agricultural systems is very scanty, confined in the published sources mainly to a few scattered references in Landa (*Relación*, 64, 87, 97), although the unpublished Spanish records of the conquest (for example, AGI, Justicia 300, Residencia Montejo, 1549) would probably yield additional fragments. Although Hellmuth ("Choltí-Lacandon [Chiapas] and Petén Ytzá Agriculture") and Freidel ("Lowland Maya Political Economy") have suggested that Spanish conquest resulted in the abandonment of large-scale intensive agriculture, the evidence presented for the existence of such systems is at best equivocal. It is in fact totally consistent with the colonial evidence for an infield-outfield combination of milpa and intensive horticulture in the sprawling town plots and around *cenotes* and *aguadas*, with rotating milpa providing the bulk of the staple foods; see chapter 4, notes 30 and 31, and chapter 6, note 42; AGI, Mexico 369, Bishop to Crown, 10 Dec. 1604, 12 July and 12 Dec. 1607; Mexico 361, Ordenanzas Governor Esquivel, 1666, no. 20.

38. Cook and Borah, *Essays* 2: 56-60 (from RY).

39. Skinner, "Marketing and Social Structure," 11.

40. Among the many complaints about the Indians' preference for living in their milpas and *milperías* and the problem of extended sojourns merging into permanent residence there, see, in addition to the material cited in note 25, Sánchez de Aguilar, *Informe*, 38, 178-180; AGI, Mexico 369, Bishop to Crown, 24 Feb. 1643, and 14 Sept. 1665; Cogolludo, Lib. 9, cap. 1; AA, Visitas pastorales 3, Parish report, Mani, 1784; Visitas pastorales 6, Parish report, Chunhuhub, 1784, and other parish reports in this series; Oficios y decretos 4, Bishop to curas and doctrineros, 5 Aug. 1786; AGI, Mexico 3168, Parecer Manuel Pacheco to Diputación Provincial, 1 March 1814. Sanders, "Cultural Ecology,"

107, and "Settlement Patterns," 79, describes the gradual process in the contemporary Valladolid region.

41. In addition to the material in chapter 4, note 46, see the house-by-house censuses for the parishes of Telchac (1805), Chancenote (1805 and 1806), and Kikil (1803), and Razón individual . . . rancho Yaxlac, Uayma, 1807, all in AA, Estadística.

42. Spalding, "Indian Rural Society," 65-67. See also Murra, "El control vertical," on the archipelago system.

43. Spalding, "Indian Rural Society," 86-90, 95.

44. See Mörner, *La corona española y los foráneos*, on the colonial segregation policy.

45. On efforts to control abuses by limiting non-Indian sojourners in the pueblos, see AGI, Indiferente 2987, Ordenanzas García de Palacio, 1584; Mexico 3048, Auto Governor, 13 June 1604; Mexico 361, Ordenanzas Governor Esquivel, 1666. See also AGI, Mexico 1037, Governor to Crown, 15 Sept. 1711; and Mexico 1035; Governor to Crown, 2 July 1723, for accounts of the various ways that the *vecino* residents harassed and exploited the Indians and suggestions that all *vecinos* should be obliged to move out of the pueblos.

46. Eva Hunt and Nash, "Local and Territorial Units," 259.

47. AGI, Mexico 3017, Representación Andrés Montero, 6 July 1763; AA, Asuntos terminados, Feliciano de Meneses to Bishop, 25 Oct. 1804.

48. Reported in AGI, Mexico, 3139, Contador real to Crown, 28 Feb. 1787.

49. AA, Visitas pastorales 3-6, Parish reports, 1782-1784.

50. AA, Visitas pastorales 4, Parish report, Teabo 1782; Visitas pastorales 5, Parish reports, Oxkutzcab, 1782, Tizimin, 1784.

51. For evidence on the clergy's laxness in visiting the dispersed settlements, see, for example, AA, Visitas pastorales 1, Visitas Seyba, Sahcabchen, Chicbul, Valladolid, Bolonchenticul, and Campeche, 1755-1757.

52. The most lurid accounts of *rancho* life are recorded in the parish reports in AA, Visitas pastorales 3 (Ticul and Mani, 1782), 4 (Teabo and Oxkutzcab, 1784), and 5 (Tizimin, Calotmul, Telchac, and Kikil, 1784). For other ecclesiastical reports on the moral evils of dispersed settlement, see note 40 and IY, Constituciones sinodales, 1722; AGI, Mexico 3168, Bishop to Crown, 28 July 1737.

53. AGI, Mexico 3168, Parecer Manuel Pacheco to Diputación Provincial, 1 March 1814. See also Mexico 3139, Contador real to Crown, 28 Feb. 1787; and AGN, Historia 498, Exp. sobre establecimiento de escuelas en Yucatan, 1790-1805, Parecer Defensor de naturales, 20 Dec. 1791.

54. AA, Visitas pastorales 3, Parish report Mani, 1782 (the Indians in the *ranchos* are "wild and untamed [montarraces]"); Parish report Ticul, 1782 (the Indians "live a life of savagery"); Visitas pastorales 4, Parish report Oxkutzcab, 1782 (on the *ranchos* "most of the Indians live among the animals in a wild state").

55. AGI, Mexico 3017, Interim Governor to Julián de Arriaga, 20 Aug. 1763. See also Mexico 361, Governor to Crown, 27 Oct. 1663; Mexico 1037, Gov-

ernor to Crown, 15 Sept. 1711; Mexico 3139, Contador real to Viceroy, 28 Feb. 1787.

56. Much ambiguity remains about the categories used, even when the clergy seemed to be making distinctions. Hacienda, *estancia*, *sitio*, and *rancho*, when not simply interchangeable, as in some of the records, were sometimes purely functional designations, denoting the type of activity carried out in the settlement rather than its status or ownership; sometimes fluid categories, with different meanings from parish to parish or within the same parish from census to census; and sometimes catch-all terms referring singly or in combination to almost any type of dispersed settlement (except for *estancia*, which I have never seen referring to anything but a cattle ranch). Patch, "Colonial Regime," 250-251, table 4.6, divides the rural Indian population into those living on Spanish-owned estates and those living in villages and hamlets, based on data from parish censuses, 1782-1785 and 1803 (AA, Visitas pastorales). Philip Thompson, "Tekanto," 24-30, tables 1.2-1.5, provides a breakdown according to pueblo, hacienda-*estancia*, *sitio*, and *rancho*, based on the same set of documents. However, the confusion over nomenclature makes a distinction between hamlets and estates highly uncertain (aside from the fact that Indians and their communities also owned estates), except for the rare censuses that provide data on ownership as well as on population of individual settlements (but then see note 65 on bogus Spanish estates). In view of the growth in both the number and the size of Spanish estates (see chapter 12) in the latter part of the eighteenth century, it is probable that estate residents had come to represent the major part of the dispersed population by independence, at least in the core region (but see Maxcanu in 1828, with 15 percent of the entire Indian population in hamlets and only 4 percent in Spanish-owned estates, according to the parish census in AA, Estadística). But I am not confident that an accurate breakdown can be made on the basis of currently available data and have therefore lumped together all dispersed residents in my figure of 35.9 percent for the years 1802-1806 (see appendix 1).

57. Gibson, *Aztecs under Spanish Rule*, 255-256. Although the debate over debts and peonage continues, the weight of evidence appears to favor the view that estates were generally able to recruit full-time and part-time labor without direct coercion, either because of a lack of alternatives for the rural population or because the estates offered freedom from community obligations or credit, or a combination of these incentives, and that debt peonage was mainly restricted to areas of very low labor supply. Among many recent works that deal with the issue of rural labor recruitment, see Bauer, "Rural Workers in Spanish America," for a general discussion; Konrad, *A Jesuit Hacienda*; Brading, *Haciendas and Ranchos*; and Tutino, "Life and Labor on North Mexican Haciendas," on New Spain; and Klein, "The State and the Labor Market," and Mörner, *Pérfil de la sociedad rural*, on Peru.

58. AA, Visitas pastorales 5, Parish report Nabalam, 1784. See for example, Asuntos terminados 2, Concurso de acreedores contra los bienes de D. Esteban Pérez, 1773, which revealed a debt of 59 pesos owed by the *vaqueros* against 318 pesos in back wages owed to them. One bishop asserted that owners lost much

money from credit advances because Indians would take off without discharging their debts (AGI, Mexico 3168, Bishop to Crown, 28 July 1737).

59. A frequent clause in the testaments preserved in the archdiocesan archives (no doubt many more examples could be found in the notarial records): for example, AA, Asuntos terminados 2, Concurso de acreedores, D. Esteban Pérez, 1773; Capellanías 1, Testamento D. Manuel de Palma, 10 Aug. 1784; Obras pías, Testamento D. Simón del Canto, 21 Feb. 1801, and Da. María Josefa Pérez Vergara, 20 April 1802. See also, AEY, Tierras 1, no. 12, Testamento José Tadeo de Quijano y Zetina, 20 June 1809. *Cofradía* estates also made cash advances to *vaqueros* and *mayorales* but sought to reduce the debts by salary deductions in installments (see, for example, AA, Libros de cofradía, Euan, Ekmul, and Xbalantun [Tipikal]).

60. The attempts and the opposition to them are outlined in AGI, Mexico 3139, Reglamento provisional, 1786; Contador real to Viceroy, 28 Feb. 1787 (also citing earlier attempts in 1774 and 1775); AA, Oficios y decretos 3, Bishop to Audiencia, 22 Nov. 1786; Asuntos terminados 5, Diligencias sobre pago de tributos de la estancia Chacsinkin, 1787.

61. For descriptions of the conditions and terms of residence of *luneros*, see AGI, Mexico 3138, Bishop to Crown, 28 July 1737; AA, Oficios y decretos 3, Bishop to Audiencia, 22 Nov. 1786; AGI, Mexico 3139, Contador real to Viceroy, 28 Feb. 1787.

62. AGI, Mexico 1035, Governor to Crown, 20 Aug. 1700; Mexico 1037, Governor to Crown, 6 March 1710, and Defensor and Procurador de indios to Crown, 15 Sept. 1711; Mexico 1039, Representación Juzgado de indios to Bishop, 1722; Mexico 3139, Contador real to Viceroy, 28 Feb. 1787: "El indio no pasa a las haciendas porque carezca de tierras en el pueblo de su naturaleza. . . . El motivo que de ordinario los lleva . . . es la vida libre y licenciosa sin obligación a tequios y cargos anuales de sus Repúblicas como independientes del cacique y justicias, sin la presencia del cura doctrinero."

63. On the hacienda Tabi, which achieved *ayuda de parroquia* status in 1765, see AA, Visitas pastorales 4, Parish report, Oxkutzcab, 1782, On Uayalceh, see Títulos de Uayalceh, Pedimento de D. Alonso Manuel Peón, 13 Feb. 1782; and AA, Oficios y decretos 7, Representación del cura de Abala, 3 Dec. 1811. AA, sections Asuntos terminados, Asuntos pendientes and Arreglos parroquiales, contain a number of other *expedientes* on *oratorios* and *ayudas de parroquia*: for example, Arreglos parroquiales 1, Representación del dueño de S. Joseph Chencoyí, 25 Feb. 1782. Another common ploy, with many examples in the same sections, was to seek to have an estate shifted to the jurisdiction of a town in a different parish on the grounds that it was closer; but the differences in distance were often so insignificant that one suspects an arrangement between the owners and the curates of the preferred parish, to leave the new parishioners in peace in exchange for acquiring additional *obvencionarios*.

64. See, for example, AA, Asuntos pendientes 2, Petición de los dueños de las haciendas Hotzuc, Yaxcopoil y Tompul, 1777, and Queja contra D. Sebastián Betancurt, 1792; Oficios y decretos 5, Queja del cura de Navalam, 1804;

Arreglos parroquiales 1, Exp. sobre que los indios de Xuxcab . . . , 1784; Oficios y decretos 6, José Gregorio del Canto to Bishop, 12 Nov. 1807, and Representación del cura de Halacho, 19 June 1809.

65. Described in detail in AGI, Mexico 3168, Bishop to Crown, 28 July 1737; and AA, Visitas pastorales 4, Parish report, Oxkutzcab, 1782.

66. Complaints from pueblo officials are reported in AGI, Mexico 1035, Governor to Crown, 15 June 1700; and Mexico 1037, Governor to Crown and Abogado and Procurador de indios to Crown, 15 Sept. 1711; and direct complaints are recorded in AGI, Mexico 1039, Visita . . . pueblos de la Costa, 1722; and Mexico 3066, Testimonio de varias presentaciones de indios, 1782 (petition from Batab and Justicias of Maxcanu, 11 May 1782). But see Cogolludo, Lib. 10, cap. 17, who alleged that *batabs* and *principales* encouraged runaways from other parishes to settle in *ranchos* and hid them there as a personal labor force.

67. A concern expressed in many of the reports and *autos de visita* in AA, Visitas pastorales 1, 1755-1757; Visitas pastorales 3, 1781; and in Oficios y decretos 3, Bishop to Audiencia of Mexico, 22 Nov. 1786.

68. The evidence for this category of migrant marginals is of two kinds. One is the data from parish registers (especially the *informaciones matrimoniales*), on *forasteros*, which often reveal a bewildering multiplicity of places of *naturalidad* and baptism for parents and siblings within the same family. The only explanation that seems to account for this evidence is that it indicates not one but sometimes several moves within a lifetime and that the moves were made by family groups rather than individuals (see note 24). The other type of evidence is the many references throughout the colonial period to the difficulty of keeping track of Indians who moved around from "pueblo to pueblo" or from "*rancho* to *rancho*" in different parishes: for example, Ordenanzas López, 1552 (Cogolludo, Lib. 5, caps. 16-19, "por andarse de un pueblo en otro hechos vagamundos"); AGI, Escribanía de cámara 318-A and 318-B, Visita que hizo . . . Flores de Aldana, 1666, 143 piezas; AA, Visitas pastorales 1, Campeche, Auto de visita, 2 April 1757; Oficios y decretos 3, Pedro de Dufau Maldonado to Bishop, 18 Oct. 1782 (arguing that runaways keep one step ahead of people searching for them); Visitas pastorales 4 and 5, Parish reports Oxkutzcab and Nabalam, 1784. See also notations on some of the 1688 parish *matrículas*, in AGI, Contaduría 920, for example, parish of Nabalam: "Como tales forasteros no tienen vecindad estable, porque suelen volverse a sus pueblos o pasarse a otros parajes."

69. See chapter 6, note 19.

70. For Spanish ideas on the Indians' motives, see, in addition to the material cited in note 68, AGI, Indiferente 2987, Ordenanzas García de Palacio, 1584; AGI, Mexico 3168, Bishop to Crown, 28 July 1737; and AA, Visitas pastorales 5, Valladolid, 1784, Testimony of the *batab* of San Marcos.

71. See chapter 8, note 22. This does not apply to the early postconquest period, when ruling lineages constituted a fairly mobile pool of *gobernadores* within their provinces (discussed in chapter 8).

72. Bauer, "The Church and Spanish American Agrarian Structures," 79. See

also Martin, *Vagabundos en la Nueva España*, on the problem of vagrancy in sixteenth-century central Mexico.

73. González Navarro, *Raza y tierra*, 57-61, 195-205, discusses postindependence labor laws.

74. See note 21 and Klein, "Hacienda and Free Community."

75. Wolf, "Closed Corporate Peasant Communities."

76. Barth, *Ethnic Groups and Boundaries*, 21.

CHAPTER 8, MAYA ELITES

1. Carrasco, "Civil-Religious Hierarchy," 493.

2. Wolf, *Sons of the Shaking Earth*, 212-213. See also, on Mexico, Gibson, *Aztecs under Spanish Rule*, 65-76, 154-185, López Sarrelangue, *Nobleza indígena de Pátzcuaro*, 83-223, and Taylor, *Landlord and Peasant*, 35-66; on Peru, see Kubler, "Quechua in the Colonial World," 376-377, and Spalding, "Kurakas and Commerce," and "Social Climbers"; and on Guatemala, see MacLeod, *Spanish Central America*, 136-142, and Sherman, *Forced Native Labor*, 266-302.

3. This is a possible interpretation of the evidence presented in note 2 and the conclusion reached by Zavala and Miranda, "Instituciones indígenas de la colonia," 60. See also Solano y Pérez-Lila, *Los mayas del siglo XVIII*, 365-366, on highland Guatemala.

4. Roys, *Indian Background*, 129-171.

5. AA, Oficios y decretos 2, Royal cédula circular, 11 Sept. 1766.

6. Peabody Museum (Harvard University), Xiu Chronicles, 1608-1817, used extensively by Roys for his study of "The Cacique System in Yucatan," in *Indian Background*, 129-171.

7. AGI, Mexico 104, Probanza Gaspar Antonio Chi, 1580; Mexico 140, Probanzas D. Juan Chan, 1601, 1619. Martínez Hernández, *Crónica de Yaxkukul*, is a kind of "relación de méritos y servicios," not submitted to the Spanish (so far as is known) but containing both genealogical credentials and an account of cooperation with the Spanish during conquest.

8. See chapter 3, note 87.

9. See Marta Hunt, "Colonial Yucatan," 385-386, 632 note 18. I have seen no one designated as an Indian in a colonial document who did not bear a Maya surname, except among *indios hidalgos* (see, for example, AA, Visitas pastorales 5, Parish census, Sisal de Valladolid, 1782). An unexplained exception is the *batab-gobernador* of Tekanto, 1703-1704, Capt. D. Agustín de Palensuela (AEY, Ayuntamiento 1, Cabildo records, Tekanto, 1683-1704), designated as an *almehen*; he may have been a mestizo.

10. AGI, Mexico 898, Contador real to Crown, 12 July 1755; Mexico 3132, Libro de cargo y data, Campeche, 1761.

11. See Philip Thompson, "Tekanto," 197-233, for a discussion of the three *indio hidalgo* families in Tekanto and their marriage ties. Thompson notes the anomalous status of the *hidalgos* but classifies them as a branch of the Maya nobility. Aside from the documents specifically outlining the distinction and its origins, the extremely uneven geographical distribution of the *indios hidalgos*,

concentrated in some towns and totally absent from others, provides a strong clue; see, for example, AGN, Historia 498, Exp. sobre establecimiento de escuelas en Yucatan, 1790-1805, Subdelegates' reports, 1790; and AEY, Censos y padrones 1, Censuses, 1811.

12. AA, Oficios y decretos 4, Bishop to Minister of the Indies, 13 Nov. 1786. AGI, Mexico 3139, Contador real to Viceroy, 28 Feb. 1787, reporting four "indiezuelos," including the "son of the *cacique* of Sotuta" (D. Ignacio Cocom).

13. AA, Exp. de hábitos, becas y órdenes, 1722-1820.

14. Except for the office of *gobernador*, the municipal government of the colonial *república de indios* was almost identical in formal structure to the *cabildos* or *ayuntamientos* of the Spanish colonial municipalities. The office of *gobernador* had already been introduced by 1552 (Ordenanzas Tomás López, 1552, in Cogolludo, Lib. 5, caps. 16-19), but the full transition to a Spanish system seems to have taken place between the López *visita* and the García de Palacio *visita*: RY, vols. 1 and 2 *passim*; "Visita García de Palacio, 1583"; AGI, Indiferente 2987, Ordenanzas García de Palacio, 1584. See Aguirre Beltrán, *Formas de gobierno indígena*, 28-57, for a description of colonial Indian government in Mexico.

15. On *ahcuchcabs*, see RY 1: 137-138, 2: 85-86, 103-104, 182-183, 211. The roles of the *ahkulels* and *holpops* are not as clearly defined, but they are mentioned in early Maya documents, such as Barrera Vázquez, *Códice de Calkini*, Martínez Hernández, *Crónica de Yaxkukul*, and the 1545 land survey of Sotuta (Roys, *Titles of Ebtun*, 424). See also RY 1: 90, 95, 187, 297; and Cogolludo, Lib. 4, cap. 5, on the *holpop*; and Philip Thompson, "Tekanto," 306-312, 315-318, 325-326, tables 5.7-5.9, for lexical evidence on the three offices. Roys, *Indian Background*, 60-64, has a useful summary of preconquest political organization.

16. On the quadripartite division in Chichen Itza and Mayapan, see Roys, *Chumayel*, 139, 140, 142; on Itzamcanac, see Scholes and Roys, *Maya-Chontal*, 54-55, 158, 390, 395.

17. "Visita García de Palacio, 1583"; TUL, Libro de Cacalchen, ff47-48, 1689-1690; AEY, Ayuntamiento 1, no. 1, Cabildo records, Tekanto, 1683-1704, contain extensive lists of *república* officials. Cárdenas Valencia, *Relación historial*, 112-113, describes local offices and government in the *repúblicas*.

18. The Maya term that the Spanish often translated as *principales* was *unicil uinicob*; see, as a typical example, AGI, Mexico 140, Petition from the pueblo of Sicpach, 12 June 1627, presented by a delegation that included in addition to the *gobernador*, *escribano*, and incumbent *cabildo* officers, four *ahcuchcabs* and eight other *unicil uinicob*, probably representing the rest of the local *principales*. Another less common term was *chuntanes* (spokesmen) as in "los regidores y principales o chunthanes de las parcialidades" (Cogolludo, Lib. 4, cap. 17; see also AGI, Mexico 886, Consulta Council of the Indies, 7 March 1722; AA, Arreglos parroquiales 1, Expedte. sobre el rancho Kambul, Pociaxum, 1810). Royal Treasury accounts also record community tribute quotas paid by "los principales" as a corporate body (for example, AGI, Mexico 3132, Libro de cargo y data, Campeche, 1761, Ramo de Tributo).

19. For titles, functions, and the relationships of authority within the hierarchy of "church servants," the most detailed sources are: AA, Real cedulario 5, Actas del capítulo provincial franciscano, May 1657; IY, Constituciones sinodales, 1722; AA, Visitas pastorales 1, Valladolid, 1755, and Mama, 1768; Visitas pastorales 4, Parish reports, Hecelchakan and Becal, 1782.

20. Collins, "*Maestros Cantores* in Yucatan," traces the links from *ahcambezah* to nineteenth-century *cruzob* priest. While *maestro cantor* was the most common term, *maestro de capilla, maestro de doctrina*, and, in early years, *maestrescuela*, were used interchangeably as well.

21. The evidence for this overlap is particularly clear for towns that have left long runs of *cofradía* records. See, for example, AA, Libro de cofradía Hocaba, 1726-1781. But see also AGI, Mexico 3066, Informaciones instruídas . . . cofradías, 1782, cuads. 5-10, in which witnesses outline their public careers.

22. Unless otherwise noted, statements concerning the political organization of the colonial Maya community and the structure and composition of the elite are based on a file of approximately 11,000 officeholders and *principales*. Slightly under 2,000 of the entries have some biographical (including genealogical) information beyond name, age, title, and residence. The main kinds of supplementary data are place of birth, age at (or date of) accession to office, other offices held, kinship relations with other officeholders and *principales* current and past, whether literate or not, and, less commonly, type and value of property owned. Although all the *repúblicas de indios* are represented, the file is weighted geographically toward the center and northwest, with especially extensive coverage for the Camino Real Alto, Sotuta, and the Costa districts and very sparse coverage for the Tihosuco district and the region immediately surrounding Campeche. Chronologically the file is also heavily weighted toward the late colonial period, reflecting the contents of the local civil and ecclesiastical archives, but with good coverage for the 1560s to 1580s, and the 1660s also.

The principal category of sources is the various sets of judicial inquiries undertaken in the Indian pueblos, which record names, titles, and usually supplementary biographical information for the Indian leaders questioned (often including *principales* not currently in office). The most detailed and complete of the civil inquiries are: AGI, Justicia 245, Residencia D. Diego Quijada, Declaraciones de los indios principales, 1565; Escribanía 318-A and 318-B, Visita que hizo a los pueblos de indios . . . Rodrigo Flores de Aldana, 1666, piezas 1-143; Escribanía 318-A, Averiguación . . . Fray Luis de Cifuentes, 1669; Mexico 366, Pueblos embargados por el gobernador, 1675 (names from these last three inquiries, 1666-1675, have been compiled, although not always accurately transcribed, by Solano y Pérez-Lila, "Autoridades municipales indígenas"); Mexico 3048, Investigación sobre repartimientos, 1755; Mexico 3066, Informaciones instruídas . . . cofradías, 1782, cuads. 5-10, 16-18. There are also many inquiries covering an incomplete portion of the towns. Among the most extensive are: AGI, Escribanía 308-A, no. 1, pieza 2, Informaciones de los indios viejos principales, 1602 (Franciscan *doctrinas*); Mexico 1035, Memoriales sobre abusos de repartimientos, 1700 (Franciscan *doctrinas*); Mexico 1036, Autos sobre repartimientos, 1711; Mexico 1039, Testimonio de visita . . . pueblos de la Costa, Tizimin y Valladolid, 1722; Testimonio de visita . . . Camino Real, 1722; Mexico 3057, Autos formados sobre la falta de tributarios, 1775, cuadernos 1 and 2. Episcopal visitations also contain similar information. The most complete sets are AA, Visitas pastorales 3-6, 1781-1784; and Visitas pastorales 9, 1803. Comparably detailed but incomplete sets are in AA, Visitas pastorales 1, 1755-1768; and AGI, Mexico 1036, Visitas pastorales, partidos of Sahcabchen-Champoton and Camino Real, 1705.

The second important category of sources consists of the various documents prepared, signed, or witnessed by the Indian officials themselves. These include petitions and letters preserved in the major civil archives and ranging from the early postconquest period (for example, a series of letters from *caciques* and *principales* to the Crown in AGI, Mexico 367, Cartas escritas a S.M., 1554-1572) to independence (most numerous in the late colonial period, in AA, Asuntos terminados and Asuntos pendientes, and AEY, Ayuntamientos and Tierras); wills (major collections listed in chapter 4, note 44); boundary surveys, such as Barrera Vázquez, *Códice de Cálkini* (listed in chapter 6, note 20), deeds of sale and a variety of other documents concerning land that are preserved in the two extant sets of *cabildo* records (Tekanto, in ANM, and Roys, *Titles of Ebtun*) and scatttered in ANM and the various *títulos de haciendas*. The *cofradía* records in AA and AC contain lists of *cofradía* officers and sometimes of *cabildo* officials as well, mainly for the eighteenth century; and a unique document in AEY, Ayuntamiento 1, no. 1, a set of election records from the town of Tekanto, 1683-1704. The final, miscellaneous category comprises the myriad Spanish records, ranging from lawsuits to house-by-house censuses that mention, with more or less biographical detail, the names of *república* and *cofradía* officers and church personnel.

23. Philip Thompson, "Tekanto," 359-363.

24. Ibid., 268-282, analyzes the data on *alcaldes* and *regidores* for Tekanto, which has especially detailed records.

25. On the overlap of *maestros cantores* and ahkins, discussed in chapter 11, see especially the material on the Landa idolatry trials in AGI, Justicia 249, Residencia Diego Quijada, 1565, ff4294-4658, and in Scholes and Adams, *Don Diego Quijada* 1: 71-129, 135-162. The major source on the appointment of the hereditary *batabs* as *gobernadores* is the *encomenderos'* reports (1579-1581) in RY, for example 1: 78, 98, 129, 148, 182, 194, 210-211, 221-222, 278, 2: 161-162, 202. On *ahcuchcabs* and *regidores*, see Cogolludo, Lib. 4, cap. 17, and chapter 5, note 60.

26. All the extensive records on Indian pueblos in the 1670 Flores de Aldana *residencia*, some of which refer back to 1657 (for example, AGI, Escribanía 318-A and 318-B, Visitas que hizo . . . Flores de Aldana, 1666, piezas 1-143) use the terms *batab* and *gobernador* interchangeably, without reference to any hereditary *batab* or *señor natural*.

27. AA, Visitas pastorales 1, Bolonchenticul, 1768; AGI, Mexico 3066, Informaciones instruídas . . . cofradias, 1782, cuad. 5 (Auto Batab and cabildo,

Ucu, 20 Jan. 1735), cuad. 6 (Testimony Cacique Bolonchencauich, 1782), cuad. 7 (Testimony Cacique et al. Dzemul, 1782), Testimonio de la real provisión, 1782 (Report by cura of Dzonotpip), Informaciones de los capitanes a guerra, 1782.

28. On presentation of election results, see, for example, AGI, Mexico 158, Testimony Escribano real, 23 Feb. 1665; AEY, Ayuntamiento 1, no. 1, Cabildo records, Tekanto, 1683-1704; AGI, Mexico 1036, Autos sobre repartimientos, 1711 (testimony on fees extorted for confirming elections).

29. A number of sources refer clearly to the "election" of *gobernadores* (and, later, *batabs*) by the *cabildo* or *principales*: AGI, Indiferente 2987, Ordenanzas García de Palacio, 1584; Sánchez de Aguilar, *Informe*, 72; AA, Oficios y decretos 4, Bishop to Josef de Gálvez, July 1784; AEY, Ayuntamiento 1, no. 28, Petition from pueblo de Espita, 29 May 1817. The "appointment" referred to in some early documents (for example, RY 2: 96-97, 175) may have been the governor's formal designation of the *principales'* choice, a procedure elucidated in AGI, Escribanía 305-A, Autos Tekax, 1610, ff213v, 219, 233; and BN, Archivo Franciscano, 55, no. 1142, Información hecha por Fr. Leonardo de Correa, 1636. An accusation against one governor of "imposing some *caciques*" suggests that such action was neither common nor accepted practice (AGI, Escribanía 315-A, Pesquisa y sumaria secreta . . . Flores de Aldana, 1670).

30. On the noble rank of the early catechists and *maestros cantores* and *naguatlatos*, see Lizana, *Historia de Yucatan*, 50-51, and this chapter, note 24.

31. On the *maestros'* control of local education, see Cogolludo, Lib. 4, cap. 18; IY, Constituciones sinodales, 1722; AGI, Mexico 3168, Bishop to Crown, 28 July 1737; AGN, Historia 498, Expedte. . . . escuelas, 1790-1805, Subdelegates' reports, 1790. On the *indios de iglesia* as a privileged, self-perpetuating caste with a monopoly of skills, see AA, Visitas pastorales 5, Parish report, Sotuta, 1784; Asuntos pendientes 2, Petition of Gregorio Ek, 1805; Asuntos terminados 10, Expedte. sobre maestro de capilla, Halacho, 1815; BN, Archivo Franciscano 55, no. 1150, Discurso, 1766 (referring to church musicians); and chapter 6, notes 52 and 60.

32. *Batab-gobernadores* and other officials were removed from office for a variety of reasons. Conspiracy and rebellion, real or alleged, were obvious grounds (see chapter 2, note 39), idolatry was another (see, in addition to the Landa idolatry trials, AGI, Mexico 369, Bishop to Crown, 11 Jan. 1686, although Cogolludo, Lib. 11, cap. 4, reports the case of a *batab* removed by the bishop and then reinstated by the governor). Both the parish clergy and local civil officials could sometimes persuade the governor to remove insubordinate or uncooperative officials (see AGI, Mexico 3053, Causa remoción cura de Becal, 1767; and AA, Visitas pastorales 5, Chancenote, 1784, concerning the "unjust removal" of a *batab* by instigation of the *comandante* of Valladolid). The recorded cases are relatively rare and as many arose from factional struggles within the elite (discussed below) as from conflicts with the Spanish authorities, supporting my contention that the Spanish pursued a hands-off policy as long as the Indian leaders (1) cooperated, and (2) commanded local support.

33. Lisón-Tolosana, *Belmonte de los Caballeros*, 54-63, 75-79, 203-208.

34. Roys discusses concepts of rulership and nobility among the pre-Columbian Maya in an appendix to *Chumayel*, 188-195.

35. TUL, Documentos de Tabi, Pox family papers, 1569-1700; AGI, Mexico 140, Probanzas D. Juan Chan, 1601, 1619; Scholes and Roys, *Maya-Chontal*, Paxbolon papers, 367-368; Xiu Chronicles, Peabody Museum, Harvard University (discussed in Roys, *Indian Background*, 129-170; see also Xiu family tree, transcribed in Roys, *Political Geography*, 65).

36. Philip Thompson, "Tekanto," 232-233.

37. While assumption of descent cannot usually be made on the basis of surname alone, Pacab was rare enough for a strong presumption that the Pacabs who ruled in Oxkutzcab, Dzan, and Muna in the decades after conquest were of the same lineage as those who figure as *principales* and sometimes *batabs* in the succeeding centuries, the last of whom on record is a D. Pedro Pacab, *teniente de batab* in 1782 and either *batab* or retired *batab* (*cacique reformado*), of Muna in 1811.

38. On medieval European kingship, see Bloch, *Feudal Society*, 383-389.

39. On elections of rulers among the Mexica, see Davies, *Aztecs*, 87, 125, 158-159, 207-208; Junta eclesiástica, Mexico, May 1532, in Llaguno, *Personalidad del indio*, 151-154. Primogeniture seems to have been a stronger rule in Texcoco and among the Mixtecs (Davies, *Aztecs*, 126-127; Spores, *Mixtec Kings*, 131-154), but see Las Casas, *Apologética historia* 2: 508, on the Verapaz region; and, for a similar system in Peru of selecting the most suitable from among ruling lineages, see Murra, "Social Structural and Economic Themes," 51. On the Yucatec Maya, where direct descent seems to have been the usual though not invariable pattern, see Landa, *Relación*, 87, 100; RY 1: 97-98, 116, 193-194, 2: 161-162; Sánchez de Aguilar, *Informe*, 140; and Roys, *Chumayel*, 189-190.

40. Gibson, *Aztecs under Spanish Rule*, 175.

41. Philip Thompson, "Tekanto," 393-397.

42. Gosner, "Soldiers of the Virgin"; Remesal, *Historia general*; Lib. 7, caps. 19-21, Lib. 8, cap. 12. The one exception was the *cacicazgo* of Chiapa, on the edge of the highlands.

43. RY 2: 211. See also the Acalan Chontal chronicle: "Nothing could be done without consulting these *principales*" (Scholes and Roys, *Maya-Chontal*, 371); and Las Casas's account of the "consejo del rey" among the Alta Verapaz Chol (*Apologética historia* 2: 511).

44. RY 1: 187; Landa, *Relación*, 26-27. But see RY 1: 297-298, for the pre-conquest precedent of local control over leadership and election from within the local group of *principales* in the absence of a provincial overlord.

45. We have especially rich information on the Huits (or Iuits) from the Landa idolatry trials in Hocaba: Scholes and Adams, *Don Diego Quijada* 1: 135-162. See also on the postconquest Pech in Ceh Pech province RY 1: 78, 129, 221-222, 278; on the Xiu, RY 1: 103, 158.

46. RY 1: 279, 281.

47. AGI, Escribanía 305-A, Autos Tekax, 1610; BN, Archivo Franciscano 55,

no. 1142, Información hecha por Fr. Leonardo de Correa, 1636. Another branch of the Xius provided a *gobernador* for the towns of Oxkutzcab and Maxcanu (Roys, *Indian Background*, p. 169, based on the Xiu Chronicles).

48. See, for example, AGI, Mexico 3066, Informaciones instruídas . . . cofradías, 1782, cuads. 5-10. With few exceptions the outsiders are from nearby towns. In the complaint lodged by the *principales* of the town of Tzotzil against their *batab*, it is clear that their major grievance was his having imposed a *forastero* from Kikil as *alcalde* when they had elected one of their own group: AGI, Escribanía 318-A, Querella de los indios principales contra D. Clemente Ek, 1670.

49. AGI, Mexico 359, Governor to Crown, 11 March 1584. For material on *batab-gobernadores* removed from office or imprisoned because of denunciations from *principales*, see chapter 6, note 86, and AGI, Mexico 1039, Testimonio de las personas que han sido puestas en prisión . . . , 30 Aug. 1722.

50. Roys, *Indian Background*, 246-247, 162, provides evidence that the officially recognized Xiu branch, settled in Yaxakumche, was unpopular locally. I would suggest that this was precisely because of their official status, which meant a lack of integration into and dependence on the support of the local gentry (see TUL, Documentos de Tabi, Pox family papers, ff49-50, on a 1594 dispute between a Xiu *gobernador* and his son and the Pox family, a long-established *principal* lineage). I would also suggest that much of the opposition noted to *caciques* in central Mexico may have represented a similar resurgence of the local gentry rather than challenges from *macehuales*.

51. The debate between and about the Cocom and the Xiu over priority of lineage was apparently a long-standing one by the time of the conquest (see, for example, 1: 161, 288). The Spanish and modern Mayanists have tended to follow the Cocom line: Landa, *Relación*, 26, 31, 40 (and 23 note 126, citing Torquemada); Roys, "Literary Sources for the History of Mayapan," and "Maya Katun Prophecies." But see Kelley, "Kakupacal and the Itzas," and Ball, "The 1977 Central College Symposium," 48-50, for recent reinterpretations.

52. On the Chel, see chapter 5, note 4; on the Pech, see Roys, *Political Geography*, 41; Martínez Hernández, *Crónica de Yaxkukul* (and its variant, "Chronicle of Chacxulubchen," in Brinton, *Maya Chronicles*; on the Canul, see Roys, *Political Geography*, 11-13, and Barrera Vázquez, *Códice de Cálkini*.

53. RY 1: 78, 129, 221-222, 278. But see RY 1: 286-287, for a list of local noble lineages in Teabo (a Ceh Pech town) who claimed descent in a direct line from ancient lords "who were in this land" and who managed to assert themselves into the *batab* category.

54. The Canuls do not seem to have been so far along in consolidating their power as the Pechs (although they had established themselves as *batabs* in Calkini and in at least eight other northern Ah Canul towns: Barrera Vázquez, *Códice de Cálkini*, 21-23, 33-35, 55, 61, 91), and perhaps had less far to fall. Canuls are found in high office only in the *parcialidad* of Dzibikal (Uman) in the late eighteenth century; since Canul was not an uncommon patronymic one can only guess at direct descent.

55. RY 1: 173, 247.

56. Landa, *Relación*, 73-74; Lizana, *Historia de Yucatan*, 50-50v.

57. The "captains of the towns" (or lords) were in general blamed for the conquest (Roys, *Chumayel*, 81), but so, in particular were the Itza—that is, the previous group of invaders or their descendants, and the leaders from the Campeche, Ah Canul, and Mani provinces who "introduced the foreigners" and were "receivers of foreigners" (pp. 84, 145-146): "It was not we who did it; it is we who pay for it today" (p. 84). The Xiu would of course have shared in the blame, as would possibly all the leaders who failed to offer the same fierce resistance as the Cocom, Cupul, and Cochuah, but the Xiu were longer established than the Canul, who were regarded as an "affliction" (p. 155). The post-conquest "restoration" could be signaled in several passages of Roys, *Chumayel*, 160, 161, which represent Christianity (that is, the coming of the Spanish) as the instrument for punishing and ending the "evil ways" of the Itza.

58. Unfortunately, the colonial documentation from eastern Yucatan is too scanty to be able to explore the relationship between legitimacy and longevity for the Cupul, who claimed the deepest roots in pre-Mayapan rulership (see the prologue, note 26). They seem to have retained preeminence in the Cupul province for some time after conquest; although a few appear in the highest posts later in the colonial period, the sample is too small to determine whether they had been eclipsed by an assertive local nobility. The scarcity of the Cupul patronymic in later censuses suggests that they may have simply faded out as a lineage, like the even smaller Cochuah family to the south, who had only a handful of survivors by the late seventeenth century (Roys, *Political Geography*, 137-138, and 9, table 1).

59. *Maestros* and *escribanos* could read and write but not everything was recorded. Genealogical information, important in and of itself for establishing lineage status and claims, was also important as a chronological framework on which to peg sequences and events that established a community's rights: see, for example, Barrera Vázquez, *Códice de Cálkini*, 73-113, in which *batabs* in the Canul province in 1595 gather together aged *ahcuchcabs* to relate the history of the area and its founding families; the oral histories of the *cofradías*, tied to founders and donors and recorded in AGI, Mexico 3066, Informaciones instruídas . . . cofradías, 1782, cuads. 5-10; and, among the many legal cases in which retired *batabs* or other elderly leaders are called on for their knowledge of family and community histories, Títulos de Uayelcheh, Testimony of D. Pascual Puch, Tecoh, 18 Oct. 1794; and AA, Expedte. sobre cofradías Telchac, 1812, Testimony of D. Pascual Dzib (*cacique reformado*, 88 years old).

60. AGI, Escribanía 305-A, Autos Tekax, 1610 (an account of the uprising is given in chapter 2).

61. Sierra O'Reilly, *Indios de Yucatan* 1: 35, 87-92, clearly consulted some of the copies extant in the mid-nineteenth century. He deplored them as of little historical value because they had suffered "mutilations" and changes in the recopying and he thought they might even have been partially invented by the friars because of the colonial dates inserted in the texts. The earliest colonial

mention I have found, aside from Landa's confiscations of manuscripts in the 1560s is AGI, Mexico 369, Memorial Bishop of Yucatan (Landa) to Crown, n.d. (1576?), informing that he had printed Christian texts in Maya in order to wean the Indians away from "muchos librillos y cuadernos viejos de mano que tenían . . . [full of] muchos horrores y grandes herejías juntamente con invocaciones de los demonios." Sánchez de Aguilar, *Informe* (written in 1613), 141-143, 181, refers to both the ancient painted codices and the colonial books transcribed from them in the Latin alphabet, with poetry, histories, and creation myths, that the Indians "keep hidden and read in their meetings" and one of which he confiscated from a *maestro cantor*. Lizana, *Historia de Yucatan*, 37-39, copies a section from a Chilam Balam prophecy, and Cogolludo, Lib. 4, cap. 7, reports that a friar saw one of these "escritos," but in general the Maya must have managed to keep them well hidden.

62. Roys, *Chumayel*, 83, 93, 102, 106, 112, 149. See also p. 75 for the account of an overthrow of one ruler by the usurper Hunac Ceel.

63. Roys, *Chumayel*, 89. Roys translates both "ahau" and "halach uinic" as "ruler," and "batab" as "chief" (Maya text, p. 25). See also p. 124: "Then the rulers of the towns shall be asked for their proofs and titles of ownership, if they know of them."

64. Roys, *Chumayel*, 91.

65. Roys, *Chumayel*, 93. See also pp. 91-92 for other nasty fates awaiting illegitimate rulers.

66. AGI, Mexico 359, Franciscans to Audiencia, 5 May 1606.

67. *Títulos* for *batabs* and other officers might be issued for new towns, but apparently only if they were voluntary "reductions" of unpacified Indians (AGI, Mexico 369, Governor to Crown, 22 Dec. 1604). Even on the frontier the town of Pich did not obtain authorization for a *batab* and a full complement of *cabildo* officers until after it was raised to *cabecera* status (AA, Arreglos parroquiales 1, Traslación y erección de cabecera de curato, 1779-1780; Visitas pastorales 4, Parish report, Pich, 1782).

68. Roys, *Chumayel*, 79 (Roys translates the "mazeualob" of the Maya text, p. 20, as "working people"). The text has a number of other references to greedy and avaricious chiefs (for example, pp. 153, 156-160), usually depicted also as provokers of internal strife and havoc ("foxes" and "moths in beehives"), that is, contrasting with the orderly rule and succession of legitimate government.

69. Philip Thompson has worked out a complex rotational system, based on a model of a quadripartite division of political groupings or territories, from a long run of over a century of *cabildo* lists for Tekanto ("Tekanto," 267-282), especially 273, table 5.4). I do not have a long enough sequence of data for any other town to test the model in any detail; but it is certainly consonant with the in-out-and-up pattern of progression through the ranks that is noticeable elsewhere, and it is also consonant with the ritual *cargo* system discussed in chapter 11. And "political deals" are also a plausible explanation for the anomalies Thompson notes in the Tekanto pattern (pp. 278-280).

70. Wealth and generosity were important criteria for leadership and public office among the pre-Columbian Maya: RY 1: 137; and Barrera Vázquez and Rendón, *Libro de los libros*, 193. Among the colonial Maya, aside from the concrete evidence of the endowments of *cofradías*, probity and skill in property management were highly stressed in Maya petitions and testimony as prerequisites for *cofradía* officers: for example, AC, Libro de cofradía de Animas, San Román; AGI, Mexico 3066, cuad. 1, Petition from Batab, justicias regidores, and principales, Kini, 14 Oct. 1781; and many of the testimonies in Informaciones instruídas . . . cofradías, 1782, cuads. 5-10, 12-16; AA, Cofradías e imposiciones, Exps. sobre cofradías, Nohcacab, 1797, Telchac, 1812-1814, Chapab, 1814. The association between political leadership and support of religious ritual will be discussed in chapter 11.

71. Compare, for example, the very businesslike and fairly typical testament of the *almehen* Nicolás Chan, pueblo of Sicpach, 6 May 1717 (IY, Documentos del sitio Suitunchen), leaving horses, *solares*, and land to his two sons, with the accounts of the various property transfers from heirless old folk, inserted in the testament of Julio Ku, 2 Feb. 1685, AEY, Tierras 1, no. 15, Litigio entre el cacique y justicias de Telchac y Francisco Sabido, 1815. See also TUL, Documentos de Tabi, Testament Juan Pox, 16 March 1569, and Testament Agustina Pox, 2 Oct. 1700; Titulos de Uayalceh, Testament D. Francisco Cen, 12 Dec. 1699, assigning property to executors in recompense for care and in trust for minor heirs.

72. Roys, *Titles of Ebtun*, 21-22, 39-49.

73. TUL, Documentos de Tabi, Pox family papers, 1569-1700 (also included are records of the decline of the Cen lineage of Yotholin, the Mul of Oxkutzcab, and the Couoh of Dzan).

74. AEY, Tierras, 1, no. 15, Litigio . . . Telchac, 1815, Testament Julio Ku, 2 Feb. 1685. I find few prominent Kus in the Costa district in the seventeenth or eighteenth century, but they were well represented among *principales* and high officers, including *batabs*, in Dzan, Muna, Pencuyut, Tekit, and Timucuy in the Sierra district.

75. AA, Cofradías e imposiciones, Exp. sobre la cofradía de Telchac, 1812 (petition from Batab to Provincial, 31 Jan. 1812, giving history of *cofradía*).

76. AEY, Tierras 1, no. 15, Litigio . . . Telchac, 1815 (petition from *cacique* and *justicias* and testimony of Francisco Sabido, 1815).

77. Gibson, *Aztecs under Spanish Rule*, 218; MacLeod, *Spanish Central America*, 141; Spalding, "Indian Rural Society," 170-173, 204-206. *Batabs* and *alcaldes* in Yucatan were also held personally responsible for the tribute and *repartimiento* quotas of *muertos y huídos*: AGI, Mexico 369, Memorial Bishop to Crown, n. d. (1576?); Mexico 1039, Testimonio de visita . . . Costa, Tizimin y Valladolid, 1722, and Testimonio de visita . . . Camino Real, 1722; Mexico 898, Oficiales reales to Crown, 20 Oct. 1745; AA, Visitas pastorales 1, Bolonchenticul, 1768; Visitas pastorales 4-6, Becal 1782, Tixcacaltuyu, 1784, Tixcacalcupul, 1784. See also Marta Hunt, "Colonial Yucatan," 497-482, on the jailing of the *cacique* of Tixkokob in 1690 for tax debts. Although this was not necessarily a unique

case, the records I have consulted refer frequently to various kinds of unauthorized physical coercion by subordinate officials—blows, whippings, confinement in stocks—but not to formal imprisonment.

78. Most of the deeds give no reason for the sale, but the Títulos de Zahe, Kisil, Chactun, and Tabi and all the volumes sampled in ANM contain deeds referring to "necesidades del común del pueblo" and "necesidad de falta de maíz." Others speak simply of "gastos de nuestra república," as a kind of general formula. Dates of famines and dates of sale would not necessarily coincide, since *batabs'* accounts were often settled only when they retired or died in office; see, for example, ANM, vol. 3, Carta de venta, Batab et al., San Francisco Extramuros, 13 June 1720 (settling the accounts of the previous *batab*, deceased); AEY, Tierras 1, no. 14, Escritura de venta, Capt. D. Blas Tamay, 26 July 1785, *cacique reformado* of Dzan.

79. See AGI, Mexico 3057, Autos formados sobre la falta de tributarios, 1775, cuads. 1 and 2; and AEY, Tierras 1, no. 15, Litigio de tierras . . . Telchac, 1815, referring to a *batab's* sale of lands after the 1769-1774 famine. (Tribute relief was granted for only two out of the five years of crop failure.)

80. Spalding, "Social Climbers," and "Indian Rural Society," 164-166, 200-201. Gibson, *Aztecs under Spanish Rule*, 156; Taylor, *Landlord and Peasant*, 49-53; and MacLeod, *Spanish Central America*, 139-140, also mention Spanish support of upwardly mobile *macehuales*.

CHAPTER 9, SURVIVAL AS A CORPORATE ENTERPRISE

1. Mintz and Wolf, "Analysis of Ritual Co-Parenthood," and Foster, "Cofradía and Compadrazgo," provide medieval European and Spanish (respectively) backgrounds and stress the contrast with Spanish America in the traditional European emphasis on the link between sponsor and sponsoree.

2. The type of occasion may differ according to class and region and is likely to be most varied in small towns. Nutini and Bell, *Ritual Kinship*, 56-60, provide a list of thirty-one possible occasions for *compadrazgo* in Indian communities in Tlaxcala.

3. None of the material on orphans cited in chapter 6, note 9, for example, mentions *padrinos*—as opposed to blood kin—as substitute parents, although the overlap may have been considerable.

4. A statistical study of contemporary Yucatan (Deshon, "Compadrazgo on a Henequen Plantation") reveals a pattern suggestive for the colonial period: *compadrazgo* ties duplicate and reinforce real kinship links when a couple functions as part of an extended family household (that is, when it does not *need* outsiders) and reach out to form a wider network when the couple is on its own. This supports the notion that among the Maya the extended family is the preferred and perhaps even necessary socioeconomic unit for survival, which people seek to recreate ritually when for some reason it is broken up or destroyed.

5. Despite Spanish efforts to force Indian men to learn weaving; see Ordenanzas Tomás López, 1552, in Cogolludo, Lib. 5, caps. 16-19.

6. According to several censuses that separate the population according to age, sex, and marital status: in AA, Estadística, Hunucma, 1813, 5.74 percent of the total Indian population age sixteen and over (4,074) were *solteros*; Tekanto, 1.16 percent (out of a total 1,922); Espita, 3.1 percent (total of 1,630).

7. On widows and widowers the figures from AA, Estadística, 1813, are: 11.5 percent for Hunucma, 12.6 percent for Tekanto, and 13.3 percent for Espita. Abandoned wives are often recorded in AA, Visitas pastorales. There is no statistical data available that I know of on the disabled, since the censuses that list *reservados* separately (for example, AA, Estadística, Relación jurada que hacen los curas, 1774) do not distinguish between exemptions for age and exemptions for disability.

8. AGN, Consolidación 4, Cuentas de la caja de consolidación, Merida, 1806-1809, yield a figure of 308,105 for ecclesiastical funds (including 100,000 pesos for the new leper hospital of San Lázaro, although 40,000 pesos of that amount in fact came from the fund of Indian *comunidades*). The list of funds "in consolidation" in AA, Cofradías generales 1816-1823, yields a figure of 198,941 (including 50,000 for San Lázaro). However, the amounts deposited in the royal Treasury represent only part of the total ecclesiastical *censos*: for example, for the Concepcionist order, only 16,210 pesos out of a total of 190,618 the order held in *censos* (AA, Administración de caudales de monjas 1, Cuentas del convento de madres monjas, 1806-1816). The diocesan records, although incomplete, suggest that 500,000 pesos of extant capital (that is, not counting amounts in default) is a conservative figure.

9. The original endowment of 3,000 pesos for cacao had been reduced to 2,250 by 1806; see AA, Obras pías, Fundación del Sr. Dr. D. Nicolás de Salazar, 1692-1796, and Cuenta general que da de la fundación . . . Salazar, 1806-1816. The total endowment for the fund for "poor Indians in the royal prison" is a generous estimate, based on a deposit of 200 pesos in the Caja de consolidación (see note 8), figured at 10 percent of the existing capital. Rather than benefit from charitable foundations, the Indians were often called upon to contribute to the support of institutions, such as the Hospicio de San Carlos for paupers in Merida and the two hospitals run by the Order of San Juan de Dios, which were in fact restricted to whites (a detail omitted in the account of the Hospicio by Cantón Rosado, "Beneficencia pública en Yucatan").

10. Accounts of episcopal finances are not well preserved in local archives, but some detailed records are included in the *expedientes* on episcopal *expolios* in AGN and AGI (for example, AGN, Clero 78, no. 1, Expolios Bishop Juan Cano Sandoval, 1695-1698; Clero 70, no. 1, Expolios Bishop Luis de Piña y Mazo, 1795-1807). The one mention of an episcopal act of charity outside the city was Bishop Ignacio de Padilla's endowment of a granary in the town of Peto with 1,000 *cargas* of maize: BL, Add. MSS, 17569, Report of visita pastoral, 1755-1757.

11. Detailed accounts of parish revenues and expenditure can be found in AGI, Escribanía 308-A, Testimonio de información a favor de los franciscanos, pieza, 16, 1660; Mexico 369, Memorial de la renta . . . Valladolid, 1694; AA,

Estadística, Relación jurada que hacen los curas, 1774, and Cuentas razonadas
. . . 1814; Cuentas de fábrica, 1784-1816, Hocaba, Chunhuhub, San Sebastián, Santiago, Seye, Sacalum, Chancenote, Ichmul, Hopelchen; AGN, Clero 70, Cuentas de los vacantes de los curatos de Chunhuhub, Tizimin, Maxcanu, Kopoma, Palizada, Tekuch y Kikil, 1795-1796.

12. On ecclesiastical efforts on behalf of famine relief, see Cogolludo, Lib. 12, cap. 21; AGI, Mexico 1035, Auto Franciscan Definitorio, 16 June 1700; Mexico 3057, Autos formados sobre la falta de tributarios, 1775, cuads. 1 and 2; AA, Oficios y decretos, Bishop to Crown, 14 Feb. 1784 (reporting on an exemplary but apparently very unusual case, the curate of Xcan, who even sold some of his own property to feed his parishioners during the 1769-1774 famine); Asuntos pendientes 3, Informe cura of Saclum, 1811.

13. In addition to the material in note 11, much correspondence on clerical incomes and expenses (with a uniform absence of the topic of alms) is contained in AA, Asuntos terminados, Asuntos pendientes, Oficios y decretos, Decretos, and Arreglos parroquiales. Another piece of indirect evidence is the lengthy argument used by Sánchez de Aguilar, *Informe*, 184-185, to persuade curates to consider the public relations benefits of a small investment to help care for sick Indians: "El cura, si quiere, con un real más de gasto cada día, puede enviar a diez enfermos un regalo [of chicken soup]. . . . El cura que cuida de los enfermos . . . es estimado, reverenciado y regalado y coge ciento por uno y el enfermo tiene en la memoria el beneficio y regalo que recibió en su enfermedad, y lo publica a todos."

14. *Encomenderos* are reported to have aided their tributaries in times of famine (see, for example, Cogolludo, Lib. 12, cap. 21; AGI, Mexico 3057, Autos formados sobre falta de tributarios, 1775), although such aid can be considered as much a financial investment as an act of charity. As the ever-pragmatic Sánchez de Aguilar noted (*Informe*, 185) in lauding the *encomenderos* who distributed their surplus maize to the Indians (at half price): "Con estos favores multiplican en hijos y va la gente en aumento."

15. On joint-family residence in the late colonial period, see AA, Estadística, house-by-house censuses for Telchac (1815), Chancenote (1805, 1806), Kikil (1803), and Bolonpoxche (1815). See also Nutini, "Nature and Treatment of Kinship," 9-10, who argues that extended family households are much more common in contemporary Mesoamerica than the scholarly literature suggests. His emphasis on the extended family as a social unit even without shared residence (pp. 16-18) is supported by Carrasco, "The Joint Family in Ancient Mexico," demonstrating, on the basis of a 1540 document from Morelos, the economic interdependence of extended families, whether living in the same household or not.

16. RY 1: 263; "Visita García de Palacio, 1583"; AGI, Mexico 361, Ordenanzas Governor Esquivel, 1666. Although I cannot recall mention of communal house building in the late colonial period, a fairly safe presumption from current practice is that it continued.

17. The *cajas de comunidad*, mentioned in RY 2: 96-97, were clearly already

constituted by the time of the *visita* of García de Palacio. Information on the early organization of the *cajas* and community finance in general is derived mainly from "Visita García de Palacio, 1583"; AGN, Tierras 2726, Autos de visita del pueblo de Espita, 1583; AGI, Indiferente 2987, Ordenanzas García de Palacio, 1584; Patronato 58, no. 1, Tasación pueblos de Nunkiní y Mococha, 12 Sept. 1585, in Probanza Juan Vázquez de Andrada, 1598; and Mexico 3167, Memorial Franciscan Provincial and Definitorio, 3 May 1586. See Lamas, *Seguridad social*, 19-105, on the colonial Mexican *caja de comunidad*, which despite Spanish influence he sees as "netamente americana y prehispánica."

18. On *derramas*, see, in addition to notes 17 and 19, AGI, Mexico 359, Governor to Crown, 15 Nov. 1700; Escribanía 305-A, Autos Tekax, 1610, Capítulos contra D. Pedro Xiu, 1609; Sánchez de Aguilar, *Informe*, 129-130; Mexico 158, Abogado de indios to Crown, 28 July 1668; Mexico 361, Ordenanzas Governor Esquivel, 1666, no. 8; Mexico 3066, Informaciones instruídas . . . cofradías, 1782, cuad. 5.

19. The main outlines of the struggle can be traced in Sánchez de Aguilar, *Informe*, 31-84; AGI, Mexico 359, Franciscan Provincial and Definitorio to Crown, 22 June 1629; Mexico 360, Governor to Crown, 12 Aug. 1635, and 27 July 1636; BN, Archivo Franciscano 55, no. 1142, Información hecha por Fr. Leonardo de Correa, Sept. 1636; AA, Oficios y decretos 2, Collection of Reales cédulas a favor de los indios (9 Nov. 1639, 24 March 1645, and 16 May 1665); Real cedulario 5, Actas del Definitorio provincial franciscano, May 1657; AGI, Mexico 1037, Auto Governor, 12 Oct. 1663, in Testimonio de autos . . . doctrina Maxcanu, 1711; Mexico 361, Defensor de indios to Crown, 19 July 1664; Mexico 158, Petition Defensor de indios to Audiencia, 1663, Testimonio de las peticiones que dieron los gobernadores, alcaldes, regidores y escribanos, 1667, and Defensor de indios to Crown, 28 July 1668.

20. The shift from *limosnas* paid from *cajas de comunidad* to *obvenciones* as a uniform head tax was formalized in IY, Constituciones sinodales, 1722, Instrucciones a los curas de indios, and Arancel diocesano, ff217-225, although it took more than a decade to enforce the change on the Franciscans; see AGI, Mexico 1040, Expedte. sobre el sínodo de Yucatan, 1725-1738.

21. AGI, Mexico 158, Defensor de indios to Crown, 28 July, 1668; Escribanía de cámara 315-A, Residencia D. Rodrigo Flores de Aldana, 1670.

22. See, for example, the Códice Sierra, an account book for the *caja de comunidad* of the pueblo of Tejupan in the Mixteca Alta, 1550-1564, transcribed in Dahlgren Jordán, "Cambios Socio-económicos," 111-119, and analyzed in Borah and Cook, "A Case History," 425-428. On Peru, see Spalding, "*Kurakas* and Commerce," 591-592. It is probable that both royal officials and modern scholars have found it so difficult to distinguish *cajas* from *cofradías* (see AGN, Cofradías y archicofradías 13, no. 5, Expedte. sobre el desarreglo de las cajas de comunidad, provincia de Nexapa, 1785; Lavrin, "Execution of the Laws of Consolidation," 41-42; Cabat, "Consolidation of 1804 in Guatemala," 28-29) because they were not distinct entities in Indian conception or practice. Lamas,

Seguridad social, 93-96, reproduces as typical an annual account (Acuchitlan, 1785), in which income from *cofradía* and *comunidad* were mixed together.

23. Described briefly in Cárdenas Valencia, *Relación historial*, 54, 85-86. *Cofradías* already existed in Mani and other major *doctrinas* by 1588 (Ciudad Real, *Relación* 2: 470), and by the 1650s Cogolludo (Lib. 4, cap. 18) tells us that all the parish *cabeceras* (numbering 51 at the time) and "muchísimos pueblos de visita" had *cofradías*. Copies of only two of the early constitutions have been preserved: one for the pueblo of Dzan, 1607, copied in AA, Visitas pastorales 3, Parish report Mani, 1782; and one for the barrio of San Román, n.d., copied at the beginning of the Libro de la cofradía de Animas, San Román, AC. But descriptions of the early rules and organization, based on early *libros de cofradía*, now lost, confirm the uniform character of the original *cofradías* as closely following the Hispanic model; see AGI, Mexico 3066, Informaciones instruídas . . . cofradías, 1782, cuads. 5-10 and 12, and the reports of the Franciscan *doctrineros*, in Testimonio de la Real Provisión, 1782.

24. Rumeu de Armas, *Historia de previsión social*, emphasizes the mutual aid aspects of *cofradías*. On the ritual aspects see, for example, Montoto, *Cofradías sevillanas*.

25. Chávez Orozco, "Orígines de la política de seguridad social"; Lamas, *Seguridad social*, 139-158. See also, on Brazil, Russel-Wood, "Black and Mulato Brotherhoods." Documentary material on Spanish-type *cofradías* in New Spain is voluminous, starting with the eighteen *tomos* of AGN, Cofradías y archicofradías, which seem to be almost entirely devoted to this more official, non-Indian type of *cofradía*. See also AGI, Mexico 2670 and 2672. For Yucatan, AA contains the libros de cofradías of Ntra. Sra. del Rosario, Ntra. Sra. de la Merced and San José, both founded by Spaniards in the cathedral; and AC, the libro de cofradía of Ntra. Sra. de la Merced, Campeche.

26. There is some evidence that this urban type of Spanish *cofradía* was also incompatible with undifferentiated peasant society in Spain, and that rural *cofradías* there have more in common with colonial "Indian" *cofradías* than with the official Spanish version; see, for sixteenth-century data, Lisón-Tolosana, *Belmonte*, 279-281; for contemporary Castile, see Freeman, *Neighbors*, 61-63, 104-106. I do not suggest derivation but rather structural affinity.

27. Gibson, *Aztecs under Spanish Rule*, 139 (and 127-132 for a description of the official and unofficial *cofradías* in the valley of Mexico). A lengthy *expediente* on Indian *cofradías* in AGN, Historia 312-314, 1775-1793, reveals close similarities in the history, organization, function, and financing throughout New Spain. See also Torre Villar, "Algunos aspectos de las cofradías" (Michoacán); Taylor, *Landlord and Peasant*, 70-71, 98, 169-170 (Oaxaca); MacLeod, *Spanish Central America*, 327-328 (Guatemala and Chiapas); and Foster "Cofradía and Compadrazgo," 19.

28. AGI, Mexico 3066, Governor to Crown, 30 April 1783, and Testimonio de la real provisión, 1782, make clear that the Indian *cofradías* came to the notice of royal officials only when a brouhaha arose over the bishop's attempted sale of *cofradía* property.

29. Unless otherwise noted, information on the income and expenditure of the *cofradías* is derived from the account books that have been preserved in diocesan archives under various titles. AA has *libros de cofradía* for the towns of Xocchel, 1702-1787 (dates given are of the actual records, not those on the spine or title page); Hocaba, 1726-1786; Tipikal (under the title of Xbalantun, the name of the *cofradía's* hacienda), 1736-1780; Euan, 1737-1781; Seye, 1743-1782; Tekom, 1747-1788; Baca, 1748-1778; Chicbul (under the title of Ntra. Sra. de Mamentel), 1758-1810; Ekmul, 1746-1781 (also contains accounts for Euan, 1799-1807); Hool, 1741-1797; Kinchil, 1797-1819. The *libro de cofradía* of the Ssmo. Cristo, Santa Ana, Merida (essentially a *vecino cofradía*) also contains some late eighteenth-century accounts for the *cofradía* of Ntra. Sra., Hunucma. AC contains cofradía books for San Román, 1685-1737; Pociaxum, 1710-1748; and Lerma, 1744-1790.

30. Most of the account books listed in note 29 begin after the modified *cofradías* were well established. For information on collective labor, *derramas*, and *repartimientos* for the *cofradías* during the transitional stage, see the oral traditions compiled in AGI, Mexico 3066, Informaciones instruídas . . . cofradías, 1782, in most detail in cuad. 5: Caucel, Ucu, Tetiz, Kinchil, Uman, Samahil, and Bolonpoxche; cuad. 7: Tunkaz, Temozon and Tekom; cuad. 9: Peto. See also the Instrumentos de fundación for the haciendas de cofradía of Ucu, 20 Jan. 1735; Caucel, 11 Feb. 1713; and Hunucma, 1730, in cuad. 17, Testimonio de varias presentaciones de indios, 1782. Even after the capital funds were developed, pueblo officials also continued to rely on *derramas* for some of the recurrent fiesta expense: IY, Constituciones sinodales, 1722.

31. See note 29. For a more detailed discussion of the growth and management of the *haciendas de cofradía*, see Farriss, "Propiedades territoriales," 164-185.

32. AA, Oficios y decretos 3, Juan José Rojo to Bishop, 2 Dec. 1786; AGI, Mexico 3167, Domingo Fajardo to Crown, 7 May 1806; AA, Oficio y decretos 6, Juan José Escalona to Secretary of bishopric, 16 Oct. 1807. See also AA, Visitas pastorales 5, Parish report Yaxcaba, 1784, referring to the economic importance of the *cofradías* during the curate's term as *vicario* of the Peten in the 1770s.

33. AA, Libros de cofradía Ntra. Sra. de Mamentel (Chicbul), 1758-1810, and Hool, 1741-1797. These trading activities are discussed in chapter 4.

34. AGI, Mexico 3168, Oficiales reales to Governor, 22 April 1813, outlining the history of the *bienes de comunidad*. On the annual yield in 1766, see BN, Archivo Franciscano 55, no. 1140, Discurso sobre la constitución, 1766; and for an official account of community finances, AGI, Mexico 3056, Protector de indios to Crown, 11 May 1770.

35. The finances and activities related to the cult of the saints are discussed in chapter 11.

36. Dirks, "Social Responses," 26-31, discusses widespread evidence that large-scale social interaction, cooperation, and sharing increase during early stages of famine, with a consequent strengthening of the sociopolitical system. Then,

depending on the duration of the crisis, the organization breaks down progressively, first atomizing into family units and finally into isolated, competing individuals.

37. DHY 2: 103-104, Bishop to Crown, 7 Sept. 1596; and AGI, Mexico 369, Bishop to Crown, 1 April 1598. The Franciscans had established hospitals in several of the major *doctrinas* but Indians refused to go because of this "superstition."

38. Colonial Maya concepts and techniques of curing are described in some detail in AA, Visitas pastorales 3-6, Parish reports, Mani and Teabo, 1782, Tixcacaltuyu, Chunhuhub, Tixcacalcupul, and Uayma, 1784; Oficios y decretos 3, Expedte. sobre indios curanderos, 1806; and AGI, Mexico 3168, Informe Bartolomé del Granado Baeza, 1 April 1813. A collection of the *ensalmos* (incantations) used for curing, referred to in these ecclesiastical reports, has been transcribed and translated in Roys, *Ritual of the Bacabs*.

39. Constituciones cofradía of Dzan, 1607, in AA, Visitas pastorales 3, Parish report Mani, 1782; AA, Real cedulario 5, Actas capítulo provincial franciscano, May 1657; IY, Constituciones sinodales, 1722; AA, Visitas pastorales 1, Bolonchenticul, 1768; Visitas pastorales 4, Parish reports, Teabo, Hecelchakan, and Becal, 1782.

40. Offered by the curate of Yaxcaba as a proven remedy against chest pains (AGI, Mexico 3168, Informe Bartolomé del Granado Baeza, 1 April 1813). Given the presumed efficacy of this and other nostrums urged by the Spanish upon the Indians (Sánchez de Aguilar, *Informe*, 123, recommended that his parishioners "drink human excrement" against snake bite), it is not surprising that the Maya so stubbornly refused Spanish "medicines" in favor of their own familiar armamentarium.

41. Arguments and evidence for the use of the cattle *estancias* as *socorros* during time of famine are uniform, with more or less detail, throughout the testimonies in AGI, Mexico 3066, Informaciones instruídas . . . cofradías, 1782, cuads. 5-10 and 12.

42. AGI, Mexico 158, Representación Abogado de indios, 1663. See also Landa, *Relación*, 96; AGI, Mexico 140, Probanzas D. Juan Chan, 1601, 1619; and Mexico 361, Ordenanzas Governor Esquivel, 1666, no. 11, on communal labor for the poor, those without kin, and other unfortunates. This practice is no doubt common to any peasant society, and even the much vaunted welfare system of the Inca empire appears to have been a similar, locally run program of working lands for the old and disabled and not a state organized system at all: Murra, "Social Structural and Economic Themes," 51.

43. AGI, Mexico 1039, Testimonio de la visita . . . Camino Real, 1723. These testimonies are the only reference I have seen to a communal sharing of tax burdens for the old, widowed, and disabled (*impedidos*), but Indian officials were, perhaps understandably, taciturn about their system of public finance and tax collection.

44. See, for example, AEY, Tierras 1, no. 1, Expedte. sobre venta de tierras

Izamal, 1730, concerning the sale of community lands to help pay the *holpatan*, technically a head tax.

45. AA, Asuntos pendientes 3, Exp. sobre reservarse de obvenciones . . . curato de Hoctun, 1810. This section contains a number of similar *expedientes* in which the issue is resolved by medical examination. The Tribunal de indios also employed a physician in Merida to examine Indians who sought exemption from tribute because of illness or incapacity (AGI, Mexico 3056, Governor to Crown, 8 Nov. 1767; AA, Oficios y decretos, Carta cordillera Bishop to Curas, 5 Aug. 1786). How this was to benefit the truly ill or disabled, unable to make the journey, is left unexplained.

46. On intercommunity boundary disputes, see chapter 6, note 20.

47. The only reference I have seen to armed strife between communities, except along the southern frontier, concerned more or less ritualized combat during Carnival: AGI, Mexico 361, Ordenanzas Governor Esquivel, 1666, no. 7.

48. Villa Rojas, "Notas sobre la tenencia de la tierra," is a useful survey of the published literature, valid in general outline except for a confusion over the two types of colonial *parcialidad*, leading to the unfounded conclusion (pp. 29-34) that the barrio type of *parcialidad* (as opposed to the relocated, subordinate town: see chapter 5) was a landholding unit.

49. The evidence is equivocal. Cárdenas Valencia, *Relación historial*, 112, describes this office as separate. But no *alcalde col* is included in the lists of *república* officers cited in chapter 8, note 22. In AEY, Tierras 1, no. 20, Litigio sobre rancho San Antonio Buluch, mensura de tierras, 1764; AGI, Mexico 3066, Informaciones instruídas . . . cofradías, 1782, cuad. 7 (Tixpeual); and Roys, *Titles of Ebtun*, 258, Conocimiento, 22 Nov. 1817, the *alcalde col* appears to be the second-ranking *alcalde*, while in AEY, Tierras 1, no. 18, Certificate cacique et al. Sotuta, 6 Jan. 1801, he appears to be the second *regidor*.

50. Information on land tenure among the Indians and on transfers of land to the Spanish is derived primarily from testaments and deeds of sale. The main collections of Indian land documents are listed in chapter 4, note 44. ANM also contains documents on land transfers among Indians, attached to deeds of sale to and among Spaniards, but the fullest and earliest records have been incorporated into the estate boundaries; see AEY, Tierras 1, no. 15 Litigio . . . Telchac, 1815 (testamente 1685); AGN, Tierras 702, Sitio Yaxche and Estancias Ixcuyum (Sicpach), 1745-1748; Tierras 833, Estancias Chalmuch, Tixcacal, and Susula (Caucel), 1758-1764; Tierras 1061, Haciendas Suitunchen and Oxchac (Caucel), 1788-1790; Tierras 1409, Hacienda Cayal (Pociaxum), 1810-1811; Tierras 1464, Sitios Opichen, Sisal, Chacsinkin, and Tepecal (Mani), 1748-1753. Another major source is Indian testimony regarding *cofradía* lands in AGI, Mexico 3066, Informaciones instruídas . . . cofradías, 1782, cuads. 5-10, 12. Copies of *instrumentos de fundación* are in AA, Asuntos terminados 9 (Cuzama, 23 Sept. 1696); AGI, Mexico 3066, Informaciones instruídas, cuad. 7 (Sicpach, 24 May 1708); cuad. 18 (Barrio de Santiago, 20 Nov. 1738); TUL, Documentos de Tabi (Pustunich, 8 April 1708).

51. By the eighteenth century the Maya were also buying and selling uncultivated bush (*kax*), as distinct from improvements to the land or *cenotes* with attached rights to land (see below), but the price, at one real for five *mecates* (Philip Thompson, "Tekanto," 118-121, table 3.3), was well below that for *milpa en roza*. The relative abundance (and therefore low value) of land even in the late colonial period is also indicated by the fact that much of the large-scale agricultural production by both the Indian elite and Spaniards was still on communal lands either rented or simply commandeered: AA, Oficios y decretos 4, Representación Abogado de indios, 25 Sept. 1781, and Bishop to Josef de Gálvez, 11 Dec. 1785; AGI, Mexico 3168, Informe Bartolomé del Granado Baeza, 1 April 1813; Sierra O'Reilly, *Indios de Yucatan* 1: 81; AGN, Consolidación 10, Exp. sobre bienes de comunidad Yucatan, Reglamento, 12 July 1797.

52. See, for example, AEY, Tierras 1, no. 4, Diligencias promovidas por Domingo Ku, 1791, in which the value of disputed fruit trees was assessed at 13 pesos 2 reales, while the *solar* itself was assessed at only 8 reales. See TUL, Documentos de Tabi, Petition Diego Pox, n.d. (1686), for an earlier dispute over fruit trees.

53. AGI, Mexico 361, Ordenanzas Governor Esquivel, 1666, no. 11; AGN, Consolidación 10, Expedte. sobre bienes de comunidad Yucatan, Reglamento para la administración de bienes de comunidad, 12 July 1797. *Solares* were sold to non-Indians: ANM contains many deeds of sale for the Merida barrios; and AEY, Tierras 1, a number of *expedientes* with deeds or references to them, for the pueblos.

54. See, for example, Roys, *Titles of Ebtun*, 130-132, Deed of sale, Cuncunal, 14 Aug. 1665: "Yo Diego Cupul . . . declaro la verdad que doy el conocimiento del paraje de un pozo mío a Don Lucas Tun el cual es cacahuatal con todos los montes que le pertenece alrededor . . . y están señalados por detrás todo con sus mojoneras . . . ."

55. Philip Thompson, "Tekanto," 118-125, tables 3.3-3.5, summarizing wills and deeds on *montes* (1726-1820), *milpa* (1725), and *sitios* (1770-1820). Documents on the town of Mani's sale of land to a Spaniard in 1753 (TUL, Documentos de Tabi, ff70-80) represent the new and old approaches: a very detailed survey by the town officials of the parcel to be sold, and a formal complaint about the survey from a Juan Cen because "when the *Justicias* asked me to declare where my *montes* ended and where the boundary markers were, I could not reply because I did not know."

56. The lands of the town of Kisil, relocated at Tzeme, were granted to Rodrigo de Escalona Pacheco in 1603 (Títulos de Kisil). Officials from surrounding pueblos were consulted, but there were no spokesmen for Kisil.

57. Documents concerning a *real merced* granted in 1633 to establish the hacienda Canicab (over the objections of the *gobernador* of Tixkokob) are summarized in Chardon, *Geographic Aspects*, 173-174. All the hacienda *títulos* I have consulted are based on purchases from the Indians rather than grants, except for Kisil (see note 56).

58. Various *cartas de venta* and inventories in ANM, vol. 3, ff25-26, 32v, 36v-

37v, 59v-97, underscore the relative cheapness of unimproved land: a *paraje* two leagues from Merida sold for 40 pesos, a female slave for 250, a male slave for 300, and an *estancia* near Conkal for 1,138 pesos (550 pesos for the *planta* and two *sitios* and the rest for livestock and 255 *mecates* of newly prepared milpa). Speculation could have been another motive for purchasing, since land could be resold at a profit, especially if a license for livestock had been obtained.

59. ANM, vol. 3, 1720-1722, ff103v-104v, Carta de venta, 17 May 1720. Another almost identical example is vol. 14, 1751-1755, ff100-102v, Carta de venta sitio San Antonio Chonlok (Conkal), 19 Jan. 1752.

60. This was among the main reasons given by Maya officials for opposing the sale of *cofradía* estates to Spaniards: AGI, Mexico 3066, Informaciones instruídas . . . cofradías, 1782; Governor to Crown, 30 April 1783.

61. Títulos de Kisil, Testimony of officials of Bolonpoxche, Uman, Samahil, Tzeme, and San Cristobal, 22 July 1603. For conflicts over cattle invasions, see, in addition to documents in Kisil and other estate records (Títulos de Kisil records further complaints in 1642 and 1661), AGI, Mexico 140, Petition gobernador et al. of Sicpach, 12 June 1627; Escribanía 306-A, no. 11, D. Bernardo de Magaña con los indios de Maxcanu, 1662-1674; Escribanía de cámara 310-A, no. 3, Pleito sobre poblar unas tierras en los partidos de Uman y Nunkini, 1697. There are also records of Spaniards, especially *encomenderos*, who took up the struggle on behalf of the Indians (AGI, Escribanía 305-A, Capt. D. Alonso de Torres con D. Gaspar León de Salazar, 1644; AGN, Tierras 483, no. 2, Cristóbal Carrillo de Albornoz contra José de la Peña, 1728-1729). Marta Hunt, "Colonial Yucatan," 404-409, suggests that the motive was to restrict competition with their own ranching enterprises.

62. AGI, Mexico 3066, Informaciones instruídas . . . cofradías, 1782, record several examples of these gifts; AEY, Tierras 1, no. 3, Documentos sobre poblar la estancia Nohcacab (Izamal), 1776-1790, concerns a later case. Bribes and intimidation help to explain the pueblo officials' acquiescence, invariably declaring either that the proposed *sitios* are savannas unfit for milpas or that the pueblo does not need the land for milpas, at the same time that they were complaining about cattle invasions and, later, land shortages; see AEY, Tierras 1, no. 18, D. Manuel Barnet con los indios de Sotuta, 1796-1804, in which the pueblo officials extracted a promise (not honored, as it turned out) from the prospective *estanciero* to kill or sell any cattle that destroyed milpas.

63. Letter summarized in AGI, Mexico 886, Consulta Council of the Indies, 7 March 1722. See also Mexico 1039, Governor to Crown, 2 July 1726, attributing the problem to the *cofradía* estates.

64. AGI, Mexico 3052, Royal cédula to Governor, 1 July 1731.

65. The rapid expansion of landed estates in the late colonial period and the reasons for it are discussed in chapter 12.

66. See, for example, AEY, Tierras 1, no. 17, Litigio sobre hacienda Holactun, 1817-1819, a *pleito* over land purchased in 1638 and 1685: the local curate of Hoctun supported the Indians' allegation that peaceful coexistence with the hacienda had lasted until 1800, when the new owner bribed the surveyor (who

confessed "en descargo de su conciencia") to enlarge the boundaries. For other similar conflicts, see AEY, Tierras 1, no. 14, Documentos del sitio San Cristóbal, 1764-1818; AA, Arreglos parroquiales 1, Exp. sobre S. Joseph Chencoyi, 1792; Asuntos terminados 9, Expedte. sobre hacienda Chunkanan, 1803-1804, and Expedte. sobre hacienda Dzotcheen, 1804; AGN, Tierras 359, no. 51, José Herrera y Francisco y José Manzanares contra Mateo y Sebastián Noh, 1804 (land purchased in 1674); Tierras 1421, no. 13, Litigio hacienda Sta. María, 1818-1819; Tierras 1425, no. 16, 17, 24, 25, and 28, *pleitos* between various haciendas and the pueblos of Yobain, Hecelchakan, Nohcacab, and Cansahcab, 1816-1821; Tierras 1426, no. 1, Denuncia de las tierras con su pozo llamado Chenku, 1817-1821. While it is true that records from the late colonial period are better preserved, we do have earlier records of conflicts over cattle. Marta Hunt, "Colonial Yucatan," 405 and 634 note 33, finds that Indian complaints that they had not intended to alienate lands begin only with the *composición de tierras* of 1726-1728 (presumably not during the *composiciones* of 1678 and 1710). Finally, the estate records themselves document the sudden appearance of disputes over boundaries, as opposed to cattle invasions: for example, Títulos de Uayalceh (most lands acquired 1657-1699, first dispute 1785); San Bernardino Chich (lands acquired 1735, first dispute 1792); Chactun (original land purchases, 1623-1700, first dispute over milpas, 1775, first dispute over boundaries, 1781).

67. AA, Asuntos terminados 3, Francisco Bravo to Bishop, 30 March 1818.

68. AEY, Tierras 1, no. 15, Litigio entre cacique y justicias of Telchac and Francisco Sabido, 1815-1816.

69. I have found no record of conflicts between the Indian communities and *castas*, but see AA, Asuntos pendientes 2, Petition from Dionisio Valdés, Caciano Nobelo and José Casanova, 1795; and AEY, Tierras 1, no. 7, Expedte. sobre paraje San Antonio, 1789-1801, for evidence that *castas*, if anything, fared worse than Indians in their encounters with Spanish *hacendados*.

70. Títulos de Chactun, Petition from D. José Manuel González to Governor, 17 June 1801. Although González (curate of the Sagrario and later Arcediano of the cathedral) acquired the estate only in 1796, the Indians had been pursuing an unremitting and on the whole successful delaying action against an attempted land grab since 1781 and were to continue their efforts, with no end in sight, until the end of the colonial period. That the threat to stir up the Indians to "poner pleitos" was considered a useful weapon in boundary disputes between *hacendados* (AA, Asuntos terminados 1, Bishop to Crown, 18 May 1782) is further evidence that these judicial challenges were not to be taken lightly.

71. Such complaints are sprinkled throughout AA, Asuntos terminados and Asuntos pendientes, and others can be found in AA, Visitas pastorales. For a particularly detailed denunciation and inquiry, see AA, Arreglos parroquiales 1, Exp. sobre permuta de curatos de Muna y Chichimila, 1782, cuad. 2, Petitions cacique y justicias de Chichimila, Xocen, Dzitnup, and Ebtun.

72. See Farriss, "Propiedades territoriales," 185-193, and below, chapter 12.

73. These jurisdictional rivalries, starting with conflicts between the Francis-

cans and civil authorities in the early postconquest period, generated a large proportion of the *expedientes* that reached the Audiencia of Mexico and the Council of the Indies. See AGI, Mexico 3051-3092, for late colonial cases from Yucatan, some of which are discussed in Farriss, *Crown and Clergy*, 23-25, 110-111, 165-167.

CHAPTER 10, THE COSMIC ORDER IN CRISIS

1. Michael Coe, "Iconology of Olmec Art," analyzes the "baby-faced jaguar" (or jaguar-faced baby) motif.

2. Visual images and written texts contain a vast amount of information about Mesoamerican "deities," but it is embedded in a symbolic system that may well be unsurpassed in its complexity and is probably no longer totally decodable. Within the limitations posed by the nature of the evidence and our own alien perceptions of it, several general studies stand out as especially illuminating as well as informative. J. Eric Thompson, *Maya History and Religion*, 159-373, is unequaled as a guide through the major domains of the lowland Maya's sacred system: ritual, gods, myths; Miller's study of the sacred imagery of the east coast Maya, *On the Edge of the Sea*, chapter 5, offers many insights of a more general nature as well. The rich conquest-period ethnographic material for the central highlands can be a helpful supplement to the scantier Yucatec data (bearing in mind regional differences), because of both the shared Mesoamerican substratum and the strong Mexican influence on Postclassic Maya "state" religion. On central Mexico, see Soustelle, *Pensée cosmologique*, and Nicholson, "Religion in Pre-Hispanic Central Mexico." Finally, Eva Hunt, *Transformation of the Hummingbird*, is a tour-de-force of structural analysis of the "transformational system" of symbolic codes, linked to the major deity (or deity cluster) Tezcatlipoca (identified with the Maya Itzamna) and therefore a major key to the grammar of Mesoamerican cosmology.

3. On Montejo's policy and practice, see the prologue, notes 29 and 30. Franciscan documents on their early missionary labors have disappeared (during the nineteenth-century secularizations, if not before). Extracts of some of the material on evangelization to 1600 were compiled by the order for a *pleito* with secular clergy, 1605-1689: AGI, Escribanía 308-A, no. 1, piezas 1, 2, 9, and 10. This same material was used by the Franciscan chroniclers, Lizana, *Historia de Yucatan*, part 2, especially pp. 42v-62, and Cogolludo, Lib. 5, caps. 1, 5-9, 14. The firsthand account by Landa, *Relación*, 67-75, is extremely cursory.

4. See the prologue note 6. The other, documented cases occurred in the southern zone of refuge.

5. See Miller, "Iconography of the Painting," on the *kusansum*, or *cuzanzum*, (living rope) symbolism.

6. For Spanish colonial accounts of these "superstitions," see Sánchez de Aguilar, *Informe*, 121-124; IY, Constituciones sinodales, 1722, Instrucciones a los curas de indios; AA, Visitas pastorales 3-6, Parish reports, Mani, Hopelchen, Teabo, Becal, and Bolonchenticul (1782), Chunhuhub, Tixcacalcupul, and Uayma (1784); AGI, Mexico 3168, Informe Bartolomé del Granado Baeza, 1 April 1813 (es-

pecially detailed). For ethnographic reports, see Brinton, "Folklore de Yucatan," and "Nagualism"; and Redfield and Villa Rojas, *Chan Kom*, especially chapters 10 and 11.

7. The first report I have seen of this new association is AGI, Mexico 3168, Informe Bartolomé del Granado Baeza, 1 April 1813. On *pauahtuns* see also Landa, *Relación*, 137-138, and notes 638-639; Roys, *Chumayel*, 110, and *Ritual of the Bacabs*, especially p. 19. What the Spanish called *misas milperas* (also called *tich* or offering) are also reported in AA, Real cedulario 5, Royal cédula to Bishop, 11 March 1764 (extracting a letter from the governor); Papeles de los señores Gala, Guerra, Carrillo y Piña, Memorial Fr. Joseph Baraona, 21 May 1770; Visitas pastorales 3-6, Parish reports, Mani, Becal, Hopelchen, Teabo (1782), Chunhuhub, Tixcacalcupul, and Uayma (1784), with details very similar to the *uhanlicol* and other milpa ceremonies described and transcribed in Redfield and Villa Rojas, *Chan Kom*, 127-144, 339-356, and Villa Rojas, *Maya of East Central Quintana Roo*, 111-117. Landa, *Relación*, scarcely mentions any aspect of private devotions, but see AGI, Justicia 249, Residencia D. Diego Quijada, 1565, cuad. 5, ff4,301-4,311, for a detailed description of what was clearly an *uhanlicol* for illness performed in the town of Chemax.

8. The distinction between Maya idolatry and superstition, although sharpening through the course of the colonial period, was already evident in the Ordenanzas of Tomás López, 1552 (Cogolludo, Lib. 5, caps, 16-19). For clerical attitudes toward Maya shamans in the late colonial period, see, in addition to note 7, AA, Oficios y decretos 5, Expedte. sobre indios curanderos, 1806; and Cuentas de Fábrica 1, Chancenote, 1784-1816, Informe cura, 1813.

9. On personal or family idols and shrines, see RY 1: 52; Landa, *Relación*, 103, 110-111, 151, 154-146, 159-160. For views on the "abandonment of the temple cult" and the "atomization of religion," see Tozzer's discussion, in Landa, *Relación*, 103-109 note 496, and p. 152 note 756; and Pollock et al., *Mayapan*, 16, 136, 267, 428.

10. Aside from the public and private rituals, and combinations thereof, described by Landa, *Relación*, 138-166, 179-184, the distinction is brought out clearly in an idolatry case in Tixcacaltuyu, involving, on the one hand, family idols kept in homes and, on the other, a large community idol (all heirlooms), the object of collective devotions: AGI, Mexico 369, Bishop to Crown, 11 Jan. 1686. Lizana, *Historia de Yucatan*, 56v-60v, describes a public sacrifice in Dzitas in 1551, aborted by Landa's timely (or untimely, depending on one's point of view) arrival to convert the populace.

11. Landa, *Relación*, 184: "Each town had the authority to sacrifice those whom the priest or *chilan* or lord thought best, and they had their public places in the temples for doing this, as if it were the most necessary thing in the world for the preservation of their public welfare."

12. The most detailed accounts of clandestine "idolatries" are the records of investigations and trials conducted by Diego de Landa, 1562, contained in the *residencia* of Diego Quijada. Many of the accounts are published in Scholes and Adams, *Don Diego Quijada* 1: 24-343, but see also the unpublished records of

investigations in the Valladolid area, 1558-1562, in AGI, Justicia 249, Residencia Quijada, 1565, cuad. 5, and an excellent summary of the early idolatry material in Scholes and Roys, "Fray Diego de Landa." Many reports on idolatries from bishops and governors to the Crown, clustered in the late sixteenth and early seventeenth centuries, are contained in Mexico 359 and 369 (but see also Bishop to Crown, 24 Feb. 1643, n.d. (c. 1646) and 11 Jan. 1686, in Mexico 369). The other major sources are RY, especially 2: 147, 190, 213; and Sánchez de Aguilar, *Informe*, an extended account of idolatries from the 1580s to 1613, much of the evidence having been uncovered or processed by the author as curate of Chancenote and later as Provisor of the diocese. On idolatries in the same period, see also Cogolludo, Lib. 11, cap. 4; and AGN, Inquisition 467, ff436-442, 1607, cited in Greenleaf, "Inquisition and the Indians," 143; and for further Inquisition records dealing peripherally with Indian idolatries, see note 25.

13. The tortures and their effects are described in Scholes and Adams, *Don Diego Quijada* 1: 24-69, Declaraciones de algunos testigos, 1562. The stretching technique (*colgar*) that suspended the witness by his wrists (sometimes with weights attached to his feet) left a particularly strong impression on the Maya, who in the 1630s still referred to that period as "el tiempo de la cuelga" (Lizana, *Historia de Yucatan*, 9) and commemorated it in Roys, *Chumayel*, 138, 152, 153. (Roys, by using the word "hang" instead of suspend, misses the connection the Maya made, p. 138, between the arrival of Bishop Toral and "when the hangings ceased." Toral put a stop to the trials.)

14. Sánchez de Aguilar, *Informe*, makes frequent reference to eastern Yucatan as more prone to idolatries, particularly the east coast and Cozumel, where the curate was supposedly drowned for his attempts to suppress pagan rites (pp. 120-121). See also, on cases of public idolatry in eastern Yucatan, AGI, Mexico 359, Governor to Crown, 11 March 1584; and, on apostasy in Bacalar and the southern zones, see the prologue, note 7.

15. Scholes and Adams, *Don Diego Quijada* 1: especially 41-128 (Procesos contra indios idólatras de Sotuta . . .), 135-162 (Información hecha en el pueblo de Homun . . .), and 162-169 (Testimonio de algunos españoles). See also, on *batabs* and *principales* in charge of the clandestine rites, Ordenanzas Tomás López, 1552, in Cogolludo, Lib. 5, caps. 16-19; Sánchez de Aguilar, *Informe*, 137-138 (on D. Andrés Cocóm of Sotuta, 1583); AGI, Mexico 359, Governor to Crown, 11 March 1584; Mexico 3048, Governor to Crown, 16 April 1585; Mexico 369, Bishop to Crown, 24 Feb. 1643; Cogolludo, Lib. 11, cap. 4 (ca. 1630). On the role of *maestros cantores* and other church personnel, see RY 2: 28, 190, 213.

16. First reported by Sánchez de Aguilar, *Informe*, 166, referring to the abandoned "cues" on the north coast around Río Lagartos. Cogolludo, Lib. 4, cap. 7, represents a later (1655) more relaxed attitude in reporting his discovery of offerings of cacao and copal in one of the "chapels" at the summit of the main pyramid at Uxmal as "some superstition or idolatry, recently committed, about which those of us there were unable to learn anything." AGI, Mexico 361, Ordenanzas Governor Esquivel, 1666, no. 6, still refers to "idolatrías . . . ado-

rando y perfumando figuras falsas" but all relegated to "cuevas, milpas y lugares ocultos y retirados." With the exception of a case discovered in 1684 (AGI, Mexico 369, Bishop to Crown, 11 Jan. 1686), these were highly furtive acts engaged in by small groups (with no further reference to idols), which the clergy could dismiss with more or less distaste as "superstitions," "memories of old errors," or not "formal idolatries": see IY, Constituciones sinodales, 1722, Instrucciones a los curas de indios; AGI, Mexico 3168, Bishop to Crown, 28 July 1737, who declared "formal idolatry" to be "entirely eradicated"; and the clerical accounts of *misas milperas* cited in note 7.

17. AGN, Inquisition 1256, no. 1, Proceso contra Pascual de los Santos Casanova, Hunucma, 1786-1787 (summarized in Uchmany de la Peña, "Cuatro casos de idolatría," 279-289). Some of the *misas milperas* referred to in colonial documents could well be *cha-chaac* ceremonies rather than private *uhanlicol* rites. For a modern version of the *cha-chaac*, see Redfield and Villa Rojas, *Chan Kom*, 138-143.

18. Indians supposedly were not forced to accept baptism, but even by official policy they were to be punished if they resisted Christian instruction and persisted in pagan practices: Ordenanzas Tomás López, 1552 (Cogolludo, Lib. 5, caps. 16-19).

19. AGI, Mexico 3168, Bishop to Crown, 28 July 1737. For a range of clerical opinions mostly, although not uniformly, pessimistic about the Indians' adherence to the faith, see AA, Visitas pastorales 3-6, Parish reports, 1782-1784, and chapter 3, note 19. Most of the reports on settlements of *indios huídos y gentiles*, listed in the prologue, notes 7, 10, and 13, stress the danger of apostasy.

20. Horton, "African Conversion," and "On the Rationality of Conversion."

21. Also seen (again not necessarily inconsistently) as a dual, male-female creative power. J. Eric Thompson, *Maya History and Religion*, 200-206, 209-233, discusses the linguistic and iconographic evidence for Hunabku as supreme creator god among the Maya, personified in Itzamna, who incorporated in his many aspects "most" (perhaps all?) of the other major Maya gods. On the Aztec Ometeotl "as the personification of godhead in the abstract," subsumed in the Tezcatlipoca complex, see Nicholson, "Religion in Pre-Hispanic Central Mexico," 411-412. For insights into the conception of the many as refractions of the one, I am indebted to Evans-Pritchard, *Nuer Religion*, chapters 2 and 3, and to Eva Hunt, *Transformation*, especially pp. 55-56. See also Hunt's discussion of the fourfold (or eightfold) manifestations of Tezcatlipoca, seen as the highland equivalent of Itzamna (pp. 120-123).

22. See, for example, Lizana, *Historia de Yucatan*, 40-41v. Maya traditions in a sense encouraged this view by claiming that they had no idolatry or idols or sacrifices before the arrival of the Mexicans and Kukulcan (RY 1: 52, 78-79, 121-122, 215, 225-226, 242-243, 254-255, 270-271), which I take to mean, purged of Christian influences, that the Mexicans introduced the proliferation of images and human sacrifice on a larger scale (and perhaps in new forms), in addition to new gods, such as Kukulcan; and that an esoteric cult of the high god and

his major Maya manifestations lost some prominence—in other words, a shift in emphasis and ritual mode.

23. On the purist stance of the Erasmians, see Bataillon, *Erasmo y España*, and its appendix, "Erasmo en el Nuevo Mundo"; and Christian, *Local Religion*, 158-165. The clergy themselves were divided (see, for example, the early conflict over the cult of the Virgin of Guadalupe, in Ricard, *Conquista espiritual*, 347-352), and in Yucatan, Franciscans and secular clergy alike promoted the cult of the saints and left enthusiastic reports of sweating and bleeding images, miraculous cures, and the other stimuli to popular devotion that the Erasmians deplored; see Sánchez de Aguilar, *Informe*, 113-114; Lizana, *Historia de Yucatan*, 17-33, 105-112; Cárdenas Valencia, *Relación historial*, 91-29, 100-101, 105-107; Cogolludo, Lib. 6, caps, 3 and 4, Lib. 9, caps. 17-21, Lib. 10, caps. 14-16, Lib. 11, caps. 1-3, 5, Lib. 12, caps, 9, 10, 12, 13, 19, 20. References to the devil (singular and plural) are legion.

24. See, for example, Sánchez de Aguilar, *Informe*, 114-118, on the famous "duende parlero," who terrorized Spaniards in the Valladolid region for decades; and the long treatise by Las Casas, *Apologética historia* 1: 449-522, on magic and the power of "demons." The rich Inquisition material for colonial Mexico has so far been quarried mainly for cases of heresy and "Judaizing," but see Aguirre Beltrán, *Medicina y magia* (and on Spain in this period, Caro Baroja, *World of the Witches*). In Yucatan, witchcraft denunciations were directed primarily against mulattoes and Indians (the latter handled in the diocesan courts), but the Spaniards reveal much of their own beliefs in their comments on and dealings with Indian magic.

25. See, for example, AGN, Inquisición 621, no. 1, Causa contra Luis Ricardo and D. Alvaro de Osorio, 1672; no. 5, Denuncias sobre brujerías y ensalmos . . . Valladolid, 1672; Inquisición 908, no. 14, Causa contra Francisco Pantoja y cómplices, 1748; Inquisición 1140, no. 2, Denuncia sobre hechicerías . . . Campeche, 1797. See also AA, Oficios y decretos 5, Expedte. sobre indios curanderos, Campeche, 1806; Papeles de los señores Gala, Guerra, Carrillo y Piña, Informe Fr. Joseph de Baraona, 21 May 1770; Visitas pastorales 4, Parish report Teabo, 1782, on *vecino* beliefs that Indians were powerful sorcerers and on *vecino* participation in Maya rituals. Belief in the power of Indian magic did not necessarily involve sharing the Indians' belief system. For example, an African slave accused of participation in idolatries did not actually take part in the ritual nor seem to have any clear idea of its particular significance to the Indians. He merely partook of some of the sacrificial food, which he regarded as having some kind of sacred power of possible benefit to him; see AGN, Inquisición 125, no. 69, Información contra Cristóbal, esclavo negro, 1582. See also Inquisición 213, no. 10, Causa contra Juan de Loria, 1467; and Inquisición 302, no. 17b, Proceso contra Juan Vela de Aguirre, encomendero, 1613-1614. In contrast, another case concerned some *pardos* who participated fully in a *chachaac* ceremony (one of them was actually the leader), who seem to have been culturally Maya (and no doubt close to pure Maya genetically): Inquisición 1177,

no. 7, Causa contra Apolonia Casanova, 1786; and Inquisición 1256, no. 1, Causa contra Pascual de los Santos Casanova, 1786-1787.

26. AGN, Inquisición 516, no. 12, Causa contra Juan de Argaez, mulato, alias Montoya, 1673. For other cases of mulattoes using Indian magic, 1612-1672, see Inquisición 297, no. 5; 360, varios, 374, no. 10; 413, no. 8; 423, no. 20; 443, no. 6.

27. AGI, Mexico 3168, Informe Bartolomé del Granado Baeza, 1 April 1813.

28. On Brazil, see Bastide, *African Religions in Brazil*, 131-133; Freyre, *Masters and Slaves*, 286-296. For the West Indies I draw on personal observation.

29. For analyses of syncretism as an historical process (as opposed to descriptions of the product, which abound in the ethnographic literature), see Madsden,"Religious Syncretism," and Jiménez Moreno, "Indians of America and Christianity," on central and northern Mexico; Nutini and Bell, *Ritual Kinship*, 287-304, on Tlaxcala; and Donald E. Thompson, "Maya Paganism and Christianity," on the Maya region, with emphasis on Yucatan.

30. Christian, *Local Religion*, discusses saints as highly localized corporate patrons and is in general a valuable guide to late sixteenth-century Spanish forms of devotion (for instance, a shifting emphasis from saints' relics to images) that represent the root stock of colonial transplants.

31. I am suggesting only a difference in emphasis and not two separate belief systems for elite and masses; see, for comparison, Horton, "On the Rationality of Conversion," part 1, p. 226, part 2, pp. 374-375.

32. Brotherston, "Continuity in Maya Writing," 249-256.

33. Lizana, *Historia de Yucatan*, 46v, 51, 55-56, mentions the lords of Campeche, Tixkumche, Uman, and Caucel and cooperation from Tutul Xiu, the lord of Mani.

34. Miller and Farriss, "Religious Syncretism," 235-240, and Roys, Scholes, and Adams, "Report and Census," summarize much of the documentation on the desultory missionary activity on Cozumel and the east coast and Maya responses to Christianity. See especially AGI, Mexico 369, Relación de Fr. Gregorio de Fuenteovejuna y Fr. Hernando Sopuerta, 15 Aug. 1573; Mexico 359, Governor to Crown, 11 March 1584; Mexico 3048, Governor to Crown, 16 April 1585; AA, Real cedulario 5, Representación . . . indios de Icab (Ecab), 6 April 1601, in Testimonio de la real ejecutoria, 22 Oct. 1681.

35. Excavation data from the Tancah chapel are summarized in Miller and Farriss, "Religious Syncretism," 229-235.

36. Cogolludo, Lib. 4, cap. 9, discusses evidence for preconquest crosses on Cozumel and early Spanish ideas on the cross as evidence for Chilam Balam prophecies of the coming of Christianity (see also Lizana, *Historia de Yucatan*, 36v-39; Roys, *Chumayel*, 148, 167, 168; RY 1: 44-45). But on the cross as the "first tree of the world," see Roys, *Chumayel*, 102, 168; Landa, *Relación*, 43, and notes 214 and 215; RY 1: 45.

37. On east-coast cults, see Miller, *On the Edge of the Sea*, chapter 5. The section of Roys, *Chumayel*, 164-169, which Roys entitles "Prophecies of a New Religion," seems to refer, among a variety of by no means mutually exclusive

interpretations, to the return of Kukulcan and of Christ in an apocalyptic Last Judgment.

38. The ratio of *visita* towns to *cabeceras* was 8.3: 1 among Franciscan *doctrinas* in 1580: DHY 2: 48-50, Memoria Fr. Hernando de Sopuerta, 1580. According to the bishop's count, the ratio was 8.9: 1 for all Indian parishes: DHY 2: 55-65, Memoria de los conventos, vicarías y pueblos, 1582. On the use of *naguatlatos* and native catechists and the question of language competence among the Franciscans (a sensitive issue in their rivalry with the secular clergy), see AGI, Mexico 369, Avisos Bishop Toral, n.d. (c. 1565), and Bishop to Crown, n.d. (c. 1599); DHY 2: 48-50, Memoria Fr. Hernando de Sopuerta, 1580; DHY 2: 70-94, Memorial Bishop to Crown, 6 Jan. 1582; DHY 2: 129-132, Bishop to Crown, 10 April 1601; "Visita García de Palacio, 1583"; Ciudad Real, *Relación* 2: 472; Sánchez de Aguilar, *Informe*, 72-73, 135, 171; Lizana, *Historia de Yucatan*, 46-46v, 58.

39. Sánchez de Aguilar, *Informe*, 35, presents a long list of the "rudiments" of Christian doctrine, which he claimed "all the Indians from childhood learn and know completely." But see AGI, Mexico 369, Avisos Bishop Toral, n.d. (c. 1565); and IY, Constituciones sinodales, 1722, Instrucciones a los curas de indios. For late colonial policy and practice in the teaching of doctrine and for assessments of the progress of Christianity among the Maya, see AGI, Mexico 3168, Bishop to Crown, 28 July 1737, and Informe Bartolomé del Granado Baeza, 1 April 1813; Papeles de los señores Gala, Guerra, Carillo y Piña, Memorial Fr. Joseph Baraona to Bishop, 21 May 1770; the section Visitas pastorales, most especially the detailed inspections and parish reports in legajos 3-6, 1782-1784; and AGN, Historia 398, Exp. sobre establecimiento de escuelas en Yucatan, 1790-1805, Informes subdelegado Campeche, 1790.

40. Roys, *Chumayel*, 82 (and, less explicitly, 155). On the umbilical cord imagery, see Miller, "Iconography of the Painting." Brotherston, "Continuity in Maya Writing," 251-252, argues for a Maya response to Christian cosmology that was not only sophisticated but also well versed in medieval biblical scholarship.

41. AGI, Mexico 359, Governor to Crown, 11 March 1584. On Cozumel as a pre-Columbian pilgrimage center, see RY 2: 54-55; Landa, *Relación*, 109, 184; Cogolludo, Lib. 4, caps. 4 and 9.

42. See the prologue, note 5.

43. AA, Libro de cofradía del pueblo de Hool, 1747-1801; Asuntos pendientes 2, Exp. sobre la obra pía perteneciente a Ntra. Sra. de Hool, 1795-1805; Oficios y decretos 5, Exp. sobre administración de bienes . . . Ntra. Sra. de Hool, 1805-1806. Bishop Ignacio de Padilla's attempt to suppress the fiesta and pilgrimage in favor of a simple, local celebration (AA, Visitas pastorales 1, Auto de visita, Campeche, 1757) was obviously unsuccessful. The shrine still draws a large number of devotees from Campeche and now Merida for the February 2 celebration.

44. Lizana, *Historia de Yucatan*, subtitled "Devocionario de Ntra. Sra. de Izmal [*sic*]," is our major source on the pre-Columbian history of the site as well as

the Christian foundation and the devotion to the cult of Our Lady of Izamal (see especially pp. 1-31v). See also Landa, *Relación*, 172-173; and RY 1: 119, 269.

45. Lizana, *Historia de Yucatan*, 20-21, 26v; AA, Cofradías e imposiciones, Solicitud de Fr. José de Esturla, 1813. For additional material on the cult (Spanish and Indian) and the pilgrimages, see Cogolludo, Lib. 6, caps. 2-4, Lib. 12, caps. 12 and 13; AGI, Mexico 1039, Governor to Crown, 2 July 1723; Mexico 3052, Royal cédula to Bishop and Governor, 1 July 1731; AA, Visitas pastorales 1, Izamal, 1764; AGI, Mexico 3066, Informaciones instruídas . . . cofradías, 1782, cuad. 7 (Izamal); and AA, Asuntos pendientes 2 and 3 and Cofradías e imposiciones, Expedte. sobre administración de bienes . . . Ntra. Sra. de Izamal, 1803-1814 (divided into three parts).

46. Cogolludo, Lib. 4, caps. 19 and 20, lists the titular patrons of *cabeceras* and *visitas*. Out of ninety-four towns for which information is available on Marian advocation, the Immaculate Conception accounted for fifty-four, the Assumption for ten, and Nativity, Dolores, Purification, Rosary, and Visitation were divided roughly equally among the rest (AGI, Mexico 3066, Informaciones instruídas . . . cofradías, 1782, cuads. 5-10).

47. Aside from the physical evidence of extant images, which are hard to date, Cogolludo, Lib. 6, caps. 2 and 4, describes some of the Our Lady images, and further data on the appearance, dress, and other adornments can be found in the *libros de cofradía* listed in chapter 9, note 29, and the *cuentas de fábrica* listed in chapter 5, notes 70 and 71.

48. *Diccionario de Motul*.

49. The Mesoamerican underworld was conceived as having nine tiers, or stages, but heaven (not actually an antithesis but rather linked in the dualistic symbolism) may also have had nine tiers rather than the generally believed thirteen; see Nicholson, "Religion in Pre-Hispanic Central Mexico," 407-408. See also J. Eric Thompson, *Maya History and Religion*, 280-282, on the nine Maya Lords of the Underworld.

50. Spanish reports on the cult of the saints are rare, except for the hagiographical accounts by Lizana, Cárdenas Valencia, and Cogolludo of miracle-working images (see note 23), which tell us more about Spanish than Indian expressions of piety. Not surprisingly, the clergy were more concerned with idolatries and other practices that they saw as pagan survivals than with more apparently orthodox forms of devotion. Nevertheless, much can be gleaned about Maya beliefs and practices from descriptions of and references to the annual round of church festivals as performed in the Indian parishes, including references to elements that the clergy perceived as idiosyncratically Maya but not necessarily objectionably pagan: see especially IY, Constituciones sinodales, 1722, Instrucciones a los curas de indios; and testimonies, parish reports and *autos de visita* in AA, Visitas pastorales 1 (1755-1764), 3-6 (1782-1784). More direct evidence of Maya attitudes and ideas about the saints can be obtained from scattered references in the Chilam Balam books, from testimony about the *cofradías* and their patrons in AGI, Mexico 3066, Informaciones instruídas

. . . cofradías, 1782, cuads. 5-10; from the *libros de cofradía* (listed in chapter 9, note 29); and from a variety of other Maya documents pertaining to the *cofradías*, ranging from deeds of endowment to the saints to petitions about the financing of fiestas, mainly in AA, Asuntos terminados and Asuntos pendientes.

51. This interpretation is not so much factually inaccurate as analytically misleading. The point is not whether Indians hid or hide images behind saints (see, for example, a report in AA, Visitas pastorales 5, Valladolid, 1784, that "idols of wax or clay" were found under the draperies of Christian saints in a local church), but whether the Indians addressed their devotions to the idols rather than the saints. My contention is that the two were fused, with or without the material presence of the idols.

52. Wallace, *Culture and Personality*, 202-206. See also idem, "Revitalization Movements"; and Berger, *Sacred Canopy*, 45-46, 50, on the loss of "plausibility structure."

53. Scholes and Adams, *Don Diego Quijada* 1: 78-79, 94, 124.

54. For material on idolatries, see notes 12, 14-16.

55. AGI, Mexico 359, Bishop to Audiencia, 2 May 1606.

56. Nutini and Bell, *Ritual Kinship*, 291-304, describe this process of fusion in colonial Tlaxcala, arguing that the friars were aware of and consciously fostered god-saint identifications, even choosing patron saints who would mesh well with local deities. The evidence for specific identifications between individual saints and deities is highly equivocal and the correlations are often strained. The Mesoamerican symbolic system was subtle, fluid, and rich enough to accommodate and reorder almost any set of superficial attributes contained in Christian hagiography and iconography. More important than any particular consonances is the merger at the more general level of collective advocates.

57. AGI, Mexico 3050, Autos criminales . . . pueblo de Cisteil, 1761.

58. AGI, Mexico 3050, Autos criminales . . . pueblo de Cisteil, 1761. Although the Maya may have preferred not to have resident clergy, they seem to have valued Christian ritual. Similar, though nonviolent, complaints can be found in AA, Visitas pastorales and Arreglos parroquiales: see, especially, Arreglos parroquiales 1, Memoriales caciques and justicias of Xocen, Dzitnup, and Ebtun, 1782.

59. Reed, *Caste War*, 48-49, 77-78, 79, 89, 95, 106, 107, 109, 133. For a detailed account of the war, including copies of manifestoes, see Baqueiro, *Ensayo histórico*; and on Christian aspects of the Speaking Cross cult, Zimmerman, "Cult of the Holy Cross," and Bricker, "Caste War of Yucatan."

60. Roys, *Chumayel*, 79, 106-107, 124-125. See also the association of greedy Spaniards with the Anti-Christ (p. 158) and the Christian God as the scourge of earlier invaders, the Itza (pp. 160, 161). The point is not so much the identity of the Maya's adversaries as the enlistment of the Christian God as a sacred force on *their* side.

61. See note 36 on the cross as "first tree of the world," the sacred *yaxche* or ceiba; and, for similar twentieth-century Maya views of the ceiba as link between heaven and earth, see Tozzer, *Comparative Study*, 154. In pre-Columbian

symbolism the cross's association with birds, serpent-birds, and sun-god signs further emphasized the sky-earth link: see Schele, "Observations on the Cross Motif," 41-43; J. Eric Thompson, *Maya History and Religion*, 213-219. It is of course possible that the sacred tree, in representing Itzamna (celestial and terrestrial aspects), was viewed as the equivalent of Christ both as personification of the divinity and as link between heaven and earth. But it is more likely that the association of the *yaxche* and the cross was via the *axis mundi* symbolism (see Eliade, *Myth of the Eternal Return*, 12-18), and that the personification of the cross was a postconquest, probably a late postconquest, development.

62. AA, Visitas pastorales 6, Parish report Chunhuhub, 1784, which also reports the Indians' special devotion to the descent from the cross. A miraculous although apparently nonspeaking cross, discovered in the *monte* outside Campeche and set up in a woman's house as a sanctuary, gave the clergy much trouble because of the rapid spread of its following: AA, Oficios y decretos 6, Diego de Solís to Secretary of Bishopric, 6 July 1807.

63. The speaking idol of Cozumel is described in RY 2: 54-55; Cogolludo, Lib. 4, cap. 9. The idea that Hunabku descended to speak through interpreters in a trance (described, for example, in the Chilam Balam of Tizimin: Roys, "Maya Katun Prophecies," 6) was given a Christian twist after conquest by one Andrés Chi of Sotuta, condemned to death in 1597, who supposedly gained a following by claiming to be "another Moses," to whom the Holy Spirit spoke, impersonated by a boy hidden in the rafters of his house: Sánchez de Aguilar, *Informe*, 138; Cogolludo, Lib. 7, cap. 15.

64. The Indians' reactions are recounted in a series of indignant reports from the parish clergy to the bishop, 1814, in AA, Estadística (filed by parish). See also AGI, Mexico 3168, Bishop to Presidente y Diputados provinciales, 22 Dec. 1813, and 12 March 1814, and Franciscan Provincial to Crown, 31 Aug. 1814. The 1812 reforms and their effect on Yucatan are discussed in chapter 12.

65. Described and transcribed with a translation in E. W. Andrews, *Balankanche*, appendixes 1 and 2.

66. Eva Hunt, in her analysis of postconquest change in the Mesoamerican symbolic system (*Transformation of the Hummingbird*, chapter 9), suggests a somewhat more complex distinction among (1) messages, which change most rapidly; (2) codes (for example, spoken language); and (3) "armatures" or cultural configurations—roughly analogous to what I call ideational structure here—which are tied most closely to basic social organization (including man's link with the physical environment) and therefore, within Mesoamerican Indian society, have been the most stable part of the system.

67. Sánchez de Aguilar, *Informe*, 153-154, 170. The apostate Maya in the Tipu region taunted visiting friars with claims that they had their own priests to celebrate mass, using tortillas and *pozole* (Cogolludo, Lib. 11, cap. 14).

68. As early as 1552 Maya lords and *principales* were enjoined not to "dare to establish on their own any church or oratory or chapel" (Ordenanzas Tomás López, in Cogolludo, Lib. 5, caps. 16-19). See also clerical reactions to the audacity of giving saints' names to idols and claiming to speak to the Holy

Spirit (AGI, Mexico 359, Bishop to Audiencia, 2 May 1606; Sánchez de Aguilar, *Informe*, 138), in the same way that in Europe the church has consistently incorporated or proscribed any relics, images, apparitions (or their sites), and other independent manifestations of the sacred.

69. Klein, "Peasant Communities in Revolt," and, for more recent studies, Wasserstrom, *Ethnic Relations in Central Chiapas*, chapter 4, and Gosner, "Soldiers of the Virgin."

70. AA, Visitas pastorales 3, Parish report Mani, 1782, recounts the history of the *cofradía*, beginning with Xiu's endowment of the *estancias* in 1602. This date is probably wrong. According to Ciudad Real, *Relación* 2: 470, the Mani *cofradía* had already been founded by 1588. There is no other Francisco de Montejo in the Xiu genealogy, only a nephew, Francisco, who lived in Yaxacumche, not Mani (Roys, *Indian Background*, 130, 150, 163). Although Landa was convinced that Xiu was the "principal cause" of the apostasies in his province (Scholes and Adams, *Don Diego Quijada* 1: 69-71, Petition Landa to Quijada, 4 July 1562), Xiu lived to protest the idolatry trials and Landa's possible reinstatement in the colony: *Cartas de Indias*, 407-410, D. Francisco de Montejo Xiu et al. to Crown, 12 April 1567.

CHAPTER 11, MAINTAINING THE COSMOS

1. AA, Papeles de los señores Gala, Guerra, Carrillo y Piña, Memorial Fr. Joseph Baraona, 21 May 1770; Visitas pastorales 4 and 5, Parish reports Hecelchakan (1782) and Chancenote (1784); AGI, Mexico 3168, Informe Bartolomé del Granado Baeza, 1 April 1813. The "indecent" songs and dances the clergy sometimes objected to (Ordenanzas Tomás López, 1552, in Cogolludo, Lib. 5, caps. 16-19; Landa, *Relación*, 128; AGI, Mexico 369, Avisos Bishop Toral, n.d. (c. 1565); Sánchez de Aguilar, *Informe*, 38; Lizana, *Historia de Yucatan*, 41) are not described in any detail, but I assume that they were derived from the sexually suggestive ones of pre-Hispanic tradition, which are still being performed today; see Bricker, *Ritual Humor*, 185-187. For other colonial references to ritual singing and/or dancing, see Landa, *Relación*, 93-94, 128, 145-148, 156-158; RY 2: 185, 195; Ciudad Real, *Relación* 2: 402-406, 410-412; Sánchez de Aguilar, *Informe*, 72, 149, 172; Cogolludo, Lib. 4, cap. 5; AGI, Mexico 361, Ordenanzas Governor Esquivel, 1666, no. 7.

2. Tozzer, *Comparative Study*, 88-89, 107, 146-147. See also, on the manufacture of idols, Landa, *Relación*, 111, 159-161 ("which they called making gods"); AGI, Mexico 3048, Governor to Crown, 16 April 1585; Mexico 359, Bustamante Andrade to Crown, 4, April 1587.

3. One of the major concerns in the complaints leveled against Spanish administration of the *cofradías* after expropriation: see AA, Cofradías e imposiciones, Petitions from Nohcacab (1797), Ticul (1803), Huhi, Sotuta, and Cuzama (1810), Telchac (1812), Chapab (1814); and Oficios y decretos, Yobain, 1806. See also Visitas pastorales 4, Tecoh, 1782, Testimony of cacique et al., Tecoh and Telchaquillo.

4. These objections and prohibitions are contained in episcopal reviews of

cofradía accounts, recorded in the Libros de cofradía (listed in chapter 9, note 29), in the *autos de visita* during tours of inspection (see, for example, AA, Visitas pastorales 3 and 4, Ticul and Becal, 1782, prohibiting bullfights); and for a general discussion, see IY, Constituciones sinodales, 1722. Similar episcopal efforts in sixteenth-century Spain to curtail fiesta expenditure on feasting and other "improprieties" are recorded in Lisón-Tolosana, *Belmonte*, 280-281; Christian, *Local Religion*, 48, 113-114, 162-166.

5. The most detailed source on feasting and on other aspects of the colonial saints' fiestas is the extant *libros de cofradía* (chapter 9, note 29), recording annual expenditure on special food, condiments, wax for candles, incense, *comedias*, gunpowder for fireworks, and other fiesta accompaniments. However, many items, such as the arbors (*ramadas*), bullfight stands, and the basic foodstuffs, were contributed by the villagers and/or *cofradía* officers and therefore do not appear in the accounts. No complete description of the colonial fiestas exists (even Stephens's accounts of village fiestas in the 1840s, in *Incidents of Travel* 1: 110-114, 122-123, 229-230, 263-264, 2: 65-72, are only fragmentary and concerned mainly with *ladino* activities). But a fairly full picture can be pieced together from a variety of sources: in addition to the *libros de cofradía*, much can be gleaned from the descriptions, admonitions, and proscriptions (apparently unavailing for the most part) in Ordenanzas Tomás López, 1522 (Cogolludo, Lib. 5, caps. 16-19); and AGI, Indiferente 2987, Ordenanzas García de Palacio, 1584; IY, Constituciones sinodales, 1722; from testimonies, parish reports, and *autos de visita* in AA, Visitas pastorales 1 (1755-1764), and 3-6 (1782-1784); and from the reports, testimonies, and petitions regarding the *cofradías* in AGI, Mexico 3066, Informaciones instruídas, 1782, cuads. 5-10, 12-18, and Testimonia de la real provisión, 1782. AA, Asuntos terminados, Asuntos pendientes, Oficios, and Oficios y decretos, contain many later colonial documents pertaining to fiestas (for example, Asuntos pendientes 2, Expedte. sobre procesión de Benditas Ánimas, 1783). Most of the references to dance (note 1) contain material on other aspects of fiestas; for other early material, see especially, "Visita García de Palacio, 1583"; Cárdenas Valencia, *Relación historial*, 85-86; Cogolludo, Lib. 4, cap. 18; and AGI, Mexico 369, Memorial de la renta . . . Valladolid, 1694.

6. J. Eric Thompson, *Maya History and Religion*, 314-319; Ruz Lhuillier, *Costumbres funerarias*, 188-192; Landa, *Relación*, 130-131. Oral traditions seem to have merged the identity of former rulers with that of deities: RY 1: 78-79, 121-122, 213, 224, 255, 259-271; Lizana, *Historia de Yucatan*, 4-4v.

7. Fulfilling obligations toward *nuestros mayores* was considered one of the primary functions of the *cofradías*: AGI, Mexico 3066, Informaciones instruídas . . . cofradías, 1782, cuads. 5-10, testimonies of community leaders.

8. Tozzer, *Comparative Study*, 157 (and on Lacandones, 47-49). Redfield and Villa Rojas, *Chan Kom*, 200, and Villa Rojas, *Maya of East Central Quintana Roo*, 150, mention a gourd placed in the grave but do not say whether it was filled with food. On placing food with the dead as pre-Hispanic custom, see Landa, *Relación*, 130; RY 2: 24.

9. Considered a dereliction of duty by some bishops (see, for example, IY,

Constituciones sinodales, 1722; AA, Visitas pastorales, 3-6, Autos de visita, 1782-1784), but openly admitted by many *curas*: see, in addition to reports and testimony in the *visitas pastorales*, AA, Estadística 1, Relación jurada que hacen los curas, 1774. There is some suggestion that even the *maestros cantores* may not have assisted at burials unless they were paid a fee: AA, Visitas pastorales 1, Valladolid, 1755; and Visitas pastorales 7, Tecoh, 1782.

10. AA, Visitas pastorales 6, Parish report Tixcacalcupul, 1784. On colonial Maya rituals, both public and domestic, surrounding death, see also Visitas pastorales 4 and 5, Parish reports Bolonchenticul (1782) and Tixcacaltuyu (1784); and AA, Oficios y decretos 5, Expedte. sobre entierros de párvulos, 1806: Oficios y decretos 6, José Gregorio del Canto to Bishop, 12 Nov. 1807; and, for basically unmodified practices in the 1930s, Redfield and Villa Rojas, *Chan Kom*, 198-202 (p. 201 for the corn-scattering procedure); and Villa Rojas, *Maya of East Central Quintana Roo*, 148-150.

11. Sánchez de Aguilar, *Informe*, 152; AGI, Mexico 369, Memorial de la renta . . . Valladolid, 1694; IY, Constituciones sinodales, 1722. According to Solano y Pérez-Lila, *Los mayas*, 360, the clergy in colonial Guatemala reported that the highland Maya would go at night to the church doors to speak to the dead and by day incense the tombs with copal. On pre-Hispanic offerings to the dead, see Landa, *Relación*, 131; Las Casas, *Apologética historia* 2: 527.

12. On food offerings made to *chaacs*, idols, and a variety of supernatural beings during the colonial period, see the material on milpa ceremonies and idolatries in chapter 10, notes 6, 7, 12, 15, and 16. On the notion of feeding the idols and/or gods, see Landa, *Relación*, 106, 114, 144-145; RY 2: 45; Sánchez de Aguilar, *Informe*, 53, 72, 133-134 (an especially explicit exposition of the link among food for the gods, ritual banquets for the devotees, and material benefits in return).

13. On food offerings, see IY, Constituciones sinodales, 1722; AA, Visitas pastorales 5, Parish report Chancenote, 1784: "No puede haber menos de superstición, pues usan poner las comidas y bebidas delante del santo." (However distasteful, the offerings were tolerated by the clergy, even encouraged, according to Sánchez de Aguilar, *Informe*, 152, because they received a portion of them as *limosnas*; these are listed quite openly as a substantial part of parish income in, for example, AGI, Mexico 369, Memorial de la renta . . . Valladolid, 1694). The *cofradía* account books record "un toro de la Virgen para la fiesta principal" as a common entry, which further supports the argument in Pohl, "Ritual Continuity and Transformation," linking the modern fiesta bullfight to the pre-Hispanic stag sacrifice.

14. See, for example, AEY Ayuntamiento 1, no. 3, Representación indios de Baca, 12 July 1790. In Roys, *Chumayel*, 107-112, 114 (34-36, 38, in Maya text), "gracia" is a metaphor both for maize and for the divinity. Sánchez de Aguilar, *Informe*, 72, refers to the Maya as "teniendo a Dios verdadero a su humano alimento [that is, maize]."

15. Tozzer, *Comparative Study*, 105-146, and plate 21, figure 1.

16. Tozzer, *Comparative Study*, 37.

17. For a detailed list of *limosnas*, see BN, Archivo franciscano 55, no. 1142, Testimonio Fr. Pedro de Burgos, Tekax, Sept. 1636; and on negotiated *limosnas*, see chapter 1, note 43. For a similar list of *limosnas* in a secularized *curato*, see AGI, Mexico 369, Memorial de la renta . . . Valladolid, 1694.

18. See chapter 9, note 19, on the conflict over *limosnas*.

19. See Cogolludo, Lib. 4, cap. 7, who is more honest than most Franciscans in conceding that by obligation the Maya "support us well" but that without the obligation, "few Indians would give us so much as an egg" (a suspicion confirmed when *obvenciones* were abolished briefly under the constitution of Cadiz in 1813-1814, while the Maya, however, continued to support their fiestas: see the register of complaints in reports made from the parish clergy, 1814, in AA, Estadística 1 and 2). Evidence on Indian objections to fiesta expenses (see, for example, AA, Real cedulario 5, Royal cédulas to Governor, 24 March 1645 and 16 May 1665) make clear that the Indians were objecting to the *limosnas* the clergy collected for themselves on the occasion of the fiesta and not to the actual expenses for the fiesta activities.

20. AA, Visitas pastorales 3, Nohcacab, 1783; AGI, Mexico 3066, Informaciones instruídas . . . cofradías, 1782, cuad. 6, Bolonchencauich. This practice was no doubt much more widespread—accepted by the Maya as customary and reported only when the usual limits were exceeded. The bishops themselves exacted a variety of "fees" from *cofradías*, aside from tithes on cattle, honey, and other *estancia* production: a 3 percent annual tax on income to pay the diocesan interpreter, a *besamanos* contribution during episcopal visitations, and an annual auditing fee (*derechos de visita*) of 4 pesos in the eighteenth century, when account books came to be kept and inspected more or less regularly; see, in addition to the *libros de cofradía* in AA, AGI, Escribanía 308-A, no. 1, pieza 4, Trasuntos de los indios de los 52 pueblos que visitó . . . el obispo . . . , 1678.

21. AA, Libro de cofradía Hocaba, autos de visita 1747-1758 (regarding the curate's embezzlement of 990 pesos from the parish's three *cofradías*); Visitas pastorales 1, 3, and 6: Usumacinta (1755), Nohcacab (1782), Chunhuhub (1784); Cofradías e imposiciones, Expedte. cofradía Huhi, 1810; AGI, Mexico 3066, Informaciones instruídas . . . cofradías, 1782, cuad. 8, Testimonies in Tunkas, Chemax, Uayma, and Kanxoc; and cuad. 12, Representaciones de los capitanes a guerra (reports from the Tizimin district all blamed the curates for heavy financial losses during the famine of 1769-1774, but it seems that the curates may have mismanaged the sale of cattle, selling on credit and failing to collect, rather than enriching themselves, as in the case of the curate of Chunhuhub). In contrast with the curates, the lay Spanish patrons appointed by the bishops to administer the Indian *cofradías* in the latter part of the eighteenth century were almost uniformly and explicitly condemned for fraudulent mismanagement: AGI, Mexico 3066, Informaciones instruídas, 1782, cuads. 5-7 (partidos of Camino Real Alto, Camino Real Bajo, and Costa), and Governor to Crown, 30 April 1783; Cofradías e imposiciones, Expedtes. on cofradías Nohcacab (1797), Cuzama (1810), Telchac (1812), Chapab (1814); Oficios y decretos 5, Exp. cofradía

Yobain, 1806; Circulares 1, Carta cordilla Bishop Estévez, 29 July 1819. For an earlier investigation, see AA, Libro de cofradía Seye, autos de visita, 1762-1764.

22. Sierra O'Reilly, *Indios de Yucatán* 1: 73-77, presents an accurate account of the *cofradías*, which he condemned from a Liberal perspective as a "rich mother lode" for the clergy at the expense of the poor Indians. But he also acknowledged that the Indians administered the *cofradías* with passionate devotion: "Era de ver el afanoso empeño de aquellos infelices en el incremento de las cofradías, trabajando asiduamente en sostenerlas e invirtiendo en ellas sus mezquinísimos ahorros" (p 74). "Cada cofradía en cada pueblo o república de indios era como la niña de sus ojos que llevaba todas sus afecciones y recibía todos sus cuidados" (p. 77).

23. IY, Constituciones sinodales, 1722, Arancel diocesano. Published by Bishop Juan Gómez de la Parada in 1723, this *arancel* remained in force with minor modifications throughout the colonial period (see AA, Aranceles): the standard fee for a fiesta sung mass was 5 pesos (with an extra 3 pesos if there was a sermon), of which 12 reales went to the *cura*, 4 reales to any assisting priest, and the remaining 3 pesos were distributed among *maestro cantor*, members of the choir, and acolytes. Individual *cofradía* account books (AA and AC) indicate some variations in fees and proportions from place to place and over time, but the point is that the Spanish clergy were not the sole beneficiaries of fiesta fees (on *maestros cantores'* fees for weddings, baptisms, and burials, see chapter 6, note 57).

24. Bishops' complaints of "lack of formality" are contained in the *libros de cofradía* (AA and AC) and in various *autos de visita* in *visitas pastorales*. See also, for example, AA, Visitas pastorales 2, Seiba, 1778, in which the curate admitted that although he had assumed the title of patron of all the parish *cofradías* he did not keep the accounts himself. Even the none-too-formal account books, dating mainly from the 1730s and preserved in AA and AC, were probably the exception. Most of the *cofradías* actually in operation were not inspected during the *visitas pastorales* and in some cases the curates themselves were ignorant of the *cofradías'* existence or learned of them only by chance: see, for example, AA, Visitas pastorales 6, Tihosuco, 1784; Cuentas de fábrica 1, Cuentas de cofradía Huhi, 1797-1804; Asuntos pendientes 2, Expedte. cofradía Xcan, 1798.

25. The poorer *cofradías* depended mainly on apiaries (*colmenares*) for their income (see, for example, AA, Libro de cofradía Tekom). For a medium-sized *estancia*, see AA, Libros de cofradía Seye, Ekmul, Xocchel, Baca. We have no income data for any of the major *cofradía* estates, some of which were sold for 5,000-6,000 pesos (the average sale price was 1,200 pesos, according to the sources cited for table 12.1) and presumably yielded commensurately large incomes.

26. AA, Decretos 2, Bando Governor, 8 Oct. 1806, prohibiting "fuegos artificiales" for the duration of the shortage.

27. Detailed records of labor and materials for construction and reconstruction are available only for the late colonial period: see especially AA, Cuentas de fábrica 1, Chancenote (1796-1816), San Sebastián (1796-1815), Seye (1811-1812), Ichmul (1799-1818), Seyba (1815-1821), Hopelchen (1804-1816). For ear-

lier, summary accounts, see AGI, Mexico 369, Bishop to Crown, 15 July 1599; Mexico 3168, Bishop to Crown, 28 July 1737 and 8 July 1769; BL, Add. MSS. 17569, Report visita pastoral, 1755-1757; AA, Oficios y decretos 4, Bishop to Crown, 14 Feb. 1784 and 1 May 1788.

28. RY 2: 30, 69, 74.

29. See, for example, AEY, Ayuntamiento 1, no. 3, Representación indios de Baca, 12 July 1790; and on objections from *cabecera* residents to contributing labor toward a *visita* church, AGN, Historia 498, Exp. sobre establecimiento de escuelas, 1790-1805, Pleito partido de la Costa (Teya), 1789-1790.

30. Draperies and vestments of imported silk were also a major expenditure: the *cofradía* of Pociaxum spent 547 pesos in 1722 on a cope, chasuble, and altar cloths of "double damask with gold fringe" (AC, Libro de cofradía Pociaxum); the much poorer *cofradía* of Xocchel, paid 69 pesos in 1753 for a silk canopy. According to Gibson, *Aztecs under Spanish Rule*, 214-215, central Mexican communities spent three-fourths or more of their total incomes on church and fiesta supplies. See also, for the sixteenth-century Mixteca Alta, Dahlgren de Jordán, "Cambios socio-económicos," 111-119, and Borah and Cook, "A Case History," 425-428; and for Michoacan, see Torre Villar, "Algunos aspectos de las cofradías," 426-433.

31. AA, Visitas pastorales 3 and 6, Parish reports Mani (1782) and Tixcacalcupul (1784). On pre-Hispanic concepts, see Michael Coe, "Death and the Ancient Maya." The notions of sin, punishment, and reward attributed to the Maya by Landa, *Relación*, 131-132, and Cogolludo, Lib. 4, cap. 7, were probably projections of Christian doctrine.

32. Redfield and Villa Rojas, *Chan Kom*, 148-151. See also Redfield, *Folk Culture of Yucatan*, 244-246, 252-254, on the "progressive individualization of the santos" and novenas as one form of modern, urban influence. The only recorded colonial *promesa* is the donation of a cow to the Santo Cristo of Ekmul in 1752, in fulfillment of a vow for the recovery of the donor's son (AGI, Mexico 3066, Informaciones instruídas . . . cofradías, 1782, cuad. 7, Ekmul). Although probably not a unique case, nevertheless, if *promesas* had been a prominent feature of colonial Maya devotion, I would expect more evidence in the written records.

33. See chapter 9, notes 24 and 25; and see BL, Add. MSS. 17569, Report on Visitas pastoral, 1755-1757, for a disapproving account of how the Yucatecan *cofradías* ("*cofradías* in name only") differed from the clergy's ideal Spanish model.

34. On Spanish rural *cofradías*, see Lisón-Tolosana, *Belmonte*, 279-281, and Freeman, *Neighbors*, 61-63. Christian, *Person and God*, discusses the two modes in Spain and the friars' not wholly successful post-Reformation efforts to emphasize personal purification and individual atonement and to promote general Marian devotions, brotherhoods, scapularies, pilgrimages, and other features the Franciscans sought to introduce into Yucatan.

35. Most of AA, Arreglos parroquiales 1, Concerns readjustments of parish boundaries, 1784-1816, and many more cases are scattered in the sections Asuntos terminados and Asuntos pendientes. For especially strong expressions of

community identification based on ancestral ties, see Arreglos parroquiales 1, Expedte. sobre que los indios de Xuxcab (Kanxoc vs. Chemax), 1784, and Expedte. sobre hacienda Bacal (Tecoh vs. Abala), 1788; Asuntos terminados 9, Expedte. sobre rancho Cumpich (Hecelchakan vs. Dzitbalche), 1804; and Asuntos terminados 10, Expedte. sobre Santa María Oxnuchbac (Espita vs. Calotmul), 1810.

36. This explains the origin of what may otherwise seem a proliferation of patron saints in some towns (see, for example, Stephens, *Incidents of Travel* 1: 228). A town might have any number of images and even so-called *cofradías* devoted to them (meaning only separate *fondos*), but only one titular saint, one Marian advocacy, and one set of *cofradía* officers, unless the town was a compound of two formerly separate settlements that retained separate *cabildos*: see, for example, on Nohcacab (referred to by Stephens), Cogolludo, Lib. 4, cap. 20; AA, Visitas pastorales 3, Nohcacab, 1782, Testimony of caciques and patrones.

37. AGI, Mexico 3066, Testimonios de la real provisión, 1782, Report on Motul. On the greatly exaggerated clerical reports of peninsula-wide Indian devotion to Izamal, see chapter 10, note 45. The cult of Our Lady of Izamal did, however, extend to the immediately surrounding area, and the pueblos of Tunkas, Sitilpech, and Teya, as corporate bodies, all donated lands to the Virgin of Izamal for *cofradía* estates: AGI, Mexico 3066, Informaciones instruídas . . . cofradías, 1782, cuad. 7, Testimony cacique and cacique reformado Izamal.

39. AA, Libro de cofradía, Ntra. Sra. de Mamentel (Chicbul), 1758-1810. See chapter 5 on the *cofradía's* trade in wax images and scapularies for cash and cacao.

39. In the late colonial period the usual fee in the pueblos was one peso for a mass, two pesos for *conducciones de santos*, one peso for novenas, and two pesos for burials, providing a full complement of violins, *chirimías*, trumpets, and drums. Izamal as a cult center was a particularly active market, and the *guardián* of the convent was accused of establishing a lucrative monopoly, hiring out the "Virgin's orchestra" for all the private *fandangos* as well, and collecting a portion of the fees: AA, Obras pías, Expedte. sobre rentas Ntra. Sra. Izamal, 1813.

40. For conflicts between the parish clergy and the *hacendados* over this issue, see, for example, Arreglos parroquiales 1, Expedte. sobre erección de ayuda de parroquia Chencoyï, 1792; Oficios 5, Representación D. Joaquín Campos, 26 April 1806; Oficios y decretos 7, Expedte. sobre ayudas de parroquia, Abala, 1811.

41. See chapter 4, note 81, on the question of divine kingship.

42. The relationship between myth and history in the ancestry of ruling lineages will surely remain a puzzle, but for some illuminating discussion, see Eliade, *Myth of the Eternal Return*; Nicholson, "Ehecatl Quetzalcoatl"; and Kubler, "Mythological Ancestries."

43. BN, Archivo franciscano 55, no. 1141, Definitorio franciscano to Comisario general, 25 June 1675, complaining that the bishop had ordained people

of "infame calidad . . . mestizos y mulatos." For evidence on the exclusion of Indians, see chapter 3, note 56.

44. On the early Franciscan schools, see chapter 3, note 40, and on the responsibilities assigned to *naguatlatos/maestros cantores*, see AGI, Mexico 369, Avisos . . . Bishop Toral, n.d. (c. 1565).

45. Scholes and Adams, *Don Diego Quijada* 1: 190-191, Auto Diego de Landa, 9 June 1562.

46. Colonial Maya handwriting is easily distinguished from Spanish in the registers. See also entries from early baptismal registers in Franciscan *doctrinas* from the 1560s to 1590s, all in Maya (at a time when few friars knew the language), in AGI, Escribanía 308-A, no. 1, pieza 9, Testimonio sobre los libros de doctrina de Kikil, Habcanul, Hunucma, and Uman, 1647. They were also supposed to keep the accounts for *limosnas* and sign the receipts, at least in the Franciscan *doctrinas*: AGI, Mexico 1037, Testimonio de autos . . . doctrinas, 1711, Decreto provincial y definidores, 6 May 1657.

47. RY 1: 117, 267, 2: 97, 133, 170-171; AGI, Indiferente 1373, Representación Bishop Montalvo, n.d. (1580s); Ciudad Real, *Relación* 2: 423, 472; AGI, Mexico 359, Franciscan Provincial and definidores to Crown; 22 Jan. 1629; Cogolludo, Lib. 4, cap. 18. According to AGI, Mexico 3168, Bishop to Crown, 28 July 1737, the staffs of every church in the province were composed entirely of Indians, except for the cathedral, which acquired a Spanish choirmaster only in 1719.

48. For evidence on the multiple responsibilities delegated to the *maestros cantores*, see AA, Real cedulario 5, Actas del Definitorio provincial franciscano, May 1657; IY, Constituciones sinodales, 1722, Instrucciones a los curas de indios; AGI, Mexico 3168, Bishop to Crown, 28 July 1737; and Visitas pastorales section in AA, 1755-1809. Bishops were sometimes shocked to find the extent to which the *maestros* were solely in charge of the ritual (*auxiliar moribundos*, burials, baptisms, rosaries) as well as the catechism, finances, and record keeping of the parishes, even in the *cabeceras* and other towns with supposedly resident clergy; AA, Visitas pastorales 1, Valladolid and Bolonchenticul, 1755; AGI, Mexico 3053, Causa remoción cura Becal, 1767.

49. See chapter 3, note 36, and in general the records of late colonial episcopal visitations in AA, Visitas pastorales 1-9, 1755-1803.

50. See AGI, Mexico 3066, Informaciones instruídas . . . cofradías, 1782, cuads. 5-10.

51. The close correlation between noble rank and leadership in the upper tier of offices in both the *repúblicas* and the *cofradías* has been discussed in chapter 8 (see especially note 22 for the sources used in the analysis of sociopolitical roles and statuses).

52. The *priostes* and *mayordomos* were not included in the permanent staff of "church servants" (see, for example, AA, Real cedulario 5, Actas del Definitorio provincial franciscano, May 1657), but were elected annually by the *cabildo* or by the incumbent *cofradía* officers (see chapter 8, note 27). Their duties were to care for the images, their *alhajas*, and candles and also to supervise the *cofradía*

estates and other property; the patrons had overall responsibility for the property, the cult, and especially the fiestas and were supposedly held liable for any deficits: IY, Constituciones sinodales, 1722, Instrucciones a los patrones . . . ; and AA, Visitas pastorales 3 and 4, Parish reports Saclum, Hecelchakan, and Bolonchenticul, 1782.

53. IY, Constituciones sinodales, 1722 (among the many "abuses" in fiesta organization the bishop sought vainly to curtail). See also, AA, Visitas pastorales 5, Parish report Chancenote, 1784.

54. See Barrera Vázquez and Rendón, *Libro de los libros*, 193, from the day prophecies of the Chilam Balam of Mani: favorable prognostications for the day sign *Eb* contain a clear statement of this notion of what might be called circular generosity, the ideal leader as rich and generous, deriving his wealth from the community as well as distributing it to the community: "Rico, cuya riqueza es de la comunidad. Buen rico. Lo de la comunidad es su hacienda. Dadivoso. Buen hombre. No será cicatero. Muy bueno."

55. See notes 1 and 5 for the chief sources on colonial fiesta ritual.

56. See, on the *ahkins* and other priestly offices, Landa, *Relación*, 27-28, 111-112; RY 2: 183-184, 210-211.

57. All the idolatry cases cited in chapter 10, notes 12, 14-16, emphasize the prominent role of the *batabs* and *principales* as custodians of the idols, as instigators and impresarios of the sacrifices, and as donors of the offerings. Ritual details and the division of function between lords and priests are most clearly revealed in the Landa trials' extensive testimonies of participants from the Sotuta, Hocaba, and Valladolid regions (Scholes and Adams, *Don Diego Quijada* 1: 71-129, 135-162; AGI, Justicia 249, Residencia Quijada, 1565). See also Ordenanzas of Tomás López, 1552 (Cogolludo, Lib. 5, caps. 16-19).

58. Presumably the *principales* who carved out hearts in the postconquest rituals corresponded to the pre-Hispanic specialists called *nacom* (Landa, *Relación*, 112, 119). But *halach uinics* and *batabs* also performed this task in the 1560s (Cocom in Sotuta and several Iuit's in Hocaba: Scholes and Adams, *Don Diego Quijada* 1: 81, 89-90, 140-141, 145-149, 154-155).

59. Juan Pech of Usil in the Sotuta province: Scholes and Adams, *Don Diego Quijada* 1: 114-119. *Maestros cantores* participated in all the other sacrifices reported in the trials. See also RY 2: 29, 190, 218; AGI, Mexico 369, Bishop to Governor, 11 Jan. 1686. The last reference I have seen to Maya "sacerdotes" (priests) in the pacified zone (as distinct from what were referred to as "aquines" [*ahkins*] among the border groups) is AGI, Mexico 359, Bishop to Audiencia, 2 May 1606. For the same dual role of *maestros cantores* as leaders of native cults in Peru, see Spalding, "Social Climbers," 659-660.

60. By the late colonial period there is some suggestion that even *maestros cantores'* knowledge may have been pure rote learning: AA, Papeles de los señores Gala, Guerra, Carrillo y Piña, Memorial Fr. Joseph Baraona, 21 May 1770.

61. Reed, *Caste War*, 161, 199, 214. That this was not such a drastic leap as one might think is indicated not only by the already-mentioned central role in

ritual and teaching of the *maestros* but also by their high rank within local society (the only other *almehen* besides the *batab* accorded the title of *yum*, or lord), with a kind of above-the-fray moral authority that no civil official possessed (see, for example, AGI, Mexico 305-A, Autos criminales, Tekax, 1610, in which only the *maestro cantor* was able to calm the town and persuade the scattered refugees to return).

62. See chapter 3, notes 99-101.

63. The late colonial clergy for the most part must have come to see these elements as innocuous, since only a handful made any complaints (see note 1). The curate of Santiago ordered a *tunkul* for the church orchestra in 1800 (AA, Cuentas de fábrica 1, Cuentas de San Sebastián, 1797-1815); and in the 1840s the curate of Tecoh got up a "dance of the Indians" (rather more Spanish than Maya by the description), accompanied by a *tunkul*, to entertain his foreign visitors (Stephens, *Incidents of Travel* 1: 81-82).

64. IY, Constituciones sinodales, 1722, Instrucciones a los curas de indios; various autos de visita in AA, Visitas pastorales, especially 1, 3, and 4 (1755, 1782); and Oficios y decretos 5, Carta cordillera Bishop to curas, 1806.

65. AGI, Mexico 886, Bishop to Crown, 4 Sept. 1701.

66. The division between donors, or patrons, and officiants was not absolute in the colonial structure. *Maestros cantores* are on record as founders of *cofradías* (AGI, Mexico 3066, Informaciones Instruídas . . . cofradías, 1782, cuad. 6, Pich, and cuad. 7, Tekanto), and even as *cofradía* patron or *prioste* (AA, Libro de Cofradía Hocaba, AGI, Mexico 3066, Informaciones instruídas, 1782, cuad. 7, Sinanche); but the overlap was rare and in these two cases the *cofradía* post had been obtained before the individual became *maestro cantor*.

67. For clerical reports of food offerings, see note 13.

68. *Comediantes* (players or entertainers) are mentioned in a number of documents also, but in only one instance were they actually paid (AC, Libro de cofradía Pociaxum, accounts for 1711-1713). The term may refer to the local, more or less amateur satirists, called *baldzam*, who were a prominent feature of fiestas (see Sánchez de Aguilar, *Informe*, 149-150); Landa, *Relación*, 93; Bricker, *Ritual Humor*, 178-187.

69. On *convites*, their occasion, participation, financing, and sociopolitical functions, see Ordenanzas Tomás López, 1552 (Cogolludo, Lib. 5, caps. 16-19); "Visita García de Palacio, 1583"; AGI, Indiferente 2987, Ordenanzas García de Palacio, 1584; Escribanía 305-A, Autos Criminales Tekax, 1610 (at the time of the riot on Shrove Tuesday, all the town officials were gathered at the house of one of the *regidores* for a *convite*); Sánchez de Aguilar, *Informe*, 150; Cogolludo, Lib. 4, caps. 5 and 18; IY, Constituciones sinodales, 1722, Instrucciones a los curas de indios; AGI, Mexico 3066, Informaciones instruídas . . . cofradías, 1782, cuad. 12, Report Capitán a guerra, Partido de la Costa, 1782; Mexico 3168, Oficiales reales to Governor, 22 April 1813.

70. Ordenanzas Tomás López, 1552 (Cogolludo, Lib. 5, caps. 16-19). The prohibition was repeated in AGI, Indiferente 2987, Ordenanzas García de Palacio, 1584.

71. Although fiesta banquets for the *común del pueblo* are often mentioned, and although some documents indicate that feasting and drinking were general among the Indians without reference to social rank (see, for example, AA, Papeles de los señores Gala, Guerra, Carrillo y Piña, Memorial Fr. Joseph Baraona, 21 May 1770; AGI, Mexico 3066, Informaciones instruídas . . . cofradías, 1782, cuad. 6, Sta. Lucía Extramuros, cuad. 7, Bokoba; Mexico 3103, Certificado D. Andrés de Zervera, 4 Oct. 1784; AA, Visitas pastorales 3-6, Parish reports, 1782-1784), there is evidence that the delicacies (cacao, lard, beef, spices) were often reserved for officers of the *cofradías* and *cabildos* and *maestros cantores* (and sometimes *cantores*, musicians, and *comediantes* as well) or the *principales* in general: AA, Libro de cofradía Xbalantun (Tipikal), and Libro de cofradía Mamentel (Chicbul); AC, Libro de cofradía Pociaxum; AGI, Mexico 3066, Informaciones instruídas . . . cofradías, 1782, cuad. 7, Tekal; Mexico 369, Memorial de la renta . . . Valladolid, 1694; AA, Estadística 1, Relación jurada que hacen los curas, 1774.

72. Cogolludo, Lib. 4, cap. 18.

73. On elections of officials, including *batabs*, see chapter 8, notes 27-29.

74. Philip Thompson, "Tekanto," 267-282, 329-333. See also chapter 8, note 22, on sources for a more extended analysis (in space and time) of colonial Maya office-holding.

75. Michael Coe, "A Model of Ancient Community Structure."

76. Landa, *Relación*, 135-150. See also Roys, *Chumayel*, 63-66 ("Ritual of the Four Quarters").

77. Michael Coe, "A Model of Ancient Community Structure," 100-107. Coe (pp. 109-110) also suggests that such a rotational system may have extended to rulers at the state level in twenty-year (*katun*) periods; see also Philip Thompson, "Tekanto," 359-363, on the possibility of similar rotations among colonial *batabs*. The Peten Itza seem to have had a quadripartite division, with four "reyezuelos" of four smaller islands subject to King Canek (Villagutierre Sotomayor, *Historia*, 306), although there is no mention of rotation in power.

78. *Diccionario Motul* and Pérez, *Diccionario de la lengua maya*. According to the *Motul*, *cuch haab*, *cuch uinal*, and *cuch katun* also refer to the burden or content of the prophecies for the particular time period, as in the books of Chilam Balam.

79. On the concept of time as a burden, each unit borne in relays by its patron or ruling deity, see J. Eric Thompson, *Maya Hieroglyphic Writing*, 12, 96, 124-128, 181, 204; and León-Portilla, *Tiempo y realidad*, 29-63; "El tiempo . . . es atributo de los dioses: ellos lo llevan a cuestas" (p. 45). Although the rituals may differ, the old calendar (*tzolkin*), the concept of year-bearers, and New Year ceremonies directed toward year-bearers have all been preserved in the Cuchumatanes region of highland Guatemala: La Farge and Byers, *Year-Bearers' People*; Lincoln, "Maya Calendar of the Ixil"; and Oakes, *Two Crosses of Todos Santos*, 99-114.

80. AA, Visitas pastorales 5, Parish report Chancenote, 1784. See also on banquets presented at the annual rotation of *cabildo* officials and/or *cofradía* officers: "Visita García de Palacio, 1583"; Sánchez de Aguilar, *Informe*, 150; AGI,

Mexico 369, Memorial de la renta . . . Valladolid, 1694. On the Dance of the Pig's Head, which can still be witnessed in Yucatecan fiestas, see Redfield and Villa Rojas, *Chan Kom*, 155, 157, 371, and Villa Rojas, *Maya of East Central Quintana Roo*, 130-131. Pohl, "Ritual Continuity and Transformation," links modern animal "sacrifice" (the fiesta bullfight) with ancient deer sacrifice.

81. Both Carrasco, "Civil-Religious Hierarchy," and Nutini and Bell, *Ritual Kinship*, 312-331, provide possible models for the colonial relationship between the civil and religious office, and they, too, lack data to support the models.

82. On the surface of things, the Spaniards' view of *caciques* and *principales* as especially prone to drunkenness was probably accurate: see, for example, AA, Papeles de los señores Gala, Guerra, Carrillo y Piña, Memorial Fr. Joseph Baraona, 21 May 1770; AGN, Consolidación 10, Expedte. sobre bienes de comunidad Yucatan, Contadores reales to Governor, 14 Nov. 1805; and AGI, Mexico 3168, Oficiales reales to Governor, 22 April 1813. What they failed to perceive is that sharing of drink was an essential aspect of their ritual functions, linked both to their mediatory role with the divinity and to the sociopolitical dynamics of elite interaction. For a clear pre-Hispanic statement of the chain of associations among drunkenness, ritual (ecstatic dance), obsequies to the divinity, and high rank, see Barrera Vázquez and Rendón, *Libro de los libros*, 213: "Embriaguez . . . cuando se contorsionan y murmuran reverencias, como corresponde a los grandes señores."

83. While the whole fiesta constituted a gift to the community, the *convites* in particular (even if the donors reserved the best for themselves) would be considered the most obvious contribution. See on the redistributive significance of fiesta *convites* offered by the Aztec *tlatoani*, Broda, "Relaciones políticas ritualizadas," 236-237, 240-241; and for colonial Michoacán, see Torre Villar, "Algunos aspectos de las cofradías," 429-434. Among the colonial Aztecs, "the fiesta was a necessity in the Indian communities, for if rulers failed to provide fiestas their people 'neither hold them in esteem nor obey them' " (Gibson, *Aztecs under Spanish Rule*, 187, quoting from Alonso de Zorita).

84. The *cargo* system or fiesta sponsorship has been described in some form or another in the ethnographic literature for many communities in Mesoamerica and is summarized in Cancian, "Political and Religious Organization." For Chiapas in particular, see Cancian, *Economics and Prestige*; and Vogt, *Zinacantan*, 246-271. For Guatemala, see Bunzel, *Chichicastenango*; Reina, *Law of the Saints*; Wagley, *Social and Religious Life*; and Nash, "Political Relationships."

85. Vogt, "Some Aspects of Zinacantan Settlement Patterns," 166-171, and *Zinacantan*, 596-599 (see also Vogt, "Genetic Model," for a theoretical rationale for the exercise); and Michael Coe, "A Model of Ancient Community Structure," 112.

86. Barbara Price, "The Burden of the Cargo," 448-449, 456-461; Kubler, "Evidencia intrínseca," 9-11. While agreeing with Kubler's general thesis that ethnographic analogy is a poor substitute for historical evidence, I find his conclusion that the *cargo* system is entirely a colonial or postindependence development also at variance with the evidence.

87. Cancian, *Economics and Prestige*. See idem, "Political and Religious Organization," 290-293, for a summary of the "equalization" and the "stratification" arguments.

88. Rus and Wasserstrom, "Civil-Religious Hierarchies in Central Chiapas."

89. AGI, Mexico 3066, Informaciones instruídas . . . cofradías, 1782, cuad. 8, Tunkas, Dzonotpip, cuad. 12, Valladolid. Once the *cajas de comunidad* were restored to the pueblos, the *república* officials drew on them for fiesta expenses to supplement the *cofradías*: AGN, Consolidación 10, Expedte. sobre bienes de comunidad Yucatan, Contadores reales to Governor, 14 Nov. 1805; AGI, Mexico 3168, Oficiales reales to Governor, 22 April 1813.

90. Torre Villar, "'Algunos aspectos de las cofradías," 434.

91. See note 85.

92. The exception was D. Felipe Chuc, *batab* of Tixcacalcupul, from a *paraje* belonging to the local *cofradía*: AGI, Mexico 3066, Testimonio de la real provisión, 1782, report on Tixcacalcupul. I do not suggest that this was the sole exception, but aside from the biographical data on officeholders (cited in chapter 8, note 22), in which political leadership is strongly correlated with town origins as well as noble birth, there were practical reasons for not entrusting high office to the, by all accounts, considerably more rustic and unsophisticated hamlet residents. Colonial leadership was not merely ceremonial, and only in the towns could one acquire the administrative, financial, and legal expertise and the experience in *vecino* ways was necessary for dealing successfully with the colonial overlords.

93. But, according to Wasserstrom, "Exchange of Saints," and *Ethnic Relations*, chapter 7, these links have begun to break down in recent decades in Zinacantan, as formerly subordinate villages, outstripping the center in population and developing economic links elsewhere, have also asserted their ceremonial independence.

Chapter 12, The Second Conquest

1. Much work on the Bourbon reforms has been published in the last few decades, most notably a series of monographs inspired directly or indirectly by Lynch, *Spanish Colonial Administration* (on the newly created viceroyalty of the Río de la Plata): for Peru, Fisher, *Government and Society*; for New Spain, Archer, *Army in Bourbon Mexico*, Brading, *Miners and Merchants*, Farriss, *Crown and Clergy*, and Hamnett, *Politics and Trade*. Brading, "Bourbon Spain and the American Empire," is an excellent summary and analysis of the recent literature. And on the Spanish background, see Herr, *Eighteenth-Century Revolution*.

2. Ranging from a squeeze on higher offices to crackdowns on tax evasion, these attacks and creole reactions to them have been amply recorded. See Lynch, *Spanish-American Revolutions*, 1-36, for a summary.

3. Certain issues involving or ultimately affecting Indians, such as the expansion of landed estates, have received much attention. But the Indians tend to figure in the discussion only tangentially (or in the desamortization of corporate property, scarcely at all). The issue of *repartimiento de efectos* in Peru and its

relationship to the Tupac Amaru rebellion is an exception: see, for a recent study, Golte, *Repartos y rebeliones*.

4. For Bourbon and early republican attacks on the church, see Farriss, *Crown and Clergy*; Hale, *Mexican Liberalism*; and Costeloe, *Church and State*.

5. The verdict is generally mixed (see, for example, Lynch, *Spanish Colonial Administration*, 172-200) but, with regard to the *repartimiento de efectos*, unequivocal on the failure of reform: Golte, *Repartos y rebeliones*; Hamnett, *Politics and Trade*, 51, 88-98, 236; and Stanley Stein, "Bureaucracy and Business."

6. The system of indirect rule in Yucatan is described in chapter 3.

7. Brading, *Merchants and Miners*, 33-92, discusses the origins, introduction, and operation of the intendant system in New Spain, with emphasis on central Mexico.

8. See, in addition to note 5, Lynch, *Spanish Colonial Administration*, 76-79; Brading, *Merchants and Miners*, 74-79; Gibson, *Aztecs under Spanish Rule*, 84-97.

9. For material on the *capitanes a guerra* (and their equivalents under various titles) and their economic activities, see chapter 1, note 55, and chapter 3, notes 6-9.

10. AEY, Ayuntamientos and Tierras, and IY, Collection Alfredo Barrera Vázquez, Documentos sueltos, contain some of these late colonial cases. The more extensive material in AA, Asuntos terminados, Asuntos pendientes, Oficios y decretos, Decretos, and Arreglos parroquiales, which covers a longer time span (beginning c. 1750, rather than c. 1790) reveals the shift more clearly. Typical examples of the new intrusiveness of local royal officials are: AA, Oficios y decretos 5, Expedte. sobre servicio personal, Tixhualahtun, 1803; and Asuntos terminados 10, Representación cacique et al. Espita, 1810. See also Roys, *Titles of Ebtun*, 370.

11. See, for example, AEY, Ayuntamiento 1, no. 3, Lucas Puc et al. to Subdelegado, 12 July 1790; Tierras 1, no. 4, Isidoro Ku et al. to Subdelegado, 1791; Tierras 1, no. 8A, Domingo Canche to Subdelegado, 14 July 1804; AGI, Mexico 3139, Expedte. . . . indios cantores, Representación Matías Bacab et al., 24 Feb. 1792; AA, Oficios y decretos 5, Representación Antonio Uitzil, 24 May 1804; Títulos de Uayalceh, Petition Esteban Yam, 1815; AA, Asuntos pendientes 3, Expedte. . . . exención de tributos y obvenciones, 1816.

12. MacLeod, *Spanish Central America*, 327, see the *cajas de comunidad* and *cofradías* as " 'broker' even 'barrier' institutions," used by the Indians to generate income to buy noninterference from the Spaniards. As it turned out in Yucatan, at any rate, both proved too tempting to leave under Indian control indefinitely.

13. Under the new system subdelegates were to get a 6 percent commission on tribute, probably the same for the *holpatan*, and 2 percent of the *comunidades* as a fee for "auditing" the accounts: AGI, Mexico 3139, Junta de Real Hacienda, 19 May 1786 (interim system); Mexico 3136, Cuentas real Caja, Campeche, 1792, Ramo Tributos; AGN, Consolidación 10, Expedte. sobre bienes de comunidad, Yucatan, 1805-1806, Reglamento para administración de cajas de comunidad, 12 July 1797 (and as an example, Cuenta y relación . . . , Tekax, 1797).

14. Roys, *Titles of Ebtun*, 396, Auto Governor, 9 July 1783 (Maya translation, including an order that the decree be recorded in all the community *cabildo* books). That the decree was actually enforced is clear from the parish reports in AA, Visitas pastorales 3-6. Those dates 1782 complain in detail about the *repartimientos* of the governor and *capitanes a guerra*; those dated 1784 either omit mention of them or state (see reports for Tixcacaltuyu, Valladolid, and Sisal) that they have ceased.

15. The most detailed case involving the clergy-subdelegate struggle, with many accusations and counteraccusations, is AGI, Mexico 3072, Causa remoción Fr. Josef Perdomo, 1790-1792. See also AA, Decretos 1, Royal cédula to Governor, 30 Jan. 1792 (concerning complaints from the *doctrinero* of Oxkutzcab); Oficios y decretos 5, correspondence between Governor Pérez and Bishop Estévez, 1804-1806, concerning a number of different cases; Oficios y decretos 6, José Gregorio del Canto to Bishop, 12 Nov. 1807. For a somewhat partisan summary of the parish clergy's resistance to the subdelegates' new judicial and administrative authority, see AGI, Mexico 3072, Governor to Crown, 18 May 1782. I do not suggest that subdelegates in Yucatan were a totally aberrant breed of local official, but they do appear to have been less extortionate than the ordinary run and certainly a marked improvement over the *capitanes a guerra*.

16. The changeover was actually decreed slightly in advance of the introduction of the intendancy-subdelegate system, as a corollary to the incorporation of *encomiendas* by the Crown, decreed in a royal *cédula* of 16 Dec. 1785: AGI, Mexico 3139, Reglamento provisional . . . para el cobro de tributos, 28 June 1786.

17. AA, Oficios y decretos 6, Josef Benito de Palma to Bishop, 26 June 1804; and several of the curates' reports in Cuentas de fábrica 1, 1797-1816. *Batabs* were still collecting *obvenciones* in the parish of Homun in 1818; AA, Asuntos pendientes 3, Francisco Bravo to Bishop, 30 March 1818.

18. AGI, Mexico 3168, Oficiales reales to Governor, 22 April 1813, quoting a royal cédula to Governor, 15 Jan. 1777. On the not totally disinterested opposition from the clergy, see AA, Visitas pastorales 3-6, Parish reports, 1782-1784; Oficios y decretos 4, Representación Abogado de Indios, 25 Sept. 1781, and Bishop to Josef de Gálvez, July 1784.

19. AA, Oficios y decretos 4, Abogado de indios to Governor, 25 Sept. 1781; AGN, Consolidación 10, Exp. sobre bienes de comunidad Yucatan, 1805-1806 (including, besides the Reglamento para la administración . . . 1797, copies of various *repúblicas'* accounts and several *pareceres* of royal officials, 1805-1806). See also the report of the Oficiales reales, 7 July 1790, with summaries of all the municipal budgets, in AGN, Historia 498, Exp. sobre el establecimiento de escuelas en Yucatan, 1790-1805.

20. The final destiny of the funds siphoned off is difficult to ascertain, since they were switched around according to where the deficits were most urgent, and various schemes were approved (for example, a 50,000 peso loan to the Royal Philippine Company) but possibly never carried out: AGI, Mexico 3066, Testimonio . . . capitales de fondos de comunidad, 1783; Mexico 3139, Gov-

ernor to Miguel Cayetano Soler, 24 Feb. 1799, and Royal cédula to Viceroy, 27 Dec. 1799; Mexico 3101, Respuesta Fiscal, Council of the Indies, 2 Feb. 1803; AGN, Consolidación 10, Exp. sobre bienes de comunidad Yucatan, Governor to Junta Real Hacienda, 23 Nov. 1805, and Consulta Audiencia of Mexico, 24 April 1806; Consolidación 12, Representación Ildefonso Maniau to Junta Superior de Consolidación, 14 Sept. 1808; AGI, Mexico 3168, Oficiales reales to Governor, 22 April 1813.

21. AGN, Consolidación 4, Cuentas de la Caja de Consolidación, Merida, 1806-1809, yields a figure of 308,105 pesos for ecclesiastical capital, including 100,000 pesos belonging to the leper hospital of San Lázaro (40,000 pesos of which had been "donated" by the Crown from the *comunidades* fund). The sum for church capital represents only partial redemption of ecclesiastical *censos* held by creoles, who were able to avoid full enforcement of the law (see chapter 9, note 8, and Lavrin, "Execution of the Laws," 38-42). Lavrin's is the first study of the consolidation laws to consider the effect on the Indians (pp. 41-42), and the consolidation records tell less than half the story, since they include neither the other outstanding (and in fact uncollected) loans to the Treasury from the *bienes de comunidad* nor the "gifts" made from the fund (see table 12.1).

22. AEY, Ayuntamiento 1, no. 28, Exp. sobre gastos de comunidad, Espita, 1817. For a similar case, see IY, Collection Alfredo Barrera Vázquez, Expedte. fondos de comunidad, Hopelchen, 1816.

23. AA, Oficios y decretos, Bishop to Cathedral chapter, 23 Sept. 1782. For a more detailed discussion of the *cofradía* expropriation and supporting documentation, see Farriss, "Propiedades territoriales," 185-193.

24. AGN, Consolidación 4, Cuentas Caja de Consolidación, Merida, 1805-1809; Consolidación 13, Principales de haciendas nombradas cofradías, 30 April 1808. The Treasury seems to have paid interest (lowered to 3 percent from the pre-consolidation rate of 5 percent) at least intermittently until independence: AA, Cofradías generales, 1816-1823 (although see Lavrin, "Execution of the Laws," 45-46).

25. Farriss, "Propiedades territoriales," 199-201. See also table 12.3 and note 28.

26. AGI, Mexico 3169, Oficiales reales to Governor, 22 April 1813; AEY, Tierras 1, no. 3, Exp. sobre hacienda de comunidad Izamal, 1790, Auto Governor, 21 Maya 1790.

27. Reported in AGI, Mexico 3066, Testimonio de real provisión, 1782. See also Sierra O'Reilly, *Indios de Yucatan* 1: 73-77, on the Indians' resentment of this "mortal blow," which he saw as a major contribution to the Caste War almost seventy years later: "No se podía inventar nada que pudiese exasperarlos más que la venta de las cofradías."

28. For expropriated *cofradía* property, annual accounts of income and expenditure are in AA, Libro cofradías, 1786-1797; Cofradías e imposiciones 1, no. 6, Razón de los sobrantes de las cofradías, 1805-1811; Cofradías generales, 1816-1823. For unsold *cofradía* estates administered under diocesan supervision, see Cofradías e imposiciones 1, no. 14, Razón de las obras pías que tienen ad-

ministratores particulares, 30 Oct. 1804. This same *legajo* and Obras pías, 1760-1842, contain many *expedientes* on particular *cofradías*, and other accounts are scattered in Asuntos pendientes, Oficios y decretos, and Cuentas de fábrica 1 (for example, Cuentas de cofradía Cuzama, 1800-1808), with more detailed accounts in the confiscated *cofradía* books (for example, Ekmul, which contains accounts for Euan, 1784-1807).

29. AA, Oficios y decretos 4, Representación Abogado de Indios, 25 Sept. 1781, Bishop to Oidor Antonio de Villaurrutia, 14 Aug. 1782, Governor to Bishop, 9 July 1782, Bishop to Josef de Gálvez, 13 Nov. 1786; AGI, Mexico 3101, Respuesta Fiscal, Council of the Indies, 2 Feb. 1803; Consolidación 10, Exp. sobre bienes de comunidad, Oficiales reales to Governor, 14 Nov. 1805; AGI, Mexico 3168, Oficiales reales to Governor, 22 April 1813; Mexico 3101, Angel Alonso de Pantiga to Crown, 3 Sept. 1814.

30. AGN, Historia 498, Exp. sobre establecimiento de escuelas en Yucatan, 1790-1805, Abogado de naturales, 24 May 1792; AGI, Mexico 3168, Actas Diputación provincial, 10-12 May 1813, and Respuesta Auditor de guerra, 26 May 1813 (the only official on record as acknowledging that the *comunidades* fund had been a fraud and a "chimera" for Indians).

31. AEY, Tierras 1, no. 3, Exp. sobre hacienda de comunidad, Izamal, Auto Governor, 21 May 1790.

32. One curate sought to soften resistance to the expropriation of *cofradía* property with the argument that the funds could support the faculty of the theological seminary so that the Indians could become "ecclesiastics, curates, even canons and bishops": AGI, Mexico 3066, Informaciones instruídas . . . cofradías, 1782, cuad. 5, Testimony Caciques Caucel and Ucu. (The Indians, whether sceptical about these blandishments or indifferent to them, insisted that they preferred their *cofradía*.) For other, less self-serving projects, see notes 33 and 34.

33. AA, Asuntos terminados 9, Auto Governor 6, Aug. 1803 (on locust control); AGN, Exp. sobre establecimiento de escuelas en Yucatan, 1790-1805. Some of the larger pueblos had schoolmasters paid from *comunidades* funds and fees from *vecinos* (see subdelegates' reports from Camino real Alto and Sierra districts). A proposal for a 6,300 peso subsidy to expand the program (Auditor de guerra, 15 March 1791) was opposed by the Procurador and the Abogado de indios (25 Jan. and 24 May 1792) and apparently never carried out.

34. On cemeteries, see AA, Oficios y decretos 5, Auto Cabildo eclesiástico, 20 March 1804, Governor to Bishop, 19 March 1805 and 20 Sept. 1806 (referring also to a vaccination program against smallpox). On medical aid, see AGN, Intendentes 70, no. 10, Governor to Viceroy, 25 Nov. 1799; on granaries and a loan program for maize purchase during shortages (that is, the Indians had to repay the subsidy, at a time when their surplus fund exceeded 350,000 pesos and was increasing annually), see AEY, Ayuntamiento 1, no. 2, Exp. sobre pósitos, 1790; AGN, Intendentes 75, Governor to Viceroy, 10 Aug. and 10 Dec. 1800, and Respuesta Fiscal civil, 18 Feb. 1801; Consolidación 10, Exp. sobre bienes de comunidad, Oficiales reales to Governor, 14 Nov. 1805.

35. Documentation on this expansion and accompanying conflicts with Indian communities is cited in chapter 9, note 66.

36. See Haring, *Spanish Empire in America*, 320-321 and 314-322, for a summary of the commercial reforms. Brading, "Bourbon Spain and the American Empire," is an excellent analysis of the Bourbon economic reforms, their genesis, and effects.

37. On exports to Caribbean ports, especially Havana, see the sources cited in table 12.5 and chapter 1, note 34.

38. Along with Mexican silver, the most spectacular late colonial growth was registered in the export agriculture (and ranching) of the "peripheral" colonies of South America and the Caribbean. See Humboldt, *Ensayo político*, 83, 505; Brading, "Bourbon Spain and the American Empire"; Lynch, *Spanish Colonial Administration*, 25-45, 162-171, (on Río de la Plata); Arcila Farías, *Economía colonial*, 256-257, 355-370 (on Venezuela). Except for Chile, however, the agricultural export boom in these other regions was directed toward European rather than intercolonial trade.

39. See note 14. The less oppressive private *repartimientos* appear to have continued to some extent, as did the traditional exports of *mantas* and beeswax. What I am suggesting is a major shift in the colony's economic base, rather than a complete switch.

40. AGI, Mexico 3139, Reglamento provisional para el cobro de tributos, 28 June 1786, and Contador real to Viceroy, 28 Feb. 1787. See also AA, Oficios y decretos 3, Governor to Provisor, 17 Nov. 1786, and Bishop to Audiencia, 22 Nov. 1786; and, for a particular example, Asuntos terminados 5, Diligencias . . . pago de tributos estancia Chacsinkin, 1787. Owners had previously paid tribute and *obvenciones* for their salaried *criados*; the new rule sought to extend the liability to the much more numerous group of *luneros*, the unsalaried tenants. the royal cédula of 16 Dec. 1785 and local documentation on its promulgation are published in "Incorporación a la Real Corona," 462-467.

41. AGI, Mexico 3061, Demostración del número de poblaciones, 15 April 1781. *Vecino* and Indian population trends are discussed in chapter 2. See also tables 2.1 and 2.3 and appendix 1 for population figures.

42. On provisioning and trade, particularly with Isla del Carmen, see AGI, Mexico 3132, Cuentas Real caja Campeche, 1796; Mexico 3138, Cargo y data Real caja Campeche, 1807; AGN, Historia 534, Diligencias . . . Presidio del Carmen, 1785.

43. Two complementry studies trace these developments: Patch, "Colonial Regime," chapter 4, deals with the late colonial expansion and shift toward cereal production; Cline, "Regionalism and Society" (published in condensed form in "The Sugar Episode" and "The Henequen Episode"), analyzes the succeeding, postindependence phases. González Navarro, *Raza y tierra*, links nineteenth-century agrarian change with the Caste War, and Strickon, "Hacienda and Plantation," is a somewhat dated but still useful summary.

44. AGI, Mexico 3057, Estado general de todos los indios tributarios, 10 Feb. 1774, recording losses of 41 percent between 1765 and 1773, including *huídos*.

The total death toll is unrecorded but may well have reached over one-third by the final tally. For further data on the famine and losses, see Mexico 3057, Autos formados sobre la falta de tributarios, 1775, cuads. 1-3.

45. See table 2.1 for these and other Indian population figures.

46. AGI, Mexico 3066, Governor to Audiencia, 30 April 1783; AA, Oficios y decretos 3, Haciendas de cofradías vendidas y su importe impuesto, n.d. (1787). The bishop's original intention had been to deposit the capital in the account of the royal Tobacco Monopoly at 4 percent (AA, Oficios y decretos 4, Bishop to Crown, 22 April 1781; Decretos 1, Bishop to Cabildo, 25 Oct. 1781), but that plan was thwarted by the governor's opposition to the sale.

47. Maya reactions to the sale are recorded in AGI, Mexico 3066, Testimonio de la real provisión, 1782 (reports by the Franciscan *doctrineros*), Informaciones instruídas . . . sobre cofradías, 1782, cuads. 5-10 (testimonies of Indian officials and *principales* in all the *partidos* except the Sierra), Testimonio de informaciones de los capitanes a guerra, 1782, cuads. 16-18 (petitions and documents presented by the pueblos of Hunucma, Tetiz, Kinchil, Ucu, Tixkokob, Maxcanu, Oxkutzcab, Chochola, and Santiago, 1781-1782).

48. On unsuccessful attempts to buy the *cofradía* estates, see AGI, Mexico 3066, Testimonio de real provisión, 1782 (reports on Mani, Dzan, and Tipikal), Informaciones instruídas . . . sobre cofradías, 1782, cuad, 7 (testimony Dzemul), cuad. 9 (testimony Yaxcaba), cuad. 10 (testimony Chikindzonot and Ekpedz); AA, Visitas pastorales 5, Parish report Teabo, 1782 (referring to the *visita* town of Chumayel). Documents on the Muna case are inserted in AA, Arreglos parroquiales 1, Exp. sobre permuta de curatos Muna y Chichimila, 1782, Autos sobre venta de la cofradía Maxal, 1780-1781. The *batab*, D. Juan Tec, paid the value of the cattle in cash (392 pesos) and the value of the planta in *censos* (500 pesos), which he must have redeemed at some point (AA, Cofradías e imposiciones 1, no. 20, Cuentas de la cofradía Maxal, Muna, 1802), before selling the estate to a Spaniard, who appears as owner in 1811: AEY, Censos 1, no. 7, Relación de los ranchos y haciendas . . . Partido de la Sierra Baja, 1811.

49. See note 47, especially for the Camino Real Alto, Costa, and Sierra districts; and AA, Visitas pastorales 4, Parish report and testimony Tecoh and Telchaquillo, 1782.

50. AGI, Mexico 1039, Governor to Crown, 2 July 1726; Mexico 3066, Testimonio de informaciones de los capitanes a guerra, 1782, report on the Partido de la Costa. See also chapter 9, note 61, on conflicts over cattle invasions of milpas.

51. AA, Oficios y decretos 4, Méritos y servicios Provisor Rafael del Castillo, 3 April 1782.

52. Some of the Indian leaders, especially in the most highly developed core region (Samahil, Bolonpoxche, Uman, Maxcanu, and Calkini in the Camino Real Alto; Izamal in the Costa; and Mani, Tecoh, and Telchaquillo in the Sierra) were presumably already experiencing the expansionist tactics of Spanish *hacendados* and therefore expressed fears of land losses at the time of the sale. The officials of Maxcanu specifically cited their struggle with the owner of the ha-

cienda Chactun (documented in the Títulos of Chactun) as the basis for their warning: "They say a Spaniard bought [the *cofradía* estate] Kumche. Well, Señor, if he bought the *cenote* with the buildings and the cattle, he need not think he has bought any *montes*. They belong to our pueblo." (AGI, Mexico 3066, cuad. 17, Representación Cacique y justicias Maxcanu, 11 May 1782).

53. See chapter 9, note 66, and, for a specific *cofradía* case, AA, Asuntos terminados 9, Exp. sobre la hacienda de cofradía Cuzama, 1803-1804. An earlier complaint concerned a *cofradía* sold in 1773 in the less densely populated district of Valladolid (AGI, Mexico 3066, Informaciones instruídas . . . sobre cofradías, 1782, cuad. 8, testimony Uayma): at the curate's urging the pueblo officials had consented to the sale of the *planta* and beehives during the famine period (1769-1774), but not to the lands, only to find that the buyer usurped a good portion of their community lands (and those belonging to neighboring Ebtun as well), including the district's only clay pit.

54. AEY, Censos 1, nos. 6-8, Relaciones de los ranchos y haciendas . . . , 1811, Sierra Baja, Sotuta, and Sierra Alta (Abala, of which Mukuyche and Uayalche were *anexos*, was traditionally a part of the Sierra but boundaries had recently been changed to include it with Sotuta). Nos. 3-5 and 8-11 of the same series contain estate censuses for the remaining districts except Tihosuco.

55. Records of production and tithe payments by individual hacienda are available in AEY, Iglesias 1, nos. 2 and 4, for the parishes of San Cristóbal (1794) and Hocaba (1795).

56. Títulos of Kisil, cuad. 2, San Bernardino Chich, 1735-1818; AEY, Tierras 1, no. 20, Litigio sobre tierras entre Da. Nicolasa de Lara y los indios de Abala, 1792-1827.

57. AGN, Consolidación 10, Expedte. sobre bienes de comunidad, 1805-1806, Reglamento para la administración . . . , 12 July 1797, art. 7; AGI, Mexico 3168, Parecer Manuel Pacheco to Diputación provincial, 1 March 1814.

58. The standard rent seems to have been five *cargas* of maize for every hundred *mecates* of milpa (see Títulos of Uayalceh, Lista de los indios que han labrado sus milpas, 1799). For later cash rents (rates not specified), see AA, Cofradías generales, 1816-1823, Razón de los que han adelantado pagos . . . estancia Petkanche, 1829.

59. AA, Libro de cofradía Tanlum, Cuentas de cofradía Sta. María (pueblo of Kinchil), 1797-1819; Oficios y decretos 5, Inventario de las cofradías Kanabchen y Chuyubchen (Kopoma and Chochola), 1805; and various *expedientes* of the management of unsold *cofradía* estates, 1790 to 1816, in AA, Cofradías e imposiciones 1.

60. Taylor, "Landed Society," 408, 409. This is not to disagree with Taylor's basic thesis that the Indians were not always and everywhere totally helpless victims of Spanish greed, as often depicted.

61. See note 55.

62. Roys, *Titles of Ebtun*.

63. The impact of the 1812 constitution of Cadiz and other legislation of the Liberal Cortes is discussed in Benson, *Mexico and the Spanish Cortes*. Rodríguez,

Cadiz Experiment, provides a more thorough analysis of the Liberal principals and their link with postindependence policies, with specific reference to Central America. On the promulgation of the constitution in Yucatan, see Rubio Mañé, "El Gobernador, Capitán General e Intendente."

64. See Cunniff, "Mexican Municipal Electoral Reform." The new municipal system was not directed specifically against the *repúblicas de indios* but was intended for all municipalities. Although promulgated throughout the empire, it was enforced with particular zeal in Yucatan, which had a strong Liberal faction (idem, 70-71).

65. For names of municipal officials, see AEY, Propios y arbitrios 1 and 2, Prospectos de arbitrios de ayuntamiento, 1813-1814 (municipal budgets of eighty-seven pueblos submitted to the Diputación provincial), and representations from a number of the constitutional *ayuntamientos* in 1813-1814, in AEY, Ayuntamientos 1; AA, Oficios y decretos 7; and AGI, Mexico 3168. Exceptions were the very heavily Indian regions of the east, where many of the pueblos had only a handful of *vecinos* and no Spanish residents at all.

66. AA, Documentos del Petén Itzá, Instrumentos de venta, Ixil, 1814 (misfiled), AEY, Propios y arbitrios 1 and 2, Prospectos de arbitrios, 1813-1814; Ayuntamientos 1, no. 6, Ayuntamiento de Champotón to Diputación provincial, 24 April 1813.

67. Sierra O'Reilly, *Indios de Yucatan,* devotes the entire second volume to an account of the 1812 reforms relating to the Indians, their local reception, and, most especially, the political maneuverings surrounding them.

68. Local authorities disagreed, however, over whether the abolition of tribute extended to the *comunidades* tax: AGI, Mexico 3168, Oficiales reales to Governor, 22 April, 1813, Respuesta Auditor de guerra, 26 May 1813, Sesión Diputación provincial, 10-12 May 1813, Parecer Manuel Pacheco to Diputación provincial, 1 March 1814, Diputación provincial to Secretario de Ultramar, 14 April 1814. See also Informe Bartolomé del Granado Baeza, 1 April 1813, on the baneful consequences of the abolition of whipping.

69. Rubio Mañé, *Sanjuanistas de Yucatan* (drawing heavily on Sierra O'Reilly, *Indios de Yucatan,* vol. 2). See also AGI, Mexico 3168, Exp. sobre que las ovenciones . . . , 1813-1814, and Bishop to Secretario de Ultramar, 1 July 1813.

70. AGI, Mexico 3168, Bishop to Diputación provincial, 22 Dec. 1813 and 12 March 1814. In addition to the curates' reports cited in note 71, see AGI, Mexico 3168, Exp. sobre . . . obvenciones, 1813-1814, which deals with Indian reactions to clerical support in general.

71. AA, Estadística, contains reports from most of the curates, Jan.-March 1814, on parish income for 1813, with appended accounts of the hardships and insolences they were suffering. See also AGI, Mexico 3168, Representación Ayuntamiento Tahdziu, 12 June 1813, Cura of Tihosuco, 7 Nov. 1813, Cura of Chichimila, 3 Jan. 1814, Vicario of Valladolid, 11 Jan. 1814, and Parecer Manuel Pacheco, 1 March 1814; AA, Asuntos pendientes 3, Cura of Hoctun to Bishop; Oficios y decretos 7, Cura of Chikindzonot to Bishop, 20 Nov. 1814.

72. González Navarro, *Raza y tierra*, 54-64.

73. Ibid., 65-67.

74. Philip Thompson,"Tekanto," 182-183, based on the notarial records of Tekanto. A similar pattern of equal bilateral inheritance is discernible in the early nineteenth-century wills of Ebtun (Roys, *Titles of Ebtun,* 327-329, 335-337, 341, 343-345, 355-357). Land continued to be inherited jointly but now daughters were included as well as sons.

75. This usage is already discernible in some of the manifestoes and correspondence of the Caste War Maya.

76. AGI, Mexico 3139, Reglamento provisional . . . cobro de tributos, 28 June 1786; AA, Oficios y decretos 4, Carta cordillera Bishop to Curas, 5 Aug. 1786; Oficios y decretos 3, Bishop to Audiencia, 22 Nov. 1786, complaining that the new system was going to make it impossible to keep track of the Indians. Tax collection continued to be organized territorially; the difference was that tribute ceased to be a corporate obligation for which the community qua community was held liable.

77. See note 11.

78. The image of peasant society as a collection of undifferentiated, egalitarian, democratic, and conflict-free communities, cooperating harmoniously in the pursuit of uniformly shared goals, has faded considerably in the face of contrary evidence from many regions. Specifically for Yucatan, Goldkind, "Social Stratification" and "Class Conflict and Caciques," has challenged Redfield's earlier portrait of Chan Kom, a village in eastern Yucatan. Significant gradations in wealth and the predominance of some wealthy families in community leadership are reminiscent of the colonial Maya social order. But there are differences, partly in degree and partly in the underlying principles that support the social order. Even in relatively undeveloped eastern Yucatan, where community organization has preserved more traditional outlines, gradations have become more subtle and wealth and power are neither derived from nor legitimated by hereditary privilege.

79. Compare the Estados de curatos, 1802 and 1828 (listing all haciendas and *ranchos* as well as pueblos), in AA, Estadística 1 and 2, and the Nómina de los curatos . . . con expresión de sus auxiliares, ranchos y capillas, 23 Nov. 1848, in AA, Estadística 3. On post-Caste War expansion in the Valladolid region (most recently into the former *cruzob* territory of the new state of Quintana Roo), see Sanders, "Cultural Ecology," 103-108; Redfield and Villa Rojas, *Chan Kom,* 22-27.

80. Wolf, "Closed Corporate Peasant Communities," 7.

81. See chapter 7, notes 62-64.

82. AGI, Mexico 3066, Informaciones instruídas . . . cofradías, 1782, testimony Yaxcaba. The residents of the town's *cofradía* estate (Kancabdzonot) objected so strongly to the change in ownership that they collected 100 pesos to purchase the hacienda and when their bid, placed via the *batab*, was refused, they packed up and moved back to town. See also Mexico 3066, Testimonio real provisión, 1782, report on Izamal. Similarly in AEY, Tierras 1, no. 20, Litigio sobre tierras . . . Abala, 1792-1827, one-third of the inhabitants of an

independent *rancho* moved away when a nearby hacienda owner claimed the *rancho* as an *anexo* in 1792, while the rest stayed to fight what they called "being enslaved"—and eventually lost.

83. Reported in AA, Estadística 1 and 2, Estados que manifiesta . . . , Jan.-March 1814: Espita, Ichmul, Izamal, Maxcanu, Teya, Tekanto. See also AGI, Mexico 3168, Auto Governor, 4 Dec. 1813, and Parecer Manuel Pacheco to Diputación provincial, 1 March 1814. Other documents (see, for example, Títulos de Uayalceh, Representación Esteban yam, 2 Dec. 1815) indicate that some Indians continued to move, although in this case only to a neighboring hacienda.

84. Strickon, "Hacienda and Plantation," 50.

85. AA, Estadística 1 and 2, Parish censuses of 1802-1806, summarized in appendix 1, yield a figure of 34.4 percent of the total Indian population living in all types of dispersed settlements. See chapter 7, note 56, on the difficulties of distinguishing among types of settlement in the documentation.

86. AGI, Mexico 1037, Governor to Crown, 15 Sept. 1711. See table 2.1 for Indian population figures.

87. AGI, Mexico 3168, Parecer Manuel Pacheco to Diputación provincial, 1 March 1814 (and compare with descriptions of hacienda life in chapter 7, note 61). The nucleation process was still far from complete at this stage, and the larger haciendas consolidated a portion of their populations into a series of subordinate nuclei designated as *ranchos anexos* rather than in one huge settlement (see, for example, Títulos de Uayalceh, with a population of 1,227 in 1806, according to AA, Estadística 1, Abala).

88. AA, Estadística 1 and 2, Estados que manifiestan . . . 1802-1828. About a third of the parish censuses in this section give a breakdown of population by individual hacienda, *estancia*, or *rancho*, as well as by pueblo, and the rest lump all of the dispersed population together. Unfortunately the hacienda censuses in AEY, Censos 1, nos. 3-11, cannot fill the gap; they list only cattle, not human, populations and there is no consistent correlation between the two.

89. See chapter 7, notes 63 and 64.

90. AA, Cofradías e imposiciones 1, no. 7, Cuentas de cofradía S. Antonio Jesús, 1810. On hacienda fiestas, see also Oficios y decretos 5, Joaquín Campos, cura of Abala, to Bishop, 26 April 1804; Oficios y decretos 7, Francisco Bravo to Bishop, 3 Dec. 1811; Arreglos parroquiales 1, Exp. sobre . . . hacienda Chencoyi, 1792.

91. González Navarro, *Raza y tierra*, 76.

92. Eligio Ancona, writing during the 1870s, quoted in ibid., 277.

93. Reed, *Caste War*, 48.

Epilogue

1. Díaz del Castillo, *Verdadera historia*; and Stephens, *Incidents of Travel*.

2. Stephens, *Incidents of Travel* 1: 120 (and also 82, 121, 203).

3. See the late Postclassic (post-1400) and mural paintings from the east-coast

sites of Tulum and Xelha, reproduced in Miller, *On the Edge of the Sea*, plates 28, 29, 31-33, and 37-40, and the possibly early postconquest mural in plate 45.

4. Rowe, "Incas under Spanish Colonial Administration," 183-187; and Phelan, *Kingdom of Quito*, 52-55. However, Kubler, "Quechua in the Colonial World," 403, argues that the Quechua had become essentially Catholic by the end of the seventeenth century.

GLOSSARY

Other Spanish and Maya words are defined in the text. (M) indicates Maya word.

aguardiente. Distilled cane liquor.

ahcuchcab (M). Official in charge of a subdivision of a town; in colonial times synonymous with *regidor.*

ahkin (M). Priest.

alcalde. Alderman, member of *cabildo.*

almehen (M). Noble.

audiencia. High court of appeal.

balche (M). Fermented beverage of honey and bark.

barrio. Subdivision of town; suburb.

batab (M). Hereditary ruler of a town.

bienes de comunidad. Community revenues on deposit in royal treasury.

cabecera. Principal town of a parish.

cabildo. Town council.

cacique. Local Indian ruler (Spanish translation of *batab*).

caja de comunidad. Municipal treasury.

capitán a guerra. Local Spanish official with military duties.

carga. Dry measure of corn, equivalent to approximately six bushels.

cargo. Burden or office; hierarchy of community civil-religious offices.

casta. Racial category denoting mixed ancestry.

cenote. Natural limestone sinkhole.

chaac (M). Rain god; milpa spirit associated with rain.

Chilam Balam (M). Literally red jaguar; Maya prophet, reputed author of Books of Chilam Balam.

cofradía. Parish confraternity dedicated to cult of one or more saints.

comal. Griddle for cooking tortillas.

compadrazgo. Ritual kinship ties between godparents and natural parents.

composiciones de tierras. Legalizations of land titles.

comunidades. Municipal head tax.

convite. Banquet.

corregidor. Local Spanish official with judicial, administrative, and fiscal duties.

criado. Indian servant or employee.

cruzob (M). Maya group, devotees of the Speaking Cross cult; descendants of Caste War rebels.

curato. Parish administered by secular clergy.

derrama. Unofficial local tax levy.

doctrina. Indian parish administered by regular clergy; also catechism classes.

doctrinero. Friar in charge of *doctrina.*

dzul (M). Foreigner, non-Indian.

ejidos. Municipal common lands.

encomienda. Grant of Indians for tribute.

encomendero. Holder of *encomienda.*

escribano. Town clerk or secretary.

estancia. Cattle ranch.

fiscal. Low-ranking Indian official.

forastero. Outsider; Indian residing outside native place.

gobernador. Appointed head of an Indian municipality.

hacienda. Large landed estate devoted to grain production and ranching.

halach uinic (M). Pre-Hispanic ruler of a province.

henequen. Fiber for cordage; also plant producing the fiber.

huipil. Long, blouse-like woman's garment.

juez español. Local Spanish official, under subdelegate.

540

katun (M). Twenty-year period.

ladino. Spanish-speaking; in modern usage, racially and/or culturally non-Indian.

limosnas. Alms; community contributions for support of clergy and liturgy.

lunero. Tenant farmer, paying a labor rent.

macehual. Indian commoner.

maestro cantor. Literally choirmaster; Indian official in charge of liturgy and catechism.

manta. Length of cotton cloth.

mayordomo. Custodian; officer of *cofradía*.

mecate. Measure of land, approximately 20 meters by 20 meters.

mestizo. Person of mixed European and Indian ancestry.

metate. Curved stone for grinding corn by hand.

milpa. Clearing in forest for planting maize; slash-and-burn or swidden agriculture.

obvenciones. Ecclesiastical head tax, analogous to tribute.

parcialidad. Ward or subdivision of town (barrio); also town annexed to another town.

pardo. Person of African-European or African-Indian ancestry.

principal. High-ranking Indian, nobleman.

Protector de Indios. Royal official in charge of defending Indian interests.

pudiente. Rich, powerful.

rancho. Hamlet.

real. Monetary unit; 8 reales = 1 peso.

regidor. Councilman, member of *cabildo*.

repartimiento. In Yucatan, forced cash advances for delivery of maize, cotton cloth, or other goods.

república de Indios. Autonomous Indian municipality.

residencia. Trial held at end of official's term.

semanero. Labor draftee.

señorío. Lordship.

servicio personal. System of forced labor, in weekly rotation.

sitio. Small rural property, usually a stock farm.

tequio. Community labor tax.

títulos. Land titles.

tun (M). Year.

vecino. Non-Indian.

vigía. Coastal lookout; lookout station.

visita. Tour of inspection; also subordinate town in a parish.

visitador. Inspector.

541

BIBLIOGRAPHY

Abernathy, Virginia. *Population Pressure and Cultural Adjustment.* New York: Human Sciences Press, 1978.

Adams, Richard E. W., ed. *The Origins of Maya Civilization.* Albuquerque: University of New Mexico Press, 1977.

Adas, Michael. "From Avoidance to Confrontation: Peasant Protest in Precolonial Southeast Asia." *Comparative Studies in Society and History* 23 (1981): 217-247.

Aguirre Beltrán, Gonzalo. *Formas de gobierno indígena.* Mexico: Imprenta Universitaria, 1953.

——. *Medicina y magia: El proceso de aculturación en la estructura colonial.* Mexico: Instituto Nacional Indigenista, 1963.

Alatas, Syed Hussein. *The Myth of the Lazy Native: A Study of the Image of Malays, Filipinos and Javanese from the 16th to the 20th Century and Its Function in the Ideology of Colonial Capitalism.* London: Frank Cass, 1973.

Ancona, Eligio. *Historia de Yucatan desde la época más remota hasta nuestros días.* 3 vols. Merida: Imprenta de Manuel Heredia Argüelles, 1878-1879.

Andrews, Anthony P. "The Salt Trade of the Maya." *Archaeology* 33 (1980): 24-33.

Andrews, E. Wyllys, IV. *Balankanche: Throne of the Jaguar Priest.* New Orleans: Middle American Research Institute, Tulane University, 1970.

Appadurai, Arjun, and Carol A. Breckenridge. "The South Indian Temple: Authority, Honor and Redistribution." *Contributions to Indian Sociology,* n.s. 10 (1976): 187-211.

Archer, Christon L. *The Army in Bourbon Mexico, 1760-1810.* Albuquerque: University of New Mexico Press, 1977.

Arcila Farías, Eduardo. *La economía colonial de Venezuela.* Mexico: Talleres Gráfica Panamerica, 1946.

——. *El siglo ilustrado en América: Reformas económicas del siglo XVIII en Nueva España.* Caracas: Ministerio de Educación, 1955.

Ashmore, Wendy, ed. *Lowland Maya Settlement Patterns.* Albuquerque: University of New Mexico Press, 1981.

Bakewell, Peter J. *Silver Mining and Society in Colonial Mexico: Zacatecas, 1546-1700.* Cambridge: Cambridge University Press, 1971.

Ball, Joseph W. "A Coordinate Approach to Northern Maya Prehistory: A.D. 700-1200." *American Antiquity* 39 (1974): 85-93.

——. "The 1977 Central College Symposium on Puuc Archaeology: A Summary View." In *The Puuc: New Perspectives,* edited by Lawrence Mills, 46-51. Pella, Iowa: Central College Press, 1979.

——. "The Rise of the Northern Maya Chiefdoms: A Socio-processual Approach." In *Origins of Civilization in the Maya Lowlands,* edited by Richard E. W. Adams, 101-132. Albuquerque: University of New Mexico Press, 1977.

Baqueiro, Serapio. *Ensayo histórico sobre las revoluciones de Yucatan desde el año*

1840 hasta 1864. 2 vols. Merida: Imprenta de Manuel Heredia Argüelles, 1878-1879.

Barrera Vázquez, Alfredo, ed. *Códice de Calkini.* Campeche: Talleres Gráficos del Estado, 1957.

———. *El libro de los cantares de Dzitbalché.* Mexico: Instituto Nacional de Anthropología e Historia, 1965.

Barrera, Vázquez, Alfredo, and Silvia Rendón, eds. *El libro de los libros de Chilam Balam.* Mexico: Fondo de Cultura Económica, 1948.

Barth, Frederick, ed. *Ethnic Groups and Boundaries: The Social Organization of Culture Difference.* Boston: Little Brown, 1969.

Bastide, Roger. *The African Religions of Brazil.* Translated by Helen Sebba. Baltimore: Johns Hopkins University Press, 1978.

Bataillon, Marcel. *Erasmo y España.* 2d ed. Mexico: Fondo de Cultura Económica, 1966.

Baudot, Georges. *Utopie et histoire au Mexique: Les premiers chroniquers de la civilisation mexicaine, 1520-1569.* Toulouse: Editions Edoard Privat, 1977.

Bauer, Arnold. "The Church and Spanish American Agrarian Structures, 1765-1865." *The Americas* 27 (1971): 78-98.

———. "Rural Workers in Spanish America: Problems of Peonage and Oppression." *Hispanic American Historical Review* 59 (1979): 34-63.

Bazant, Jan. "Evolución de la industria textil poblana (1544-1845)." *Historia Mexicana* 7 (1965): 473-516.

Becker, Marshall J. 'Moieties in Ancient Mesoamerica: Inferences on Teotihuacan Social Structure." *American Indian Quarterly* 2 (1975-1976): 217-236, 315-330.

Beidelman, Thomas O. "Swazi Royal Ritual." *Africa* 36 (1966): 373-405.

Beltrán de Santa Rosa María, Pedro. *Arte del Idioma Maya reducido a sucintas reglas y semilexicon yucateca* (1742). Merida: Imprenta de J. D. Espinosa, 1859.

Bennassar, Bartolomé. *The Spanish Character: Attitudes and Mentalities from the 16th to the 19th Century.* Berkeley: University of California Press, 1979.

Benson, Nettie Lee, ed. *Mexico and the Spanish Cortes, 1810-1822.* Austin: University of Texas Press, 1966.

Berger, Peter L. *The Sacred Canopy: Elements of a Sociological Theory of Religion.* Garden City, N.Y.: Doubleday, Anchor Press, 1969.

Berlin, Heinrich. "El glifo 'emblema' en las inscripciones mayas." *Journal de le Société de Américanistes,* n.s. 46 (1958): 111-119.

Blanton, Richard E. *Monte Albán: Settlement Patterns at the Ancient Zapotec Capital.* New York: Academic Press, 1978.

Bloch, Marc. *Feudal Society.* Chicago: University of Chicago Press, 1961.

Borah, Woodrow. "The Historical Demography of Aboriginal and Colonial America: An Attempt at Perspective." In *The Native Population of the Americas in 1492,* edited by William M. Denevan, 13-34. Madison: University of Wisconsin Press, 1976.

Borah, Woodrow, and Sherburne F. Cook. *The Aboriginal Population of Central*

Mexico on the Eve of the Spanish Conquest. Ibero-Americana no. 45. Berkeley: University of California Press, 1963.

———. "A Case History of the Transition from Pre-colonial to the Colonial Period in Mexico: Santiago Tejupan." In *Social Fabric and Spatial Structure in Colonial Latin America*, edited by David L. Robinson, 409-432. Ann Arbor, Michigan: University Microfilms for Syracuse University, 1979.

Boserup, Ester. *The Conditions of Agricultural Growth: The Economics of Agrarian Change under Population Pressure.* Chicago: University of Chicago Press, 1965.

Boxer, Charles R. *Race Relations in the Portuguese Colonial Empire, 1415-1825.* Oxford: Clarendon Press, 1963.

Brading, David A. "Bourbon Spain and the American Empire." In *Cambridge History of Latin America,* edited by Leslie Bethel. Cambridge: Cambridge University Press, in press.

———. "La estructura de la producción agrícola en el Bajío de 1700 a 1850." *Historia Mexicana* 23 (1973): 197-237.

———. *Haciendas and Ranchos in the Mexican Bajío: León, 1700-1800.* Cambridge: Cambridge University Press, 1978.

———. *Miners and Merchants in Bourbon Mexico, 1763-1810.* Cambridge: Cambridge University Press, 1971.

Bricker, Victoria R. "The Caste War of Yucatan: The History of a Myth and the Myth of History." In *Anthropology and History in Yucatan,* edited by Grant D. Jones, 251-258. Austin: University of Texas Press, 1977.

———. *Ritual Humor in Highland Chiapas.* Austin: University of Texas Press, 1973.

Brinton, Daniel G. *El Folklore de Yucatan.* Translated and edited by Alfredo Barrera Vázquez. Merida: Ediciones del Gobierno del Estado, 1976.

———. *The Maya Chronicles* (1882). Reprint. New York: AMS Press, 1969.

———. "Nagualism: A Study in Native American Folklore and History." *Proceedings of the American Philosophical Society* 33 (1894): 1-65.

Broda, Johanna. "Relaciones políticas ritualizadas: El ritual como expresión de una ideología." In *Economía política e ideología en el Mexico prehispánico,* edited by Pedro Carrasco and Johanna Broda, 221-255. Mexico: Editorial Nueva Imagen, 1978.

Brotherston, Gordon. "Continuity in Maya Writing: New Readings of Two Passages in the Book of Chilam Balam of Chumayel." In *Maya Archaeology and Ethnohistory,* edited by Norman Hammond and Gordon R. Willey, 241-258. Austin: University of Texas Press, 1979.

Brown, Paula. "From Anarchy to Satrapy." *American Anthropologist* 65 (1963): 1-15.

Bunzel, Ruth. *Chichicastenango: A Guatemalan Village.* Publications of the American Ethnological Society, no. 12. Seattle: University of Washington Press, 1952.

Burke, Peter. *Popular Culture in Early Modern Europe.* New York: Harper and Row, 1978.

545

Cabat, Geoffrey A. "The Consolidation of 1804 in Guatemala." *The Americas* 28 (1971): 20-38.

Campbell, Lyle, John J. Justeson, and William C. Norman. "Foreign Influence on Lowland Maya Language and Script." In *Interdisciplinary Approaches to the Study of Mesoamerican Highland-Lowland Interaction*, edited by Arthur G. Miller. Washington: Dumbarton Oaks, in press.

Cancian, Frank. *Economics and Prestige in a Maya Community: The Religious Cargo System in Zinacantan*. Stanford: Stanford University Press, 1968.

————. "Political and Religious Organizations." In *Handbook of Middle American Indians* 6; 283-298. Austin: University of Texas Press, 1967.

Cantón Rosado, Francisco. "La beneficencia pública en Yucatán durante la época colonial." *Anales de la Sociedad de Geografía e Historia* 14 (1938): 495-504.

Cárdenas Valencia, Francisco de. *Relación historial eclesiástica de la provincia de Yucatán de la Nueva España escrita en el año de 1639*. Mexico: Editorial Porrua, 1937.

Cardós de M., Amalia. *El comercio de los mayas antiguos*. Mexico: Escuela Nacional de Antropología e Historia, 1959.

Carneiro, Robert. "Political Expansion as an Expression of the Principle of Competitive Exclusion." In *Origins of the State: The Anthropology of Political Evolution*, edited by Ronald Cohen and Elman R. Service, 205-223. Philadelphia, Institute for the Study of Human Issues, 1978.

————. "A Theory of the Origin of the State." *Science* 169 (1970): 733-738.

Caro Baroja, Julio. *The World of the Witches*. Chicago: University of Chicago Press, 1964.

Carrasco, Pedro. "The Civil-Religious Hierarchy in Mesoamerican Communities: Pre-Spanish Background and Colonial Development." *American Anthropologist* 63 (1961): 483-497.

————. "The Joint Family in Ancient Mexico: The Case of Molotla." In *Essays on Mexican Kinship*, edited by Hugo G. Nutini, Pedro Carrasco and James M. Taggart, 45-64. Pittsburgh: University of Pittsburgh Press, 1976.

Cartas de Indias. Madrid: Ministerio de Fomento, Imprenta de Manuel G. Hernández, 1877.

Catálogo de construcciones religiosas del estado de Yucatan. 2 vols. Mexico: Secretaría de Hacienda y Crédito Público, 1945.

Chamberlain, Robert S. *The Conquest and Colonization of Yucatan, 1517-1550*. Washington: Carnegie Institution, 1948.

————. *The Pre-Conquest Tribute and Service System of the Maya as Preparation for the Spanish Repartimiento-Encomienda in Yucatan*. University of Miami Hispanic-American Studies, no. 10. Coral Gables, Florida: University of Miami Press, 1951.

Chance, John K. *Race and Class in Colonial Oaxaca*. Stanford: Stanford University Press, 1978.

Chapman, Anne. "Port of Trade Enclaves in Aztec and Maya Civilizations." In *Trade and Market in Early Empires*, edited by Karl Polanyi, C. M. Arensberg, and H. W. Pearson, 114-153. New York: The Free Press, 1957.

Chardon, Roland E. P. *Geographic Aspects of Plantation Agriculture in Yucatan.* Washington: National Academy of Sciences, 1961.

Chávez Orozco, Luis. "Orígenes de la política de seguridad social." *Historia Mexicana* 16 (1966): 155-183.

Chevalier, François. *La formation des grands domaines au Mexique.* Paris: Institut d'Ethnologie, 1952.

——, ed. *Instrucciones a los hermanos jesuítas administradores de haciendas.* Mexico: Universidad Nacional Autónoma de Mexico, 1950.

Christian, William A., Jr. *Local Religion in Sixteenth-Century Spain.* Princeton: Princeton University Press, 1980.

——. *Person and God in a Spanish Valley.* New York: Seminar Press, 1972.

Ciudad Real, Antonio de. *Relación de las cosas que sucedieron al R. P. Comisario General Fray Alonso Ponce . . .* (1588). In *Colección de documentos inéditos para la historia de España,* vols. 57 and 58. Madrid: Imprenta de la Viuda de Calero. 1872.

Cline, Howard F. "Civil Congregations of the Indians in New Spain, 1598-1606." *Hispanic American Historical Review* 29 (1949): 349-369.

——. "The Henequen Episode in Yucatan, 1830-1890." *Inter-American Economic Affairs* 2 (1948): 30-51.

——. "Regionalism and Society in Yucatan, 1825-1850." Ph.D. dissertation, Harvard University, 1947.

——. "The Sugar Episode in Yucatan, 1815-1850." *Inter-American Economic Affairs* 1 (1947-1948): 79-100.

Codex Pérez: see Craine, Eugene R., and Reginald C. Reindorp.

Código de derecho canónico. Madrid: Editorial Católica, 1957.

Coe, Michael D. *America's First Civilization.* New York: American Heritage, 1968.

——. "Death and the Ancient Maya." In *Death and the Afterlife in Pre-Columbian America,* edited by Elizabeth P. Benson, 87-104. Washington: Dumbarton Oaks, 1975.

——. "The Iconology of Olmec Art." In *The Iconography of Middle American Sculpture,* by Ignacio Bernal, et al., 1-12. New York: Metropolitan Museum of Art, 1973.

——. "A Model of Ancient Community Structure in the Maya Lowlands." *Southwestern Journal of Anthropology* 21 (1965): 97-114.

——. "Social Typology and the Tropical Forest Civilizations." *Comparative Studies in Society and History* 4 (1961): 65-85.

Coe, William R. *Tikal: A Handbook of the Ancient Maya Ruins.* Philadelphia: University Museum, University of Pennsylvania, 1967.

Coggins, Clemency C. "Painting and Drawing Styles at Tikal." Ph.D. dissertation, Harvard University, 1975.

Cogolludo, Diego López de. *Historia de Yucatan* (1654). Madrid: J. García Infanzón, 1688.

Cohen, Abner. "Drama and Politics in the Development of a London Carnival." *Man,* n.s. 15 (1980): 65-87.

547

Cohen, Abner. "A Polyethnic London Carnival as a Contested Cultural Performance." Paper presented at the Ethnohistory Workshop, University of Pennsylvania, Philadelphia, 1981.

Cohen, Mark N. *The Food Crisis in Prehistory: Overpopulation and the Origins of Agriculture.* New Haven: Yale University Press, 1977.

Collins, Anne C. "The *Maestros Cantores* in Yucatan." In *Anthropology and History in Yucatan*, edited by Grant D. Jones, 233-247. Austin: University of Texas Press, 1977.

Connell, Kenneth H. *Irish Peasant Society: Four Historical Essays.* Oxford: Clarendon Press, 1968.

Cook, Sherburne F., and Woodrow Borah. *Essays in Population History: Mexico and the Caribbean.* 3 vols. Berkeley: University of California Press, 1972-1979.

————. *The Indian Population of Central Mexico, 1531-1610.* Berkeley: University of California Press, 1960.

Cortés, Hernán. *Cartas de relación* (1522-1525). Edited by Manuel Alcalá. Mexico: Editorial Porrua, 1963.

Costeloe, Michael P. *Church and State in Independent Mexico: A Study of the Patronage Debate, 1821-1857.* London: Royal Historical Society, 1978.

Cowgill, George L. "On Causes and Consequences of Ancient and Modern Population Changes." *American Anthropologist* 77 (1974): 505-555.

————. "Teotihuacan, Internal Militaristic Competition, and the Fall of the Classic Maya." In *Archaeology and Ethnohistory*, edited by Norman Hammond, 52-62. Austin: University of Texas Press, 1979.

Craine, Eugene R., and Reginald C. Reindorp, eds. *The Codex Perez and the Book of Chilam Balam of Mani.* Norman: University of Oklahoma Press, 1979.

Culbert, T. Patrick, ed. *The Maya Collapse.* Albuquerque: University of New Mexico Press, 1973.

Cunniff, Roger L. "Mexican Municipal Electoral Reform, 1810-1822." In *Mexico and the Spanish Cortes*, edited by Nettie Lee Benson, 59-86. Austin: University of Texas Press, 1966.

Dahlgren Jordán, Bárbara. "Cambios socio-económicos registrados a mediados del siglo XVI en un pueblo de la Mixteca Alta, Oaxaca, Mexico." In *Actes du XLIIᵉ Congrès International des Américanistes, Paris, 1976* 8: 103-119. Paris: Société des Américanistes, 1979.

Davies, Nigel. *The Aztecs: A History.* London: Macmillan, 1973.

Davis, Natalie Z. *Society and Culture in Early Modern France.* Stanford: Stanford University Press, 1975.

Denevan, William M., ed. *The Native Population of the Americas in 1492.* Madison: University of Wisconsin Press, 1976.

Deshon, Shirley K. "Compadrazgo on a Henequen Hacienda in Yucatan: A Structural Re-evaluation." *American Anthropologist* 65 (1963): 574-583.

Díaz del Castillo, Bernal. *Verdadera historia de la conquista de la Nueva España*

(1554?-1568). Edited by Joaquín Ramiro Cabañas. 2 vols. Mexico: Editorial Porrua, 1968.

Diccionario de Motul maya-español, atribuído a Fray Antonio de Ciudad Real . . . (late 1500s). Edited by Juan Martínez Hernández. Merida: Talleres de la Compañía Tipográfica Yucateca, 1929.

Dirks, Robert. "Social Responses during Severe Food Shortages and Famine." *Current Anthropology* 21 (1980): 21-44.

Domínguez Ortiz, Antonio. *La sociedad española en el siglo XVII.* 2 vols. Madrid: Consejo Superior de Investigaciones Científicas, 1963-1970.

Douglas, Mary. *Purity and Danger.* London: Routledge and Kegan Paul, 1966.

Dumond, D. E. "Independent Maya of the Late Nineteenth Century: Chiefdoms and Power Politics." In *Anthropology and History in Yucatan*, edited by Grant D. Jones, 103-138. Austin: University of Texas Press, 1977.

Durkheim, Emile. *The Division of Labor in Society.* Translated by G. Simpson. New York: Macmillan, 1933.

Eggan, Fred. "The Maya Kinship System and Cross-cousin Marriage." *American Anthropologist* 36 (1934): 188-202.

Eliade, Mircea. *The Myth of the Eternal Return, or Cosmos and History.* Princeton: Princeton University Press, 1954.

Eugenio Martínez, María Angeles. *La defensa de Tabasco, 1600-1717.* Seville: Escuela de Estudios Hispano-Americanos, 1971.

Evans-Pritchard, E. E. *Nuer Religion.* Oxford: Oxford University Press, 1956.

――――. *Witchcraft, Oracles and Magic among the Azande.* Oxford: Clarendon Press, 1937.

Fallers, Lloyd, *Bantu Bureaucracy.* Cambridge, England: W. Heffer, 1956.

Farriss, Nancy M. *Crown and Clergy in Colonial Mexico, 1759-1821: The Crisis of Ecclesiastical Privilege.* London: The Athlone Press, 1968.

――――. "Nucleation versus Dispersal: The Dynamics of Population Movement in Colonial Yucatan." *Hispanic American Historical Review* 58 (1978): 187-216.

――――. "Propiedades territoriales en Yucatán en la época colonial: Algunas observaciones acerca de la pobreza española y la autonomía indígena." *Historia Mexicana* 30 (1980): 153-208.

Faust, Drew G. "Culture, Conflict and Community: The Meaning of Power on an Ante-bellum Plantation." *Journal of Social History* 14 (1980): 83-98.

Fernández de Recas, Guillermo, ed. *Cacicazgos y nobiliario indígena de la Nueva España.* Mexico: Universidad Nacional Autónoma de Mexico, 1961.

Figuera, Guillermo. *La formación del clero indígena en la historia eclesiástica de América, 1500-1810.* Caracas: Archivo General de la Nación, 1965.

Fisher, John. *Government and Society in Colonial Peru.* London: The Athlone Press, 1970.

Flores Caballero, Romeo. *La contrarrevolución en la independencia: Los españoles en la vida política, social y económica de México (1804-1838).* Mexico: El Colegio de Mexico, 1969.

Florescano, Enrique. *Precios de maíz y crisis agrícolas en México, 1708 1810.* Mexico, El Colegio de Mexico, 1969.

Foster, George M. "Cofradía and Compadrazgo in Spain and Spanish America." *Southwestern Journal of Anthropology* 9 (1953): 1-28.

——. *Culture and Conquest: America's Spanish Heritage.* Chicago: Quadrangle Press, 1960.

——. "What is Folk Culture?" *American Anthropologist* 55 (1953): 159-173.

Frank, Andre Gundar. *Capitalism and Underdevelopment in Latin America: Historical Studies of Chile and Brazil.* 2d rev. ed. New York: Monthly Review Press, 1969.

Freeman, Susan Tax. *Neighbors: The Social Contract in a Castilian Hamlet.* Chicago: University of Chicago Press, 1970.

Freidel, David A. "Lowland Maya Political Economy: Historical and Archaeological Perspectives in Light of Intensive Agriculture." In *Spaniards and Indians in Southeastern Mesoamerica,* edited by Murdo J. MacLeod and Robert Wasserstrom. Lincoln: University of Nebraska Press, 1983.

——. "The Political Economics of Residential Dispersion among the Lowland Maya." In *Lowland Maya Settlement Patterns,* edited by Wendy Ashmore, 372-382. Albuquerque: University of New Mexico Press, 1981.

Freyre, Gilberto. *The Masters and the Slaves.* Translated by Samuel Putnam. New York: Alfred A. Knopf, 1964.

Fried, Morton. *The Evolution of Political Society.* New York: Random House, 1967.

García Bernal, Manuela Cristina. *La sociedad de Yucatán, 1700-1750,* Seville: Escuela de Estudios Hispano-Americanos, 1972.

——. "La visita de Fray Luis de Cifuentes, obispo de Yucatán." *Anuario de Estudios Americanos* 29 (1972): 229-260.

——. *Yucatán: Población y encomienda bajo los Austrias.* Seville: Escuela de Estudios Hispano-Americanos, 1978.

Geary, Patrick J. "The Nine-Century Relic Trade: A Response to Popular Piety?" In *Religion and the People, 800-1700,* edited by James Obelkevich, 8-19. Chapel Hill: University of North Carolina Press, 1979.

Geertz, Clifford. "Form and Variation in Balinese Village Structure." *American Anthropologist* 61 (1959): 912-1012.

——. *Negara: The Theatre State in Nineteenth-Century Bali.* Princeton: Princeton University Press, 1980.

Genovese, Eugene E. *Roll, Jordan, Roll.* New York: Random House, 1972.

Gerhard, Peter. *The Southeast Frontier of New Spain.* Princeton: Princeton University Press, 1979.

Gibson, Charles. *The Aztecs under Spanish Rule: A History of the Indians of the Valley of Mexico, 1519-1810.* Stanford: Stanford University Press, 1964.

Gilman, Antonio. "The Development of Social Stratification in Bronze Age Europe." *Current Anthropology* 22 (1981): 1-23.

Gluckman, Max. *Rituals of Rebellion in South-East Africa.* Manchester: Manchester University Press, 1954.

550

Goldkind, Victor. "Class Conflict and Caciques in Chan Kom." *Southwestern Journal of Anthropology* 22 (1969): 325-345.

―――. "Social Stratification in the Peasant Community: Redfield's Chan Kom Revisited." *American Anthropologist* 67 (1965): 863-884.

Golte, Jürgen. *Repartos y rebeliones: Tupac Amaru y las contradicciones de la economía nacional.* Lima: Instituto de Estudios Peruanos, 1980.

Gómez Canedo, Lino. "Fray Lorenzo de Bienvenida y los orígenes de las misiones de Yucatan (1537-1564)." *Revista de la Universidad de Yucatan* 18 (1976): 46-68.

González Cicero, Stella María. *Perspectiva religiosa en Yucatán, 1515-1571.* Mexico: El Colegio de Mexico, 1978.

González Navarro, Moisés. *Raza y tierra: La guerra de castas y el henequén.* Mexico: El Colegio de Mexico, 1970.

Gosner, Kevin. "Soldiers of the Virgin: An Ethnohistorical Analysis of the Tzeltal Revolt of 1712 in Highland Chiapas." Ph.D. dissertation, University of Pennsylvania, 1983.

―――. "Uman Parish: Open, Corporate Communities in Eighteenth-Century Yucatan." Paper presented to the Association of American Geographers, Philadelphia, 1979.

Graham, Ian, and Eric Von Euw. *Corpus of Maya Hieroglyphic Inscriptions.* Cambridge: Peabody Museum, Harvard University, 1975.

Greenleaf, Richard E. "The Inquisition and the Indians on New Spain: A Study in Jurisdictional Confusion." *The Americas* 22 (1965): 138-166.

Gutman, Herbert G. "Work, Culture, and Society in Industrializing America, 1815-1919." *American Historical Review* 78 (1973): 531-587.

Hale, Charles A. *Mexican Liberalism in the Age of Mora, 1821-1853.* New Haven: Yale University Press, 1968.

Hamilton, Earl J. *American Treasure and the Price Revolution in Spain, 1501-1650.* Cambridge: Harvard University Press, 1934.

Hammond, Norman, and Wendy Ashmore. "Lowland Maya Settlement: Geographical and Chronological Frameworks." In *Lowland Maya Settlement Patterns,* edited by Wendy Ashmore, 19-36. Albuquerque: University of New Mexico Press, 1981.

Hamnett, Brian R. "The Appropriation of Mexican Church Wealth by the Spanish Bourbon Government: The 'Consolidación of Vales Reales', 1805-1809." *Journal of Latin American Studies* 1 (1969): 85-113.

―――. *Politics and Trade in Southern Mexico, 1750-1821.* Cambridge: Cambridge University Press, 1971.

Haring, Clarence H. *The Spanish Empire in America.* 2d ed. New York: Harcourt, Brace & World, 1963.

Harrison, Brian. *Drink and the Victorians: The Temperance Question in England, 1815-1872.* Pittsburgh: University of Pittsburgh Press, 1971.

Harrison, Peter D., and B. L. Turner II, eds. *Pre-Hispanic Maya Agriculture.* Albuquerque: University of New Mexico Press, 1978.

Harvey, Herbert R. "Religious Networks of Central Mexico." *Geoscience and Man* 21 (1980): 135-140.

Haviland, William A. "Dynastic Genealogies from Tikal, Guatemala: Implications for Descent and Political Organization." *American Antiquity* 42 (1977): 61-67.

————. "A New Population Estimate for Tikal, Guatemala." *American Antiquity* 34 (1969): 429-433.

————. "Rules of Descent in Sixteenth-Century Yucatan." *Estudios de Cultura Náhuatl* 9 (1973): 135-150.

Hellmuth, Nicholas M. "Choltí-Lacandon (Chiapas) and Petén-Ytzá Agriculture, Settlement Pattern and Population." In *Social Process in Maya Prehistory*, edited by Norman Hammond, 421-448. London: Academic Press, 1977.

————. "Progreso y notas sobre la investigación etnohistórica de las tierras bajas mayas de los siglos XVI a XIX." *América Indígena* 32 (1972): 172-244.

————. "Some Notes on the Ytza, Quejache, Verapaz Chol and Toquegua Maya: A Progress Report on Ethnohistory Research Conducted in Seville, June-August 1971." New Haven, Conn. Mimeographed.

Hemming, John. *Red Gold: The Conquest of the Brazilian Indians, 1500-1760.* Cambridge: Harvard University Press, 1978.

Hernández, Pablo. *Misiones del Paraguay: Organización social de las doctrinas guaraníes de la Compañía de Jesús.* 2 vols. Barcelona: Gustavo Gili, 1913.

Herr, Richard. *The Eighteenth-Century Revolution in Spain.* Princeton: Princeton University Press, 1958.

Heston, Alan W., and Tom G. Kessinger. "Toward a Paradigm for Peasant Economies." Paper presented to the Association for Asian Studies, San Francisco, 1975.

Hiemert, Alan. "Puritanism, the Wilderness and the Frontier." *New England Quarterly* 26 (1958): 361-382.

Horton, Robin. "African Conversion." *Africa* 41 (1971): 85-108.

————. "On the Rationality of Conversion." *Africa* 45 (1975): 219-235, 373-399.

Huddleston, Lee E. *Origins of the American Indians: European Concepts, 1492-1729.* Austin: University of Texas Press, 1967.

Huerta, María Teresa, and Patricia Palacios, eds. *Rebeliones indígenas de la época colonial.* Mexico: Instituto Nacional de Antropología e Historia, 1976.

Humboldt, Alexander von. *Ensayo político sobre el reino de la Nueva España* (1808). 7th Spanish ed. Edited by Juan A. Ortega Medina. Mexico: Editorial Porrua, 1966.

Hunt, Eva M. *Transformation of the Hummingbird: Cultural Roots of a Zinacantecan Mythical Poem.* Ithaca: Cornell University Press, 1977.

Hunt, Eva, and June Nash. "Local and Territorial Units." In *Handbook of Middle American Indians* 6: 253-282. Austin: University of Texas Press, 1967.

Hunt, Marta E. "Colonial Yucatan: Town and Region in the Seventeenth Century." Ph.D. dissertation, University of California, Los Angeles, 1974.

————. "Processes of the Development of Yucatan, 1600-1700." In *Provinces of*

Early Mexico, edited by Ida Altman and James Lockhart, 33-62. Los Angeles: UCLA Latin American Center, 1976.

"Incorporación a la Real Corona de las encomiendas de la provincia de Yucatan. Distritos de las Reales Cajas de Merida y Campeche, 1785." *Boletín del Archivo General de la Nación* 9 (1938): 456-569.

Isaacman, Allen. *Mozambique: The Africanization of a European Institution, the Zambezi Prazos, 1750-1902*. Madison: University of Wisconsin Press, 1972.

Jiménez Moreno, Wigberto. "The Indians of America and Christianity." *The Americas* 14 (1958): 411-431.

Jones, Christopher. "Inauguration Dates of Three Late Classic Rulers of Tikal, Guatemala." *American Antiquity* 42 (1977): 28-60.

————. "Tikal as a Trading Center: Why It Rose and Fell." Paper presented at the 43rd International Congress of Americanists, Vancouver, 1979.

Jones, Grant D. "Agriculture and Trade in the Colonial Period Central Maya Lowlands." In *Maya Subsistence: Studies in Memory of Dennis E. Puleston*, edited by Kent V. Flannery, 275-293. New York: Academic Press, 1982.

————. "The Last Maya Frontiers of Colonial Yucatan." In *Spaniards and Indians in Southeastern Mesoamerica*, edited by Murdo J. MacLeod and Robert Wasserstom. Lincoln: University of Nebraska Press, 1983.

————. "Levels of Settlement Alliance among the San Pedro Maya of Western Belize and Eastern Petén, 1857-1936." In *Anthropology and History in Yucatan*, edited by Grant D. Jones, 139-189. Austin: University of Texas Press, 1977.

————. "Revolution and Continuity in Santa Cruz Society." *American Ethnologist* 1 (1974): 659-683.

————. "Southern Lowland Maya Political Organization: A Model of Change from Protohistoric through Colonial Times." In *Actes du XLIIe Congrès International des Américanistes, Paris, 1976* 8: 83-94. Paris: Société des Américanistes, 1979.

Juan, Jorge, and Antonio de Ulloa. *Noticias secretas de América*. London: Imprenta de R. Taylor, 1826.

Kelley, David H. "Glyphic Evidence for a Dynastic Sequence at Quirigua, Guatemala." *American Antiquity* 17 (1962): 323-335.

————. "Kakupacal and the Itzas." *Estudios de Cultura Maya* 7 (1968): 255-268.

Klein, Herbert S. "Hacienda and Free Community in Eighteenth-Century Alto Peru: A Demographic Study of the Aymara Population of the Districts of Chulumani and Pacajes in 1786." *Journal of Latin American Studies* 7 (1975): 193-220.

————. "Peasant Communities in Revolt: The Tzeltal Republic of 1712." *Pacific Historical Review* 35 (1966): 247-264.

————. "The State and the Labor Market in Rural Bolivia in the Colonial and Early Republican Period." In *Essays on Politics and Society in Colonial Latin America*, edited by Karen Spalding. Newark, Delaware: Latin American Studies Program, University of Delaware, 1982.

Kluckhohn, Clyde. *Navajo Witchcraft*. Cambridge: Peabody Museum, Harvard University, 1944.

Konrad, Herman W. *A Jesuit Hacienda in Colonial Mexico: Santa Lucía, 1576-1767*. Stanford: Stanford University Press, 1980.

Kubler, George A. "La evidencia intrínseca y la analogía etnológica en el estudio de las religiones mesoamericanas." In *La religión en Mesoamérica*, edited by Jaime Litvak King and Noemí Castillo Tejero, 1-24. Mexico: Sociedad Mexicana de Antropología, 1972.

———. *Mexican Architecture of the Sixteenth Century*. 2 vols. New Haven: Yale University Press, 1948.

———. "Mythological Ancestries in Classic Maya Inscriptions." In *Primera Mesa Redonda de Palenque*. Part 2, edited by Merle G. Robertson, 23-33. Pebble Beach, California: Robert Louis Stevenson School, 1974.

———. "On the Colonial Extinction of the Motifs of Pre-Columbian Art." In *Essays in Pre-Columbian Art and Archaeology*, by Samuel K. Lothrop et al., 14-34. Cambridge: Peabody Museum of American Archaeology and Ethnology, Harvard University, 1961.

———. "The Quechua in the Colonial World." In *Handbook of South American Indians* 2: 331-410. Washington: Smithsonian Institution, 1946.

———. *The Shape of Time: Remarks on the History of Things*. New Haven: Yale University Press, 1962.

———. *Studies in Classic Maya Iconography*. New Haven: Connecticut Academy of Arts and Sciences, 1969.

Kula, Witold. *An Economic Theory of the Feudal System: Towards a Model of the Polish Economy, 1500-1800*. London: Humanities Press, 1976.

Kurjack, Edward B. *Prehistoric Lowland Maya Community and Social Organization: A Case Study at Dzibilchaltun, Yucatan, Mexico*. New Orleans: Middle American Research Institute, Tulane University, 1974.

Kurjack, Edward B., and E. Wyllys Andrews, V. "Early Boundary Maintenance in Northwest Yucatan, Mexico." *American Antiquity* 41 (1976): 318-325.

Kurjack, Edward B., and Silvia Garza T. "Pre-Columbian Community Form and Distribution in the Northern Maya Area." In *Lowland Maya Settlement Patterns*, edited by Wendy Ashmore, 287-332. Albuquerque: University of New Mexico Press, 1981.

LaFarge, Oliver, and Douglas S. Byers. *The Year-Bearer's People*. New Orleans: Middle American Research Institute, Tulane University, 1931.

Lamas, Adolfo. *Seguridad Social en la Nueva España*. Mexico: Universidad Nacional Autónoma de Mexico, 1964.

Landa, Diego de. *Landa's Relación de las cosas de Yucatan*. Translated and edited by Alfred M. Tozzer. Cambridge: Peabody Museum of American Archaeology and Ethnology, Harvard University, 1941.

Lange, Frederick W. "Una reevaluación de la población del norte de Yucatán en el tiempo del contacto español, 1528." *América Indígena* 31 (1971): 117-139.

Las Casas, Bartolomé de. *Apologética historia de las Indias* (c. 1550). Edited by Edmundo O'Gorman. 2 vols. Mexico: Universidad Nacional Autónoma de Mexico, 1967.

Lavrin, Asunción. "The Execution of the Laws of 'Consolidación' in New Spain: Economic Aims and Results." *Hispanic American Historical Review* 53 (1973): 27-49.

Lee, Thomas A., Jr., and Carlos Navarrete, eds. *Mesoamerican Communication Routes and Cultural Contacts*. Provo, Utah: New World Archaeological Foundation, Brigham Young University, 1978.

Lees, Lynn. "Mid-Victorian Migration and the Irish Family Economy." *Victorian Studies* 20 (1976): 25-43.

León-Portilla, Miguel. *Tiempo y realidad en el pensamiento maya*. Mexico: Universidad Nacional Autónoma de Mexico, 1968.

―――, ed. *Visión de los vencidos: Relaciones indígenas de la conquista*. Mexico: Universidad Nacional Autónoma de Mexico, 1959.

Lewis, Herbert S. "Warfare and the Origin of the State: Another Formulation." In *The Study of the State*, edited by Henri J. M. Claessen and Peter Skalnik, 201-221. The Hague: Mouton, 1981.

Lincoln, J. Steward. "The Maya Calendar of the Ixil of Guatemala." In *Contributions to American Anthropology and History* 7: 97-128. Washington: Carnegie Institution, 1942.

Lisón-Tolosana, Carmelo. *Belmonte de los Caballeros*. Oxford: Oxford University Press, 1966.

Lizana, Bernardo de. *Historia de Yucatan: Devocionario de Nuestra Señora de Izmal y conquista espiritual* (1633). 2d ed. Mexico: Museo Nacional, 1893.

Llaguno, José. *La personalidad jurídica del indio y el III Concilio Provincial Mexicano (1585)*. Mexico: Editorial Porrua, 1963.

Lockhart, James. *Spanish Peru, 1532-1560: A Colonial Society*. Madison: University of Wisconsin Press, 1968.

López de Cogolludo, Diego: see Cogolludo, Diego López de.

López Sarrelangue, Delfina E. *La nobleza indígena de Pátzcuaro en la época virreinal*. Mexico: Universidad Nacional Autónoma de Mexico, 1965.

Lynch, John. *The Spanish-American Revolutions, 1808-1826*. New York: W. W. Norton, 1973.

―――. *Spain under the Habsburgs*. 2 vols. Oxford: Basil Blackwell, 1964-1969.

―――. *Spanish Colonial Administration, 1782-1810: The Intendant System in the Viceroyalty of the Río de la Plata*. London: The Athlone Press, 1958.

MacBryde, Felix W. *Cultural and Historical Geography of Southwest Guatemala*. Washington: Smithsonian Institution, 1947.

MacLeod, Murdo J. "Ethnic Relations and Indian Society in the Province of Guatemala, 1620-1800." In *Spaniards and Indians in Southwestern Mesoamerica*, edited by Murdo J. MacLeod and Robert Wasserstrom. Lincoln: University of Nebraska Press, in press.

―――. "Forms and Types of Work and the Acculturation of the Colonial Indian of Mesoamerica: Some Preliminary Observations." In *El trabajo y los trabajadores en la historia de Mexico,* edited by Elsa C. Frost et al., 75-92. Mexico City and Tucson: El Colegio de México and University of Arizona Press, 1979.

―――. *Spanish Central America: A Socio-Economic History, 1520-1720.* Berkeley: University of California Press, 1973.

MacLeod, Murdo J., and Robert Wasserstrom, eds. *Spaniards and Indians in Southeastern Mesoamerica: Essays on the History of Ethnic Relations.* Lincoln: University of Nebraska Press, 1983.

Madsden, William. "Religious Syncretism." In *Handbook of Middle American Indians* 6: 369-492. Austin: University of Texas Press, 1967.

Marcus, Joyce. *Emblem and State in the Classic Maya Lowlands: An Epigraphic Approach to Territorial Organization.* Washington: Dumbarton Oaks, 1976.

Martin, Norman F. *Los vagabundos en la Nueva España, siglo XVI.* Mexico: Editorial Jus, 1957.

Martínez Hernández, Juan, ed. *Crónica de Yaxkukul.* Merida: Talleres de la Compañía Tipográfica Yucateca, 1926.

Matheny, Ray T. "Maya Lowland Hydraulic Systems." *Science* 193 (1976): 639-646.

Means, Philip A. *History of the Spanish Conquest of Yucatan and of the Itzas.* Cambridge: Peabody Museum, Harvard University, 1917.

Meggers, Betty J. "Environmental Limitations on the Development of Culture." *American Anthropologist* 56 (1954): 801-824.

Memmi, Albert. *Dominated Man.* New York: Grossman, 1968.

"Merida de Yucatan." *Artes de Mexico,* nos. 169-170 (1970).

Miles, S. W. "The Sixteenth-Century Pokom-Maya: A Documentary Analysis of Social Structure and Archaeological Setting." *Transactions of the American Philosophical Society,* n.s. 47, pt. 4: 731-781. Philadelphia: American Philosophical Society, 1957.

―――. "Summary of Pre-conquest Ethnology of the Guatemalan Chiapas Highlands and Pacific Slopes." In *Handbook of Middle American Indians* 2: 237-275. Austin: University of Texas Press, 1965.

Miller, Arthur G. "Captains of the Itza: Unpublished Mural Evidence from Chichén Itzá." In *Social Process in Maya Prehistory,* edited by Norman Hammond, 197-225. London: Academic Press, 1977.

―――. "The Iconography of the Painting in the Temple of the Diving God, Tulum, Quintana Roo, Mexico: The Twisted Cords." In *Mesoamerican Archaeology: New Approaches,* edited by Norman Hammond, 167-186. London: Duckworth, 1974.

―――. "The Little Descent: Manifest Destiny from the East." In *Actes du XLIIᵉ Congrès des Américanistes, Paris, 1976* 8: 221-236. Paris: Société des Américanistes, 1979.

―――. "The Maya and the Sea: Trade and Cult at Tancah and Tulum, Quintana Roo, Mexico." In *The Sea in the Pre-Columbian World,* edited by Elizabeth P. Benson, 97-138. Washington: Dumbarton Oaks, 1977.

—. *On the Edge of the Sea: Mural Painting at Tancah-Tulum, Quintana Roo, Mexico.* Washington: Dumbarton Oaks, 1982.

Miller, Arthur G., and Nancy M. Farriss. "Religious Syncretism in Colonial Yucatan: The Archaeological and Ethnohistorical Evidence from Tancah, Quintana Roo." In *Maya Archaeology and Ethnohistory,* edited by Norman Hammond and Gordon R. Willey, 223-240. Austin: University of Texas Press, 1979.

Mintz, Sidney W., and Eric R. Wolf. "An Analysis of Ritual Co-Parenthood (Compadrazgo)." *Southwestern Journal of Anthropology* 6 (1950): 341-368.

Miranda, José. *La función económica del encomendero en los orígenes del régimen colonial: Nueva España (1525-1531).* Mexico: Universidad Nacional Autónoma de Mexico, 1965.

Molina Solís, Juan Francisco. *Historia de Yucatan durante la dominación española.* 3 vols. Merida: Imprenta de la Lotería del Estado, 1904-1913.

Montoto, Santiago. *Cofradías sevillanas.* Seville: Universidad de Sevilla, 1976.

Morley, Sylvanus G. *The Ancient Maya.* 3d ed. Revised by G. W. Brainerd. Stanford: Stanford University Press, 1956.

Mörner, Magnus. *La corona española y los foráneos en los pueblos de indios de América.* Stockholm: Instituto de Estudios Ibero-Americanos, 1970.

—. *Pérfil de la sociedad rural del Cuzco a fines de la colonia.* Lima: Universidad del Pacífico, 1978.

Morris, Michael. "Ethno-Linguistic Systems in the Southern Maya Area: A Case Study in Natural Regions as the Spatial Organization of Ecological and Communicative Relations." M.A. thesis, University of Pennsylvania, 1973.

Morse, Richard M., ed. *The Bandeirantes: The Historical Role of the Brazilian Pathfinders.* New York: Knopf, Borzoi Books, 1965.

Murra, John V. "El control vertical de un máximo de pisos ecológicos de las sociedades andinas." Reprinted in *Formaciones económicas y políticas del mundo andino,* by John V. Murra, 59-115. Lima: Instituto de Estudios Peruanos, 1975.

—. "Social Structural and Economic Themes in Andean Ethnohistory." *Anthropological Quarterly* 34 (1961): 47-59.

Nash, Manning. "Political Relations in Guatemala." *Social and Economic Studies* 7 (1958): 65-75.

Nicholson, Henry B. "Ehecatl Quetzalcoatl vs. Topiltzin Quetzalcoatl of Tollan: A Problem in Mesoamerican Religion and History." In *Actes du XLIIe Congrès International des Américanistes, Paris, 1976* 6: 36-47. Paris: Société des Américanistes, 1979.

—. "The Mixteca-Puebla Concept in Mesoamerican Archaeology: A Reexamination." In *Man and Cultures: Selected Papers from the Fifth International Congress of Anthropological and Ethnographical Sciences,* edited by Anthony F. C. Wallace, 612-617. Philadelphia: University of Pennsylvania Press, 1960.

—. "Religion in Pre-Hispanic Central Mexico." In *Handbook of Middle American Indians* 10: 395-466. Austin: University of Texas Press, 1971.

557

Nutini, Hugo G. "The Nature and Treatment of Kinship in Mesoamerica." In *Essays on Mexican Kinship,* edited by Hugo G. Nutini, Pedro Carrasco, and James M. Taggart, 3-27. Pittsburgh: University of Pittsburgh Press, 1976.

Nutini, Hugo G., and Betty Bell. *Ritual Kinship: The Structure and Historical Development of the Compadrazgo System in Rural Tlaxcala.* Princeton: Princeton University Press, 1980.

Nuttall, Zelia. "Royal Ordinances concerning the Layout of New Towns." *Hispanic American Historical Review* 4 (1921): 743-753.

Oakes, Maud. *The Two Crosses of Todos Santos: Survivals of Mayan Religious Ritual.* New York: Pantheon, 1951.

Oviedo y Valdés, Gonzalo Fernández de. *Historia general y natural de las Indias* (1535-1547). 4 vols., Madrid: Real Academia de la Historia, 1851-1855.

"Papeles relativos a la visita del oidor Dr. Diego García de Palacio, año de 1583." *Boletín del Archivo General de la Nación* 11 (1940): 385-483.

Pares, Richard. *War and Trade in the West Indies, 1739-1763.* Oxford: Clarendon Press, 1936.

Patch, Robert W. "A Colonial Regime: Maya and Spaniard in Yucatan." Ph.D. dissertation, Princeton University, 1979.

—. "La formación de estancias y haciendas en Yucatán durante la colonia." *Boletín de la Escuela de Ciencias Antropológicas de la Universidad de Yucatan* 4 (1976): 21-61.

—. "Haciendas and Markets in Colonial Yucatan." Paper presented at the 43rd International Congress of Americanists, Vancouver, 1979.

Pearce, Roy H. *The Savages of America: A Study of the Indian and the Idea of Civilization.* Baltimore: Johns Hopkins University Press, 1953.

Pérez, Juan Pío. *Diccionario de la lengua Maya.* Merida: Imprenta Literaria de Juan Molina Solís, 1866-1877.

Phelan, John L. *The Hispanization of the Philippines: Spanish Aims and Filipino Responses, 1565-1700.* Madison: University of Wisconsin Press, 1967.

—. *The Kingdom of Quito in the Seventeenth Century: Bureaucratic Politics in the Spanish Empire.* Madison: University of Wisconsin Press, 1967.

Plumstead, A. W., ed. *The Wall and the Garden: Selected Massachusetts Election Sermons, 1670-1775.* Minneapolis: University of Minnesota Press, 1968.

Pohl, Mary. "Ritual Continuity and Transformation in Mesoamerica: Reconstructing the Ancient Maya 'Cuch' Ritual." *American Antiquity* 46 (1981): 513-529.

Pollock, Harry E. D., Ralph L. Roys, Tatiana Proskouriakoff, and A. Ledyard Smith. *Mayapan, Yucatan, Mexico.* Washington: Carnegie Institution, 1962.

Price, Barbara J. "The Burden of the 'Cargo': Ethnographical Models and Archaeological Inference." In *Mesoamerican Archaeology: New Approaches,* edited by Norman Hammond, 445-465. London: Duckworth, 1974.

—. "Secondary State Formation: An Explanatory Model." In *Origins of the State,* edited by Ronald Cohen and Elman R. Service, 161-186. Philadelphia: Institute for the Study of Human Issues, 1978.

—. "Shifts in Production and Organization: A Cluster-Interaction Model." *Current Anthropology* 18 (1977): 209-233.

Price, Richard, ed. *Maroon Societies: Rebel Slave Communities in the Americas.* Garden City, N.Y.: Doubleday, Anchor Books, 1973.

Priestley, Herbert I. *José de Gálvez, Visitador General of New Spain (1765-1771).* Berkeley: University of California Press, 1916.

Proskouriakoff, Tatiana. "Historical Data in the Inscriptions of Yaxchilan." *Estudios de Cultura Maya* 3 (1964): 177-201.

————. "Historical Implications of a Pattern of Dates at Piedras Negras, Guatemala." *American Antiquity* 25 (1960): 454-475.

Puleston, Dennis E. "Terracing, Raised Fields, and Tree Cropping in the Maya Lowlands: A New Perspective on the Geography of Power." In *Pre-Hispanic Maya Agriculture*, edited by Peter D. Harrison and B. L. Turner, II, 225-245. Albuquerque: University of New Mexico Press, 1978.

Puleston, Dennis E., and Donald W. Callender, Jr. "Defensive Earthworks at Tikal." *Expedition* 9 (1967): 40-48.

Radell, David R. "The Indian Slave Trade and Population of Nicaragua during the Sixteenth Century." In *The Native Population of the Americas in 1492*, edited by William M. Denevan, 67-76. Madison: University of Wisconsin Press, 1976.

Rathje, William L. "Classic Maya Development and Denouement: A Research Design." In *The Classic Maya Collapse*, edited by T. Patrick Culbert, 405-454. Albuquerque: University of New Mexico Press, 1973.

————. "The Origin and Development of Lowland Classic Maya Civilization." *American Antiquity* 36 (1971): 275-285.

————. "Praise the Gods and Pass the Metates: A Hypothesis of the Development of Lowland Rainforest Civilizations in Middle America." In *Contemporary Archaeology*, edited by M. P. Leone, 365-392. Carbondale: Southern Illinois University Press, 1972.

————. "The Tikal Connection." In *The Origins of Maya Civilization*, edited by Richard E. W. Adams, 373-382. Albuquerque: University of New Mexico Press, 1977.

Recopilación de leyes de los reynos de las Indias. 4 vols. Madrid: Julián de Paredes, 1681.

Redfield, Robert. *The Folk Culture of Yucatan.* Chicago: University of Chicago Press, 1941.

————. "The Folk Society." *American Journal of Sociology* 52 (1947): 293-308.

Redfield, Robert, and Alfonso Villa Rojas. *Chan Kom: A Maya Village.* Washington: Carnegie Institution, 1934.

Reed, Nelson, *The Caste War of Yucatan.* Stanford: Stanford University Press, 1964.

Reina, Ruben E. *The Law of the Saints: A Pokomam Pueblo and Its Community Culture.* Indianapolis: Bobbs-Merrill, 1966.

"Relaciones de Yucatan." In *Colección de documentos inéditos relativos al descubrimiento, conquista y organización de las antiguas posesiones de Ultramar*, n.s. vols. 11 and 13. Madrid: Real Academia de la Historia, 1898-1900.

Remesal, Antonio de. *Historia general de las Indias Occidentales, y particular de la governación de Chiapa y Guatemala (1619).* 2 vols. Guatemala: Tipografía Nacional, 1932.

Ricard, Robert. *La conquista espiritual de México*. Translated by Angel María Garibay. Mexico: Editorial Jus, 1947.

Ríos, Eduardo Enrique. "La rebelión de Canek, Yucatan, 1761." *Boletín de la Sociedad Mexicana de Geografía y Estadística* 54 (1940): 483-495.

Robertson, Donald. "The Tulum Murals: The International Style of the Late Postclassic." In *Verhandlungen des XXXVIII Internationalen Amerikanisten- kongresses, Stuttgart-München, 1968* 2: 77-88. Munich: Kommissionsverlag Klaus Renner, 1970.

Robertson, Merle Green, ed. *The Art, Iconography and Dynastic History of Pa- lenque.* Part 3. Proceedings of the Segunda Mesa Redonda de Palenque. Pebble Beach, California: Robert Louis Stevenson School, 1976.

―――. *Primera Mesa Redonda de Palenque.* Parts 1 and 2. Pebble Beach, Califor- nia: Robert Louis Stevenson School, 1974.

Robinson, David J. "Indian Migration in Eighteenth-Century Yucatan." Paper presented at the 43rd International Congress of Americanists, Vancouver, 1979.

Robinson, David J., and Carolyn G. McGovern. "La migración regional yu- cateca en la época colonial: El caso de San Francisco Umán." *Historia Me- xicana* 30 (1980): 99-125.

Rodgers, Daniel T. "Tradition, Modernity and the American Industrial Worker: Reflections and Critique." *Journal of Interdisciplinary History* 7 (1977): 655- 681.

Rodríguez, Mario. *The Cádiz Experiment in Central America, 1808-1826.* Berke- ley: University of California Press, 1978.

Rosaldo, Renato I., Jr. "The Rhetoric of Control: Ilongots Viewed as Natural Bandits and Wild Indians." In *The Reversible World: Symbolic Inversion in Art and Society*, edited by Barbara Babcock, 240-257. Ithaca: Cornell Uni- versity Press, 1978.

Rosenblat, Angel. *La población de América en 1492: Viejos y nuevos cálculos.* Mex- ico: El Colegio de Mexico, 1967.

Rowe, John H. "The Incas under Spanish Colonial Institutions." *Hispanic Amer- ican Historical Review* 37 (1957): 155-199.

Roys, Ralph L. "Conquest Sites and the Subsequent Destruction of Maya Ar- chitecture in the Interior of Northern Yucatan." *Contributions to American Anthropology and History* 11:129-182. Washington: Carnegie Institution, 1952.

―――. *The Ethno-Botany of the Maya.* New Orleans: Middle American Re- search Institute, Tulane University, 1931.

―――. *The Indian Background of Colonial Yucatan* (1943). Reprinted. Norman: University of Oklahoma Press, 1972.

―――. "Literary Sources for the History of Mayapan." In *Mayapan, Yucatan, Mexico*, by Harry E. D. Pollock et al., 24-86. Washington: Carnegie Insti- tution, 1962.

―――. "Lowland Maya Native Society at Spanish Contact." In *Handbook of Middle American Indians* 3: 659-678. Austin: University of Texas Press, 1965.

————. "Personal Names of the Maya of Yucatan." In *Contributions to American Anthropology and History* 6: 31-48. Washington: Carnegie Institution, 1940.

————. *The Political Geography of the Yucatan Maya*. Washington: Carnegie Institution, 1957.

————, ed. *The Book of Chilam Balam of Chumayel*. 2d ed. Norman: University of Oklahoma Press, 1967.

————, ed. "The Maya Katun Prophecies of the Books of Chilam Balam. Series I." In *Contributions to American Anthropology and History* 12: 1-60. Washington: Carnegie Institution, 1960.

————, ed. "The Prophecies for the Maya Tuns or Years in the Books of Chilam Balam of Tizimin and Mani." In *Contributions to American Anthropology and History* 10: 157-186. Washington: Carnegie Institution, 1949.

————, ed. *Ritual of the Bacabs*. Norman: University of Oklahoma Press, 1965.

————, ed. *The Titles of Ebtun*. Washington: Carnegie Institution, 1939.

Roys, Ralph L., France V. Scholes, and Eleanor B. Adams, eds. "Census and Inspection of the Town of Pencuyut, Yucatan, in 1583 by Diego García de Palacio, oidor of the Audiencia of Guatemala." *Ethnohistory* 6 (1959): 195-225.

————. "Report and Census of the Indians of Cozumel, 1570." In *Contributions to American Anthropology and History* 6: 1-30. Washington: Carnegie Institution, 1940.

Rubio Mañé, J. Ignacio. "El Gobernador, Capitán General e Intendente de Yucatán, Mariscal don Manuel Artazo y Barral, y la Jura de la Constitución Española en Mérida, el año de 1812." *Boletín del Archivo General de la Nación*, n.s. 9 (1968): 45-170.

————. *Los sanjuanistas de Yucatán: Manuel Jiménez Solís, el Padre Justis*. Mexico: Archivo General de la Nación, 1971.

Rumeu de Armas, Antonio. *Historia de la previsión social en España: Cofradías, gremios, hermandades, montes píos*. Madrid: Editorial Revista de Derecho Privado, 1944.

Ruppert, Karl, J. Eric S. Thompson, and Tatiana Proskouriakoff. *Bonampak, Chiapas, Mexico*. Washington: Carnegie Institution, 1955.

Rus, Jan, and Robert Wasserstrom. "Civil-Religious Hierarchies in Central Chiapas: A Critical Perspective." *American Ethnologist* 7 (1980): 466-478.

Russell-Wood, A.J.R. "Black and Mulatto Brotherhoods in Colonial Brazil: A Study in Collective Behavior." *Hispanic American Historical Review* 54 (1974): 567-602.

Ruz Lhuillier, Alberto. *Costumbres funerarias de los antiguos mayas*. Mexico: Universidad Nacional Autónoma de Mexico, Seminario de Cultura Maya, 1968.

Sabloff, Jeremy A., and David A. Freidel. "A Model of a Pre-Columbian Trading Center." In *Ancient Civilization and Trade*, edited by Jeremy A. Sabloff and C. C. Lamberg-Karlovsky, 369-408. Albuquerque: University of New Mexico Press, 1975.

Sabloff, Jeremy A., and William L. Rathje. "The Rise of a Maya Merchant Class." *Scientific American* 233 (1975): 72-82.

Sánchez de Aguilar, Pedro. *Informe contra idolorum cultores del obispado de Yucatan dirigido al Rey N. Señor en su Real Consejo de las Indias* (c. 1613). 3d ed. Merida: Imprenta Triay e Hijos, 1937.

Sánchez Albornoz, Nicolás. *El indio en el Alto Perú a fines del siglo XVIII.* Lima: Seminario de Historia Rural Andina, 1973.

Sanchiz Ochoa, Pilar. "Cambio cultural dirigido en el siglo XVI: El oidor Tomás López y su 'planificación' de cambio para los indios de Guatemala." *Étnica: Revista de Antropología* 12 (1976): 129-148.

Sanders, William T. "The Central Mexican Symbiotic Region: A Study in Prehistoric Settlement Patterns." In *Prehistoric Settlement Patterns in the New World*, edited by Gordon R. Willey, 115-127. New York: Viking Fund, 1956.

————. "Classic Maya Settlement Patterns and Ethnographic Analogy." In *Lowland Maya Settlement Patterns*, edited by Wendy Ashmore, 351-369. Albuquerque: University of New Mexico Press, 1981.

————. "The Cultural Ecology of the Lowland Maya: A Reevaluation." In *The Classic Maya Collapse*, edited by T. Patrick Culbert, 345-365. Albuquerque: University of New Mexico Press, 1973.

————. "Cultural Ecology of the Maya Lowlands." *Estudios de Cultura Maya* 3 and 4 (1962-1963): 79-121, 203-241.

————. "Environmental Heterogeneity and the Evolution of Lowland Maya Civilization." In *The Origins of Maya Civilization*, edited by Richard E. W. Adams, 287-297. Albuquerque: University of New Mexico Press, 1977.

————. "The Jolly Green Giant in Tenth-Century Yucatan, Or Fact and Fancy in Classic Maya Agriculture." *Reviews in Anthropology* 6 (1969): 493-506.

————. "The Population of the Central Mexican Symbiotic Region, the Basin of Mexico, and the Teotihuacan Valley in the Sixteenth Century." In *The Native Population of America in 1492*, edited by William A. Denevan, 85-150. Madison: University of Wisconsin Press, 1976.

————. "Settlement Patterns." In *Handbook of Middle American Indians* 6: 53-86. Austin: University of Texas Press, 1967.

Sanders, William T., Jeffrey R. Parsons, and Robert Santley. *The Basin of Mexico: Ecological Processes in the Evolution of a Civilization.* New York: Academic Press, 1979.

Sanders, William T., and Barbara J. Price. *Mesoamerica: The Evolution of a Civilization.* New York: Random House, 1968.

Sarmiento, Domingo F. *Civilización y barbarie: La vida de Juan Facundo Quiroga.* Santiago de Chile: Imprenta del Progreso, 1845.

Scardaville, Michael C. "Alcohol Abuse and Tavern Reform in Late Colonial Mexico City." *Hispanic American Historical Review* 60 (1980), 643-671.

Schele, Linda, "Accession Iconography of Chan-Bahlum in the Group of the Cross at Palenque." In *The Art, Iconography and Dynastic History of Palenque*, edited by Merle G. Robertson, 9-34. Pebble Beach, California: Robert Louis Stevenson School, 1976.

————. "Observations on the Cross Motif at Palenque." In *Primera Mesa Re-*

donda de Palenque, Part 1, edited by Merle G. Robertson, 41-61. Pebble Beach, California: Robert Louis Stevenson School, 1974.

Scholes, France V., and Eleanor B. Adams, eds. *Don Diego Quijada, Alcalde Mayor de Yucatán, 1561-1565.* 2 vols. Mexico: Editorial Porrua, 1938.

Scholes, France V., Carlos R. Menéndez, J. Ignacio Rubio Mañé, and Eleanor B. Adams, eds. *Documentos para la historia de Yucatán.* 3 vols., Merida: Compañía Tipográfica Yucateca, 1936-1938.

Scholes, France V., and Ralph L. Roys. "Fray Diego de Landa and the Problem of Idolatry in Yucatan." *In Cooperation in Research*, 585-620. Washington: Carnegie Institution, 1938.

————. *The Maya Chontal Indians of Acalan-Tixchel: A Contribution to the History and Ethnography of the Yucatan Peninsula* (1948). 2d ed. Norman: University of Oklahoma Press, 1968.

Scholes, France V., and J. Eric S. Thompson. "The Francisco Pérez 'Probanza' of 1654-1656 and the 'Matrícula' of Tipu (Belize)." In *Anthropology and History in Yucatan*, edited by Grant D. Jones, 43-68. Austin: University of Texas Press, 1977.

Scott, James C. *The Moral Economy of the Peasants: Rebellion and Subsistence in South-East Asia.* New Haven: Yale University Press, 1976.

Selby, Henry A. *Zapotec Deviance: The Convergence of Folk and Modern Sociology.* Austin: University of Texas Press, 1974.

Sharer, Robert J. "The Maya Collapse Revisited: Internal and External Perspectives." In *Social Process in Maya Prehistory*, edited by Norman Hammond, 531-552. London: Academic Press, 1977.

Sharer, Robert J., Christopher Jones, and Wendy Ashmore. *Quirigua Reports.* Vol. 2. Philadelphia: University Museum, University of Pennsylvania, in press.

Sherman, William L. *Forced Native Labor in Sixteenth-Century Central America.* Lincoln: University of Nebraska Press, 1979.

Siemens, Alfred H., and Dennis E. Puleston. "Ridged Fields and Associated Features in Southern Campeche: New Perspectives on the Lowland Maya." *American Antiquity* 37 (1972): 228-239.

Sierra O'Reilly, Justo. *Los indios de Yucatán* (1848-1851). Edited by Carlos R. Menéndez. 2 vols. Merida: Compañía Tipográfica Yucateca, 1954-1957.

Skinner, G. William. "Marketing and Social Structure in Rural China." *Journal of Asian Studies* 24 (1964-1965): 3-43, 195-228, 363-399.

Solano y Pérez-Lila, Francisco. "Autoridades municipales indígenas de Yucatan (1657-1677)." *Revista de la Universidad de Yucatan* 17 (1975): 65-128.

————. *Los mayas del siglo XVIII: Pervivencia y transformación de la sociedad indígena guatemalteca durante la administración borbónica.* Madrid: Ediciones Cultura Hispánica, 1974.

————. "La población indígena de Yucatan, 1500-1650." *Anuario de Estudios Americanos* 28 (1971): 165-200.

Soustelle, Jacques. *La pensée cosmologique des anciens Mexicains.* Paris: Hermann, 1940.

Spalding, Karen. "Indian Rural Society in Colonial Peru: The Example of Huarochirí." Ph.D. dissertation, University of California, Berkeley, 1967.

———. "*Kurakas* and Commerce: A Chapter in the Evolution of Andean Society." *Hispanic American Historical Review* 53 (1973): 581-599.

———. "Social Climbers: Changing Patterns of Mobility among the Indians of Colonial Peru." *Hispanic American Historical Review* 50 (1970): 645-664.

Spores, Ronald. *The Mixtec Kings and Their People.* Norman: University of Oklahoma Press. 1967.

Stein, Mark Aurel. *Innermost Asia: Detailed report of Explorations in Central Asia, Kan-su and Eastern Iran.* 4 vols. Oxford: Clarendon Press, 1928.

Stein, Stanley J. "Bureaucracy and Business in the Spanish Empire, 1759-1804: Failure of A Bourbon Reform in Mexico and Peru." *Hispanic American Historical Review* 61 (1981): 2-28.

Stein, Stanley J. and Barbara H. Stein. *The Colonial Heritage of Latin America: Essays on Economic Dependence in Perspective.* New York: Oxford University Press, 1970.

Stephens, John L. *Incidents of Travel in Yucatan* (1843). 2 vols. New York: Dover Press, 1963.

Strickon, Arnold. "Hacienda and Plantation in Yucatan: An Historical-Ecological Consideration of the Folk-Urban Continuum in Yucatan." *América Indígena* 25 (1965); 35-65.

Sumption, Jonathan. *Pilgrimage: An Image of Medieval Religion.* London: Faber and Faber, 1975.

Tambiah, S. J. *World Conqueror and World Renouncer: A Study of Buddhism and Polity in Thailand against a Historical Background.* Cambridge: Cambridge University Press, 1976.

Taylor, William B. *Drinking, Homicide and Rebellion in Colonial Mexican Villages.* Stanford: Stanford University Press, 1979.

———. "Landed Society in New Spain: A View from the South." *Hispanic American Historical Review* 54 (1974): 387-413.

———. *Landlord and Peasant in Colonial Oaxaca.* Stanford: Stanford University Press, 1972.

Thompson, Donald E. "Maya Paganism and Christianity: A History of the Fusion of Two Religions." In *Middle American Research Institute Publication* 19: 1-36. New Orleans: Middle American Research Institute, Tulane University, 1954.

Thompson, E. P. "The Moral Economy of the English Crowd in the 18th Century." *Past and Present* 50 (1971): 76-136.

———. "Time, Work-Discipline and Industrial Capitalism." *Past and Present* 38 (1967); 56-97.

Thompson, J. Eric S. *Maya Hieroglyphic Writing: An Introduction.* 2d ed. Norman: University of Oklahoma Press, 1960.

———. *The Rise and Fall of Maya Civilization.* 2d ed. Norman: University of Oklahoma Press, 1966.

————. *Maya History and Religion.* Norman: University of Oklahoma Press, 1970.

————. "Maya Rulers of the Classic Period and the Divine Right of Kings." In *The Iconography of Middle American Sculpture,* by Ignacio Bernal et al., 52-71. New York: Metropolitan Museum of Art, 1973.

————. "A Proposal for Constituting a Maya Subgroup, Cultural and Linguistic, in the Peten and Adjacent Regions." In *Anthropology and History in Yucatan,* edited by Grant D. Jones, 3-42. Austin: University of Texas Press, 1977.

Thompson, Philip C. "Tekanto in the Eighteenth Century." Ph.D. dissertation, Tulane University, 1978.

Tibesar, Antonine S. "The Lima Pastors, 1750-1820: Their Origins and Studies as Taken from Their Autobiographies." *The Americas* 28 (1971), 39-51.

Torre Villar, Ernesto de la. "Algunos aspectos de las cofradías y la propiedad territorial en Michoacán." *Jahrbuch für Geschichte von Staat, Wirtschaft und Gesellschaft LateinoAmerikas* 4 (1967): 410-439.

Toussaint, Manuel. *Colonial Art in Mexico.* Austin: University of Texas Press, 1967.

Tozzer, Alfred M. *Chichen Itza and Its Cenote of Sacrifice: A Comparative Study of Contemporaneous Maya and Toltec.* 2 vols. Cambridge: Peabody Museum, Harvard University, 1957.

————. *A Comparative Study of the Mayas and the Lacandones.* New York: Macmillan, 1907.

————. *A Maya Grammar.* Cambridge: Peabody Museum, Harvard University, 1921.

Trens, Manuel B. *Historia de Chiapas desde los tiempos más remotos.* Mexico: Impresora S. Turanzas del Valle, 1942.

Turner, B. L., II. "Prehistoric Intensive Agriculture in the Mayan Lowlands." *Science* 185 (1974): 118-124.

Turner, B. L., II, and Peter D. Harrison. "Comment on William T. Sanders' Review of *Pre-Hispanic Maya Agriculture.*" *Reviews in Anthropology* 16 (1979): 544-555.

————. "Implications from Agriculture for Maya Prehistory." In *Pre-Hispanic Maya Agriculture,* edited by Peter D. Harrison and B. L. Turner II, 337-373. Albuquerque: University of New Mexico Press, 1978.

Turner, John K. *Barbarous Mexico.* Chicago: Charles H. Kerr, 1911.

Tutino, John. "Life and Labor on North Mexican Haciendas: The Querétaro-San Luis Potosí Region, 1775-1810." In *El trabajo y los trabajadores en la historia de Mexico,* edited by Elsa C. Frost et al., 339-378. Mexico City and Tucson: El Colegio de Mexico and University of Arizona Press, 1979.

Uchmany de la Peña, Eva A. "Cuatro casos de idolatría en el area maya ante el Tribunal de la Inquisición." *Estudios de Cultura Maya* 6 (1967): 267-300.

Van Young, Eric. "Urban Market and Hinterland: Guadalajara and Its Region in the Eighteenth Century." *Hispanic American Historical Review* 59 (1979): 593-635.

Vicens Vives, Jaime. *An Economic History of Spain*. Princeton: Princeton University Press, 1969.

Villa Rojas, Alfonso. *The Maya of East Central Quintana Roo*. Washington: Carnegie Institution, 1945.

———. "Notas sobre la tenencia de la tierra entre los mayas de la antigüedad." *Estudios de Cultura Maya* 1 (1961): 21-46.

Villagutierre Sotomayor, Juan de. *Historia de la conquista de la provincia de el Itza* (1701). Guatemala: Sociedad de Geografía e Historia, Tipografía Nacional, 1933.

Villamarín, Juan A., and Judith E. Villamarín. "Chibcha Settlement under Spanish Rule, 1537-1810." In *Social Fabric and Spatial Structure in Colonial Latin America*, edited by David J. Robinson, 25-84. Ann Arbor: University Microfilms for Syracuse University, 1979.

"Visita García de Palacio, 1583": See "Papeles relativos a la visita . . ."

Vogt, Evon Z. "The Genetic Model and Maya Cultural Development." In *Desarrollo Cultural de los mayas*, 2d ed., edited by Evon Z. Vogt and Alberto Ruz Lhuillier, 9-48. Mexico: Universidad Nacional Autónoma de Mexico, 1971.

———. "Some Aspects of Zinacantan Settlement Patterns and Ceremonial Organization." In *Settlement Archaeology*, edited by K. C. Chang, 154-171. Palo Alto, California: National Press Books, 1968.

———. *Zinacantan: A Maya Community in the Highlands of Chiapas*. Cambridge: Harvard University Press, Belknap Press, 1969.

Wachtel, Nathan. *The Vision of the Vanquished: The Spanish Conquest of Peru through Indian Eyes*. New York: Barnes and Noble, 1977.

Wagley, Charles. *The Social and Religious Life of a Guatemalan Village*. Memoirs of the American Anthropological Association, no. 71. Menasha, Wisconsin: American Anthropological Association, 1949.

Wagner, Helmuth O. "Subsistence Potential and Population Density of the Maya on the Yucatan Peninsula and Causes for the Decline in Population in the Fifteenth Century." In *Verhandlungen des XXXVIII Internationalen Amerikanistenkongresses, Stuttgart-München, 1968*, 1: 185-191. Munich: Kommissionsverlag Klaus Renner, 1970.

Wagner, Henry R., ed. *The Discovery of New Spain in 1518, by Juan de Grijalva*. Berkeley, California: Cortés Society, 1942.

———. *The Discovery of Yucatan, by Francisco Hernández de Córdoba*. Berkeley, California: Cortés Society, 1942.

Wallace, Anthony F. C. *Culture and Personality*. New York: Random House, 1961.

———. "Revitalization Movements." *American Anthropologist* 58 (1956): 264-281.

Wasserstrom, Robert. *Ethnic Relations in Central Chiapas, 1528-1975*. Berkeley: University of California Press, 1983.

———. "The exchange of Saints in Zinacantan: The Socioeconomic Bases of Religious Change in Southern Mexico." *Ethnology* 17 (1978): 187-210.

BIBLIOGRAPHY

Wauchope, Robert. *Modern Maya Houses: A Study of Their Archaeological Significance*. Washington: Carnegie Institution, 1938.
Webb, Malcolm C. "The Flag Follows Trade: An Essay on the Necessary Interaction of Military and Commercial Factors in State Formation." In *Ancient Civilization and Trade*, edited by Jeremy A. Sabloff and C. C. Lamberg-Karlovsky, 155-209. Albuquerque: University of New Mexico Press,
1975.
Webster, David L. *Defensive Earthworks at Becan, Campeche, Mexico: Implications
for Maya Warfare*. New Orleans: Middle American Research Institute, Tu-
lane University, 1976.
———. "Warfare and the Evolution of Maya Civilization." In *The Origins of
Maya Civilization*, edited by Richard E. W. Adams, 335-372. Albuquerque:
University of New Mexico Press, 1977.
Weisser, Michael R. *The Peasants of the Montes*. Chicago: University of Chicago
Press, 1976.
Wheatley, Paul. *The Pivot of the Four Quarters: A Preliminary Inquiry into the
Origins and Character of the Ancient Chinese City*. Chicago: Aldine, 1971.
Weidner, Donald. "Forced Labor in Colonial Peru." *The Americas* 16 (1960):
358-378.
Willey, Gordon R. "External Influences on the Lowland Maya: 1940 and 1975
Perspectives." In *Social Process in Maya Prehistory*, edited by Norman Ham-
mond, 57-75. London: Academic Press, 1977.
Willey, Gordon R. and William R. Bullard, Jr. "Prehistoric Settlement Patterns
in the Maya Lowlands." In *Handbook of Middle American Indians* 2: 360-377.
Austin: University of Texas Press, 1965.
Willey, Gordon R., and Demitri B. Shimkin. "The Maya Collapse: A Summary
View." In *The Classic Maya Collapse*, edited by T. Patrick Culbert, 457-
501. Albuquerque: University of New Mexico Press, 1973.
Wolf, Eric R. "Closed Corporate Peasant Communities in Mesoamerica and
Central Java." *Southwestern Journal of Anthropology* 13 (1957): 1-18.
———. *Sons of the Shaking Earth*. Chicago: University of Chicago Press, Phoe-
nix Books, 1959.
Wrigley, E. A. *Population and History*. New York: McGraw-Hill, 1969.
Zavala, Silvio, and José Miranda. "Instituciones indígenas en la colonia." In
Métodos y resultados de la politica indigenista en Mexico, by Alfonso Caso et
al., 29-112. Mexico City: Instituto Nacional Indigenista, 1954.
Zimmerman, Charlotte. "The Cult of the Holy Cross: An Analysis of Cos-
mology and Catholicism in Quintana Roo." *History of Religions* 3 (1963):
50-71.
Zuckerman, Michael. *Peaceable Kingdoms: New England Towns in the Eighteenth
Century*. New York: Knopf, 1970.
———. "Pilgrims in the Wilderness: Community, Modernity and the Maypole
at Merry Mount." *New England Historical Quarterly* 50 (1977): 255-277.

INDEX

Abala, 373, 374
Acalan, 98, 121, 153
Acculturation, models of, 110, 113. *See also* Hispanization
Africans: and caste system, 103, 107, 176; immigration of, 108, 258, 298; religious beliefs of, 298; as slaves, 104, 107, 176; in total population, 65, 109
Agriculture, commercial: early development of, 34-36, 47, 54-56, 85, 216; engaged in, by clergy, 45, 178-180, 182; engaged in, by Indians, 45, 178-180, 182, 266-267; expansion of, 47, 221, 367-371, 373-374, 379, 382, 384; outside of haciendas, 53-54, 55, 95-96, 374. *See also Estancias; Haciendas*
Agriculture, subsistence. *See* Milpa agriculture
Aguadas, ownership of, 180, 275
Aguardiente (cane liquor): consumption of, 45, 195-197, 322; royal monopoly, 54, 197
Ahcambezah, 233, 340. See also *Maestros cantores*
Ah Canul (province), 21, 245
Ahcuchcabs, 163, 232, 242, 248, 345-347
Ahkinchel (province), 148, 245
Ahkins, 233, 290, 340-341. *See also* Priests, Maya
Ahkulels, 232
Alcabala, 82
Alcalde col, 273
Alcaldes, Indian, 232, 234, 241, 273, 344-345
Alguaciles, 232-234
All Saints' Day, and ancestor cult, 311, 323, 328, 332
Almehen, 177, 238, 239, 379. *See also* Nobility, Maya
Ancestors: cult of, 173, 322-323, 328, 332; obligations to, 135, 250, 251, 262, 323
Andes. *See* Peru
Apiculture, Maya wealth from, 179, 180, 185, 267
Ascensión, Bay of, 76
Audiencia (Ayuntamiento), 159, 327, 361-362

Audiencia of Guatemala, 123
Audiencia of Mexico, 88, 264, 372
Auditor de guerra, 88
Ayuda de parroquia, 216, 384
Aztecs: *calpulli* system of, 137; conquest of, 12, 15, 20; and drunkenness, 196, 198; and evangelization, 307; hereditary rule among, 240, 245, 333; at Xicalango, 21. *See also* Mexicans; Mexico, central

Bacalar: and Caste War, 19; as military outpost, 14, 18, 66-67, 89, 267, 370
Balamcanche (Balankanche), grotto of, 317
Balche: as offering, 313; as ritual drink, 196, 322, 323, 340
Banquets (*convites*): and elite politics, 250, 343-344, 346, 347; and intercommunity ties, 152, 157, 344; in religious festivals, 321-324, 332, 339-347
Baptism: and *compadrazgo*, 106, 257-258; by Maya assistants, 213, 336; of Maya lords, 24, 106, 287, 298; and naming practices, 94
Barrios, Indian: and Canek revolt, 68-69, 157; migration to, 104, 109, 202-204; and urban markets, 45, 104; *vecinos* in, 104, 106-107
Batabs: and administration of justice, 357-358; and Caste War, 386; economic status of, 165, 177, 178-179, 252, 372; and *gobernadores*, 232, 235, 243, 246, 248; labor service to, 183, 184, 249, 263, 270; military expeditions of, 175; as colonial rulers, 192, 194, 281; as Prehispanic rulers, 140, 142, 151, 232; ritual role, 290, 340, 343; status and privileges of, 229, 233, 237-238; succession of, 233-234, 236, 240-244, 249, 344; and tax collection, 184-185, 205, 359. *See also* Indian officials; Rulers, Maya; Uz, Fernando
Bauer, Arnold, 221
Becal, 283
Beeswax: collected in forest, 157, 263, 292, 332; exported, 18, 39, 43, 120; Maya wealth from, 134, 179, 180, 185;

573

Library of Congress Cataloging in Publication Data

Farriss, Nancy M. (Nancy Marguerite), 1938-
Maya society under colonial rule.

Bibliography: p.   Includes index.
1. Mayas—History. 2. Mayas—Social conditions.
3. Mexico—Social conditions—To 1810. 4. Acculturation
—Mexico. 5. Indians of Mexico—Yucatán—History.
6. Indians of Mexico—Yucatán—Social conditions.
I. Title.
F1435.F28 1984   972'.6500497   83-43071
ISBN 0-691-07668-5 (alk. paper)
ISBN 0-691-10158-2 (lim. pbk. ed.)